Eritrea

Eritrea at a Crossroads

A Narrative of Triumph, Betrayal and Hope

Andebrhan Welde Giorgis

Strategic Book Publishing and Rights Co.

Strategic Book Publishing and Rights Co.
12620 FM 1960, Suite A4-507
Houston TX 77065
www.sbpra.com

ISBN: 978-1-62857-331-2

In Memory of the Martyrs
Who Fell so that
Eritrea Would Rise and Thrive
And that
The Eritrean People Would Be Free

Contents

Foreword
by
Glenys Kinnock

In 1991, the Eritrean liberation forces marched into Asmera, the capital city of Eritrea, ending three decades of a war waged against Ethiopia. Two years later, the triumphant freedom fighters conducted an internationally-monitored referendum, the outcome of which formalised Eritrea's status as an independent sovereign state.

This was a time of hope and of anticipation of a better future by people who, as I saw for myself when I visited Eritrea in March 1988, made extraordinary advances in education, childcare, medicine and agriculture – and this in spite of waging a relentless, brutal war.

I met many Eritrean idealists like Andebrhan, the author of this book – who subsequently has become a close and dear friend - whose life has been dedicated to promoting, and supporting, the people of Eritrea, and the promise which liberation offered.

After peace eventually came he and others wasted no time in formulating sound economic and social policies designed to guide rehabilitation and the reconstruction of the war-ravaged economy and infrastructure. The Government sponsored a Commission that, through a process involving the broad participation of the population, drafted a

Constitution that established sound governance structures, and fundamental rights which had the potential to become the foundation for the country's future laws and policies. Everything was, it seemed, in place as the Eritrean people anticipated, at last, a peaceful and secure future.

The tragedy is that the independence celebrations in May 1993 can hardly be further from what has become the reality of Eritrea now - where torture, arbitrary arrest and severe restrictions on freedom of expression, and association are the norm.

Elections have not taken place since independence in 1993 and the Constitution has not been implemented, and political parties are not allowed. President Isaias Afwerki has been in office for twenty two years – presiding over a country where access to justice does not exist and where there is imprisonment without trial.

The author of this book, "Eritrea at a Crossroads", Andebrhan Welde Giorgis has lived through it all - the armed struggle, post-independence, and the profound disappointment which has followed. He had left Harvard University to join the struggle of his people for independence in the early 1970s and I saw how effective, committed, and courageous Andebrhan is when I spent time with him during the war, and later when he was the Ambassador to the European Union, and I was an MEP. He has an impressive record, which has shown his unfailing integrity, courage and devotion to the wellbeing of the Eritrean people.

"Eritrea at a Crossroads" is both a personal story and a unique exposé of the failings of a Government which has brought misery and suffering to its people. In the various leadership positions which Andebrhan has held in the post-independence Government, he has worked to build viable institutions and protect the fundamental rights of the Eritrean people. His frustration, regret and disappointment are evident when you read the chapters towards the end of the book. This is an insider's personal story, and interpretation of events - which exposes how the country's President, once viewed as one of a new breed of African leaders, went on to purge many of his former comrades, suppress dissent and civil liberties, and draw political power into his own hands. Now, as we know and as the author points out, the Eritrean people's right to democracy, human rights and social justice are being rigorously denied.

This book certainly has helped me to understand more about the challenges facing Africa, and Eritrea, and provides much needed information about a crisis festering in Africa. It is a welcome and timely publication, and I trust will provide Eritreans with the evidence they need to hear about one of the most secretive and repressive regimes in the world.

Baroness Kinnock of Holyhead

Preface

The inspiration for this book stems from a desire to contribute to the existing body of knowledge about Eritrea and the Eritrean people, both historical and contemporary, as well as to the internal debate on the future of Eritrea, from the perspective of an Eritrean freedom fighter. I had initially wanted to write about the Eritrean experience of self-reliance in waging the armed struggle for self-determination and in the pursuit of peacetime reconstruction and development as a world-historic heritage of peoples fighting oppression, underdevelopment and poverty while aspiring to advance freedom, democracy and prosperity. Undoubtedly, the Eritrean experience embraces an array of commendable achievements offset by lamentable failures.

My preoccupation with the daily chores of life in public service delayed the realisation of my initial project. In due course, elements of the book gathered as a study on *Nation Building, State Construction and Development in Africa: The Case of Eritrea*. Published by the German Foundation *Friedrich Ebert Stiftung* in April 2010, the study was presented to the Parliamentary Working Committee on Africa of the Social Democratic Party, Deutsche Bundestag (German Parliament), in Berlin on 6 May 2010. Since the situation in the new State of Eritrea has steadily deteriorated, failing the will of the heroes of the war of national liberation and thwarting the aspirations, hopes and expectations of the Eritrean people, the work eventually evolved into *Eritrea at a Crossroads: A Narrative of Triumph, Betrayal and Hope*.

Coming out at the start of the third decade of Eritrea's independence, the book seeks to shed some light on the fundamental disparity between the ideals and objectives of the historic struggle for liberation, on the one hand, and the reality of independence, demonstrating the failed policies and practices of a dysfunctional government, on the other.

The greater part of my adult life revolved around the axis of Eritrea's struggle for freedom, democracy and prosperity. Set against this backdrop of lifelong engagement, the discourse portrays my own personal perspective enriched by primary and secondary sources, neatly sifted through the prism of an insider's knowledge and insight. It recounts general events as they unfolded and particular ones which I lived through in a specific Eritrean setting during the armed struggle and after independence. This work addresses issues that have matured and become ripe for open discussion without compromising Eritrea's national security (as distinct from regime security), the drive for internal change, or the safety of former comrades-in-arms and colleagues. I set these red lines for the work in constant commitment to the interest of Eritrea, to my former fellow freedom fighters, and to the ideals for which we put our lives on the line.

Eritrea at a Crossroads: A Narrative of Triumph, Betrayal and Hope aims to stimulate informed political debate regarding the prevailing situation in Eritrea and the way forward for the country and its people. Beyond Eritrea, it is intended to contribute to greater knowledge, deeper understanding and more rigorous debate of the root causes and key drivers of the essential fragility of the prototype contemporary African state, as demonstrated by recent developments in North and West Africa, and to a better appreciation of the challenges facing its reconstitution. It is a sad commentary that, fifty years after the accession to independence that marked the end of the colonial era, the typical African state remains fragile, dysfunctional and irrelevant to the wellbeing of its citizens. Overcoming the malaise would require restoring its legitimacy, establishing responsive governance and building institutional capacity to deliver.

I am very grateful to several colleagues and friends who reviewed the text of various chapters and offered helpful comments. Avoiding mention in respect of their request, I deeply thank all of them anonymously. I am very grateful to my colleagues, Professor Stefaan Smis and Professor Joachim Koops of *Vrije Universiteit Brusssel* (Free University of Brussels), and my friend Peter Alexiadis of *Gibson, Dunn & Crutcher LLP,* for their helpful comments and advice. I am especially grateful to two compatriot friends and two former comrades-in-arms who, for the moment, will remain anonymous, for their review of the entire manuscript, valuable comments, and suggestions. But any errors in fact, analysis or interpretation are my sole responsibility.

Special thanks to Joëlle Aflalo, always there for me in true friendship and constant support.

Last, but foremost, I am deeply indebted to my family. My sons Johannes, Abraham and Azazi, and my wife Alganesh, provided vital inspiration and indispensable support. Alganesh's constant advice, assistance and encouragement made the work possible.

About the Author

A mbassador Andebrhan Welde Giorgis is a member of the Board and Senior Adviser of the European Centre for Electoral Support (ECES), a Senior Expert in the Peace and Security Section of the Global Governance Institute (GGI) and an Adjunct Professor of Diplomacy, African Politics and International Relations at Vesalius College, Free University of Brussels (VUB) where he is also a research fellow. He has extensive experience as a freedom fighter, scholar, central banker, diplomat, international negotiator, and political consultant with particular expertise in peace, security and development issues.

Andebrhan is a veteran of the war for Eritrea's liberation and a founding member of the central committee of the Eritrean People's Liberation Front (EPLF) and the People's Front for Democracy and Justice (PFDJ). Upon independence, he served *inter alia*, as: President of the University of Asmera; Governor of the Bank of Eritrea; member of the Eritrean National Assembly; Ambassador to the EU, Belgium, France, Luxembourg, the Netherlands, Portugal, Spain and the United Kingdom, and Permanent Representative to the International Maritime Organisation and UNESCO; Eritrea's Special Envoy to the African Great Lakes region; and Commissioner for Coordination with the UN Mission in Eritrea and Ethiopia (UNMEE). After dissociating from the government of Eritrea in 2006, Andebrhan worked as Senior Advisor for the Africa Programme of the International Crisis Group and advised the European Commission for the Preparation of an EU Strategy for the Horn of Africa.

Andebrhan holds a BSc and MBA from the University of Colorado, conducted doctoral studies at Harvard University and has published several articles. He speaks Tigrinya, Amharic, Arabic, English and French.

Abbreviations

ACP	African, Caribbean and Pacific Group of States
ACP-EU	African, Caribbean and Pacific –European Union
AFS	American Field Service
ALF	Afar Liberation Front
ALCE	Association of Love of the Country of Eritrea
ARS	Alliance for the Re-liberation of Somalia
AU	African Union
AUEE	Association of the Unity of Eritrea and Ethiopia
BC	Before Christ
BMA	British Military Administration
CDR	Commander
CENTCOM	Central Command (US)
CIA	Central Intelligence Agency (US)
CLI	Cost of Living Index
CPA	Cotonou Partnership Agreement
CPI	Consumer Price Index
CPSU	Communist Party of the Soviet Union
DRC	Democratic Republic of Congo
DSRSG	Deputy Special Representative of the Secretary General

EBI	Eritrean Bloc for Independence
EDF	Eritrean Defence Forces
EDF	European Development Fund
EDP	Eritreans for Democracy and Peace in North America
EEBC	Eritrea-Ethiopia Boundary Commission
EFLE	Eritreans for Liberation in Europe
EFLNA	Eritreans for Liberation in North America
ELA	Eritreans Liberation Army
ELF	Eritrean Liberation Front
ELF-PLF	Eritrean Liberation Front-People's Liberation Forces
ELF-RC	Eritrean Liberation Front-Revolutionary Council
ELO	Ethiopian Liaison Office
ELP	Eritrean Labour Party
EOC	Eritrean Orthodox Church
EOSA	Eritrean Old Soldiers Association
EPAs	Economic Partnership Agreements
EPDM	Ethiopian People's Democratic Movement
EPLA	Eritrean People's Liberation Army
EPLF	Eritrean People's Liberation Forces/Front
EPRDF	Ethiopian People's Revolutionary Democratic Front
EPRP	Eritrean People's Revolutionary Party
EPRP	Ethiopian People's Revolutionary Party
ERN	Eritrean Nakfa
ESECE	Eritrean Secondary Education Certificate Examination
ESP	Eritrean Socialist Party
ESRA	Ethiopian Second Revolutionary Army
ETB	Ethiopian Birr

EU	European Union
FC	Force Commander
FDI	Foreign Direct Investment
FDRE	Federal democratic Republic of Ethiopia
GHG	Greenhouse Gas
GHoA	Greater Horn of Africa
GUES	General Union of Eritrean Students
GUEW	General Union of Eritrean Workers
HIV/AIDS	Human Immunodeficiency Virus/Acquired Immunodeficiency Syndrome
IB	Independence Bloc
ICRC	International Committee of the Red Cross
IDA	International Development Association (World Bank)
IDPs	Internally displaced persons
IFC	International Finance Corporation (World Bank Group)
IGAD	Inter-Governmental Authority on Development
IMO	International Maritime Organisation
ICU	Islamic Courts Union (Somalia)
JAES	Joint Africa-EU Strategy
MACC	Mine Action Coordinating Centre
MEISON	All-Ethiopia Socialist Movement
ML	Moslem League (Eritrea)
MLWP	Moslem League of the Western Province
NAM	Non-Aligned Movement
NDP	National Democratic Programme (EPLF)
NDR	National Democratic Revolution
NEPF	National Economic Policy Framework
NEP	New Eritrea Party
NEPIP	New Eritrea Pro-Italy Party

NLA	National Liberation Army (Algeria)
NLF	National Liberation Front (Algeria)
NP	Nationalist Party
NUESY	National Union of Eritrean Students and Youth
NUEW	National Union of Eritrean Women
NUEW	National Union of Eritrean Workers
OAU	Organisation of African Unity
OETM	Occupied Enemy Territory Administration
OLF	Oromo Liberation Front
PCA	Permanent Court of Arbitration
PDS	Presidential Disinformation Service
PENA	Provisional Eritrean National Assembly
PFDJ	People's Front for Democracy and Justice
PHG	Provisional Head of Government
PMAC	Provisional Military Administrative Council
PPP	Purchasing Power Parity
PSC	Provisional State Council
RECs	Regional Economic Communities
RSTC	Red Sea Trading Corporation
SALF	Somali Abo Liberation Front
SCF	Steadfastness and Confrontation Front
SG	Secretary General
SLF	Sidama Liberation Front
SRSG	Special Representative of the Secretary General
TTS	Teachers' Training School
TPLF	Tigray People's Liberation Front
TNA	Transitional National Assembly
UK	United Kingdom of Great Britain and Northern Ireland
UN	United Nations

UNESCO	United Nations Educational, Scientific and Cultural Organisation
UNMEE	UN Mission in Eritrea and Ethiopia
US	United States
USA	United States of America
USAID	United States Agency for International Development
UP	Unionist Party (Eritrea)
WSLF	Western Somali Liberation Front

Maps

CHAPTER 1

Introduction

Eritrea, a small country with a strategic location in the volatile Horn of Africa, won liberation in 1991 through an armed struggle that had lasted 30 years, and declared independence in 1993 following a referendum. Having waged an epic struggle however, Eritrea today is littered with the shards of broken expectations, broken promises and broken hopes of freedom, justice, and progress. Twenty-two years past *de facto* independence, the Eritrean people continue to endure and Eritrea's youth strive to escape the caprices of despotic rule, harsh oppression and perennial insecurity. Wrong policy choices and wasted opportunities have forfeited Eritrea's potential to grow into a prosperous regional *entrepôt* and hub of industry, commerce and services and, instead, immersed it in a state of abject poverty and comprehensive isolation.

The land of modern Eritrea has a long history as a cradle and hub of the old Axumite civilisation. *Eritrea at a Crossroads: A Narrative of Triumph, Betrayal and Hope* presents a brief outline of the evolution of Eritrea as an upshot of the colonial implant of the Westphalian order on African soil. It sketches Eritrea's long journey to self-determination, impeded by constant acts of external intervention. It narrates a story of heroic triumph in struggle and of dismal failure in victory. It assesses the record of the post-independence government and makes the case for renewal and the reconstruction of a functional democratic state to meet the age-old yearnings of the Eritrean people for peace, freedom, justice and prosperity via real empowerment. As the alpha of eighteen chapters, *Chapter 1: Introduction* provides a concise summary of each succeeding chapter.

Chapter 2: The Making of Eritrea presents a brief profile of the land and the people of Eritrea, taking a glimpse at the ancient history of the region, and asserts that the Eritreans, like all other African peoples, existed in history long before the moment of their contact with Europe and the Europeans. It provides a bird's eye view of the evolution of the region's pre-colonial history and traces the matrix of constant invasions, population movements, migrations and intermingling that forged the mosaic of peoples, cultures and languages that make up Eritrea. It describes the reality of a fragmented territory from the decline of the Kingdom of Axum, through the centuries, to the advent of the European scramble for Africa and the colonial era.

The Making of Eritrea describes the Italian conquest, subjugation and unification of the territory into a single entity under colonial rule. It recounts the forging of the Eritrean state and the rise of an overarching distinctive Eritrean national identity as a product of the dialectics of colonialism and the resistance of the colonised. It highlights the crucial regional and global ramifications of Italy's defeat in Eritrea, signifying the dismantling of Mussolin's *Africa Orientale Italiana* and the paving of the way to the reversal of fortunes of Rommel's *Deutsches Afrika Korps*, the German surrender in North Africa and the ultimate Allied victory in World

War II. Further, it underscores that Eritrea, having served as a crucial battleground in the 'great fight' between the forces of global 'fascism and liberal democracy' on African soil and as a significant cornerstone in the construction of the Allied victory, was abandoned and betrayed by the Allied Powers.

The plan to partition Eritrea, divide its people and destroy its identity, and the plunder of its productive assets that retarded its development, under the British Military Administration are covered in *Chapter 3: A Plan to Dismember Eritrea*. The chapter describes the awakening of the Eritrean people's aspirations for self-determination, the chain of events that unfolded, and the resultant turbulence whose severe 'stresses and strains' brought Eritrea to the brink of chaos and extinction, leaving lasting scars on the Eritrean psyche and body politic. It also portrays the rise of organised national political activity and the blend of British intrigues, Ethiopian interference, and Big Power caprices. This dynamic thwarted Eritrea's legitimate claim to decolonisation and sowed the seeds of long-term conflict that beset Eritrea and Ethiopia and disturbed the security and stability of the Horn of Africa as a whole.

The interplay of geopolitical factors and the ambitions and rivalry of the Big Powers that blocked Eritrea's quest for decolonisation while appeasing Ethiopia's claims by using the UN to impose a federal union with Ethiopia against the wishes of the Eritrean people, are considered in *Chapter 4: Transition From European to African Colonialism*. The chapter describes how the UN violated the principle of self-determination, facilitated Eritrea's continued domination by an oppressive power with an African face that damaged long-term Ethio-Eritrean relations. Further, it underscores Ethiopia's systematic and reckless subversion of the Federal

Act and the tacit complicity of the UN in the incorporation of Eritrea into the Ethiopian Empire, fuelling popular indignation and fomenting the Eritrean armed struggle for self-determination.

The legitimacy in international law of the right of self-determination, in the dual sense of the right of a nation and the right of a people, and the applicability of the principle to the case of Eritrea as such, are outlined in *Chapter 5: The Arduous Struggle for Self-Determination*. This chapter bares the UN failure to uphold its own Charter and declarations with respect to Eritrea's legitimate claim to, and active struggle for, the right of self-determination. In addition, it stresses the role of external intervention, in the context of a complex web of geopolitical interests and shifting alliances, as a complicating factor in the evolution of modern Eritrean history.

The chapter sketches the rise of a distinctive shared identity as the driving force of Eritrean nationalism, the resurgence of the Eritrean national movement, the dynamics of the ensuing political and military struggles, the tortuous internal developments and the unfolding of the difficult drive to dislodge foreign domination. Further, it highlights the resistance, sacrifices, and triumph of the Eritrean people that challenged successive superpower intervention and defeated Ethiopian occupation. Finally, it hails the historic exercise of the right to self-determination of Eritrea as a nation availed by military victory while underscoring the inability of independence to allow for the exercise of the right of self-determination of Eritrea as a people.

Chapter 6: State Construction and Development depicts the initial commitment of the nascent state to construct a democratic government based on the rule of law as the 'foundation of economic growth, social harmony and progress'. It hails the pledge to establish a constitutional political system that respects democratic principles, human rights and civil liberties. Further, the chapter features the promise to rehabilitate and develop a 'modern, technologically advanced, and internationally competitive economy within the next two decades' to enhance the "standard and quality of life of the Eritrean people'. More specifically, it assesses the project to establish a unitary, secular, united, democratic and developmental state, and contrasts the declared policies and actual practices of the Eritrean government since independence.

The indelible link between Eritrea's domestic and foreign policy and its impact on the evolution of the state are featured in *Chapter 7: Self-Reliance and the Coupon Economy*. The chapter notes the positive external environment and the outpouring of international goodwill and support that greeted the advent of independent Eritrea, appreciates the great opportunity that this offered for constructive engagement, and appraises the regime's imprudent and counterproductive policy responses to the devastating domestic repercussions of the border war with Ethiopia. It unveils the deliberate pursuit of regime stability at the expense of the paramount national interest and bares the use of self-reliance as a euphemism for the external isolation of the country.

Further, the chapter describes the institution and operations of the political economy of rationing in the context of a contracting economy in crisis that has delivered a declining standard of living for the people. It probes the abysmal failure to manage a national economy, or to mobilise domestic and external resources, to cater to the most basic subsistence needs of a small national population. Finally, it appraises the essential fragility of the Eritrean economy primarily as the outcome of the government's wrong policies, gross incompetence, and wasteful management of the country's human and material resources.

Chapter 8: The Scourge of Indefinite National Service affirms the importance of rules-based, duration-specific and well-applied programme of national service to build a reliable reserve force as an element of national defence strategy. It lauds the role of a reserve force, as an alternative to a large standing army, to supplement a small professional army in the event of need and to participate at times in meaningful development projects implemented in accordance with planned national priorities. It notes the practice of voluntary service that evolved as a tradition among Eritrean youth during the war of national liberation and the complementary role played by forced recruitment as an instrument of wartime mobilisation.

Further, the chapter reviews the Proclamation of National Service in terms of the waste, the opportunity cost, the loss of legitimacy, the crisis of mass exodus and the devastation caused by abuses in implementing the programme. It exposes the illegal practice of endless active national service, carried out without due remuneration, as a scourge afflicting Eritrean youth, destroying the nuclear family and draining Eritrean society. In particular, it deplores the colossal misuse of the nation's most productive manpower resources that cast a pall over its future.

Disagreements and disputes in the internal relations of an organisation are normal and should be treated as such through dialogue. That is the focus of *Chapter 9: Resort to Force as a Default Mode.* The chapter analyses the historical and structural causes of the resort to force as a default mode and the recurrent use of coercion, in the form of suspension, demotion, transfer, detention, torture or elimination, as an arbiter of internal discord during the armed struggle. It dissects the extension of the use of coercion in the form of arbitrary arrests, indefinite detentions, systematic torture and extrajudicial killings after independence as a persistent government practice. Against this backdrop, it describes the rise of dissent within the historical leadership of the EPLF, the ensuing confrontations, the arbitrary detention of senior government officials and journalists, and the banning of the private press to suppress dissent and independent opinion.

Further, the chapter deplores the regime's suppression of internal criticism and elimination of political dissent, burying the victims alive in the desolate *Irairo* prison, to forestall resistance and intimidate the protagonists of Eritrea's historic struggle for freedom into reluctant submission to dictatorship through the demonstrative effects of arbitrary arrest, indefinite detention and solitary confinement, with tragic consequences for the country. It sketches the accumulation of power in the Presidency, the marginalisation of key institutions and the consequent rise of 'one man rule', with its sequel of rampant political corruption and abuse. The chapter highlights the unrestrained use of coercion as an instrument of political repression afflicting Eritrea today.

Chapter 10: Disconnect between Policy and Practice contrasts the policies and practices of the government in terms of the establishment of a constitutional, democratic and developmental state capable of promoting political participation, gender equality, and religious freedom. Using the policy instruments provided by the National Charter, the Macro-Policy paper and the ratified Constitution as benchmarks, the chapter exposes the existence of an enormous disparity between the stated policies and actual practices of the government. Linking the unfortunate political, economic and social reality prevailing in Eritrea today to this disparity, it concludes that its root cause is structural and its remedy lies in national renewal.

Some of the recent literature on the nature of the postcolonial state in Africa is reviewed in *Chapter 11: The African State in Crisis* in order to ground the Eritrean experience in state construction and development in the African setting. The chapter highlights the European heritage of the state system in Africa and interrogates its suitability to the socio-economic conditions of African society. It notes the impacts of slavery, colonialism and the Cold War on Africa's development. Slavery robbed Africa of millions of its most productive work force, drained its creative energy, and sapped its potential to develop. Colonialism plundered Africa's natural and human resources and disrupted its indigenous progression. The Cold War turned Africa into an ideological battleground, disoriented its priorities, and destabilised its polities.

Further, the chapter notes how the African state, as a graft of the European state system rooted in the industrial and political revolutions in Europe, gave rise to anti-colonial nationalism and Pan-Africanism that fuelled the drive to independence, and ended up inheriting the authoritarian features of the colonial state. It explores how these features led to the failure of the postcolonial state to build functional governance, establish stability, achieve sustainable development, and deliver public wellbeing for most of its citizens. The chapter notes that the prototype African state faces a deep crisis of legitimacy, delivery and relevance and, as recent events in North and West Africa have shown, remains dysfunctional, repressive and fragile.

Chapter 12: Eritrea: The Future of Africa that Works contrasts the historical colonialist and nationalist narratives, on the one hand, and the official and dissenting perspectives within the nationalist narrative, on the other. It contends that Eritrea's record has not borne out the optimism of sympathetic observers, like Abdulrahman Babu, that independent Eritrea would deliver democratic development and prosperity where other African states had failed. The chapter asserts that the regime has not lived up to the progressive goals of the struggle and the ideals of the freedom fighters that animated Babu's enthusiasm. It admits that, far from representing the *future of Africa that works*, Eritrea manifests the authoritarian features of the prototype African state, with its attendant crises of legitimacy, delivery and relevance.

The origins, formation national role of the Eritrean diaspora are described in *Chapter 13: Engaging the Diaspora*. It explains how interstate conflicts and domestic repression have driven more and more people out of the country to join the diaspora since the start of the border war with Ethiopia in 1998 and the government's crackdown in September 2001. It also describes how the relative size, wealth, educational attainment and close attachment to the home country have made the Eritrean diaspora a source of sizeable remittances and a significant player in the political, economic and social life of the country.

The chapter notes that a more conducive political and economic space would enable the Eritrean diaspora to use its multiple linkages and resources to promote investment and make a more effective contribution to national development. It also signals the need for the diaspora to transcend the old political and social divides, unify its politics, and reposition its focus on the drive for change. The chapter emphasises the patriotic duty of political activists, movements, and media outlets to distinguish between the interests of the State and the regime, and the potential of the diaspora to play a catalytic role in the effort to bring about change, reconstruct a democratic state, and transform society through constructive engagement and collaborative action.

The writer speaks of the formative influences on his political perspective and dedication to the cause of the liberation, reconstruction and development of Eritrea and the progress, prosperity and wellbeing of the people in *Chapter 14: In the Service of Eritrea*. The chapter highlights his efforts to revitalise the University of Asmera as a centre of higher learning and applied research and institute the Bank of Eritrea as a functional central bank. It also touches on his work in Eritrea's diplomatic service. Further, it recounts the role of constant presidential interference in disrupting the effort to build institutions and undermining mission delivery.

Post-independence issues of war and peace between Eritrea and Ethiopia are covered in *Chapter 15: An Avoidable War*. The chapter notes the various missed opportunities, during and after the war, to agree on the colonial treaty border and secure durable peace. It traces the slide towards an unnecessary war between former allies, the human tragedy of the deportations, the evolution and devastation of the war, and the international effort to end hostilities.

The chapter tells the story of the unravelling of an old, pervasive and problematic relationship burdened by a difficult narrative of conquest, war and conflict, often impacted by the intricacies of shared ethnic and cultural affinity straddling a common border, and closely bound by mutual economic and strategic interests. Further, it affirms the potential of the multiple pillars of the Ethio-Eritrean relationship to serve as levers of durable political cooperation, drivers of economic integration, and anchors of regional peace and security.

The role of the writer as Commissioner and the UN Mission in Eritrea and Ethiopia (UNMEE) in the effort to implement the Agreement on Cessation of Hostilities is described in *Chapter 16: An Uneasy Truce*. The chapter notes the failure of the parties to resolve key operational issues, of the UN Security Council to address them, and of the UN and the AU to honour their commitment to enforce the agreement, precipitating the inauspicious termination of UNMEE's mission and turning a potentially successful peace building operation into a fiasco.

Chapter 17: Securing the Peace between Eritrea and Ethiopia crystallises the key provisions of, and the effort to implement, the Algiers Agreement. It notes the omission of the Inquiry Commission and the creation of the Claims and Boundary commissions. It summarises the final damage awards of the Claims Commission, the territorial significance of the delimitation decision of the Boundary Commission, and its virtual demarcation of the boundary. In addition, it assesses the role of the parties in terms of the respect of their treaty obligations under the agreement and in the failure to achieve durable peace between Eritrea and Ethiopia.

Further, the chapter notes the lack of convergence of interest, unity of purpose, and coherence of policy that has hampered the effort of the UN Security Council to help Eritrea and Ethiopia achieve peace. It stresses the need for the full implementation of the Algiers Agreements; and for Ethiopia's unconditional recognition of the border, as demarcated by the EEBC and respect of Eritrea's territorial integrity to ease a troubled historical memory, and secure a stable peace and normal relations in the interests of the fraternal peoples.

The concluding chapter, *Chapter 18: We Didn't Do It for This* expresses the author's sense of profound deception and disappointment, shared by many veterans of the independence war, at the present predicament of Eritrea and the Eritrean people. It decries the betrayal of the Eritrean people by their own government, the desertion of the promises of freedom, democracy, justice, and prosperity, for which the armed struggle was fought and great sacrifices made. The chapter signals the need for a fundamental rethinking of Eritrean politics and for reform to reconstruct a functional state, in line with the ethos and transformational goals of the armed struggle.

CHAPTER 2

The Making of Eritrea

Until the lion has his own historians, the tale of the hunt will always belong to the hunter. - African proverb[1]

It is often the case that history is 'made', narrated and interpreted by the powers that be or the victors of the moment in a manner that suits their purposes and glorifies their feats. The annals of human history attest that the victims of colonial, neocolonial, or domestic oppression are too busy enduring or protesting their suffering to write their story. This phenomenon partly explains the notion held by some that Africa and the Africans only entered "history" at the point of their contact with Europe and the

---

[1] The story of a hunter who revelled in his bountiful game obtained through the unsung efforts of a lion. The proverb has slight variations in different parts of Africa. Among the Ewe-mina in Benin, Ghana, and Togo: *"Until the lion has his or her own storyteller, the hunter will always have the best part of the story"*. Among the Igbo, Nigeria: *"Until lions have their own historians, tales of the hunt shall always glorify the hunter"*. In Kenya and Zimbabwe: *"Until lions start writing down their own stories, the hunters will always be the heroes"*. 2006 African Proverbs of the Month http://www.afriprov.org/index.php/african-proverb-of-the-month/32-2006proverbs.html.

Europeans. This chapter aims to trace the evolution of the region to place Eritrea and the Eritreans in their historical and geopolitical context and to help dispel this erroneous view and, by extension, of Africa and the Africans.

A glance at the region's ancient history highlights the phenomenon of constant population movements, displacements, migrations, and intermingling that created the mosaic of peoples and cultures that is Eritrea today. It also reveals the reality of a fragmented Eritrea from the decline of the power of Axum to the advent of European colonialism in the Horn of Africa. For a brief period preceding the European scramble for Africa, the territory of modern Eritrea became a battleground for regional hegemony between expanding Egypt and emergent Abyssinia.

Decisive Abyssinian military victory in the Eritrean Central Plateau could not displace overwhelming Egyptian presence in the Barka Lowlands, the Bogos region (Senhit) and the Red Sea Coastal Plains. The Mahdist revolt in the Sudan and the intrusion of the European colonial venture aborted the Ethio-Egyptian geopolitical contest in the region. Italian conquest occasioned the subjection and unification of the territory into a single political entity under a centralised colonial administration. Along with all its wrongdoings and residual benefits, colonial conquest resulted in the creation of Eritrea as a nation state and the emergence of an overarching distinctive Eritrean national identity.

2.1 The Land and the People

Bounded by the Red Sea in the east, Djibouti and Ethiopia in the south, and Sudan in the west and north, Eritrea is a small country that occupies a strategic location on the northern saddle of the Horn of Africa along the southwestern shores of the Red Sea. Along with Djibouti and Yemen, Eritrea commands the southern entrance to the Red Sea through the Strait of Bab el Mandeb, or the Gate of Lament. It adjoins the vital international shipping lanes of the Red Sea linking the Mediterranean Sea and the Indian Ocean. Its land and sea territory straddles one of the world's busiest and most critical maritime routes. Its proximity to the oil-rich but highly volatile Middle East further enhances Eritrea's strategic location.

Map 1: *Eritrea's location in the Horn of Africa* http://www. eritrea.be/old/eritrea-geography.htm

Eritrea has an area of about 125,000 km² and an estimated population of 5.5 million, including its diaspora. Endowed with rich marine resources, its relatively extensive territorial waters are dotted with some 354 islands and islets. The country has the longest aggregate coastline among the Red Sea littoral states. Its landmass comprises the Central Plateau or Highlands (the *Kebessa*) and the Northern Highlands, the Western Lowlands (the *Metaht*), and the Red Sea Coastal Plains. These distinct topographic features bestow Eritrea with some of the most beautiful landscapes, pristine waters and coral reefs in the world.

Mainly a Christian population interspersed with small Muslim minorities inhabits the densely populated Central Plateau, with its undulating plains and rugged mountains rising up to 3,180 metres at the highest peak of Emba Soira. Largely a Muslim population with small Christian minorities inhabits the relatively sparsely populated Coastal Plains, Northern Highlands, and Western Lowlands, with an elevation that ranges from below sea level to two thousand five hundred metres. Despite its small size, Eritrea exhibits great diversity and represents a mosaic of nationalities, ethnic groups, languages, religions, and topographic features.

The people of Eritrea and their constituent nationalities have historically evolved from three ancient races that inhabited both flanks of the Red Sea Basin in North East Africa and Arabia Felix: the Semitic, the Hamitic (Cushitic), and the Nilotic.[2] The Nilotic peoples, the earliest inhabitants of Eritrea, had moved from their original forest home in southeastern Sudan to the Gash-Setit Basin about 2000 BC

---

[2] Mebrahtu, Simon, Eritrea: Constitutional, Legislative and Administrative Provisions Concerning Indigenous Peoples, Country Report of the Research Project by the International Labour Organisation and the African Commission on Human and Peoples' Rights, 2009. http://www.chr.up.ac.za/chr_old/ indigenous/country_reports/Country_reports_Eritrea.pdf

and, from there, proceeded to settle in the Central Plateau.[3] Subsequently, Hamitic pastoralists hailing from northern Sudan invaded the Northern Highlands and the Barka Lowlands, subdued or ousted the Nilotic inhabitants, and spread along the coastal plains, extending all the way to eastern Ethiopia and Somalia.[4] Around 1000 BC, Semitic Sabaeans from the South Arabian highlands crossed the Red Sea and colonised the Central Plateau.[5]

The Sabaeans introduced a more advanced level of political organisation, agricultural techniques, masonry, and maritime commerce. They intermingled with the Hamitic population in the Plateau, established the Kingdom of Axum "during the first century of the Christian era" and, in reference to their 'hybrid ancestry', acquired the name 'Habash' or 'mixed' from which the term 'Abyssinia' derives.[6] The advent of a new wave of immigrants from South Arabia followed; the Himyarites entrenched "a Semitic culture among the plateau communities and, with it, the classical Ethiopic language of Ge'ez."[7] The power and influence of Axum extended to the Hamitic tribes outside the Plateau, "as a consequence of which the less remote abandoned their harsh Hamitic dialects for the soft Semitic Ge'ez of their Axumite rulers."[8]

As the kingdom expanded and developed into a great hub of international commerce, it attracted people from its

---

[3]   Trevaskis, G.K.N., Eritrea: A Colony in Transition: 1941-1952, Oxford University Press, London, 1960, p.4.

[4]   Ibid., p. 4.

[5]   Ibid., p. 4.

[6]   Ibid., p. 4-5.

[7]   Ibid., p. 5.

[8]   Ibid., p. 5.

trading partners of the ancient world, such as Arabia, Egypt, Greece, Rome, Persia, India and Byzantium.[9] While using Greek as the official language of the court and as the lingua franca at the cosmopolitan port city of Adulis, the Axumites embraced Christianity as the state religion during the first third of the third century A.D. and spread their Semitic culture and language[10] among the local Hamitic population. They also introduced terrace farming to conserve soil and water, built dams and cisterns to store water, constructed aqueducts and canals to channel water from the mountain streams into the crop fields, and minted gold, silver and bronze coins to facilitate commercial exchange.

Following the decline of Axum, the Central Plateau, the Northern Highlands, and the Barka Lowlands remained under the dominion of the Hamitic Beja tribes; the Afar (Denkel), a kindred Hamitic people, occupied the southern coastal strip; while the Nilotics continued to inhabit the Gash-Setit Basin. The Beja tribes, unlike their Sabaean predecessors, lacked the knowledge and political maturity needed to organise and maintain an ordered society. This was a period when "'Eritrea' was abandoned to anarchy."[11]

In turn, the earliest recorded invasion from the south overwhelmed the Beja. During the fourteenth and fifteenth centuries, groups of Hamitic Agaw from Lasta and Abyssinians from Denbya and Tigray carried out successive invasions of the Central Plateau and spread to its periphery.[12]

---

[9]   The Kingdom of Aksum, African Civilizations, pp. 225-229.
[10]   Egypt, Meroë and Axum were the only ancient African kingdoms to have developed their own written languages.
[11]   Trevaskis, G.K.N., 1960, p. 6.
[12]   Ibid., p. 6.

The Agaw invasion marked the first known northward population movement from present-day Ethiopia to modern Eritrea, while the immigration of the Abyssinians signified the first return of groups of descendants of the Axumites to the original home of their ancestors. The latest arrivals to the territory, the Rashaida, are Bedouin Arabs who migrated from the Arabian Peninsula and settled on the Eritrean (and Sudanese) Red Sea coast in the late 1860s.[13] Their migration into the African side of the Red Sea coincided with the Italian advent in the Bay of Asseb and the start of the colonial conquest of Eritrea.

Along with the waves of invasions, periodic movements, and continuous intermingling, three distinct language groups have evolved, reflecting the racial roots of the Eritrean people: Nilotic, Hamitic, and Semitic. The Semitic group comprises the Tigrinya (48 per cent of the total population), the Tigre (35 per cent), and the Rashaida (1 per cent). The Hamitic group comprises the Afar (4 per cent of the total population), the Saho (3 per cent), the Bilen (2 per cent), and the Hidareb (2 per cent). The Nilotic group comprises the Kunama (3 per cent of the total population) and the Nara (2 per cent).[14]

Attesting to the broader impact of historical migrations and population movements, the three language groups also exist outside Eritrea scattered around six countries in the region. The Cushitic (Hamitic) group embraces the Afar

---

[13] Young, William C., The Rashayida Arabs vs. the State: The Impact of European Colonialism on a Small-Scale Society in Sudan and Eritrea, Journal of Colonialism & Colonial History, Baltimore: Fall 2008, Vol. 9, Issue 2.

[14] Ibid., p. 3

in Djibouti and Ethiopia; the Agaw, the Saho, the Hadiya, the Kambata, the Gedeo, and the Oromo in Ethiopia; the Somali in Djibouti, Ethiopia, Somalia, and Kenya; and the Oromo in Ethiopia and Kenya. The Nilotic group embraces the Kunama, the Gumuz, and the Manjangir in Ethiopia; and the Annuak and the Nuer in Ethiopia and South Sudan. The Semitic group embraces the Amhara, the Tigrinya, the Gurage, and the Harari in Ethiopia; and the Tigre in the Sudan.[15]

In addition to the heritage of three racial and language groups, Eritrea is home to three religious communities, namely, Animist,[16] Christian, and Muslim, which have coexisted for millennia, for the most part, in peace and harmony. The Tigrinya are 93 per cent Christian and 7 per cent Muslim (*Jeberti*). The Bilen are 30 per cent Christian and 70 per cent Muslim. The Afar, Hidareb, Nara, and Rashaida are entirely Muslim. The Saho are 97 per cent Muslim and 3 per cent Christian (*Irob*). The Tigre are mostly Muslim, with a small Christian minority (*Mensae*). The Baza or Kunama are mostly Muslim and Animist, with a small Christian minority.[17]

2.2 A Glimpse at Pre-Colonial History

The people and territory of Eritrea existed long before the advent of Europe and the Europeans in Africa. Archaeologists

---

[15] Adejumboli, Saheed A., 2007, p. 8.
[16] Animism is an indigenous religion with a set of monotheistic beliefs but without the formal hierarchies and rites of Christianity and Islam practiced among a small minority of the Kunama people in southwestern Eritrea.
[17] Pateman, Roy, 1990.

20

have found evidence of one of the oldest pre-human presences and human habitation in contemporary Eritrea, dating back to the eighth millennium BC.[18] The name Eritrea derives from the Greek word for Red, Ἐρυθράς *(Eruthros)*.[19] The territory of modern Eritrea formed the "core" of the Axumite Empire which "attained its greatest power from the fourth to the sixth centuries"[20] A.D. and extended across present-day Ethiopia, northern Sudan, southern Egypt, southern Saudi Arabia, Yemen, Djibouti, and northwestern Somalia.[21]

Adulis, situated south of Massawa on the Gulf of Zula at the geographic middle of Eritrea's Red Sea coastline, was the Kingdom of Axum's principal port and main trading centre. During the seventh century A.D., the power and influence of Axum "declined as a direct consequence of the Arab invasion of Egypt" which forced the Hamitic Beja tribes of eastern Egypt and northern Sudan to move southwards and push their kinsmen already in the Northern Highlands and the Barka Lowlands on to the Central Highlands.[22] The Beja invasion, followed by the expansion of Islam into the coastal areas and the destruction of Adulis in 710 A.D., cut off Axum from access to the sea, disrupted its vital maritime trade and

---

[18]   History of Eritrea, http://www.eritrea.be/old/eritrea-history.htm

[19]   The Erythrean Sea, in Greek, Ἐρυθρά Θάλασσα means the Red Sea. The Periplus Erythrean Sea, Περίπλους τῆς Ἐρυθράς Θαλάσσης or Periplus Maris Erythrea, was a handbook for ancient navigation attributed to Ptolemaic or Roman Egypt.

[20]   Trevaskis, G.K.N., 1960, p. 5.

[21]   Turchin, Peter and Jonathan M. Adams and Thomas D. Hall: East-West Orientation of Historical Empires, University of Connecticut, November 2004 http://www.eeb.uconn.edu/people/turchin/PDF/Latitude.pdf

[22]   Trevaskis, G.K.N., 1960, p. 5.

led to the decline of its civilisation that had thrived for about 800 years. The loss of Adulis and the Red Sea littoral to nascent Islam forced the Christian Axumites to withdraw southwards to the isolation of their highland bastions.

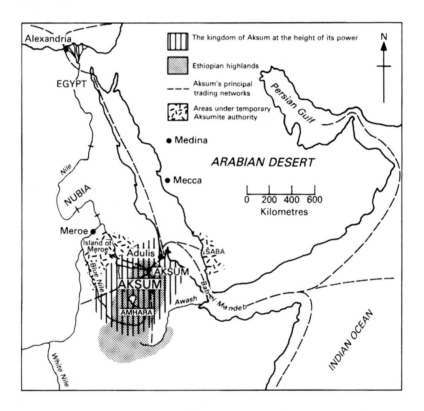

Map 2: Ancient Axum (A.D. 100-700) *History of Africa,* Kevin Shillington, p. 69 (2005)

Located at the core of this region of rich history and diverse cultures, Eritrea has for millennia, been at the crossroads of migrations, invasions, civilizations, and commerce, both within northeast Africa and between northeast Africa, the northeastern Mediterranean basin, Asia Minor, Arabia Felix, and Persia. Its history has been characterised by "constant migrations - immigrations from without and migrations from place to place within the country."[23] The Erythrean Sea served as the main conduit of trade for the Phoenicians, Greeks, Romans, Turks, and Persians with the region as well as with civilisations further east on both flanks of the Arabian Sea and the Persian Gulf.[24]

Furthermore, the region has seen extended, if discontinuous and sporadic, periods of local suzerainty with expanding or contracting dominions and shifting borders, varying degrees of dominance, and constantly changing epicentres of power in what is today Eritrea, Ethiopia and the Sudan. Over the thirteen centuries, from the fall of the Kingdom of Axum to the advent of the European colonial era, powerful kingdoms that rose and fell in today's northern Ethiopia or eastern Sudan carried out invasions, made incursions or established intermittent rule over large areas in modern day southern, western or northern Eritrea.

Yet, none of these kingdoms managed to establish full control over the entire territory of present day Eritrea. Nor did any of them represent a continuity of the Kingdom of Axum in terms of territory, political system or lineage, despite the convenient myth of the Solomonic dynasty, perpetuated by whoever occupies the Abyssinian throne and a compliant

---

[23] Nadel, S.F., *Land Tenure on the Eritrean Plateau*, Africa: Journal of International African Institute, 1946, 16(1), p. 2. http://www.jstor.org/pss/1156534

[24] Almedom, Astier M., Re-reading the Short and Long-Rigged History of Eritrea 1941-1952: Back to the Future, *Nordic Journal of African Studies* 15(2): 103–142 (2006), p. 105. http://www.njas.helsinki.fi/pdf-files/vol15num2/almedom.pdf.

feudal aristocracy. The pre-colonial history of Eritrea actually records the history of fragmented constituent regions, on the one hand, and the history of the scramble of external forces for their control and domination, on the other. Thus, aside from the Ethiopian claim verging on legend, no contemporary state in the region today can justifiably claim to be the direct heir of the old Axumite Kingdom.

At the time when the 'Amhara kingdom of Abyssinia'[25] emerged in today's northcentral Ethiopia in 1270, "six and a half centuries" after the downfall of Axum, "the whole of Eritrea was still under the Beja confederacy."[26] For another six centuries, from the emergence of Abyssinia to the eve of the Italian conquest, much of the territory of contemporary Eritrea stayed largely fragmented. The Barka Lowlands, the Northern Highlands, and the Coastal Plains were subjected to Funj or Turkish domination.

During much of this extended period in the region's pre-colonial history, from the fifteenth to the eighteenth centuries, the Central Plateau formed the core of what was

---

[25]   The first mention of *Habesha* appears in "a Sabaean South Arabian inscription ca. 200 AD" referring to the people and territory of the Kingdom of Axum. http://www.urbandictionary.com/define. php?term=Habesha. Abyssinian or *Habesha*, in the local vernacular, is a generic term used to self-identify or to refer to the Semitic-speaking peoples of Eritrea and Ethiopia. Broadly, it includes the Tigre and Tigrinya in Eritrea and the Amhara, Gurage, Harari and Tigrinya in Ethiopia. Abyssinia also refers to Ethiopia prior to the nineteenth century or parts of Eritrea and Ethiopia or, narrowly, to the people and territory of the Eritrean and Ethiopia plateaux today.

[26]   Yohannes, Okbazghi, Eritrea: A Pawn in World Politics, University of Florida Press, 1991, p. 30.

variously known as the *Medre Geez* (the Land of the Free), the *Medre Bahri* (the Land of the Sea), or the *Mereb Mlash* (Beyond the Mereb).[27] It enjoyed sovereignty under the rule of the *Bahre-Negasi* (King of the Sea).[28] Despite recurring and reciprocal incursions across the Mereb, the Eritrean highlands and the western and coastal lowlands remained separate from Abyssinia.[29] The Scottish explorer James Bruce, who set out from Massawa to trace the source of the Blue Nile in Lake Tana in 1770 reported that the "*Medre-Bahri* and Abyssinia were distinctly separate political entities constantly at war with each other."[30]

Later writers also attest that the *Medre Bahri* existed as an independent entity essentially autonomous of, and in continuous conflict with, Abyssinia. This was particularly the case during the most relevant epoch of the last century and a half of the pre-colonial period. This spanned Abyssinia's *zemene mesafint*, or 'the era of the princes' (1769-1855), and the reigns of the three architects of modern Ethiopia – the emperors

---

[27] Pateman, Roy, Eritrea: Even the Stones Are Burning, Red Sea Press, 1990. [Author's note: The Mereb River separates a part of the central Eritrean plateau, the *Kebessa*, from the Ethiopian region of Tigray and forms part of the natural as well as the 1900 Italo-Ethiopian colonial treaty border between present-day Eritrea and Ethiopia.]

[28] Haile, Semere, *Historical Background to the Ethiopia-Eritrea Conflict*, The Long Struggle of Eritrea for Independence and Constructive Peace, Lionel Cliffe and Basil Davidson (eds.), The Red Sea Press, Trenton: NJ, 1988, p. 12-13.

[29] Reid, Richard, *The Trans-Mereb Experience: Perceptions of the Historical Relationship between Eritrea and Ethiopia*, Journal of Eastern African Studies, 2007, 1:2, p. 246.

[30] Yohannes, Okbazghi, 1991, p. 31.

Tewodros, Yohannes, and Menelik,[31] during which "the area of modern-day Eritrea was clearly autonomous from, if not wholly independent of, any central government to the south."[32]

The region of the Trans-Mereb, linked by primordial relations of common ethnicity, culture and traditions, shared "a history of violence and warfare". Moreover, "war and 'rebellion' in Tigray often spilled across the Mereb and necessarily involved the Eritrean highlands, where local rulers would take refuge from imperial armies dispatched from the 'Abyssinian' heartland;" but "the area north of the Mereb was one over which more powerful rulers further south had no lasting control."[33] The pre-colonial history of the region from the early sixteenth to the late nineteenth centuries was however, marked not only by conflict with the south but also by the encroachment of hostile forces in the east hailing from a faraway place beyond the sea.

Ottoman Turkey seized Massawa and the northeastern coastal plains in 1557. Subsequently, it invaded the central plateau, the heartland of the *Medre Bahri* and occupied it "for twenty years until driven out during the last quarter of the sixteenth century."[34] The Ottomans maintained firm control over Massawa and its environs under the autonomous authority of the *Naib*, the hereditary local 'Lieutenant or Deputy of the Sultan' of Constantinople,[35] and posed a

---

[31] The three kings dominated Abyssinia's central and northern regions from the mid-1850s to the early 1900s.
[32] Reid, Richard, 2007, 1:2, pp. 240-241, referencing Pateman (1990) and Haile (1988).
[33] Ibid., p. 243.
[34] Ibid., pp. 32-34.
[35] D'Avray, Anthony, Lords of the Red Sea: The History of a Red Sea Society from the Sixteenth to the Nineteenth Centuries,

constant threat to the *Medre Bahri* until their replacement by the Egyptians. Having occupied the Barka Lowlands and the Gash-Setit Basin and established the military garrison in Keren, *khedivate* Egypt extended its authority to Massawa and the coastal areas by 1872.[36]

Keenly aware of the geopolitical imperative, the *Bahre-Negasi* made shifting alliances with their co-religionist Christian Abyssinian rulers, or the Ottoman Turks and their Muslim vassals in the coastal plains. They were able to ward off constant threats to the political or cultural survival of the *Medre Bahri* from the east or the south and maintain their autonomy by helping sustain a favourable regional balance of power. *Bahre-Negasi* Issak, for instance, supported the Abyssinians when besieged in their highland strongholds by invading Muslim forces hailing from the Sultanate of Adal and "made a significant military contribution to the defeat of Ahmed Gragn (Ahmed ibn Ibrahim al-Ghazi) in the sixteenth century."[37] On another occasion, he enlisted the support of the forces of the *Naib* for his invasion of Tigray in 1578.[38]

For the most part, the *Medre Bahri* was largely able to fend off attacks from the south and east and maintain its uneasy autonomy. Massawa and the northeastern coastal plains remained under successive Turkish and Egyptian domination for over three and half centuries prior to the advent of the Italians. Prior to the Turkish encroachment, the southeastern coastal plains of Denkel had constituted

---

Wiesbaden, Harrassowitz, 1996, p.4.

[36] Trevaskis, G.K.N., 1960, p. 7.

[37] Yohannes, Okbazghi, 1991, p. 31.

[38] Pollera, Alberto, The Native Peoples of Eritrea, Red Sea Press, 2001, p.48.

part of the Sultanate of Adal, which included modern Djibouti, parts of present day Somalia and the northeastern region of today's Ethiopia from 1415 to 1555.[39]

The decline of the Funj Empire (1504-1821) in the Sudan, which dominated today's northern and western Eritrea as well, enabled *khedivate* Egypt, driven by the desire to control the headwaters of the Nile River and the vital trade routes of the Red Sea, to expand southwards and seize eastern Sudan. Using Kassala as a base, it occupied the Gash-Setit Basin and the Bogos region in the mid-1880s.[40] Having secured its hold over Massawa and these areas, Egypt set its sights on the Central Plateau and coveted Abyssinia itself. The same year, Yohannes, a Tigrayan chieftain, became emperor of Abyssinia and set his sights on the Central Plateau and the Red Sea coast as well. Egypt and Abyssinia were thus set on a 'collision course' over what is today Eritrea.[41]

Their forces collided in the Central Plateau, or the *kebessa*, the core of the old *Medre Bahri*. The short but bloody confrontation between Egypt and Abyssinia for control of Eritrea unfolded at a time when the region faced internal fragmentation and external encroachment. On the eve of the Italian conquest, Egypt set out to scale the eastern escarpment while Abyssinia, using a stratagem that combined military incursion, fuelling local rivalry and outright deception, invaded across the Mereb and established tenuous control over the *kebessa*.[42]

---

[39]   Trevaskis, G.K.N., 1960, p. 7-8.

[40]   Longrigg, Stephen H., A Short History of Eritrea, Oxford Clarendon Press, 1945.

[41]   Trevaskis, G.K.N., 1960, p. 7.

[42]   Resistance from Raesi Welde-Mikael of Hamasien, Dejach Bahta Hagos of Akele Guzai, Fitewrari Kiflu of Seraye and Kentiba Hamid

In the process, Egypt and Abyssinia turned the Central Plateau into a battlefield and fought pitched battles in Gindae (1874), Gundet (1875) and Gurae (1876) for control of Eritrea.[43] Decisive Abyssinian victory led to a brief domination of the Central Plateau. With their contest overtaken by the Sudanese Mahdist rebellion in the west and the Italian incursion in the east, however, neither Egypt nor Abyssinia was able to establish permanent occupation or impose its hegemony over the Eritrean plateau or the entire territory of Eritrea.

Nevertheless, Eritrean and Ethiopian narratives render conflicting and often "polemical and polarised" readings and analyses of the early history of Eritrea and the nature of the relationship between Eritrea and Ethiopia prior to the Italian conquest.[44] The Ethiopian narrative uses pre-colonial history to "demonstrate Ethiopia's historical control over the region of Eritrea - and in particular the Red Sea coast", while the Eritrean narrative uses it to "challenge this 'Ethiocentric' interpretation and prove the long-standing 'independence' of the region."[45]

The Mereb, Belesa and Muna Rivers which bound the southern flank of the Central Plateau form only the central sector of the border between contemporary Eritrea and Ethiopia. The Central Plateau forms only part of Eritrea. Hence, breaching the Mereb-Belesa-Muna divide and brief

---

of Habab and peasant revolt hindered Yohnnes' effective control of the central plateau.

[43] Longrigg, Stephen H., 1945, pp. 32-35.

[44] Reid, Richard, The Trans-Mereb Experience: Perceptions of the Historical Relationship between Eritrea and Ethiopia, Journal of Eastern African Studies, 2007, 1: 2, 238-255, p. 239.

[45] Ibid., p. 239-240.

military occupation of the central plateau does not constitute *historical control over Eritrea or the Red Sea coast.* The short-lived Ethiopian military encroachment across the Mereb-Belesa-Muna bore absolutely no geopolitical significance to the Coastal Plains, the Western Lowlands, or the Northern Highlands of Eritrea, which remained largely under Egyptian control. Otherwise, there was neither the permanent occupation of the territory of Eritrea nor the absorption of its identity by the invaders from south of the Mereb-Belesa-Muna divide, attesting to the contentious character of the pre-colonial Ethio-Eritrean relationship.

Accordingly, Ethiopia's more recent claims, even in the context of the abortive Ethio-Egyptian military contest for control of the territory of present-day Eritrea on the eve of the Italian conquest, are tenuous at best. Abyssinia was at no time prior to the European colonial scramble for Africa during the last quarter of the nineteenth century in control of the entire territory of modern-day Eritrea or of contemporary Ethiopia. Nor was Eritrea an integral part of Ethiopia, as the two countries did not exist as such during the pre-colonial history of the region.

During the early period of the European colonial scramble for Africa, resurgent Abyssinia was both a victim and a perpetrator of colonial aggression. Having warded off Italian aggression in 1895-96, it expanded through wars of conquest in collusion and rivalry with the European colonial powers to occupy and subjugate historically non-Abyssinian territories to assume its present formation. Menelik, the King of Shoa who succeeded Yohannes as Emperor of Abyssinia in 1889, invaded and annexed Oromia, Harar, Wellega, Wellamo, Jimma, Kaffa, and Gommu and doubled "the territory under his control, occupying as many areas as were seized by the European powers in the scramble for territories in the northeastern region."[46]

Menelik signed the Treaty of Wichale with Italy in 1889 whereby, among other things, Italy "officially recognised Menelik as emperor of Abyssinia and also granted his state duty-free privileges for any goods passing through the port of Massawa."[47] Menelik showed no interest in the territory 'Beyond the Mereb'. He connived with the Italians, who proceeded to occupy the Plateau and colonise Eritrea with his approval.[48] At the same time, Menelik adroitly exploited European rivalry and ambitions in the region to procure modern arms, acquire territories, and secure diplomatic recognition. The European scramble for Africa thus coincided with the emergence, territorial expansion, and political consolidation of the Abyssinian Empire.

In brief, modern Eritrea constituted the core of the Axumite Kingdom. The collapse of Axum, however, irrevocably severed the territory of Eritrea *per se* from any enduring association with the political entities that periodically sprang up, thrived or declined to its south, including Tigray with which the Central Plateau shares close ethnic, linguistic, and cultural affinity. In the main and for the most part, Eritrea remained a fragmented region, often partly autonomous and partly dominated. Legend aside, the Eritrean Red Sea coast had existed independent of Ethiopia from the fall of Axum to the late nineteenth century, as a

---

[46] Adejumboli, Saheed A., The History of Ethiopia, Westport, Connecticut & London: Greenwood Press, 2007, p. 28. http://mindseyedub.com/Ethiopia.pdf

[47] Ibid., p. 29.

[48] Trevaskis, G.K.N., 1960, p. 8.

region of contention or a battleground of rival foreign forces (Beja, Funj, Turkey, Egypt, and Abyssinia).

On balance, therefore, the historical record contests the general Ethiopian claims of control and Eritrean assertions of independence as being untenable, "as no state prior to the 1890s resembled the polities called by those names (Ethiopia and Eritrea) today."[49] In any case, the region's pre-colonial history cannot undo the reality of a well-developed and distinctive Eritrean national identity, detract from the legitimacy of the case for Eritrean independence, or undermine the authenticity of contemporary Eritrean statehood. Indeed, history affirms that the modern states of Africa, including Eritrea and Ethiopia, as geopolitical entities, are products of the European colonial project sanctioned by the Berlin Conference.[50]

2.3 Advent of Italian Colonial Rule

Jomo Kenyatta, the first Prime Minister and President of independent Kenya, is credited with the following famous statement:

> *When the Missionaries arrived, the Africans had the Land and the Missionaries had the Bible. They taught how to pray with our eyes closed. When we opened them, they had the Land and we had the Bible.*[51]

---

[49]   Reid, Richard, 2007, p. 240.

[50]   See for example, Tesfagiorgis, Gebre H. "Approaches to Resolve the Conflict Between Eritrea and Ethiopia," in ERITREAN STUDIES REVIEW, Vol. 3, No.2, Special Issue, 1999," pp. 39-165.

[51]   Tyehimba, Ras, Of Land and Injustice: The Colonial Legacy of Kenya. http://www.africaspeaks.com/kenya/20082006.html

As in many parts of Africa, missionaries were the precursors of colonial conquest in Eritrea and land was the prime target of the Italian project of settler colonisation. Italian settlement in Eritrea was conceived and pursued as a solution to the perennial population pressure in southern Italy and Sicily, in particular. With its Mediterranean-like hospitable climate, Eritrea was billed to serve as a territorial extension of Italy in Africa and the fertile land expropriated from its rightful owners to create space for Italian immigrant settlers. As in Zimbabwe, Kenya and South Africa, the people bitterly resisted dispossession, for Eritreans have a deep attachment to ancestral or communal land as an inalienable birth right, a basis of identity and a source of livelihood.

The opening of the Suez Canal in 1869 transformed the Red Sea into a major maritime route linking Europe with the Middle East and the Far East, without having to navigate around the Cape of Good Hope. This lent the Red Sea a new strategic significance and fuelled Anglo-French competition for its control. Britain held sway over its northern gateway through its Egyptian Protectorate and took hold of Aden while France set a foothold in Obock (today's Djibouti). Britain and France faced each other across the Strait of Bab el Mandeb at the southern entrance to the Red Sea. In the context of the growing Franco-British rivalry for hegemony over the Red Sea and its strategic commercial lanes, the British prodded Italy to occupy Eritrea.[52]

Italian invasion of Eritrea followed the arrival of Roman Catholic missionaries in Massawa and Asseb and their penetration of the hinterland. An Italian missionary, Father Giuseppe Sapeto, implored Italy to establish a presence "on

---

[52]   Trevaskis, G.K.N., 1960, p. 8.

the vital sea route" and arranged the purchase of the Bay of Asseb, nominally by the Rubatinno Shipping Company, from the local Sultan for 8,100 Maria Theresa dollars in November 1869.[53] He fixed similar deals with the Sultan of Rahaita in 1879 and 1880 to include the areas adjacent to Asseb Bay, and the company transferred the enlarged territory to the Italian state in 1882.[54] Having thus initiated its colonial venture in Africa, Italy concluded a 'treaty of peace and friendship' with Mohamed Hanfire, the Sultan of Asseb, on 15 March 1883.

Italian troops occupied Asseb and Beilul, some 40 km further north, in January 1885 and, egged on by the British to forestall French expansion into the region from their foothold in Djibouti, proceeded to take over Massawa from the Egyptians without a fight in the beginning of February 1885.[55] Three weeks later, on 26 February 1885, the newly concluded Berlin Act formally recognised Italy's claim to Eritrea.[56] Yet, it took the Italian army another four years of sporadic fighting and heavy losses to traverse the narrow coastal plains, scale the steep eastern escarpment of the Central Plateau, and subdue the entire territory.

Italian effort to extend control from the coastal strip around Massawa into the hinterland faced stiff resistance and suffered disastrous setbacks, most notably at Dogali, 30 km inland, on 26 January 1887. An Abyssinian force under the command of Raesi Alula, the chief of the general staff of Emperor Yohannes' army, ambushed and virtually decimated

---

[53] Longrigg, Stephen H., 1945, pp. 112 – 113.
[54] Ibid., p. 113.
[55] Ibid., p. 113.
[56] Almedom, A., 2006, p. 106.

an Italian battalion sent to reinforce the embattled fort at Saati. The toll: 430 officers and men, including their commander, Colonel De Cristoforis, killed and 110 wounded.[57]

Despite suffering serious setbacks initially, the invading Italian army eventually prevailed and managed to advance into the hinterland, conquering the central plateau and the western lowlands by the end of 1889. Subsequently, Italy formally proclaimed Eritrea into being on the 1st of January 1890 as its dominion, with Massawa as its capital. Thus, Italy established its first-born (*primo genito*) African colony under the name of Eritrea just twenty years after the capture of Rome on 20 September 1870 concluded its own unification (*il Risorgimento*) into a nation state and barely five years after the Berlin Conference.

Italy set out to consolidate its stranglehold over the colony through ruthless suppression of all opposition. The resistance and revolts against Italian colonial rule, while heroic, were mostly localised, largely uncoordinated and routinely crushed. The last and most serious challenge to confront Italy's colonial project in Eritrea was the notable revolt led by *Dejazmach* Bahta Hagos. Declaring that "the Italians curse us, seize our land; I want to free you... let us drive the Italians out and be our own masters,"[58] he led an insurgent force of 1,600 men and rose up to avenge the

[57] Finaldi, Giuseppe, *Italy's Scramble for Africa from Dogali to Adowa* in John Dickie, John Foot & Frank M. Snowdon (edts.) Disastro! Disasters in Italy since 1860: Culture, Policy and Society, PALGRAVE™, New York, 2002, p. 81-82.

[58] Caulk, Richard, *Black snake, white snake: Bahta Hagos and his revolt against Italian overrule in Eritrea, 1894,* in Donald Crummey, *Banditry, Rebellion, & Social Protest in Africa,* African Writers Series, Heinemann, 1986.

"rights trampled on by the Italians".[59] The death of Bahta Hagos at the celebrated Battle of Halay on 19 December 1894 marked the defeat of the rebellion. It also signified the end of organised armed opposition to the Italian occupation of Eritrea.

Superior military technology and organisation enabled the Italian army to crush the resistance and colonise Eritrea. However, local opposition and sporadic resistance to the Italian occupation continued unabated. To stabilise its domination, Italy incarcerated, on the notorious prison island of Nakura in the Dahlak Archipelago, executed, exiled to Italy, or simply made to disappear hundreds of Eritrean notables and patriots who opposed or defied its colonial rule.[60]

Not satiated with the conquest of Eritrea, Italy invaded Ethiopia. Its attempts to extend its dominion across the Mereb-Belesa-Muna divide into Ethiopia were, however, thwarted by its disastrous military defeats at Emba Alaje (December 1895) and Adwa (March 1896) in Tigray. The great victory at Adwa, in particular, where a defending African army decisively crushed an invading European army, represented "the first major African victory over a European country since Hannibal's time two thousand years earlier."[61]

---

[59] Pankhurst, Sylvia, *Eritrea on the Eve: the Past and Future of Italy's 'first-born' colony, Ethiopia's Ancient Sea Province*, New Times and Ethiopia News Books, Walthamstow Press Ltd., Walthamstow, 1952

[60] Kidane, Aida, an Eritrean researcher, has documented the names of 300 Eritrean political prisoners in Nakura who were executed, incarcerated or exiled by the Italian colonial regime during the 'pre-1900' period alone. *The Prisoners of Nakura*, 19 February 2001. http://www.ehrea.org/PrisonerNakuraCentury.pdf.

[61] Harris, Joseph E., Africans and their History, Revised Edition, New American Library, New York and Scarborough, Ontario: 1987, pp.

The historic victory shocked Europe, caused the collapse of the Italian government in Rome and helped secure, along with the rivalry among Britain, France and Italy in the Horn of Africa, Ethiopia's independence and the grudging recognition of its sovereignty by Italy and the major European colonial powers.

2.4 The Colonial Legacy

Following the Italian conquest, a series of treaties signed between Italy, on the one hand, and Ethiopia, France and Great Britain, on the other, delimited Eritrea's borders at the turn of the nineteenth century.[62] These colonial treaty borders have remained essentially unchanged except for

---

176-177. It must be stated in deference to historical fact, however, that the first great victory of an African army over a European army, after Hannibal's, occurred about a decade earlier when the Sudanese Mahdist army routed General Gordon's British colonial army in Khartoum, at the confluence of the Blue and White Niles, in January 1885. Unlike the case for Ethiopia, however, the absence of European rivalry for the colonial domination of the Sudan allowed the British to eventually subdue the Mahdist resistance and establish the Anglo-Egyptian Condominium of the Sudan by September 1898.

[62] Eritrea's boundary with Ethiopia was defined by the Ethio-Italian treaties of 1900, 1902 and 1908. Eritrea's boundary with Djibouti was defined by the Franco-Italian Protocols of 1900 and 1901, the Franco-Ethiopian Convention of 1897, the Franco-Ethiopian Protocol of 1954 and the Franco-Ethiopian Additional Protocols of 1954 while the 1935 Franco-Italian Treaty was not ratified by France. Eritrea's boundary with the Sudan was delimited by the Anglo-Italian agreements of December 1898, June 1899, April 1901, and November 1901 and the Anglo-Italian-Ethiopian agreement of May 1902.

the duration of Benito Mussolini's short-lived Italian East Africa, or *Africa Orientale Italiana*, when the inclusion of Tigray and most of Wello in Ethiopia greatly expanded Eritrea, and the revisions wrought by the Eritrea-Ethiopia Boundary Commission in 2002.[63]

Italian colonisation gave Eritrea its present geopolitical formation, bringing together a hitherto fragmented territory and diverse population under a single central administration. In doing so, it unleashed new social forces. The experience of common oppression under alien rule led to the development of a distinctive Eritrean national identity and a shared psychological makeup.[64]

Italy amalgamated nine nationalities, or ethnic groups, three religious communities, and three distinct topographic regions into a single colonial entity under a unified imperial administration. Once it secured its conquest of Eritrea, it established a centralised colonial state with extremely repressive machinery to administer, control and exploit the country. Having entrenched its stranglehold, it set out to modernise the colony to prepare it for Italian settlement and to use its strategic location as a launching pad for its wars of colonial conquest in Africa. Ports, a railroad, roads, hotels, schools, hospitals, factories, etc., were built and Eritrea served as a springboard (and Eritreans as cannon fodder) for the invasion of Ethiopia, Libya, and Somalia.

---

[63] See Chapter 17 of this book.

[64] For a detailed treatment of Eritrean national identity and right to independence, see, Tesfagiorgis, Gebre H., "Self-determination: Its Evolution and Practice by the United Nations and Its Application to the Case of Eritrea," in WISCONSIN INTERNATIONAL LAW JOURNAL, Vol. 6, No. 1, Fall 1987, pp.75-127.

Like the British in Kenya or Southern Rhodesia (Zimbabwe) or the Boers in South Africa, Italy set out to create a settler colony in Eritrea. Declaring land as *terra domeniale* or State property, it expropriated large tracts of land in total disregard of indigenous land rights to settle poor farmers from southern Italy.[65] Immigrant settlers established concession farms and plantations on the most fertile lands, taken away from their rightful owners without compensation. The manner, scale, and repercussions of land expropriation for use by Italian immigrant settlers in violation of indigenous Eritrean land rights was the subject of complaint even by the Italian Governor, Ferdinando Martini, recorded in the colonial government's 1913 annual report:

> *In my previous report I did not conceal the serious consequences of the hasty appropriations of land by the State and particularly of those lands which were taken without any account being taken of local customary rights. Native opinion cannot understand how the Government is able to appropriate lands which have always been private property.*[66]

All land formally belonged to the colonial state by 1926, effectively disenfranchising the people. Immigration into the colony was encouraged and the number of Italian settlers in

---

[65] Italy declared nearly half of the territory of Eritrea *terra domeniale* through land laws issued in 1909 and 1923. Land in traditional Eritrean society belonged to the people, either privately owned by an extended family (*risti*) as in the Central Plateau or collectively claimed by a clan as in the other parts of the country. The Italians introduced *diessa* in many villages in the Central Plateau, changing family ownership of land to communal village ownership

[66] Quoted in Trevaskis, G.K.N., 1960, p. 54.

Eritrea grew from 3,949 in 1905 to 76,000 in 1939, comprising 10.3 percent of the total Eritrean population of 740,000 at the time.[67] As land constituted the source of livelihood for virtually all Eritreans, dispossession forced much of the population into wage labour and military conscription.

With the influx of Italian settlers came architects, engineers, artisans, farmers, etc. They drew up master plans, designed structures, and used cheap Eritrean labour to build modern transport and communication facilities; construct laboratories, hotels, quarries, mines and irrigation projects; and establish shoe and textile factories, concession farms, and food and beverage processing plants. Experimenting with modernist, avant-garde style architecture banned in Italy under the fascist regime, they invested Asmera with some of the finest and most beautiful designs creating "one of the highest concentrations of Modern architecture in the world."[68]

Between 1936 and 1941, Italy's Fascist rulers transformed Eritrea into one of the most industrialized, modern colonies in Africa. [...]Asmara became an Art Deco laboratory during the 1930s for designs that seemed, well, just too out there for mainland Italy. Rationalism, Novecento, neo-Classicism, neo-Baroque and monumentalism are among the varied avant-garde styles played with here. The result today is hundreds of aging, sherbet-coloured buildings.[69]

---

[67] Podestà, Gian L., L'emigrazione italiana in Africa orientale http://www.ilcornodafrica.it/rds-01emigrazione.pdf.

[68] Denison, Edward, RenGuang Yu and Gebremedhin, Naigzy, Asmara: Africa's Secret Modernist City, Merrell, London and New York, 2003, p.16.

[69] Jeoffrey Gettleman The New York Times Media Group, Eritrea's Surreal Mix of War and Art Deco, International Herald Tribune, 8

The Italians introduced state-of-the-art urban design, city planning and construction, bequeathing Asmera with superb art deco designs, modernist architecture and magnificent structures. This signified Benito Mussolini's dream of building a second Roman Empire and symbolised Rome's *civilising mission* in Africa. Asmera, which replaced Massawa as Eritrea's capital in 1897, stood out as an ideal model of a well-planned modern city featuring impressive architecture, with its beautiful villas and graceful mansions, pedestrian pavements, wide boulevards lined with indigenous *shibakha* and palm trees, paved streets, piazzas, boutiques, bars, restaurants and cafés. It could boast of "more traffic lights than Rome did when the city was being built".[70]

These remain enduring relics of the fascist phase of Italian colonial legacy in Eritrea. A recent publication, *Asmara: Africa's Secret Modernist City*, presents a brief history of the city and an impressive pictorial review of its main modernist buildings. Despite the loss of their 'lustre and shine' to the attrition of 'time, weather and neglect', Eritrean government sponsored exhibitions occasionally showcase photographs of Asmera's modernist architecture abroad.

Italy also built a modern transport infrastructure in Eritrea. The construction of the road and railway network linking the port city of Massawa to Asmera, and westwards to Keren, Agordat and Tesseney (road) and Bisha (railway), with its magnificent scenery, sharp curves, nerve racking

---

October 2008.

[70] Santoianni, Vittorio, *Il Razionalismo nelle colonie italiane 1928-1943 La «nuova architettura» delle Terre d'Oltremar* (Italian Architectural Planification of Asmara), 2008, p. 64-66 http://www.fedoa.unina.it/1881/1/Santoianni_Progettazione_Architettonica.pdf

switchbacks, picturesque bridges and breath-taking tunnels, remains a living testament to the marvels of the feat of Italian engineering and Eritrean labour. Massawa harbour and its facilities were considerably modernised. In addition, the Italians built a 75-km long aerial tramway, the Asmera-Massawa Cableway (*La Teleferica Massaua-Asmara*), which "in one leap more than doubled the commercial traffic between the sea and the interior."[71]

Eritrea's rapid transformation facilitated the colonial control of territory, the settlement of Italian immigrants, and the conquest of new colonies. It catered to the military requirements of rapid and efficient mobility, logistics and supply for the Italian invading army. It also enabled the extraction of raw materials, the exploitation of resources, and the provision of amenities to the colonial military and civilian elite, and the increasing number of Italian settlers.

The railway, the roads and the cableway enabled the fast movement of war materiel, supplies, and food for the colonial army and the growing Italian settler community as well as the rapid transport of troops, arms and provisions from Massawa to the interior. They also facilitated the logistic preparations for the 1935 invasion of Ethiopia. Following the conquest of Ethiopia, a state-of-the-art asphalted road linked Asmera with Addis Ababa, the new capital city of *Africa Orientale Italiana*, via both Gonder and Dessie, and onwards with Mogadishu, Somalia. A similar road linked Eritrea's southern port of Asseb with Addis Ababa via Dessie.

---

[71] La Teleferica Massaua-Asmara http://www.trainweb.org/italeritrea/teleferica1.htm

But, the "racist and exploitative" nature of the colonial system that treated "Africans as inferior to Europeans"[72] ensured the exclusion of Eritreans from the benefits of modernisation. The Italian colonial regime enacted racial laws aimed to ensure the separation of the races, grant special privileges to Italian settlers, espouse white superiority, and discriminate against Eritreans and other indigenous Africans in the colony. In the 1930s, it introduced the first system of racial apartheid on African soil in Eritrea. Under the policy of strict racial segregation, the much applauded and prided edifices of the fascist era in Asmera, for instance, were all located in the European sections of the city. They were reserved for the exclusive service of the 53,000 Italian residents out of the capital's total population of 98,000.[73]

Confined to the crowded, sprawling slums with their narrow and dirty alleys in the 'native' quarters without proper health and sanitary services, Eritreans had no access to tap water, private toilet or sewerage facilities.[74] These poor districts in the capital continue to languish in a similar state of neglect, want, and decay to this day.[75] The fact that the entire city suffers from frequent and prolonged power outages and water supply stoppages has compounded the situation for the residents of the slums.

---

[72] Davidson, Basil, 1989, p. 5.

[73] 1939 Italian Census on Eritrea http://www.italyrevisited.org/photo/Migration_and_Immigration/world/1/page20

[74] Eritreans were pejoratively referred to as the 'natives' by both the Italian and British colonizers.

[75] The Transitional Government torpedoed a German aid project worked out with the Municipality of Asmera in 1994 to rebuild one of the city's major slum areas, Aba Shawl.

Otherwise, located on the crest of the Central Plateau, on the northwestern rim of the Great African Rift Valley, Eritrea's capital city enjoys perennial spring-like weather and year-round mild temperature averaging 16^0 Celsius. At an altitude of 2,450 metres, Asmera stands out as the capital city with the highest elevation in Africa. It took the Italians barely six years (1935-41) to build the now widely acclaimed former European quarters of the city through the efficient combination of Italian architectural and engineering knowhow and Eritrean labour and materials, other than the "Portland cement and reinforcing iron bars."[76] Regarded as the jewel in the crown of Italy's East Africa Empire, Asmera was nicknamed *Piccola Roma,* or Little Rome, for the Italianate façade of many of its buildings.[77]

The establishment of the colonial state, the construction of public works, the development of physical infrastructure, the building of new industrial structures, the installation of factories, and the ensuing Eritrean acquisition of basic vocational skills through on-the-job apprenticeships were some of the tangible benefits accruing from Italian colonialism in Eritrea. Moreover, Italy introduced urban amenities, a modern lifestyle and the quintessential Italian staple of pasta, albeit with limited access for Eritreans. These unintended residual benefits of 'Rome's civilising mission in Africa' were however, accompanied by an awful legacy of colonial oppression, economic exploitation and racial

---

[76] Gebremedhin, Naigzy, Asmara, Africa's Modernist City, Paper prepared for the African Perspectives: Dialogue on Urbanism and Architecture, The Faculty of Architecture, TU, Delft 6-8 December 2007.

[77] Vittorio Santoianni, 2008.

subjugation that treated Eritreans as inferior, second-class citizens in their own country.

Further, countless young Eritrean men were uprooted from their homes and forcibly conscripted to serve as *askari* (soldiers) in the Italian colonial army. In the 1930s, a staggering "40 per cent of the male Eritreans able to fight were enrolled in the colonial Italian army."[78] Italy used poorly trained Eritrean *askari* as cannon fodder in its wars of invasion against Somalia, Libya and Ethiopia. With the alignment of Italy with the Axis Powers after the outbreak of the Second World War, Eritrean *askari* also served in the war against British forces in Somaliland, Kenya, and the Anglo-Egyptian Condominium of the Sudan.

Compiled aggregate figures on the grand size of the Eritrean contingent of the Italian colonial army and the total figure of Eritrean casualties sustained fighting Italy's colonial wars in Africa are hard to come by in the public domain. However, patchy data indicate that hundreds of thousands of *askari* fought in the Battle of Adwa and in the conquests of Somalia, Libya, and Ethiopia, during the period between the mid-1890s and 1941. About 150,000 *askari* served in the Italian colonial army during the 1935-41 occupation of Ethiopia,[79] with 60,000 deployed, and 5,000 killed in the initial invasion alone.[80]

---

[78] History of Eritrean Ascari (in Italian) http://www.italiaeritrea.org/africus/dasaro/dasaro_sfilarono.htm

[79] Schroeder, Gunter, The Eritrean Economy in Historical Perspective, presentation at a conference on Eritrea's Economic Survival, Royal Institute of International Relations, London, 20 April 2007 http://www.chathamhouse.org/sites/default/files/public/Research/Africa/200407eritrea.pdf

[80] Nicolle, David, The Italian Invasion of Abyssinia 1935-36, Osprey Publishing Ltd, Oxford, 1997

Around 60,000 Eritreans fought and built infrastructure during the Italian invasion of Libya from 1911 to 1932. The death toll of Eritrean and Ethiopian *askari* in the Battle of Keren in the spring of 1941 was 9,000.[81] In all, tens of thousands of Eritrean *askari* perished in Italy's military campaigns in Africa.

Adding insult to injury, Eritrean soldiers serving in the Italian colonial army suffered from racial discrimination and inequality. Maltreatment of the *askari* was particularly harsh after the rise to power of Mussolini's fascist regime in 1922. Often forced to take "the lead during the attacks" and fighting with "great valour" in the battlefield, discrimination denied the *askari* any positions of responsibility and barred them from rising to the ranks of commissioned officers.[82]

Further, the *askari* endured brutal treatment, physical assault, and verbal abuse because of their skin colour on a daily basis. Colonial repression and the colour bar however, worked as a double-edged sword. The common experience of ill treatment and humiliation based on race and colour stirred a kind of 'solidarity of the oppressed', thus cementing their awareness of unity in suffering and sharpened their distinctive shared national identity as Eritreans.

Colonial education, as one of the tools of imperial Europe's 'civilising mission' in Africa, often aimed to "produce graduates needed for the colonial bureaucracy."[83] This was especially the case with British and French colonial

---

[81] Rovighi, Alberto, *Le Operazione in Africa Orientale*, Vol. 1, Officio StoricaSME, Rome, 1995, p. 256; *Gli Italiani in Africa Orientale*, Vol. 3, p. 433.

[82] Ibid., p. 435.

[83] Langohr, Vickie, Colonial Education Systems and The Spread of Local Religious Movements: The Cases of British Egypt and Punjab http://faculty.virginia.edu/mesp/Langohr-paper.pdf

schooling in most of their overseas territories. Italian colonial education in Eritrea, however, represented an exception to the norm set by its British and French counterparts in most of their African colonies. Italy deliberately denied the Eritrean people access to modern education and technology and sought to hold them in a state of subjugation through an institutionalised policy that fostered ignorance and isolation.

During its first three and half decades, Italian colonial rule denied Eritreans any access to public education, preferring to keep them illiterate and innumerate. A few Italian Catholic and Swedish Protestant missionary schools provided private education. After the introduction of public education in the 1920s, schools operated under rules of strict racial segregation and restriction of access for Eritreans beyond the fourth grade. The regime not only denied Eritreans opportunities to basic education but it also closed "the only schools which aspired to more normal standards" in 1932.[84] At the height of Mussolini's East Africa Empire at the turn of the 1930s, there were "only 20 schools for Eritreans" with a total enrollment of "4,177 students".[85]

The limited schooling offered aimed to teach rudimentary knowledge of the Italian language and the story of prominent Italians, train basic skills, and produce menial workers. There was nothing in the curriculum for Eritreans about Eritrea and the Eritrean people or the rest of the world. Colonial education aimed to glorify Italian history and civilisation,

---

[84] Ibid., p.33.

[85] These shools were run by the Swedish Evangelical Mission. See: Eritrea - History & Background http://education.stateuniversity. com/pages/434/Eritrea-HISTORY-BACKGROUND.html.

teach Eritreans to say *si* (yes) and *babiene* (OK), and groom
obedient local servants. The Director of Education, Andrea
Festa, in a confidential directive to Italian headmasters in
Eritrea in 1938 stated that:

> *By the end of the fourth year, the Eritrean student should*
> *be able to speak our language moderately well; he should*
> *know the four arithmetical operations within normal limits;*
> *he should be a convinced propagandist of hygiene; and of*
> *history he should know only the names of those who have*
> *made Italy great.*[86]

Italy's early defeat in World War II cut short the exclusive
enjoyment by the colonial officials and Italian immigrant
settlers of the much-celebrated public works, structural
vestiges and cultural relics of the fascist era. Whatever
residual benefits accrued to Eritreans were merely marginal
and totally unintended. The fascist policy of stringent
separation of the races kept the modern facilities and urban
amenities strictly off limits to Eritreans, who laboured to
build them with much blood, sweat and toil at very low
wages.

In brief, Italian colonial rule carved up Eritrea, forged
a centralised colonial state and created a vibrant modern
economic sector. In the process, it released new social
forces, helped create a new *Eritrean-ness* with an awareness
of a common condition and a distinctive shared identity
that evolved to transcend ethnic, religious or regional
affiliations. An Eritrean national identity started to take
root and Eritrean nationalism began to emerge in reaction

---

[86]   Trevaskis, G.K.N., 1960, p.33.

to Italian colonial domination. The stern system of racial subjugation imposed under Mussolini's fascist *Second Roman Empire* operated to accelerate and cement that process.

2.5 Fall of Italian Colonial Rule

Italian colonial rule lasted from 1890 until 1941, when Allied forces under British command invaded Eritrea via the Anglo-Egyptian Sudan and eventually defeated fascist Italy's army in East Africa. British victory had, in the eyes of the long victimised Eritreans, deflated the pompous vanity of Italian fascism and shattered Italian prestige. Fed by decades of maltreatment and harsh racial discrimination, deep-seated Eritrean resentment set in motion a new political dynamic that degraded the political, economic and social status of the Italians in Eritrea.

During the war, the British had spread 'promises' for a free Eritrea flying its own 'national flag' via "leaflets sprinkled by the RAF," urging Eritreans and the *askari*, in particular, to abandon their posts, rise up against the Italian oppressors and collaborate with the Allies in favour of freedom.[87] The promises stirred hopes of liberation and raised expectations of independence. Among other things, they induced 6,000 Eritrean *askari* to forsake their units in Keren. The sizable show of 'disloyalty' provoked an enraged Italian command to disband forty Eritrean battalions.[88] Although most remained loyal and fought bravely and well until Italy's final surrender, the desertion and dispersal of large numbers of Eritrean

---

[87] Wrong, M., 2005, p. 98.
[88] Steer, George L., *Sealed and Delivered: A Book on the Abyssinian Campaign*, London: Hodder and Stoughton, 1942, p. 175.

askari helped lower Italian morale, weaken their defences, and ensure a very narrow but extremely significant victory for the Allied Forces in Keren.

Won "by a hair's breadth" and secured "within a whisper of calling off the assault",[89] the victory ended Italy's occupation of Eritrea, Ethiopia and Somalia; dismantled Mussolini's East Africa Empire; marked a turning point for the Allies in the entire East and North Africa theatre; and shaped the course of combat that determined the outcome of the global war. Crucially, it helped secure British control of the Nile Basin, the Suez Canal, the Strait of Bab el Mandeb and, therefore, the vital shipping lanes of the Red Sea, and proved decisive for Allied fortunes in North Africa, the Middle East, the Far East, and Europe.[90] The Battle of Keren had, indeed, reverberated far and wide and catapulted the hitherto little known Eritrean town into world-historic prominence, immortalised in the dreaded memories of its survivors.

Surrounded by stunningly picturesque, rugged and undulating mountain peaks, Keren lies at the intersection of Eritrea's varied topographic regions and the crossroads of its diverse cultures. Approached from the west, as the Allied forces initially did, the town's location represents an impregnable natural fortress guarding the gateway to Asmera at the peak of the Central Plateau, with the winding road along the narrow Tunkulahas gorge as the only path of access. The stakes were thus very high, the confrontation fierce, the fighting resolute and the toll in human life quite heavy. "The regiments and battalions sent to fight in Keren [...] were the

---

[89] Wrong, 2005, p. 95
[90] Steer, 1942, p. 183.

best Italy could muster" and delivered "Italy's most spirited performance in the Second World War".[91]

Both sides battled hard. For British veterans of the Eritrea Campaign who also fought "in the deserts of North Africa, the streets of European cities and the jungles of Burma" during the war, "the fighting in Keren was the most dreadful they ever experienced.[92] 'Physically, by World War II standards, it was sheer hell. NOTHING I met in nine months as a company commander in NW Europe compared with it.'"[93] In a *do-or-die* contest that lasted 54 days (2 February-27 March 1941), both sides fought well and sustained heavy losses, "more than 50,000 casualties"[94] in total including 3,120 Italian and about 9,000 Eritrean and Ethiopian *askari* killed.[95]

An Italian naval officer later attested to the importance of the battle of Keren for the overall Allied effort in East and North Africa and the particularly stiff resistance mounted in the city's defence: "The battle of Keren ... was one of the best episodes of the Italian military history. The Italian and *Askari* battalions initially managed to repel Gen. Platt's divisions fighting with great decision and effectiveness."[96] He asserts that strenuous Italian and *Askari* resistance in Keren, aided

[91] Wrong, 2005, p. 88

[92] Ibid., p. 82

[93] Major John Searight of the Royal Fusiliers, in a post-war letter quoted in Michela Wrong, 2005, p. 82.

[94] Wrong, 2005, p. 95

[95] Rovighi, Alberto, *Le Operazione in Africa Orientale*, Vol. 1, Officio StoricaSME, Rome, 1995, p. 256; *Gli Italiani in Africa Orientale*, Vol. 3, p. 433.

[96] Marino, Lt CDR Francesco (Italian Navy), Military Operations in the Italian East Africa, 1935-1941: Conquest and Defeat,

by the nature of the terrain that hampered the effective use of British artillery, tanks and aviation, seriously compromised the entire British strategy in the Mediterranean. He ascribes the eventual collapse of the Italian defences of Keren to exhaustion and lack of provisions.

In Marino's words: "Fifty days of privations of food, rest, and supply resulted in a breakdown of Italian defensive line," led to the easy conquest of Asmera on the 1ˢᵗ of April, and the seizure of Massawa on the 8ᵗʰ of April, thereby neutralising "the Italian fleet in the Red Sea" and achieving "the British strategic objective of East Africa."[97] Adequate logistics, supplies and reinforcements could, perhaps, have prolonged the confrontation and dented the momentum of the Allied war effort in the Africa theatre. Nevertheless, it is highly improbable that they could have affected the ultimate outcome of the battle or the war.

Thirty-six years later, Keren was the scene of yet another decisive battle, this time the locus of a gruelling confrontation between the forces of Eritrean liberation and Ethiopian occupation. In a brilliant seventy-two hour operation (5-8 July 1977), the Eritrean People's Liberation Army (EPLA) completely encircled and routed a much larger Ethiopian army. For the first time in the history of the armed struggle, the EPLA captured seven battlefield tanks and several heavy artillery and mortar pieces.

Based mainly on conversations with Ibrahim Afa, the chief architect of that splendid victory, the author and Ahmed Baduri narrated the planning and execution of

---

USMC Command and Staff College, 15 April 2009, p. 22. italian Navy

[97] Ibid., p. 22-23.

the operation in Vanguard.[98] A former marine cadet of the Ethiopian Navy and trained in Cuba after joining the ELF, Ibrahim[99] was a member of the political bureau and standing committee, secretary of the military committee, and head of the Department of Military Training of the EPLF. Effectively, he was the chief of the general staff and the principal military strategist of the EPLA until his killing in 1985 during the Ethiopian seventh or stealthy offensive (*selahta werar*).

The second Battle of Keren was comparatively brief. It was, however, as intense and potentially as momentous as the first. It took place at a time when the Eritrean armed struggle was making steady progress in 'liberating the land and the people step by step'. At that crucial juncture, the triumph in Keren signified the consolidation and expansion of the EPLA's consecutive earlier victories in Karora, Nakfa, and Afabet in January, March, and April of 1977, respectively, and marked an important milestone in the Eritrean war of national liberation.

---

[98] Eritrean People's Liberation Front, *Reportage: The Battle of Keren*, Vanguard, Official Monthly Organ, August 1977, Volume II, No. 5, pp. 13-21. [Vanguard was published in Tigrinya, Arabic and English. At that stage, Ahmed wrote in Arabic and I wrote in Tigrinya. Together, we translated the Arabic articles into Tigrinya and vice versa, as neither of us could work alone in the other language. When we finished the reciprocal translation, Ahmed edited the Arabic version while I did the Tigrinya version and translated it into English for simultaneous publication and internal and external distribution from Fah, the EPLF rear base in Sahel in the Northern Highlands of Eritrea.]

[99] In Eritrea, we use the first name, Ibrahim, in this case; and the surname only for purposes of full identification.

There was a striking similarity in the significance of the two events, joined in space but separate in time. In as much as the earlier Allied victory heralded the demise of Italy's imperial rule in Africa, the later EPLA victory signified the probable demise of imperial Ethiopian occupation of Eritrea. Were it not for the massive Soviet-led intervention in support of the Ethiopian counter-offensive that followed in mid-1978, the Eritrean victory in Keren would have spelled the defeat and imminent termination of Ethiopian domination of Eritrea.

The first Battle of Keren paved the way for Eritrea to serve as a strategic rear base of air and naval logistics for Allied operations against Rommel's German Africa Corps in the crucial battles of El Alamein (Egypt) and Tobruq (Libya) until the German surrender in North Africa in May 1943.[100] According to Michela Wrong's lucid rendition:

> *Eritrea's surrender freed up the troops Wavell desperately needed... to fight Rommel. Had Keren not fallen when it did, British morale, bruised by Dunkirk and the Blitz, might never have recovered. Its conquest was a small but crucial part in turning the tide of the Second World War, from a position where a vast Nazi empire seemed a certainty to a point where Allied victory was for the first time conceivable.*[101]

Most of the casualties of the war for East Africa, mainly fought and principally decided in Keren, were Eritreans: tens

---

[100] The Battle of El Alamein http://www.historylearningsite.co.uk/battle_of_el_alamein.htm
[101] Wrong, 2005, p. 97

of thousands perished in combat or as collateral damage of allied aerial and artillery bombardments. However, the epic battle "was plotted, planned and ultimately capitalised on in the capitals of Axis and Allied powers."[102] Eritrea was merely a 'proxy location' of the crucial campaign in the 'great fight' between the forces of global fascism and liberal democracy on African soil. Once the war was over, the Allied Powers, having used it as a significant cornerstone in the construction of their victory, abandoned, betrayed, and subjected Eritrea to further European occupation. As the next chapter describes, the British in particular, had condemned the territory and its people for disintegration.

---

[102]   Ibid., p. 81.

CHAPTER 3

A Plan to Dismember Eritrea

Ethnically disunited and economically non-viable, there is no good reason for preserving it (Eritrea) as an administrative unit... The right solution would seem to be to dismember it along its natural lines of cleavage. - British draft resolution, UN General Assembly, May 1949

In treating the former Italian colony as an occupied enemy territory and placing it under military administration, the British reneged on their wartime promise to help free Eritrea. British rule (1941-1952) featured systematic attempts to divide the country, plunder its assets, impede its development, and destroy its identity. The period 1945-50, in particular, was one of great turbulence and severe 'stresses and strains' that brought Eritrea to the brink of chaos, tested the unity of its body politic, and threatened its very survival as a united territory.

Concomitantly, it was a transformative period characterised by the rise of political awakening, a new opportunity for self-expression, and a licence for organised partisan activity. It witnessed persistent Eritrean aspirations for self-determination and demands for independence. Yet, the combination of British machinations and Ethiopian interference, abetted by the betrayal of the Big Powers, thwarted Eritrea's legitimate claim to decolonisation. Unfortunately, the outcome sowed the seeds of long-term conflict, insecurity, and instability that continue to haunt the peoples of Eritrea, Ethiopia, and the Horn of Africa to this day.

3.1 British Military Occupation

Despite the wartime promises that had generated popular expectations for delivery from foreign domination, the British placed Eritrea, along with Ethiopia and Somalia, under Occupied Enemy Territory Administration (OETA). Sir Philip Mitchell, a South African-born and Africa-veteran British colonial official, ran the OETA from Nairobi, Kenya.[103] Freedom for Eritrea was not part of the British agenda in waging the war in East Africa and it soon became clear that the British had no intention to honour their initial pledge. To the dismay of the Eritrean people, the chain of events revealed that the calculus of the strategic goals fought for in the war did not entertain their wishes or consider their interests. Far from liberation, the British design aimed to dismember Eritrea, divide the Eritrean people, and erase Eritrean national identity.

There is a telling anecdote in Eritrea about a British captain who, following the decisive victory of the Allies in Keren, met an old woman on the road while leading his company of

---

[103] Vestal, Theodore M., *Consequences of the British Occupation of Ethiopia during World War II*, Rediscovering the British Empire, Barry Ward (eds.), Melbourne, FL: Krieger, 2001. http://fp.okstate.edu/vestal/ BookReview/consequences____.htm.

soldiers on the march along Mussolini's Imperial Way toward Asmera. In Eritrean custom, ululation is a celebration of joy marking the occasion of a significant family or social event. The elderly woman, garbed in traditional dress, greeted the column of soldiers on the march with spontaneous ululation, celebrating the victory in anticipation of deliverance from Italian subjugation. The captain rudely interrupted the jubilant woman "in mid-flow" with a one-liner: "I didn't do it for you, nigger".[104] The officer's cynical riposte epitomised the British attitude towards Eritrea and the Eritrean people at the time.

With its surrender, Italy lost its colonies in the Horn of Africa. In a stroke, the sun set forever on Mussolini's crumbling new Roman Empire. British occupation was formalised as part of the spoils of war. However, it retained the "fascists in high office;" maintained the "fascist colour bar intact;" and sanctioned the continued display of the sign, "*Vietato per Nativi*" (Prohibited for Natives), "over the front doors of Cafés, cinemas, restaurants and hotels." It "divided Eritrea's populace by ethnicity, religion, region, language and locality, in order to divide and rule;" and "committed grave injustices against the Eritrean people."[105] It also retained the racial system of separate hospital beds for Eritreans and Europeans.[106] "To the inhabitants of Eritrea, the change in regime brought little apparent change in the system of government."[107]

---

[104]   Ibid., p. 99

[105]   Pankhurst, E. Sylvia, as quoted in Assfaw Berihun, Sylvia Pankhurst: Citizen of the World (undated), pp. 11-13. http://www.ethiosun. com/sylviapank.pdf.

[106]   Four Power Commission Report, p. 72-74.

[107]   Trevaskis, 1960, p. 29.

Placing Eritrea under military occupation displayed a cynical betrayal of trust, initiating the first in a long series of international betrayals of Eritrea and its people that were to follow suit in the future. Stephen Longrigg, Chief Military Administrator, admitted that much in his first annual report on the Occupied Enemy Territory of Eritrea when he stated that the British inability or unwillingness to keep their promise was a cause of complaints by the 'natives', in a sniping reference to the Eritreans:

> *We had unfortunately made promises or half-promises before the occupation which we have been unable (or not always willing) to implement, thereby giving the natives some grounds for complaints.*[108]

However, the worst was yet to come in the plan to partition Eritrea, as the next section illustrates.

3.2 The British Partition Plan

Not content with occupation, the British government schemed to divide Eritrea. In a step that revealed marked contrast between word and deed, the British conceived and strove to put in place a plan whose implementation would have made Eritrea "disappear as a political unit completely from the map."[109] The plan essentially aimed to split Eritrea

---

[108] Longrigg, Stephen H., Half Yearly Report by the Military Administrator on the Occupied Enemy Territory of Eritrea: From the Period 1st January to 30th June 1942, Asmara: Eritrea, July 29, 1942, p. 6-7.

[109] Longrigg, Stephen H., 1945, Preface.

between Ethiopia and the Anglo-Egyptian Sudan, mainly but not exclusively, along sectarian and regional lines.

Globally, a major shift in the international balance of power was underway. The Axis Powers were losing the war. Within the Allied camp, the might of the British Empire was waning while the United States of America (USA) was rising to the pinnacle as the new world power. In Eritrea's immediate neighbourhood across the Red Sea, Saudi Arabia and North Yemen were independent states while South Yemen remained under British occupation. On the African side, Djibouti was under French control, the then Anglo-Egyptian Condominium of the Sudan was effectively a British colony, and Ethiopia had only recently been liberated from Italian occupation and subsequently put under British tutelage.

The original idea of the plan was to divide Eritrea into three parts.[110] Incorporate the predominantly Muslim inhabited Western Lowlands, Northern Highlands, and northern third of the Coastal Plains into the Anglo-Egyptian Sudan. Unite the predominantly Christian inhabited Central Plateau, the mostly Muslim inhabited central Coastal Plains, and the port of Massawa with a Tigray 'state or province', 'administered by a European power' under the 'nominal sovereignty of the Emperor', and cede Denkel and the port of Asseb to Ethiopia. An initial variant envisaged retention of British control over the capital of Asmera and main port city of Massawa linked by a corridor with Sudan.

First conceived in 1942 and adopted on 18 May 1943, the partition plan was the brainchild of a certain British Committee on Ethiopia. Chaired by Lord Moyne, Deputy

---

[110]   Ibid., pp. 174-5.

Resident Minister of State in Cairo, the committee included Colonel Stephen Longrigg, Military Administrator of Eritrea, Mr. Robert G. Howe, British Ambassador to Ethiopia, and General William Platt, Commander of Allied Forces during the Eritrea Campaign.[111] The scheme underwent subsequent modifications of detail but retained its central feature of dismembering Eritrea until it became official British policy in April 1946. The British tabled it for resolution during the third session of the UN General Assembly in May 1949 as follows:

> *Ethnically disunited and economically non-viable, there is no good reason for preserving it (Eritrea) as an administrative unit under any form of administration, whether under Individual Trusteeship or restored Italian rule. The right solution would seem to be to dismember it along its natural lines of cleavage.*[112]

World War II in the European theatre formally ended on 8 May 1945. The leaders of the three victorious powers, Winston Churchill, Joseph Stalin, and Harry Truman, met in Potsdam, Germany, from 17 July to 2 August 1945. They agreed to establish a council of foreign ministers comprising the three countries plus France and China with a mandate to conclude a peace treaty with Italy and decide the future of its former colonies. The Council of Ministers held its first meeting in London from 11 September to 2 October 1945

---

[111] Tesfai, Alemseged, Aynfelale, 2001, p. 42-45.
[112] The Secretary of State for Foreign Affairs, Memorandum to the British Cabinet, 18 April 1946, p. 14, British National Archives (BNA).

and its second meeting in Paris from 25 April to 16 May 1946. The British formally proposed the plan to partition Eritrea at the Paris meeting of the Council of Ministers.

Inability to resolve differences over the colonial question and competing national ambitions over the former Italian possessions protracted the negotiations on the terms of a peace treaty with Italy. Reached on 10 February 1947, the agreement came into effect on 15 September 1947. The treaty provided for Italy's renunciation of title to its former colonies and their joint disposal by the Four Powers within one year. In the event that the council of ministers failed to agree, they would refer the matter to the UN General Assembly for resolution.

As the council could not agree, it sent a Commission of Inquiry to the territories to "ascertain the wishes of the local population" and report on the "political, economic and social conditions in each colony."[113] The Four Power Commission visited Eritrea from 12 November 1947 to 3 January 1948 and its report "revealed a sharp difference of opinion between the British and Americans, on one side, and the Russians and French, on the other."[114] As the discord persisted, the Four Powers abandoned the effort to reach agreement and, on 15 September 1948, referred the matter to the United Nations for decision.

The peace treaty transformed Italy from an 'enemy' into a 'co-belligerent' country and allowed it a voice in the disposal of its former colonies. In the beginning, Italy strongly opposed the British plan to partition its oldest colony and, instead, advocated immediate independence for

---

[113]   Four Power Commission Report 1948, Appendix 1.
[114]   Trevaskis, G.K.N., 1960, p. 89.

Eritrea. Nevertheless, it ultimately agreed, in a *volte-face*, to back the partition plan as a *quid pro quo* for British support for a proposal to grant Italy trusteeships in Somalia and Tripolitania.[115] Subsequent to the 10 May 1949 agreement between the British and Italian foreign ministers, Ernest Bevin and Carlo Sforza, to co-sponsor the proposal during the fourth session of the UN General Assembly, the project became the Bevin-Sforza Plan.

The Bevin-Sforza Plan proposed a composite resolution on the disposal of the former Italian colonies. It proposed to grant independence to Somalia after a period of ten years of Italian trusteeship; to grant independence to Libya after a period of ten years of trusteeship, with the three provinces of Tripolitania, Cyrenaica and Fezzan placed under Italian, British and French trusteeships, respectively; and to partition Eritrea between Ethiopia and the Sudan. The First Committee adopted the resolution, jointly sponsored by Britain and Italy. In considering the draft composite resolution on 17 May 1949, the UN General Assembly voted first on the proposal for each territory and then on the resolution as a whole.

Voting on the proposal for each territory, the UN General Assembly adopted the proposal to partition Eritrea with 37 in favour, 11 against and 10 abstentions. It adopted the proposal to grant Libya independence after 10 years of trusteeship with 48 in favour, 10 against and 1 abstention; the sub-proposal to establish British trusteeship over the Libyan province of Cyrenaica with 36 in favour, 17 against and 6 abstentions. It also adopted the sub-proposal to establish French trusteeship over the Libyan province of Fezzan with

---

[115]   Trevaskis, G.K.N., 1960, p. 93.

36 in favour, 15 against and 7 abstentions.[116] However, the proposal to place Somalia under Italian trusteeship and the sub-proposal to establish Italian trusteeship over Tripolitania, which had triggered anti-Italian riots in the Libyan province, fell short of one vote to obtain the required two-thirds majority.[117]

The separate rounds of voting resolved the disposal of Eritrea and the two Libyan provinces of Cyrenaica and Fezzan but left the fates of Somalia and the third Libyan province of Tripolitania pending. Under the circumstances, the General Assembly decided to disregard the outcome of the separate balloting and reconsider the resolution on the disposal of the former Italian colonies as a whole. Accordingly, it reconsidered the Bevin-Sforza Plan as a package and rejected it, with 37 votes against, 14 in favour and 7 abstentions.[118]

The defeat of the Bevin-Sforza plan spared Eritrea dismemberment by a fateful single vote: that of the delegate of Haiti cast in opposition to the proposed Italian trusteeship in Somalia and Tripolitania. Crucial as it was for the retention of Eritrea's territorial unity, however, the rejection of the Bevin-Sforza plan *per se* advanced neither the country's prospects for immediate decolonisation nor its people's legitimate aspirations for independence. It merely postponed the issue of the disposal of Eritrea and kept its fate uncertain. Nor did it make the British give up the partition plan, kept in reserve, as 'Plan B' should the UN reject the

---

[116] UN General Assembly, 17 May 1949. http://www.un.org/documents/ga/res/3/ares3.htm.

[117] Ibid.

[118] Ibid.

pending draft resolution for the federation of Eritrea with Ethiopia.[119]

A UN Commission, comprising delegates from Burma, Guatemala, Norway, Pakistan, and South Africa, was subsequently set up to review the question of Eritrea and propose a solution for the future of the country taking the following three considerations into account:

> (a) *the wishes and welfare of the inhabitants of Eritrea, including the views of the various racial, religious and political groups of the provinces of the territory and the capacity of the peple for self-government; (b) the interests of peace and security in East Africa; and (c) the rights and claims of Ethiopia based on geographical, historical, ethnic or economic reasons, including in particular Ethiopia's legitimate need for adequate access to the sea.*[120]

The contradictions inherent in the terms of its mandate constrained the work of the UN Commission on Eritrea. Consequently, its report failed to reconcile the conflicting interests of the Four Powers, to ascertain the real wishes of the Eritrean people, or to determine the economic viability of the territory and the capacity of its people for self-government. Actually, the Commission submitted two separate reports and three sets of proposals for a solution.[121]

---

[119]   This was agreed by the British Cabinet under Prime Minister Clement Attlee on 6 September 1950, BNA.

[120]   UNGA Resolution 289C (IV).

[121]   Report of the United Nations Commission for Eritrea, General Assembly, Official Records: 5th session, Supplement no. 8 (A/1285), 1950.

The delegates of Guatemala and Pakistan presented a joint report and proposed a ten-year UN trusteeship followed by independence, in line with the wishes of the 'great majority of the population'. The delegates of Norway, Burma, and South Africa presented a combined report and two different proposals. The Norwegian delegate proposed union with Ethiopia, except for the Western Province, which would remain under British administration and eventually allowed to decide between union with Ethiopia or the Sudan. The delegates of Burma and South Africa proposed that Eritrea 'be a self-governing unit federated with Ethiopia under the sovereignty of the Ethiopian Crown', a compromise between independence and union with Ethiopia. In the final analysis, the failure of the UN Commission to present a joint report and a single proposal on the future of Eritrea placed the matter in the hands of the Big Powers, whose divergent geopolitical interests obstructed consensus on the way forward.

3.3 British Policy of Destabilisation

As Frantz Fanon had aptly observed, the colonial system seeks to systematically destroy the "national culture" and promote a culture of 'regionalism' and 'separatism' in contest with the culture of unity of the colonised people, in the service of colonial domination.[122] In an apparent affirmation of Fanon's premise, the British drew up the plan to divide Eritrea based on ethnic, regional and religious factors. The scheme was designed to foster 'separateness', prompt the

---

[122] Fanon, Frantz, The Wretched of the Earth, New York: Grove Press, Inc., 1963, p. 73, 191.

budding national movement to resort to region/religion as a mobilising principle, and induce the formation of political parties along regional, ethnic and/or religious lines.

Having concocted the plan, the British Military Administration (BMA) schemed to define the terms of reference and drive the internal debate on the future of Eritrea in a manner designed to foster ethnic, regional and religious schisms within the nationalist movement and to prepare the ground for the partition of the country. In October 1943, the chief British military administrator announced that Eritreans would henceforth, be allowed to discuss the political affairs of their country and express opinions on its future in an organised way, spurring intense jockeying and a flurry of activities for the formation of political parties.[123]

In August 1944, Brigadier Longrigg authored an ingenious article under the guise of an Eritrean Tigrinya speaking Christian highlander and had it translated and published in the BMA-run Tigrinya weekly, *Semunawi Gazetta*.[124] The article depicted Eritrea as intricately divided between two main regions, peoples and cultures: the highlands inhabited by Tigrinya-speaking Christians and the lowlands inhabited by mostly Tigre or Arabic-speaking Moslems. Disguising the British design with the garb of Eritrean 'desires', the article opined that the lowlanders wished to unite with the Sudan with whom they share educational, commercial and religious affinity. It also opined that the highlanders wished to unite and establish one country with the Tigrayans in northern Ethiopia with whom they share ethnic, religious, cultural,

---

[123]   Tesfai, Alemseged, Aynfelale, 2001, pp. 103-104.
[124]   Semunawi Gazetta, N⁰. 3/101, August 1944.

historical, educational and traditional affinity and a common Axumite heritage.

The article aimed to prepare the groundwork for the execution of the British plan to partition Eritrea. It sought to direct national debate, and split the Eritrean body politic, along regional, religious, and linguistic lines; and drive a wedge between Highlander and Lowlander, Christian and Muslim, and Tigrinya and Tigre/Arabic speaker. It set the stage for the formation of political parties based on sub-national affiliation; and encourage the use of sectarian considerations as the underlying mobilising principle of political organisation in order to undermine national unity, divide the country, and facilitate the realisation of the partition plan.

The advocacy of a greater Tigray state and cession of western Eritrea to the Sudan was designed to sow national discord and division along sectarian lines. It targeted the unity of the Eritrean people and the territorial integrity of Eritrea. Partition would reverse the historical process of colonial state formation, undo the dynamics of the making of Eritrea, and erase Eritrean national identity. Hence, the Italians accused the British of pursuing a deliberate policy of divide and rule (*divide et impera*) in encouraging the Unionists in the Plateau and the Moslem League in the Lowlands; introducing Arabic and Tigrinya into the school system; impoverishing the territory; and promoting communal strife in the service of the partition plan.[125]

The British authorities connived to widen social divisions, incite religious friction, antagonise inter-communal relations, and poison the political climate. They undertook measures

---

[125]   Trevaskis, G.K.N., 1960, p. 78-79.

harmful to national unity and communal harmony while allowing the disruption of public order and security by failing, for instance, to prevent violence by Moslem Sudanese soldiers that targeted Christian civilians. In the same vein, reluctance to confront Ethiopian-backed armed political banditry that conducted an overt campaign of assassinations, intimidation, and threats against prominent leaders and supporters of the Independence Bloc fuelled insecurity, vitiated peaceful political contest, and stoked social tension. The uncanny mix of fostering sectarian politics and failing to prevent partisan violence aimed to stir popular indignation, incite religious animosities, and undermine the unity of the nationalist movement.

3.4 The British Pillage of Eritrea

The British Government, "together with 16 other governments of the United Nations and the French Committee had signed a formal declaration to combat and defeat Axis plundering of occupied Europe" on 5 January 1943 and "reserved all rights to declare invalid any transfers of, or dealings with, all kinds of property, rights, and interests in the Nazi-occupied territories".[126] The very same British Government, however, allowed the plunder of British-occupied Eritrea as fair game, sanctioning one set of standards for behaviour in 'Nazi-occupied Europe' and another set of standards for behaviour in 'British-occupied Eritrea'.

The BMA orchestrated the wholesale pillage and destruction of Eritrea's industries, productive assets and

---

[126] Inter-Allied Declaration Against Acts of Dispossession Committed in Territories under Enemy Occupation or Control, pp. 443-444. http://www.ushmm.org/assets/documents/usa/i-17.pdf

vital properties. In an operation described as "a disgrace to British civilisation,"[127] the British systematically plundered, dismantled and destroyed millions of US dollars' worth of Eritrean assets. They dismantled and sold industrial installations, equipment, cranes, docks, buildings, warehouses, stores, bridges, factories, machinery, ships, and facilities in Asmera, Massawa, Dekemhare, Gurae, Mai Habar, Asseb, Zula, etc.[128] What the Italians created and built in Eritrea for colonial grandeur and glory, the British looted and ruined for colonial spoils!

Notable items of loot included the Asmera-Massawa Cableway, the mobile docks in Massawa, 16 large ships, and a variety of stocks worth USD 20 m taken from stores in several cities and peddled abroad. The BMA sold a mobile dock to Pakistan for BPS 500,000, and most of the other assets to India, Pakistan, Saudi Arabia, Sudan and Yemen, and to Italian and Arab traders in the Middle East. Arguably, Eritrea could establish a reliable estimate of the total value of the pillage and reserve "all rights to declare invalid" the "transfers of and dealings with" all the properties in British-occupied Eritrea. It could lodge a legitimate claim to due compensation from the British Government for the present value of the assets lost to plunder and demolition, executed under the auspices of the British Military Administration.

The British were well aware of Eritrea's economic prospects. The *Asmera Industrial Exhibition* of 1943 advertised Eritrea's potential as a supplier of industrial goods for the

---

[127] Pankhurst, Sylvia, Eritrea on the Eve, Woodward Green, London, 1952, p.13, 15-16
[128] Tesfai, Alemseged, Aynfelale, 2001, p. 138-139.

large Middle East market. The value of Eritrea's exports grew by about 240 per cent within the next two years, from BPS 494,000 in 1943 to BPS 1,678,000 in 1945.[129] Instead of enhancing this potential, the British requisitioned "the plant and equipment essential for development"[130] and "prevented economic development as a means of furthering British hopes of partition."[131]

At the time, cotton production comprised the 'most valuable agricultural asset', while earlier prospecting had established the presence of substantial mineral deposits in Eritrea. The British purposely paralysed the agricultural, agro-industrial and mining sectors, while restricting the prospecting of gold whose extraction could have revitalised the economy. They also subverted efforts to exploit other mineral resources, and discarded the production of cotton in order to engender economic depression.[132] Making matters worse, the British imposed "heavy and severe" income, property and municipality taxes in utter disregard of the population's low and diminishing levels of income and ability to pay.[133] They also made Eritreans pay school and hospital fees and special annual contributions to help run the colonial administration.

The upshot of general plunder, destruction of industrial and transport assets, and heavy taxation represented the colonial transfer of wealth, both direct and indirect, from Eritrea to Great Britain. This, along with the engineered

---

[129] Four Power Commission Report, Appendix 64B.

[130] Trevaskis, G.K.N., 1960, p. 77.

[131] Ibid., p. 100.

[132] Ibid., p. 78.

[133] Ibid., pp. 43-45.

economic depression, led to an abrupt decline and regression of Eritrea's hitherto thriving and relatively developed modern economic sector whose foundations had been laid by the Italians. The immediate impact of the British pillage and paralysis of the Eritrean economy was mass unemployment, impoverishment and social discord.

Besides profiteering from the spoils of war, plunder served as an integral element of the overall strategy to destabilise Eritrea. Contrived decline would furnish fresh evidence of the economic unfeasibility of independence. These machinations sought to support the logic behind the partition plan. An Eritrea that was economically unviable, politically unstable and socially discordant would be an unlikely candidate for independent statehood and an easy prey for dismemberment in the malleable tribunal of international diplomacy.

The British cited the engineered economic distress, political discord, and social volatility as arguments of Eritrean weakness, and presented them as evidence of the economic and political unviability of Eritrean independence. Ironically, this happened during the twilight of the British Empire and in the aftermath of Ethiopia's liberation from Italian occupation, when 'the wind of change' for national independence was in the offing. These schemes managed to influence the shape and orientation of Eritrean political organisation and deepen its social divides. They also managed to create a misguided constituency for the union project with Ethiopia, but ultimately failed to produce support for the partition plan to split Eritrea.

A nascent nationalist movement that demanded independence for a united Eritrea, intact within its colonial treaty borders, emerged in opposition to these manoeuvres.

It articulated the popular aversion to the partition plan and hostility to the union project. The burgeoning Eritrean nationalist movement challenged British imperial interests and Ethiopian expansionist designs. Opposition to the partition plan, in particular, galvanised Eritrean public opinion in defence of a common destiny, reinforced popular awareness of a shared national identity, and catalysed the nationalist resistance movement.

3.5 Imperial Ethiopian Interference

While the Big Powers vied for Eritrea for its strategic location and treated it as a pawn in the global geopolitical chessboard, Ethiopia coveted to take possession of Eritrea primarily in order to obtain an outlet to the Red Sea. Driven by an overarching desire to gain maritime access through acquiring the whole of Eritrea, or parts thereof, Ethiopia pursued a two-pronged policy during the debate on the disposal of Eritrea as a former Italian colony. It pressed a false historical claim and demanded the 'return of its lost territory' in its entirety, on the one hand, while it gave support to the British partition plan during the 4th Session of the UN General Assembly, on the other.[134] Ethiopia even coerced the leaders of Eritrea's Unionist Party to declare their support for the partition plan before the UN Inquiry Commission,[135] without the knowledge and consent of the party's membership, in its desire to obtain a part of the Eritrean coastline.

---

[134] FO 371/73842, 20 April 1949; Tesfai, Alemseged, 2001, pp. 346-347.

[135] Tesfai, Alemseged, 2001, p. 456.

The Ethiopian and British governments worked in concert opposing Eritrean independence. Imperial Ethiopian interference in the internal affairs of Eritrea unfolded more often in collusion than in collision with imperial British intrigues. With the connivance of the BMA, Ethiopia worked to enflame religious tensions, instigate sectarian strife, and prompt social conflict in Eritrea in pursuit of territorial aggrandisement. The shared British-Ethiopian objective was to perpetuate foreign domination of Eritrea, irrespective of whether kept intact or split apart.

With the help of a small band of Eritrean collaborators, Ethiopia created, nurtured and used a vassal political movement, the Unionist Party (UP), to agitate for union with Ethiopia and subvert Eritrean aspirations for self-determination. The UP championed the Ethiopian cause and its leaders became "servants of the Ethiopian Government."[136]."[137] Its cardinal task was to subvert the independence movement and deliver Eritrea to Ethiopia in the name of union through bribery, coercion, and violence.

In pursuit of this objective, the UP collaborated in the elimination of prominent leaders and partisans of the independence movement through hired *agents provocateurs* and armed political bandits.[138] Under the cover of the UP, Ethiopia unleashed "an organised campaign of terrorism and intimidation" and assassinated eighteen supporters of the Independence Bloc (IB) between October 1949 and February 1950 alone.[139] The violent campaign of political

---

[136]   Trevaskis, G.K.N., 1960, p. 74.
[137]   Trevaskis, G.K.N., 1960, p. 74.
[138]   Tesfai, Alemseged, 2001, pp. 274-290 and 498-501.
[139]   Trevaskis, G.K.N., 1960, p. 96.

banditry aimed to decapitate the IB, paralyse its political work and terrorise the Eritrean people into submission to the Ethiopian project.[140] The campaign immersed Eritrea in a state of anarchy and, for the first time in its modern history, incited religious friction that pitted Christians and Muslims against each other, and tore neighbouring communities asunder in a general strife that engulfed much of the country and brought its people to the brink of disaster.[141]

The state of strife and insecurity caused by Ethiopian sponsored terrorism under the watch of the British was so grave that the UN Commissioner, Anze Matienzo, on mission to prepare the transition from British rule to Eritrean self-government, in accordance with the provisions of the federal resolution, had to suspend his work on 1 May 1951, stating that:

> *I do not believe it advisable to begin these consultations at a time when the population, which desires peace and security above all else, is in danger. Furthermore, I do not think it proper that I should travel about the country flying the flag of the United Nations, on roads stained with the blood of people attacked by terrorists.*[142]

---

[140] Prominent leaders of the Independence Bloc murdered included Blata Kahsay Malu (12 February 1949), Sheikh Abdelkader Kebire (27 March 1949), Asmatch Berhe Gebrekidan (16 May 1950), Azmach Abdelkader Jabir (15 June 1950), and Signor Vittorio Longhi (20 July 1950). Ato Weldeab Weldemariam survived a total of seven assassination attempts between 1947 and 1953 before fleeing the country for exile in Cairo, Egypt.

[141] Ibid., p. 109.

[142] *Progress Report of the United Nations Commissioner in Eritrea during 1951* (A/1959), p. 177.

Ethiopia found another tool in the Eritrean Orthodox Church (EOC). In abdication of its spiritual mission, the EOC acted as the 'godfather' of the UP and the nemesis of the IB by resorting to religious extortion and blackmail. Under the leadership Abuna Marcos,[143] its monasteries, churches, feast days, priests and sermons became purveyors of imperial interference and agents of Ethiopian propaganda.[144] The Church threatened excommunication and denial of "baptism, marriage, burial, communion and absolution" services to members of the IB and their families in the service of the Ethiopian cause.[145] It zealously worked to spread 'spiritual' fear and insecurity over its devout followers with the aim of inhibiting their support for the independence movement and forcing their allegiance to the unionist camp.

These adverse conditions notwithstanding, however, resurgent Eritrean nationalism firmly and consistently opposed both the British partition plan and the Ethiopian union project, and stood for the preservation of the country's territorial unity and accession to independence. The partition plan ultimately failed in the UN General Assembly by the slimmest of margins and the union project failed. Nevertheless, resolution of the question of the future of Eritrea had to wait and the legitimate demand for

---

[143] There were two main reasons for the Patriarch's avid support for union with Ethiopia. First, the Church hoped that Ethiopian rule would restore its former large land estates lost to domeniale under the Italians. Second, Abuna Marcos, who had been ordained by an Italian puppet Archbishop for his loyalty to the Italians during the occupation of Ethiopia, was anxious to retain his See as the Bishop of Eritrea and Tigray under Ethiopian rule.

[144] Trevaskis, G.K.N., 1960, pp. 59-61.

[145] Ibid., p. 96.

independence subsequently denied. The interplay of British intrigues, Ethiopian territorial ambitions and Big Power rivalry vis-à-vis the disposal of the ex-Italian colony eventually dimmed Eritrea's prospects for immediate self-determination and put the country's aspirations for decolonisation on hold.

3.6 Eritrean Aspirations for Freedom

Even after the formal substitution of Italian rule, the BMA continued to follow Italian colonial policy in Eritrea by retaining the deeply hated fascist colonial officials in office in their pre-war posts, implementing racial segregation, and perpetrating discrimination against Eritreans. The situation angered Eritreans who had expected not only to be relieved of the indignity of fascist rule but also to replace the Italians in running their country's affairs and receive equal treatment in the issuance of trade licences, grants of land and the setting up business ventures.

The maintenance of *de facto* Italian domination, with the reviled fascists holding high office and wielding real power under the BMA incensed many Eritreans. Adding insult to injury, the fascists carried out brutal acts of retribution with vengeance against Eritreans for 'disloyalty' during the war. Abusive and vindictive Italian behaviour aggravated public discontent and lent new impetus to Eritrean aspirations for self-government. Some Eritrean notables, intellectuals and businessmen responded by forming small discussion groups and organising secret meetings with the aim to defend the dignity, demand racial equality, protect the human rights and social interests of the Eritrean people, and deliberate on the future of the country.

The retention of Italian jurisdiction, courts and judges (until 1950) as well as Italian officials, carabineri and Sudanese soldiers in the police and security services under the BMA caused great popular indignation and palpable tension that led to several violent incidents between May 1941 and August 1946. Pankhurst,[146] Tesfai,[147] and Trevaskis[148] have recounted these incidents in detail. Suffice it here to mention just a few of the many such episodes.

On 4 May 1941, members of the Eritrean colonial police allowed to continue in service under the BMA sent a delegation of twenty unarmed representatives to the British police headquarters in Asmera to plead their case for the payment of arrears in salaries not received for three months prior to the Italian surrender. An Italian rather than a British officer met them on arrival and, piqued by their 'temerity' to complain and claim back pay, ordered the Italian carabineers under his command to open fire, killing one representative and dispersing the rest.

The carabineers gave chase to the fleeing police representatives and shot dead another police officer near the city centre. Angry spectators pursued the attacking carabineers and surrounded the church where they took refuge. Only the intervention of the same British soldiers, who had failed to protect the Eritrean police officers in flight, saved the predators, now turned 'prey'.

The murder of the two Eritrean police officers by Italian carabineers under the authority of the BMA caused

---

[146] Pankhurst, Sylvia, British Policy in Eritrea and Northern Ethiopia, Woodward Green, London, 1945, p. 3-4.
[147] Tesfai, Alemseged, 2001, pp. 27-36 and 65-68.
[148] Trevaskis, G.K.N., 1960, pp. 67- 68.

widespread public anger and dismay. It catalysed the secret formation of the first Eritrean quasi-political national organisation. Small clandestine groups, that had already begun to coalesce, met that evening to consider the situation and decided to establish an association forthwith. They thus set up the Association of Love of the Country of Eritrea (ALCE)[149] in Asmera on 5 May 1941 as the first collective formation in the history of Eritrea with a national scope cutting across traditional social divides.

The ALCE called for the holding of a peaceful public demonstration in protest of the killings on the same day to coincide with its own planned inauguration. More than 4,000 people demonstrated in front of the BMA headquarters. A delegation met with the Chief Military Administrator and made a firm but civil representation stating that the Eritrean people expected the British government to honour its wartime promise of freedom and independence and spare them from continued colonial domination.

In reply, Brigadier Kennedy-Cook merely stated that he had taken note of their statement and declined making direct comments on the content of the petition. He then went on to declare that the demonstration was illegal, that the protesters should disperse instantly and go home, and that there would be no such public meetings in the future without prior permit from the police. The demonstrators ignored the order to disperse and, instead, marched in an orderly and peaceful manner to all the churches and main mosque in Asmera and held prayers.

The indirect response was swift and hostile to the development of political opposition. The BMA declared

---

[149] ማሕበር ፍቕሪ ሃገር ኤርትራ (*Mahber Fikri Hager Ertra*).

a ban on protest demonstrations without 'police permit' and on any public gathering of more than two or three persons as of that day. The loose structure and naiveté of the leadership of the ALCE, whose unity began to unravel under the impact of Brigadier Stephen Longrigg's anonymous article,[150] dented its ability to mount an effective challenge to the British injunction. In addition, it lacked the clarity of perspective and political maturity to articulate Eritrean aspirations for freedom, guide the constructive development of national politics, and marshal a coherent nationalist drive towards independence.

About three months later, in August 1941, scuffles broke out between Sudanese soldiers and Eritrean civilians in Massawa, causing the death of 15 persons on both sides. Similar clashes occurred in the port city on eight and 20 January 1943, involving Eritrean police officers and civilians, Italian officers, and Sudanese soldiers and workers, resulting in 21 people dead and 20 wounded. Most of the casualties were unarmed Eritrean civilians.

The worst incident occurred in downtown Asmera on 28 August 1946. Some Sudanese soldiers got involved in an argument with a group of Eritreans. A Sudanese soldier died in the ensuing brawl. When the news reached their barracks on the outskirts of the capital, 70-armed Sudanese soldiers arrived on the scene and, in reprisal, started a shooting spree that targeted Christian Eritreans and lasted for two hours. In all, 46 civilians and 3 Sudanese soldiers died, while 70 civilians and 13 soldiers sustained injuries.

The fact that regular soldiers of the BMA could go on a shooting spree killing unarmed civilians at will for two hours

---

[150]   Teasfai, Alemseged, 2001, p. 119.

in the heart of the capital suggested British complicity and caused great consternation and bitterness. The massacre triggered considerable public indignation and brought "bitter disillusionment" with the British occupation to the fore; pushing many deeply aggrieved Christian Eritreans in the Central Plateau to view union with Ethiopia as a better alternative to "alien European rule."[151] The UP and the Church exploited the incident and the resulting grievances to the hilt to advance the unionist project.

The British authorities, who had conveniently grounded the Eritrean police just in time, apparently to disable them from reacting in defence of the unarmed victims, failed to prevent the attacks or to bring the killers to account in the aftermath of the cold-blooded murders. The massacre of innocent Christian civilians by Muslim Sudanese soldiers in the service of the British and the failure to render justice enraged Christian and Muslim Eritreans alike. Despite the wave of a 'common grief and indignation,' the incident injected religion into the political landscape and, for a fleeting moment, prompted an accord between the leaders of the nationalist and unionist factions to work for "an autonomous state within the framework of the Ethiopian Empire."[152] Apart from this 'short lived and soon forgotten' compromise, however, the incident failed to inflame religious tensions in defiance of British expectations.

The killings of unarmed Eritrean police officers and civilians by Italian carabineers and Sudanese soldiers infuriated many Eritreans and generated deep resentment of British rule. The fact that justice was not done in any of the

---

[151] Trevaskis, G.K.N., 1960, p. 68.
[152] Ibid., p. 74.

wrongdoings made the negative repercussions worse. The religious overtones of the Sudanese incident, in particular, had divisive ramifications that helped to strengthen sectarian tendencies in the nascent Eritrean political movement.

A brief survey of the main political developments in Eritrea in the 1940s would be incomplete without mention of the revolutionary events that shook the very foundations of feudal society in the Northern Highlands, the Western Lowlands, and the Northeastern Plains. A harsh system of semi-pastoral serfdom forced the masses of Tigre peasants and nomads to pay onerous taxes, dues and tithes to traditional chiefs of aristocratic *Shumagle* families.[153] The Italian colonial administration had tried to mollify serf uprisings since the 1920s, when the Tigre of Biet Almeda in Sahel had refused to pay taxes to Biet Asgede chiefs, through petty reforms.[154]

The revolt resumed in 1941 when Tigre serfs of Ad Teklies refused to pay the traditional tithes and taxes to the chiefs and demanded complete emancipation. Their determination to put an end to the old relations of production that allowed the exploitation of the majority by a tiny minority set a profound social upheaval in motion. The uprising gained momentum, embraced all the Tigre clans in Sahel and, after the December 1945 peace agreement that ended the 1942-45 Beni Amer-Hidareb conflict, spread to Barka, Senhit and Semhar, unifying the 90 per cent of the Tigre serfs against the 10 per cent aristocratic families in a systemic resistance to serfdom.[155]

---

[153] The chiefly families include the Deglel of the Beni Amer, the Kentibay of the Habab, the Shum of the Maria Tselam and Maria Keyah, and the Naib in Semhar.

[154] Tesfai, Alemseged, 2001, pp. 69-74.

[155] Trevaskis, G.K.N., 1960, p. 71-72.

The revolt posed a dilemma for the British. Letting the uprising run its course promised real emancipation that would undermine the colonial system while forcible suppression risked violent revolt that would threaten administrative control. In the end, the British decreed an 'incongruous compromise' that allowed the chiefs and *shumagle* to 'retain their political authority' but made the payment of serf 'dues and services' voluntary.[156] This proved unworkable and failed to stem the surging tide of the popular desire for freedom and eventually forced the British to agree to the demand to resurrect the old Tigre tribes and clans as a way of dismantling the chiefly privileges rather than radically reforming the system.

The struggle for emancipation had a significant impact on the evolution of Eritrean politics. The Tigre serfs gained unity and solidarity in a common yearning for freedom while the chiefs and *shumagle* found unity in mutual defence of their old privileges. The conscious pursuit of their conflicting interests would lead these two rival forces to align themselves with opposite political camps during the formative years of the struggle for independence. The serfs furnished the main political support base of the Moslem League while the chieftain families supported the UP.

3.7 Formation of Political Parties

The BMA lifted the ban on political activity and allowed freedom of expression in October 1943,[157] officially allowing the formation of political parties in October 1946, after

---

156   Ibid., p. 71.
157   Tesfai, Alemseged, 2001, pp. 103-104

the decision of the Four Power Commission to investigate the wishes of the Eritrean people regarding the future of Eritrea.[158] This encouraged open debate on the future of the country and catalysed the initiation of political associations. Yet, British scheming and Ethiopian interference induced internal rifts that led to the split of the ALCE into rival political camps: pro-independence and pro-Ethiopia. The BMA initially favoured the pro-Ethiopia forces and granted them permission to organise while denying similar permission to the proponents of independence.[159]

The divisions eventually materialised in the formation of three main political associations – the Moslem League (ML) and the Liberal Progressive Party (LPP) on one side, and the UP on the other, pursuing two fundamentally opposed ultimate objectives: independence versus union with Ethiopia. These political parties were essentially organised along geographic and religious lines: Highlands vs. Lowlands, Christians vs. Muslims, although real party affiliation and political goals cut across ethnic, regional and religious divides. Further splits resulted in the creation of more political parties, with the following list comprising the main formations: the ML, the UP, the LPP, the Pro-Italy Party (PIP), and the New Eritrea Pro-Italy Party (NEPIP).

Established in Keren on 4 December 1946, with Islam as its organising principle, the ML held its first substantive discussions on the future of Eritrea on 21 January 1947.[160] The predominantly Muslim inhabited regions of western, northern, eastern and southeastern Eritrea and the Muslim

---

[158]   Trevaskis, G.K.N., 1960, pp. 68-69.
[159]   Tesfai, Alemseged, 2001, p. 106.
[160]   Trevaskis, G.K.N., 1960, pp. 74-75.

populations in the urban centres formed the main base of its support. The ML firmly opposed partition or union with Ethiopia and called for the independence of Eritrea within its 1935 borders immediately, or following a ten-year period of international trusteeship.

The ML played a pivotal role in the articulation of Eritrean aspirations for self-determination, catalysed the development of Eritrean nationalism, and spearheaded the quest for independence. Under the able and farsighted leadership of Sheikh Ibrahim Sultan, it actively sought alliance with the LPP in opposition to the partition plan and the union project and in consistent support of Eritrea's territorial unity and independence. Under British and Ethiopian interference, pressure, and enticement, the ML split four-ways: the ML, the Nationalist Party (NP), the Moslem League of the Western Province (MLWP), and the Independent Moslem League of Massawa (IML-M). Even with its power and influence waning subsequent to this fragmentation, the ML maintained a firm nationalist stance and continued to champion the cause of Eritrean independence.

The breakup of the ML added region to religion as an organising principle in Eritrean politics. It reduced the support base of the ML to pockets in the Northern Highlands, the eastern fringes of the Central Plateau, the Coastal Plains and the cities of Asmera and Massawa. Support for the MLWP was confined to western Eritrea where it had a large following. It initially called for the independence of the Western Province; briefly entertained the partition plan; and switched from the nationalist bloc to the unionist camp. The IML-M found small support in eastern and central Eritrea, mainly around Massawa and Keren. It deserted the nationalist bloc and supported union with Ethiopia. The

IML-M later re-joined the Independence Bloc. Support for the NP was limited to the port city of Massawa and its environs in Semhar.

Established in Asmera in December 1946, the UP was an offshoot of the Association of the Unity of Ethiopia and Eritrea (AUEE) and a splinter of the ALCE. Dedicated to uniting Eritrea with Ethiopia, the UAEE was formed in Addis Ababa on 27 February 1944 by senior Eritrean officials serving in Haile Selassie's government under the sponsorship and behind-the-scenes direction of the Emperor's private secretary (minister of the pen),[161] and infiltrated the ALCE. Eritrean officials serving in the Ethiopian government went on mission to Asmera and potential Eritrean recruits for the unionist cause invited from Asmera to Addis Ababa. Ethiopia used Eritreans in its service and under its pay to undermine the legitimate demand for Eritrean self-determination and establish its domination over Eritrea.

The British allowed the opening of an Ethiopian Liaison Office (ELO) headed by an army colonel, Nega Haile Selassie, in Asmera in March 1946. This enabled Ethiopia to exercise direct authority and tight control over the leadership of the UP and to organise, plan, and direct the campaign of political violence against the proponents and supporters of Eritrean independence. Complemented by a direct line that linked the Emperor's private secretary to the field operations of banditry via Adwa in Tigray,[162] the ELO served as the general headquarters for Ethiopia's state sponsored campaign of terrorism and assassinations.[163] British records show that

---

[161]   Tesfai, Alemseged, 2001, pp. 113-119.
[162]   Ibid., p. 283.
[163]   Ibid., pp. 274-301.

Ethiopia's growing interference in Eritrea's internal affairs began to change the lack of sympathy for association with Ethiopia that prevailed prior to 1943.[164] With Ethiopian political support, funds, and direction, the UP began to gain adherents in the Central Plateau among followers of the EOC and the feudal chiefs, both Christian and Muslim, throughout the country.

The use of political coercion and religious blackmail extracted much of the support for the UP in the Central Plateau. Nevertheless, it also had some genuine support among those who, fearful of a return of Italian or a continuation of British rule, truly believed that "Eritrea's and their interests would be better served under Ethiopian than under European rule."[165] To those who opposed the restoration or continuation of one or the other European rule were added a few "aspirants to chieftainship" and "chiefs, headmen, nobility who had lost sinecures"; the UP was otherwise "not supported by the mass of the population" in the countryside.[166]

Sustained, driven and manipulated by Ethiopia, the UP became an instrument of its strategy in Eritrea. In collaboration with the top hierarchy of the EOC, it provided cover for Ethiopian subversion of the independence movement through open banditry and the introduction of religious and regional animosities to the political divide in Eritrea. This targeted the unity of the Eritrean people and strove to drive a wedge mainly between Christians and Muslims, highlanders and lowlanders, and supporters and opponents of independence.

---

[164]   Ibid., p. 84.
[165]   Trevaskis, G.K.N., 1960, p. 130.
[166]   Ibid., p. 62.

Founded in Adi Keih on 18 February 1947, the LPP issued from a movement for independence launched in 1943, a year that coincided with the outbreak of the first Weyane uprising in eastern and southern Tigray in opposition to Shoan (Amhara) domination. Despite its impressive initial successes, the revolt failed with the help of British military assistance. Both Longrigg and Trevaskis allude to links between rebel leader Blata Haile Mariam Redda and LPP stalwarts Raesi Tessema Asberom and Ato Weldeab Welde Mariam in support of the British instigated concept of a 'greater Tigray' bringing together the union of Tigray and Eritrea, or Tigray-Tigrigny.[167] The idea has its origins in the incorporation of Tigray into Eritrea under Mussolini's *Africa Orientale Italiana* during the Italian occupation of Ethiopia from 1935 to 1941.

Covertly conceived in the beginning of 1945 by prominent Christians and Muslims opposed to union with Ethiopia, the LPP issued from the split in the ALCE. Its founders pledged, respectively under the Bible and the Koran, to preserve the unity of Eritrea, to strengthen the solidarity of the Eritrean people, and to fight for the independence of a united Eritrea.[168] They sent representatives to all of Eritrea's provinces, starting with the Western Province, to collect signatures of support under the banner of 'Eritrea for the Eritreans'.

The LPP shunned religion as an organising principle and its initial formation was inclusive of Christians and Muslims in the capital and the Central Plateau, which

---

[167] Ibid., pp. 63-64.
[168] Ato Weldeab Weldemariam in an interview quoted in Tesfai, Alemseged, 2001, p. 128-129.

constituted its main support base. The defection of many of its founding Muslim members to the ML and the UP, however, reduced it to a largely Christian organisation. Sharing similar political principles and objectives, the LPP and the ML had virtually identical programmes, drawn up in mutual consultation. Both parties pledged to work in mutual respect, close cooperation and patriotic solidarity. Further, they had established an umbrella organisation that however, they failed to operationalize. In effect, religion was the only factor that prevented the LPP and the ML from forming a united party and justified their existence as separate entities. However, the split of the Liberal Unionist Party (LUP), which abandoned the cause of independence and advocated 'conditional union' with Ethiopia, later weakened the LPP.

The New Eritrea Pro-Italy Party (NEPIP) came into being in Asmara in July 1947 as the political face of the Eritrean Old Soldiers Association (EOSA), formed the previous March. Former *askari*, Italian settlers, and half-castes made up its main support base. The NEPIP was essentially a creation of Italian intervention and grouped together social forces that hankered for the return of Italian rule or trusteeship. After the defeat of the Bevin-Sforza Plan, the merger of the NEPIP and the EOSA formed the New Eritrea Party (NEP), which aligned itself with the nationalist camp and joined ranks with the ML and the LPP to organise an Independence Bloc committed to the immediate independence of Eritrea.

The ML, the LPP and the NEP established the Eritrean Bloc for Independence (EBI) on 19 June 1949. Leaders of the ML, LPP, NEP and the Italo-Eritrean Association met on 4 July 1949 and set up a council whose unanimous decisions would be binding on all its members. An enlarged EBI held the largest ever meeting in Asmera on 22 July 1949 and, rejecting any and any ideas of partition or union, proclaimed its objective to be the immediate independence of a united Eritrea, within its present borders, and the establishment of a democratic state.[169]

3.8 British Intrigues and Ethiopian Subversion

The unity and common political platform of the EIB constituted 'substantial and firm opposition' to the unionist project, transformed the nationalist movement into a potent force able to rally the majority of the Eritrean people for independence, and enjoyed the "support of the majority of the population."[170] The EIB generated a groundswell of popular support for independence while the UP rapidly lost ground and faced the prospect of mass defections. A confidential British report at the time estimated that the EIB would garner 75 per cent of the popular vote, in the event of a plebiscite on the future of Eritrea.[171]

In desperation, Ethiopia and the UP riverted to terrorist attacks against the leaders and supporters of the EIB and unleashed a brutal campaign of political assassination, violence and intimidation unprecedented in the history of the country.[172] Those who could not be bribed or intimidated had to be physically eliminated. This persuaded or compelled many to desert the EIB to save their skin. Imperial Ethiopian subversion turned small Eritrea into a battlefield and sowed

---

[169]   Tesfai, Alemseged, 2001, pp. 358-368.
[170]   Trevaskis, G.K.N., 1960, p. 94.
[171]   US Department of State, Incoming Telegram Control 8528, No. 171, 19 August 1949.
[172]   Trevaskis, G.K.N., 1960, p. 76.

chaos and disorder under the watch of the mighty British Empire.

State-sponsored violence, and the concomitant instigation of sectarian and regional discord, aimed to undermine the unity of the nationalist movement and destabilise the occupied territory. The pillage of the productive assets, and the attendant economic stagnation, operated to further impoverish the country. These subversive acts of destabilisation were intended to buttress the argument that Eritrea lacked the economic viability and political stability to merit independence, thereby garnering international support for the partition plan.

State-sponsored violence, and the concomitant instigation of sectarian and regional discord, aimed to undermine the unity of the nationalist movement and destabilise the occupied territory. The pillage of the productive assets, and the attendant economic stagnation, operated to impoverish the country. These subversive acts of destabilisation aimed to buttress the argument that Eritrea lacked the economic viability and political stability to merit independence, thereby garnering international support for the partition plan.

Despite its claims of a 'civilising mission', the colonial system never intended to benefit the subject peoples. It spread the myth of European superiority and African inferiority and fostered divisions among its victims in order to advance its interests and objectives. The initiation of the politics of sectarian, ethnic and regional division, the plunder of industrial assets, and the contrived economic slump remain the salient vestiges of the legacy of BMA in Eritrea.

Even so, it was not without its residual benefits. The expansion of access to primary education and the introduction of education beyond the elementary level stand out as a major legacy. The British had, by 1950, set up 59 primary schools and 1 middle school.[173] In total, there were 100 primary, 14 middle and 2 secondary schools enrolling 13,500, 1,200 and 167 pupils, respectively, and 30 Eritreans pursuing higher learning abroad at the time the British left Eritrea in September 1952.[174] In addition, the British initiated the publication of newspapers that provided Eritreans with a forum to express their opinions and exchange views, even if initially confined to cultural and social issues. Further, the formation of political parties and the ensuing debate on the future of the country stimulated the awakening and growth of political consciousness among the people and the rise of the Eritrean nationalist movement.

In some respects, the contours of Eritrea's political landscape, including the initial split and final configuration of the main political parties that emerged, reflected the contradictions inherent in Eritrean society. Even more ominously, they also demonstrated the vulnerability of Eritrea's social divides to the machinations of foreign, particularly Ethiopian, intervention in the internal affairs of its people. Despite the structural and induced weaknesses, however, the emergence of the two main strands of political parties during the second half of the 1940s catalysed a vibrant political climate that allowed the conduct of robust debate on the future of the country.

In retrospect, it is plausible to contend that the nascent Eritrean nationalist movement could, if left alone, have developed sufficient coherence of perspective, unity of purpose, and solidarity of action to lead the Eritrean people to national independence. Even under the divisive machinations

---

[173] Four Power Commission Report, p. 71.
[174] Trevaskis, G.K.N., 1960, p. 129.

of external interference, the nationalist movement managed to make a quantum leap from *ad hoc* and localised resistance against colonial oppression to an organised nationwide struggle for independence. It overcame the devastation, stresses and strains of organised political violence to survive and keep the torch aflame in the search for freedom.

The nationalist project persevered in the face of adversity from without and division from within. Even while deeply discordant in many respects, the political discourse of the 1940s expressed firm opposition to partition, articulated a strong popular desire for freedom and, in the main, generated a preponderant voice in support of the demand for the independence of a united Eritrea. Crucially, its resilience drew the battle lines between the pro- and anti-independence forces into sharper focus and helped keep Eritrean aspirations for freedom alive. This resilience was however, put to a new and a more strident test, as the following chapter shows.

CHAPTER 4

Transition from European to African Colonialism

[T]he strategic interests of the United States in the Red Sea Basin and world peace make it necessary that the country [Eritrea] be linked with our ally Ethiopia. - John F. Dulles

Geography has bestowed Eritrea with a pivotal location in one of the world's most strategic and volatile regions, at the interface of the Horn of Africa and the Arabian Peninsula. The Red Sea forms a critical bridge between East and West and a vital lifeline of commercial, economic, and cultural interaction between Europe, Africa, and Asia, making Eritrea the natural gateway to the vast Ethiopian and Sudanese hinterlands. This location has lent the country a special geopolitical significance, attracting the interest and rivalry of external powers as an enduring feature of its political history and a defining factor of its post-World War II evolution.

Following the onset of the Cold War, this strategic location attracted the ambitions and rivalry of the Big Powers whose machinations subverted Eritrea's march along the crest of the first wave of decolonisation. Of the three former Italian colonies brought under British occupation, Eritrea alone did not gain independence. Its federation with Ethiopia in 1952 contradicted the free wishes of the majority of its people. Still, when the UN adopted the federal resolution, most Eritreans were prepared to cooperate to make the federation work.

Ethiopia, however, subverted the federal arrangement, incapacitated its key institutions and dismantled the federation itself. With the connivance of the US and its Western allies, Ethiopia annexed Eritrea on 14 November 1962 and declared it its 14th province. Moreover, the UN and the international community acquiesced in Ethiopia's annexation and imposition of direct rule over Eritrea, in flagrant violation of the UN federal resolution.

In retrospect, it should have been obvious from the outset that, federating a small country armed with a modern constitution, the trappings of democratic self-government with a large country steeped in feudal anachronism, and the prerogatives of divine right would be incompatible. The anomaly delivered an essentially stillborn federal scheme. At the UN, Sheikh Ibrahim Sultan made a passionate plea to consider the express wishes of the Eritrean people and prophetic warnings that Eritreans would not acquiesce in a new form of oppression. Had the world powers heeded his message, the peoples of Eritrea, Ethiopia, and the Horn of Africa could perhaps, be spared the suffering, the turmoil, and the insecurity that followed the last six decades.

4.1 Access to the Sea as a Pillar of Cooperation

Viewed against the backdrop of the colonial experience, even if the Ethiopian version of Eritrean history that portrays Eritrea as an integral part of pre-colonial Ethiopia were true - which in fact is not - it would still not justify the case for the 'return' of Eritrea or the UN decision to federate Eritrea with Ethiopia. Nor would Ethiopia's desire for access to the sea ever be a sufficient rationale to justify the destabilisation and eventual annexation of Eritrea. Securing access to the sea or transit services *per se* does not, or should not require the political or territorial control of a neighbouring state. It is a facility that a landlocked and a littoral state can negotiate, sort out its technical modalities, and arrange its procedures through bilateral discussion based on mutual economic and commercial benefits.

Fourteen other landlocked countries in Africa and, indeed, Ethiopia itself, have brokered amicable bilateral commercial arrangements for safe passage in transit and secure access to port services with one or more of their maritime neighbours. Otherwise, under no circumstances can a country's political desire or economic need for access to the sea justify encroachment on the legitimate right of self-determination or territorial integrity of another. In this regard, what I stated in reply to a question from Ms Louise Graham at a conference in London on 9 November 1985, under a different set of circumstances holds, equally true today:

> *Access to the sea is important but it is not indispensable to the survival, wellbeing and prosperity of a country. And it cannot be used to justify the aggression of a powerful neighbour against a weaker one. [...]Ethiopia cannot try to justify its aggression against Eritrea on the grounds that it needs access to the sea. [...Ethiopia and Eritrea] could reach*

mutually beneficial agreements as to the use of our port facilities.[175]

Despite the events that have transpired since the outbreak of the 1998-2000 Ethio-Eritrean war, subsequent developments have confirmed the validity of the assertion that peaceful coexistence and commercial cooperation are not only desirable but also possible between Eritrea and Ethiopia. This is borne out by several developments that have occurred since 1991:

First, the firm support for Eritrea's right of self-determination in principle, and the recognition of Eritrean independence in practice, by the ruling Ethiopian People's Revolutionary Democratic Front (EPRDF) government in power since 1991. Ethiopia was the first country to recognise the State of Eritrea at the time of the declaration of independence, pursuant to the outcome of the referendum on self-determination

Second, the conclusion of the Transit and Port Services Agreement between Eritrea and Ethiopia in 1993 providing for, *inter alia*, the use of the Eritrean ports of Massawa and Asseb as transit ports for Ethiopia and the facilitation of the speedy movement of goods in transit across Eritrea.[176] The agreement served the economic, commercial and financial interests of both countries until the outbreak of hostilities

---

[175] Giorgis, Andebrhan W., *The Current Situation in Eritrea and the Way Forward* in Eritrea: The Way Forward, Proceedings of a Conference on Eritrea organised by the United Nations Association on the 9th November 1985, Russell Press Ltd., London, 1986, p. 55.

[176] Governments of Ethiopia and Eritrea: Transit and Port Services Agreement between the Transitional Government of Ethiopia and the Government of the State of Eritrea, 29 September 1993.

rendered it void in 1998. Otherwise, during the brief period of amicable relations, Ethiopia enjoyed preferential access to Eritrea's ports while Eritrea earned large revenues from port services, albeit denominated in Ethiopian Birr.

Third, the vital lessons learned from the experience of cordial and cooperative relations during the period 1991-1998 that neither political nor territorial control of Eritrea, or parts thereof, was necessary to secure Ethiopia's overland transit and maritime access to the Red Sea through Eritrea. The vagaries of regional geopolitics aside, considerations of geographic proximity, road infrastructure, and comparative cost make Massawa the port of choice for north-central Ethiopia, and Asseb for the Ethiopian hinterland further south.

Fourth, the current demonstration that Ethiopia is able to use, though at significantly higher financial cost, other ports in the region, such as Djibouti, Berbera, Mombasa and Port Sudan, and achieve relatively high rates of economic growth without the use of Eritrea's ports.

As former US president Bill Clinton would say, it is a matter of arithmetic. Eritrea's ports represent valuable assets capable of generating large income for Eritrea and providing cost-effective services for Ethiopia as exit and entry points for the bulk of its foreign trade. In this rapidly changing era of growing global interdependence, it is in the vital interest of both countries to work out a bilateral arrangement of port and transit services to mutual benefit. In the context of reconciliation and amicable relations, Ethiopia's use of Eritrea's assets as facilities of transit and maritime access has the potential to serve as a major pillar of cooperation and an essential bridge to stimulate greater economic integration between the two countries.

4.2 The Geopolitical Setting

Outside intervention, chronic conflict, and perennial insecurity have blighted the Horn of Africa proper and the southern Red Sea Basin, where Eritrea holds a vital location, for the last sixty years. As a result, the region has suffered from the absence of economic growth and, therefore, the prevalence of extreme poverty. More recently, this highly strategic region has been embroiled in the vagaries of the so-called *war on terror*, and has seen an upsurge in external intervention, cross-border interference, the rise of militant political Islam, and the growth of maritime piracy. All along, foreign interference has been a significant destabilising factor feeding the region's highly complex conflict matrix.

During the height of World War II, the US, which soon replaced the UK as the principal world power, occupied Radio Marina in Asmera in 1942 for use as a wartime communications base. It also established the Kagnew Station, a crucial military and intelligence communications base in 1953. The altitude and suitable location of Asmera along the same longitude as Moscow gave the US military base a unique advantage to eavesdrop on the Kremlin. Eritrea thus became a critical link in the chain of the postwar US strategy for the defence of the Middle East and the southern Mediterranean against the threat of expansion of Soviet influence.

The establishment of Kagnew Station ushered in American involvement in the affairs of Eritrea and set the stage for US engagement in the region with its enormous long-term destabilising effects. Against the backdrop of an evolving Big Power rivalry vis-à-vis the disposal of Italy's ex-colonies, US desire to retain the extremely vital base led, a decade later, to a policy decision that subordinated Eritrea's legitimate right to self-determination and the long-term stability of the region to US strategic interests, in the context of the Cold War. In the telling words of John F. Dulles, the then US Representative to the Fifth Session of the UN General Assembly:

> *From the point of view of justice, the opinion of the Eritrean people must receive consideration. Nevertheless, the strategic interests of the United States in the Red Sea Basin and world peace make it necessary that the country [Eritrea] be linked with our ally Ethiopia.*[177]

Ignoring a confidential British report[178] in its possession, which revealed that about 75 per cent of Eritreans wanted independence, the US sponsored, and the UN General Assembly adopted, Resolution 390 (V)A(1950) on 2 December 1950, providing for the federation of Eritrea as an autonomous unit with Ethiopia.[179] The denial of Eritrea's legitimate right to full self-government, despite the warning that "the people of Eritrea will not accept the dominance of Ethiopia,"[180] sowed the seeds of the thirty-year Ethio-Eritrean war (1961-1991). Ethiopia's annexation, in abrogation of the

---

[177]   Dulles, John Foster, United States Representative to the Fifth General Assembly of the United Nations, December 1950.

[178]   US Department of State, Incoming Telegram Control 8528, No. 171, 19 August 1949.

[179]   UN General Assembly, 5th Session, 2 December 1950 http://www.un.org/documents/ga/res/5/ares5.htm

[180]   Sheikh Ibrahim Sultan, one of the leaders of the Eritrean Independence Block, in a statement to the 5th Session of the UN General Assembly in December 1950.

UN resolution ten years after its entry into force, with US complicity and UN acquiescence, stirred Eritrean resistance and provoked one of the longest and bloodiest wars of national liberation in modern African history.

General Western opposition to decolonisation persisted not just in Eritrea but also elsewhere in Africa and Southern Africa, in particular. The West provided tacit support to the apartheid regime in South Africa, discreet support to Portugal's colonial war effort in Angola, Guinea Bissau and Cape Verde, and Mozambique until the fall of the Salazar dictatorship, and covert support for the white supremacist regime in Southern Rhodesia in violation of the mandatory UN sanctions.[181] In direct opposition, the Soviet Bloc extended support to the anti-apartheid and national liberation movements in Africa and Southern Africa, in particular.

As the Cold War deepened, Ethiopia formed the 'southern tier' of a US cordon of 'containment of the Soviet Union' across the Middle East,[182] which was subsequently punctured by the establishment of countervailing Soviet footholds in Somalia and South Yemen, dominating both flanks of the Strait of Bab el Mandeb. Ethiopia was waging war on three fronts: in Eritrea to suppress a national liberation movement; inside Ethiopia to suppress ethnic and regional revolts, particularly in Tigray, Oromia and the Ogaden; and against Somali irredentism aimed to unite all ethnic Somali inhabited territories in a single Somali state.

As a direct effect of the colonial partition of the Horn of Africa, more than 5 m ethnic Somalis live in Ethiopia,

---

[181] Oudes, Bruce, Zimbabwe Independent, 4-10 February 2011, p.15.
[182] Woodward, Peter, US Foreign Policy and the Horn of Africa, Ashgate Publishing Ltd., Hampshire, England, 2006, p.19

Kenya and Djibouti while later displacement and migration produced a Somali diaspora of over 5 m spread around the world.[183] Somalia's ambitions to undo the fragmentation wrought by colonialism and unite all Somali inhabited lands, including the Ogaden and Haud in eastern Ethiopia, the former French Somaliland of Djibouti, and the North-eastern Frontier District of Kenya, in a Greater Somalia, fuelled regional tensions. Discord among the states in the region created a fertile ground for external intervention in the context of the Cold War.

There thus emerged a new configuration of regional and international alignments with periodically shifting combinations. The US and Israel actively supported Ethiopia with the provision of arms, military advisors and training in its attempt to crush the Eritrean insurgency. The Eritrean resistance drew the tacit support of several regional allies of the Soviet Union, such as Syria, Iraq, Libya, and South Yemen; the Palestinian organisations and the Lebanese nationalist movement; and certain conservative Arab states, such as Kuwait, the United Arab Emirates (UAE), and Saudi Arabia. Outside the region, the Eritrean struggle received a one-off training support from the People's Republic of China and Cuba.

Meanwhile, the conflict between Ethiopia and Somalia, which degenerated into open warfare in 1964, in 1977-78, and in 1982, fuelled an arms race in the Horn of Africa, with the US and the Soviet Union, and their respective

---

[183] Danish Ministry of Foreign Affairs, Policy Paper for Denmark's Engagement in Somalia, August 2009 http://www.afrika.um.dk/ NR/rdonlyres/4534134B-6930-4357-8209-A2FCD53FA6BF/0/ Policy_Paper_Denmark_Somalia_ENG.pdf

allies, supplying weapons to their client states in the region. Further, certain allies of the superpowers, notably Israel, Cuba, South Yemen, and Libya, intensified their involvement in the internal and regional conflicts in shifting alignments. These allies provided, often at the behest or with the connivance of the superpowers, military advisors, training, or combat personnel to the protagonists in the region's interstate or intrastate wars. All this contributed to the long-term destabilisation of the Horn of Africa.

The West, particularly the US and Israel, supported Ethiopia in its wars against Eritrea and Somalia while the Soviet Union and its allies supported Somalia until 1975. In turn, Somalia, along with South Yemen and, sporadically, Libya, supported the Eritrean liberation movement. External support had crucial political, diplomatic, and military components and, to a significant extent, explained the shifting military balance between the warring parties.

In the mid-1970s, the Soviet Union switched sides and, along with its allies, including East Germany, Cuba, South Yemen, and Libya, propped up Ethiopia until 1991, while the US and its Arab allies supported Somalia. At the same time, Somalia continued to support the Eritrean liberation movement and Ethiopian armed insurgent movements until the demise of the dictatorial regimes of Ziad Barre in Somalia and Mengistu in Ethiopia in 1991.

Enmeshed in the East-West rivalry of the Cold War and racked by interstate wars, intrastate conflicts and internecine strife, the Horn of Africa became a battleground of proxy warfare. Trapped in the geopolitics of superpower rivalry, Eritrea, Ethiopia, and Somalia remained hubs of violent conflict and external interference until the fall of the Berlin Wall and the collapse of the Soviet Union. Shifting regional and global alignments operated, among other things, to prolong the war, and escalate the scale and level of fighting, between Eritrea and Ethiopia, destabilise the Horn of Africa, and make the entire region extremely volatile and insecure.

4.3 Federation of Eritrea with Ethiopia

Decided without the consideration of the interests, the participation, and the consent of the Eritrean people, the 1950 UN resolution provided for the federation of Eritrea as an autonomous unit with Ethiopia, under the sovereignty of the Ethiopian crown. It contradicted the fundamental principle of the right of colonised and dependent peoples to self-government. Even though it upheld the unity and territorial integrity of Eritrea, the federal resolution essentially constituted a denial of the Eritrean people's legitimate right of self-determination, and served merely as a prelude to imperial Ethiopian domination.

It is conceivable that a genuine federal arrangement could have thrived and served the mutual interests of Eritrea and Ethiopia. The UN resolution did not, however, provide for a federation of two co-equal states managing their respective internal affairs and sharing responsibility for federal business. Despite the UN Commissioner's recommendation that an Imperial Federal Council with equal representation be set up,[184] in reality there were no provisions or attempts to constitute and operationalize joint bodies or supranational federal organs. The Ethiopian government itself was the federal government. Ethiopia was given charge of Eritrea's defence, foreign affairs, finance and currency, interstate and

---

[184] Final Report of the UN Commissioner for Eritrea, A/2188.

international trade, and communications. The federation allowed Eritrea no say in these vital matters of national interest, security and wellbeing, confining its authority strictly to internal affairs.

On paper, the federal arrangement granted Eritrea: an autonomous democratic government with its own flag, official seal and coat of arms; an elected chief executive, an elective legislature, and an independent judiciary; and full autonomy in the management of its internal affairs, such as taxation, education, health, agriculture, and domestic commerce. It provided for: a system of government based on democratic principles, the rule of law and respect for human rights; an Eritrean constitution with guarantees of fundamental rights, basic freedoms and civil liberties, such as freedom of expression, freedom of the press, freedom of association, freedom of peaceful assembly, and freedom of conscience, faith and belief;[185] and a federal act that

---

[185] Constitution of Eritrea, 1952, Final Report of the United Nations Commissioner in Eritrea, General Assembly Official Records: Seventh Session Supplement N0 15 (A/2188), pp. 76-89. The UN-drafted Constitution of Eritrea was duly ratified by the 68-member Eritrean Representative Assembly elected in March 1952 to consider the Federal Constitution. The 68 members represented 68 constituencies of approximately 15,000 electorates each. Direct elections by secret ballot were held in Asmera and Massawa. Elsewhere, village and family groups elected representatives to regional electoral colleges which, in turn, elected regional representatives by secret ballot. Upon ratification of the Constitution, the Representative Assembly became the Eritrean Assembly and confirmed the establishment of the first Government of Eritrea jointly formed by the Unionist Party (32 seats) and the Moslem League of the Western Province (15 seats), with the

sanctioned competitive politics in a framework of exclusive male suffrage.

Drafted by the UN Commissioner for Eritrea, adopted by the Eritrean Representative Assembly (10 July 1952), and ratified by the emperor of Ethiopia (11 September 1952), Eritrea's federal constitution provided for statutory checks and balances among the legislative, executive, and judiciary organs. It provided for an Eritrean Assembly, elected by the people; a Chief Executive, elected by the Eritrean Assembly; and an independent judiciary made up of a supreme court, a high court and district courts.[186] The Chief Executive would appoint cabinet secretaries, on the confirmation of and answerable to the Eritrean Assembly, to take charge of government departments and, on the recommendation of the President of the Eritrean Assembly, appoint qualified judges.[187] The civil service commission would appoint all other officials.

While granting Eritrea the trappings of a modern democratic system, the arrangement also granted Ethiopia

---

Democratic Bloc (18 seats) constituting the main parliamentary opposition. Trevaskis, G.K.N., 1960, pp. 119-120.

[186] The Supreme Court would be a court of final appeal, the judge of questions involving the jurisdiction of other courts, and the sole authority for interpreting the Constitution. The High Court would be a court of criminal issues and an appeal court in the first instance from the district courts. The district courts would enjoy unlimited jurisdiction in all civil and criminal issues, with the exception of cases reserved for the High Court.

[187] All judges of the Supreme Court and at least 50 percent of the judges of the high court were to be legal practitioners, or the holders of law degrees for a minimum of seven years. Trevaskis, G.K.N., 1960, pp. 121-123.

sovereignty over the federation. Ethiopia, however, was an anachronistic feudal empire whose absolute monarch claimed to be the 'Elect of God' and ruled by 'divine right'. Basic rights, civil liberties and democratic principles, fully enshrined in the Eritrean constitution, were alien concepts to Ethiopia's 1931 constitution and merely formal addenda to its revised 1955 constitution. It smacked of anomaly to put an autonomous state, granted a democratic constitution, under the authority of a feudal emperor vested by celestial power.

Evidently, the stark contrast between the archaic and the modern systems of government and principles of governance manifest in the constitutions and prevailing political cultures of Ethiopia and Eritrea at the time reduced the federation into an incongruous arrangement. There prevailed an intrinsic contradiction, an irreconcilable mismatch, between feudal absolutism and imperial prerogatives, on the one hand, and fundamental freedoms and inalienable rights under autonomous self-rule, on the other. The inherent incompatibility of government by divine right and governance by democratic mandate rendered the federal arrangement untenable from the very beginning and doomed it to ultimate failure.

Put into effect on 15 September 1952, federation represented an imposed compromise between independence and union with Ethiopia. It gave closure to a particularly turbulent period in Eritrean history that featured the spectre of dismemberment and anarchy. It was against the backdrop of such unprecedented political turmoil that the independence camp reluctantly acquiesced to federation as the lesser evil vis-à-vis partition, European rule, or union. Ethiopia and the Eritrean unionists also grudgingly accepted it as a better alternative to independence.

At a peace conference held barely a month after its adoption by the UN, leaders of the unionist and independence camps agreed to reconcile and make peace, accepted the federation as a *fait accompli*, and pledged to cooperate to make the compromise arrangement work.[188] The independence camp, in particular, expressed a genuine desire to promote and implement the federation and, as a gesture of commitment, changed its name from the Independence Bloc to the Eritrean Democratic Party (EDP), signalling the end of the struggle for independence and the beginning of the struggle for democracy within the federal union. It thus seems that, despite its serious shortcomings, the federation could have endured had Ethiopia prudently sustained rather than recklessly subverted it.

4.4 Abrogation of the Federation

The absence of credible institutional constraints or enforceable instruments of safeguard seems to have been deliberately planned by the authors of UN Resolution 390 A(V) and condoned by the realpolitik of international complicity. Federation divested Eritrea of national sovereignty and the prerogative to develop a capacity for self-defence without, at the same time, availing internal or external checks against any infringement on its autonomy. Ethiopia exploited this structural weakness to constantly intervene in Eritrea's internal affairs, despite the fact that its interference directly contravened the letter and spirit of the UN federal resolution.

---

[188] The peace conference (Gubae Selam) was held in Asmara on 31 December 1950 with 4 000 participants. For a detailed exposition of the peace conference, see Tesfai, A., *Aynfelale*, p. 158.

Ostensibly relying on the 'good will of the Emperor' to keep his pledge to safeguard the integrity of the Federal Act and the Eritrean constitution, the arrangement offered Ethiopia the prospect to democratise its political system, modernise its economy, and make the association work.

Instead, Ethiopia chose to forfeit the opportunity to build a viable federal association; decided to abandon any pretense to observe Eritrean autonomy; and opted to drag Eritrea down rather than to lift itself up. It openly flouted the guarantees to let Eritrea freely manage its internal affairs. For instance, when members of the Eritrean Assembly protested Ethiopian encroachment on Eritrean domestic jurisdiction, they were bluntly told that:

> *There are no internal or external affairs as far as the office of His Imperial Majesty's representative is concerned, as there shall be none in the future. The affairs of Eritrea concern Ethiopia as a whole and the Emperor.*[189]

A blatant lack of imperial restraint allowed the playing out of Ethiopia's hegemonic ambitions and unravelled the federation. It was not enough that Ethiopia gained sovereignty over Eritrea, access to the sea, and control of Eritrea's finances, ports, foreign affairs, and international trade! Nay, Eritrea had to be totally swallowed and all traces of its special status completely erased as a matter of urgency.

---

[189] Address of the Emperor's representative in Eritrea to the Eritrean Assembly, 22 March 1955, quoted in Eritrean Liberation Front, *Eritrea: The National Democratic Revolution versus Ethiopian Expansionism*, (Beirut: ELF Foreign Information Centre, 1979), p. 24.

Barely three years into the federation, Ethiopia forced the resignation of Eritrea's elected Chief Executive for standing up against its transgressions of the Federal Act, and appointed an Eritrean official of its government in his place. Once it imposed a docile 'Chief Executive' eager to do its bidding, Ethiopia accelerated the demise of the federation.

Ethiopia's disregard of repeated petitions and protests and heavy-handed interference disaffected and alienated most Eritreans. While using the UP as the main instrument of intervention in the internal affairs of Eritrea to corrode Eritrean autonomy, Ethiopia disposed of, marginalised, betrayed, and alienated even its most loyal erstwhile collaborators in the UP and the MLWE, and turned them into staunch federalists who resisted its encroachment and defended Eritrea's prerogatives. Increasingly, Ethiopia's betrayal cornered its former unionist allies into open opposition, driving many to join the ranks of the emerging independence movement.[190]

---

[190] The Unionist Party and the Moslem League of the Western Province were coalition partners in the first pro-union Government of Eritrea formed when the federation came into effect. Tedla Bairu, the leader of the UP, became the first Chief Executive of Eritrea while Ali Mussa Radai, the leader of the MLWP, became the first President of the Eritrean Assembly. Both, the Chief Executive of Eritrea and the President of the Eritrean Assembly, were forced to resign in 1955 under heavy Ethiopian pressure. Idris Mohamed Adem, the second President of the Eritrean Assembly, was also forced to resign in 1957, fled into exile in 1959 and became the first chairman of the Supreme Council of the Eritrean Liberation Front (ELF) upon its establishment in Cairo in July 1960 and was instrumental in persuading Hamid Idris Awate to start the armed struggle in 1961 under the banner of the ELF. Tedla Bairu, the first

Elsewhere in Africa, the process of decolonisation was facilitated by the use of the principle of self-determination as a powerful instrument in waging and legitimising national resistance to European colonialism, and attaining self-rule through the proclamation of independence. In the case of Eritrea, this principle was set aside; the UN federal resolution served merely as a smokescreen for the substitution of a new form of African colonial rule for the old form of European colonial system in contravention of the principle of self-determination. Through the agency of the UN, Eritrea became a sacrificial lamb on the altar of federation in the interest of US strategic interests in the region. Deprived of the prerogative to establish its own foreign relations and made dependent for, among other things, its finances and defence on Ethiopia, Eritrea finally became the victim of brazen military occupation.

The UN imposition of the Ethio-Eritrean federation and acquiescence in its abrogation, therefore, violated the principle of self-determination and sowed the seeds of conflict between the two neighbours. Ethiopia's strategy proved counter-productive, as its actions enflamed Eritrean public opinion, incited popular indignation and galvanised support for the armed struggle for liberation. The following chapter explores further the legitimacy of the Eritrean people's right to self-determination, and describes the long, difficult and protracted struggle waged to create the conditions for its exercise.

Chief Executive of Eritrea later joined the ELF and became vice-chairman of the Supreme Council in 1967.

CHAPTER 5

The Arduous Struggle for Self-Determination

All peoples have the right of self-determination. - International Covenant on Civil and Political Rights

The right of self-determination refers to the right of a nation to independence and the right of a people to a government of their free choice. The two rights are complementary and international law upholds the legitimacy of the principle of self-determination in its dual meaning. This chapter asserts the applicability of the principle of self-determination, as embedded in the UN Charter and reinforced by subsequent UN General Assembly declarations, to the case of Eritrea both as a nation and as a people. Accordingly, it comments on the failure of the United Nations and the international community to apply the principle of the right of self-determination with respect to Eritrea's legitimate claim to the same right, and to support the just and long struggle of the Eritrean people to assert their legitimate right of self-determination.

Further, the chapter scans the evolution of the political resistance of the Eritrean people, as it extended to military struggle. It recounts the tortuous internal development of the armed struggle for liberation and underscores the final military victory that made the exercise of the right of national self-determination possible. Finally, the chapter explains the failure of independence, which is the outcome of the exercise of the right of self-determination of Eritrea as a nation, to allow the exercise of the right of self-determination of Eritrea as a people.

5.1 The Right to Self-Determination in International Law

International law affirms, "*All peoples have the right of self-determination*" which allow them to *freely determine their political status* and manage *their economic, social and cultural* affairs.[191] The principle of self-determination is enshrined in the UN Charter, the International Covenant on Civil and Political Rights, and the International Covenant on Economic, Social and Cultural Rights as a fundamental human right. Likewise, the International Court of Justice endorses the right to self-determination, underlining that the outcome of the exercise must be the "result of the freely expressed wishes of the territory's peoples."[192] UN General Assembly declarations on self-determination lent the principle legal force in international law and further strengthened the legitimacy of the right of nations and peoples to self-determination.

The UN Declaration on the Granting of Independence to Colonial Countries and Peoples affirms, "All peoples have the right to self-determination," to "freely determine their

---

[191] *The International Covenant on Civil and Political Rights; the International Covenant on Economic, Social and Cultural Rights*, Article 1, paragraph 1.

[192] International Court of Justice, Advisory Opinion on Western Sahara, 16 October 1975.

political status and freely pursue their economic, social and cultural development." It stresses the urgent need to end to the colonial system to enable all colonial peoples and dependent territories to attain "complete independence and freedom".[193] The UN Declaration on Principles of International Law reaffirms "the principle of equal rights and self-determination of peoples enshrined in the Charter of the United Nations." It underscores the importance of applying that principle in order to promote "friendly relations and cooperation among states" and end colonialism. Further, it specifies the modes of a people's exercise of the right to self-determination.[194]

Giving force to the statement of political principles enshrined in the UN Charter, subsequent UN resolutions and practice on decolonisation have gradually transformed the principle of the right of peoples to self-determination "into legal rules calling for the independence of colonial territories".[195] Essentially, the principle of self-determination affirms the inherent right of a colonised people or a

---

[193] UN General Assembly Resolution 1514 (XV), 14 December 1960.

[194] UN General Assembly Resolution 2625 (XXV), 24 October 1970.

[195] Smis, Stefaan, *The Legal Status of International Land Boundaries in Africa*, in Politics of Identity and Economics of Conflict in the Great Lakes Region, Ruddy Doom & Jan Gorus (eds.), Brussels: VUB Press, 2000, p. 197. *See*, for an overview of the UN involvement with self-determination and decolonisation, e.g., RIGO SUREDA, A., The Evolution of the Right of Self-Determination: A study of United Nations Practice (Leiden, A.W. Sijthoff, 1973); GROS ESPIELL, G., The Right to Self-Determination. Implementation of United Nations Resolutions, UN Doc. E/CN.4/Sub. 2/405/Rev. 1(1980); CRISTESCU, A., The Right to Self-Determination: Historical and Current Developments on the Basis of United Nations Instruments, E/CN.4/Sub. 2/404/Rev. 1(1981).

dependent territory to freely determine their political destiny and advance their economic, social and cultural development. The following represents an apt summation of the dual meaning of the principle of self-determination:

> *Politically, self-determination has come to connote two types of rights which complement each other: (1) the right of a people to self-determination, and (2) the right of a nation to self-determination.*
>
> *First, 'the right of a people to self-determination' has come to mean the right of a people to have a government resulting from its own free choice without any external or internal domination...*
>
> *Second, 'the right of a nation to self-determination' has come to mean the right of a nation to independence, and is perhaps the more significant operational definition of self-determination.*[196]

The right of a people to self-termination signifies their right, in an independent state, to decide the mode of the political organisation of their society, to choose freely their own government, to participate in the democratic process of governance, and to manage their economic, social and cultural affairs. The right of a nation to self-determination signifies its right to freely dissociate from, or associate with, an independent state. More specifically, it means the right to freely secede and establish an independent sovereign

---

[196] Tesfagiorgis, Gebre Hiwet, Self-Determination: Its Evolution and Practice by the United Nations and Its Application to the Case of Eritrea, Wisconsin International Law Journal, Vol. 6, No. 1, June 1988, p. 79.

state, or to freely associate with an independent state. The right of free association implies the right to integrate with the independent state, or to set up its own structures of autonomous self-government in order to safeguard and/or advance its special political, economic, social and cultural rights or interests.

The first perspective found its historic expression in the American and French revolutions in the second half of the eighteenth century; the second perspective found its historic expression in the national movements in Europe during World War I and in the anti-colonial movements in Africa and the Third World during and post-World War II. The national movements in Europe catalysed the creation of independent states out of the old Austro-Hungarian and Russian empires, while the anti-colonial movements in Africa, Asia, and Latin America spearheaded the processes of decolonisation that resulted in the establishment of various independent states.[197]

As explained in the preceding chapters, colonial rule forged Eritrea. Italian, British and Ethiopian domination represented infringements of the right of the Eritrean people to self-determination under the UN Charter and relevant UN declarations. Further, Ethiopia's war to suppress the legitimate struggle of the Eritrean people for self-determination and independence posed a threat to regional peace and security.

Constituted either as "a colonial people," or as "a people subjected to foreign domination", the Eritrean people merited the exercise "of their right to self-determination." As such, the Eritrean "claim to self-determination and

---

[197]   Ibid., p. 79-80.

independence," both as a people and as a nation, possessed "a legal basis grounded in the applied principle of self-determination as defined, and as should be applied, by the United Nations."[198]

Despite the solid political and legal foundation of the Eritrean claim to self-determination under the UN Charter and subsequent UN declarations, resolutions and practice, the UN and the broader international community ignored Eritrea's legitimate right of, and just struggle for, self-determination and the sufferings of the Eritrean people for several decades. Yet:

> *Of all the people who, since the Second World War, have been the victims of Great Power rivalries and ambitions, perhaps the one with the greatest claim for consideration is the people of Eritrea. Nevertheless, no nation has yet been willing to raise the issue of the rights of this people in the United Nations. The truth is that the 'Eritrean question' is a source of embarrassment both to the UN itself and to almost all 'interested parties'.*[199]

5.2 The Dialectics of Repression and Resistance

Colonial rule and the fight for self-determination have effectively reduced much of the modern history of Eritrea into one of successive confrontations between the forces of foreign domination and those of national resistance. This

---

[198] Ibid., p. 125.
[199] International Commission of Jurists, *Review of the International Commission of Jurists*, No. 26, June 1981.

history is replete with betrayal, tragedy, and suffering, on the one hand, and with heroism, self-sacrifice, and triumph, on the other. Further, Eritrea has, at critical moments in its contemporary history, been betrayed by the powers that be and its people subjected to wanton injustice and suffering duplicated, sadly, by the current regime.

The British reneged on their initial promise of liberation and merely replaced the Italians during World War II. The victorious Allied Powers failed to agree on the disposal of the former Italian colony. The US and its allies used the UN to thwart Eritrean aspirations for decolonisation and federate Eritrea with Ethiopia in the pursuit of strategic geopolitical interests.

When the federation came into effect, Ethiopia defaulted on its commitment to the Federal Act, abrogated the federation, and annexed Eritrea. The UN triple-crossed Eritrea: it violated the precepts of its own Charter when it resolved to deny Eritrea and its people the right of self-determination; it failed to discharge its responsibility to protect the federation when Ethiopia abolished it, despite its pledge that it "would remain an international instrument and, if violated, the General Assembly could be seized of the matter;"[200] and it ignored the struggle, plight, and suffering of the Eritrean people during thirty years of Ethiopia's relentless war.

Ignoring the basic fact that federation represented a reluctant compromise for most Eritreans in the first place, Ethiopia emasculated the Eritrean Government, nullified Eritrea's autonomy, and undercut its economy. It constrained

---

[200] Report of the Special Political Commission of the general Assembly, December 11-12, 1952, A/2188, ▯ 101.

Eritrea's domestic income tax revenues and expropriated its share of revenues from customs and excise duty. It outlawed political parties, banned labour syndicates, and muzzled the press. It shut down, or forced the relocation of, Eritrean factories to Ethiopia to weaken the economy and the labour movement.[201] Further, Ethiopia replaced 'Government of Eritrea' by 'Eritrean Administration'; barred Eritrea's official seals, coat of arms, flag and languages; and seized Eritrea. The occupation violated the UN federal resolution, breached international law, contravened the UN Charter and relevant UN declarations and resolutions, and contradicted UN practice in similar cases elsewhere, such as those of Namibia, Western Sahara, East Timor and Belize.[202]

Eritrean political parties, cabinet secretaries, and Assemblymen repeatedly protested, and tried to resist, Ethiopia's transgressions and interference in Eritrea's internal affairs. Eritrean workers and students staged repeated demonstrations, strikes and boycotts in protest. All proved to no avail, as the UN turned a blind eye. The forcible suppression of the general strike of Eritrean workers in Asmera in March 1958, in particular, demonstrated the futility of peaceful protest in the face of harsh repression, and pointed to armed resistance as the only option left to redress Ethiopia's violations and overcome its violence.

---

[201] The number of factories in Eritrea decreased from 165 in 1958 to 83 in 1961, resulting in large-scale unemployment and mass migration of Eritrean workers to the Sudan, the Middle East and Ethiopia in search of employment. See Tesfagiorgis G., Mussie, Eritrea, Greenwood Publishing Group, 2010, p. 62.

[202] *See*, e.g., Tesfagiorgis, Gebre Hiwet, 1987, pp. 94-127, for an excellent comparative analysis of the five cases.

Imperial ambitions to acquire territory and secure access to the sea drove Ethiopian policy towards Eritrea. Having failed to achieve its aims at the UN, Ethiopia used the federation as a means to recoup its initial loss and incorporate Eritrea. Otherwise, it had no intention to honour its international obligations or to respect the Federal Act, as its later actions swept aside any lingering doubts about its designs for Eritrea. However, as the following section explains, Ethiopia's actions backfired and served to revive Eritrean nationalist aspirations for independence, stiffen Eritrean resistance, and fan the flames of the armed struggle for liberation.

5.3 Armed Struggle as Political Resistance

Imposition of imperial rule and harsh repression left the Eritrean nationalist movement no choice but to take up arms in self-defence. The conviction that continued peaceful resistance in the face of Ethiopia's use of brute force to suppress the nationalist protest would be suicidal informed the decision to resort to armed struggle. The belief that the international community had abandoned the Eritrean case reinforced the move. The premise that peaceful means alone would not achieve Eritrea's independence, that it was necessary to confront Ethiopian violence with armed resistance, sustained it. The Eritrean Liberation Movement (ELM) was established in Port Sudan in September 1958 and, two years later, in July 1960, the Eritrean Liberation Front (ELF) in Cairo, each with the aim to liberate Eritrea from Ethiopian rule through military action.

Better known as *Mahber Shewate* in Tigrinya and *Harekat Tahrir Eritrea*, or simply *Hareka* in Arabic, the ELM was a clandestine political association organised in secret cells of seven members each. Its aim was to liberate Eritrea, consolidate the unity of the Eritrean people, and establish a democratic state. As a secular nationalist organisation, the ELM enjoyed widespread support among Muslim and Christian Eritreans in the Sudan, Eritrea, and Ethiopia. It viewed the Eritrean struggle as an integral part of the anti-colonial and anti-imperialist struggles of the peoples of Africa, Asia, and Latin America.[203] When its plan to seize power through popular insurrection failed, it set out to prepare the groundwork for armed struggle.

The call to arms came as an extension of political resistance. Consistent with the notion that "War is a mere continuation of policy by other means,"[204] the Eritrean armed struggle for self-determination constituted the continuation of the previous policy of political resistance, but by military means. The deadly repercussions of the politics of peaceful protest had brought home to the leaders of the nationalist movement the futility of pacific resistance. The war of national liberation emerged as a political instrument of effective defiance of state violence and, therefore, legitimate action of self-defence in pursuit of the right of self-determination.

In effect, the armed struggle for liberation started as a necessary instrument of a policy of national survival. With

---

[203] The ELM was led by one of Eritrea's unsung heroes, Mohamed Said Naud, a former member of the Sudanese Communist Party, who wrote a book in Arabic in 1996, *Harekat Tahrir Eritrea: Alhaqiqa Weltar'ikh* (Eritrean Liberation Movement: The Truth and the History) and died in Asmera in September 2010.

[204] General Carl von Clausewitz, On War, Book I, Chapter 1, Sec. 24,The Complete Translation by Colonel J.J. Graham, Published by N. Trübner, London, 1873 http://www.clausewitz.com/readings/OnWar1873/TOC.htm

all avenues of peaceful protest leading to a dead end, armed resistance was the only means left to counter aggressive Ethiopian fire with defensive Eritrean fire, and prevent Ethiopia from suppressing the Eritrean national movement into oblivion. The decisive transition from peaceful protest to armed struggle, combining active political resistance with military self-defence, enabled the nascent Eritrean nationalist movement to thrive, kept the quest for self-determination alive, and paved the way to eventual independence.

On 1 September 1961, Hamid Idris Awate led, at the behest of Idris Mohamed Adem, a few fighters to declare the birth of the armed struggle for national liberation under the banner of the Eritrean Liberation Front (ELF).[205] Fired in self-defence against an Ethiopian force, at Mount Adal in the Gash-Barka Lowlands, the sounds of the first shots reverberated in the hearts and minds of many Eritreans at home and in exile. Gradually, the ragtag band of a handful of fighters of the ELF attracted support and recruits from among Eritrean veterans of the Sudanese army, members of the Eritrean Police Force, growing numbers of young Eritrean peasants and workers from the rural and urban areas, and Eritrean students from the Middle East.

---

[205]   Idris Mohamed Adem was one of the leaders of the Moslem League of Western Eritrea which split from the Moslem League of Eritrea in 1949 in opposition to Sheikh Ibrahim Sultan's democratic and progressive nationalist perspective and allied itself with the Unionist Party to form the first Government of Eritrea under the federation. He served as the president of the Eritrean National Assembly from 1955 to 1957 and fled Eritrea in 1959 for exile in Cairo where he became the founding leader of the Eritrean Liberation Front (ELF) in 1960.

Meanwhile, the ELM had also deployed fighters in the field soon after the ELF had started armed struggle. The ELF Supreme Council was unprepared to contemplate cooperation with, and reluctant to allow the emergence of a potential rival with a secular and progressive world view, a more inclusive political appeal, and a wider social base. Under the pretext that the Eritrean struggle could not accommodate more-than-one armed organisation, the ELF decided to liquidate the much smaller ELM by military means. Finally, ELF forces encircled and wiped out ELM fighters at Ila Tsaeda, deep in the mountains of northern Sahel, in 1965.

During the period from 1961-1968, the ELF attracted many recruits and its military wing, the Eritrean Liberation Army (ELA), evolved into a strong guerrilla force that attacked, harassed and wearied the Ethiopian occupation army throughout much of rural Eritrea. Despite the sectarian outlook, makeup, and politics of its leadership, the Front grew in size, swelling the ranks of the ELA. The overall composition of the fighters steadily evolved to reflect the general ethnic, religious, regional, and social diversity of Eritrean society. In 1965, the Supreme Council of the ELF set up the Revolutionary Command, based in Kassala, eastern Sudan, and reorganized the ELA into five autonomous territorial divisions based on ethnic and regional affiliation and deployed them essentially in the geographic areas of their origin.

The ELA's five regional divisions comprised: the First Division, deployed in the then Barka and Gash provinces in western and southwestern Eritrea; the Second Division, deployed in the then Senhit and Sahel provinces in northern and northeastern Eritrea;

the Third Division, deployed in the then Akele-Guzai and Seraye provinces in southern Eritrea; the Fourth Division, deployed in the then Semhar and Denkel provinces in eastern and southeastern Eritrea; and the Fifth Division, which was created in 1966, deployed in the then Hamasien province in central Eritrea. This reorganisation, purportedly, intended to facilitate the mobilisation of support and the recruitment of volunteers for the armed struggle.

This organisational model was ostensibly, drawn from the Algerian war of independence (1954-1962). The ELA's regional divisions duplicated the military regions, or *wilayat,* of the *Armée de Libération Nationale* (ALN) or the National Liberation Army (NLA), the military wing of the *Front de Libération Nationale* (FLN) or the National Liberation Front (NLF). The *wilayat* were set up as clandestine military networks, between March and October 1954, to prepare for the war of independence. On 1 November 1954, the ALN launched the war with simultaneous military operations against the French colonial army in Algeria's six military regions.

By 1956, the French had deployed over 400,000 troops in Algeria. There followed a brutal military campaign that managed to virtually suppress the military resistance of the Algerian National Liberation Army by 1959 at the cost of over a million civilian casualties who were overwhelmingly Algerian. However, growing public and political opposition to the war on the home front brought about a dramatic reversal of the French colonial position. General Charles De Gaulle, the then president of France, declared self-determination for Algeria and opened negotiations with the FLN. The successful conclusion of the Evian

Accords paved the way to the independence of Algeria in 1962.[206]

The leadership's attempt to replicate the Algerian model in Eritrea, given that the specific settings in the two countries were asymmetrical in many respects, was inopportune and, in the end, proved detrimental to the unity of the ELF and the development of the Eritrean struggle. The regional divisions evolved into virtual fiefdoms of their commanders who, in turn, were associated with rival members of the factionalised leadership of the ELF based outside the country - the Supreme Council in Cairo, Egypt, and the Revolutionary Command in Kassala. Favouritism and differential treatment of units in terms of the provision of arms, supplies and privileges fuelled resentment and undermined solidarity. Steeped in the parochial politics of regional, religious and ethnic calculus, the ELF leadership failed to rise to the challenges of inclusive politics and ensuring inner cohesion and unity of the fighters so essential for the conduct of effective warfare. As a result, the Front faced internal dissent, rivalry and tension regarding questions of leadership, organisation and strategy.

There emerged a reform movement aimed to remodel the ELF from within. It sought to unify the zonal divisions, base the leadership of the Front inside the Field, and respect the human rights of the civilian population. This movement led to the first meeting of the commanders and political commissars of the five zones in Aredaib in June 1968. The Third, Fourth and Fifth Divisions held the second meeting

---

[206] See, e.g., Horne, Sir Alistair, A Savage War of Peace: Algeria 1954-1962, Viking Adult (First Edition), 27 March 1978 for a detailed account of the Algerian war of independence.

of delegates in Anseba in September 1968. The commanders of the First and Second Divisions, who reportedly, at the behest of their backers in Kassala and Cairo, had asked for a postponement, did not participate in the meeting. The Anseba Conference established the 'Unity of the Three' under a single Provisional Revolutionary Command.

The third meeting, or the Adobha Conference, was convened between the 'Unity of the Three' and the First and Second Divisions in August 1969. It established a new provisional leadership, the General Command (al *Qiada al Ama*), to be based inside Eritrea. The General Command, made up of 38 members - 18 from the 'Unity of the Three' and 20 from the First and Second Divisions, at the insistence of the latter two – was to replace the external leadership based in Kassala and Cairo, pending the convening of a national congress. The General Command, however, was unable to function independently of the external leadership, maintain its cohesion, and extricate the Front from the simmering internal problem.

Beleaguered by political rivalry, weakened by internal strife, and unable to resolve the crisis through peaceful dialogue, the General Command resorted to acts of forcible suppression and presided over the implosion of the Front. In the turmoil that followed, the Front eventually split four ways in 1970: the Eritrean Liberation Front-General Command (ELF-GC), the parent front; the Eritrean Liberation Front-People's Liberation Forces (ELF-PLF1) that regrouped in Seduha Ella, Denkel; the Eritrean Independence Party,[207] or the ELF-PLF2, that regrouped in Ala, Akele Guzai; and

---

[207] Selfi Natsnet Ertra in Tigrinya.

the Eritrean Liberation Forces (ELF-Obel) that regrouped in Obel, Barka.

Following the convening of its Awate Military Conference in March 1971, the ELF-General Command held its first National Congress in Arr, Barka, in October-November 1971, and changed its name to the Eritrean Liberation Front-Revolutionary Council (ELF-RC). Declaring, once again, that the Eritrean revolution cannot tolerate the presence of more-than-one armed organisation in the Field, it set out to implement a divisive, 'liquidationist' resolution adopted by the Congress. The ELF-RC denounced the dissident factions as the 'counter-revolution' and warned them to return to the fold or risk annihilation.

When the dissidents rejected the warning and called, instead, for dialogue to resolve the internal, or secondary, contradictions of the struggle, the ELF-RC declared war to liquidate the 'counter-revolution' by force. In response, the three-hounded factions agreed to resist and work together, regrouped their forces in Sahel, and established a United Front to avoid piecemeal elimination by the ELF-RC. Outnumbered and outgunned in the effort to avoid annihilation, the United Front eventually coalesced to form the Eritrean People's Liberation Forces (EPLF) in 1973, drew up a plan for more coordinated self-defence, and adapted the strategy of a protracted people's war to liberate the land and the people. The fratricidal civil war, often pitting literally brother against brother, fought with vengeance, caused thousands of casualties on both sides, and left a bitter legacy with lingering scars on the Eritrean body politic.

Despite recurring attempts and intermittent agreements (1975, 1977, and 1979) to cease internecine fire and forge a common front against the primary Ethiopian enemy, unity proved elusive. The civil war lasted, on and off, for ten years until the forces of the ELF-RC, undercut by internal discord, were defeated and pushed out of Eritrea into eastern Sudan, in August 1981, through coordinated EPLF-TPLF military action. Once in the Sudan, the ELF disintegrated into rival factions one of which, the ELF-Central Command (Sagem), returned to the Field and merged with the EPLF in its Second and Unity Congress in 1987. For about ten years following the displacement of the ELF into the Sudan, the EPLF remained the sole force operating in the Eritrean Field until the total defeat of the Ethiopian army in 1991. During that decade, Eritrean efforts and military assets were, for the first time since the start of the civil war in 1972, directed solely against the Ethiopian occupation army.

By the end of 1977 and the beginning of 1978, Eritrean liberation forces of the EPLF and the ELF had liberated the entire countryside and most towns, including mainland Massawa.[208] The Ethiopian army was isolated and besieged in its remaining garrisons in Barentu, Adi Keih, Asseb, the island sections of Massawa, and Asmera. Total victory for the still splintered Eritrean liberation movement seemed within reach. However, that was not to be. A new menace cast an ominous shadow over the Eritrean horizon: massive external intervention. Preparations for a large-scale Soviet backed Ethiopian counter-offensive were approaching completion, whose launch would impede immediate victory, reverse

---

[208] The Ethiopian army was able to hold on to the island sections of the port city with the support of the Soviet navy which kept shelling EPLA positions from its base on Dahlak Kebir Island in the Dahlak Archipelago and warships operating from waters closer off shore overlooking Massawa.

the recent spectacular gains of the Eritrean revolution, and prolong the war for another thirteen years.

5.4 Choosing between Bad and Worse

As explained in the section on *The Geopolitical Setting*, Ethiopia under Emperor Haile Selassie was a staunch ally of the West, in general, and of the United States, in particular, while its regional arch rival, 'Socialist' Somalia aligned itself with the Soviet Camp. When the Ethiopian military junta, the Provisional Military Administrative Council (PMAC), or the Derg, seized power in 1974 under the slogan of 'Ethiopia First' and declared its commitment to 'Ethiopian Socialism' in 1976, the Soviet Union abandoned Somalia and switched its support to Ethiopia. There followed a massive airlift of Soviet arms, the deployment of Soviet Russian and East German military advisors and Cuban and South Yemeni troops in support of the Ethiopian wars with Somalia and in Eritrea.

The unleashing of the mammoth Soviet-backed Ethiopian counter-offensive forced the Eritrean liberation fronts to make a strategic retreat during the second half of 1978. At the time, it was a painful blow to the Eritrean liberation movement in general, and Eritrea's freedom fighters in particular, to turn back from the very gates of Asmera and abandon the people and relinquish the land liberated at considerable sacrifice. The undulating flatlands of the Central Plateau and the vast plains of the Western Lowlands, in particular, offered great advantage to the mechanized and heavy armour of the Ethiopian army in contrast to the relatively lightly armed Eritrean liberation forces. Only the rugged terrain of the Northern Highlands would neutralise this comparative advantage and help level the playing field for the Eritrean resistance to thwart the onslaught of the Ethiopian army.

The Eritrean liberation fronts faced a difficult choice between bad and worse. The strategic retreat staved off positional warfare on unfavourable terrain and foiled the plan of the Ethiopian military regime to deal a debilitating blow to the Eritrean revolution. But, the counter-offensive unleashed by Ethiopia's Soviet supported and numerically superior forces on several fronts had to be dented and their advance delayed in order to allow for an orderly retreat of the liberation army. Several pitched battles were fought to stall the counter-offensive, notably in Massawa, Gerhu Sernay (Tigray), Enda Giorgis (Mereb), Shambuko, Om Hajer, Ingerne (Akurdet), Elabered (Keren), and Maamide (Afabet). The sieges of Adi Keih, Asmera, Barentu, and Massawa were lifted, the Asmera-Massawa and the Mereb-Mendefera roads reopened, and all the liberated cities and towns, save Nakfa, were abandoned. As ELF and EPLF forces, fighting separate and uncoordinated battles, withdrew, Ethiopian troops reoccupied Adi Quala, Afabet, Ali Gidir, Akurdet, Dekemhare, Digsa, Gindae, Mendefera, Omhajer, Tessenei, etc.

In the gruelling battles of the first and second offensives during the summer and autumn of 1978, the Ethiopian army was able to gain considerable ground at the expense of both the ELF and the EPLF while sustaining, in the process, staggering losses in men and materiel. Both cannons and cannon fodder, of which there was no shortage, were dispensable. There were replenishments of weapons and foot soldiers aplenty from a willing Soviet Union and a compelled Ethiopian peasantry, respectively. The paramount objective was to 'eradicate the secessionist bandits once and for all.'

The all-out counter-offensive would continue irrespective of the human toll or material losses incurred. Unable to organise a coordinated resistance in the Eritrea-Ethiopia borderlands, the two fronts quickly ceded territory, mostly in the relatively flat terrain of the southern, central and western parts of the country, and withdrew the bulk of their forces to the rugged north and north-west. However, both fronts maintained limited presence throughout much of Eritrea and continued to carry out significant mobile and guerrilla operations behind the main enemy lines and around the reoccupied cities.

In the Derg's scheme of things, the capture of Keren in the middle of the Anseba Valley, where the Central Plateau, the Northern Highlands, the Western Lowlands, and the eastern Coastal Plains interconnect, would hem in, tighten the noose on, and strangle the Eritrean resistance. With the ELF severely weakened and practically marginalised in the aftermath of the initial Ethiopian counter-offensive, the Ethiopian army concentrated its forces against the EPLF. Both sides in the conflict and the outside world were well aware of the symbolic significance of Keren as the largest liberated city and the unofficial capital of the EPLF since July 1977. Large Ethiopian forces were dispatched to encircle and cut off all access routes to and out of the strategic city. They were engaged by determined forces and scuttled on the approaches to Keren from Asmera, Massawa, and Akurdet at Elabered, Maamide, and Ingerne, respectively.

The stakes were very high in these fierce and fateful zero-sum confrontations. Fresh Ethiopian reinforcements rushed and deployed in haste proved to no avail. These do-or-die battles stalled the advance of the invading army and enabled the orderly evacuation of the city and retreat of the liberation army. Civilians at risk of Ethiopian reprisals, wounded combatants, and Ethiopian prisoners of war (POWs) were withdrawn and vital supplies and equipment retrieved and hauled from or via Keren to the sanctuary of the rear base in Sahel.

The outcome depended more on military intelligence and wit rather than on gross force. Success in these battles enabled the execution of an orderly withdrawal, virtually intact, of the main body of the Eritrean People's Liberation Army (EPLA), its quasi civilian auxiliary departments, and heavy armaments and munitions from the hitherto liberated urban and rural areas to the impregnable EPLF stronghold in Sahel. The defensive victories secured through a conscious spirit of heroic self-sacrifice, resolute determination, and extraordinary solidarity, were crucial to the survival and continuity of the struggle, boosted the morale of the EPLA, and undermined that of the invading Ethiopian army. They stand out in comparable significance at that critical juncture in the evolution of the armed struggle and shall forever remain engraved in the collective memory of the veterans of Eritrea's war of independence.

At the tactical level, the EPLA won, and had to win, these crucial battles. The imperative of self-preservation offered no other choice. Strategically, however, it could not sustain the fighting, or the level of casualties it entailed, on that scale and intensity of combat. The Eritrean resistance army was greatly outnumbered and outgunned. It risked being overstretched, outflanked, and overwhelmed by Colonel Mengistu's huge army, beefed up by South Yemeni and Cuban army contingents and Soviet officers under the command of Field Marshal Vasily I. Petrov, first deputy commander-in-chief of the ground forces of the Soviet army at the time. The pro-

Soviet Arab states in the Steadfastness and Confrontation Front (SCF) were divided in their stance vis-à-vis the counter-offensive: Algeria, Iraq and Syria continued their firm support of the Eritrean struggle while South Yemen sent mechanised units, Libya served as a bridgehead for the Soviet airlift of armaments and provided political and material support, and the Palestine Liberation Organisation (PLO) gave propaganda help to the Ethiopian military.

Having conclusively won the infernal confrontation at Elabered and compelled the Ethiopian forces to disengage and flee back towards Asmera, the triumphant EPLA units withdrew towards Keren and onwards to Sahel. Meanwhile, other units were locked in fierce combat at Ingerne to the west and at Maamide to the east of Keren. Other units rushed to the north to confront and thwart Ethiopian forces which had opened a new front along the northeastern coast of Sahel, threatening to penetrate the rear base and cut off its road and sea links to, and supply lines from, the Sudan and the outside world.

Taken by surprise at the withdrawal of the EPLA from Elabered after having scored a stunning victory, the Soviet field marshal is said to have reported to the General Secretariat of the Communist Party of the Soviet Union (CPSU)[209] in

---

[209] Support for Colonel Mengistu's military regime or its counter-offensive against the Eritrean liberation movement was not unanimous in Moscow. Some members of the central committee of the Communist Party of the Soviet Union (CPSU) reportedly opposed the Soviet role and sympathised with the Eritrean liberation movement. One such sympathiser was said to have confided the contents of the field marshal's report to an Eritrean student in Moscow who later joined the EPLF and recounted the story.

Moscow that a resistance army that employed such a military strategy and battlefield tactics could not be defeated. It had dawned on him that the Eritrean People's Liberation Front possessed the prowess to adjust the strategy and tactics of resistance to the changing balance of military forces. But it was the capture in battle of three Russian colonels ten years later and the advent of *Glasnost* and *Perestroika* under President Mikhail Gorbachev, rather than the field marshal's sober assessment, that persuaded the Soviet Union to reconsider and downgrade its military support to the Ethiopian junta's aggressive but losing campaign against the Eritrean liberation movement.

The EPLA pursued the strategy of a 'protracted people's war' developed by Mao Zedong in China and Vo Nguyen Giap in Vietnam, and adapted it to the particular circumstances of Eritrea. The distinctive motto of the EPLF was "Liberate the Land and the People Step by Step". The liberation of the occupied territory and the emancipation of the oppressed people were to proceed in tandem. The EPLA planned its operations carefully, choosing the time and place of engagement, to inflict maximum damage on the huge invading army and minimise its own losses. When the going got rough, it readily exchanged territory for time to conserve its forces, preserve its assets, and consolidate its military capability. At a critical turning point in the struggle, superior morale, competent operational command, impeccable military intelligence, and intimate familiarity with the terrain more than compensated for the smaller size, inferior equipment, and significantly less firepower of the Eritrean forces.

With the completion of the strategic retreat, the bulk of the EPLA was deployed along an extensive network of bunkers, trenches, ditches, and fortifications, built along the mountain ridges stretching inland from the coastal plains to the western lowlands, in the defence of the rear base in Sahel. The remainder was scattered throughout the rest of the country in small mobile and guerrilla formations. In the bitter war of attrition that ensued for ten years, the EPLA thwarted eight major offensives (*werarat*) between 1978 and 1985, and brought the Ethiopian war machine to a screeching halt.[210]

The EPLA waged four kinds of warfare simultaneously: trench warfare to defend its rear base and liberated areas; mobile warfare to overrun fortified enemy garrisons in the contested areas; guerrilla warfare to harass enemy forces and disrupt their supply and communication lines; and special warfare to destroy or damage strategic military assets in the occupied cities, such as the naval base in Massawa and the air force base in Asmera. The aggregate impact of the combined operations battered the once mighty Ethiopian army, drained its finest units, and infected its rank and file with war fatigue and low morale. A sense of the impossibility of an Ethiopian military victory in Eritrea permeated the Ethiopian high command, dented its internal cohesion, and fanned a hesitant mindset that robbed it of military initiative and resolution. Increasingly, a final Ethiopian defeat seemed only a matter of time to both sides.

---

[210] The first offensive was launched in July-August 1978, the second in October-November 1978, the third in January-February 1979, the fourth in March-April 1979, the fifth in July 1979, the sixth (Red Star) in February-June 1982, the seventh (*selahta werar*) in March-August 1983, and the eighth (*bahr negash*) in October-December 1985.

5.5 A New Shift in the Military Balance

The changing dynamics of the war on the ground, and the battle of willpower that drove it, diminished the morale, weakened the resolve and reduced the combat effectiveness of the Ethiopian army while enhancing those of the EPLA. The EPLA grew in strength, ability, and confidence. It evolved into a highly disciplined fighting force, developed an effective military capability as it captured more sophisticated armaments, munitions, logistics and communications equipment, and gained new recruits, both voluntary and forced.

Incrementally, the war was fought to a stalemate and the fortunes of the contending armies eventually reversed. Amassing an arsenal of over 200 battlefield tanks and armoured vehicles, hundreds of artillery pieces and mortar launchers, and a growing fleet of homemade speedboats ingeniously fitted with medium and heavy armaments, the EPLA had developed into the seventh best equipped army in Africa towards the end of the war.[211] The EPLA was able to dismantle the Ethiopian navy, neutralise the Ethiopian air force, and route the Ethiopian army, setting Eritrea's territory, waters and skies free of foreign occupation once and for all.

The demise of the *Nadew* Command in March 1988 signified a decisive shift in the military balance of forces in favour of the Eritrean struggle. Composed of three infantry divisions and a mechanised brigade, *Nadew*, which means "demolish" in Amharic, was the largest, best trained

---

[211] According to Roy Pateman, Eritrea: Even the Stones Are Burning (The Red Sea Press: 1990, p. 121), the first six countries are: Angola, Egypt, Ethiopia, Mozambique, Nigeria and South Africa.

and best equipped of the four commands or army corps of the Ethiopian Second Revolutionary Army (ESRA). Headquartered in Asmera and spearheaded by the *Nadew* Command, the ESRA was tasked with annihilating the Eritrean liberation movement.

Based in Afabet at the crossroads of Nakfa, Keren, and Massawa, and the approach to the northern escarpment of the Central Plateau, *Nadew*'s specific mission was to recapture liberated Nakfa, the symbolic capital of the EPLF and the gateway to the vital rear and base areas in the Front's Sahel stronghold. In a three-day lightening operation, spanning from 17 to 20 March 1988, *Nadew*, the backbone of the Ethiopian Second Revolutionary Army primed to demolish Eritrean resistance, was itself demolished, its assets and equipment seized virtually intact, and three of its Soviet Russian military mentors taken prisoner, the first time since the Second World War that Russian colonels were captured in combat.

The historic victory in the Battle of Afabet was described at the time by a world famous British historian as the most significant victory of any liberation movement since the great Vietnamese victory against the French colonial army at Dien Bien Phu in 1954[212] and by a Canadian journalist as the largest battle in Africa since the decisive Allied victory against the Axis armies at El Alamein in Egypt in 1942.[213] The

---

[212] Conversations of the author with Basil Davidson in Ararb, Eritrea, after the latter's visit to Afabet in the immediate aftermath of the battle, echoed later in a BBC interview and a subsequent article in Cliffe, L. & Davidson, B., (eds.) The Long Struggle of Eritrea for Independence and Constructive Peace, 1988.

[213] Worthington, Peter, *Needless War Engulfs a Unique African Oasis*, Toronto Sun, 27 December 1998.

destruction of the *Nadew* Command sent shockwaves across the Ethiopian political and military leadership, marked a decisive shift in the military balance of forces in favour of the Eritrean national army, and changed the course of the war.

In a fundamental sense, the demolition of the *Nadew Command* and the attendant capture of the senior Russian military officers compelled the Kremlin to rethink the calculus of Soviet military intervention in the Ethio-Eritrean war. Further, the decisive victory attracted a laudatory message from the TPLF leadership that prompted an immediate rapprochement and the resumption of military cooperation with the EPLF. The renewed EPLF-TPLF alliance provided for the deployment of sizeable EPLA mechanised and infantry units that enabled the TPLF to seize Shire Enda Selassie, following previous botched attempts, and engineered the long joint march to Addis Ababa. There is no question that the instant geostrategic impact of the remarkable victory in Afabet paved the way for a new matrix of regional and international relations.

For the EPLA, the crucial victory heralded the opening salvo of the strategic offensive toward the complete liberation of the country. Subsequent Eritrean military advance was, however, slowed down by the redeployment of the bulk of the Ethiopian First Revolutionary Army from the Ogaden in the Eastern Front with Somalia to reinforce the battered Ethiopian Second Revolutionary Army in the Eritrean theatre. This followed a hastily concluded rapprochement between Addis Ababa and Mogadishu in the context of the rapidly declining fortunes of the hitherto mutually hostile regimes. The new Ethio-Somali entente served to delay, but could not prevent, the demise of the Derg's army in Eritrea and its rule in Ethiopia.

The fresh Ethiopian reinforcements had helped thwart the immediate liberation of Keren and Dekemhare. Nevertheless, the closing salvos of the EPLA's strategic offensive launched in Afabet spelled the looming demise of the Derg's Ethiopian army and the impending termination of Ethiopian occupation of Eritrea. The brilliant victory signalled the beginning of the end of Soviet military support to Ethiopia, as Moscow opened a new line of communication with the EPLF to negotiate the release of its POW officers.

Overall, the Eritrean war of independence lasted virtually thirty long years. The people waged a difficult political and military struggle to affirm their legitimate right of self-determination and to redress the injustice done by the Big Powers and Ethiopia. It was an unequal struggle that pitted the Eritrean liberation forces against the imperial Ethiopian army and its many and strong foreign backers. It was a war that unleashed the destructive energy of modern conventional weapons against the people and the land with unbridled ferocity, compelling an eyewitness to observe that 'even the stones are burning' in Eritrea.[214] That the Eritrean people won remains a living testament to their determination, perseverance, and resilience in the face of great odds.

Made possible at a staggering cost in human life and suffering, liberation constitutes a historic feat and a great achievement for the Eritrean people. The war killed more than 65,000 freedom fighters, disabled about 10,000 combatants, and made over 90,000 children orphans.[215] The death toll

---

[214] Pateman, Roy, Eritrea: Even the Stones Are Burning, The red Sea Press, First Edition 1990.

[215] The officially declared number of martyrs does not include hundreds of freedom fighters, perhaps more, who were executed

amounts to over two per cent of the then population of the country. Although there is no detailed record of the non-combat casualties and civil damage, the war also killed tens of thousands of civilians, decimated scores of entire families, and razed hundreds of villages to the ground.[216] Further, the war displaced and dispersed as refugees about one million people, representing over a quarter of the then total population. Virtually every family contributed to the hard-won victory and to the long list of martyrs and disabled war veterans. In relative per capita terms, the people of Eritrea paid a very high price in blood, toil and treasure.

Beyond the huge casualties and immense damage that still scar the Eritrean demographic and physical landscape, the war destroyed the country, ruined its infrastructure, devastated its economy, disrupted its social fabric, dispersed its communities, and tore its families apart.

5.6 Solidarity amidst Isolation

The outright defeat of the Ethiopian army and the triumphant entry of the EPLA into Asmera on the 24th of May 1991 signified the end of the war. The victorious fighters marched into a joyous reception by an ecstatic and ululating population. The armed struggle achieved victory against

---

or made to disappear under various pretexts or missing in action throughout the duration of the war.

[216] Much of the Eritrean countryside is littered with the ruins of burnt down villages and Eritreans are saddled with the dreadful memories of Ethiopian massacres in Ad Ibrihim, Ad Omer, Ad Shuma, Akurdet, Basikdera, Elabered, Geleb, Hazemo, Hirgigo, Korokon, Mogoraib, Omhajer, Ona, Shebah, She'eb, Wekidba, etc.

overwhelming odds. Over three decades, the Eritrean people had to fight Ethiopian occupation, overcome internal strife and civil war, and confront an array of powerful enemies allied with Ethiopia. Further, Eritrea's war of independence had to contend with the apathy of the United Nations, the general hostility of the Organisation of African Unity (OAU), the forerunner of the African Union (AU), and an international conspiracy of silence, complicity, and isolation.

Well aware that the war of independence would be won, on the battlefield in Eritrea, primarily through the efforts and sacrifices of the Eritrean people, the EPLF nevertheless sought international support and solidarity to complement the national struggle and to help prepare a receptive global response to victory. Moreover, in spite of the apathy, or even downright hostility of the official organs of the international community, mainly the United Nations, the Non-Aligned Movement (NAM), and the OAU, the Eritrean people's resistance enjoyed significant support and solidarity at the level of informed international public opinion.

Indeed, the Eritrean struggle benefited from the revolutionary solidarity of several national liberation movements in Africa and the Middle East. It received the support of civic groups, human rights advocates, and humanitarian organisations in the Middle East, Europe, the Americas, and Australia. Further, it won the acclaim and admiration of many visiting journalists, writers and prominent personalities the world over. The Eritrean people and freedom fighters drew great moral satisfaction from such international support and solidarity.

The list includes opinion setters and renowned scholar-activist-practitioners like Abdulrahman Babu; famous historians like Basil Davidson; celebrated authors like

Thomas Keneally; leading politicians like Glenys and Neil Kinnock, and Uschi Eid; prominent scholar-activists like Ruth First; Nobel laureates like Gabriel Garcia Márquez[217] and José Manuel Ramos-Horta; and revolutionary leaders like Amilcar Cabral and Samora Machel. These and many other leading lights firmly supported and strongly advocated the cause of Eritrean independence. I had the privilege to meet all, and I have the good fortune to remain in friendship with some, of them.

At the regional level, the Eritrean liberation struggle received virtually universal support from the Arab states, liberation movements and civic organisations. In contrast, most of Africa was indifferent. Ever beholden to the mix of hospitality and intimidation of its Ethiopian hosts, the OAU ignored Eritrean appeals for support and remained hostile to the Eritrean liberation movement up to the end of the war. Under the pretext of non-interference in internal affairs and the sanctity of colonial borders, it conveniently overlooked the fact that Ethiopian annexation violated the colonial treaty border between Eritrea and Ethiopia.

Despite the general hostility of the OAU, there were times when the Eritrean issue reverberated in the halls and corridors of its assembly. To their credit, OAU member states, such as Tunisia, Libya, and Morocco, had raised the Eritrean question at different OAU summits of heads of state and government. Except for angry Ethiopian reactions, each of these interventions met stony silence. Otherwise, the Eritrean question was, to the discredit of the premier pan-

---

[217] Gabriel Garcia Márquez, who was also a close friend of Fidel Castro, was instrumental in the suspension of Cuban intervention against the Eritrean liberation movement in 1978.

African organisation, never addressed by the OAU that, like the UN, ignored the struggle and suffering of the Eritrean people during the first three decades of its existence.

This did not however mean that there was no support for the Eritrean question among other OAU member states. In fact, several African leaders had expressed, in separate meetings with EPLF representatives, support for the Eritrean struggle for self-determination. I had the opportunity, as a member or leader of visiting EPLF delegations, to witness expressions of such support in meetings with Ahmed Sékou Touré of Guinea-Conakry, Léopold Sédar Senghor of Senegal, Mohamed Siad Barre of Somalia, France-Albert René of Seychelles, Didier Ratsiraka of Madagascar, and Samora Machel of Mozambique.

Somalia was the sole African state to officially support, facilitate international mobility, and extend political and material assistance to the Eritrean liberation movement. Certain images and presidential remarks have remained vividly imprinted in my memory to this day. The persona of President Ahmed Sékou Touré impressed, while the warm welcome he extended our delegation moved, me very much. Meeting us in the company of his principal cabinet ministers, Sékou Touré called the Eritrean struggle the 'pride of Africa' and promised full Guinean political and diplomatic support for the just struggle of the Eritrean people at regional and international forums. Much as Sékou Touré's disposition and stance had impressed me however, his domestic record and the poverty I observed in and around Conakry disappointed me.

I met Samora Machel in Freetown, Sierra Leone, on the margins of the 1980 OAU Summit of Heads of State, and his then foreign minister Joaquim Chissano. He was forthright and forceful in his expression of support for the cause of Eritrean independence. I readily identified with and deeply admired Samora Machel, not just, because he referred to the Eritrean struggle as the 'lions of Africa', but for the force of his commitment to the revolutionary ideal and the vitality of his youthful energy. Much as I admired Samora Machel then, his premature death later on deeply saddened me.

There were three EPLF missions to Antananarivo during the late 1970s and early 1980s, in two of which I participated. The aim was to solicit the government of Madagascar to raise the Eritrean question and advocate the case for the Eritrean people's right to self-determination at the OAU, the UN, and the Non-Aligned Movement. President Ratsiraka's response to our request was quite candid and telling in a troubling way.

He stated that, while he fully sympathised with the legitimate struggle of the Eritrean people and would readily support Eritrean self-determination if raised at the regional and international forums, Madagascar could not be the first country to raise the issue because of its dependence on the Soviet Union for arms. Our conversations with Ratsiraka and his frank depiction of his government's predicament, in particular, gave me the first insight into the structural weakness of the typical postcolonial African state whose ability to determine its own foreign policy was constrained by its dependence on external aid.

Closer to home, the Eritrean liberation movement considered the building of an independent Eritrea and the construction of a democratic Ethiopia inseparable, and established relations of mutual support and solidarity with progressive opposition movements in Ethiopia. Accordingly, the EPLF established relations with the Ethiopian People's

Revolutionary Party (EPRP) in 1970 and with the TPLF in 1976. Besides, it maintained ties with the Ethiopian People's Democratic Movement (EPDM), the Western Somali Liberation Front (WSLF), the Sidama Liberation Front (SLF), the Afar Liberation Front (ALF), the Oromo Liberation Front (OLF), the Somali Abo Liberation Front (SALF), and the All-Ethiopia Socialist Movement (MEISON). These relations were based on the recognition of the right of the Eritrean people to self-determination and the common commitment to fight the oppressive Ethiopian state.

When the EPRP was founded in 1972, the EPLF provided its first group of fighters with military training, arms, and escort to their initial base in Assimba in the rugged mountainous terrain of northern Tigray. By 1976, relations between the two organisations had developed to the level of engaging in joint military action against the Ethiopian army. They were, however, terminated in 1977 due to the divergence of views on the nature and appropriate resolution of the Eritrean question. The EPLF held that the Eritrean question was a colonial one, and its resolution lay in the exercise of the right to self-determination via independence, while the EPRP maintained that the Eritrean question was a national one that should be resolved through the exercise of the right to self-determination within the framework of a united democratic Ethiopia.

Even though the EPLF maintained cordial ties with several progressive Ethiopian opposition movements, the most important relationship evolved with the TPLF, followed later by that with the OLF. Similar to its initial support for the EPRP, the EPLF provided military training, arms, and personnel from among its Tigrayan-Eritrean fighters, like Mehari Tekle and Yemane Kidane (Jamaica), to the newly established TPLF in 1976. The TPLF emulated the EPLF, replicated its structure and the two fronts developed close relations. Over time, the EPLF trained and armed several thousands of Tigrayan recruits for the TPLF. In 1981, the TPLF joined forces with the EPLF to defeat and displace the ELF from Eritrea and TPLF forces fought alongside the EPLF against the Derg's 1982 *Red Star* or 6th offensive.

Nevertheless, constant tension underlay the EPLF-TPLF relationship. The objective of the TPLF was the establishment of a "Republic of Greater Tigray" whose geographic boundaries would incorporate large areas of Eritrea and whose definition of a "Tigrayan" included the majority of the Eritrean population.[218] At the outset, the national question and the national struggle were paramount and the secession of Tigray the ultimate objective for the TPLF. In contrast, the EPLF maintained that while the solution to the national question lay in the right to self-determination, secession would be an incorrect and an impractical solution in the specific conditions of Ethiopia.[219] The EPLF contended that regional autonomy allowing for the unity of the oppressed nationalities on the basis of equality within the territorial integrity of Ethiopia would provide for a just and durable solution to the national question in Ethiopia.

More specifically, the EPLF asserted that there was neither a historical basis nor a socioeconomic justification for the claim to Tigrayan independence and that the TPLF should, instead, fight for regional autonomy within the

---

[218] Tigray People's Liberation Front, Manifesto 1976.

[219] EPLF, "The EPLF and its Relations with Democratic Movements in Ethiopia", *Adulis* (monthtly organ of the EPLF), Vol. 1, No. 11, May 1985.

framework of the liberation and democratic transformation of Ethiopia as a whole. The TPLF resented the EPLF prescription that would limit the scope of the right of self-determination of Tigray. The resulting friction, accentuated by the strains inherent in the historical relationship between Tigray and Eritrea, along with a clash of divergent military strategies and ideological visions, led to an open conflict. In spite of the bitter polemical dispute and simmering tensions that accompanied the severance of relations and all collaboration between the EPLF and the TPLF from 1985 to 1988, the two fronts resumed mutual cooperation following the demise of the *Nadew Command* in Afabet and bolstered the alliance that ultimately toppled the Ethiopian military junta in 1991.

In addition to the EPRP and the TPLF, the EPLF provided military training and assistance to the OLF. It armed and handed over thousands of Ethiopian Oromo POWs who agreed to join the Front. Arms and trainees passed through eastern Sudan in transit from Eritrea to the OLF area of operations in southern Ethiopia. Furthermore, in January 1990, sizable EDF forces fought their way through SPLA positions on the Sudan-Ethiopia border at Kurmuk and, in coordination with the OLF, overran the Ethiopian army garrison in Assosa, Wellega, southwestern Ethiopia.

Beyond the Arab World, Africa, and Ethiopia, the Eritrean struggle for self-determination also enjoyed the support and solidarity of several major political parties.in Western Europe. The French Socialist and Gaullist parties, the British Labour and Liberal Democratic parties, the principal Italian and Norwegian political parties, the German Social Democratic and Green parties, and the Swedish Social Democratic Party were among those which officially recognised the right of the

Eritrean people to self-determination. On balance, therefore, the Eritrean struggle enjoyed the moral and political support of much of the progressive world.

Undoubtedly, Ethiopia's war of aggression against Eritrea was the largest and most devastating war in the modern history of the Horn of Africa, surpassed in scale and intensity only by the 1998-2000 Ethio-Eritrean border war. Its impact shook Ethiopia and reverberated throughout the region. Its evolution set in motion an inexorable process of internal ferment and revolt that destabilised the feudal foundations of the Ethiopian Empire and paved the way for the demise of two successive regimes: first the imperial regime of Emperor Haile Selassie, and second the military regime of Colonel Mengistu Haile Mariam.

While it lasted, the war pitted two of Africa's poorest nations, wrought enormous damage to both countries, hindered their socioeconomic development, and caused immense suffering to their peoples. When it ended, it ushered in the decolonisation of Eritrea and the liberation of Ethiopia from the Derg regime's brutal military dictatorship. The overthrow of the Derg and the demise of its huge army were the product of the joint struggles of the Eritrean and Ethiopian liberation movements, and the collective sacrifices of the Eritrean and Ethiopian peoples.

Following the historic victory at Afabet, the EPLF and the TPLF abruptly patched up the feud that had disrupted their relations from 1985 to 1988, and resumed cooperation, an alliance that enabled them to dismantle the Derg and scuttle its war machine. As the EPLA inched towards Massawa, Asmera, and Asseb, some of its units fought alongside TPLF and, later, EPRDF (the umbrella organisation of Ethiopian opposition groups) troops, from Shire Endaselassie in northern Tigray, near the Ethiopia-Eritrea border, all the way to Addis Ababa. Unit after unit, the Ethiopian army crumbled on all fronts and Colonel Mengistu Hailemariam fled to Zimbabwe as the allied EPLF and EPRDF forces closed in on the capital. The insurgent armies liberated Asmera and Addis Ababa on 24 and 27 May 1991, respectively.

5.7 Eritrea Independent at Last

The shared victory of the Eritrean and Ethiopian liberation movements prompted a radical shift in the traditional balance of power in Ethiopia, and potentially in the entire region of the Horn of Africa, and changed the configuration of Ethiopian politics for a long time to come. Ethiopia was an anachronistic feudal empire reeling under an absolute monarch who ruled by 'divine right' until 1974, when a brutal military dictatorship took over. The seizure of power by the insurgent EPRDF in 1991, at the conclusion of the protracted war of national liberation in Eritrea and a long civil war in Ethiopia, marked the end of the highly centralised imperial Ethiopian state that progressive Ethiopians characterised as 'a prison of nations and nationalities'.

The ascent of the EPRDF government shattered the open-air prison that was the semi-feudal empire-state, reconfigured Ethiopian politics and signified a radical shift in the country's century-old internal power relations. The liberation of Eritrea from the yoke of Ethiopian oppression created the possibility for the liberation of Ethiopia itself. The defeat of the military dictatorship in Addis Ababa and the consequent breakup of the colonial bondage in Eritrea ended the regime of oppression in both countries. The EPRDF instituted a system of ethnic federalism, a decentralised federation of ethnically defined regional states, based on a parliamentary system of government at the federal and state levels. The hitherto "imprisoned nations and nationalities" of Ethiopia were reorganised into new regional states with a constitutional guarantee of equality and the right to self-determination, up to and including secession.[220]

The stage was thus set for the establishment of democratic and developmental states in Ethiopia and Eritrea. Both governments were committed not only to democratising their respective societies but also to support each other to become stable, democratic and good neighbours through the promotion of close cooperative relations in the political, economic, social, and cultural spheres. This heralded the prospect of a new era of peace, stability, and cooperation between Eritrea and Ethiopia, with a potential to serve as a nucleus for political cooperation and regional integration in the Horn of Africa.

With its foundations firmly laid in rural Eritrea, the armed struggle resonated increasingly louder among a restive population in the cities, urban centres and diaspora communities outside the country. It gradually gained ground and gathered momentum as the war became ever extended. As described above, the insurgency developed from small hit-and-run attacks against isolated Ethiopian garrisons and extended supply lines in the early years into a formidable

---

[220] Article 39(1) of the 1995 Constitution of the Federal Democratic Republic of Ethiopia states that "every Nation, Nationality and People in Ethiopia has unconditional right to self-determination including the right to secession" whileArticle 39(3) guarantees that "every Nation, Nationality and People in Ethiopia has the right to a full measure of self-government which includes the right to establish institutions of government in the territory that it inhabits and to equitable representation in state and Federal governments".

mix of guerrilla, conventional, mobile, and special warfare that eventually enveloped the entire country and swept away Ethiopian occupation.

As the movement grew in size, outreach and scale of operations, the burgeoning Eritrean liberation army overcame serious afflictions of internal division, survived a fratricidal civil war, withstood regional isolation, and defied superpower intervention. Over the course of three decades, punctuated by periods of advance and setback, the Eritrean liberation movement challenged, stalemated, and ultimately defeated the Ethiopian occupation army. In the process, it rid Eritrea of foreign domination for the last time, and helped Ethiopia overthrow both imperial despotism and military dictatorship.

Outright military victory in 1991 ended the war, marked Eritrea's liberation from Ethiopian occupation, and paved the way for the formal declaration of sovereign independence. The momentous event signified the triumph of the lonely and long march of the Eritrean people to freedom and justice. Finally, the brilliant triumph created the conditions that enabled Eritrea as a nation to exercise the right of self-determination and to acquire a new international status as a sovereign state. Accession to independence generated a very high level of national excitement verging on euphoria, and triggered an explosion of optimism, setting the country ablaze with the flames of hope and expectation. In the hearts and minds of the Eritrean people, it promised the vindication of the huge sacrifices made on the way and signalled the advent of a new dawn heralding a bright future shining with peace, freedom, democracy and prosperity.

The improbable military victory made the liberation and *de facto* independence of the country possible in 1991. After a century of colonial domination, half a century of political resistance, and three decades of military struggle, the time had come for the people of Eritrea to freely exercise the right of self-determination as a nation and as a people, and reap the fruits of liberty. In a free and fair referendum conducted from 23 to 25 April 1993, and observed by several international and regional organisations, the Eritrean people decided in favour of sovereign statehood by an overwhelming majority of 99.8 per cent. The historic exercise of the right of self-determination of Eritrea as a nation ushered in *de jure* independence, proclaimed the birth of an independent sovereign state, and determined the international status of Eritrea.

At the same time, sovereign statehood provided the Eritrean people with an opportunity to freely choose their own government, chart their future, embark on a new democratic dispensation, manage their affairs in their own best interest, and build a prosperous and fair society. As a basis for the exercise of their right of self-determination as a people, independence heralded the prospect of a new era of freedom, peace and security for Eritrea with democracy, justice and prosperity for its people. It offered the new Eritrea and its people the possibility to develop, thrive, and prosper in peace and freedom.

The EPLF had issued, in November 1980, a seven-point proposal to hold a referendum in Eritrea to bring about a peaceful solution to the Eritrean question in accordance with the principle of the right of peoples to self-determination under the supervision of an international commission acceptable to both sides.[221] In contrast to the Derg's *Nine Point Policy of*

---

[221] Eritrean People's Liberation Front, Proposals for a Referendum in Eritrea, 21 November 1980.

Regional Autonomy on Eritrea, announced in March 1976, which restricted the exercise of the right to self-determination to 'regional autonomy' within Ethiopia, the EPLF proposal provided for a free choice between full independence, federal association with Ethiopia, or regional autonomy.

The Derg's policy of regional autonomy represented a ploy to cover up its effort to resolve the Eritrean question by military means and force the surrender of the Eritrean struggle. On the other hand, the EPLF proposal laid the legal basis for the peaceful resolution of the Eritrean question. Predictably, the Derg rejected the proposal. Its overthrow by military means created the conditions, and paved the way for the conduct of the referendum after the liberation. Accordingly, the referendum was organised by the Provisional Government of Eritrea (PGE) with the blessing of the new EPRDF government in Ethiopia and monitored by the United Nations in April 1993. As the outcome of the vote was a foregone conclusion, the ballot gave a choice between '*Yes*' or '*No*' for '*Independence*'. Had the outcome been '*No*', the two options of association with Ethiopia could have come into play in a second stage in line with the EPLF's original proposal to allow the Eritrean people to determine their future.

For the people and freedom fighters, the liberation from Ethiopia set the stage for the creation of a free and sovereign state, founded on a progressive constitution that sanctions the separation of powers and enshrines the rule of law, democratic principles, and respect for human rights. As the expression of the free exercise of national self-determination, independence represented a great historic achievement for Eritrea and its people. It opened the way for the emergence of a free, democratic, and prosperous state at peace with itself and with its neighbours.

In a nutshell, liberation was pursued as a stepping stone for independence; independence was sought to enable the creation of a new democratic state whose hallmarks would be the pursuit of liberty, progress, and prosperity for the people, under a government constituted on the basis of the free exercise of the Eritrean people's right to self-determination. Together, liberation and independence gave promise to an Eritrea capable of rebuilding from the ruins, healing the wounds, and bridging the divides caused by the war.

As the victorious movement that dismantled Ethiopian colonial rule, the EPLF established the Provisional Government of Eritrea (PGE) in 1991. It formed the Transitional Government of Eritrea (TGE) in 1993, subsequent to the expressed wishes of the great majority of the people for independence in the referendum in exercise of the right of national self-determination. The EPLF initially relied on the legitimacy of its revolutionary credentials, backed by the might of the EPLA, to fill in the political vacuum created by the demise of Ethiopian occupation. The exercise of the people's right of self-determination, in the form of free and fair elections, pending an interim period of four years, would bring a constitutional government into being.

The following chapters will examine the consequences of the failure to complement the free exercise of the right of Eritrea to self-determination with the right of the people to choose their own government, to determine the evolution of the Eritrean state, and to manage their political, economic, and social affairs.

CHAPTER 6

State Construction and Development

Our object in the construction of the state is the greatest happiness of the whole, and not that of any one class. - Plato

The preceding chapter stressed that Eritreans fought the armed struggle to secure the right to self-determination, as a nation and as a people. In line with the political programme of the EPLF, independent Eritrea adopted a National Charter,[222] a Macro-Policy paper[223] and a Constitution.[224] The *National Charter* articulates the vision of a free, democratic, and prosperous Eritrea. The *Macro-Policy* provides a coherent economic policy framework to rehabilitate the economy, catalyse sustainable development, and generate prosperity with social justice. The *Constitution* lays down the legal foundation of the Eritrean State. These policy instruments aimed to establish a constitutional

---

[222] Eritrean People's Liberation Front (EPLF), A National Charter for Eritrea: For a Democratic, Just and Prosperous Future, Third Congress, Nakfa, February 1994.

[223] Government of the State of Eritrea, *Macro-Policy*, Asmera, November 1994.

[224] Constitution of Eritrea, 23 May 1997.

government, build a democratic state, and construct an advanced economy. Their underlying set of ideals, principles, and objectives, given life during the brief interlude of peace and stability that reigned from May 1991 to May 1998, epitomised considerable optimism, great expectations, and enormous promise for Eritrea and the Eritrean people.

During the last decade of the thirty-year war of independence, Eritrea under the EPLF possessed a formidable liberation army. It also owned elaborate quasi-civilian departments that managed an extensive network of administrative and social services throughout the liberated areas and operated several liaison offices abroad. The Front's organisational regime functioned very much like a state-in-waiting. However, although it was in virtual control of the defined national territory of Eritrea and maintained offices of foreign representation, the EPLF regime of the 1980s lacked the juridical attributes necessary for international recognition, consistent with the terms of the 1933 Montevideo Convention on Rights and Duties of States.

According to the Montevideo Convention, "a state is characterised by: (a) a permanent population; (b) a defined territory; (c) a government; and (d) the capacity to enter into relations with the other states."[225] Eritrea possessed the attributes of a permanent population and a defined territory upon its establishment as a colonial state and acquired a government upon its liberation in 1991. Furthermore,

---

[225]   Smis, Stefaan, *The Legal Status of International Land Boundaries in Africa*, in Politics of Identity and Economics of Conflict in the Great Lakes Region, Ruddy Doom & Jan Gorus (eds.), Brussels: VUB Press, 2000, p. 191-192, in reference to the Montevideo Convention on Rights and Duties of States, 23 December 1933, Article 1 165 *League of Nations Treaty Series*, p.19.

it acquired the characteristic of the capacity to enter into relations with the other states at the conclusion of the referendum, conducted on 23-25 April 1993, and subsequent declaration of independence on 27 April 1993.[226]

In view of the quite remarkable political, social and economic achievements of the EPLF under difficult wartime conditions, liberation and accession to statehood gave rise to high expectations among the people and friends of Eritrea for comparable, if not better, performance in peacetime reconstruction and development. There prevailed great anticipation that Eritrea would build on the revolutionary achievements of the war of independence to establish an effective, efficient and functional state able to meet the challenges of constitutional government, democratic governance and sustainable development. Equipped with the abovementioned political, economic and legal policy instruments, the new state had a great opportunity to blaze a new path towards real emancipation, democracy, and prosperity.

6.1 Essential Policy Instruments

Upon liberation, the EPLF formed the Provisional Government of Eritrea pending the holding of a referendum, the formal

---

[226] The referendum was conducted on the single question of "Do you want Eritrea to be an independent and sovereign country?" The UN Observer Mission to Verify the Referendum in Eritrea (UNOVER) declared the conduct of the referendum free and fair and verified the ballot results of 99.8 % 'Yes', 0.17 % 'No', and 0.03 % 'Uncounted' in a voter turnout of 98.2 %, representing 1,154,001 out of 1,174,654 registered voters (A/48/283, 11 August 1993), paragraphs 52-53. Eritrea thus effectively exercised its right of self-determination as a nation.

declaration of independence and the establishment of a constitutional government.[227] That government consisted of the Eritrean National Assembly (ENA), an interim legislative organ constituted of the EPLF Central Committee (CC); the State Council, an interim executive organ composed of the secretaries of the various sectoral departments; and the Eritrean courts as a judicial organ that would function independently of the legislative and executive branches. The Secretary General of the EPLF CC was designated the Secretary General of the Government, the Chairman of the State Council, the Chairman of the National Assembly, and the Commander-in-Chief of the armed forces.

Upon formal accession to sovereign statehood, the establishment of the transitional government, the Government of Eritrea, superseded the provisional government. Issued on the eve of the formal declaration of independence, Proclamation 37/1993 drew up the structure, established the powers, and defined the functions of the transitional government.[228] Subsequently, Proclamation 42/1993 stated the specific functions of the newly established ministries, commissions, authorities and agencies, and vested them with the requisite statutory authority to facilitate the performance of their respective functions.[229]

The transitional government would be composed of the National Assembly as the legislative body, the Council of State or cabinet of ministers as the executive branch,

[227] Provisional Government of Eritrea, Gazette of Eritrean Laws: Proclamation 23/1992, No.5, Asmera, 22/5/1992.

[228] Provisional Government of Eritrea, Gazette of Eritrean Laws: Proclamation 37/1993, No.6, Asmera, 19 May 1993.

[229] Provisional Government of Eritrea, Gazette of Eritrean Laws: Proclamation 42/1993, No.8, Asmera, 1 July 1993.

and the judicial organ made be up of the civil, special, and military courts. As the supreme representative of the people vested with the highest authority, the transitional National Assembly would elect the state president, and confirm the members of the cabinet and heads of diplomatic missions. The three branches of the government would exercise their respective statutory mandates within the framework of a functional balance. However, the president would also serve as the chair of the legislative body, an arrangement that vested considerable authority in the presidency in violation of the principle of the separation of powers.

The National Assembly would convene in regular meetings every six months, or in extraordinary meetings at the behest of the president or the request of two-thirds of its members, as required. The Council of State, chaired by the president and accountable to the National Assembly, would serve as the highest authority between sessions of the National Assembly. The president would serve as the highest authority between meetings of the cabinet of ministers.

The transitional government was mandated to, *inter alia*, safeguard the fundamental freedoms and basic rights of the people, defend the unity and territorial integrity of the country, and ensure justice, peace, and stability. It was set up for an interim period of maximum four years, pending the adoption of a constitution, the holding of national elections, and the creation of a freely and fairly elected democratic government in accordance with the provisions of the Constitution.

Surviving members of the EPLF Central Committee, elected in the second congress of 1987, and 60 members from outside of the leadership of the Front, constituted the transitional Eritrean National Assembly. The 60 other persons were made up of 30 members selected from the ten provincial assemblies, 10 women members and 20 other members from outside the EPLF. Most of the non-EPLF appointees were former senior cadres and members of the leaderships of different factions of the Eritrean Liberation Front (ELF).

As the supreme legal authority and repository of legitimate power during the transition period of four years, pending the establishment of a democratically elected constitutional government, the National Assembly would oversee the work of the executive branch. It would enable the adoption of a state constitution, the promulgation of a national press code, and the creation of legislation on the formation of political parties and political organisations. In addition, it would expedite all necessary measures to facilitate the transition to a constitutional order by 1997. After the third congress of the EPLF in 1994, the reconstituted National Assembly comprised 150 members, embracing the 75 members of the new central council of the People's Front for Democracy and Justice (PFDJ), the successor of the EPLF, and 75 members elected by the Front's regional committees. It also retained its transitional mandate.

As mentioned in the chapter above, the EPLF had, immediately after independence, articulated, in *A National Charter for Eritrea*, its vision of establishing a free, democratic and prosperous Eritrea on the ruins of the colonial state. Further, the Transitional Government issued a policy document entitled *Macro-Policy*, which set out a coherent macroeconomic policy framework to rehabilitate the economy. The overriding objective of the Macro-Policy paper was to achieve rapid national reconstruction, ensure sustainable development and generate prosperity with social justice. To cap and entrench the political vision found in the National Charter and the economic policy framework articulated in the Macro-Policy paper, a national *Constitution* was drafted and duly ratified in May 1997 to serve as the legal foundation of the State of Eritrea.

The set of political, economic and legal precepts, values and objectives underpinning the three documents aimed to provide policy guidance to support the effort to rebuild the country, construct the state, and kick-start the economy. The Constitution defined the structure of government, set up institutional checks and balances, and provided guarantees of individual freedom, political rights, and civil liberties. Following a finite period of transition lasting for four years (1993-1997), the conduct of national, regional and local elections would allow the people to democratically elect their leaders and establish government units at all levels.

The National Charter outlined a holistic vision of Eritrea, encapsulated in six basic goals and six guiding principles. The six basic goals are national harmony, political democracy, economic and social development, social justice, cultural revival, and regional and international cooperation. The six basic principles are national unity, active participation of the people, the decisive role of the human factor, struggle for social justice, self-reliance, and a strong relationship between the people and the leadership. The National Charter embedded democracy, justice, and prosperity as essential elements for the improvement of the human condition of the Eritrean people.

More specifically, the National Charter pledged the creation of a *constitutional political system* that respects the rule of law and ensures basic human rights and fundamental freedoms. It promised *national constitutional system* that reflects the history, development and specificity of Eritrean society and ensures unity, balanced development, national independence and security. It also pledged a *democratic constitutional system* based on the full range of democratic principles. The National Charter enunciated the values, principles, and objectives of a new Eritrea in line with the ethos of the armed struggle and the aspirations of the Eritrean people.[230]

The *Macro-Policy* paper crystallised the essential conclusions of a series of brainstorming sessions on development strategy and policy. The initial exercise, chaired by the President, involved extensive participation of senior officials from the key economic ministries and the central bank.[231] It availed an economic policy framework conducive to the rapid rebuilding and sustainable development of the country. The new Eritrea rising from the ravages of war faced, *inter alia*, the task of rehabilitating a ruined economy, rebuilding a damaged physical and social infrastructure, demobilising and reintegrating former fighters, and organising the repatriation and reintegration of refugees from neighbouring countries.

The macroeconomic policy paper identified the rehabilitation, reconstruction and development of the economy, ravaged by war and neglect, as the most serious challenge facing Eritrea at the time of liberation. To remedy the situation and make up for lost time, the Macro-Policy

---

[230] In other words, the principles of accountability, transparency, pluralism and tolerance. See EPLF, A National Charter for Eritrea, p. 19-24.

[231] The governor of the central bank and two senior officials of the ministry of finance were entrusted with crystallising the framework.

framework set the overall national development objective as "the creation of a modern, technologically advanced and internationally competitive economy within the next two decades."[232]

Agricultural growth, export oriented industry and services, tourism, an international financial services centre, and extensive human capital formation, were to serve as the principal drivers of national development. In addition, the macro-policy paper identified as priorities the creation of an advanced public health care system, a social welfare safety net, protection and restoration of the environment, a decentralised and democratic political system, domestic peace and stability, harmony with neighbours, and respect for human rights. These constituted essential conditions for sustainable development and the betterment of the people's standard of living.

The Macro-Policy paper stipulated that the private sector would be the leading economic actor and the main engine of growth in the new Eritrea.[233] Microeconomic and business operations were to be its exclusive preserve. The role of the government would be regulation, supervision, research, and human resource development. Its central economic function would be to provide the necessary stimulus and supplement to the efforts of the private sector. The "establishment of an efficient, outward looking, and private sector-led market economy" was to be the core objective of economic policy and the centrepiece of development strategy.[234]

---

[232] Government of the State of Eritrea, *Macro-Policy*, Asmera, November 1994, p. 10.
[233] Ibid, p. 15.
[234] Ibid, p. 12.

Furthermore, the macroeconomic policy framework aimed to define the roles and interface of the private and public sectors in the national economy and to clarify the question of property rights to nurture entrepreneurship and encourage the full participation of private enterprises in economic development. This aimed to promote the private sector, stimulate private investment, both domestic and foreign, and achieve rapid economic recovery and sustainable growth to enhance the "standard and quality of life of the Eritrean people."[235] Further, the programme of economic reform would to initiate the transition to a market economy, with the formulation of the National Economic Policy Framework (NEPF) in 1998 reinforcing the development vision of a market-based and export-oriented economy.

The ratification of the Constitution of Eritrea in 1997 represented an important milestone for the introduction of democratic institutions of governance. As a living document framed in broad terms, the Constitution forms the legal foundation on which the State of Eritrea rests. The *Preamble* affirms the Constitution as the fundamental law of the State as the covenant between the people and the government. It is the source of all laws, government legitimacy, and the basis for the protection of the freedoms, rights and dignity of the Eritrean people.

The Constitution establishes the legislature, the executive organ, and the judiciary as three coequal branches of government, defines their principal functions, and delimits their respective powers to ensure institutional checks and balances. It affirms the head of the executive as head of state and government as well as commander-in-chief of the

---

[235]   Ibid, p.14.

armed and security forces, but corrects the previous anomaly of the head of the executive also serving as the head of the legislature. It sanctions the national defence and security forces of the country to owe allegiance to the Constitution and to a duly established constitutional government.

As the legal foundation of the State, the Constitution provides the basis for state construction in accordance with democratic principles and the rule of law; stipulates the "establishment of a democratic order" as the "foundation of economic growth, social harmony and progress;"[236] and advocates the creation of a political system embedded in universal democratic values.

At the time of independence, Eritrea stood impoverished by the combined effects of a century of foreign occupation, a history of colonial plunder and neglect, and the devastation of a protracted war of national liberation. It was the firm conviction that liberty, dignity and prosperity would remain elusive dreams under continued Ethiopian occupation that drove tens of thousands of Eritrean youth to the field, lent the armed resistance a powerful new impetus and ensured final victory. Having suffered from oppression, poverty and deprivation for so long and forced to sacrifice so much to reclaim their country, the great majority of the Eritrean people entertained high hopes and great expectations that independence would be a prelude to a better life of freedom, democracy and prosperity in peace and security.

The political, economic and legal policy frameworks would guide the pursuit of these long-held legitimate aspirations of the people. The National Charter proclaimed the basic goals, guiding principles and political system for

---

[236] Constitution of Eritrea (Article 7), p. 6. Preamble, p. III.

a new democratic state. The Constitution laid the basis and defined the main pillars of a democratic state based on the rule of law and committed to the protection of fundamental freedoms and basic rights. The Macro-Policy paper promised to create an economic order conducive to rapid reconstruction of the damaged infrastructure and swift rehabilitation of the ruined economy, pursue sustainable development, and improve public wellbeing. In combination, these instruments equipped the Government with the policy guidance needed to consolidate nation building and deliver emancipation, democracy and progress.

The imperative to expedite the complex, dynamic and interconnected processes of nation-building, state construction and balanced development required the government to make several key policy choices and to adopt a set of measures that would define the essential character of the emerging Eritrean state in its various institutional, ethical and industrial dimensions.

6.2 A Unitary Eritrean State

Upon independence in 1993, Eritrea's formerly nine provinces were reorganised into ten, including Asmera, the state capital. Eritrea adopted the model of a unitary state, with decentralised administration and significant power devolving to the provinces. The government declared land state property in 1994 and, in 1996, reorganised the state into six administrative zones or *zobas*, 59 subzones or *neus zobas*, and 701 administrative locales or *kebabis*.[237]

---

[237] The 701 administrative locales or *kebabis* regroup 2006 villages and village clusters.

The administrative regions were ostensibly, constructed around catchment basins and drawn up based on considerations of population size, resource base, development potential, and the easing of traditional land disputes. The configuration of considerable ethnic, religious and regional overlap in five of the six regions aimed to promote a strong Eritrean national identity that transcends regional, religious and ethnic affiliation in the service of consolidating nation-building, state construction and sustainable development.

Each region would have an autonomous administration, an appointed administrator acting as the regional executive, an elected assembly functioning as the regional legislature, and regional, sub-regional, and local courts serving as integral parts of an independent judiciary. Decentralisation would allow the devolution of power, the democratisation of the decision-making process, and the consolidation of national unity in diversity. The exercise of real autonomy would facilitate grassroots involvement at the regional (*zoba*), sub-regional (*neus zoba*), and local (*kebabi*) levels to enable the people to determine and manage their day-to-day affairs.

One of the principal objectives of the administrative reorganization of the country into regions, sub-regions, and locales was to provide for the devolution of power and to promote participatory politics at the three layers of local government, in tandem with the unitary structures of the state. Emulating the traditional *baito* (assembly) system of local governance that functioned in much of pre-colonial and colonial Eritrea (prior to Ethiopian rule under the *Derg*), democratically elected representatives of the people would constitute the *baitos* or assemblies. The *baitos* would serve as vital deliberative organs and repositories of real power with oversight functions over the executive bodies at the three levels of local government.

6.3 Land and Internal Mobility

Eritrean society holds land in great value as the source of economic livelihood, the basis of identity and the reference point of affiliation. An intricate link between land, village, and community defines identity and sense of belonging. Under the conventional system of land tenure, land generally belonged to the village or clan and its use for farming, grazing, or forestry managed as private property under family and/ or communal ownership. Under the system of communal ownership in parts of the Central Plateau, for instance, the village assembly, or *baito adi*, determined the allocation and use of land among members of the village community. In traditional Eritrean society, the village, or *adi*, is the locus of identity and the nucleus of community. Eritreans also use *adi* as a generic reference for Eritrea as a whole, in normal conversation or common parlance.

Modern Eritrea has endured three waves of nationalisation that established state ownership of land and effectively disenfranchised the people. First, during the Italian era when the colonial regime issued land laws in 1909 and 1923 that declared land *terra domeniale*, or State property, in violation of local land rights and expropriated vast tracts without compensation to their rightful owners. Second, during the Ethiopian military regime when the *Derg* issued a proclamation of land reform in 1975 and nationalised all land and urban housing. And third, during the period after independence when the Eritrean government, following in the footsteps of the Italian and Ethiopian colonial regimes, issued the Land Proclamation of 1994 that declared all land and urban housing to be state property.

The Proclamation declares land state property and authorises the government to regulate the system of land ownership, land tenure, land use and management. Specifically, it empowers the state to determine the distribution, allocation, and expropriation of land, with provisions for due compensation to its rightful owners or users, for various purposes. These purposes include development, national reconstruction, and housing (*tiesa* land); giving Eritreans leases or usufruct rights; and defining the powers and duties of the Land Commission, charged with the responsibility for the implementation of the new system of land tenure directly under the auspices of the president.[238]

Given rational and prudent management, Eritrea possesses sufficient land for housing, farming, grazing, national parks, forestry, urban, and industrial use to ensure the balanced development, prosperity, and enjoyment of the country's relatively small population. In practice, however, the presidency has disbanded the Land Commission as an autonomous agency and taken over its task. The government expropriates agricultural and grazing land without compensation, allots land and urban housing in an arbitrary manner, delays the allocation of land for residential purposes, and wantonly obstructs the construction of new urban housing. A recent government editorial disseminated through the state owned media openly concedes the prevalence of gross abuse and rampant corruption in the management, allocation and use of land, including

---

[238] Government of the State of Eritrea, Land Proclamation (No. 58/1994), 24 August 1994.

the illegal allotment and sale of land and urban housing facilitated through corrupt administrative, banking and lending practices and the laundering of criminally acquired dirty money.[239]

The war of national liberation was, among other things, fought for land, liberty and livelihood. Linked by a symbiotic bond, the land and the people are inseparable. Land appropriation without due compensation violates the property rights of the people and disregards the interests of the community. The land issue in Eritrea today has become an integral part of the general demand for change to restore the machinery of government and the vital resources of the country to the people. Restitution of land ownership and management to the people would end rampant government abuse in its allocation, rationalise its use to meet the basic needs of the people, and help to resolve the acute shortage of housing in Eritrea's capital and main urban centres. Further, it would stem the forcible resettlement of people, with its attendant problems in terms of the rights and wellbeing of both the forced settlers and the disowned host communities.

Eritreans forced to flee the country during the armed struggle for liberation or the border war with Ethiopia, and living as refugees outside the country, have an inalienable right to return home and resettle in their original communities or locales of their choice. The government has also an obligation to facilitate their repatriation, assist their rehabilitation, and help them build a new life. A tripartite arrangement, involving the Eritrean and Sudanese governments and the United Nations High Commission for Refugees (UNHCR),

---

[239] ሓዳስ ኤርትራ፡ "መሬት ናይ መንግስቲ'ዩ": 25 መስከረም 2012: ገጽ 2:: [Hadas Ertra, *Land Belongs to the State*, 25 September 2012, p. 2.]

was undertaken in the mid-1990s to repatriate, resettle, and reintegrate Eritrean refugees from the Sudan. Several thousands were able to return and resettle in selected areas mostly in the fertile Gash-Setit Basin, either on their own or under the tripartite programme prior to its interruption.

At the same time, any Eritrean has a right to live, work or own property in a locality of his/her choice within the country. As elsewhere in the developed and developing world, economic development and growing urbanisation are bound to induce internal population movements in search of better opportunities. Internal mobility is a natural consequence of modernisation driven by the dynamic interplay of domestic economic growth and the pursuit of individual self-interest. Allowed to run its course, it stimulates further growth, promotes greater social interaction and exerts positive demographic effects on the occupational, ethnic and religious mix of the population in the different regions of the country, and helps to cement national unity. However, it also follows that such movement transpires without external coercion.

Unfortunately, the government has forced some people to leave their villages in the Central Plateau and relocate in the Gash-Setit Basin. Such a policy of forcible resettlement raises serious concerns of justice and equity in two respects. First, it is ethically wrong and counter-productive to uproot people from their accustomed habitat and forcibly resettle them. Second, it is wrong and unjust to deprive people of their traditional grazing lands to make room for the new settlers without offering due redress. Certain autocratic and totalitarian regimes have carried out forcible resettlements of populations under various political or economic pretexts. Experience shows, however, that the forcible resettlement of populations is generally unwarranted, often fails to deliver its declared objectives, and invariably creates more problems than it resolves.

6.4 A Secular Eritrean State

Eritrean society is diverse, with overlapping ethnic, regional and religious affiliations in several localities. For millennia, peaceful religious coexistence, with Animist, Christian and Muslim people enjoying freedom of faith and worship, has generally been part of the cultural heritage. For most of the modern history of the country, living together in mutual respect, tolerance, and harmony has been a way of life consistent with the teachings of the great world religions of Christianity and Islam which prescribe 'a moral code of conduct' that promotes harmonious peaceful coexistence among people of different faiths. This historical religious coexistence faces new challenges, pressures and strains today from a volatile neighbourhood troubled by the ramifications of the so-called *war on terror* and the emergence of militant political Islamist groups with a radical agenda committed to the creation of clerical states.

Regionally in the Horn of Africa as well, Christianity, Islam and Animism have generally coexisted in a state of mutual tolerance and internal peace for the most part of a thousand and a half years. Presently however, the region's traditionally dominant Sunni Islam is undergoing a new and violent schism between tolerant traditional Sufism and aggressive revolutionary Salafism, with avowed or suspected links to global jihad. Militant political Islam in Somalia, in particular, operates to aggravate a state of civil conflict, instability, and insecurity.

The politicisation of religion, or the use of religion as an instrument for the pursuit of political objectives, sows sectarian strife and antagonises both Christian-Muslim and Muslim-Muslim relations. The readiness of militant political Islamist movements to use religious violence to set up Islamic states based on *Sharia*, or Islamic law, poses a real threat to the stability and security of established states in the region. In particular, the commitment to enforce the strict application of *Sharia* as a basis of gender relations and 'a system of corporal and capital punishment' on society as a whole curtails fundamental human rights and jeopardises the peaceful coexistence, cohesion, and harmony of the concerned communities, both Muslim and multi-religious.

Contrary to clericalism, whose tenets seek to combine religion and politics in government, secularism advocates the separation of state and politics from religion, and insists on the exclusion of religious rationales in civic affairs and in public education. Further, it espouses freedom from religious rule, freedom from state intervention in religious matters, freedom from religious persecution, and freedom from the imposition of official religion. A secular state committed to safeguarding the separation of religion from politics and education, while also upholding the equality of all religions under the rule of law, is an essential ingredient for consolidating national unity, cultivating enlightened citizenship, and constructing a democratic society in a multi-religious and multidenominational state, such as Eritrea.

Secularism, inspired by a Marxist-Leninist world outlook, was the hallmark of the EPLF. During the long struggle for national liberation, the Front's secularist stance ensured the equal treatment of fighters, irrespective of religious affiliation, and made a significant contribution to reinforcing the cohesion of purpose, both within its ranks and among the population in the broader society characterised by religious diversity. Such internal cohesion and unity were critical to the successful execution of the war and its triumphant conclusion.

Building on the experience of the armed struggle for national liberation, Eritrea, upon independence, opted for a secular state that separates politics and education from religion. The ratified constitution guaranteed freedom of religion and belief. Faithful observance of these precepts would facilitate the construction of a secular state committed to the separation of religion and politics and non-interference in religious affairs.

The separation of politics and religion would also ensure equality among the different religions and religious denominations in Eritrea. Likewise, the separation of public education and religion would help promote a shared civic secular culture of mutual respect, tolerance, and affinity among all citizens, irrespective of religious affiliation. A national system of enlightened public education would eradicate ignorance as the mainstay of prejudice, strengthen solidarity, and foster harmony. The rapid expansion of nation-wide opportunities for secular education at all levels would nurture literate and enlightened citizens, for whom religion is a private affair and politics a public domain.

6.5 A United Eritrean State

The story of its making, as recounted in Chapter 2, tells that Eritrea, like virtually all African states today, is a product of the colonial experience. Italy conquered the territory, created a single entity, built unified public administration, and introduced new forces and relations of production. In the process, colonial rule unleashed new social forces, bred a shared national identity, and fanned Eritrean nationalism. Extension of Italian policy under British rule intensified Eritrean yearnings for freedom. In brief, the dialectics of oppression and resistance crystallised an awareness of a common condition and a sense of a shared identity that evolved to transcend ethnic, linguistic, religious, and regional affiliation in the context of a new *Eritrean-ness*.

During and post-World War II, the majority of the Eritrean people aspired for independence. Once their aspirations for independence failed to materialise, they had begrudgingly come to terms with federation as the lesser evil to alternatives of the country's partition between the Anglo-Egyptian Sudan and Ethiopia, incorporation into Ethiopia, or return to Italian rule under the guise of a possible UN trusteeship. Hence, Ethiopia's creeping subversion of Eritrea's federal status stirred vigorous opposition. Discontent set in and spread even among its former unionist supporters. Ethiopia's eventual repudiation of the federation and unlawful annexation served to bolster Eritrean resistance and entrench the demand for independence.

The reluctance of the international community to heed Eritrean protests against Ethiopia's incremental dismantling of the federation and the failure of the UN *to be seized of the matter,* as provided for in the federal resolution,[240] fuelled growing Eritrean opposition. The futility of peaceful protest in the face of brutal repression became starkly clear to the nationalist movement. This led to the eruption of the armed

---

[240]   UN Resolution 390(A), 1950.

resistance on 1 September 1961, prior to Ethiopia's formal annexation on 14 November 1962.

The war of independence helped to forge a strong Eritrean national identity and buttress a potent Eritrean nationalism. A hardened Eritrean nationalism, in turn, became the driving force of the armed resistance. The potency of Eritrean nationalism lent the struggle a degree of vigour and tenacity at critical moments of extraordinary difficulty, which carried it through to victory against the odds. Its strength and resilience successfully challenged the myth of Ethiopian historical hegemony, the might of Ethiopia's military machine, and the onslaught of its full-scale offensives sustained by its numerous benefactors. It also overcame the active hostility of the superpowers and their allies, the acquiescence of the UN and the OAU, and the machinations of regional states. Further, it laid a strong basis for the consolidation of nation building, the construction of a viable state, and the development of a vibrant national economy.

Meanwhile, constant population movements, both voluntary and involuntary, have created considerable intermingling and overlap in habitat among Eritrea's diverse ethnic, linguistic, and religious communities. The resultant mosaic manifests itself in an increasingly bilingual or trilingual population with multiple ethnic, religious, and regional demographics, especially in the cities and semi-urban areas. The last fifty years of war-related displacement and resettlement have accentuated this feature of the Eritrean population.

Eritrean nationalism and nationality are coextensive with the territory delimited by the country's colonial treaty borders. Eritreans, like many peoples the world over, share primordial relations with their immediate neighbours across international boundaries. Crystallised by the dialectics of colonialism and resistance, a common experience within the confines of these delineated borders had, however, the effect of defining a collective Eritrean nationality that transcends ethnic, linguistic, national, religious, and regional affiliation in a shared feeling of Eritrean-ness.

The progressive codification of Eritrean nationality by birth, for persons of Eritrean origin who were resident in Eritrea in 1933, and by naturalisation, for those persons of non-Eritrean origin who entered and lived in the country in 1934, and as later embedded in the Eritrean Nationality Proclamation which gave legal force to the historical evolution of a shared Eritrean identity.[241] Further, the provisional government promised to strengthen nation building, in ways that included the commitment to promote the equality of nationalities, languages, and genders.

The ratified Constitution guarantees the equality of all Eritrean nationalities and languages and names no official language. While Arabic and Tigrinya are designated compulsory subjects at elementary level, each nationality has the right to use and develop its own language, culture and traditions. The government formalised the EPLF's longstanding "mother tongue" policy, initiated and developed during the war, in the delivery of primary education and use of Arabic and Tigrinya, along with English, as working languages. The Front had also experimented with Latin transliteration to devise a common script for use by all Eritrean languages, including the main languages of Tigrinya

---

[241]   Provisional Government of Eritrea, *Gazette of Eritrean Law: Proclamation 21/1992, No. 3*, Asmera, 6 April 1992, p. 1-4.

and Tigre. Mercifully, the mindless project to discard the Geez[242] alphabet and replace it with the Latin alphabet atrophied.

The Italians introduced formal schooling limited to the fourth grade, with Italian as the medium of instruction. The British replaced the use of Italian by Tigrinya or Arabic in primary schools, depending on whether the local population was mainly Christian or Muslim, and used English as a medium of instruction in middle school, then grades five to eight. The choice of language at the primary level, allegedly informed by local educational committees, was in line with the British plan to partition Eritrea. During the federation, the Government of Eritrea sustained the use of Arabic and Tigrinya and added the instruction of Amharic, Ethiopia's official language, in middle and secondary schools. After the annexation, Ethiopia abolished Tigrinya and Arabic and replaced them with Amharic. During the war of national liberation, the two fronts, the ELF and the EPLF, used both Arabic and Tigrinya as working languages.

Today, Eritrea's multiple nationalities or ethnic groups are, in principle, free to use their own mother tongue, or a language of their choice, as a medium of instruction at the primary level, namely, the first five years of schooling. Geez, Arabic, or Latin transliteration provides scripts for the hitherto unwritten languages. The teaching of Arabic, English, and Tigrinya is mandatory at the primary level,

---

[242] Geez is an ancient South Semitic language that developed in today's Eritrea and northern Ethiopia. It was the official language of the Kingdom of Axum and the Abyssinian imperial court. It remains in use in the liturgy of the Eritrean and Ethiopian Orthodox Tewahdo Churches, the Ethiopian Catholic Church and the Beta Israel Jewish community.

while English is the medium of instruction beyond primary school. The state-run radio and television programmes broadcast in five Eritrean languages while the state-owned print media publish in Arabic, Tigre, Tigrinya, and English.

The government's policy of instruction in the mother tongue, or a language of choice, has considerable merit. First, the use of one's language is an inalienable right. Second, educational experts maintain that schooling in the mother tongue facilitates early learning of reading and writing skills and enables better comprehension of academic content. A child's use of first language offers definite pedagogical advantages over 'submersion' through an alien second language. Third, use and development of the mother tongue serve an important function in the preservation of ethnic identity, folklore, and cultural heritage.

Nevertheless, the mother tongue policy has caused resentment among some Eritreans schooled in Arabic who, upon return home, find themselves marginalised vis-à-vis Tigrinya and English speakers in the public job market. The policy has also attracted criticism, particularly from proponents of the use of Arabic as a medium of instruction in schools where the local population is mostly Muslim. Such critics advocate the abandonment of the use of the mother tongue as a medium of instruction for the non-Tigrinya ethnic groups and, instead, the adoption of Arabic as a unifying factor to strengthen Moslem solidarity in order to 'counteract growing Christian Tigrinya domination'.

The injection of a religious dimension into political life has made the issue a highly emotive one and the dialogue has become extremely polarised. The discussion that started with the brief flowering of the private press in 2000-2001, even if aborted through ruthless suppression at home, has continued to flourish in the diaspora via the unrestricted domain of cyberspace. Nevertheless, there is a need for caution not to over-promote such narrow concerns, important as they might be from the point of view of equity, to dominate the legitimate and broader political debate on the future of Eritrea.

History offers instances that show the futility or disastrous consequence of the political use of religion as a basis of national identity or sectarian solidarity. The religious inspired breakup of Pakistan from India in 1947 is a case in point. Religious uniformity did not prevent the subsequent civil war and secession of the former East Pakistan, resulting in the creation of Bangladesh in 1971. The fragility and state of constant insecurity of the Pakistani state, and the extreme volatility of contemporary Pakistani politics and state-society relations, attest that religion cannot be a viable basis of national solidarity among diverse ethnic communities. In this connection, it is quite striking that the *ulema* "had opposed the creation of Pakistan"[243] and that most sectarian violence today is Muslim-on-Muslim, as shown in the cases of Afghanistan, Egypt, Iraq, Libya, Mali, Pakistan, Somalia, Sudan, Syria, etc.

It is quite illustrative that the attempt to equate the Arabic language with Islam and impose an Islamic and Arab identity on an essentially diverse majority non-Arab African population has provoked a bloody struggle for self-determination whose exercise has resulted in the partition of, and the continuing crisis in, the Sudan. Beyond our

---

[243] Rashid, Ahmed, Descent into Chaos: How the War against Islamic Extremism Is Being Lost in Pakistan, Afghanistan and Central Asia, the Penguin Group, London, 2008, p. 235.

region, it is noteworthy that the vast majority of the world's Muslims do not speak Arabic, the language of the original writing of the Holy Quran, just as the vast majority of the world's Christians do not speak Hebrew, Aramaic, or Greek, the languages of the original writing of the Holy Bible.

At the same time, experience shows that normally people would not opt to use an alien language in place of their own. In fact, they would usually resist efforts to impose one on them. Given a choice, people would usually prefer to speak and use their first language. Further, besides being an undeniable right, language is primarily the principal medium of self-expression, a means of communal communication, and a vehicle of cultural survival.

Irrespective of its scientific or political merits or demerits however, use of first language should be, neither banned nor imposed. Whether any nationality or ethnic group would use the first or a second language as a medium of instruction at the primary level should be a choice left to it. The issue is too weighty and its implications for linguistic rights and national cohesion too serious to succumb to the preferences of self-appointed spokespersons with vested short-term or parochial interests on either side of the divide. As a matter of basic principle and inalienable right, it should be left to the concerned nationality or ethnic group to choose, without external pressure or interference affecting such a choice.

Beyond a general statement of principle affirming the unassailable right, however, each Eritrean nationality or ethnic group must be availed of the opportunity to freely decide, in a political climate that provides credible democratic space, whether to use its first language or choose a second language as a medium of instruction at the elementary level. The choice must then be upheld to build on the culture of peaceful coexistence and mutual respect, reinforced by an ability to speak one or more languages of contiguous neighbours. This distinct feature has traditionally facilitated communication and fostered cooperation among Eritrea's diverse ethnic, linguistic, and religious communities.

6.6 A Democratic Eritrean State

Freedom, democracy and prosperity were among the core objectives of the armed struggle. Reflecting the legitimate aspirations of the Eritrean people, the National Charter proclaimed that Eritrea would be a democratic state with participatory politics at the national, regional and local levels. This included a clear commitment to democracy and the rule of law; a society governed by democratic principles, institutions and culture; popular participation in decision-making; and a constitutional government accountable to the people.[244] The exercise of participatory politics would allow the people to have a voice in the making of public policy and decisions, manage their affairs, strengthen their unity in diversity, and foster responsive government.

Democracy means many things to many people. The debate on democracy, or what constitutes a democratic state, is replete with discord and contention, both at the theoretical and normative levels. Within the 'democratic' family of values, there exist concepts of liberal democracy, socialist democracy, communist democracy, or guided democracy. Each prototype has also its own internal variants. Many strands, embracing several variants and differing perspectives of democracy, coexist within the neoliberal world of the West

---

[244]   EPLF, National Charter for Eritrea, p. 21.

itself. The fact that national regimes of the political right and left, respectively espousing the model of the liberal state or the social state, periodically alternate in the assumption and exercise of state power as a function of parliamentary majority, does not change the basic understanding.

Further, there prevails a reality of inconsistency and double standards vis-à-vis the policies and practices of neoliberal democracy in the West that arise from the conflict inherent between proclaimed values and real interests. The disparity between professed values and real interests undermines the credibility of the Western model of democracy or good governance for the Global South. Some in the Global South, including states in Africa, use this discrepancy to malign the very essence of democracy and cast aspersions on its desirability or workability in their circumstances. Certain undemocratic regimes often go further to exploit the West's apparent hypocrisy and double standards to lend justification to their authoritarian rule in the name of safeguarding national sovereignty and policy independence.

The object here is not to dwell on the different perspectives on democracy or the wide discrepancy that prevails between the preaching and practice of democracy; nor is it to pander to the West's pontificating about democracy or to echo the countervailing disdain for it expressed by some in the Global South. It is rather to press home the point that, despite its imperfections or practical shortcomings as a system, the integration of modern democratic principles with traditional African governance structures and cultural values to create and consolidate a democratic system of governance offers the best hope for the prototype postcolonial African state to overcome its present crisis and to regain legitimacy and the ability to deliver. This is particularly essential for the reconstitution of the Eritrean State.

But this observation comes with an important caveat. The discourse on democracy lacks consensus and the global practice remains divergent. There is no 'one size fits all' formula of democracy for use as a model by all states. Yet, there are generally accepted basic principles that underpin a democratic system. These principles include the rule of law; respect for fundamental freedoms; protection of basic rights, including minority rights; popular participation in the governance process; and transparency and accountability of public policy and decision making. Each state must creatively adopt these fundamental principles to suit the specific requirements of its historical evolution, socioeconomic conditions and cultural values. The forms of adaptation may vary, but the application of the essential principles must remain the same.

Georges Nzongola-Ntalaja defines democratic governance as "the management of societal affairs in accordance with the universal principles of democracy as a system of rule that maximizes popular consent and participation, the legitimacy and accountability of rulers and the responsiveness of the latter to the expressed interests and needs of the public".[245] Accordingly, it has three attributes: first, as an end and as a means; second, as a process; and third, as a form of politics based on universal principles. In brief, democratic

---

[245] Nzongola-Ntalaja, Georges, *Democratic Governance and Human Rights in the International Framework*, Keynote Address, Helsinki, 15 June 2004 http://www.undp.org/oslocentre/docs04/ DEMOCRATIC_GOVERNANCE_AND_HUMAN%20 RIGHTS_IN_THE_INTERNATIONAL_FRAMEWORK.pdf

governance is a moral imperative consistent with human aspirations for freedom and a better political order with social justice; a constant process of opening up an inclusive political space for all; and a political practice based on the rule of law, legitimacy, and accountability.

A democratic system of government embeds several key features. It sustains an institutionalised electoral process that enables the conduct of regular, fair and credible elections to allow citizens to choose freely their leaders and governments. It safeguards *equality of citizens* and ensures uniform rights and obligations under the law. Beyond mere declarations of formal equality, a democratic system avails citizens of equitable access to opportunities, resources, and amenities for all to be able to actualise their individual potential and satisfy their basic human needs.[246]

In a democratic state, legitimacy of power is manifested in the exercise of authority derived from the consent of the governed and sustained by their active participation in the governance process. Democratic governance ensures efficiency, accountability and transparency in policy and decision making and in the management of state assets and resources. A democratic state strives to deliver public wellbeing that improves socioeconomic conditions, leads to a rising standard of living and a better quality of life, at least for the majority of the people.

---

[246] This characterisation of a democratic state is adopted from a paper (unpublished) by the author: *Contradictions in the Relationship: Democracy - Governance - Stability?* presented at an Observatoire de l'Afrique Conférence on Strengthening Cooperation between Europe and Africa on Democratic Reform, Brussels, 12 October 2010.

Political pluralism signifies another essential feature of a democratic system of government. The National Charter envisions a pluralist Eritrean state with a multiparty system to foster healthy political competition, promote robust popular participation, and ensure accountable, transparent, and effective government. The ratified Constitution guarantees fundamental freedoms and basic rights, including the freedom of association and the freedom of expression to allow the emergence of pluralist politics. Pluralism precludes the rise of political monopoly by a single party, front, movement, or group, and provides for the peaceful mediation of the various conflicting interests of diverse political, social, and civic groups in society.

The accumulation of state power by a single political movement, group, or person tends to take life out of the political process, stifle democratic participation, breed corruption, and lead to eventual dictatorship. Conversely, political pluralism tends to sanction inclusive political parties, independent media, autonomous civil society organisations and non-state actors to operate freely. By allowing the existence of multiple poles of power and influence in society, political pluralism mediates social conflict, injects certain vibrancy to the political process, enhances democratic accountability and transparency, and helps to counter corruption.

Civil society, with its variety and scope of organisations, can play a constructive role in the promotion, exercise, and consolidation of democratic rule in states like Eritrea. Civil society actors could mediate or facilitate dialogue between the state and diverse social interest groups, and help moderate or restrain potential abuses and excesses of the state and its agencies. Their engagement in developmental activities could complement the efforts of the state in service delivery, while their desire to play an advocacy role could help in the defence of the public interest. To thrive and remain relevant, however, they should stay focussed on fulfilling their specific mandate and avoid the tendency to pose as representatives of society or as substitutes of legitimate state authority, especially in the context of fragile or failing states.

Likewise, a free press is an essential feature of a pluralist democratic state, with its role often likened to that of 'the third estate' in pre-revolutionary France. The print and broadcast media provide a forum to disseminate and exchange information and to enlighten the general public about current issues of interest; some also play the role of a gadfly and critical public informer. A free and responsible press can serve to inform the public, stimulate public awareness of, and conversation on, vital national issues, and help to nurture a culture of peaceful dialogue among different political forces and interest groups in society. To this end, a press code was adopted in 1996 to serve these essential functions in an emerging Eritrean democratic state.

6.7 Gender Equality

There is an old Chinese saying that "women hold up half the sky." The proverb signifies the equal share of women with men in the cooperative effort to sustain our planet for the collective benefit of human society. Despite their equal contribution to the sustenance of human life on earth, however, women have generally been, and are, discriminated against or marginalised in most of traditional and much of modern society. In Eritrea as well, women work as much and as hard as men do, or even more so, for the upkeep of the household and the sustenance of society. Yet, the status of women in Eritrean society has been subordinate to that of men, with women facing discriminatory treatment in the family, unequal access to opportunities, and marginalisation in the political, economic, social, and cultural life of the country.

During the war of national liberation, the EPLF viewed the fight for gender equality and the empowerment of women as an integral part of the overall struggle for a just and democratic society. Safeguarding the social rights of women constituted one of the main pillars of its National Democratic Programme. As Eritrean women joined the armed struggle in increasing numbers in the 1970s, the motto of 'equality through equal participation' and the demands of the war of independence for an increasingly larger fighting force helped break all traditional barriers and allowed them full equality to serve with men in virtually all spheres of life in the field. All traditional and legal barriers to gender equality disappeared. It all seemed at the time that the emancipation and empowerment of women was within reach.

As the war progressed and the participation of women increased, the National Union of Eritrean Women (NUEW) emerged as a mass organisation of the EPLF in 1979. The NUEW operated to mobilise and organise Eritrean women workers, students, and homemakers at home and in the diaspora in support of the struggle for liberation. Eritrean women workers in the diaspora - in the Sudan, the Middle East, Europe, and North America - raised substantial funds from their relatively meagre earnings and donated to the Front. Furthermore, women in the Ethiopian-occupied cities and contested areas, organised in underground cells, played a vital role in the Front's intelligence gathering, clandestine lines of communication, and urban operations.

The level of mobilisation of Eritrean women in support of the armed struggle was considerable. Women constituted about a third of the combatants, particularly during the last dozen years of the war. With the traditional barriers to gender equality swept aside by the paramount need for numbers in a lopsided combat against a much larger enemy, the scope of women's participation and the quality of their contributions to the war of independence were truly remarkable. Women served alongside men as doctors, teachers, nurses, midwives, laboratory technicians, barefoot doctors, mass organisers, frontline commanders, etc. Truly, the active participation and crucial role of Eritrean women helped secure the victory of the armed struggle.

In recognition of this effort, the National Charter pledges the equality of all Eritrean citizens irrespective of regional origin, ethnic or linguistic identity, religious affiliation, or gender. The ratified Constitution bans all forms of discrimination and guarantees gender equality in all spheres of national life. It proscribed all barriers to gender inequality and prescribed the right of women to equality with men. Further, the stated mission of the NUEW is to defend the rights and ensure equal participation of women in all spheres of national life and to advocate equal access to opportunities for education and employment with equal pay for equal work.

6.8 A Developmental Eritrean State

A consensus had evolved and a pledge made, among the leadership and senior cadres of the EPLF, that an independent Eritrea would be a developmental state committed to rapid, balanced and sustainable economic growth. Since the second congress in 1987, the EPLF had abandoned its infatuation with the ideology of 'scientific socialism' and the tenets of a command economy, proclaiming its intention to establish a democratic state with a mixed economic system after the liberation.[247] Accordingly, the drawing up and adoption of the National Charter, the Macro-Policy paper and the Constitution following independence confirmed the Front's loyalty to the ideological shift signalled in 1987 and the transitional government's commitment to a developmental state within the framework of a mixed economy.

As a rule, a developmental state is a pragmatic rather than an ideological construct. In a strict sense, it espouses neither capitalism nor socialism, but a brand of a mixed economic system. The mixed economy combines elements of the capitalist and socialist systems. It allows the operations of private enterprise and centralised economic planning, enabling market forces and government regulation to coexist and work together to promote sustainable economic development. It charts a path and implements a plan of development somewhere between "a free market capitalist economic system and centrally planned economic system," or "a plan-rational capitalist system, 'conjoining private ownership with state guidance.'"[248] A developmental state could, as in the experience of the "Asian Tigers", create and regulate the "seamless web of political, bureaucratic, and

---

[247] Following the 1987 second congress, the Eritrean People's Revolutionary Party (EPRP), the clandestine party that constituted the Marxist-Leninist core of the EPLF as the 'vanguard' of the Eritrean revolution, changed its name to the Eritrean Socialist Party (ESP).

[248] Woo-Cumings, Meredith (ed.), The Developmental State, Cornell University Press, 1999, p. 2.

moneyed influences"[249] that structure and determine the content and pattern of economic life in a market driven economy.

The hallmark of the developmental state is state intervention in the economy that fosters strong partnership and effective coordination of the public and private sectors in the service of rapid and sustainable development. The developmental state is typically, but not necessarily or invariably, authoritarian. Experience furnishes three criteria that distinguish the developmental state, whether democratic or authoritarian, from all others: first, the clear formulation of development objectives; second, the establishment of competent institutional structures to pursue the stated objectives; and third, the effective delivery of improved public wellbeing, a higher standard of living and an enhanced human condition for the majority of its citizenry.

It is possible to envisage the construction of a state that combines both democratic and developmental features, and Eritrea at the time of its independence had a unique opportunity to become such a state. Subsequent to the adoptions of the National Charter and the Macro-Policy paper, the transitional government of Eritrea proclaimed its intention to follow Singapore as a model. Effective emulation of Singapore's successful development strategy would turn Eritrea into an 'African Singapore'. Virtually every '*who is who*' in the government and the ruling Front visited the small island city state in the mid-1990s to observe the *modus operandi* of the Singaporean model, witness its achievements, and learn from its experience. In those days, there was

---

[249]   Johnson, Chalmers, MITI and the Japanese Miracle: The Growth of Industrial Policy 1925-1975, Stanford University Press, 1982.

much excitement and anticipation in the air, sustained by enthusiastic statements of senior government officials and vented by considerable coverage in the local media.

Singapore is strategically located at the tip of the Malay Peninsula. Its population, comprising mainly of ethnic Chinese, Malays, Indians, Peranakans, and Eurasians, is also multiracial and multi-religious. At the time of its independence in 1965, Singapore had no natural resources, no adequate water supply, no defence capability, no unified national identity, and no promising prospects.[250] It had tense relations with its much bigger and more powerful neighbours, Malaysia and Indonesia. Its redeeming feature lay in an enlightened leadership committed to meritocracy and dedicated to effecting rapid economic and social transformation, forging a strong national identity and building unity in diversity through the protection of minority rights.[251]

Adopting a brand of 'guided democracy', the government of Singapore instituted an efficient, accountable and transparent system of public administration and civil service based on meritocracy. It devised and implemented an export-oriented development strategy conducive to the participation of domestic capital and the inflow of direct foreign investment and expertise; and built a modern service sector led by banking, financial, and port services. In addition, it established strong state enterprises with

---

[250] US Library of Congress, Singapore Country Studies: *Two Decades of Independence* http://countrystudies.us/singapore/11.htm

[251] Peebles, Gavin and Peter Wilson, Economic Growth and Development in Singapore: Past and Future, Cheltenham, UK: Edward Elgar, 2002

competent management to provide infrastructure for public utilities and services; expanded high quality tertiary education to generate the knowledge and skills needed to develop a modern economy driven by 'high-tech' sectors; and promoted free trade, cordial relations, and peace with its neighbours.

By 1984, nineteen years after independence, Singapore had: achieved remarkable economic growth with low inflation and full employment; come out of impoverishment into prosperity; overcome communal strife and attained domestic tranquillity; cultivated cordial relations with its neighbours; and evolved into a significant player in the promotion of regional cooperation, security, and solidarity.[252] The Singaporean economy has continued to grow, providing the population with a very high standard of living. In terms of GDP (PPP) per capita, Singapore has become the fifth wealthiest country in the world, with its official foreign exchange reserves standing at US$ 170.3 billion as of January 2009.[253]

There exists enormous dissimilarity in size of territory and population, as well as in resource base and racial diversity, between Eritrea and Singapore. Nevertheless, the adoption of the Singaporean political, economic, and social model could possibly have enabled Eritrea to duplicate Singapore's successful experience in nation-building, state construction, and economic development. In retrospect, however, the transitional government's infatuation with the Singaporean model seems to have been nothing

---

[252]   US Library of Congress, Singapore Country Studies
[253]   US Library of Congress, Singapore Country Studies: *Two Decades of Independence*

more than a publicity stunt for public consumption. For the Government of Eritrea clearly lacked what it takes to implement such a model successfully, including political will, leadership quality, functional institutions, accountable and transparent public administration, meritocracy in the civil service, etc., to transform the country into an African Singapore.

In brief, the vision, objectives, principles and values enshrined in the National Charter, the Macro-Policy paper and the Constitution of Eritrea conferred upon the transitional government the necessary legal instruments, economic guidelines, and political legitimacy to enable it to transform Eritrea into a free, democratic, and developmental state. The triad of political, economic and legal frameworks provided the young government with the key policy guidelines and normative standards it needed to pursue the goals of nation building, state construction and socioeconomic development. In the beginning, there were high hopes and great expectations that the promise of a bright future would materialise through efficient performance of the functions of state and actual delivery of a higher standard of living and a better quality of life.

Twenty-two years on, it is fair to interrogate whether the present Government of Eritrea has followed its own script and made effective use of the prescribed policy instruments to develop the country and emancipate the people. It is quite legitimate to probe whether the Government has raised the standard of living, improved the quality of life and uplifted the human condition of the people. In other words, has independence ushered in a functional state able to deliver freedom, progress, and prosperity for the Eritrean people? Despite the lofty promises embedded in the triad of documents and the great expectations they generated, the ensuing chapters show the dismal record of a dysfunctional state whose actual practice has diverged from its stated policy in every domain, with disastrous consequences for Eritrea and its people.

CHAPTER 7

Self-Reliance and the Coupon Economy

Your government, which we considered our own and expected to serve us well, is the worst one that has ruled Eritrea during my long life. – Negash Tesfagaber, an Eritrean elder

The record of independent Eritrea's first government in terms of its treatment of the people is, in many respects, quite comparable to that of successive colonial regimes. Ruthless suppression of dissent within its own ranks and harsh treatment of the population at large stand out as distinctive features of the present regime. Indeed, the consequences of its utter disregard for the rule of law, its propensity for pervasive control, and general maladministration with respect to the wellbeing of the Eritrean people are unprecedented. In the words of an Eritrean elder:

> *I grew up in my village during the Italian era. I was conscripted into the colonial army and fought in Tripoli [Libya] and Ethiopia. When the Italians were defeated, I went back to my village and lived as a farmer during the British, the federal and the Ethiopian periods. None of the colonisers was good to us; none looked after our interests. However, we are worse off today. People cannot find work*

here in Asmera or the other towns. You take our children away and you do not even pay them for their labours. We have to take care of their young wives and children in our old age. Your government, which we considered our own and expected to serve us well, is the worst one that has ruled Eritrea during my long life.[254]

7.1 Imprudent Policy Responses

Rehabilitating the dilapidated physical and social infrastructure of the country and healing, the wounds wrought by the war of national liberation had barely started when the border war with Ethiopia erupted in 1998 and reversed the process of reconstruction. The Eritrean economy has yet to recover from the negative impact of the 1998-2000 war and its devastating domestic political repercussions. Not only did it inflict an enormous loss of human life on a population already bled white in a long war and impose a huge financial burden on a weak and struggling economy, but it also diverted national focus from development.

Moreover, it caused untold human suffering and immense physical destruction of infrastructure and property, especially in the borderlands. The third and final Ethiopian offensive, which ended with the occupation of large swathes of territory in the central and western sectors and the displacement of about a quarter of the entire population of the country, was particularly devastating to the Eritrean people and destructive of the Eritrean economy. Overall, the

---

[254] Conversations of the author with an Eritrean elder, Ato Negash Tesfagaber, Asmera, 4 September 2001 (author's translation from the original Tigrinya).

direct damage of the war to Eritrea's productive and social assets, estimated at US$580 million, amounted to about 90 per cent of the country's 1999 GDP.[255]

In addition, the war and the subsequent state of 'no war, no peace' since 2000 have resulted in, among other things, the complete severance of bilateral economic and trade relations between the two countries, including the suspension of Ethiopia's use of Eritrean ports. Sealing off the common border and cutting off longstanding and highly complementary economic and commercial ties have produced a 'lose-lose' scenario for both sides. The attendant economic losses and financial costs have been biting for both Eritrea and Ethiopia.

Eritrea's ports are the best-suited and most cost effective venues of transit for the bulk of Ethiopia's foreign trade. They are closer to its main population and production centres and, therefore, less expensive to use. Its non-use of Eritrean ports since the outbreak of the war and its use, instead, of more distant and more expensive ports in the neighbourhood has cost Ethiopia substantially greater amounts in transport, transit and services fees.

Ethiopia's non-use of Eritrean ports is a double-edged sword that slashes the purse strings of both countries. Eritrea has also lost considerable annual revenues from transit and port services fees as well as the export market for approximately 80 per cent (at pre-war levels) of its industrial products, plus the source of the bulk of its imports of raw materials and staple agricultural commodities. Further, the forcible closure of the long common frontier of the two countries

---

[255] Erritrea – European Community: Country Strategy Paper and National Indicative Programme for the Period of 2002 – 2007, p. 8.

has deprived the straddling borderland communities of the benefits of normal cross-border economic interaction and commercial exchange of local produce which generally filtered through to the interior of both countries prior to the war.

The war and its consequences, including the closure of the common border, have entailed additional disadvantages and further weakened the Eritrean economy. Ethiopia uprooted long settled communities that originally hailed from Eritrea, and expelled them from their long established villages in the hitherto remote, uninhabited, and inhospitable wilderness across the border in northwestern Ethiopia. In addition, it shut off Eritrean nomadic pastoralists in the western half of the country, in particular, from the seasonal use of traditional grazing lands and watering holes around and across the common border. Moreover, the Eritrean economy has lost a significant flow of remittances in cash and in kind because of the deportation of tens of thousands of relatively well to do Eritreans and Eritrean Ethiopians from Ethiopia.

The Eritrean government's policy responses to the domestic consequences of the war and its aftermath have however, inflicted greater harm on the Eritrean body politic and the Eritrean economy than the direct damage to physical and social infrastructure and the economic costs of the war. Using the frozen conflict as a pretext, the government suspended all preparatory processes already underway towards the establishment of a democratic system of governance, detained several senior officials and journalists, and banned the private press. It took these measures to suppress internal political dissent and to pre-empt demands for change in the president's manner of conducting the affairs of state. Further, it abandoned the macroeconomic policy framework, marginalised the economic role of the private sector, imposed open-ended active national service, and placed the application of the ratified Constitution on hold.

At home, the government's draconian measures operated, among other things, to nip any internal political dissent in the bud, to obstruct the drive towards the evolution of a democratic system of government, and to stall the engine of the Eritrean economy. As a result, the political and economic situation in Eritrea grew from bad to worse. Externally, the harsh measures complicated the country's relations with the West and main development partners, especially the US, the EU, and key EU Member States. Several attempts to persuade Eritrea to redress its domestic situation and improve its external relations failed, as the government proved unwilling to treat the case of the continued detention of the former officials and journalists in accordance with due process, lift the ban on the private press, and implement the ratified Constitution.

The reluctance, or inability, of the Eritrean government to follow normal legal procedures to prosecute or set free the accused detainees, in particular, transformed the 'internal' issues into issues of wider concern on the grounds of the country's international commitments to uphold the rule of law, democratic principles, and respect for human rights. Eritrea's development partners and the EU, in particular, invoked standard policy and political dialogue in order to persuade the government to address these issues in accordance with the rule of law as per its contractual obligation under the Cotonou Agreement, effectively making some degree of progress in the bilateral dialogue a *de facto* conditionality for the disbursement of allocated funds.

Lack of progress in the EU-Eritrea policy and political dialogue within the framework of the Cotonou Agreement first slowed down and eventually dried up actual disbursement of already committed European Development Fund (EDF) resources to the country. Putting on a bold face, government officials and the state media have presented the country's strained relations and waning development cooperation with the West as the outcome of Eritrea's vital defence of its policy of self-reliance and independence of decision-making. In reality, the fallout from the government's policy responses to the domestic events that unfolded in the aftermath of the war, and the external reaction that they provoked in the West, have operated to isolate the country and suspend the Eritrean economy in alternating modes of stagnation and decline.

7.2 Self-Reliance as a Euphemism for Isolation

Self-reliance was first introduced as a guiding moral principle in life by Ralph Waldo Emerson, the American philosopher and essayist, during the first half of the nineteenth century. In his essay on self-reliance, Emerson propounded the need for individuals to shun conformity and false consistency and follow their own instincts or ideas.[256] In its original religious inspiration, the concept of self-reliance signified a

---

[256] Emerson, Ralph Waldo, Essays: First Series: Essay II Self-Reliance, 1841. Emerson first introduced self-reliance as a philosophy as part of a sermon delivered in September 1830. This was followed by his presentation of a series of lectures on the philosophy of history at the Masonic Temple in Boston, which were published as a collection of essays on self-reliance in 1841. http://www.emersoncentral.com/selfreliance.htm

moral disposition for persons to manage their own affairs independent of the intervention or will of outsiders. In its Emersonian conception, it literally means to 'pull oneself up by one's own boot straps' without external assistance.

In essence, self-reliance as a political philosophy emphasises the 'moral worth of the individual' and the values of self-dependence and independence in pursuing one's objectives, desires and interests free of any external interference. The philosophy takes the human individual as the focal point and primary agent; dependence on one's own capabilities, resources, or judgment as its principal orientation; and maintenance of an independent course of action as the centerpiece of policy, in the struggle for liberation.

In a broad sense, the launch of the armed struggle in 1961 signified the adoption of self-reliance in the pursuit of liberation through the military mobilisation of the Eritrean people and the pooling together of their material resources in organised resistance to Ethiopian subversion. But the decision to launch the armed struggle was taken in exasperation at the failure of the UN to intervene, rather than out of a preference to preclude its interference, in support of Eritrean autonomy. In fact, both Eritrean liberation fronts, the ELF and the EPLF, petitioned the UN for intervention on several occasions and consistently appealed to various members and elements of the international community for solidarity with, support for, and assistance to the struggle of the Eritrean people for self-determination.

Despite the active official hostility of the then superpowers and their respective allies, there gradually evolved significant international solidarity with and support for the just cause of the Eritrean people. In due course, governments, regional inter-governmental organisations, political parties, international tribunals, national liberation movements, professional associations, civil society organisations (CSOs), non-governmental organisations (NGOs), humanitarian aid agencies, prominent personalities, professionals, etc., declared their political solidarity with the legitimate aspirations of the Eritrean people for liberation. Moreover, they extended vital moral, political, and material support to the Eritrean liberation movement.

Many parliamentarians, political activists, journalists, and cineastes visited the liberated areas of Eritrea. Upon return home, they recounted what they saw in the field of struggle and advocated for greater and wider international support for the Eritrean cause. I remember very well how warmly we welcomed them during their visits and how the news, reports and commentaries they disseminated about our struggle through the international media were regularly monitored, eagerly exchanged, and avidly consumed among our cadres and freedom fighters. International solidarity, support, and assistance, though relatively limited in substance and scope, were crucial in spreading the legitimacy of the Eritrean struggle and boosting the morale of the Eritrean people and freedom fighters.

However, the relative inadequacy of external assistance had, right from the outset, engendered the need for the Eritrean People's Liberation Front to rely mainly on the resources of Eritrea and its people. Outside assistance could, even if it were forthcoming on a larger scale, only complement internal efforts, resources, and capabilities. It was quite clear that the successful execution of the war of national liberation required, first and foremost, the total mobilisation of the human and material resources of the

Eritrean people. Further, the policy of self-reliance, adopted out of necessity, was creatively applied in the field to turn the Ethiopian occupation army into the main supplier of the Eritrean liberation army.

Relying on the resilience and determination to make the supreme sacrifice of its combatants, the EPLA used the military tactics of enveloping Ethiopian garrisons, coordinated pincer movements, and lightening attacks against the besieged enemy troops. The Front's policy of humane treatment of prisoners of war (POWs) encouraged large numbers of encircled Ethiopian officers and men to surrender and hand over their weapons rather than resist to the finish. In this way, the EPLA paid dearly in life and limb to turn Ethiopian garrisons in Eritrea into its supply depots and seize whole cashes of arms, munitions, and provisions virtually intact.

As an extension of the efforts in the Field, primary reliance on the resources and capabilities of the Eritrean people demanded the maximum mobilisation of the nation's human and material resources. In a fundamental sense, self-reliance entailed engaging the full participation of the Eritrean people living inside and outside the country as the surest means of sustaining the armed struggle, maintaining the movement's independence of policy and decision-making and, ultimately, securing national liberation as the prelude to independence. At the same time, international solidarity was keenly sought, external material and military support actively solicited, and any forthcoming assistance warmly welcomed, and put to good use.

Self-reliance did not preclude the search for external assistance during the war of national liberation. Quite the contrary, the EPLF actively solicited outside material support and military assistance. Whenever availed, it used external assistance effectively to fill in the gaps in its military assets, augment its resources, strengthen its capabilities, and lead the war of national independence to victory. The principle of self-reliance thus signified the dependence, first and foremost, on one's own decisions, efforts, resources, and capabilities in waging the armed struggle for liberation. In turn, its ability to achieve a degree of self-reliance enabled the EPLF to withstand external pressures, maintain the independence of its policy and decisions, and successfully navigate through the labyrinth of byzantine regional politics.

International solidarity, support, and assistance, prudently used as an extension of the self-reliant effort, were instrumental in the successful management of the internal conduct and external politics of the war of national liberation. Similarly, international support, development cooperation, and technical assistance could contribute to the effort to reconstruct the Eritrean economy and develop the country within the framework of the principle of self-reliance.

7.3 Foreign Policy as an Extension of Self-Reliance

"Foreign policy is just an extension of domestic policy... dictated by domestic concerns".[257] Rather than being a mere extension, however, the substance of foreign policy is highly dependent on and quite reflective of domestic

---

[257] Pascual, Jr., Federico D., Simple Equation: Foreign Policy Just an Extension of Domestic Policy, (The Philippine Star) Postscipt, 20 July 2004. http://www.philstar.com/Article.aspx?articleId=258150.

policy, thus indicating a close relationship between the internal developments in a country and its external policies. States have a perennial national interest in establishing and maintaining normal diplomatic ties and pursuing peaceful, friendly and cooperative relations with all other states, irrespective of political and economic systems or relations with third countries. Rational foreign policy always serves paramount national interests. To paraphrase the famous words of Lord Palmerston, a former British prime minister: States have no permanent friends or permanent enemies; they have only permanent interests.[258]

Governments may pursue foreign policy in the general interest of the nation-state or in the narrow interest of regime stability in the international system. Regardless of the motivation, it is in the vital interest of states to maintain amicable relations with all other states, in general, and the key global actors, in particular. Most crucially, states have strategic interests with their proximate neighbours, with whom they are destined to live together by geography. A nation's vital and strategic interests are thus, best served through the pursuit of peaceful coexistence and cooperative relations. Isolation is, by no means, a viable option in our globalised world.

At the time of independence, Eritrea's relations with the outside world began on a positive note. A number of countries that, at different stages, had supported the Ethiopian war

---

[258] He is reputed to have said that "Britain had no eternal allies and no perpetual enemies, only interests that were eternal and perpetual." quoted in David Brown, Palmerston and the Politics of Foreign Policy, 1846-1855 (Manchester: Manchester University Press, 2002), pp. 82-83.

effort against the Eritrean liberation movement, most notably the US, Israel, Russia, Cuba and Libya, readily recognised and established diplomatic relations with the new state. The EPLF, which set up the Transitional Government of Eritrea upon independence, in turn, abandoned its liberation era revolutionary rhetoric of opposition to US imperialism and Israeli Zionism, which reflected a response to US and Israeli military support for Ethiopia rather than a genuine commitment to an anti-imperialist or anti-Zionist ideology. The Front had also abandoned its claim to a natural alliance with the Socialist Camp in reaction to massive Soviet military support for Ethiopia.

The EPLF government was set to pursue pragmatic domestic and foreign policies in the service of Eritrea's national interest. The international community was also well disposed toward the new state. There was an outpouring of virtually universal goodwill and readiness to extend a helping hand to the new nation and to provide a peace dividend, reinforced by a sense of guilt for past wrongs committed against Eritrea and the cause of Eritrean self-determination. For instance, Italy, the former colonial power, whose officials were, as late as the summer of 1988, "persuaded that Eritrea would never be capable of gaining independence from Ethiopian domination by the force of its weapons," topped the list of donors in allocating 210 billion Lire and delivering 140 billion Lire in development cooperation to Eritrea between 1992 and 1998.[259]

---

[259]   Del Boca, Angelo, *The Myths, Suppressions, Denials, and Defaults of Italian Colonialism* in Patrizia Palumbo, (ed.) A Place in the Sun: Africa in Italian Colonial Culture from Post-Unification to the

Starting afresh, Eritrea had a great opportunity to formulate and pursue domestic and foreign policies conducive to overcoming the formidable challenges of state construction, institution building and economic reconstruction. The maintenance of a favourable external climate in the service of its paramount national interests required the adoption of a prudent foreign policy and proactive diplomacy. The ordeal of its struggle and the circumstances of its birth in defiance of the powers that be availed Eritrea of international goodwill and support to be capitalised on and built upon to promote cordial relations, foster economic cooperation, and encourage foreign direct investment (FDI) in order to bolster its efforts to reconstruct and grow its economy.

In reality, however, intermittent difficult relations and proxy warfare with the Sudan, a maritime skirmish with Yemen, a devastating war trailed by a frozen conflict with Ethiopia, and a border standoff with Djibouti have marred Eritrea's first two decades of independent statehood. Discord and disputes are a normal aspect of the relations among nations and the root causes of conflict with its neighbours were not solely of Eritrea's making. However, the regime's propensity to shun timely dialogue and fast antagonise relations reveals the dynamic interplay of the domestic and foreign policy nexus and the close relationship between Eritrea's internal politics and external policies. An authoritarian default mode that short-circuits internal debate and uses coercion to silence divergent opinion or to stifle dissent within the Front and the government at home extends to the tendency to bypass judicious dialogue and

Present, University of California Press, Berkeley, Los Angeles, London: 2003, p. 29.

prompt military confrontation in the treatment of normal disputes with hitherto friendly neighbours.

As during the period of the armed struggle for national liberation, Eritrea currently finds itself regionally and globally isolated. However, there is an important distinction: the isolation during the armed struggle was imposed and involuntary while that of the present is partly unforced and self-induced. The authoritarian default mode leaves no room for discussion, analysis, or impact assessment of decisions. Such a disposition has plunged Eritrea's internal politics into a mindless muddle of policy reversals, harmful forfeitures, and brutal repression and its foreign policy reflects a series of missed opportunities and a jumble of erratic reflexes that immerse the country in a constant state of tension, hostility, and isolation. Eritrea's isolation during the independence war was solely the outcome of an international geopolitical calculus. Today, the government's domestic actions and foreign policy responses are the main drivers of its isolation.

Its current regional and international isolation exerts a powerful negative impact on Eritrea's national development, prosperity and security, both now and for the near future. In the age of a globalised world where competitive interdependence is the name of the game and investment and trade fuel economic growth, no country, no matter how large, rich or developed, can go it alone or thrive in isolation. No individual nation on its own, least of all undeveloped and impoverished Eritrea is capable of achieving economic self-sufficiency or prosperity. The imperative of effective mobilisation of national resources and the concentration of effort in the service of tangible national development, security and prosperity, necessarily requires proactive political engagement, diplomatic interaction, and economic cooperation within the framework of regional peace and stability.

7.4 Eritrea-US Relations

The ice of historical hostility of US policy to Eritrean independence had started to thaw by the late 1980s. The US encouraged negotiations between Ethiopia's Derg regime and the EPLF towards achieving a political solution to the Eritrean problem in apparent anticipation of an inevitable Eritrean military victory.[260] Faced with an imminent *fait accompli*, the US, which emerged as the sole superpower after the collapse of the former Soviet Union at the turn of the 1990s, initiated formal engagement with the leaderships of the Eritrean and Tigrayan liberation movements in London in May 1991. It sought initially to negotiate the outcome of the war in favour of retaining the unity of the Ethiopian state in a new construction. Having won the war however, the liberation movements had their way. The US then tried to mediate post-war arrangements and influence the new transition to power in Addis Ababa and Asmera.

Resetting its relations with the new nation, the US reopened its former consulate in Asmera in August 1992 and recognised Eritrea as an independent state on 27 April 1993. The two countries established diplomatic relations on 11 June 1993 and their bilateral relations grew steadily warmer

---

[260] Former US president Jimmy Carter started mediating peace negotiations between representatives of the EPLF and the government of the then People's Republic of Ethiopia at his Carter Center in Atlanta in September 1989.

and closer. The US viewed Eritrea as an emerging democratic state, provided military, development and humanitarian assistance, and sought to promote democracy, economic renewal, and regional stability. When the border war broke out with Ethiopia in 1998, the US tried, unsuccessfully, to mediate an end to the conflict and eventually brokered the Algiers Agreement between the two countries in 2000.

On its part, the government of Eritrea strove to cultivate warm relations and establish a close alliance with the US. It supported US foreign policy objectives and the deployment of US troops in the Horn of Africa. Senior commanders of the US Central Command (CENTCOM) regularly visited Asmera for meetings with the president and the ministers of defence and foreign affairs. It was indicative of the burgeoning Eritrea-US relationship that President Isaias Afwerki described his meetings with US CENTCOM Commander General Tommy Franks and US Secretary of Defence Donald Rumsfeld (welcomed with a red carpet in a ceremony befitting a head of state) in December 2002 as 'superb' and added:

> *I share the strategic view of the Americans in the region. French forces in Djibouti have been a stabilising factor, and US troops would add to that. You need outside powers to keep order here. It sounds colonialist, but I am only being realistic.*[261]

Eritrea also made common cause with the US against the National Islamic Front (NIF) regime in response to the

---

[261] Kaplan, Robert, *A Tale of Two Colonies*, Atlantic Monthly, April 2003, p. 46-53.

latter's sponsorship of the militant Eritrean Islamic Jihad (EIJ) and support for its cross-border armed operations. *Al Qaida's* founder had set up base in Khartoum, which had become the regional venue of the Islamic Peoples' Congress under the auspices of Osama bin Laden, Ayman al-Zawahiri, Mohamed Atef, et.al. With US blessing, Asmera hosted, in June 1995, the founding conference of the National Democratic Alliance (NDA), a coalition of Sudanese opposition groups, including the Sudan People's Liberation Movement/Army (SPLM/A). In a breach of normal diplomatic protocol, Eritrea also handed the NDA the premises of the Embassy of the Republic of the Sudan in Asmera to serve as its headquarters.

Besides, Eritrea provided armed groups within the NDA, which conducted military operations in the east and south of the country and, later, the Darfuri insurgency in the west, with significant political, financial and military assistance. The NDA aimed to topple the NIF government and seize power in Khartoum. Further, Eritrea served as a linchpin in a US-backed tripartite military alliance with Ethiopia and Uganda that provided active support to the SPLM/A, including direct military intervention, to counter the militant Islamic regime's subversive regional activities.

Moreover, the government abandoned the commitment to pursue a foreign policy of peace and non-alignment, enshrined in the EPLF National Democratic Programme, and offered its territory for use as US bases. The government openly courted the US and Isaias tried hard to ingratiate himself with the Bush administration. Eritrea became one of only two African countries, along with Ethiopia, to join the US-led 'Coalition of the Willing' for the invasion of Iraq in 2003, carried out under the pretext of non-existent 'weapons of mass destruction' and fabricated links to al Qaida. Further, Eritrea pledged active cooperation in the so-called 'war on terror' and lobbied the US government hard to set up military and naval bases on Eritrean territory as ideal staging grounds for the wars in Iraq and Afghanistan.

Well aware that the US generally subordinates its declared foreign policy concerns for issues of democracy or human rights to its strategic interests in the region, President Isaias predicated his offer on the calculus that the US would not forego the prospect to use Eritrea's pivotal location and, therefore, could ill-afford to alienate him by insisting on any conditionality. The US, for its part, seriously considered and would have accepted the offer of military bases in Eritrea except for one problem: the Eritrean government's continued detention of two Eritrean employees of the US Embassy in Asmera. Insisting that the issue was an internal matter, as if Eritreans have no right to due process, Isaias adamantly refused to grant repeated US requests and demarches to either bring the two detainees to trial before a court of law or release them forthwith.

Beneath a façade of normalcy, therefore, US-Eritrea relations were coming under increasing strain because of the impasse. Following a telephone plea from the new Secretary of State at the time, President Isaias railed that 'people in the State Department have entrapped him [Colin Powell] in their position' and mused bafflement at 'their preoccupation with petty issues' while 'we are offering them strategic partnership on big issues'.[262] He thought that as long as he stood with the US on the big regional issues, Washington would turn

---

[262] Conversation of the author with the President, 7 July 2003, Asmera, Eritrea.

a blind eye on his autocratic rule, no matter his abuses, and continue with business as usual. Improbable reports from the Eritrean embassy in Washington might have abetted miscalculation that US State Department opposition would not deter the US Defence Department from establishing a military base in Eritrea.[263]

There are, in the context of infighting, situations of strategic US interest in which the department of defence does override the department of state and impose its views on US policy. However, Eritrea's was not such a case. Adopting a winning or a losing policy response is generally a matter of judgment. Whether out of lack of general understanding of the internal dynamics driving and determining US foreign policy towards Eritrea at the time, proper grasp of the import of the issue at hand to America's self-image, or reckless disregard of the potential fallout of obstinacy on Eritrea's paramount national interest, President Isaias played his cards wrong. His policy response failed to either appreciate or care that a refusal to release or bring to trial the two jailed US embassy employees would damage Eritrea's relations with the US.

Albeit all Eritrean detainees deserved due legal process, the issue of the detention of US embassy personnel without charge or trial was not only inconsistent with stated US foreign policy objectives in Eritrea, but it also represented an affront to American prestige and an offense to US sensibilities. In the end, failure to resolve the deadlock resulted in the

---

[263]   The reports indicated that it was only the US State Department that was hostile to Eritrea while the US Defence Department, the US National Security Council, and the US National Security Agency were favourable.

rejection of the offer of military bases and prompted the reversal of fortunes that has shaped the negative evolution in US-Eritrea relations. Further, the antagonisation of the bilateral relationship triggered an unjustifiable retaliatory shift in the US position on the boundary issue that has contributed to keeping on hold the physical demarcation of the Ethio-Eritrea boundary.

The US selection of Ethiopia and Kenya as anchor states for US regional security strategy in the Greater Horn of Africa (GHoA) created an additional irritant. President Isaias viewed this as a decision that marginalises Eritrea and favours Ethiopia in the region at a time when the two countries maintained hostile relations and the US could have acted as an honest broker to help implement border demarcation and facilitate reconciliation. Annual US State Department Human Rights Reports, routinely castigating Eritrea's violations of human rights, including the detention of the former senior officials and journalists without charge or trial, caused more consternation and provoked reaction in kind. The stinging public criticism of the US by the president and the state media further strained bilateral relations.

In an initiative to resolve the impasse regarding the jailed US embassy employees and reset bilateral relations, Ambassador Donald Yamamoto visited Eritrea in 2005 and held talks with President Isaias Afwerki. In return for the release or formal charge of the two detainees, the US envoy promised strategic US cooperation in the form of sizeable financial and technical assistance to develop Eritrea's water resources, or any chosen sector, and support for the demarcation of the border with Ethiopia. In response to his question as to whether the two detainees were still alive, they were whisked from solitary confinement in Irairo and brought to Asmera to be shown to Ambassador Yamamoto and his delegation.

President Isaias insisted that the US first enforce the border demarcation; and the release of the prisoners and strengthening of bilateral cooperation would follow. He was concerned that putting on trial or releasing the detained US embassy employees would create a precedent and lead to more demands and increased pressure for similar treatment of the detained former senior officials and journalists. The US duly promised to do so and, a few weeks later, issued a statement calling on Ethiopia to cooperate for the demarcation of the boundary. According to a well-placed EU official in Brussels, the US statement and its implied possible rapprochement in US-Eritrea relations had caused palpable anxiety in the Ethiopian government.

However, there was no reciprocal move or signal of willingness to address the question of the jailed embassy staff. The impasse continued and Eritrea, in a display of pique, requested the US to stop providing development assistance and food aid and close the US Agency for International Development (USAID) office in Asmera in 2005. Putting regime stability above national interest, the Eritrean government missed an excellent opportunity for rapprochement and close cooperation with the US and forfeited the promise of effective support for the demarcation of the boundary with Ethiopia and the attendant restitution of Eritrea's territorial integrity.

Upping the ante, Isaias embarked on a collision course and unleashed a wave of criticism of the US, denigrating US domestic and foreign policy, in the state-owned media. Setting the tone and leading the fray in his periodic staged interviews with the state media, he accused the US of abetting Ethiopian aggression and the US Central Intelligence Agency (CIA) of conspiring to overthrow him. His attacks, echoed by the state media, grew more frequent and increasingly vitriolic, portraying the US as the "historic enemy of Eritrea".

Lacking a capacity for strategic calculation and diplomatic tact to seize the moment, the government of Eritrea missed another excellent opportunity to reset Eritrea-US relations in 2009. The new Obama administration and US Secretary of State Hillary Clinton, in particular, who had visited Eritrea as First Lady in 1997 and made positive remarks about her meeting with President Isaias Afwerki in her 2003 book, Living History,[264] had undertaken direct and indirect overtures. Several intermediaries, including Norway, friendly EU officials and EU member states, such as Germany, Italy and The Netherlands, tried to reach out and reengage with the government of Eritrea. Isaias rejected these overtures, refused to reengage with the new US administration, and opted for the continued isolation of the country.[265]

As Eritrea-US relations grew more strained, the US government has more than reciprocated in spite and hostility in response to the Eritrean president's rebuff of its overtures to

---

[264]   Clinton, Hillary Rodham, Living History, Simon & Schuster, 9 June 2003, p. 405. Mrs Clinton graciously states that Isaias had given up his university studies to fight in the resistance while he, in fact, left after 'Christmas graduation', a term used to describe the status of freshman students who failed to make it beyond the first semester.

[265]   The author's conversations with an adviser of German Chancellor Angela Merkel in Berlin in May 2009, with a senior official of the Belgian Ministry of Foreign Affairs in Brussels in November 2009 and with senior EU officials in Brussels in June 2009.

re-engage with the country. It abetted Ethiopia's intransigence on the issue of boundary demarcation, and used its political and diplomatic clout to shield it from international censure and pressure to comply with its treaty obligations under the Algiers Agreement. Further, the US maintained its criticism of the domestic and regional policies of the Eritrean regime, in general, and its alleged continued support to militant Islamist insurgents in Somalia, in particular. Finally, the US, in an apparent display of double standards, singled out Eritrea in its support of the imposition of UN sanctions for geopolitical infractions that are by no means unique to the Eritrean government in the region.

7.5 Eritrea-EU Cooperation

The EU provided the largest source of Eritrea's overseas development assistance (ODA). Cooperation between Eritrea and the EU is undertaken in the framework of the Cotonou Partnership Agreement (CPA) between the African, Caribbean and Pacific Group of States and the EU (ACP-EU) and stands on three pillars. These pillars are preferential economic and trade relations, policy and political dialogue, and development cooperation. The first pillar aims to promote Eritrea-EU economic and trade cooperation through reciprocal free access for their goods and services to each other's respective markets.

The second pillar provides for Eritrea-EU engagement in policy and political dialogue at the level of state authorities, civil society organisations (CSOs), and non-state actors (NSAs) based on the mutually agreed fundamental and essential elements underpinning the ACP-EU CPA. As a signatory to the CPA, Eritrea had agreed that "comprehensive, balanced and deep political dialogue leading to commitments on both sides", covering all the objectives, interests and concerns of the Partnership, focused on "specific political issues of mutual concern or of general significance", and "conducted in a flexible manner", in a "formal or informal" setting "within and outside the institutional framework" underpins its relations with the EU.[266]

The third pillar of EU-Eritrea partnership, development cooperation, is based on the principle of national ownership of Eritrea's development strategy and guided by a contractual commitment on the fundamental and essential elements enshrined in the CPA:

> *Respect for human rights and fundamental freedoms, including respect for fundamental social rights, democracy based on the rule of law and transparent and accountable governance are an integral part of sustainable development... Respect for human rights, democratic principles and the rule of law, which underpin the ACP-EU Partnership, shall underpin the domestic and international policies of the Parties and constitute the essential elements of this Agreement.[267]*

By mutual agreement, EU-Eritrea development cooperation aims to promote sustainable economic and social development, the gradual integration of the Eritrean economy into the world economy, and the reduction and

---

[266] Africa - Caribbean - Pacific - European Union, ACP-EU Partnership Agreement, Cotonou, 23 June 2000 as revised in Luxembourg n 25 June 2005, Article 8, p. 8.
[267] Ibid., Article 9, pp. 8-9.

eventual eradication of poverty. Eritrea had drawn up a macroeconomic policy framework designed to rebuild the economic and social structures ruined by thirty years of war and promote economic growth and sustainable development via an outward-oriented and private sector-led market economy. As Eritrea proved unable to advance past the first phase, however, EU development cooperation remained focused mainly on a programme of support to post-conflict rehabilitation and reconstruction.

These include policies affecting: social and transport infrastructure reconstruction; humanitarian aid and demining programmes; the reintegration of demobilised fighters, internally diplaced persons (IDPs), repatriated refugees, and disabled war veterans; the restoration of macroeconomic stability and the realisation of the country's potential; and the development of long-term strategies in the food security, transport, and education sectors to relax the main structural constraints to Eritrea's development.

To this end, the EU allocated €337.5 million programmable financial resources to Eritrea under four successive European Development Funds (EDFs), namely, the 7th EDF (1991-1995), the 8th EDF (1995-2000), the 9th EDF (2002-2007), and the 10th EDF (2009-2013).[268] EDF resources are grants that, unlike loans, need not be repaid. Eritrea could have proactively engaged with the EU and effectively utilised this quite substantial financial and technical assistance to bolster its efforts towards economic growth in line with its own priorities.

---

[268] An aggregate of the A-Envelope and B-Envelope allocations compiled and cumulated by the author from the Eritrea - European Community Country Strategy Papers and National Indicative Programmes for the four periods.

The programmable financial assistance that the EU had earmarked for Eritrea, its allocation among priority development sectors and the modality of its implementation were, unlike the actual disbursements, completely untied and always decided by mutual agreement. Apart from the binding commitments to the fundamental principles and essential elements of the CPA, there were no preconditions or strings attached that impinged on Eritrea's legitimate claim to policy independence, self-reliance, or ownership of national development programme. Even so, Eritrea did not manage to secure timely disbursement and ensure effective use of the bulk of the availed EDF resources. Among the notable causes of the relatively low levels of disbursement were Eritrea's low institutional and absorption capacity, complex EU procedures and red tape, and the president's often impulsive and irrational decisions that impeded the implementation of agreed deals or ongoing projects through constant disruption and discontinuity.

To cite but one such case: in Libreville, in November 1997, Jean Ping, then Gabon's Minister of Planning and Co-President of the ACP-EU Council of Ministers, asked me why Eritrea has decided to refuse its 9th EDF allocation and withdraw from the ACP Group. When I, as Eritrea's ambassador to the EU and delegate to the ACP-EU Council of Ministers, expressed surprise and denied any knowledge of the story, he brought me a copy of a letter addressed to him and signed by Berhane Abrehe, then National Authorising Officer (NAO) in the Office of the President.[269] The gist of the letter was that Eritrea had decided to decline its national

---

[269] The National Authorising Officer (NAO) is a senior government official appointed by each ACP state to represent it in all the

envelope of €96.8 m under the 9th EDF, as it had made the transition from rehabilitation to development and wished, henceforth, to receive aid in the form of loans rather than grants. I later learned that the minister of foreign affairs and the minister of finance were also unaware of the matter.

While in Asmera in January 1998, I asked President Isaias why the government had opted not to avail itself of the EU's €96.8 m aid grant and to withdraw from the ACP Group. He replied that there was no such decision. When I mentioned that a letter was sent from his office to that effect, he responded that he did not know about it. I told him that I had a copy of the letter and could show him if he wished to see it. I looked him in the eye and he fell silent. I then asked him if he would let me restore the allocation and he said, "Okay, go ahead and try if you can".

It is said that ambassadors, who often serve as glorified messengers, lie for their governments. Unless they prefer to resign in protest, they are, at times, instructed to lie or to misrepresent facts in the 'national interest'. It is thus not surprising that President John F. Kennedy once referred to Adlai E. Stevenson, the US ambassador to the UN at the time of the Cuban Missile Crisis in October 1962, as "my official liar."[270] Diplomats frequently use spin to juggle facts and avoid outright lying. In my situation on this specific case, I did not want to see Eritrea forfeit the €96.8 m grant or abandon the solidarity of the ACP family and the privileged partnership of the EU. I needed to unravel

---

operations financed through the European Development Fund (EDF).

[270] United States History: Bay of Pigs Invasion http://www.u-s-history. com/pages/h1765.html.

the adverse decision in the service of Eritrea's national interest.

Back in Brussels, I met and discussed the matter with Poul Nielsen and Philip Lowe, then EU Development Commissioner and Director General of Development (DG DEV), respectively. Both were well disposed towards Eritrea and ready to help salvage the situation. By way of 'face saving', I argued that Eritrea was endeavouring to rebuild and develop its economy fast so as to make up for lost time and recover from the devastation of the long war; that the letter from the president's office was merely an overreaction to the prolonged delays entailed in the complex procedures for the disbursement of EDF resources that had the effect of holding back funding for agreed projects and retarding implementation of Eritrea's national development programme; and that, otherwise, Eritrea needed and highly valued EU assistance to speed up its on-going efforts of economic reconstruction and sustainable development.

As a way forward, I proposed that the EU transfer its development assistance in the form of direct budget and balance of payments support, instead of the then prevalent project-based aid. I argued that budget and balance of payments support would minimise the time lag between the commitment and the disbursement of EDF allocations and address Eritrea's concerns. There was a consensus that direct budget and balance of payments support would permit faster disbursement and more effective utilisation of EU aid. The Commission eventually agreed, in principle, to ignore the letter and channel assistance via direct budget and balance of payments support. The agreement represented a big breakthrough; but, there was a problem. Use of the two instruments required the existence of published national budget and foreign trade statistics, which Eritrea still lacked, to serve as frames of reference for execution in line with stringent standards of accountability and transparency in the management of public finance.

I informed the president and the NAO of the outcome of my discussions with the Commission and sent them a jointly initialised memo crystallising our conclusions, which was welcomed forthwith. The face-saving exercise worked and, despite its delaying effects, the damage was undone and Eritrea was offered the prospect of direct and speedy access to the 9th and future EDFs. The gathering momentum was, however, scuttled by the outbreak of the border war with Ethiopia in May 1998, before the accompanying measures could be worked out and the mode of execution agreed. In the event of hostilities, the standing rules of EU development cooperation bar the initiation of disbursements for new programmes, in contrast for programmes that are already in the pipeline, for either belligerent nation.

The end of hostilities in 2000 opened up the prospect for the speedy funding of Eritrea's 9th EDF allocation through a programme of direct budget and balance of payments support. Apart from the inability to produce published budget and trade data, the lack of focused and coherent engagement contributed to the failure to exploit the opportunity. Discontinuity in Eritrea's representation in Brussels accentuated the negative effects of the absence of institutional memory at the ministerial and ambassadorial levels. Eritrea had four successive ambassadors, each of whom had to pass through a slow protocolar process of formal accreditation within a span of less than two and a half years between September 1999 and February 2002.[271]

All this delayed the working out of the modalities for the provision of direct budget and balance of payments support. Further, the process was brought to an abrupt halt in September 2001. The EU recalled its head of delegation and suspended development assistance to Eritrea in response to the detention of the former senior government officials and journalists, the crackdown on the private press, and the expulsion of the Italian ambassador and local representative of the rotating EU Presidency in Asmera for protesting the government's measures on behalf of the EU.

The suspension was lifted and EU development cooperation with Eritrea resumed following months of intensive discussions and the signing of a Cooperation Strategy in November 2002. Commitments made during my discussions with the Commission in Brussels, in particular, that the government of Eritrea would duly address the issues arising from the drastic measures taken on 18 September 2001 helped conclude the agreement. EU-Eritrea relations started to improve. Budget and balance of payments support

---

[271] Having designated nine heads of mission between 1991 and 2010, Eritrea holds the record for the highest turnover of ambassadors in Brussels for the period. Apart from the learning curve, this had its adverse effects, as each designate must wait for an agrément from the host country, go through a process of accreditation after arriving at the post, and start at the bottom of the diplomatic seniority ladder once accredited. In contrast, Ethiopia, whose receipt of substantial EU aid serves as the bogus upon which the president accuses the EU of partiality, maintains prudent and interactive relations with the EU and had only two ambassadors in Brussels during the same period.

was confirmed as the preferred instrument for funding of Eritrea's allocation of EDF resources.

But there were impediments to progress in EU-Eritrea cooperation. The partaking of students in military training during their last year of high school in Sawa raised issues of the eligibility of the education sector for EU assistance; the absence of a published government budget raised concerns of transparency and accountability in the use of EDF funds for budget support; and the lack of foreign trade data raised questions of the feasibility of balance of payments support. The idea was finally laid to rest after the killings of national service evaders, who were rounded up and detained at the Adi Abeto military prison in November 2004. The incident provoked strong EU condemnation and caused new strains in EU-Eritrea relations.

Most crucially, the impasse in EU-Eritrea policy and political dialogue had persisted for over ten years. The bilateral dialogue had failed to make progress. The EU was unable to deliver on the key Eritrean demand of boundary demarcation. The Eritrean government resorted to obfuscation and refused to budge in on the principal issues of EU concern, namely, the case of the detained former senior officials and journalists, the ban on the private press, the implementation of the ratified Constitution, the application of the proclamation on regional decentralisation, the holding of national elections and the improvement of the macroeconomic situation. Repeated EU initiatives and efforts to advance the stalled process through diplomatic demarches, political declarations, high level representations and special missions failed to bear fruit.

The president has persistently insisted that the detention of the former senior officials and journalists is an internal matter and would be dealt with in the 'Eritrean way'. At the same time, certain senior PFDJ officials have, in response to questions in various seminars for Eritreans in the diaspora, repeatedly echoed the president's stance that the case of the political detainees would be handled in the 'Eritrean way', as if Eritreans were not entitled to the application of due process, the rule of law, or the proper administration of justice. Indeed, the government has acted as if the non-implementation of the Constitution gives it licence to violate the constitutional guarantees of basic human rights and fundamental liberties with impunity.

Further, the regime's arguments seemed very oblivious of the fact that Eritrea's accession to the CPA and subscription of its fundamental principles and essential elements had transformed the denial of the rule of law and due process from a seemingly simple Eritrean affair to a weighty matter of broader international concern. The phenomenon of indefinite detention without charge or trial has exposed the meaning of the 'Eritrean way' as the presumption of guilty as accused, without discharging the burden of proof, a mere euphemism for extra-judicial elimination. The government's handling of the case denies credence to a different interpretation.

The government's reluctance to address these critical issues has contributed to the political paralysis, economic stagnation, and external isolation of the country. In the specific setting of the Cotonou Agreement, it has bogged down policy and political dialogue between Eritrea and the EU, stalled EU-Eritrea relations, and risked the cessation of sizeable EU financial and technical assistance to the detriment of the Eritrean State. Inability to resolve the outstanding issues tabled in the long drawn out process of policy and political dialogue, coupled with Eritrea's objection to an inclusion of support for the International Criminal Court (ICC), finally culminated in the formal termination of EU development aid to Eritrea in November 2011. Characteristically, the Eritrean government has packaged the adverse outcome as an affirmation of its self-reliance and the independence its policy and decision.

Despite the rhetoric of self-reliance shrouded in non-transparency, there prevails a situation of substantial and growing dependence on foreign aid and a heavy burden of domestic and foreign indebtedness. In reality, the government's claims of self-reliant development stand in stark contrast to its heavy external dependence: aggregate donor support represented 34 per cent of public sector output, which constituted 80 per cent of GDP in 2002-2003, and amounted to 27.2 per cent of GDP; the country's public debt, estimated at 32 per cent of GDP in 2002, making up more than 300 per cent of the net present value of exports, is twice the level of the Heavily Indebted Poor Countries (HIPC) eligibility criteria of 150 per cent; and debt servicing consumed 23 per cent of the value of exports in 2002.[272] More recent data indicate that foreign aid has risen to 29 per cent of GDP, ranking Eritrea as the third most aid-dependent national economy in the world after that of Sao Tome and Principe (75.2 per cent) and Guinea-Bissau (37.3 per cent).[273]

---

[272] Draft Joint Annual Report on European Commission/State of Eritrea Cooperation, 16 April 2003, p. 7.

273 Economy Statistics > Aid as % of GDP (most recent) by country. http://www.nationmaster.com/graph/eco_aid_as_of_gdp-economy-aid-as-of-gdp

The extreme preoccupation of the domestic policy of the Eritrean government with regime security has dictated the pursuit of a foreign policy geared to serving the narrow interest of regime stability at the expense of the overarching welfare of the Eritrean nation-state. Overall, the policy of self-reliance successfully pursued during the war of independence has, in an apparent distortion of its initial application, turned into a euphemism for the country's privation and debilitating international and regional isolation. The situation is compounded by a reluctance to engage in effective political dialogue with development partners, which arises, at least in part, from the government's obsession with, and fear of loss of, control that submitting to the rule of law and opening up to real accountability and transparency may entail.

In abandoning the Macro-Policy paper and the National Economic Policy Framework (NEPF) in favour of an overly centralised economic command, the regime has imposed a coupon economy that demeans the dignity of the people, as discussed below.

7.6 The Shame of the Coupon Economy

The government's tight control of the daily life of the people and use of access to basic needs as a political weapon of repression find one of its ugliest manifestations in the institution of a system of rationing of essential consumer goods and foodstuffs. Basic necessities, such as bread, flour, tomato paste, milk, sugar, coffee, tea, soap, cooking oil, kerosene, etc., are rationed on a strict quota system that involves three actors: the government, the *kebele*, and the ruling People's Front for Democracy and Justice (PFDJ).

The *kebele* is a neighbourhood association created by and inherited from Ethiopia's *Derg* era as the smallest unit of local administration, similar to a ward, in which membership and assessed contributions are compulsory. The *Derg*'s military regime created the *kebele* as an instrument of control and used it to register people, raise funds, spy on the population, and follow their daily activities. Under the prevailing system of rationing, the government determines the amount of rations for families according to the size of a household. The *kebele* collects the assessed donations and issues the coupons for the rations. The Front provides supplies through its so-called 'Rational Shops'[274] that sell the rations to the people in the neighbourhood in accordance with the coupons presented.

Coupons are earned monthly through demonstrations of 'good' citizenship, not automatically availed. To receive coupons, families and persons must be in good standing in terms of Front affiliation, regular attendance of mandatory meetings of the local cells of the Front, and payment of membership dues and assessed donations to the Front. Other requirements include contributions for and presence in celebrations of national holidays, timely payment of and steady participation in an assortment of other 'voluntary' contributions in cash and in kind, etc. Failure to comply with any of these and a miscellany of kindred other obligations disqualifies a family or a person from entitlement to coupons and, therefore, of access to rations.

Families or persons that pass the test of scrutiny receive their coupons at the office of the *kebele*. After getting their coupons, people line up in long queues and wait for many

---

[274] Known as *Rita'awi Dkuanat* in Tigrinya, which literally means Rational Shops in English.

hours to fetch their monthly rations of basic necessities. To maximise their chances of getting their rations on the following day, many people start queuing on the eve just before midnight in the hope that they can take delivery of their allotments by noon. The waiting in the biting night cold of the Eritrean highlands often extends to late afternoon or even to the next day. Long files of people have become a common sight in Asmera and Eritrea's major cities and towns. Chronic shortage of essential goods is the norm and rations are irregular, with some items supplied only every other month, and often every two or even three months. Availability of the provisions in the 'rational shops' often depends on the amounts confiscated from petty traders.

Family rations are based on the size or number of members of a household. A family of seven members, for instance, receives the following rations when supplies are available: twenty five kilogrammes of sorghum every two months; five litres of cooking oil, one hundred grams of tea, seventy grams of tomato paste, three and half kilogrammes of pasta, nine kilogrammes of sugar and one kilogramme of coffee per month; and ten litres of kerosene every six to eight months. Each family is also allotted a daily ration of one small loaf of bread per person. Often, the rations are irregular and hardly sufficient to meet the basic daily needs of families.

Made up mostly of confiscated property and often totally unavailable for prolonged periods, the items rationed are of insufficient quantity and substandard quality. Their cost is quite high relative to household disposable incomes. Such a package of monthly rations costs about Eritrean Nakfa (ERN) 1,600 and must be paid up front. Even so, obtaining the allotted rations involves a lot of hardship and aggravation.

Just as in the case of buying their daily quotas of bread and other rationed necessities, people stand in long lines for hours to buy the additional bread, milk, and other needed items in privately owned parallel shops at substantially higher prices.

Mass unemployment prevails across the country, and most people do not earn any income at all. With the private sector virtually disabled and housing construction ordered to a standstill, resulting in the suspension of work on many building projects at different levels of progress, the stagnant government and Front bureaucracies are the major employers. The existing salary and wage scales are extremely low. The average salary of a senior government or Front official is about ERN 2,000, that of a middle level government or Front employee about ERN 1,200, and that of a national service conscript ERN 500 per month. In contrast, the ERN 1,600 paid for the package of rationed items is quite hefty and burdensome.

Depending on a family's level of income, the ration takes up the entire, most or even more than the salaries or wages of the great majority of households. Worse still, it is often not enough to sustain life at the minimum threshold. To survive, families must supplement the rations with additional purchases from private shops at exorbitant black market prices. In addition to the cost of other essential items of consumption, such as meat, vegetables, fruits, spices, etc., there are regular bills to pay for rent, transport, firewood, electricity, water, etc., even when the supply of water and electricity is unavailable, as is the case most of the time. The combination of very low or no incomes, acute shortages of basic commodities, and spiralling prices depresses the standard of living and downgrades the quality of life.

Rations, inadequate as they may be, are not even available to the vast majority of the people, namely, the more than eighty per cent of the population who live on subsistence agriculture in the rural areas. Moreover, peasant farmers are not free to sell their produce in the open market. They are allowed to sell them only in the captive market of the Front-owned 'rational shops' at prices arbitrarily fixed below the real market price to allow for ample profit margins to be made at the point of resale. They must then buy the items they need at relatively high prices in the open or black market. Families of subsistence farmers face double jeopardy: low sales prices for their agricultural produce in the captive market and high purchase price for the items they need to buy in the open or black market. Such an indirect dual penalty exacerbates rural poverty.

The state of Eritrea's economy and the condition of its people show the wasteful, inefficient and demeaning features of the coupon economy. Designed to serve an obnoxious control function, the blight of indignity it inflicts on the people is a daily curse that is deliberate. Its operation enables the regime to determine people's access to food, decide what they eat, and in what quality and quantity. It also allows it to monitor and control the internal movements of people. Worse still, the coupon economy keeps the people constantly on edge, with their thoughts and energies totally preoccupied with the endless anxieties of daily survival. Further, it enables the regime to use food insecurity as a means to enforce compliance with *kebele* directives and Front obligations. In brief, the coupon economy is an instrument of population control imposed by a government obsessed with the pursuit of its own security and survival at any cost while the fear of incarceration or deprivation forces the people to endure its caprices.

The hapless combination of political diktat, a command economy, and a policy of repression at home and confrontation abroad, compounded by general mismanagement, have: led to the misuse of the country's productive assets and resources; deterred domestic and foreign direct investment; provoked international isolation; and squandered Eritrea's golden opportunity to attain economic growth, pursue sustainable development and create wealth. The consequences are, as the next section describes, an inevitable shrinking of the Eritrean economy in real terms, large-scale unemployment, and widespread poverty, causing a steadily declining standard of living for the great majority of the population.

7.7 A Contracting Economy in Crisis

Published and publicly accessible government statistics on the Eritrean economy are unavailable. In addition to constraining informed public policy and decision-making, the absence of reliable and comprehensive primary macroeconomic data, such as national income accounts, public revenues and expenditures, employment figures, consumer price indexes, population census, demographic characteristics, balance of payments statistics, real exchange rates, etc., makes the quantitative assessment of the condition and performance of the Eritrean economy difficult. Such difficulty compels us to rely upon figures compiled by credible international sources for key economic indicators on the state of the Eritrean economy.

Latest available reports from the International Monetary Fund (IMF),[275] the World Bank (WB)[276] and the United

---

[275] IMF Executive Board Concludes 2009 Article IV Consultation with the State of Eritrea, PIN No. 09/13, December 11, 2009. http://www.imf.org/external/np/sec/pn/2009/pn09133.htm.

[276] World Bank Indicators Database: Eritrea Country Profile, September 2009. http://ddp-ext.worldbank.org/ext/ddpreports/

Nations Development Programme (UNDP),[277] portray Eritrea as one of the least developed and poorest countries in the world. A Gross National Income (GNI) per capita of USD 300 (Atlas method) ranks Eritrea among the lowest in Africa. The country's Gross Domestic Product (GDP) at constant market prices shrank by an estimated 9.8 per cent in 2008 while the Consumer Price Index (CPI) rose by 30.2 per cent.

These reports and the associated data show the profile of a sharply contracting economy in crisis: unsustainable levels of fiscal and balance of payments deficits; external debt distress; double-digit inflation; and an acute shortage of foreign exchange reserves. Spiralling inflation keeps prices soaring and deflates the purchasing power of the *Nakfa* (Eritrean currency), depresses the living standards of civil servants and workers earning declining real incomes under fixed salary and wage scales prescribed in 1996, and exacerbates income disparities.

Worse still, the mixture of high general unemployment and token stipends paid to conscripts doing civil service jobs or deployed on development projects under indefinite active national service makes the purchase of basic necessities unaffordable. The inability of the large number of unemployed people to find work and earn any income in a stagnant job market and the low pay of those employed block access even to the meagre daily rations for essential

---

ViewSharedReport?&CF=1&REPORT_ID=9147&REQUEST_TYPE=VIEWADVANCED&HF=N&WSP=N.

[277] United Nations Development Programme (UNDP), *Human Development Report 2009* http://hdrstats.undp.org/en/countries/country_fact_sheets/cty_fs_ERI.html.

subsistence goods. The general expansion and deepening of poverty has reduced people to passive objects grappling with life at the margins, fully absorbed in the preoccupation for the next meal.

A GDP per capita ranking of 177 out of 182 countries and a Human Development Index (HDI) ranking of 165 out of 182 in 2007 place Eritrea at the lowest rungs of the development ladder.[278] Over half of the country's population lives on less than US$1 per day and about a third subsists in a state of extreme poverty, defined as a daily intake of less than 2,000 calories.[279] Although the government routinely denies the existence of famine in the country, the plain fact is that the prevalence of severe impoverishment translates into extreme deprivation, malnutrition and hunger with few parallels in the annals of modern Eritrean history. The Global Hunger Index (GHI) combines undernourishment (the proportion of undernourished people as a percentage of the population), child underweight (the proportion of children under age five who are underweight, which is one indicator of malnutrition), and child mortality (the mortality rate of children under age five), with equal weights as an indicator of hunger. The 2012 GHI gives Eritrea an alarming score of 34.4, just between Haiti's 30.8 and Burundi's 37.1.[280]

---

[278] United Nations Development Programme (UNDP), *Human Development Report 2009*.

[279] IMF Executive Board Concludes 2009 Article IV Consultation with the State of Eritrea

[280] 2012 Global Hunger Index: The Challenge of Hunger: Ensuring Sustainable Food Security under Land, Water and Energy Stresses, p. 19. http://www.ifpri.org/sites/default/files/publications/ghi12.pdf

General malnutrition afflicts 64 percent of the Eritrean population; the per capita daily calorie intake is 1,587 and the per capita daily protein intake (% kcl) is 12; 30 per cent of Eritrean children are malnourished and underweight while 48 per cent are malnourished and stunting; and the child mortality rate stands at 55 per 1,000.[281] Only approximately 1.5 per cent of the people in rural areas have access to safe sanitation and about 58 per cent to a source of clean water.[282] The lack of real economic growth and gainful employment has widened and deepened poverty all over the country and caused chronic food insecurity. Neither government claims of success nor restrictions of access to information can hide the fact that famine stalks Eritrea today.

Instead of alleviating poverty, government policy worsens the state of impoverishment. The relegation of the private sector has discouraged domestic and foreign direct investment, stifled economic activity in the productive sectors and diminished national output. Further, tight government control and strict restriction on domestic population and commodity movements, enforced through security checkpoints and roadblocks that long dotted the main transport arteries of the country at regular intervals, have shackled normal economic and business activity.

A special government body set up in 1994 to privatise state enterprises ended up overseeing the eventual transfer of direct or indirect ownership of most of them to the Front at no cost. Freely acquired, the Front's 'parastatals'

---

[281]   Food and Agriculture Organisation of the United Nations Country Briefs, 7 July 2011 http://www.fao.org/countries/55528/en/eri/

[282]   Eritrea guide, OneWorld.net, quoting UNICEF http://uk.oneworld.net/guides/eritrea/development

enjoy privileged access to public financial resources, foreign exchange reserves, and *de facto* tax exemptions.[283] Headed and staffed by mostly incompetent but 'loyal' personnel, the management of their operations is subject to constant political interference. Consequently, they are inefficient. Furthermore, they are ultimately accountable to nobody but the president. The complete absence of regular financial reports and external audit betrays a lack of accountability and transparency.

A similar lack of accountability and transparency characterises the government's arbitrary granting of title to land, public housing, and access to credit and business licences to selected beneficiaries. Another form of corruption involves the practice of non-competitive award of exclusive contracts for the import of certain commodities by the Red Sea Trading Corporation's (RSTC). The recurring exhortations against 'corruption' by the state media and the government's revealing frequent arrests of senior managers of the Front-owned RSTC on corruption charges confirm a widely held suspicion of rampant corruption prevalent in high places.

Under the aegis of a crude system of economic command imposed since 2001, the government has disparaged normal business practice and failed to create a viable legal

---

[283] Stefanos Seyum, a founding member of the EPLF and PFDJ central committees, and under detention in solitary confinement since 18 September 2001, was dismissed as Director General of the Ministry of Finance's Department of Inland Revenue for criticising, at a meeting of the central committee, the non-payment of corporate income taxes by the Red Sea Trading Corporation and the Front's other parastatals.

economy.[284] The parastatals monopolise economic activity and dominate the national economy. Their incompetent management and monopoly position cause them to perform very poorly, operate under capacity, and produce inferior quality goods in insufficient quantities that often fall short of meeting even the small level of domestic demand. The combination of control and shortages has generated a burgeoning black market and a parallel economy characterised by corruption.

As a corollary, the government has discouraged foreign direct investment, aborted viable investment projects, and restricted the scope of domestic private enterprise. For instance, it rejected an attractive offer for a partnership with Lufthansa to build a viable national airline and obstructed a Mercedes-Benz project to set up an automobile assembly plant in Dekemhare. Moreover, it disrupted a budding fruit and flower farm in Adi Nefas and a promising seawater fish farm in Massawa, and let the Elabered agricultural estate deteriorate.

Following its crackdown of internal dissent in 2001, the regime has given priority to the retention of tight control of every aspect of national business activity and the daily economic life of the population at the expense of national development. Its misplaced priorities have diminished industrial, agricultural, and fisheries production and brought housing construction to a standstill. Constant talk of strategic

---

[284] Formal restrictions on trade have allowed certain groups, with links to, in partnership with or protection from people in high places in the army and security apparatus, to thrive in an underworld economy of smuggling, contraband, random confiscations from petty traders, and human trafficking.

national development plans and hollow claims of success cannot be a substitute for real progress. The government's misguided policies have created chronic shortages of basic housing, commodities and services, including beverages and food items, reduced gainful employment, and degraded the overall human condition of the people.

The resulting economic stagnation of the country has caused mass unemployment, both real and disguised, in the form of systemic idleness and underemployment perpetrated by active national service. The decline in overall economic activity has substantially reduced government revenues from income taxes, excise levies and import-export customs duties. The government regularly claims successful implementation of development projects and promises progress in achieving food security. On the contrary, the prevailing situation in the country, gauged by the available key economic and social indicators, shows an economy in tatters and a population reeling under conditions of grinding poverty. No rhetorical claims can hide the manifest suffering of the people under chronic shortages of food, water, power, and fuel and widespread malnutrition.

The government has used self-reliance and policy independence as tools of deception to cover up its inability to pursue rational domestic and foreign policies that serve the overarching interests of the country and deliver essential goods and services for the sustenance of the people. The situation is made worse by its unwillingness to undertake or engage in constructive political dialogue, both at home and overseas, that leads to firm commitments to reform, opens up the path to renewal and sustains cooperative relations. As we approach a quarter-century of sovereign statehood, it is a telling indictment to the regime that Eritrea possesses no: functional state organs; viable institutions of higher learning; operative national air carrier; serviceable shipping lines; effective land transport system; viable national electricity grid; or sustainable water supply system. Globally, the government has been unable to implement a programme of self-reliant national development, deliver prosperity, or achieve social justice.

In sum, the institution of the political economy of rationing at the turn of the third millennium symbolises an abysmal failure to manage a tiny national economy or to use state resources to cater to the most basic needs of a small population. The extreme fragility of the economy is mainly an outcome of the wrong policies and administrative incompetence of the government. The failure to organise the provision of the necessities and the delivery of essential services for the great majority of the people is primarily a function of the government's wasteful management of the country's labour resources and material assets. The following chapter deals with a prime example of the colossal misuse and squandering of the nation's most productive human potential, casting a pall over the future of the country.

CHAPTER 8

The Scourge of Indefinite National Service

When there is no enemy within, the enemies outside cannot hurt you. - African proverb

National service is typically an obligation of citizenship required of all young men between the age of eighteen and late twenties in many of the world's developed, emerging or developing countries. Originally conceived as an instrument of wartime mobilisation or an element of national defence strategy, it invariably entails some form of military training and active military and/or alternative civilian service. Generally, national service is a programme of mandatory military service, or compulsory conscription that usually lasts between one and two years. Most states allow reserved professions, such as the clergy, or special exemption for conscientious objection. There are only two countries, Israel and Eritrea, which require women to serve along with men in their programmes of mandatory military service.

Eritrea is a small country in terms of the size of both its territory and population. After Djibouti, it is the second smallest state in the Horn of Africa. In addition, Eritrea shares a highly volatile, conflict-riven, and insecure region with its comparatively much bigger land and maritime neighbours, notably, Ethiopia, the Sudan, Saudi Arabia and Yemen. It is also, like most of its neighbours, a poor developing country with a predominantly traditional rural economy based on subsistence agriculture and pastoralism. Afflicted by a turbulent history of successive colonial incursions, the physical devastation and social disruption of a long war of national liberation, and the debilitating consequences of the border war and subsequently frozen conflict with Ethiopia, its people yearn for peace, security and prosperity.

As a strategically located littoral state, Eritrea has the potential to become an entrepôt and a prosperous hub of regional commerce, industry and services, including tourism, transport, port, communications, and financial services *à la* Singapore. As a small state, its national security interests are best served by the pursuit of a policy of sustainable development, peaceful coexistence, political cooperation, and regional integration. As a poor developing country, it does not need, nor can it afford, a large standing army. Its national defence and security needs would be best served by building a small corps of highly trained and well equipped modern professional army, navy and air force, complemented by a large trained reserve army, *à la* Switzerland, capable of rapid mobilisation and deployment at short notice whenever necessary.

8.1 Voluntary versus Forced Service

The practice of voluntary military service evolved as a tradition among Eritrean youth during the war of independence. Tens of thousands of people freely joined the armed struggle to fight in the war with no remuneration. During the first eighteen years of the war, joining the armed struggle was voluntary. Although people were urged, directly or indirectly, to join the war, there was no formal compulsion. After 1979, however, Eritrean youth, both men and women, were compelled to join the liberation movements and fight for national liberation. Forced recruitment for military service was thus introduced in Eritrea as an instrument of wartime mobilisation and effectively practiced for more than a decade prior to the liberation from Ethiopia.

Pouring out of its impregnable rear base in the mountainous fortress of Sahel, portrayed as Eritrea's 'Yenan' in the EPLF folklore of the time, like an unrelenting torrent in mid-1977, the EPLA, along with the ELF's Eritrean Liberation Army (ELA), had, within a year, liberated virtually the entire territory of Eritrea, including most of the cities, towns and population centres. The Northern Highlands, the Western Lowlands, other than the garrison in Barentu, the Central Plateau, other than the town of Adi Keih in the south and the capital of Asmera in the centre, and the Coastal Plains, except for the southern port of Asseb and the island sections of the port of Massawa, were freed from Ethiopian occupation.

The liberation of the capital Asmera, besieged on all sides by a narrow and tightening 'ring of fire', appeared within our grasp, and the deliverance of the entire country from Ethiopian occupation seemed within sight. We, the freedom fighters, and our people had taken imminent triumph for granted. Our expectations of a swift victory were, however, thwarted by a sudden reversal in the military balance of forces following the large-scale Ethiopian counter-offensive, backed by the then Soviet Union and its allies. In response to the adverse battlefield situation, the EPLF introduced compulsory military service and began forcibly rounding up and recruiting young men and women of fighting age from the liberated and semi-liberated areas.

The fast chain of military victories, during 1977-1978, had greatly replenished the EPLA's arsenal of light, medium and heavy weapons and significantly augmented its size and firepower. But the battles had also taken their human toll, resulting in heavy casualties that depleted the rank and file of several units. The need to reinforce the liberation army and consolidate control over the extensive newly liberated areas required extra manpower. Besides, the rapid expansion of the theatre of operations and the significant extension of the lines of confrontation overstretched the military assets of the EPLF and thinned the strategic reserves of the EPLA.

Ethiopia's deployment of sizeable additional forces and launching of consecutive large-scale offensives on multiple fronts overextended the EPLA. The cold logic of numbers, the great difference that numbers make in a protracted and multi-pronged combat pitting unequal forces against one another, was made starkly clear to the Eritrean leadership and military command during and after the strategic retreat in 1978. Lacking in sufficient reinforcements, the much smaller Eritrean liberation armies were put on the defensive by the much larger Ethiopian aggressor army, beefed up by an abundant influx of fresh reinforcements.

The EPLA had remained an all-volunteer army. Casualties were running high. The flow of new recruits from the occupied cities and main population centres was dwindling, partly due to the remoteness of our Sahel rear base and the near complete Ethiopian encirclement. With the ELF effectively marginalised, the Ethiopian strategy focused on the effort to contain, isolate and annihilate the armed struggle by encircling and preventing the EPLF from recruiting new fighters and bleeding the EPLA white while continuously replenishing and reinforcing its own army. To counter the Ethiopian strategy and sustain the resistance by ensuring a continuous inflow of new recruits, the EPLF had adopted forcible recruitment in 1979 and sustained it until 1991.

Forced recruitment was instrumental in thwarting Ethiopia's large counter-offensives, foiling its military strategy of containment and annihilation, and ensuring the survival and ultimate victory of Eritrean resistance. The preservation and constant replenishment of its manpower via forced call up enabled the EPLF to overcome the blitz of the large Ethiopian army and its foreign allies in the late 1970s and early 1980s. Mandatory military service made a substantial contribution to the victory of the war of independence and has become a distinctive feature of the new state.

8.2 Proclamation of National Service

Having served the liberation movement so well during the last dozen years of the war, there were factors that supported the resumption of mandatory military service through formal proclamation in peacetime. At the time of independence, the capital city Asmera and the major towns were home to large numbers of unemployed and unemployable youth. There were no employment opportunities in an economy ruined by war and colonial neglect. The closure of the first and only university in Eritrea and the removal of its staff and assets to Agarfa[285] in southern Ethiopia, and the general

---

[285] The Derg regime had moved the University of Asmera to Agarfa, a small settlement located west of the Shebelle River in the Bale zone

degradation of the standard of education under the Derg regime, had deprived the young men and women of any possibility to develop their intellectual potential and acquire the knowledge and skills needed for gainful employment.

In the absence of proper education, functional skills, and opportunities for employment, a large number of urban youth lived on hand-outs from friends and family members in the diaspora. The dependence on remittances fostered a lifestyle that undermined the traditional Eritrean work ethic and sense of personal discipline. This undesirable state of affairs called for addressing the problem through the adoption of national service as a strategic instrument of self-reliance to help imbue the youth with an appreciation of the value of labour and self-sufficiency.

There was another and, perhaps a more pressing reason, for the government to introduce national service in peacetime as an instrument of a strategy of regime security. In May 1993, on the eve of the formal declaration of independence, units of the EPLA in Asmera had mounted a protest that was later, treated as a mutiny. The protesters went to government headquarters, took hold of the then Secretary General of the Provisional Government, and current president, and force-marched him to a meeting at the city's main football stadium. Joined by an influx of supporters and sympathisers in the spontaneous gathering, they presented several grievances and demanded immediate remedies. The Secretary General was let free to go only after he, typically whenever cornered or saw dire threats to his authority, bowed down to the pressure, acknowledged the legitimacy of the demands raised, and promised to fulfil them.

---

of Oromia in southern Ethiopia.

Once the situation calmed down and the provisional government regained control, the promises were set aside. The suspected ringleaders and principal supporters of the protest were hunted down, rounded up, and jailed at the Italian-built, maximum-security prison, in Adi Quala, a town near the border with Ethiopia. Characteristically, they were tortured, condemned to harsh prison terms without due process, and summarily discharged from the army.

Having meted out severe and excessive punishment on the protesters, viewed as potential rebels, the leadership of the Front and the government, in general, and the Secretary General, in particular, had taken their cue. The protest of armed fighters shook the would-be president and set the alarm on the spectre of a future coup d'état by 'disloyal' elements of the EPLA. The incident brought home the potential value of national military service to establish a citizen's reserve army as a useful counter-weight to the regular army.

It was against the general backdrop of these compelling factors that the transitional government proclaimed, albeit without internal debate, a programme of national service in 1995, providing for "compulsory active national service" for all Eritreans "from the age of eighteen to forty years". The programme consists of "six months of training, [...] twelve months of active military service and development chores in military forces for a total of eighteen months [...] and compulsory duty of serving [...] until the expiry of fifty years of age under mobilisation or emergency situation directives."[286] It allows no reserved professions or special exemptions.

---

[286] Government of Eritrea, Gazette of Eritrean Laws: Proclamation 82/1995, No.11, Asmera, 23 October 1995.

According to the decree, the objectives of national service are to create a strong reserve army, comprising active national and reserve military services, imbue the youth with the ethos of the armed struggle, cultivate strong discipline, inculcate work ethic, provide vocational training, promote economic development, and foster national unity. The ratified Constitution of Eritrea codifies completion of national service as a duty of all citizens (Article 25.3). In principle, the objectives of national service, as originally conceived, are commendable.

Designed to pursue these general objectives, the programme of national service embodied certain noble features of service to the nation in its conception and its adoption initially enjoyed a groundswell of support among the people and the youth, in particular. The crucial role that national service conscripts played in the defence of the country during the border war with Ethiopia in 1998-2000 demonstrated the imperative of the programme.

Furthermore, properly planned and effectively executed in accordance with the provisions of the proclamation and consistent with Eritrean cultural values of fairness and justice, national service could perform significant transformative social and political functions. It could also facilitate learning practical skills, cultivate a comparatively more cosmopolitan quasi-urban lifestyle, and nurture national unity in diversity among the youth.

8.3 Erosion of Legitimacy

Total disregard for the core provisions of the proclamation has rendered national service open-ended and undermined its legitimacy. It has deployed and kept the bulk of Eritrea's able-bodied men and women between eighteen and fifty years of age in a Sisyphean project, toiling without producing commensurate value. Along with the militarisation of the so-called *Warsai-Ykealo National Development Campaign,* indefinite active national service has operated to turn Eritrea into a garrison state on a false war footing, regiment its society and immerse the country in a self-destructive undertaking, with the ensuing inertia wasting away the creative energy of its most productive human resources and scarce economic assets.

The distinctive blend of inadequate planning, patent administrative deficiencies, and lack of proper oversight have eroded support for the programme. Some of the implementing bodies at the national and regional levels, which proved dysfunctional even while they lasted, have turned defunct, leading to rampant abuse. Forcible call up has routinely entailed unwarranted house searches of families and needlessly aggressive and forcible bouts of periodic roundups. Post recruitment, compulsory national service is characterised by gross abuses of conscripts during both military training in Sawa and subsequent deployment in active national service.

This has given rise to widespread reluctance to serve among conscripts. Conversely, evaders and deserters are subject to extremely harsh treatment and their families wronged with excessively severe punishment. The unjustified and unreasonable punishment dealt out to families of adult children gone missing under the watch of the government, in particular, evokes a story told about an incident involving the mother of a top Chinese ballet dancer who defected to the United States in 1979. When Chinese government officials paid a visit to the defector's family and blamed the mother for his defection, the peasant woman is reported to have angrily retorted:

> *How could you blame me? You, the government took my son away! From the age of eleven you were responsible for his upbringing! Now, you are asking me what have I done? You have lost my son. You are responsible!* [287]

Embarrassed, the Chinese officials turned speechless, left, and never bothered the family again.

There are discernible similarities between the regimes in China in the 1970s and in Eritrea in the 2000s and 2010s. Unlike the Chinese officials of yesteryear, however, present Eritrean officials have no such compunction or show no such implicit sense of responsibility. They readily detain and penalize families whose adult children evade national service or flee the country.

Families of adult children imprisoned on such pretexts are given, a choice between continued detention or paying ERN 50,000 per child.[288] It is quite indicative of the predatory nature of the regime that it imposes this penalty for every missing national service conscript while it allotted only ERN 10,000 as compensation for every combatant killed in the war of national liberation. Eritrea's lesser officials are under strict orders to mete out collective punishment on families whose adult children flee from or dodge open-ended

---

[287] Li Cunxin, Mao's Last Dancer, Penguin Books Australia, 2003, p. 308.

[288] The ERN 50,000 fine is equivalent to US$ 3,333.00 at the official exchange rate, an amount more than eleven times the country's annual per capita income of US$ 300.

military service. Anything that could signal an admission of responsibility would have severe consequences.

More ominously, the statutory period of eighteen months for national service - comprising six months of military training and twelve months for active military service and compulsory duty on public works, development projects or civil service jobs - underwent indefinite extension, in flagrant violation of the provisions of the Proclamation. Effectively, the imposition of open-ended compulsory military duty has turned indefinite active national service into the abyss of a dark alley without a window of escape for conscripts. Such flagrant abuses have, over time, incensed large sections of the population.

Indeed, the perpetration of indefinite active national service has generated deep-seated resentment among the people. It has antagonised the youth, depreciated their commitment to the noble ideal of service to the nation, and provoked widespread resistance. Further, the prevailing system of open-ended active national service has tainted the legitimacy of national service and caused a huge flight of labour and brain drain, thus compromising the imperative of national development, defence, and security in a fundamental and strategic sense.

8.4 The Waste of Student Summer Work Camps

Prior to their eligibility to the physical and mental drudgery of endless active national service, secondary school students are subject to the waste of mandatory summer work camps initiated in 1994. Applicable also to university students until the closure of the University of Asmera, the programme dispatches the students to the countryside at the end of each school year, ostensibly to help enhance the welfare of rural communities and improve the environment through terracing and reforestation. The random deployment, however, typically lacks proper planning, advance preparations, adequate resources, and essential follow-up to make a difference.

Conversely, the programme denies the adolescents essential parental guidance and the respite of normal family life during their summer recess. It also deprives families of subsistence farmers in rural communities the vital helping hand of their teenage children during the cultivation season. Further, without the drudgery of summer work camps, some high school students could find summer jobs and internships, and chip in some cash to help sustain their needy families.

About 80 per cent of the people live in the countryside and are engaged in subsistence agriculture, agro-pastoralism, and pastoralism. In such a rural-based subsistence economy, families need the hand of every member to look after their herds of livestock, to help with work in their crop fields, or to tend their vegetable gardens during the rainy season. The mandatory consignment to the summer work camps thus harms the wellbeing of secondary school children and diminishes the economic welfare of the families of subsistence farmers and pastoralists. Furthermore, despite official claims to the contrary, the student summer work camp has failed to improve the environment or produce tangible benefits to rural society.

After 'graduation' from the mandatory summer work camps, secondary school students from all over the country are, in effect, initiated into the military component of national service. At the end of their eleventh grade, students enrol in the isolated military training camp in Sawa to complete the newly added twelfth grade as the last year of high school. The original idea was to extend high school instruction up to the twelfth grade in order to improve the qualification of the students for university education. As Eritrea's secondary schools lacked the capacity to accommodate the planned extension, however, Sawa was selected for its facilities as a temporary solution, pending a short period of adjustment to enable the secondary schools to prepare for the transition (by acquiring the additional teachers, equipment, and classroom space needed).

Once in Sawa, students undergo political and military instruction in regimented formations. Contrary to the original plan, twelfth grade enrolment became regularised in Sawa. Initiation to militarised life at the tender age of their teens, separated from their close-knit families, deprives the students of normal family upbringing that is so essential in their formative years.

Likewise, teachers live away from their families in the remote and sequestered military camp in the far west of the country. Family members need special permits to visit the isolated camp school. The regimented life of students and teachers alike in Sawa deprives them of the comfort and support of normal family life and of the benefits of parent-teacher consultations.

This, coupled with the lack of an appropriate syllabus and adequate school facilities, such as a library and science laboratories worth their names, fosters alienation, diminishes aspirations for educational achievement, and undermines the pursuit of academic excellence. Upon completion of the final year of secondary school in Sawa, students sit for matriculation in the Eritrean Secondary Education Certificate Examination (ESECE). Those not assigned to the assortment of militarised colleges and institutes that serve as low-rate substitutes for the university are, consigned to indefinite active national service.

Eritrea's best and greatest asset is its youth. Generations of youth have made national liberation possible and independence sustainable, through struggle, toil and sacrifice. The youth represent the future of the country. To waste their formative years, to misuse their productive energies, and to deny them proper upbringing, education and training is tantamount to squandering the opportunity to actualise their human potential and enable them to make a greater contribution to society. The acquisition of knowledge, technical knowhow, and professional expertise is essential to building the country's human capital, without which long-term national security, sustainable development, and social progress would be impossible.

The effective closure of the first and only university in the country and the trivialisation of tertiary education have accompanied open-ended active national service. In an age of globalisation, higher education has emerged as the principal agent of social transformation and mobility, while knowledge has become the primary capital of the modern economy. Yet, the combination of the closure of the university, the militarisation of education beyond the eleventh grade, and the consignment of most high school graduates to indefinite national service has worked to downgrade tertiary education, hinder human resource development, and constrain the acquisition of knowledge, professional skills, and technical expertise.

This has frustrated the aspirations of the great majority of multiple generations of college age youth for proper higher learning as a path to self-fulfilment and a better life. At the same time, the country is made to forfeit their potential contribution to its development. Clearly, these features operate to retard the progress of Eritrean society, weaken the country's long-term regional competitive position, and compromise its future prosperity in an increasingly knowledge based global economy.

8.5 Linking Infrastructure to Development

Systemic aversion to applying standard engineering norms and misuse of professional expertise have damaged the effectiveness of national service and dented its contribution to development. Above all, its output lacks linkages to real economic growth and social progress capable of bringing about tangible improvement in the living conditions of the people. Ignoring its glaring deficiencies, the government and the State-owned media make a lot of fanfare in praise of the alleged contribution of national service to the 'great achievements scored' in the reconstruction and building of physical and social infrastructure as a great success story. There is, of course, an element of truth, or rather some half-truths, in the claim.

There has been a substantial increase in the reconstruction of roads and feeder roads, the building of schools, hospitals, health centres, and clinics, and in the establishment of concession farms - all made possible by the employment of the essentially unremunerated labour of national service conscripts. The expansion in physical infrastructure has resulted in a corresponding extension in basic medical services and school enrolment at the elementary, middle and secondary school levels throughout the country. As the government has neglected or subverted the development of the human factor, however, qualitative improvements in staffing, service delivery capacity, or essential support facilities have lagged significantly behind such quantitative growth. Further, the extensive flight of teachers, doctors, and health workers, has hit the education and health sectors particularly hard and made a bad situation worse.[289]

Infrastructure construction *per se* does not constitute national development. It is a means to accelerate economic growth and increase the stock of available goods and services to society to raise the standard of living and improve the quality of life of the people. Otherwise, it is not an end in itself. Infrastructure is a necessary but an insufficient condition for development. It provides the basis for rapid and sustainable development when it operates to stimulate increasing production in agriculture, industry, and services; enable greater movement of people, goods, and services throughout the country; and consolidate national economic integration.

Physical infrastructure must promote domestic mobility of the factors of production, stimulate economic interaction, and enhance commercial exchange. Social infrastructure must generate human capital, the knowledge, skills and knowhow that catalyse the creation of wealth via the production of a rising stock of goods and services for the enjoyment of society. As the ultimate objective of all endeavours is to improve the human condition, physical and

---

[289] Teachers make up the largest group of professional escapees. Members of other professions are also fleeing the country in large numbers. For instance, a group of fifteen medical doctors and other professionals, including the regional director of public health, the representative of the ministry in the administrative region and a surgeon, fled from the Gash-Barka region and sought asylum in the Sudan in one single day in July 2011.

social infrastructure must engender an increasing output of available goods and services, a higher standard of living, a better quality of life, and greater wellbeing for the majority of the people.

This is definitely not the case in Eritrea today. The rehabilitation of the Italian-built narrow gauge railroad between Asmera and Massawa, completed at considerable cost to the country, bears little economic significance and, has for instance, not yielded an increase in the travel of people or in the flow of goods and services between the capital and the port city. Likewise, the reconstruction of the old Italian-built roads, rough tracks and feeder roads has not fostered better economic interaction or contributed to greater commercial exchange among the different regions of the country. The unstudied, defective repair or building of micro-dams has not resulted in any hydropower generation, greater agricultural production, or enhanced food security, as rapid siltation diminishes their holding capacities and long-term utility.

As if the general lack of economic development were not enough, the government has erected barriers to domestic trade and commercial exchange and established checkpoints where public and private transport vehicles are stopped, and searched and where carry-on goods, including small quantities of cereals, flour and other semi-processed food items, are routinely confiscated en route to their destinations. The government's strange restriction of the free passage of people and the free movement of goods, products and services from one region to another and from the rural areas to the cities within the country, diminishes the utility of such physical infrastructure construction and its contribution to increased economic interaction, growth, and prosperity.

In addition, the absence of significant public or private investment in research and the productive sector has denied the possibility that infrastructure reconstruction could ultimately lead to development and prosperity. The indefinite deployment and use of national service conscripts in infrastructure construction has not brought about significant innovation in the engineering works, improvement in economic productivity, or any enhancement in the standard of living. Further, the delivery of substandard products, irreparable damage to the environment, and lack of cost effectiveness have compromised quantitative progress in infrastructure construction. The only consolation, in the anguished words of a then senior government colleague, is that "we may be able to redo them properly one day."

Despite the government's pledge to protect and restore the integrity of the natural environment, indefinite active national service has operated to compound the damage caused by drought and war to Eritrea's habitats. The total reliance of the Ethiopian army, and the Eritrean liberation armies, for building shelter, fortifying trenches, generating energy (fuel wood and charcoal) and providing for general daily sustenance during the thirty-year war of independence, had caused immense destruction to the country's dwindling forestry, water and wildlife resources.

As a result, the vegetative and forest cover of the country has dwindled from 30 per cent a century ago to about 13.5 per cent of the total land area today.[290] The long war decimated pockets of thick natural forest in the Northern

---

[290] FAO Corporate Document Repository, Country Report – Eritrea http://www.fao.org/docrep/003/x6782e/X6782E01. htm#TopOfPage

Highlands, like the Darekal Valley in the Halhal region of Bogos, the lush green banks of the Anseba, Barka, and Gash rivers, and patches of eucalyptus plantations in the Central Highlands. The border war aggravated deforestation.

The reforestation campaign launched immediately after independence has floundered. More deforestation has occurred during the last twenty-two years to provide for the daily sustenance needs of a general population completely dependent on the bounties of its immediate environs for housing construction and energy supply. The continued encampment of the national service conscripts and the bulk of the Eritrean Defence Forces (EDF) in the countryside and their similar dependence on the scant forest resources, further depleted by the sustenance needs of the coterie of armed regional opposition groups that use Eritrea as sanctuary, has exacerbated an already fragile ecology. The combined effect of these factors has decimated Eritrea's fauna and flora, diminished the size and diversity of its wildlife population and degraded its environment. Several areas of the country have lost their forest cover, wooded hills and valleys laid bare, and formerly perennial water springs and streams turned dry.

Thus, indefinite active national service, far from catalysing national development, has exerted a powerful negative impact on the state of the Eritrean economy and the welfare of the Eritrean people. It has robbed private agriculture and animal husbandry, the mainstay of the national and household economies, as well as industry and services, of vital work force. Played out in the setting of a stagnant economy paralysed by economic autarky, unlimited active national service has resulted in diminished domestic production, ruined the livelihoods of many families, and contributed to an acute shortage of basic necessities and the impoverishment of society.

Active national service conscripts work in Front- or army-owned commercial farms, in the civil service, in road building, dam construction, and other public works projects. The absence of a well-planned, comprehensive national development programme with ordered priorities often translates into undertaking such projects without the bother of blue prints, feasibility studies, or environmental impact assessments.

8.6 Opportunity Cost of National Service

The concept of opportunity cost is used to evaluate the economic cost and benefit of one decision vis-à-vis another decision of resource use. Given a rational allocation of scarce resources with multiple uses, it is a measure of the cost of the next best alternative use relative to the cost of a selected alternative use or, conversely, the benefit forgone in the next best alternative use relative to the selected alternative use of a resource. Committing Eritrean youth to indefinite active national service in contrast, for instance, to enabling them fulfil finite national service, complementing a comprehensive national development programme with ordered priorities, and allowing human capital formation through quality education and meaningful vocational training, would have different cost and benefit outcomes or implications for the country.

There prevails a pervasive self-serving scorn for the educated among certain senior Front and government officials. An anti-intellectual strand, mainly driven by a sense of 'sour grapes' for having foregone university education was systematically nurtured by the top EPLF leadership during the period of the armed struggle. Such systemic contempt abets the common practice of misallocation of professional and technical expertise of most conscripts under active national service. This breeds reliance on amateurish trial and error approaches in the conduct of the engineering works, entailing enormous waste of time, resources, and opportunities.

The general practice of keeping professionals on active national service idle, underutilising their skills, or deploying them on misplaced development priorities entails huge opportunity costs. Irrational and unviable projects squander limited national resources. These include sugar plantations in dry and semi-arid areas watered through drip-irrigation from deep-drilled underground wells pumped out by diesel-powered engines. The low value of the final product does not even compensate for the high cost of the diesel consumed in the process.

The expertise, skills, and labour of active national service participants and the accessory state assets are scarce national resources. As such, they have an alternative use and, therefore, create an opportunity cost for the country. These costs are measurable in terms of their costs and benefits foregone from their most rational use, full utilisation, and gainful employment under a comprehensive programme of national development.

8.7 The 'Silent Crisis' of Mass Exodus

Most Eritreans have a deep attachment to, and strong love of, their country and, in an earlier era, young men and women had flocked to the bush in their tens of thousands to fight for freedom. Driven by hope for a better future, they left their homes and families, or returned from the diaspora, in droves, ready to make the supreme sacrifice. The loss of hope today has brought about a significant reversal in fortunes. Since the beginning of the 2000s, the youth have fled the country in increasingly large numbers. An apparently persistent and growing resistance to endless active national service has triggered widespread evasion and forced a significant mass of youth to vote with their feet and flee the homeland at great risk to their lives.

The UN High Commissioner for Refugees (UNHCR) has reported that around 220,000 Eritreans, about 5 per cent of the population, had fled the country by early 2011, and depicts the on-going exodus of Eritrean refugees as a "silent crisis".[291] Recent reports indicate that approximately 3,000 young Eritrean men and women cross the border into Ethiopia (1,000 to 1,300) and Sudan (1,600 to 1,800) each month.[292] These figures signify that the *silent crisis* has already taken a heavy toll of the country's population. It would continue unless, its causes are removed, costing Eritrea an estimated 36,000 of its most productive labour force annually. The magnitude of such an exodus surpasses that of the waves of refugees during the country's darkest periods

---

[291]   UN Office for the Coordination of Humanitarian Affairs: IRIN, 21 December 2011 http://www.irinnews.org/.

[292]   Copnall, James, *Eritrea: The land its citizens want to forget*, BBC News, 21 December 2009 http://news.bbc.co.uk/2/hi/africa/8393376. stm?utm_source=twitterfeed&utm_medium=twitter; UN Office for the Coordination of Humanitarian Affairs: IRIN, 21 December 2011; and private conversations of the author with European diplomats in the region.

of war and colonial domination under both Emperor Haile Selassie and Colonel Mengistu.

These figures exclude the quite significant and steadily rising number of relatively privileged professionals and business people, and senior and mid-level government officials, leaving the country to escape the state of insecurity and repression under the regime's tyranny. Some of Eritrea's finest athletes and sports stars, including its best national football players, have used the chance to represent the country abroad to go missing and escape the harsh conditions in the country. In this way alone, Eritrea has lost at least 58 of its top football players and athletes to defection between May 2006 and November 2012.[293] The government's imposition, in 2007, of a required deposit of ERN 100,000 (about US$ 6,700) for all travelling athletes prior to leaving the country and policy of strict surveillance by the official entourage while overseas have done little to curb the trend. This was shown by the defection of several athletes, including the bearer of the national flag, of the Eritrean team to the London Olympic Games of 2012.

It is unfortunate and, in many ways, quite tragic that the country, in its third decade of independence, is emptying of its youth and undergoing a huge brain drain. At present, Eritrea has become the source of the biggest number of

---

[293] Thirty-five players of the Eritrean national football team (six in Angola in March 2007, twelve in Kenya in December 2009 and seventeen, along with their team doctor, in Uganda in November 2012), seventeen players of the Red Sea FC football club (four in Kenya in May 2006 and thirteen in Tanzania in July 2011), and six members of Eritrea's national athletics team (in the UK in December 2008) have absconded, sought political asylum and resumed their football and athletic careers in Europe, North America and Australia.

asylum seekers and refugees per capita in the world. In this regard, there are persistent allegations that elements of the government and military often facilitate the flight of refugees to neighbouring countries in exchange for money, making fortunes out of their misery. Certain agents of the regime and rings of operators with links to the regime stand accused of involvement or complicity in illicit human trafficking.

Several reports by Amnesty International, Human Rights Watch, the US State Department, the UN Monitoring Group on Somalia and Eritrea, etc., implicate certain military and security officers in the smuggling of persons out of the country and the facilitation of illegal immigration to neighbouring countries for profit.[294] The government routinely denies such reports. On the other hand, many Eritrean escapees have stated that their journeys from the capital Asmera all the way to the Eritrea-Sudan border were arranged via land cruisers bearing government or army registration plates in exchange for the payment of US$3,000, or Eritrean Nakfa equivalent, per person. The same escapees also claim that, despite the regime of strict control and tight enforcement in place, the drivers of such vehicles carrying passengers being smuggled out of the country navigate their way through the various military checkpoints that dot the long roads from Asmera to the border crossings.

Once they manage to cross the border on their own or with the help of costly and often dangerous smugglers,

---

294 Report of the Monitoring Group on Somalia and Eritrea pursuant to Security Council resolution 1916 (2010), 18 July 2011(S/2011/433) http://www.un.org/ga/search/view_doc. asp?symbol=S/2011/433; U.S. State Department Trafficking in Persons Report, June, 2009 http://gvnet.com/humantrafficking/ Eritrea-2.htm; Human Rights Watch World Report 2012: Eritrea http://www.hrw.org/world-report-2012/world-report-2012-eritrea.

most escapees are camped as refugees in Eritrea's immediate and Greater Horn of Africa neighbours, namely, Ethiopia, Sudan, Djibouti, South Sudan, Kenya, and Uganda. These countries are often used as temporary way stations on the long, perilous, and improbable journey through circuitous routes to Israel, North Africa, Europe, and North America. Eritreans are also found scattered as refugees, exiles, and immigrants across the sea in Yemen, Saudi Arabia, Israel and the wider Middle East; in East, North, Central and Southern Africa; and in Europe, North America, and Australia.

Many have perished on the way, succumbing to desert heat and dehydration trying to trek the Sahara Desert or drowning trying to cross the Red Sea, the Gulf of Aden, or the Mediterranean Sea in transit to the Middle East and Europe. As the book went to press, the horrific death of about 350 Eritreans off the coast of the Italian island of Lampedusa represented the latest tragedy in this seemingly unending saga. Furthermore, those who make it to the Sinai Desert in Egypt en route to Israel are held as bonded labour, abused, and tortured by their illicit Bedouin traffickers, with the alleged collaboration of Egyptian security agents, in extortion of more money. According to a CNN documentary broadcast on 21 September 2012, showing graphic and gruesome photos of abandoned corpses, more than 4,000 young Eritreans have been murdered or left to die in the Sinai Desert after extraction of their body organs for sale by associated criminal gangs operating with the collaboration of medical doctors in Cairo.[295]

---

[295] A Stand in the Sinai: A CNN Freedom Project Documentary, first aired on 21 September 2012. http://cnnpressroom.blogs.

The desperate search for respite from an endless agony, rather than the gravitational pull of the Global North, or 'going for a picnic', drives tens of thousands of young Eritreans to dare death from 'shoot to kill' orders at Eritrean border crossings, exhaustion in the trans-Sahara trek, drowning in the sea, brutal murder, or deadly harvest of body organs in the Sinai Desert.[296] The present government has, through the perpetration of a wretched economic situation, indefinite active national service, and harsh repression, turned Eritrea into an earthly inferno and made life insufferable for its people. This has rendered the country unsuitable and insecure to live in for its people and provoked mass exodus, especially of young men and women.

8.8 Open-Ended National Service

The illegal practice of indefinite active national service, undertaken without due compensation, has become an affliction without a respite in sight. It afflicts multiple generations of Eritreans in the context of an undeclared state of emergency. The regime has placed the country in a phoney war footing and a permanent state of siege to unleash a silent war on its youth. Open-ended active national service has robbed Eritrea's young men and women of their prime

---

cnn.com/2012/08/28/a-stand-in-the-sinai-a-cnn-freedom-project-documentary/.

[296] In response to a question on why thousands of young Eritreans were fleeing the country, President Isaias Afwerki, cynically stated that "They are going for a picnic. They will come back one day." Talk to Al Jazeera English with correspondent Jane Dutton, updated on 19 February 2010. http://www.youtube.com/watch?v=O0uQwODNkTA

years, deprived them of normal family life, disrupted the development of their intellectual potential, and denied them a future. Its impact is ruining the nuclear family and denting the progress of society.

The programme has reduced families of conscripts, especially those without access to remittances from the diaspora, to destitution. Such conscripts, deployed without appropriate remuneration, are unable to provide for their families, or to protect them from privation, out of their token monthly stipends. Sadly, Eritrean society teems with broken and destitute families whose breadwinners languish in what has become *de facto* modern-day servitude.

Apart from the persistent allegations of involvement in illegal human trafficking, it seems that the present government deliberately perpetrates this plight and sustains the exodus of the youth as a sort of safety valve to mass unemployment and potential protest. It is quite apparent that the government acquiesces in the mass flight of youth to take refuge abroad. It cannot be otherwise, as the ruling Front and the government are well aware that indefinite active national service is driving the youth to flee en masse and draining the country of its most promising manpower and brainpower, thereby undermining its development and sapping its future potential. There is no question that the government could remove the cause and redress the situation by simply adhering to the terms of the proclamation.

Indefinite active national service has become the scourge of Eritrea's youth, forcing their flight in alarming numbers. Pervasive insecurity, fed by periodic roundups at random intervals, arbitrary arrests, and routine harassments in city streets or at checkpoints on the roads has roundly disillusioned them, irrevocably shaken their loyalty to the regime, and undermined their confidence in the country's prospects. It was the hope of a better future that inspired Eritrean youth yesteryear to flock to the battlefield to fight for freedom and sustained them through the incredible hardships and sacrifices of the struggle. The desperation of endless servitude drives them today to flee home en masse and risk their lives on the way out of the country at border crossings, across desert trails, or in the depths of treacherous sea passages.

The uncanny combination of the militarisation of the state, the regimentation of society, and the imposition of endless active national service has dealt a serious blow to the fabric of Eritrean society and its traditional socioeconomic institutions, without offering viable remedies or substitutes. The compulsory use of conscript labour without remuneration has, in particular, prevented Eritrea's youth from earning their livelihoods and building families, thereby, unleashing a frontal assault on the nuclear family, the foundation of Eritrean society.

In practice, the application of national service is strictly compulsory for eligible men and women resident inside the country while it is voluntary for residents abroad. In addition, Eritreans living outside the country who, for one reason or another, volunteer to do national service are exempt from indefinite active national service. They are free to leave after completing the legally prescribed period of one year and a half. Moreover, in the event that they choose to stay after the completion of military training, they get preferential placement in government ministries and agencies in the relative comfort and ease of urban life facilitated by regular parental remittances. Such an inconsistent practice is clearly discriminatory.

Generally, the children of the poor endure the most of indefinite active national service. Many families who have the necessary wherewithal manage to bribe their way through the extreme difficulty of getting exit visas and arrange for the 'legal' departure of their children from the country to Europe and North America. In addition, the absence of proper supervision during implementation under the general situation of low salaries and high inflation has encouraged corrupt practices in the ranks of the army officer corps that allow national service participants from relatively well-to-do families to buy their way out of the drudgery via 'demobilisation' for the bribe of ERN 50,000.

Under the present circumstances, national service, implemented in contravention of the terms of the proclamation for the vast majority of eligible Eritreans, has become an end in itself, used as an instrument of extortion, repression, and control. It has evolved into a central element of a strategy of survival of an authoritarian, and increasingly oppressive, regime bent on keeping the youth in thrall and national development on hold. The regime's arbitrary extension of the duration of active national service beyond the legally specified eighteen months breaks the law, strips it of legitimacy, and violates the basic human rights of conscripts. Further, the absence of due compensation reduces the conscripts to a state of virtual servitude.

National service is an obligation of citizenship established by proclamation. Its objectives are clear, its terms specific, and its duration delimited. Its initial design as a feasible means to a noble end was commendable. Nevertheless, open-ended active national service, as currently practiced, is illegal, unjust, and illegitimate. Its consequences are disruptive to the development potential and prospects of normal life for generations of Eritrean men and women. Tens of thousands of Eritrean youth have amply demonstrated their opposition to the present form and mode of its implementation through acts of life-risking disobedience. As part of the maelstrom of the general Eritrean crisis, the illegitimacy of indefinite active national service, with its pervasive negative impact on society, has indisputably become a central issue directly linked to the wider question of the transition of Eritrea to a democratic system of government.

CHAPTER 9

Resort to Force as a Default Mode

[L]et not your rage or malice destroy a life – for indeed, he who does not value it, does not himself deserve it. - Leonardo da Vinci

The justness and legitimacy of Eritrea's claim to self-determination and the feats of its people's armed struggle for liberation have been amply publicised by many writers. There is, however, an aspect of the history of the war of national liberation often glossed over in most of these works: the constant use of force as a means to settle internal disputes. This chapter aims to fill this gap by addressing the use of force to sew discord during the armed struggle, and its persistence after independence. It skims the rise of dissent within the cohesive historical leadership of the EPLF and the dispute that followed the closure of internal communication. Further, it recounts the rise of dissention, the detention of several key Front and government leaders, the accumulation of power in the presidency, and the consequent rise of 'one man rule' in the country.

Discord, disputes, and dissention in the internal relations or interaction of an organisation are normal aspects of politics as a struggle for power. Their existence is not, nor should it be, an issue. The issue is how to treat them to mediate the internal power struggle constructively. In the case of Eritrea, those at the helm of power at various stages of the national war shunned dialogue as a means to resolve disputes and build consensus, and frequently resorted to force to silence dissent seen to be a threat to their political power. In the context of the changing conditions of a life dominated by the brutality of war, the liberation movements used violence to quell dissent in their ranks or eliminate rival groups.[297] This took many forms: suspension, demotion, or transfer and, in the worst cases, detention, torture, or outright elimination of freedom fighters.

There is, of course, nothing uniquely Eritrean about the use of force to resolve political discord. The practice is as old as the evolution of organised human society itself. The strong have usually relied on the use of force to impose their power, enforce their will, or advance their interests over the weak. Indeed, it appears an inescapable aspect of human nature that, in the absence of proper institutional checks and balances, whoever acquires a monopoly of the instruments of violence tends to utilise them to defend self-interest or to prevent threats to one's position of power. Repeatedly done during the armed struggle in the past, the forcible suppression of dissent has evolved into an institutionalised practice of the present Eritrean government.

9.1 Force as an Arbiter of Discord

The history of Eritrea's armed struggle is replete with manifestations of internal power struggle and incidences of

---

[297] These include the Eritrean Liberation Front (ELF), the Eritrean Liberation Front-People's Liberation Forces (ELF-PLF) and the Eritrean People's Liberation Forces/Front (EPLF).

the use of force to suppress the dissenting voices of political challenge and eliminate rival political movements or groups. The leadership of the ELF, the Front that started the armed struggle in 1961, and that of the EPLF, the Front that won the war in 1991, viewed critical thought as a threat and sought to suppress it, or eliminate its proponents. The ELF used military force to liquidate rival armed groups, or to eliminate dissident elements within its ranks from the mid-1960s to the early 1980s. The ELF-PLF and its successor, the EPLF, also used force to eliminate internal dissent and suppress political opposition whenever expedient.

Despite the fact that the ELF and the ELM shared the goal of liberating Eritrea from Ethiopian occupation, the former wiped out the latter in 1965. Rationally, it would have been in their mutual interest, and to the advantage of their joint national struggle, to resolve their differences and coordinate their efforts against the common enemy. Yet, there was no peaceful attempt to find common ground or to mediate their political struggle for supremacy in the Eritrean arena. Relying on the same logic that affirms the precept that war is the extension of politics by other means, the ELF used force to crush the internal rectification movement in 1970, and to eliminate the three factions that eventually regrouped to form the EPLF. Further, It resorted to military action to: liquidate the EPLF, igniting the civil war that lasted intermittently from 1972 to 1981; to suppress another internal reform movement in 1977;[298] and to crush the ELF-

---

[298]   The ELF dubbed the movement as *falul,* a Tigrinya term for anarchist. In July 1977, about 1,500 strong of the fighters targeted for attack left the ELF and joined the EPLF. They were a formidable military contingent. Camped adjacent to the Revolution or Zero School at

PLF, which had tried to constitute itself as a third liberation front, in 1978.

For its part, the EPLF resorted to the forcible suppression of the internal dissent that arose within the Eritrean Liberation Front-People's Liberation Forces 2 (ELF-PLF2) group in 1973. The dissident movement, which characterised the PLF2 leadership as undemocratic and challenged its authoritarian style, listed several functional deficiencies and abuses of fighters and advocated corrective democratic reforms, was baptised *Menkae* and described as 'destructive' in a special pamphlet.[299] The word *menkae* literally means bat in Tigrinya. It has a second meaning, used as a pejorative reference to a left-handed person who, in contrast, is also fondly nick-named *aba gray*. For, in Eritrean tradition, 'right' is usually associated with good and 'left' with bad.

The use of the label *menkae* was intended to indicate the group's clandestine nocturnal activities and secretive

---

the foothills of Mount Zagré in Sahel, they were reoriented to the EPLF by three members of the central committee: Mahmud Ahmed (Sherifo), Beraki Gebreselassie and the author. The orientation course consisted of seminars covering the history of the Eritrean armed struggle, the gender question, the non-capitalist path of development and the national democratic revolution. Upon completion of the course, they built a road linking Zero to Bilikat, the EPLF training camp for women and the *fitewrari* (underage recruits), before being deployed to the various units of the EPLA. Many of them fell fighting valiantly in the battles on the ascent of the eastern escarpment from Gahtielay to *Sei Deci* towards Asmera, in the plains of Semhar and on the salty swamps of Salina during the first battle for the liberation of Massawa in the fall of 1977.

[299] Afwerki,Isaias, Destructive Movement (ኣዕናዊ ምንቅስቃስ), selectively disseminated among EPLF cadres, fighters, and members of mass organisations abroad in 1973.

meetings conducted under cover of darkness and to malign its political ideology as extreme 'leftist'. The leaders and many supporters of the movement were incarcerated at *Halewa Sewra,*[300] or Security of the Revolution in Fah, Sahel. A committee appointed by Isaias Afwerki and chaired by Ibrahim Afa was set up to review their case and it was announced during the first EPLF congress in January 1977 that its key leaders were condemned to death.[301] A longtime Italian observer and friend of the Eritrean armed struggle has characterised the forcible suppression of the movement as a "dark chapter in the history of the EPLF".[302]

Fighters branded 'leftists' (*menkae*), 'rightists' (*yemanawian*), 'deviants' (*zmbulat*) or 'Ethiopian or CIA agents' (*jasusat*), were picked up from their units, interned in *Halewa Sewra* and often executed without due process. Recurring incidents of physical elimination of real or imagined political opponents and violent suppression of dissent set a pattern of dispute settlement and conflict resolution that afflicted the Eritrean liberation movement as represented by both the ELF and the EPLF. The use of force as an arbiter of discord or as a means to intimidate people to conform has survived the armed struggle and has evolved as a persistent practice of the present governance system. The government has used force to suppress internal dissent, subdue domestic opposition, and enforce submission to its

---

[300] The EPLF security organ during the war, which became part of the ministry of interior after independence.

[301] The list included Afwerki Teklu, Habteselassie Gebremedhin, Mussie Tesfamicael, Russom (pharmacist), Tareke Yehdego, and Yohannes Sebahtu.

[302] Poscia, Stefano, Eritrea: Colonia Tradita (Eritrea: A Colony Betrayed), Roma: Edizione Associate, 1989.

political hegemony. The following six notable cases illustrate a pattern of systematic and persistent use of force to quell dissent:

First, the incarceration and harsh punishment of the ringleaders and principal supporters of the protest of freedom fighters in Asmera in May 1993, demanding due compensation and improvement in the conditions of their continued military service after independence and, ultimately, the democratisation of the Front's internal decision making process.

Second, the killings and imprisonment of disabled war veterans in July 1994 for protesting and demanding an improvement in their living conditions at the isolated Mai Habar camp located between the towns of Nefasit and Dekemhare.

Third, the internment of about 2,000 university students in Wia in August 2001 for refusing to sign up to the mandatory summer work programme in protest of the terms of deployment and the arrest of the president of their student union. They were collected from dormitories and the city streets, kept in the city's main football stadium overnight, and taken to Wia, about 30 km southwest of Massawa, in one of the hottest, most desolate and least hospitable locations in the world. The internment camp lacked adequate food, water, shelter and medical care. Two of the students reportedly died of heat stroke immediately after internment.

Fourth, the arrest, in September 2001, and indefinite detention, in a state of solitary confinement in Iraïro, of dissident former senior government officials, military officers, and journalists.

Fifth, the round-up, detention and killing of national service evaders at the Adi Abeto military prison on the outskirts of Asmera on 4 November 2004. About 16,000 'national service deserters and dodgers' were picked up from homes, offices and the street and crammed into the prison where several detainees were gunned down for protesting their treatment.[303]

Sixth, the numerous cases of disappearance and/or detention of suspected regime critics taken from home, work, or the street. Nobody, including their families, friends or colleagues, knows their whereabouts.

The issue of dissident former government officials in particular, warrants further discussion. The rise of the highest profile internal political dissent and its forcible suppression followed the end of the border war with Ethiopia. To begin with, there prevailed considerable misgivings among senior members of the PFDJ Central Council about the outbreak and escalation of hostilities with Ethiopia in 1998. The avoidability of the war aside, the Central Council and the National Assembly, like the public, were merely informed of the eruption of hostilities *ex post facto.* Meanwhile, the president had 'frozen' or cast aside the historical champions of the Eritrean high command and military intelligence at a time when the prevention of war and, once it started, its successful persecution required the deployment of their acumen and competence.

The Eritrean and Ethiopian armies enjoyed overall numerical parity. However, critical failures of leadership and intelligence allowed, during the third offensive in

---

[303] According to an internal presidential memo circulated among senior Front and Government officials following the incident, 10,000 were from the Operation Zones, 3,000 from the ministries, 2,000 students and 200 Ethiopians.

particular, the Ethiopian army to outflank the Eritrean army and breach its defences on the Mereb-Setit Front, to seize commanding positions on the Mereb-Alitena Front, and to occupy large swathes of sovereign Eritrean territory in the central and southwestern parts of the country. These serious setbacks brought to the fore the simmering discontent with, and growing criticism of, the president's personalisation of power among senior government officials excluded from the policy and decision making process, especially with regards to the eruption and conduct of the war. The relegated officials included the chief architects of the military strategy and tactics of the victorious war of national liberation.

The aftermath of the border war had set internal dynamics in motion that wrecked the unity of the Front and diverted the course of the evolving political process in the country. Solidarity gave way to dissidence. A reign of repression began with the detention of senior officials and the purge of their suspected supporters in the Front, the government and the army. The drive to establish a constitutional government and a pluralist political system came to a halt.

A constructive response to the discreet criticism, aired informally at the outset and more formally later on, could have averted the political disaster that followed the forcible repression of the internal dissent. Unfortunately, however, the president reacted to the internal criticism, initially made in private, by ignoring the pleas and admonition of his colleagues, at first, and demoting or suspending them from their ministerial or army posts, later. In an intolerant and stubborn reaction to prudent efforts to address the growing concerns internally, he opted for a policy of hardheaded confrontation and forced the issue to become public. For the first time since the founding of the EPLF central committee in January 1977, there appeared an irrevocable crack in the façade of unity in the historical leadership of the EPLF within the PFDJ central council.

Beyond the government and the Front, the reverberations of the political dispute within the top leadership resonated at home and abroad with ominous implications for the future of the country. At the time of writing, the Eritrean body politic has yet to recover from the systemic damage caused by the president's authoritarian response to the legitimate criticism of his increasingly autocratic style of leadership, impulsive decision-making, and incompetent management of the affairs of state and of the border war with Ethiopia, in particular. The failure to address the core issues of concern, and reform the Front and the government, led to the eventual imposition of an open system of 'one man rule' on the country.

On the political front at home and the diplomatic arena abroad, the regime's regressive measures tainted its legitimacy, eclipsed the legal finality of the delimitation decision of the Eritrea-Ethiopia Boundary Commission (EEBC), and took the edge off Eritrea's moral high ground vis-à-vis Ethiopia's obstruction of the work to demarcate the boundary. Subsequent international reaction to these developments and rising preoccupation with the 'war on terror' brought about a new realignment of forces in the region that cast a shadow of isolation over Eritrea. Predictably, Ethiopia took advantage of the situation not only to avoid effective criticism for its violation of the Algiers Agreements but also to further isolate Eritrea.

Ethiopia exploited the government of Eritrea's domestic reverses, internal weakness and external isolation to escape censure and avert pressure for its defiance of international law and relevant UN Security Council resolutions. With the tacit support of the US, it manoeuvred to enlist UN acquiescence in its non-compliance with its treaty obligations to implement the demarcation of the boundary in accordance with the EEBC's "final and binding" ruling. Meanwhile, Djibouti accused Eritrea of violating its territory while Eritrea rejected the accusation and denied the existence of any problem between the two neighbours. Despite its previous refusal to acknowledge the issue, however, Eritrea later made a turnabout and accepted Qatari mediation on the dispute on condition that neither Djibouti nor Qatar publicise the agreement. The turnabout, however, came too late to spare the country from punitive measures.

Clueless about the adverse geo-political consequences of its total isolation, the dire implications of sanctions for the country, and the enormous difficulty in getting sanctions removed once imposed, the regime virtually dared the UN Security Council by insisting on its blanket denial and refusal to heed its repeated resolutions and warnings. The government's pathetic behaviour allowed Ethiopia to scheme not only to deflect attention from its continued defiance of the EEBC's mandatory ruling but also to further isolate Eritrea. Addis Ababa capitalised on Eritrea's self-suspension of membership in IGAD and the AU to mobilise unanimous support for a resolution calling for UN sanctions against Eritrea by the two regional bodies.

In a rare heeding of 'AU calls', the UN Security Council imposed sanctions on Eritrea[304] on the basis of allegations

---

[304] United Nations Security Council Resolution 1907(2009), 23 December 2009. http://www.un.org/apps/news/story.asp?NewsID=33337&Cr=somali&Cr1=

of providing military aid to Somali Islamist insurgents and refusal to comply with calls to demilitarise the border and address the standoff with Djibouti.[305] In contrast, it failed to censure or impose sanctions on Ethiopia for defying the Algiers treaty and several Council resolutions calling for the physical demarcation of the border with Eritrea. Rather than highlighting the unresolved border issue with Ethiopia, the hapless regime succeeded only in further isolating itself and

---

[305] The governments of Eritrea and Ethiopia had long supported a shifting mix of Somalia's rival warring factions. Following the Ethiopian invasion of Somalia in December 2006, Eritrea hosted the leaders of the Islamic Courts Union (ICU) and the newly created Alliance for the Re-liberation of Somalia (ARS) in Asmera. It also probably continued to support some of the ICU's rival factions, including those that waged a militant Islamist insurgency against Somalia's Transitional Federal Government (TFG) and the Ethiopian occupation. However, the initial charges were largely unsubstantiated and lacked corroborative evidence. The author's discussion with members of the UN Panel in Nairobi, Kenya, on 22 February 2007 revealed that much of the information came from a hostile and, therefore, suspect source and subsequent events cast doubt on its credibility or accuracy. If there were, for instance, about "2,000 Eritrean troops" aiding Somali insurgents, as the UN Panel Report alleged, what happened to them during and after the 2006 Ethiopian invasion of Somalia? As regards the problem with Djibouti, the allegation that Eritrea was in occupation of Djiboutian territory is not borne out by the terms of the 1900 Rome treaties that delineated the boundary between the then Italian Eritrea and French Somaliland. What Eritrea did was militarise, for internal political reasons, what has been a demilitarised area. Having thus violated the colonial agreement, however, Eritrea denied the existence of any problem and spurned all bilateral, regional and international attempts to resolve the dispute until it reversed position in silence and accepted Qatari mediation on the matter.

eclipsing Ethiopia's brazen occupation of sovereign Eritrean territory. The regime's self-destructive behaviour aside, however, the UN Security Council, once again, double-crossed Eritrea, underscored its double standards and undermined its own authority.

Proactively addressing the issues raised would have contained the dissent in-house and preserved the internal unity of the Front and the government. A positive response to the attempts by the new US administration, including through the intermediary of friendly European interlocutors, to re-engage, and a heeding of its warnings to desist from supporting militant Islamist insurgents in Somalia or making a credible rebuttal of the allegations, could have prevented the worsening of Eritrea-US relations. A policy of responsive governance at home and prudent engagement abroad could have averted Resolution 1907, with the dire implications of its arms ban for the country's national defence capability in a volatile and conflict-ridden region.

The *de facto* suspension of the PFDJ Central Council and the National Assembly to spite the legitimate assertion of their statutory mandates disabled the key organs of internal consultation and consensus building. The subsequent arrogation of their powers by the president closed off all avenues of internal dialogue and discussion. The following section highlights some aspects of the development of the EPLF to help shed light on the evolution of this destructive phenomenon.

9.2 The Historical Setting

The parochial domestic politics of the leadership of the ELF and, as an extension, its external misrepresentation of Eritrea as an Arab and Moslem country, germinated the seeds of its own destruction. Its sectarian policy and structure failed to accommodate the diversity of Eritrean society, provide a common home for all its fighters, and to galvanize a unified national effort in the liberation struggle. The reorganization and territorial deployment of the Eritrean Liberation Army (ELA) in 1965 into *wilayat* or zonal divisions on the basis of ethnic and regional affiliation fanned discord and undermined the cohesion and unity of command of the ELA. The failure of the rectification movement in 1968-1969 to bring the autonomous zonal divisions together as an integrated fighting force under a unified command aggravated the situation.

The factionalised leadership unleashed sectarian repression that shattered the unity of the Front, triggered sizeable desertions and posed a grave threat to the progress of the armed struggle. Prior to the splintering of the ELF in 1970, there had evolved a broad awareness of the need to build a cohesive political nucleus to amend the fragmentation and factionalism of its leadership and command structure. The idea to establish a revolutionary vanguard party capable of forging the unity of the fighters was, however, overtaken by the turmoil that engulfed the Eritrean Field in the wake of the Front's implosion and subsequent division into four factions.[306]

---

[306] The four factions were the ELF-RC, the ELF-PLF1, the ELF-PLF2, and the Eritrean Liberation Forces (ELF-Obel). The would-be reformers were also splintered four-ways, leading to the eventual crystallisation of the Eritrean Labour Party (ELP) within the Eritrean Liberation Front-Revolutionary Council (ELF-RC) and the Eritrean People's Revolutionary Party (EPRP) within the Eritrean People's Liberation Forces (EPLF). In general, the ELP

The establishment of the EPRP was inspired by the Maoist doctrine of a vanguard party to lead a protracted people's war of national liberation and a peasant-based national democratic revolution to victory. Armed with the Marxist-Leninist ideology of scientific socialism, it aimed to provide a progressive world view and a common basis for political unity among its leaders and cadres. The decision to launch it within the PLF1 and PLF2, which were formed out of the split from the ELF, was made in 1971; its evolution was instrumental in bringing the two groups under a unified command in 1973; it formalised its structure, drew up its programme and constituted a distinct party leadership in a conference in 1975, convening its first congress in 1976.

Right from the outset, the EPRP used Marxist-Leninist analysis, tinged with Maoist doctrine, as an organising principle. In turn, the socialist ideals of progress, equality and justice would serve as a mobilising force to forge a core of progressive cadres and unify the ranks of the Eritrean liberation struggle. Such unity would transcend regional, religious or ethnic affiliation. As the revolutionary vanguard, the party would guide the armed struggle, promote the unity of the Front and strengthen the cohesion of the liberation army. Like the superorganism of a bee colony, the EPRP would embody collective consciousness and intelligence,

---

adopted the Soviet supported model of the 'Non-Capitalist Path of Development' while the EPRP adopted the Chinese inspired model of the 'National Democratic Revolution' as the path to socialism. As I have no direct knowledge on the internal structure and evolution of the ELP and researching its history is beyond the scope of my present work, I will focus here on the EPRP for two reasons: First, I knew it first hand as a member for seventeen years; and second, its dictatorial legacy is in power in Eritrea today.

permeated through the agency of the EPLF, to foster solidarity, discipline and conformity. These attributes often induced unquestioning obedience to authority among its members. The party would also forge and lead an alliance of workers and peasants in a national democratic revolution (NDR) that would serve as an intermediate stage for the eventual establishment of a socialist state in Eritrea.

The EPRP adopted a highly centralised, top-heavy and tightly controlled structure in line with Leninist organizational principles. The structure was simple, double-layered and efficient. The EPRP existed as a clandestine organisation within the EPLF and operated in small cells permeating all military and paramilitary units in a pyramidal formation with the secretary general at the apex. Meeting under night darkness, each party cell elected its secretary and the secretaries of the cells elected the secretary of the branch, with the branch secretaries electing the zonal committee. The secretaries of the party cells formed party branch committees and the secretaries of the party branch committees formed the party zonal committees. The secretaries at each level convened the regular meetings of the cells and branch committees in absolute secrecy.

The zonal committees were convened by, and answerable to, the secretary general (SG) of the party, elected by the party congress. Detailed situation reports of each unit of the Front in the rear base, the combat zone, and behind enemy lines, including personnel assessments classifying the fighters into layers of categories in terms of their political attitude and loyalty to the leadership of the Front, flowed regularly upwards, with party directives flowing downwards. In the main, the Central Committee (CC) of the party, elected by the party congress, constituted the EPLF Political Bureau. In the name of democratic centralism, the CC was the nominal repository of power. In practice, the overarching focus on the war, the structure of the party, and the infrequency of regular meetings allowed the SG to wield considerable power and to exercise effective control of the Party and the Front in the name of the CC.

The party zonal committees, branch committees and cells constituted the invisible link between the Party and the Front as well as between the leadership and the base in both organisations. Operating in secrecy within and, often, parallel to the formal structures of the Front and the liberation army, they served as forums for internal consensus-building, agencies of political intelligence and control within the Party and the Front. On the downside, the Party's covert parallel structures functioned to, among other things, inhibit free expression, encourage conformity of views, ensure strict adherence to the Party line fed from the top, ostracise dissent, and enforce iron discipline throughout the Party, the Front and the liberation army.

The leading organs of the EPLF were constituted of members of the CC of the EPRP: the Standing Committee, the highest executive organ of the Front; the Political Committee embraced the quasi-civilian departments of the EPLF; and the Military Committee grouped its purely military departments.[307] The parallel structures of the Party and the Front, under the overall direction of the Political

---

[307] The Standing Committee comprised the Secretary General, the Deputy Secretary General, and the secretaries of the respective political and military committees of the Central Committee, namely, Romedan Mohamed Nur, Isaias Afwerki, Haile Weldensae, and Ibrahim Afa.

Bureau, reinforced centralised control of the Front, unified command of the liberation army, and tightened the cohesion of the politico-military organisation.

Under the EPRP's ideological guidance, the EPLF characterised the Eritrean struggle as a progressive national democratic revolution whose friends were the socialist countries, all progressive forces, and the workers and oppressed peoples of the world, while it identified its enemies as Ethiopian colonialism, US imperialism, Israeli Zionism and internal reaction. It viewed the socialist camp as the natural or strategic ally of the continuous national and democratic revolution to liberate Eritrea from Ethiopian occupation and to carry out the socioeconomic transformation of an independent Eritrean state. The EPLF viewed the Eritrean struggle as an integral part of the national liberation movement in the Third World and the overall international struggle for liberation, democracy, justice and progress.

In its second and last congress in 1986, fifteen years after its initiation, the EPRP was renamed the Eritrean Socialist Party (ESP), moderated its militant Marxist-Leninist rhetoric, and proclaimed its commitment to the pursuit of political pluralism and a mixed economic system in an independent Eritrea. This shift was formalised in the second congress of the EPLF in 1987. The secretary general of the ESP became the secretary general of the EPLF, with the standing, political, and military committees abolished. Despite the change in name, the ESP continued to function in the same manner as the EPRP until the liberation of Eritrea in 1991. It lay virtually dormant during the first three years of the liberation until the holding of a secret general meeting in Valineki, on the outskirts of Asmera, prior to the third EPLF congress in 1994, at which the secretary general announced that the ESP would be disbanded.

A few years later, a close observer of the Eritrean scene postulated that the third and last EPLF congress, which changed the name of the Front to the People's Front for Democracy and Justice (PFDJ), made a decision to convert the Front "into a mass political movement".[308] On the contrary, however, the 1994 congress represented a veritable coup by the secretary general of the Party and the Front against his most prominent and mostly younger potential rivals in the old guard of the EPRP/ESP and the EPLF. Isaias Afwerki effectively relegated them in the guise of injecting new blood into the leadership of the Front. He plotted the definitive political retirement of Romedan Mohamed Nur, the first secretary general of the EPLF, and the removal of all but three of the former members of the CC of the EPRP/ESP and the politburo of the EPLF from the executive arm of the PFDJ, of which he remained the secretary general.[309]

---

[308] Connell, Dan, *Inside the EPLF: The Origins of the 'People's Party' & its Role in the Liberation of Eritrea*, Review of African Political Economy (September 2001), Vol. 28, No. 89, p. 345. http://www.roape. org/089/03.html

[309] Using an *ad hoc* committee, made up of Romedan Mohamed Nur and Mahmud Ahmed (Sherifo), as a cover, Isaias selected a list for the executive body of the Front that included only Alamin Mohamed Said and Ali Said Abdella from the old guard. He relegated Berhane Gebrezgiabher, Haile Weldensae (Drue), Mahmud Ahmed (Sherifo), Mesfin Hagos, Mohamed Said Bareh, Ogbe Abraha, Petros Solomon, and Sebhat Efrem to the Central Council. There was opposition to two candidates in the list; Mesfin Hagos replaced one, by insistence from the floor, and Hagos Gebrehiwet (Kisha) the other, by the *ad hoc* committee.

Isaias alleged that his fellow colleagues in the Party CC and Front politburo have become too decadent and unfit to retain their positions of leadership. If decadence had indeed taken over the highest organ of the Party and the Front, its core must have lay at the apex. Although some cadres tried to force debate on the issue, I found it quite perplexing that none of the accused challenged his accusations. Had they stood up to refute and counter his allegations, they could have garnered the necessary support, including the author's, to foil his coup. Instead, divided and stung, they kept silent and two of them served, at his behest, as an ad hoc committee to 'finalise' the list of the members of the Front's new executive committee and central council.

The third congress of the EPLF replaced most of the historical leaders of the Party and the Front, signified an apparent shift in the Front's internal power relations and facilitated the concentration of the decision-making process into the hands of the secretary general of the Front. Effectively, the PFDJ represented the relegation of the old guard of the EPRP/ESP and the EPLF. Their replacement, mostly by novices and upstarts who lacked the experience, stature, and confidence to stand up to and countervail Isaias's careerist ambitions to accumulate and monopolise power, paved the way for his complete domination and control of the leading Front and state organs. Further, it heralded a shift in the country's domestic and foreign policy orientation.

The disbanding of the ESP and the advent of the PFDJ set the stage for the steady concentration and personalisation of power, leading to a 'one man show'. This development had three negative consequences. First, it hindered the transition of the EPLF from a movement fighting a war of liberation with an operational mind-set of tight secrecy and security into a governing Front managing the affairs of state with democratic accountability and transparency in peacetime. Second, it impeded the envisioned qualitative transformation of the Eritrean People's Liberation Army (EPLA) into a professional Eritrean Defence Forces (EDF), the modernisation of its assets and capability and the rationalisation of its command and control structures. Third, it obstructed the building of efficient and functional civil service machinery out of the national liberation war veterans and the remnants of the Ethiopian colonial bureaucracy.

Indeed, the predominance of Isaias's careerist ambitions and associated political calculus has subordinated the Front to his whims and resulted in its acquiescence in the institution of an authoritarian and repressive regime unable to undertake democratic state construction or to deliver sustainable development. The combined effect of careerism and mediocrity has subverted the evolution of the EDF into an effective national army with a unified chain of command dedicated to the defence of the land and the people. In the process, it has undermined the EPLA's legacy of operational autonomy, dented its legendary combat effectiveness, and weakened its ability to defend the integrity and sovereignty of Eritrea's territory. Further, limitations of professional, financial and institutional capacity have constrained equipping the EDF with more advanced conventional weapons and sophisticated defence and surveillance systems.

In the main, the Eritrean security apparatus, with the EDF at its core, is the proud heir of the EPLA, formed and steeled in the crucible of war as an instrument of liberation. Ironically, the historic mission of the Eritrean defence and security forces has been diverted from the liberation and defence of the people to an instrument of repression in the hands of an authoritarian regime. This has come about as an offshoot of the failure to forge the EDF into a modern national army with the requisite professional commitment to the rule of law; internal cohesion to fend off presidential ploys of 'divide and rule'; and unity of command to assert the integrity of its mission in defence of the sovereignty and freedom of the people.

Operating under the tight grip of Isaias, the PFDJ has thus been unable to transform the EPLF from a tightly controlled, highly disciplined and deeply secretive politico-military organisation into a transparent political organisation at the helm of state power that embraces the rule of law, adheres to democratic principles and tolerates political pluralism. An authoritarian structure that functioned in accordance with the precepts of democratic centralism may have proved efficient in executing a war of national resistance but became ill suited to participatory decision-making in peacetime. In short, the Front has succumbed to Isaias's complete control as a mere instrument of his absolute power and failed to adjust its wartime *modus operandi* to the imperative of running the affairs of state in the interest of the State and the people.

Clearly, what were remarkable assets during the armed struggle became debilitating liabilities after the liberation. Secrecy was necessary for survival and imperative for the efficient execution of the war; by contrast, transparency is essential for the democratic and accountable management of the affairs of state. The PFDJ's incarnation of the EPLF's highly centralised internal workings developed under difficult conditions of war has negated collegial decision-making, undermined the rule of law, and contravened democratic principles in matters of peacetime public policy and action. Its inability to respond to demands for change, to accommodate internal criticism or to accept the legitimacy of political dissent has wrecked its unity. Its reduction to a mere instrument of the arbitrary and callous exercise of personalised power has dented its legitimacy.

Isaias's deep-seated hostility to any functional structure, institutionalisation, and meritocracy has foreclosed the evolution of rational policy- and decision-making processes in public affairs. This, in turn, has fostered mediocrity in the higher ranks of the Front, the government, the civil service, and the army high command. Despite official denials, the prevailing lack of transparency and accountability has fostered a state of widespread alienation and encouraged endemic political and economic corruption at all levels.

The overarching objective to win the war against a much larger Ethiopian occupation army that possessed superior military assets and resources required firm unity of command, singularity of purpose, and iron discipline. The state of military regimentation under conditions of tight secrecy and strict control cultivated a mind-set that sanctioned severe restrictions on self-expression and freedom of association, condoned flagrant violations of basic democratic, civic and human rights, and turned a blind eye on ruthless suppression of deviant thought, behaviour, or action. Perceived as a threat to internal cohesion or a challenge to the leadership of the clandestine party, ideas originating outside the party or dissenting opinion inside the party met with ruthless suppressed. There prevailed a state of general acquiescence to this policy under the rationale that "the end justifies the means", a legacy that continues to haunt Eritrea today.

The Party's (and Front's) tradition of a top-heavy authoritarian structure has been inimical to the democratic impulse. The drive to inculcate conformity of thought, banish divergent ideas, and control things 'top-down' that permeated the Party and Front organisations has hindered the development of a democratic political culture conducive to independent thinking and free expression. The PFDJ, like its precursor, the EPLF, has thus remained a highly centralised and a strictly 'top-down' organisation. The SG, who is also head of state and president of the National Assembly, exercises absolute power and tight control of its decision-making process.

In brief, the absence of regular meetings of the key Front organs leads to the imposition of decisions without any discussion. The highly centralised policy and decision-making process lacks democratic content, transparency, and accountability. This allowed the president to respond with subterfuge and ruthless repression, instead of addressing the central issues of public concern through the prescribed procedures within the relevant institutional organs.

9.3 The Confrontation

The principal critics of the president were his staunchest supporters and chief collaborators, some of whom idolised and lionised him as the 'Lenin of Africa' during the war of national liberation.[310] Their loyal support, constantly reinforced by his playing them one against the other, enabled Isaias to seize, retain, and dominate the leadership of the Party, the Front, the State, and the Army. They were among the founding members of the central committee of the EPRP and the central committee and political bureau of the EPLF.

---

[310] Conversation of the author with a member of the EPLF politbureau (now in detention), Arag, July 1979.

During the armed liberation struggle, meetings of the Party and Front CCs occurred at long and irregular intervals, often due to the fluidity of the war situation. Front and army units submitted their activity and situation reports to the secretary general. The SG set the agenda and presented compiled reports in the Party and Front CC meetings. The meetings of the Party CC always preceded those of the Front CC. Carefully choreographed to ensure a uniform perspective and bar divergent opinion; the proceedings often eschewed or shelved real discussion of substantive or sensitive issues. This led to the adoption of decisions and resolutions by consensus, with binding effect in the context of the Marxist-Leninist tenet of democratic centralism.

In between the infrequent meetings, members of the political bureau and the CCs of both the Party and the Front entrusted with leading the various units of the Front and the army had wide latitude and exercised real operational autonomy in their respective areas of competence under Isaias's overall leadership. Geographic dispersion, physical separation, infrequent contact, and the drudgery and vulnerability to enemy decoding of enciphered radio messaging rendered centralised control untenable. Independence concentrated and brought the EPLF/ESP leadership together in Asmera and facilitated constant contact and direct communication. This enabled the SG of the Provisional Government, and later the President of the Transitional Government, to interfere in the routine work of the ministries and government agencies.

Ministers grew increasingly unhappy with his frequent meddling in the internal affairs of their ministries and of being by-passed or marginalised in their own turfs. Their attempts to embed themselves centre stage and assert their ministerial functions prompted constant reshuffles. The escalation of presidential interference directly, and indirectly through the central office of the PFDJ after the Front's third congress, further undermined the authority of ministers and made their positions more precarious. I will cite three instances to illustrate the point.

First, in December 1994, the president severed Eritrea's diplomatic relations with the Sudan, without consulting or informing the then minister of foreign affairs. Petros Solomon was quite incensed to learn of the event from international media reports, and had to fend off requests for interview pending formal verification with Asmera while on mission in Europe.

Second, in August 1999, the president instructed Alamin Mohamed Said, the secretary of the PFDJ, to coordinate the Front's intrusion into the work of the ministry of foreign affairs with the then foreign minister. This prompted Haile Weldensae (Drue), to retort that such "misguided interference would undermine the mandate of the ministry and the ambassadors, and hinder the institutional method of work we wish to build".[311]

Third, in September 2000, the president notified Haile Weldensae (Drue) that he was relieved of his post as minister of foreign affairs and assigned as minister of trade and industry and reminded him to handover the responsibility and duties of the ministry of foreign affairs to Ali Said

---

[311] Letter from Haile Weldensae, Minister of Foreign Affairs to Isaias Afwerki, President of the State of Eritrea, 25 August 1999 (MFA/ A1/114/99) [author's translation from the original Tigrinya].

Abdella.[312] On finding the note on his desk upon his return from mission abroad, Haile expressed misgivings about the reshuffle, especially at that critical stage in the peace process when Eritrea was in the midst of negotiations of the Algiers Peace Agreement with Ethiopia, questioned the very need for the reshuffle, and alluded to the president's ulterior motives for doing so.[313]

Constant presidential interference through the Front, in particular, fostered rivalry between the ministers (the 'old guard') and their erstwhile *protégés* in the central office (the 'new blood'); caused duplication and inefficiency; and fanned resentment and growing discontent.

In the aftermath of the unexpected Ethiopian capture of Badme during its second offensive in February 1999, the president publicly admitted to the commission of certain mistakes and promised to institute corrective measures. There were, however, no corrective measures and repeated attempts to retake Badme failed, despite the high casualties sustained. Ministers and senior officials excluded from the planning and conduct of the war became very critical of the president's incompetent management of the war and grew more disgruntled, in private, with his increasingly arbitrary, erratic, and fruitless military decisions.

Driven by a strong desire to preserve the unity of the Front and the Government during a time of crisis, the senior officials discreetly pleaded with the president, in private

---

[312] A two-sentence note from Isaias Afwerki to Haile Weldetensae, copied to Ali Said Abdella, 23 September 2000 [author's translation from the original Tigrinya].

[313] Letter from Haile Weldensae, Minister of Foreign Affairs to Isaias Afwerki, President of the State of Eritrea, 28 September 2000 (MFA/A1/164/00) [author's translation from the original Tigrinya].

conversations and in writing, to change his ways and engage in consultations. However, their personal pleas proved to no avail. For instance, General Ogbe Abraha, the then chief-of-staff of the EDF, wrote the President a letter, dated 27 November 1999, in which he, after reassuring him of his continued high regard, shared issues of concern that his senior colleagues raised and griped about. The letter summarised the gist of the complaints to the effect that the president was: making decisions alone without consulting his colleagues; undermining the development of institutions by interfering in their internal affairs; and jeopardising national security and alienating Eritrea's friends and supporters by pursuing haphazard and erratic policies. Moreover, it suggested the prudent tackling of the objects of complaint without further delay.

General Ogbe's letter proposed convening a meeting of the seasoned former members of the political bureau, rather than the entire cabinet that, in his view, included novices of doubtful contribution, in order to prevent the bad situation from getting worse. President Isaias's letter of reply, dated 9 December 1999, feigned amazement, evaded discussion of the substantive issues in question and raised a series of argumentative, police-like peripheral questions. Two further written exchanges reproduced a similar case of 'dialogue of the deaf'.[314]

The growing discontent gradually led to an open clash, but still in-house, during the eighth meeting of the PFDJ

---

[314] General Ogbe Abrha's letter to President Isaias Afwerki dated 27 November 1999, the President's reply dated 9 December 1999 and two subsequent exchanges read by the president at the meeting of the Central Council held in August-September 2000.

CC, held from 31 August to 2 September 2000. This marked the first ever overtly critical conversation that generated a heated debate within the historical leadership of the EPLF in the CC of the PFDJ. The president faced concrete, direct and substantive criticism, accusing him of mismanaging the affairs of state and displaying an increasingly autocratic style of leadership. Put on the defensive and unable to present a coherent and credible justification of his conduct and actions, the president resorted to subterfuge and blackmail to muzzle the debate. With the Rubicon crossed, however, there was to be no turning back.

The criticism centred on the need to convene regular meetings of the CC to allow broader participation in policy and decision-making and clearly set the delineation of authority and division of functions between the Front and the government to ensure accountability and transparency. There were demands for a review of the first decade of independence, in general, and an appraisal of the conduct of the border war and the peace process with Ethiopia, in particular. There were also calls for an immediate launch of preparations to lay the groundwork for the implementation of the ratified constitution and the expeditious convening of the long overdue fourth congress of the PFDJ. The ultimate aim of these demands was to conclude the transitional period and establish a constitutional government committed to the rule of law, democratic principles and respect for civil liberties and human rights.

The Ethiopian capture of Badme had shattered the aura of invincibility of the EPLA, exposed the structural weaknesses in the Eritrean operational command and military intelligence capability, and raised the spectre of further setbacks. There was thus the need for an urgent review of the strategy, tactics and execution of the war in order to better equip and strengthen the combat effectiveness of the Eritrean Defence Forces. Despite broad support for these legitimate demands, the president scorned them under the pretext that the situation was not conducive to holding regular meetings and formal consultations.

The even more significant reversals of the third and last Ethiopian offensive in May-June 2000 had resulted in the seizure of large areas of Eritrean territory in the central and western sectors and the displacement of about a third of the Eritrean population. With the end of the war and the signing of the Agreement on the Cessation of Hostilities in June, the ninth meeting of the PFDJ CC in August-September 2000 witnessed the upping of the ante. The critics reiterated the need for a thorough review of the conduct of the war, the expeditious convening of the overdue fourth congress of the Front, the speedy conduct of national elections to establish a constitutional order, and the strengthening of the country's military and diplomatic capability.

The president manoeuvred to weather the storm through inaction. The desire for change and reform, however, persisted and the call for action pursued with added vigour during the thirteenth meeting of the National Assembly held in September-October 2000. Allergic to any criticism and ever-watchful to internal threats to the predominance of his power, President Isaias, instead of acceding to the legitimate demands of his senior colleagues for a proper evaluation and renewal, countered with an underhanded attack against them.

He orchestrated a smear campaign maligning the integrity and patriotism of the historical leaders of the EPLF and current senior government officials, hitherto his most trusted and loyal right-hand men, through the upstarts in the central office of the PFDJ. The campaign was carried out in selected small group meetings and special seminars for the leading cadres of the Front accusing the high officials, behind their backs, of 'regionalism and treason', insinuating that they were acting as a 'fifth column' giving succour to the enemy, and threatening action to silence their criticism. The insidious campaign caused considerable consternation within the Front and, as word leaked, serious indignation and concern spread among the broader Eritrean public. Senior Front officials quashed demands for a proper debate of the issues at the appropriate organs of the Front and the government where the accused could also air their views.

Meanwhile, the dissident senior officials began to overcome their reciprocal distrust and rivalry, meticulously cultivated in a Machiavellian manner over many years, and to openly exchange views and discuss issues among themselves. They grew bolder and more vocal in their criticism of the president, still expressed in a guarded manner and within the limits of discretion in the privacy of trusted colleagues. They gradually became key members of an informal group of senior government officials and Front leaders who raised questions about the effects of the lack of transparency, accountability and participation in the crucial decisions of war and peace. They aimed to reverse the president's growing authoritarian style of leadership.

As the president had failed to convene the regular meetings of the CC of the Front and the Eritrean National Assembly, the senior Front and government officials repeatedly urged him, in his capacity as the secretary general of the PFDJ and the chair of the National Assembly, to do so. When he refused, the senior officials initiated the collection of signatures from members of the CC in February 2001 to petition the president to convene the long overdue meetings. The petition was legal, allowed under the Front's constitution and, therefore, legitimate. Like several other colleagues in the CC, I recognised the need and supported the demand for change but disagreed with the approach taken. Given Isaias's character and hold on the security apparatus, I considered the petition highly unlikely to produce the convening of the CC to address the outstanding issues and stressed the imperative for a swift move to neutralise his power base and deter his predictable suppressive reaction.

In late afternoon of the day the signing of the petition was undertaken, a key insurgent leader had come to my office at the Commission with the intention to get me and another colleague to sign. However, the president had just called me to his office and I had to leave while the leader met with my colleague. On arrival, I gathered that a certain member of the CC who refused to sign the petition when approached had informed the President's Office and a concerted effort was already set in high gear to dissuade other members from signing. Asked to help in the effort, I politely declined, explaining that the CC members I could raise the matter with are ones that I knew would not be signing the petition anyway, because they shared my reservations regarding the efficacy of the approach taken. On my way out, I stated that I would call and discuss the matter with a certain CC member; a close friend whose political perspective and position on the way to bring about change I knew to be similar to mine, which I did.

I also learned later that a certain member of the CC who refused to sign the petition by the same key leader who had come to see me at the Commission reported to the president, afterwards, the content of his conversation with the key leader. The following day, the president took the reporting member along with him to Sawa where he instructed him to present what he had told him the previous day to a hastily convened meeting of senior army commanders with the gibe: *Let him tell you what this people are doing!* The move aimed to malign the motives of the group and secure the support of the army officers.

At the behest of the president, the PFDJ central office issued a circular that warned members of the CC not to sign the petition. The use of pressure led certain members who had already signed the petition to retract their signatures. With the drive to collect signatures subverted, the planned petition aborted the same day. The senior officials responded by a counter-circular in March 2001, accusing the president of "conducting himself in an illegal and unconstitutional manner" and calling for the convening of meetings of the CC and the National Assembly to address the outstanding issues. The president rejected their call with the curt reply that "you are making a mistake". The senior officials addressed a second letter. The president rejected the second request, invoking the same rejoinder and removing them from their ministerial posts. Dismissal from office did not, however, silence the dissent nor resolve the problem.

Certain senior officials raised the allure of splitting the PFDJ into two parties to foster political competition. I continued to meet with, discuss the state of play, and brief the key dissidents on the situation in the TSZ. I cautioned that time was of the essence lest Isaias outmanoeuvre them and subvert the demand for change using the security forces. A key insurgent leader confidently assured me that they got majority support in the army high command and had the 'cowardly [Isaias] pretty much cornered'. My probing for details to gauge the alignment of forces confirmed his assessment. In the deck and reeling from political isolation in the higher ranks of the government and the Front, only the lack of swift and decisive action on the part of his senior critics allowed Isaias to regain control, retain power, and nip the idea of reform in the bud by the hairbreadth during the crucial interlude following the third offensive.

Surrounded by mediocre and unscrupulous yes-men and self-seeking eager informants who pander to his whims and tell him what he liked to hear, the president gradually lost touch of the real world around him and dipped into a make-believe world of personal grandeur. His growing isolation mirrored enemies everywhere and made him more suspicious of independent opinion, less tolerant of divergent views and harsher in his treatment of dissenters and critics. His demeanour of false modesty could no longer conceal his crass arrogance and insatiable hunger for power, while the combination of his unrestrained impulsiveness and lack of scruples humiliated his colleagues and inflicted colossal damage in every sphere of national life.

This attitude fanned a budding sense, hardened by his handling of the relations with the Sudan, the dispute with Yemen and the conflict with Ethiopia, that he had outlived his usefulness. Increasingly, most of the veteran senior leaders and prominent cadres of the Front saw Isaias as a liability to the country and as a real obstacle to its peaceful democratic development, a view widespread in the general Eritrean body politic. With the serious military reverses following the launch of Ethiopia's third offensive, talk among some of the historical leaders about the need for him to let go, or to be forced out, of power had started to move from the grapevine into the open. Nevertheless, this was just an idea, rather than a concrete plan of action, exchanged in confidential conversations among several senior officials in exasperation. They reportedly shared the idea with Senator Rino Serri, the EU Special Representative, and requested him to pass it on to the Ethiopian government as a quid pro quo for ceasing its offensive, with adverse implications on state security.

Nevertheless, the general aim of the officials, as portrayed in private conversations at the time, was not to oust or replace Isaias as president but to constrain his powers and restrain his singular decision-making, especially concerning issues of national defence and security. The idea was for CC of the PFDJ to constitute a special body, sanctioned by the National Assembly, to serve as a 'national security council' to advise the president. The council would be provisional, pending the convening of the Fourth Congress of the Front that would elect a new leadership and subsequently, through the agency of the National Assembly, a new state president.

Once dismissed from office, the signatories of the petition were 'frozen' and denied access to public resources and facilities. Isaias has long used the tactics of arbitrary dismissal and extended suspension from active duty, of veteran fighters and senior Front, government and army officials as a weapon of punishment for suspected disloyalty or the slightest hint of dissent or critical opinion with the acquiescence of the rest. Such suspensions happen on the basis of unverified and often vindictive reports of informants, who include jealous colleagues.

This practice of 'freezing' public servants leaves hundreds of government and military officials frozen from active duty for years with regular pay. Barred from seeking alternative jobs, 'frozen' officials are let to languish in forced idleness.

They are denied the dignity that comes with work and the satisfaction of creating value through working. Intended to humiliate and render the victims subservient to the president's whims, is a double-edged sword that deprives the State of the benefit of their productive services and depletes its treasury through the issue of unearned paychecks of salaries for doing nothing. The practice affirms that Isaias has no qualms about squandering the nation's scarce human and financial resources.

This arbitrary, abusive and wasteful practice, allowed to run its course during the war of national liberation and continued after independence, was rarely applied to sitting ministers until that time. They had, up until that moment, felt immune to its usage and remained indifferent to the injustices meted out against their comrades-in-arms and colleagues. Not expecting to find themselves on the receiving end, the former senior Front leaders and high government officials generally acquiesced in 'freezing' until it also happened to them. Having appeased the entrenchment of the practice, they themselves were not spared. It was business as usual when their turn came to be frozen, in a case of "what goes around comes around".

What followed is history. The president, as stated above, refused to heed the repeated pleas to convene a meeting of the CC or the National Assembly in order to discuss the burning issues facing the country. In the absence of internal forums for dialogue and discussion at the highest organs of the Front or the government, the initially discreet protest became public and generated considerable attention. It received extensive coverage in the private newspapers, mainly through direct press interviews or commentaries by the critics and dissenters.

The public followed the revelations of the open split with keen interest and a deep sense of apprehension. Some elders tried to mediate with a view to finding a common ground between the protagonists, but the president rejected their initiative and put them in jail. Then came the 'Black September' of Eritrean politics, setting a terrible winter of discontent: security agents descended on the homes of the dissenters, picked them up in the wee hours of the morning and hauled them to detention in contravention of their parliamentary immunity as members of the Eritrean National Assembly. There followed a purge of hundreds of suspected supporters or sympathisers of the detained former senior officials in the middle echelons of the Front, the government and the army and their similar arrest and detention in total disregard of due process.[315]

The president made the charges against the former senior Front and government officials and military officers in a prepared report read to the last session of the Eritrean National Assembly in February 2002, five months after their arrest. The now 'frozen' National Assembly rubber-stamped the tendentious and unsubstantiated accusations and acquiesced in the arbitrary detention of the accused dissenters *ex post facto*. The state media orchestrated an extensive smear campaign to malign the detainees. The emasculated judiciary has remained silent in the face of the indefinite incarceration and solitary confinement of the victims without charge or trial and the common occurrence of arbitrary arrests and sudden disappearances.

---

[315] Conversations of the author with a member of the PFDJ executive committee, Asmera, January 2005.

The government employs repression to root out political opposition, diversity of thought, and dissenting opinion. Otherwise, the former senior officials broke no national or international law in wishing to see the president out of power. They merely advanced political views critical of his increasingly autocratic style of leadership and advocated reform to democratise the policy and decision-making process in the management of the affairs of state. They intended to institute measures that would allow the CC of the PFDJ and the Eritrean National Assembly to perform their legitimate oversight functions over the management of the affairs of state at the Front and government levels and help constrain rash actions that impinge on national security.

Indeed, they are honourable men and women, ardent patriots who devoted their prime years to fighting for Eritrea's freedom and serving the cause of its reconstruction and development. Even though some of them were among the chief historical props of Isaias's growing power, they had come to realise the urgency of curbing its detrimental use. Unfortunately, the attempt was too hesitant at the outset, came too late, and proved too ineffective in the end. Consequently, their dream of democratic reform turned into the nightmare of indefinite solitary confinement. The next section will highlight their fateful detention, along with several journalists, aimed to crush their dissent and put an end to the idea of reform, with dire consequences for Eritrea.

9.4 Detention to Suppress Dissent

The early hours of the morning of 18 September 2001, exactly a week after the atrocities of 9/11 that sent shockwaves across the globe, witnessed the arrest of eleven senior Front, government, and army officials, who had signed the petition to convene a meeting of the CC, on the direct orders of President Isaias. The victims included nearly all the top surviving historical leaders of the armed struggle comprising, in effect, the core of the most prominent political and military leadership of the EPLF. They also included some of the most senior officials of Eritrea's provisional and transitional governments: cabinet ministers, members of the National Assembly, regional administrators, army generals, ambassadors, and other high officials.[316]

---

[316] Mahmud Ahmed (Sherifo), Haile Weldensae (Drue), Petros Solomon, Berhane Gebrezgiabher and Ogbe Abraha were members of the EPLF central committee (CC) and political bureau from 1977 to 1994 and the PFDJ central council (CC) from 1994-2001; Beraki Gebreselassie and Estifanos Seyum were members of the EPLF and PFDJ CCs from 1977 to 2001; Germano Nati, Saleh Kekia and Hamid Himed were members of the EPLF and the PFDJ CCs from 1987 to 2001; and Aster Fesshatsion was a member of the PFDJ CC from 1994 to 2001. All eleven detainees were members of the Transitional Eritrean National Assembly. In addition, Mahmud Ahmed served as minister of froreign affairs and local government; Haile Weldensae as minister of finanace, foreign affairs, and trade and industry; Petros Solomon as minister of defence, foreign affairs, and fisheries; Gen. Ogbe Abraha as minister of trade and industry, and chief staff in the ministry of defence; Maj. Gen. Berhane Gerezgiher as commander of the EDF ground forces and minister of trade and industry; Beraki Gebreselassie as minister of education, information, and ambassador to Germany; Brig. Gen. Estifanos Seyum as director general of inland revenue in the ministry of finance and head of finance in the ministry of defence; Saleh Kekia as director of the prsident's office and minister of transport and communications; Germano Nati as administrator of Gash-Barka region; Aster Fesshatsion as director general in the ministry of social affairs: Hamid Himed as member of the PFDJ

In addition, Isaias ordered the arrest of ten journalists who had provided press coverage to the dissenting perspective and published interviews with the senior officials critical of the president's leadership.[317] Their arrest in late September followed their protest of the closure of the private press. A special committee, established later, to review their case found that the detained journalists were merely doing their normal professional work, and had committed no violations or crimes indictable under the Press Code of Eritrea. Accordingly, the committee recommended releasing the detained journalists and lifting the ban on the private press.[318]

Isaias has condemned the detained senior officials and journalists to languish in solitary confinement without the benefit of due process, formal charge, or trial before a court of law. He has denied them the right to give their version of events in self-defence; interact with anyone and with each other; and visitation by family, friends, or human rights monitors. He has severed their external links completely and virtually buried them alive in an isolated prison camp. They have not, to date been acknowledged, seen, or heard from. The regime has withheld information regarding their

---

executive committee, ambassador to the Sudan, and director general of Middle East desk in the ministry of foreign affairs.

[317] Seyum Tsehaye, Fessehaye Yohannes, Yusuf Mohamed Ali, Medhanie Haile, Dawit Habtemicael, Amanuel Asrat, Said Abubaker, Mattewos Habteab and Temesgen Gebreyesus.

[318] The president, who had set up the committee under pressure, characteristically shelved its recommendations. The committee comprised Mahmud Ali Jabra, Mohamed Ali Omaru, Naizgi Kiflu, Tesfai Gebreselassie (China), Yemane Gebreab (Monkey), and the author.

condition and refused to deny or confirm repeated reports that most of them have died under harsh prison conditions. If this is the case, it is a tragedy of epic proportions.

Their inhumane treatment blights the memory of our martyrs and the vision of freedom that inspired generations of Eritreans. Article 17 of the ratified Constitution guarantees the right of *habeas corpus* and the Penal Code of Eritrea limits detention without charge to 30 days. The accusations levelled by the president that the former senior officials had conspired to overthrow him and had committed crimes of defeatism, treason, raising untimely questions, criminalising the president through the private media, corruption, and abuse of power and public resources, remain arbitrary charges that lack legal force unless duly substantiated in a court of law.[319] Their indefinite incarceration, unjustified even if, the charges were proven right, violates the basicl legal principle of the 'presumption of innocence until proven guilty'. In the words of a famous British leader, "The power of the Executive to cast a man into prison without formulating any charge known to the law, and particularly to deny him the judgment of his peers, is in the highest degree odious and is the foundation of all totalitarian government."[320]

The unexpected capture of Barentu and Ethiopia's rapid military gains in the Western Sector had induced a loss of composure and caused great anxiety in the Eritrean body politic, including in the ranks of the senior leadership of

---

[319] Prepared report presented by the president to the last meeting of the Eritrean National Assembly in February 2002, five months after the detention of the senior officials in September 2001.

[320] Winston Churchill, as quoted in *In The Highest Degree Odious: Detention Without Trial in Wartime Britain* (1992), by A. W. B. Simpson.

the government and the Front. The fact that the president kept ministers and senior officials in the dark accentuated the uncertainty regarding the evolving situation in the battlefield. The absence of formal communication fostered uncertainty and fuelled all kinds of speculation about the unfolding reality on the ground.

The discernible lack of leadership able to provide an official compass at that critical moment of national shock and uncertainty represented a systemic failure for which the president bears direct responsibility. The chain of events that unfolded on the ground during that fateful episode of military reversal confirms his culpability. In retrospect, there is ample evidence that the president's accusations are analogous to a case of 'a thief crying thief'. After all, that the president failed at that critical moment to act in a presidential manner, demonstrated a lack of leadership, and personified defeatism was common knowledge among members of the PFDJ CC, the cabinet of ministers, and the EDF high command.

When the Ethiopian army made significant advances in the central and western sectors, captured Barentu, the capital of the Gash-Barka Region, and occupied large areas of Eritrean territory during the height of the third round of the war, the president instructed bank officials to evacuate the money in the vaults from Asmera to Afabet in Sahel. Perhaps too humiliated to announce it himself, he directed Haile Weldensae (Drue), the then foreign minister, to break the news of the fall of Barentu to a stunned Eritrean public on Eri-TV. I asked a reluctant Drue, "Why you?" and advised him to tell Isaias to own up and do it himself. He replied, "How can I?" Further, Isaias ordered the EDF to retreat from the Bure Front and abandon the defence of Asseb.

Luckily, for Eritrea and, to the credit of brave frontline commanders and combatants of the EDF who disobeyed his orders, fought valiantly, and firmly stood their ground, the defences of Asseb held firm. The central and western fronts were stabilised following a strategic redeployment of the EDF to new defensive positions, adopted when a panicky president summoned the relegated leaders *ex post facto* for informal consultations. Paradoxically however, those who helped save the day were later, detained and remain virtually 'buried alive' in the regime's dungeons.

Having seized control of the Eritrean state and personalised power, Isaias has used the security apparatus as a tool of *Stasi*-style[321] repression to silence criticism, bully independent opinion, punish divergent views, criminalise dissent and crush opposition, whether real or imagined. There abound reports of arrests and missing persons, taken away and never heard from again.[322] Accountable to nobody but the president, the security services have created a pervasive state of fear and insecurity that spares nobody. The regime's resort to a shifting mix of brutal repression, harassment and intimidation is designed to ensure the docile submission of officials and citizens alike and to severely punish any manifestation of non-conformist behaviour.

In the case of the detained former senior officials, the president has acted as the accuser, judge and executioner

---

[321] The *Stasi* was the secret police of the then German Democratic Republic (East Germany).

[322] Former fighters and officials under indefinite detention include: Beteweded Abraha, Ermias Debessay (Papayo), Brig. Gen. Habtezion Hadgu (Commander of the Eritrean Airforce), Aster Yohannes (wife of Petros Solomon), Miriam Hagos, Senait Debessay, Feron Weldu, Kiros Tesfamicael (Awer), and Tesfai Gebreab (Gomera).

without evidence or reference to the law. The political detainees are presumed guilty as accused and held in indefinite solitary confinement under inhumane conditions. Having crucified them on the altar of repression, the government provides no information about their status or situation. The president has long suspended the PFDJ CC and the Eritrean National Assembly and emasculated the High Court. The absence of countervailing constraints to the exercise of arbitrary power has given Isaias's 'dark side', which thrives in the pain of those he condemns to freezing, torture or death, free rein to trample on the basic rights and civil liberties of the people and condemn many Eritrean patriots to extinction.

The government stands accused of widespread and systematic use of physical and mental torture against detainees. The repeated accusations seem to be generally credible, borne out by the testimonies of torture victims, several of whom have recounted their ordeal to the author in confidential private conversations. UN and international human rights organisations have also reported that Eritrean political prisoners and prisoners of conscience are subject to systematic and widespread physical and mental torture.[323] The UN Human Rights Council (UNHRC) has strongly condemned "the continued widespread and systematic violations of human rights committed by the Eritrean authorities, including arbitrary executions,

---

323 Amnesty International, Annual Report 2011, The State of the World's Human Rights: Eritrea. http://www.amnesty.org/en/region/eritrea/report-2011#section-44-8 and Human Rights Watch, State Repression and Indefinite Conscription in Eritrea, 16 April 2009. http://www.hrw.org/en/reports/2009/04/16/service-life-0

enforced disappearances and systematic use of torture"[324] and appointed a Special Rapporteur on the human rights situation in Eritrea. Predictably, the Eritrean government refused to cooperate with the Special Rapporteur, describing the Council's decision as politically motivated. The Special Rapporteur's first report to the UNHRC and the UN General Assembly, delivers:

> [A]n overview of the most serious human rights concerns in Eritrea, including cases of extrajudicial killing, enforced disappearance and incommunicado detention, arbitrary arrest and detention, torture, inhumane prison conditions, indefinite national service, and lack of freedom of expression and opinion, assembly, association, religious belief and movement.[325]

Routine denials aside, the regime combines coercion, forced disappearance, indefinite detention and torture to intimidate people and perpetrate its rule. According to reliable first hand reports, the regime uses various forms, tools and techniques of physical and mental torture. Complete isolation in solitary confinement causes depression. Starvation and malnutrition emaciate the victims to the bone. Exposure to scorching heat during the day and numbing cold during the night in the purpose-built desert dungeons like *Irairo* or the

---

[324] UN Human Rights Council: Resolution A/HRC/20/L19, Geneva, Switzerland, 06 July 2012 http://www.ohchr.org/en/NewsEvents/Pages/DisplayNews.aspx?NewsID=12329&LangID=E.

[325] Report of the Special Rapporteur on the situation of human rights in Eritrea, Sheila B. Keetharuth, 23 May 2013. http://www.ohchr.org/Documents/HRBodies/HRCouncil/RegularSession/Session23/A.HRC.23.53_ENG.pdf

underground and shipping container prisons that dot the country. Mental inertness induced through the continued denial of intellectual activity and deprivation of access to all forms of public media. Some might never get to see the light of day because they know too many of Isaias's darkest secrets.

The tribulation of prolonged suffering endured in utter isolation, coupled with wanton neglect of proper medical attention, raises serious concerns and legitimate questions about the state of the physical wellbeing and mental health of the surviving victims. The consequences of twelve years, and still counting, of life in solitary confinement and deprivation remain totally unknown. If one day the political detainees are able to get out of their infernal cells and see the light of day in freedom, their survival of the ordeal would be a testament to the durability of the human spirit and its capacity to overcome adversity under dire situations.

Eighteen more journalists arrested after the initial crack down remain under indefinite detention without charge or trial.[326] The ban on the private press has restored the government's previous monopoly and tight control of the media, making it the sole provider of news, analysis and commentary. The state media use this monopoly to reconstruct the history of the armed struggle, expunge the role of the former senior officials in the war of national liberation, and erase their memory altogether. This represents an insidious attempt, by Isaias and his overeager

---

[326] According to the New York based Committee to Protect Journalists (CPJ), the continued imprisonment of 28 journalists makes Eritrea the top jailor of journalists in Africa with a continental 52 journalists in prison. Sudan Tribune, 13 December 2011. http://www.sudantribune.com/Africa-jailed-52-journalists-most,40976.

cronies, to cleanse the archives, reconstruct documents, and revise history.

9.5 Concentration of Power

The proclamation establishing the Transitional Government of Eritrea provides for a functional division of powers among three branches. However, the suspension of the legislature and the emasculation of the judiciary have resulted in the accumulation of power in the office of the presidency. Structural and institutional weaknesses of the Front and the Government have allowed Isaias to impose the supremacy of power over law and to exercise absolute dominion over the political, economic and social life of the country. Irrevocably wedded to the Maoist dictum that "Political power grows out of the barrel of a gun", the power of his presidency depends not on the consent of the people but on his control and coercive use of the defence and security forces to suppress internal opposition and to intimidate the people into submission.

Absolute power has enabled the President to treat the state as his private fiefdom. He uses, and enables the Front, to access state resources without restraint. Public and private assets, resources and affairs are intermingled. He subverted an effort to identify, segregate, and institutionalise the assets and resources of the government and the Front.[327] He regards himself as the 'rightful' ruler of the country, behaves as its

---

[327] A four-member committee set up in 1994 to separate the assets and resources of the government and the Front was, disbanded before finishing its work. Chaired by Haile Weldensae (Drue), the minister of finance, the committee included Berhane Habtemariam, the auditor-general, Habtemariam Berhe, the official in charge of the

owner, and dispenses with the people, land, and properties at his discretion. He appoints, suspends, or dismisses senior government officials and civil servants at will. The criterion is personal loyalty measured by blind obedience, rather than service, competence or merit. His impulsive abuse of power allows him even to deny the burial of the remains of veteran freedom fighters in their ancestral homeland.

Isaias has suspended the key Front and state organs and impeded the development of a functional state apparatus, effective public institutions, and rational decision-making mechanisms. He disregards formal organisational hierarchies and institutional structures, routinely interferes in the chain of command at the higher and middle echelons of the armed forces, ministries and government agencies, and often operates through individuals who hold no formal position or function in the hierarchy of the Front, the government or the army. The use of parallel informal structures blurs accountability, breeds corruption and hampers effective mission delivery.

Despite the launch of the Civil Service Administration in 1998, the constitutional provision (Article 11) for an "efficient, effective and accountable" civil service remains little more than ink on paper. A weak state bureaucracy, undeveloped institutions, lack of meritocracy and the precedence given to loyalty over competence have fostered mediocrity, undermined institutional capacity-building and hindered adequate service delivery. The absence of accountability and transparency, against the backdrop of low salaries, spiralling inflation and extreme poverty, has abetted the abuse of power and the spread of corruption.

Front's foreign currency accounts then based in Rome, and the governor of the central bank (the author).

The rapid turnover of ministers, senior officials, regional administrators, and army officers exacerbates these consequences. The president treats them as private employees and appoints, suspends or fires them at whim. Arbitrary transfers from one post to another, demotion, dismissal or suspension aim to forestall the rise of autonomous power centres. The climate of general instability that permeates the higher echelons of the government, the civil service and the army causes uncertainty, disaffection and inefficiency.

Elected Secretary General of the Provisional Government in 1991 by the EPLF CC and President of the Transitional Government in 1993 by the Transitional National Assembly, pending national elections within a maximum period of four years, Isaias continues to hold the reins of power in violation of the accord. He has proven himself neither accountable to the citizens nor replaceable by the people through democratic elections. The imposition of arbitrary rule, the 'freezing' of the CC and the National Assembly for over twelve years and the suspension of national elections for over sixteen years, and counting, have tainted the legitimacy of his presidency.

During the war, Isaias played a key role as the leader of the EPRP and the EPLF, which he, to a considerable extent, forged in his own image via meticulous tactics of 'divide and rule', tight control and ruthless suppression of dissent. He was warmly welcomed at liberation as the leader of a victorious armed struggle and embraced as a war hero by an adoring population. He was, also well regarded internationally as an able leader who guided the armed struggle to victory against great odds. The Clinton administration for instance, branded him in the mid-1990s as one of a new breed of leaders of an African renaissance.

Driven by careerist ambitions and afflicted by an authoritarian disposition, however, Isaias has long succumbed to his dark side and imposed autocratic rule. He has undergone an inexorable makeover from a once charismatic leader into a detested despot, save for a coterie of henchmen at home and a handful of "Johnny-come-lately" sycophants in the diaspora who are unable or unwilling to distinguish between the interests of the country and the people, on the one hand, and those of the regime, on the other.

Isaias has nobody but himself to blame for alienating the Eritrean people, being politically isolated at home and abroad, and leading the country into stagnation. He is a shrewd, street-smart tactician capable of manipulating people; but without the vital complement of his former comrades-in-arms, he lacks a sense of strategy and long-term vision. He has absorbed Maoist dogma, internalised Machiavellian scheming, and mastered the intricacies of Eritrean society.

Equipped with such an array of tools, Isaias has exploited the weaknesses of the EPLF leadership and the historical context of a society lacking in political and social structures capable of inhibiting the subversion of the noble aims of the armed struggle and the profound aspirations of the people. He has betrayed the trust his former comrades and fellow fighters reposed on him. His tactics have enabled him to dominate the Front, monopolise state power and control the small world around him. At the same time, his inept strategy has turned him into a blind alley and entrapped his regime in a comprehensive failure that has produced general impoverishment, alienation and mass exodus at home and isolation and international sanctions abroad.

This makeover has coincided with the display of extraordinary cruelty surpassing, in the oral narrative of

Eritrean folklore, the sadism of the notorious *gzat turki* or the 'rule of the Turks'. Indeed, the tyranny of the regime, the brutality of its suppression of dissent, and the severity of its repressive rule have few parallels, both in scope and intensity, in the annals of the turbulent history of modern Eritrea. Consumed by a supreme desire to stay in power at any cost, Eritrea's self-appointed *de facto* president-for-life has bitten the hand that fed him. Ever ungrateful and ungracious, he has been unwilling to govern by the law, unable to serve the interests of the State, and uninterested in improving the lot of the people.

As in the case of many other dictators in history, his relations with colleagues and former comrades-in-arms reflect deep distrust, all-consuming jealousy, and treachery. His careerist ambition and obsession for control find expression in the constant surveillance, marginalisation or elimination of potential rivals by accusing them of sedition and treachery in collusion with foreign enemies, such as the US Central Intelligence Agency (CIA), his favourite bogey. He sees no need for evidence or due process; it is enough just to label and point an accusing finger. The list of victims of his obsession with power and insatiable appetite for control includes some of the most prominent leaders of Eritrea's armed struggle for liberation.

Devoid of an iota of compassion, haunted by chronic suspicion and possessed of a delusion of grandeur, Isaias has no real friends or advisers, only disposable tools: messengers, informants, 'court' jesters, or drinking companions.[328] He

---

[328]   The title, 'adviser to the president', does not match the function of the Front officials holding it. Its use, along with another fictitious post, 'chairman of the parliamentary committee on foreign affairs',

has marginalised, incarcerated, 'frozen', or driven into exile many of the principal leaders, prominent cadres and veteran fighters of the war of liberation and chief architects of its remarkable victory. This has caused widespread popular consternation with his rule. Isaias presides over a society where self-identity is deeply rooted in paternal ancestry and which, despite its enthusiastic initial embrace, he knows he has alienated and feels no longer accepts him. He has thus turned a non-issue into an issue in his mind's eye, because of which he suffers from a rejection complex verging on identity crisis that occasionally surfaces when under the influence of alcohol or seized of drunken brawls.[329]

Selfish to the core, fixated on his grudges, and vindictive in the extreme, Isaias is ruthless in his punishment of 'disloyalty' or persecution of dissent. No one is spared or forgiven; not even his most loyal henchmen and erstwhile closest comrades-in-arms. He is a control freak obsessed with keeping a tight grip on everything. Further, he is prone to betray, abuse, and brutalise his colleagues and plunge Eritrea

---

in lieu of 'head of the PFDJ department of political affairs', is traceable to a ploy in 1999 to embellish the CV and enhance the candidacy of Yemane Gebreab (Monkey), who held no formal government position, for the presidency of the ACP Assembly. Otherwise, 'Mr Know-It-All', who has become paranoid to the point of distrusting even his own shadow, uses no advisers. More and more arrogant and aloof, Isaias considers himself an expert on everything, and listens increasingly less and less to anybody.

[329] In one such incident, Isaias blurted, "I know that you call me Agame (the name of a district in Tigray misused in popular parlance as a pejorative reference to people of Tigrayan origin) behind my back. I will show you! I will take this country down as I put it up." [ብድሕረይ፡ ዓጋመ ክም እትብሉኒ እፈልጥ እየ። ክርእየኩም'የ! ነዛ ዓዲ፡ ከም'ታ ዘምጻእኩዋ ከጥፍእ እየ።]

into the abyss trying to preserve his power. His wilful policies betray cavernous hatred, his wanton actions portray barely disguised contempt, and his uncouth utterances seethe with unabashed spite of the Eritrean people. Increasingly, the consequences and prospective legacy of his administration seem to evoke an old Eritrean adage, "a donkey that said, 'may the grass never grow here once I pass away'".

The Isaias regime has abused and down casted Eritrean society. The Eritrean predicament is unique. To many friends of Eritrea, it is an 'enigma shrouded in mystery' and, indeed, a matter of supreme irony that the struggle waged to liberate Eritrea from foreign oppression has ended up in installing a regime that perpetrates even more brutal repression. It has virtually *buried alive* several prominent dissenters and critics to crush the democratic impulse through the force of example. The regime has managed to forestall resistance to its oppression and intimidate many of the protagonists of that impressive struggle for freedom, who retain a critical stance and an independent perspective, into reluctant acquiescence in its dictatorial ways through the demonstrative effects of arbitrary arrest, indefinite detention, and solitary confinement.

Inexorably, therefore, the forcible suppression of dissent and removal of opposition had evolved into the default mode of conflict resolution of the Eritrean liberation fronts (both the ELF and the EPLF). Regrettably, the malignant practice that bedevilled the evolution of the armed struggle has given rise to a political culture of extreme intolerance of pluralism that disparages independent thought, criminalises divergent opinion and equates dissent with treason and treachery in post-independence Eritrea.

This practice continues to haunt Eritrean politics with tragic consequences for many patriots, their families and Eritrean society as a whole. It has frustrated the realisation of the enduring aspirations of the Eritrean people for freedom, democracy, and prosperity. The suspension, marginalisation or emasculation of institutions, and the concentration of power in the presidency that have allowed the unrestrained use of coercion have also facilitated the wide disparity that exists between the policy and practice of the government addressed in the following chapter.

CHAPTER 10

Disconnect between Policy and Practice

Power tends to corrupt, and absolute power corrupts absolutely. - Lord Acton

The National Charter, the Macro-Policy paper and the Constitution of Eritrea are consistent with the objectives of the National Democratic Programme of the Eritrean People's Liberation Front (EPLF), the Front that led the armed struggle for liberation to victory and formed the government upon independence. These policy instruments set the overall framework to guide the integral process of nation-building, state construction and sustainable development in the new Eritrea. They aimed to enable the government to build a constitutional, democratic and developmental state able to deliver the rule of law, responsive governance, and prosperity.

The objectives enunciated in the trio were all fine on paper, agreeable in principle and achievable in practice. Using these objectives as criteria, this chapter examines the evolution of the real situation on the ground. Specifically, it assesses whether the Eritrean government has been faithful to the ethos of the armed struggle and the aims articulated in the tri-documents in terms of the convergence or divergence of actual practice and stated policy.

Even then, neither policy nor practice is an end in itself. For the ultimate aim of all rational endeavours is to improve the human condition in terms of achieving a higher standard of living and a wider space of freedom. Boosting economic growth to create wealth, generate prosperity and enhance the quality of life is one of the core functions of responsible government while the ability or inability to do so is the principal measure of a government's performance. A British historian once stated that the most important idea to emerge from the history of political thought is "the ideal that government is to be judged by results"[330] while a famous French philosopher asserted that a good government is one that improves the quality of life of its people.[331]

Delivery of a better quality of life for the people would thus enhance the legitimacy of the state. The upshot would nurture the people's sense of affinity with the state and ownership of the political system. On the other hand, poor performance, failure to deliver results and incapacity to improve the livelihood of the people would demonstrate the irrelevance of the state to the wellbeing of society and undermine its legitimacy.

10.1 Establishing a Constitutional State

The National Charter and the Constitution of Eritrea pledged the creation of a constitutional state and a democratic system of government founded on the rule of

---

[330] Parkinson, Cyril Northcote, *The Evolution of Political Thought*, Boston, Houghton Mifflin Co., 1958, p. 310.

[331] Rousseau, Jean-Jacques, "On the Social Contract", quoted in C. Northcote Parkinson, *The Evolution of Political Thought*, op. cit., pp. 205 and 311.

law. According to Proclamation 37/1993, No. 6 (Asmera, 19 May 1993), the ratification of the Constitution signalled the end of the transitional period and the advent of representative government. There was great anticipation that the timely application of the Constitution would inaugurate a new democratic dispensation and sanction the exercise of legitimate power based on the rule of law.

The Constitution of Eritrea, *inter alia*, determines the structure, defines the authority, enumerates the functions, and delimits the powers of the executive, legislative and judiciary branches of the government. It guarantees the fundamental freedoms, proclaims the basic rights, and specifies the national duties of the people and requires the state to safeguard them. The Constitution would to serve as the legal foundation of the Eritrean State, the repository of the sovereignty of the people, and the source of all legitimate authority. It vests supreme legislative power, including the issuance of proclamations, the promulgation of legislation on domestic and foreign policy, the ratification of international treaties and agreements, in the National Assembly.

The Constitution remains unimplemented, the National Assembly suspended, and the judiciary marginalised. The State operates in a legal vacuum, with no 'compact' between the government and the people. The absence of any semblance of a separation of powers and the entrenchment of an omnipotent executive have stripped the people of sovereign power and abetted the usurpation of the historic triumph of the Eritrean people. The Special Court has arrogated the powers of the High Court,[332] undercutting

---

[332] The former president of the High Court, Teame Beyene, dismissed in 2001 for criticising the creation of the Special Court and

the ability of the courts to freely adjudicate criminal and civil cases and administer justice, jeopardising the safety of citizens, and condoning the abuse of their basic human rights. This has effectively reduced the government to a single overpowering presidency that dominates all political life, with unrestrained powers to use the state apparatus as an instrument of suppression. The purposeful obstruction of building viable state structures and functional institutions has allowed free rein to dictatorial decision-making.

The *de facto* suspension of the central council of the ruling People's Front for Democracy and Justice (PFDJ) since September 2000 has closed the sole forum of internal consultation and conversation among the senior leadership of the Front.[333] Likewise, the *de facto* suspension of the National Assembly since October 2000[334] has nullified the role of the legislature in the governance process and denied the Eritrean people an essential voice in running the affairs of state. The consequent rise of the rule of men has exposed the people to the flagrant abuse of their rights, freedoms and dignity without recourse for redress.

---

presidential interference in the work of the judiciary, remains 'frozen'.

[333] The eighth and last meeting of the Central Council, the legislative body of the PFDJ, took place from the 31st of August to the 2nd of September 2000.

[334] The 13th session of the National Assembly - the last one attended by all constituent members of the PFDJ CC - met from 29 September to 02 October 2000. The 14th and very last session after the 18 September arrest of 11 of its members met from 29 January to 2 February 2002 to hear the president's accusations against its former members detained in violation of their parliamentary immunity.

The unwarranted and indefinite political detention of senior officials, journalists and prisoners of conscience constitutes a grave violation of basic human rights and the negation of the rule of law (*état de droits*). To the detriment of the State, the anguish of its people and the disappointment of its long-time friends, the closing years of the first decade of Eritrea's independence have witnessed the rapid contraction of the political space for democratic debate within the Front, the Government and the larger society. Eventually, the complete closure of the political space paved the way to the inexorable imposition and consolidation of authoritarian rule and foreclosed Eritrea's immediate prospects for a constitutional state founded on the rule of law, committed to democratic principles and bound by social contract.

10.2 Building a Democratic System of Government

The first objective of the eleven-point EPLF National Democratic Programme (NDP), adopted in its first congress in 1977, is the establishment of a democratic state. The Front's second and unity congress in 1987 reaffirmed the goal to establish a democratic state committed to a decentralised form of government and a participatory system of pluralist politics. Further, it pledged that the state will protect the Eritrean people's democratic rights of freedom of speech, freedom of the press, freedom of assembly, freedom of worship and freedom of peaceful demonstration.

Some of the principal attributes that distinguish a democratic from a non-democratic state are: the commitment to the rule of law; respect for fundamental freedoms; protection of basic rights, including minority rights; political pluralism; popular participation in the governance process; and transparency and accountability of public policy and action. The trinity of policy instruments envisage the creative adaptation of these essential principles to suit the specific requirements of Eritrea's historical evolution, traditional governance structures, socioeconomic conditions and cultural values to create and consolidate a democratic system of government.

The EPLF's desire to integrate Eritrean cultural values of governance with modern systems of public administration was clear in the early attempts of the Provisional Government of Eritrea (PGE) to adapt traditional customary laws governing administration and adjudication to the evolving structures of local government.[335] Its commitment to modern pluralist democracy was also evident in the initial efforts of the PGE to inform and educate the population, through the official media and a series of pamphlets issued in 1992, about pluralist systems, political parties, governance systems, civic duties, voting and participatory politics.[336] The adoption of the tri-documents lent a new impetus to the drive to establish a democratic Eritrean state. A draft Proclamation of Political Parties and Political Organisations was drawn up,[337] an election proclamation adopted [338] and a national electoral commission established.[339]

---

[335] Provisional Government of Eritrea, Negarit Gazeta, 1, 15 September 1991.

[336] Provisional Government of Eritrea, Department of Media and Culture, *State, Government and Party*, Asmera, December 1992, pp. 1-56.

[337] Draft Proclamation of Political Parties and Political Organisations of Eritrea, February 2001.

[338] Election Proclamation of Eritrea, January 2002.

[339] National Elections Commission of Eritrea, 2001.

The internal rift within the top leadership of the ruling Front and the president's reassertion and eventual monopolisation of authority through the brutal suppression of the tentative effort to democratise the policy and decision-making process and to establish accountable government put the ratification of the draft Proclamation of Political Parties and Political Organisations on hold. This dealt a fatal blow to the project of multiparty politics and the establishment of a democratic system of government in Eritrea. Much as the ratification of the Constitution has not resulted in its implementation, the adoption of an electoral law and the setting up of an electoral commission have not led to elections. Eritrea today remains under the grip of an all-powerful presidency using the People's Front for Democracy and Justice (PFDJ), formerly the EPLF, as an instrument of pervasive domination and tight control.

Operating under the direct command of the president, the PFDJ holds complete sway over the Eritrean political, economic, social and cultural landscape. No political, civic, trade or media organisations exist in the country outside the orbit of its hegemony. There also exists no room for local civil society or non-state actors in the PFDJ scheme of things. The appearance of private newspapers, four years following the adoption of the press code in 1996, had broken the government's monopoly over the local print media. During its year-long existence from September 2000 to September 2001, the nascent private press had effectively resisted PFDJ patronage and the fruits of its independent work caught the imagination of the Eritrean public.

For a brief 'Eritrean Spring', the private press served as a medium of vibrant debate of national, regional and global issues. There was much excitement and enthusiasm in the air; people rushed to get copies of their favourite newspapers from street vendors before having breakfast or going to work early in the morning. Many people started their daily conversations with a discussion of the main issues of the moment given coverage by the newspapers. One fateful Tuesday morning, 18 September 2001, all that was no more! The private newspapers vanished and several of their editors went to jail a few days later. Although they remain in prison, and some of them are reportedly dead, they have not been charged or brought before a court of law.

The lack of a domestic climate conducive to the initiation and conduct of autonomous political, media, civic and cultural activity has led only to the proliferation of political, civic, and cultural opposition groups and media outlets in the diaspora. The concentration of power has induced corruption. The absence of a published budget and proper accounting of government revenues and expenditures raises legitimate questions regarding the government's management of Eritrea's public finances. In the absence of parliamentary oversight and mandatory budgetary constraints, the president uses his absolute powers over government and Front institutions to dispense state resources at will. Direct control over the treasury, the central bank, the commercial bank and the Front's parastatals gives him unfettered access to the financial resources and foreign exchange reserves of the country, often causing their random dispersal and depletion.

National economic decisions, issues of public finance, and inflows of overseas development assistance are, conducted in secrecy. There is no public information on the amounts of foreign aid received, on the size of the country's domestic or foreign debt, on the Front's investment ventures overseas, or on the government's allocations for an assortment of foreign non-state actors from and in the neighbourhood. Such a state of affairs subverts the democratic imperative of accountability and transparency in managing the national economy, state assets and national resources, domestic and foreign policy, and economic and financial operations.

The government's crackdown on the private press, coupled with its tight control over the official media, has denied the Eritrean people the right to independent information and news analysis. Furthermore, banning the 'third estate' has precluded its constructive contribution to the democratic development of Eritrean society. Having regained monopoly, the state media serve mainly to embellish mundane happenings; obscure important local, regional and global events; and propagate generally skewed, often imprudent and highly partisan commentaries.

The state media constantly con the people with fears of an impending threat to national security from an array of foreign enemies, most notably the US and its *"Wayane* servants" (reference to the Ethiopian government). They also serve as a forum for the periodic dissemination of tendentious, redundant and self-contradictory monologues of the president, on an assortment of preselected 'national, regional and international' issues and events, principally targeted at captive audiences at home and 'true believers' abroad. Most of the daily news and views in the government owned media deal with what the president, the ministries, and managers of the Front parastatals do, however mundane, exaggerated, or even concocted.[340]

---

[340] An editorial in the state-owned Tigrinya daily, Hadas Ertra (Vol. 21, No. 84, Friday 25 November 2011), that bears the imprint

The EPLF had eschewed the cult of personality during the war in the Field as well as during the first few years of independence. Upon monopolising power, the president has used his personal control of, and heavily invested in, the government-owned media to reverse that tradition. He has egged on the state media to glorify and meticulously cultivate his personality cult, exalting him to the status of a demi-god. At his behest, the state media not only flatter the president but also present a rosy image of an otherwise bleak and worsening political, economic and social situation in the country to divert attention from the people's terrible predicament.

It seems that the regime's ministry of information, with its Orwellian substitute of "Serving the Truth" for its mendacious propaganda, has no clue that the age of the information revolution and globalisation has effectively 'deinstitutionalised' news and reduced the government into just another news maker. Thanks to the widespread availability of satellite television, the internet and the vast cyberspace outside the realm of state control, its views on a given subject or analyses of events are no longer the only ones on the offer. Despite its persistent but unsuccessful attempts to restrict access to these alternative sources of news, information and comments, the government has virtually lost its monopoly and must compete for audience and attention with other newsmakers, including its opponents, in an increasingly unfavourable terrain.

---

of Isaias's pen in a 'tongue in cheek', bemoans the fading of the EPLF values of letting deeds speak for themselves. It scolds senior officials, including ministers, regional administrators and PFDJ executive committee members, for the on-going practice of complete exaggeration or fabrication of fictitious performance.

There thus exist no independent media, political pluralism or autonomous civil society organisations on the ground that could stand up as a counter-weight to injurious government policy and action on critical issues of national concern in present-day Eritrea. There is no tolerance of dissent or even divergent opinion. The government suppresses freedom of expression and association and bans all rival political activity inside the country, driving opposition underground or abroad. The inability of the government to avail a forum for democratic dialogue to express and mediate the competing viewpoints, interests and equities poses a threat to the long-term stability of the country. Monopoly of power, absence of internal democracy in the Front, the government and the society at large, practices of exclusion and economic mismanagement have engendered an internal political crisis, widened the cracks in the Eritrean body politic and further fragmented Eritrea's political landscape.

Eritrea has entered the third decade of its post-independence era. Nevertheless, the commitment to a democratic system of government proclaimed in the EPLF National Democratic Programme (NDP), the National Charter of Eritrea, the Macro-Policy framework and the Constitution of Eritrea has not materialised. The country ranked 46th out of 53 countries on the Mo Ibrahim Index of African Governance for 2009.[341] Based on indicative measures of "delivery of public goods and services to citizens by government and non-state actors", the Index assesses governance quality using the four general criteria of safety

---

[341] Mo Ibrahim Foundation, *The Mo Ibrahim Index of African Governance*, 05 October 2009. http://www.moibrahimfoundation. org/en/media/get/20091004_eritrea.pdf.

and rule of law; participation and human rights; sustainable economic opportunity; and human development. Eritrea scored well below the continental average in all the four categories of governance quality.[342]

Far from being a democratic state, Eritrea today is an authoritarian state par excellence. Democratic principles, institutions and practices are lacking and, in their place, lurk political tyranny and economic autarky. The complete absence of representative organs and rule of law in Eritrea today is alien to the traditional structures of public administration and management of the Eritrean society, whether in the Kebessa (Highlands) or in the Metaht (Lowlands) regions. Reneging on the promises of freedom and democracy that sustained the armed struggle, the regime has unleashed an infernal mill of oppression crushing the people with tyranny; grinding their humanity with repression; suffocating their spirit with intimidation, fear and insecurity; and driving them into mass exodus without parallel in the annals of modern Eritrean history.

10.3 Instituting Participatory Politics

The territorial reorganisation of the country in 1996 had, as one of its principal objectives, the creation of a decentralised and democratic political system to enable the people to constitute their government at all levels, to manage their political, economic and social affairs, and to have an effective voice in the making of policies and decisions affecting their lives. This affirmed the Front's proclaimed commitment to the construction of a democratic state and the promotion

---

[342] Ibid.

of participatory politics at the national, regional and local levels. An inclusive participatory process would reinforce the creation of an accountable and functional regime committed to democratic principles and governing in accordance with the law.

The territorial reorganisation has however, not resulted in administrative autonomy. The absence of regular elections, the discretionary appointment of administrators by the head of the executive branch of the central government, and the dependence of the *baitos* (or people's assemblies) on the regional administrators for financial resources, including their work expenses, undermine the envisioned deliberative role, legislative mandate and oversight functions of the *baitos* and divest them of real power. Thus, administrative decentralisation without devolution of corresponding political authority and provision for autonomous financial resources to the representative regional and local bodies has ruled out participatory politics at the grassroots level. The discrepancy between stated policy and actual practice has undermined the process of nation building, state construction and sustainable development.

The regional *baitos* thus lack the political, operational and financial autonomy to fulfil their representative duties, expedite their legislative mandate and exercise their oversight functions over the executive branches. To the extent that they assemble in session, they act as mere rubberstamps for the regional administrators. Instead of enabling real decentralisation of state authority, as was originally intended, the territorial reorganisation of the country has merely facilitated the institution of top-down political control from Asmera.

The lack of real decentralisation and the weak capacity of the regions have effectively precluded the participation of local communities in the policy and decision making process. In reality, there exist parallel government, Front and security structures that extend from the centre to the village level and dominate virtually all aspects of political, economic, social and cultural life. Such pervasive control stretches its tentacles to the celebration of national and religious holidays and the provision of family coupons that give access to rations of necessities.

Besides, the restructuring of the country has created certain practical problems for the people. Under this arrangement, people in the far-flung corners of the new administrative zones and sub-zones must trek long distances to the now 'remote' regional or sub-regional capitals to conduct official business or address routine concerns. For instance, residents of the outskirts of Asmera are required to travel to Massawa, Keren, Barentu or Mendefera, the capitals of their respective new administrative regions. The state of inconvenience entailed is similar for people in other parts of the country similarly affected by the territorial reorganisation.

The absence of efficient and affordable transport and communication services aggravates the difficulties encountered. Further, lack of expeditious handling and resolution by the relevant state authorities leaves even petty cases pending for extended periods, often involving repeated adjournments and several trips to the regional or sub-regional capitals. This occasions the added hardship of recurrent costs and lost days of work in the context of an impoverished and labour starved rural economy dependent on subsistence agriculture and pastoralism.

The territorial reorganisation of the country into six regions was imposed from the 'top down', without due consultation of the people or assessment of its impact on their livelihood. In fact, the dissolution of the historical provinces and districts and the haphazard reconfiguration of the constituent units and seats of local administration faced popular disfavour, protest and outright opposition, especially in parts of the south and west of the country. The negative effects have only reinforced the original misgivings about the whole affair.

The use of the regional structures to reinforce central control, rather than to facilitate grassroots participation, and the practical problems arising from the associated systemic weaknesses, functional limitations and administrative deficiencies have negated the envisioned benefits of the territorial reorganisation of the country. They have also provoked a backlash among the most affected sectors of the population that one cannot wish away or suppress into oblivion. There is thus a need for a future democratic Eritrean government to reconsider the issue in earnest.

When the time comes, it would be in the interest of national cohesion to undertake democratic popular consultations either to confirm the new regions and sub-regions or restore the historical provinces and districts, intact or modified. Reconsideration would be imperative, especially in view of the failure of the territorial reorganisation to promote participatory politics, a democratic system of local government or economic growth. The Eritrean people deserve a decisive say in the process either directly or through their duly constituted representative organs.

10.4 Ensuring Gender Equality

Women make up roughly half of Eritrean society and hold half of its skies. The significant participation of women in the armed struggle was one of the crucial factors for its victory; yet, independence has brought them neither liberation nor equality with men. Traditional norms of inequality continue to define the status of the vast majority of Eritrean women. The much-anticipated transformation of gender relations and empowerment of women in society have yet to happen. A statement by a fourteen-year veteran of the armed struggle for liberation echoes the post-independence condition and feeling of many former EPLF fellow women fighters:

> *After all we did in the struggle. We contributed more than the men. Now women fighters have many problems. After all we did, it is like being thrown away.*[343]

An event that transpired immediately after the liberation was quite illustrative of the disposition of the new government toward the gender issue and the vulnerability of women in independent Eritrea. The provisional government sponsored, through the agency of private contractors accountable to nobody, former women fighters to work as house cleaners in Lebanon, Kuwait, Qatar, and the United Arab Emirates (UAE) in the Middle East. There were no safeguards for their social rights or provisions for their protection against the inevitable abuses and horrible mistreatments that later afflicted many of them in the hands of unscrupulous employers.

There is another case that is illustrative of the prospects for women in the new Eritrea. Demobilised women ex-fighters

---

[343] Quoted by Bernal, Victoria, Equality to Die for?: Women Guerrilla Fighters and Eritrea's Cultural Revolution, Political and Legal Anthropology Review: Vol. 23, No. 2, November 2000, p. 61. http://www.socsci.uci.edu/~vbernal/bio/Bernal-POLAR.pdf

whose spouses were government or Front officials were, denied the opportunity to set up small business enterprises while the same was not true for demobilised men ex-fighters. Likewise, the restriction did not apply to civilian spouses of government or Front officials. Generally understood to have emanated from a verbal directive of the president, no rational explanation was, given for this arbitrary and discriminatory practice.

The denial of equal opportunity that targets women former fighters constitutes a flagrant violation of the basic right to gender equality. It also impedes their reintegration as productive members of civil society. In addition, banning demilitarised women from engaging in civilian private business activity hinders their efforts to achieve economic independence and improve their livelihoods and the lot of their families.

Furthermore, there are persistent, credible reports of gross and flagrant abuses of women national service conscripts during training and deployment in active national service. Eritrean women did not fight and make great sacrifices in the war of national liberation in order to face abuse, discrimination, or denial of the right to establish, own and operate businesses on their own right in their country, or to become migrant house cleaners or menial workers in the Middle East. Just like their men counterparts, Eritrean women fought to help liberate their country, reconstruct their society, build normal families, and make the new Eritrea a better and a more prosperous place to live in for its people - men, women and children.

There is a sense that the EPLF did not transform gender relations during the war but merely repressed the domestic and erased the feminine in women; it integrated "women into the EPLF not simply as the equals of men, but as male equivalents."[344] After the end of the war, the domestic and the feminine have resurged, allowing male dominance to reassert its traditional position in Eritrean society.

The National Union of Eritrean Women (NUEW), much like the National Union of Eritrean Workers (NUEW) and the National Union of Eritrean Youth and Students (NUEYS), lacks the leeway to develop as an autonomous civil society organisation dedicated to the promotion of the welfare and special interests of women. It has retained its original role as the mass organisation of the ruling PFDJ. The NUEW functions mainly to mobilise recruitment to Union membership and ensure the compliance of its members with Front and government policies and directives, no matter how abusive, oppressive or discriminatory to women.

Thus, despite yesteryear's narrative of the EPLF's commitment to the emancipation of women and the attainment of gender equality, the subordinate position of women to men, including that of former freedom fighters, in Eritrean society today remains deeply ensconced in its traditional enclave. Women who fought side by side with men as equals during the war of independence find themselves marginalised in the society and the family. They lack the power and the capacity for initiative to change their unenviable position in a stagnant society.

The problem is systemic. The NUEW lacks the organisational autonomy and the political clout to challenge the entrenched patriarchal social structure and fulfill its pledge to defend the rights and ensure the equality of women. The token appointment of a handful of women to ministerial and

---

[344] Bernal, Victoria, 2000, pp. 61-62.

senior government posts, in the absence of effective gender mainstreaming, does not change the subordinate position of the vast majority of women. Surely, Eritrean women and men did not fight shoulder-to-shoulder during the war expecting to see the retention of the patriarchal order and the inferior status of women in the family and society after the liberation.

As the issue of the equality and empowerment of women is part of the general question of democracy and development, the situation of Eritrean women cannot improve in isolation from the overall condition of the larger society. The removal of legal barriers to the inequality of women is an essential first step; but it is not sufficient to ensure gender equality without additional accompanying measures. In this context, the government's general disregard for the rule of law represents the primary impediment to the equality of women. Traditional gender relations and the inferior status of women in Eritrean society are thus bound to persist until the restitution of the rule of law and the realisation of significant socioeconomic progress.

Even in the tiny modernised sector, Eritrean society in general, and the typical Eritrean household in particular, remain bastions of patriarchy, gender-based division of labour and male privileges. Overall, lack of access to meaningful tertiary education, economic growth, gainful employment opportunities and social progress continues to hinder the advancement of women and the enhancement of their status in Eritrean society. It has made the reinsertion of demobilised former women (and men) combatants into gainful civilian life, the emancipation of women and the realisation of gender equality particularly difficult.

10.5 Constructing a Secular State

Despite the pledge to construct a secular state with constitutional guarantees of the "right to freedom of thought, conscience and belief"[345] and the separation of state and religion, there exist state interference in religious affairs, close oversight of church and mosque activities, and coercive attempts to influence the religious choice of citizens. The government recognises only the established Christian churches[346] and Sunni (Sufi) Islam, criminalises the new sects and disenfranchises their followers. It requires the new sects to 'register' but keeps filed requests to 'register' on hold and cracks down on their ritual activities pending 'registration', with adherents often detained without charge or trial for extended periods of time.

The state meddles in the management of the internal affairs of the Church and the Mosque and supervises their religious activities at home and abroad. Such unwarranted intervention contravenes one of the basic tenets of secularism, namely, the separation of state and religion, and fuels resentment and discord. Resistance to heavy-handed state interference has resulted, among other things, in the protest and subsequent dismissal and continuing house arrest of the duly ordained Patriarch of the Eritrean Orthodox Tewahdo Church as well as the detention of several priests in 2006.[347]

---

[345] Constitution of Eritrea, Article 19.1, p.16.

[346] The Eritrean Orthodox Tewahdo Church, the Roman Catholic Church, and the Eritrean Evangelical Church.

[347] The former Patriarch of the Eritrean Orthodox Tewahdo Church, His Holiness Abune Antonios, dismissed from office and placed under house arrest for resisting government interference in the Church's religious affairs.

State meddling in religious affairs has also been a divisive factor polarising the Eritrean diaspora between supporters and opponents of government imposed or sanctioned priests to minister in their established overseas community churches.

The claims of a secular policy notwithstanding, therefore, the government routinely intervenes in the affairs of religion and religious institutions. It bans, disenfranchises or discriminates against certain religious groups and sects. It tries to influence the religious choice and activities of the people and implant the tentacles of its domination in the spiritual domain as well. In its obsession to control religious life, the regime is increasing the risk of religious polarisation and playing with fire. Persistent state interference in religious affairs, relegation of certain religious sects, and discriminatory treatment of particular religious groups may provide ammunition, support and recruits to militant political movements that use religion as a mobilising principle to the detriment of long-term national cohesion.

Despite its commendable tradition of pious tolerance, Eritrea is not completely devoid of religious extremism. Militant political Islamist groups with a radical agenda have sprung from the remnants of the former Eritrean Liberation Front (ELF) in the Sudan in the late 1980s and early 1990s. Instigated by external jihadist forces, based outside the country, and active among sympathetic elements of Eritrea's Muslim Diaspora, these small and constantly splintering militant Islamist groups operate openly in Ethiopia and clandestinely in the Sudan and in Eritrea. In May 2009, the Eritrean Islamic Jihad Movement (EIJM), the Eritrean Islamic Salvation Movement (al-*Islah*), the Eritrean Liberation Front (ELF-National Council), and the Eritrean

Federal Democratic Movement (EFDM) agreed to form the Eritrean Solidarity Front (ESF), under the Ethiopia-based opposition umbrella Eritrean Democratic Alliance (EDA).[348]

Mainstream Islam in Eritrea, like mainstream Christianity, prescribes a moral code of conduct as a way of virtuous life for adherents, eschews overt political activity, and seeks harmonious coexistence of Muslims and Christians in equality in all aspects of national life. It sanctions the secular state, endorses the precedence of secular jurisdiction over Islamic law and advocates the flexible application of *sharia* in certain civil and family matters with the mutual consent of the concerned parties. Militant political Islam, on the other hand, rejects the secular state, aims to establish an Islamic state under *sharia* in its place, and operates to antagonise Muslim-Muslim as well as Muslim-Christian relations.

The practice of state supervision of religion and heavy-handed interference in religious affairs, coupled with the repression of dissent and the absence of a medium for the peaceful expression of grievances, could alienate both the Christian and Muslim populations, politicise religion and fuel religious extremism. Rising popular discontent could find expression in religious ferment. In this context, the worsening domestic repression, the lack of gainful employment opportunities, and the country's present regional and international isolation could strengthen the hands of militant political Islam and help it gain support and recruits.

---

[348] Prior to the merger, the EIJM and al-*Islah* conducted sporadic hit-and-run attacks, carried out ambushes and laid landmines on roads in southwestern Eritrea, from bases in Ethiopia. The Eritrean Islamic Congress and al-*Nahda* have declined the call to join the alliance.

Upholding the integrity of the secular state in a democratic system of government thus offers the best option to ensure the separation of religion and politics and guarantee religious equality and freedom of worship for all. The injection of religion into politics and the codification of sectarian features in the construction of the state could be a recipe for future instability. It would operate to polarise Eritrean society, insert a malignant thorn in the flesh of its body politic, and turn Eritrea into a permanently dysfunctional state. It is thus highly imperative that Eritrea avoids falling victim to the mixture of sectarian politics, social fragmentation and external interferences that has fanned the flames of national discord and reproduced a debilitated state like Lebanon.

10.6 Constituting a Developmental State

The end of the war of liberation found Eritrea's economy shattered, its infrastructure ruined, its social fabric disrupted and its people impoverished. At the time of independence, the country had to start building virtually from scratch. There were no viable colonial administrative structures to inherit, functional institutions to provide sorely needed public services, or budgetary resources to finance government operations and run the affairs of state. The remarkable feat of winning the war of liberation against all odds had given the new Eritrea the confidence and determination to set out to create a modern, advanced and competitive economy within a span of two decades.

Despite the devastation of the long war, Eritrea inaugurated statehood with several advantages that signified a potential to rapidly modernise the economy and uplift the human condition: Primarily, a united, resourceful and enterprising people, with a shared culture that values hard work. Second, a reliable corps of professional, technical and skilled personnel with exemplary commitment and devotion to public service steeled in the crucible of a difficult struggle and steeped in the wartime tradition of asceticism, discipline and self-reliance. Third, a relatively large number of highly educated and well trained professionals in a united and patriotic diaspora ready to serve and participate in the effort to reconstruct and jumpstart the economy. Fourth, Eritrea had the rare financial blessing of zero national debts. Fifth, it had considerable reserves of public goodwill and political capital at the national, regional, and global levels.

Geographically, Eritrea occupies a strategic location amenable to transforming the country into a centre of services - port, transport, communications, financial, tourist, etc., as well as a regional hub of industrial processing and commercial exchange. Eritrea's two major ports of Massawa and Asseb adjoining the busy waterways of the Red Sea represent great assets capable of making a significant contribution to national development. They could also provide vital transit trade services to the region, especially to Ethiopia, South Sudan and the Sudan. Even more lucratively, Eritrea's ports are ideally located to serve as transhipment ports for maritime traffic between Western Europe and the Mediterranean basin, on the one hand, and the Middle East, South East Asia and the Far East, on the other. Furthermore, Eritrea's relatively ample endowment of agricultural, mineral and marine resources avail it a potential to achieve rapid and sustainable development and ensure food security for its relatively small population.

The potential to harness these advantages gave Eritrea a unique opportunity to combine self-reliance with proactive international cooperation and blaze a new trail of rapid economic growth and developmental state construction. However, despite the timely formulation of the necessary policy instruments embodied in the tri-documents, reinforced later by the National Economic Policy Framework (NEPF), the government failed to establish competent institutional structures, follow its own policy guidelines and pursue its stated goals. The promise of an advanced, competitive and prosperous economy capable of delivering improved public wellbeing and a better quality of life for the majority of the people failed to materialise.

Erratic policies and disruptive practices have deterred domestic capital formation and foreign direct investment. Subsistence agriculture and traditional animal husbandry, essentially in their age-old forms, persist as the mainstay of the national economy. Eritrea's two major ports remain underutilised or virtually idle, foregoing hundreds of millions of US dollars' worth in lost annual revenues. The country continues to languish in the lowest rungs of the global development ladder while the great majority of its people live under extreme poverty. The state of abject poverty, mass unemployment and indefinite active national service continue to drive tens of thousands of young Eritreans yearly into exile. Eritrea's actual record since independence displays neither the general contours nor the distinctive features of a developmental state. The vision of a free, democratic and prosperous Eritrean state shimmering in the mind's eye of the tri-documents has turned into a mirage, getting more remote and elusive by the day.

Using the frozen conflict with Ethiopia as a pretext, the government has abandoned the tri-documents and imposed a command economy under the pervasive domination of parastatals mostly owned by the ruling People's Front for Democracy and Justice (PFDJ). It has pursued an outmoded Maoist ideology[349] whose rigid doctrine has been modified, its political precepts substantially reformed and its economic tenets long discarded to pave the way for a rising China. The government's imprudent policies and mismanagement have caused productivity to decline, the economy to contract and the standard of living to deteriorate.

Despite constant talks of 'strategic development plans', the regime oversees a stagnant command economy so severely mismanaged that opportunities for real growth have been lost. As a result, extreme poverty has engulfed all layers of Eritrean society but the handful of predators allied with the Front's parastatals and the military high brass. The government arbitrarily expropriates prime cereal producing fields, forces elements of collectivisation on farmlands and often dictates to peasant farmers what crops they should grow. Besides, it takes away a good portion of their harvest at a government-set price, significantly lower than the market price, to be resold at higher prices in the Front-owned 'rational shops'. This operates to discourage farmers, diminish overall agricultural production and impoverish rural communities.

---

[349] Wikileaks has exposed a report that President Isaias berated the Chinese ambassador in Asmera for China's embrace of market capitalism and the Chinese ambassador remarked that Isaias internalised Maoist ideology and "learned all the wrong things" when he went to China for political training at the height of the Cultural Revolution in the late 1960s. Ambassador Ronald K. McMullen, *Bio Notes on Eritrean President Isaias Afwerki*, Cable 08Asmara543, http://wikileaks.blogs.linkbucks.com/archives/2055

Further, the Front uses the Red Sea Trading Corporation to conduct rather bizarre commercial operations that are exceedingly predatory. Upon arrival in the port of Massawa, imported goods are shipped inland, intact in their containers, to Tessenei in the extreme west of the country as if for export to the Sudan and sold to itinerant petty traders for resale in Asmera and the other Eritrean cities and towns. Under the weird trade regime, exorbitant transit and mark-up charges borne by end-users push consumer prices sky high and feed spiralling inflation.

The regime does not publish macroeconomic data and it is, in fact, allergic to the use of metrics because they expose its dismal record in terms of concrete economic growth or human welfare. IMF and World Bank statistics portray the economy between 1993 and 2010 in three distinctive profiles.[350] First, an economy that grew at an average annual rate of 7 per cent during 1993-1996, and 8 per cent in 1997, in real terms. Second, an economy that suffered from a sharp drop in growth to 1.8 per cent in 1998, zero growth in 1999 and a negative growth of minus 13.1 per cent in 2000. Third, an economy set on a fluctuating decline that ranged from a short-lived recovery of 9.2 per cent growth in 2001 to negative 9.8 per cent in 2008 and to 2.2 per cent in 2010. Further, the IMF and World Bank data show that the population grew

---

[350] The Wold Bank, Eritrea: Country Data Profile, 2010 http://ddpext.worldbank.org/ext/ddpreports/ViewShared Report?REPORT_ID=9147&REQUEST_TYPE=VIEW ADVANCED&DIMENSIONS=78 \IMF, Eritrea: Key Economic Developments, 1993-2002 http://www.imf.org/external/pubs/ ft/wp/2004/wp0407.pdf IMF, Eritrea: Selected Economic and Financial Indicators, 1998-2003 http://www.imf.org/external/ np/sec/pn/2005/pn0518.htm.

within a range of 3.0 to 3.8 per cent and GDP per capita registered a negative rate of growth during the same period.

The sharp economic decline of 13.1 per cent was a direct result of the war's sudden disruption of the development effort, severe damage to the country's economic and social infrastructure, and massive displacement affecting over one-third of the population. The rapid recovery to 9.2 per cent growth in 2001 signified the economy's resilience and ability to quickly absorb the shocks of the war and move forward. However, the government's abandonment of the macroeconomic policy framework as of 2001 ended the relatively sound and prudent economic policies of the first decade of independence and operated to reverse the post-war economic recovery.

This had disastrous repercussions on the economy and public welfare. Government diktat and the Front's privileged domination of a command economy have squeezed out the private sector, marginalised the small entrepreneurial and professional class and dried up foreign direct investment (FDI), except in the mining and cement sectors. The result is low and falling productivity, high domestic and foreign indebtedness, acute shortages of necessities, disruption of electricity and water supplies, soaring inflation, mass unemployment, and widespread impoverishment. A declining economy in the face of a growing population has aggravated poverty, diminished the standard of living, and exacerbated the human condition. The mix of constant state propaganda and mendacious and incoherent sophistry, orchestrated in the form of periodic presidential interviews on the state-owned media, can hardly beautify the ugly reality of the present political, economic, and social malaise afflicting the people.

There are indications that the development of the country's extractive industry would drive high levels of economic growth. The economy was for instance, forecast to grow by 17 per cent in 2011, riding on the back of the commercial production of gold.[351] It was, also projected to grow by 6 per cent in 2012 and by 7 per cent in 2013.[352] The expected 17 percent growth rate in 2011 was later revised to 8.5 per cent and the initial estimate of gold production at the Bisha mine for 2012 adjusted down by about 50 per cent.[353] The planned start of copper production in 2013 could also provide an additional boost to economic growth.

The expansion of gold and copper mining and extraction of the country's already established high grade base metal deposits augur well for future growth. *Per se*, the predicted expansion of the economy, driven by a booming mining sector, is good news for the country, especially if the forecast materialises. The absence of accountable and transparent management of state assets and national resources however raises legitimate questions whether the mining boom would translate into greater prosperity for the country providing for a higher standard of living and a better quality of life for the people or turn out to be a resource curse.

The government has squandered an excellent opportunity to develop and transform Eritrea into a regional hub of industry and services. A very high level of unemployment has pushed people to flock into the informal economy and

---

[351] The Economist Intelligence Uint, 16 December 2010.

[352] Market Research Report: Country Report Eritrea 1st Quarter 2012.

[353] Reuters Africa, UPDATE 1-Nevsun cuts Eritrea gold mine output view for 2012, 7 February 2012. http://af.reuters.com/article/eritreaNews/idAFL4E8D75JT20120207

induced the pauperisation of the majority of the people. Presidential and Front interferences deliberately subverted efforts to create a vibrant financial sector and establish an accountable, robust, and transparent system of financial management. Actually, the regime's reluctance and inability to utilise, indeed its abandonment of the instruments put at its disposal by the tri-documents have, in the main, shaped the contours and determined the general trajectory of the country's economic underdevelopment, authoritarian government, and extreme poverty.

To date, the government has presided over the imposition of the coupon economy and a rise in extreme poverty in the country across all regions and virtually all strata of society. Rampant unemployment and a shrinking economy with large fiscal, domestic and external imbalances have overburdened the people with ever widening and deepening poverty. This is the outcome of the government's failed economic policies and mismanagement, aggravated by an *insatiable presidential urge to control everything*, including the daily food intake of citizens and the free movement of people, goods and services within the country.

10.7 Divergent Policy and Practice

An objective appraisal of the regime's record reveals that its performance does not measure up to its declared objectives. It shows significant divergence between stated policy and actual practice. Mindless and stingy suffocation of the economy under incompetent management has arrested its productive potential, squeezed the nascent middle class, generated mass unemployment and caused large-scale impoverishment. Harsh domestic repression, ruinous regional conflicts and wanton international isolation have worsened the situation. A state of pervasive political and economic repression has resulted in the unprecedented exodus of Eritrea's professional class, entrepreneurial elite and youth in search of a freer life and better opportunities abroad.

In sum, the present regime has been unable to overcome the dictatorial legacy of the colonial past, to establish a constitutional state and institute an inclusive and participatory system of democratic governance. Lack of tangible economic growth has resulted in mass unemployment, immersed the vast majority of the people in a morass of extreme poverty, and created daily scenes of long lines for a ration of necessities, including substandard loaves of bread and diluted powdered milk in the urban areas. Further, inability to avoid or settle disastrous conflicts or adhere to acceptable norms of diplomatic conduct has encumbered the country with debilitating regional and international isolation and the imposition of UN sanctions.

The initial high hopes and promises that the long coveted and hard won independence of Eritrea would lead to the emergence of a democratic, developmental and progressive state have not transpired. Lamentably, the historical record and the prevailing state of affairs reveal marked disconnect between the declared policy and real performance of the transitional government. There exists a clear dichotomy between the vision of a free, democratic and prosperous Eritrea enunciated in the tri-documents and the actual reality of an enchained, oppressed and impoverished Eritrea under the sway of an authoritarian, patrimonial and predatory regime gone awry. The rise of dictatorship has thwarted the country's peaceful democratic development and frustrated the people's aspirations for emancipation, security and prosperity.

Some may argue that the period used to evaluate Eritrea's performance record is insufficient. After all, twenty-two years *per se* is not a long time in the life of a country. However, twenty years was the timeframe that the government had set for itself in the Macro-Policy paper to create "a modern, technologically advanced and internationally competitive economy within the next two decades." In addition, if Singapore, which is relatively less-endowed with natural resources and which was less well-placed at independence in terms of national cohesion and social harmony than Eritrea, has done it within twenty years, it is appropriate to ask, why not Eritrea within twenty-two years?

One might also argue that the border war with Ethiopia and its aftermath are the main cause of Eritrea's present problems. It is true that the period since 1998 has witnessed the border war with Ethiopia (1998-2000) and the subsequent state of neither peace nor war that has prevailed. The war was a veritable disaster, indeed. It caused huge loss of life, enormous destruction of infrastructure and property, significant disruption of agricultural production in the country's granaries, and produced a massive humanitarian crisis. The war displaced over one million people in the border areas, created an estimated 100,000 refugees and produced about 75,000 expellees uprooted from Ethiopia. In sum, it consumed considerable resources, damaged infrastructure, disrupted the development agenda, and diverted national focus.

The war and its aftermath warped Eritrea's peaceful development and contributed significantly to the present malaise in the country. Nevertheless, these are neither the sole nor the decisive factors that explain Eritrea's current predicament. Feigning total preoccupation with national security, the government used the resultant state of '*no war, no peace*' as a pretext to engineer a mind-set of a state of siege and extend the transition to a democratic system of governance beyond the prescribed four years with dire consequences for the country and the people.

It put the application of the ratified Constitution on hold and paralysed the political process through brutal suppression of discordant discourse. This has undermined its legitimacy. Further, it subverted its ability to deliver through relegation of key state institutions and the closure of the economic space for the private sector in violation of the agreed precepts of prudent economic policy and the desertion of the goals of the liberation struggle. Further, the government has closed the space for internal debate within the leadership of the Front and the government, incarcerated senior officials without due process indefinitely and clamped down on the nascent private press. In brief, the government has become openly authoritarian.

It ruthlessly suppressed internal dissent and perpetrated gross abuses of human rights, including arbitrary arrests, torture and the brutal treatment in solitary confinement of prominent political detainees, journalists and prisoners of conscience. It set up an extensive domestic spy network to inform on and sow distrust among the people, suppress independent thought and muzzle criticism. Besides, the government has imposed indefinite active national service, closed the only university in the country and trivialised education and tertiary education, in particular. Further, it has adopted a conflictual stance at home and projected a bellicose posture abroad.

All this has consumed Eritrea's energy, blurred its national priorities and sapped its political, economic and social development potential, producing a huge disparity between stated policy and actual practice. The imposition of a despotic and reclusive regime unable to build functional and effective structures of public administration has undermined the government's capacity to achieve the objectives of liberation, battered its domestic support base and eroded its legitimacy. The emergence of a dysfunctional state has damaged the image of the country, diminished its regional standing and engendered its international isolation.

Otherwise, it is plausible to imagine a scenario in which the dynamic interaction of three timely undertakings could have enabled Eritrea to avoid the long-term negative impact of the war, forestall external isolation, and secure border demarcation through Ethiopia's compliance under concerted international persuasion. First, allowing internal debate among the senior Front and government leaders, with popular participation, to build domestic consensus and bring about national political renewal. Second, conducting timely and appropriate bilateral consultations or accepting third party mediation to settle disputes by peaceful means before they turn into violent conflicts. Third, engaging in constructive dialogue with partners to sustain normal diplomatic relations and promote cooperative political and economic relations in the national interest.

Adhering to the National Charter, applying the Macro-Policy framework and implementing the ratified Constitution could have effectively enabled Eritrea to avert or constructively address the internal political crisis, to prevent conflict or overcome the consequences of the war, and to meet the challenges of reconstruction and development. Deserting the ideals of the armed struggle in practice, however, the government has opted to abandon rather than to make use of these policy instruments, and to flout the legitimacy they confer. Lacking in strategic vision, it has failed to address the challenges of the moment, missed opportunities at critical stages, and invited eventual isolation. Indeed, the government has forfeited the establishment of a constitutional order, failed to build viable state institutions, and defied the rule of law at home.

It is a sad commentary that nearly a quarter-century of independence has not delivered a better Eritrea for its people. Worse still, it has ushered in an authoritarian government which has proved unwilling to safeguard the basic rights and fundamental liberties of the Eritrean people and unable to cater to their aspirations for freedom, democracy and prosperity. The PFDJ regime has lost credibility and legitimacy. The failure to deliver on its declared agenda has undermined the nation building, state construction and development project. Consequently, the Eritrean state has been unable to build domestic consensus, promote unity of purpose and galvanise national effort toward democratic development, sustainable growth and prosperity.

Thus, to argue that the war and the frozen conflict with Ethiopia are solely responsible for Eritrea's dire present situation is to ignore the primacy of the dynamics of internal factors and seek to externalise the consequences of failure to devise and pursue a proactive policy that could have enabled the country to successfully rise up to the challenges. It is quite apparent therefore that the situation in Eritrea today is primarily the product of the policy decisions that the government has made and the policy choices that it has forfeited.

There can thus be no denying that the conspicuous disparity between the stated policies and actual practices of the government, whose effects are so vividly manifest in the unfortunate political, economic and social malaise afflicting Eritrea today, is self-made. The root cause is structural and lies squarely within Eritrea itself; and so does the solution. Disconnecting policy and practice has as the next chapter explains, detracted Eritrea from avoiding the African crisis.

CHAPTER 11

The African State in Crisis

[T]he modern African state remains largely irrelevant to the needs, interests, and aspirations of the people. - Agbese and Kieh

This chapter presents a concise appraisal of some of the recent literature on, and the emergence and nature of, the postcolonial state in Africa to place the Eritrean experience in state construction and development in the African context. In concise terms, the bulk of the existing literature and most of the academic debate on the emergence and nature of the postcolonial state in Africa dwell on the European heritage of the state system, and on the interrogation of its suitability to the socioeconomic conditions of African societies. In the main, the discourse on the African state has focused on its European legacy and absorbed in the effort to explain its record of failure to deliver a democratic system of government, sustainable development, and prosperity for the majority of its citizens. Moreover, it is characterised by "the absence of a coherent theoretical and methodological corps [*core*]" and acute division "concerning their analysis, definition and explanation of the African State."[354] As Redie further observed:

> Basically, the debate on the postcolonial state revolves around the European origin of the state system inherited by Africa, and its appropriateness to the socio-cultural reality of African societies. Since the onset of the independence of African societies two dominant paradigms have characterised the debate on the postcolonial state in Africa. These can be identified as the one, which rationalises the relevance of the European state system, and another which attributes the cause for the crisis of the African state to its European origin.[355]

The lack of coherence of theory, and the variance in analysis and description, of the state have in turn, engendered discord in the explanation of the causes of state fragility or state failure, and in the prescription for its remedy.[356] Affiliation with

---

[354] Bereketeab, Redie, State Building in Post-Liberation Eritrea: Challenges, Achievements and Potentials, Adonis & Abbey Publishers Ltd., London, 2009, p.13.

[355] Ibid., p. 14.

[356] See Azarya, Victor, Reordering State-Society Relations, Incorporation and Disengagement, The Precarious Balance: State-Society Relations in Africa, Rothschild & Chazan (eds.), 1988; Calhoun, Craig, Nationalism, Open University Press, Buckingham, 1997; Davidson, Basil, The Black Man's Burden: Africa and the Curse of the Nation-State, James Currey, London, 1992; First, Ruth, Colonialism and the Formation of the African States, States and Societies, David Held et al(eds.), Oxford, 1983; Markakis, John, National and Class Conflicts in the Horn of Africa, Cambridge, 1987; Mazrui, Ali, Francophone Nations and English-Speaking States: Imperial Ethnicity and African Political formation, States Versus Ethnic Claims: African Policy Dilemma, Rothchild & Olorunsola (eds.), Westview Press,

different approaches or schools of thought and the "diversity of the continent and the complexity of events taking place there" could be among the factors affecting the apparent disagreement in approach and discourse.[357] A perspective that considers the historical factors and the resultant interplay of the exogenous and indigenous forces that brought about the implantation of the state system and shaped the evolution of the postcolonial state in Africa may help provide a more consensual explanation of the crisis besetting the continent and point the way forward to its remedy.

"Africa is probably the oldest continent" and the "birthplace of mankind."[358] Confirmed as the original home of *Homo sapiens* and the cradle of civilisation, it possesses a very rich history of old and diverse cultures. Endowed with abundance and variety of natural resources, Africa has a large, young and fast growing population. For about five and half centuries, however, the trajectory of its autonomous development was dented and warped by the intervention of nascent Europe: the slave trade followed by the colonial venture and the Cold War.

11.1 Snafus of Africa's Development

Slavery deracinated, brutalised, dehumanised millions of Africans, and reduced them to exchangeable private property

---

Boulder, 1983; Young, Crawford, The African Colonial State in Comparative Perspective, Yale University Press, New Haven, 1994.

[357] Chabal, Patrick & Jean-Pascal Daloz, *Africa Works: Disorder as Political Instrument,* Indianapolis: The International African Institute and Indiana University Press, 1999.

[358] Davidson, Basil, Modern Africa: A Social and Political History, 2nd, Longman Group UK Ltd 1989, p. 3.

in the form of 'captive labour'. An enduring reminder of man's appalling inhumanity to his fellow man, the slave trade was not only inhumane and morally repugnant, but it was also socially disruptive and economically injurious to Africa. The slave trade took 11,232,000 Africans via the transatlantic route to the New World and 50,000 to Europe and the Atlantic islands between 1450 and 1900.[359] The slave trade uprooted 18,320,000 Africans: 17,500,000 shipped and 820,000 dead awaiting shipment in African ports.[360]

In terms of opportunity cost, slavery deprived Africa of the benefits of the productive labour and potential contribution to its indigenous development of the millions taken away from their homes in their prime years and exported overseas, and constituted a major cause of its stagnation. Besides, slavery ushered in "modern Africa's dependence on the 'world system' of trade and wealth-transfer" to the enduring detriment of the continent.[361] The surplus created by the slave trade and using slave labour in the New World represented Africa's loss and Europe's gain. Adding insult to injury, the descendants of African slaves were, despite their pioneering and considerable contribution to the development of Europe and the Americas, subjected to pervasive racial discrimination and harsh oppression for centuries in their new destinations.

The catastrophe of slavery gave way to the calamity of colonialism that spelled the undoing of Africa. Sanctioned

---

[359] Lovejoy, Paul E., Transformations in Slavery: A History of Slavery in Africa, Cambridge University Press, 2000, Tables 2.1 & 3.1, pp. 26 and 47.

[360] Meltzer, Milton, Slavery: A World History, Da Capo Press, 1993.

[361] Davidson, Basil, 1989, p. 49.

by the Berlin Conference of 1884-85, the colonial system gave the continent its present geopolitical configuration. Driven by ascending Europe's rising demand for African labour, raw materials, minerals and markets, the Berlin Conference laid the groundwork for the European scramble, colonial conquest, and territorial partition of the *Dark Continent.* "Europe invaded Africa, took possession of Africa, and divided Africa into colonies of Europe."[362]

Existing at different levels of pre-capitalist development for the most part, pre-colonial African society lacked the necessary economic surplus to provide for the emergence of indigenous ruling classes capable of state formation and territorial defence. Although most Africans tried to fend off European encroachment, they lacked the organisation, technology, and cohesion necessary to resist the colonial onslaught. In the aftermath of occupation, European conquest created the colonial state as an apparatus to pacify local resistance, subjugate the 'natives', and extract surplus primarily for the benefit of colonial settlers and the colonial metropolis.

The partition and sharing out of the continent by seven European colonial powers carved up, constituted, and forged the modern nation states of Africa.[363] The new state frontiers, drawn without regard to the interests of the affected populations, often artificially split same communities into two or three different colonial systems. The creation of a modern economic sector and a centralised administrative system accompanied the brutal political subjugation, racial

---

[362] Lovejoy, Paul E., 2000, p.4.

[363] The seven European colonial powers were Belgium, France, Germany, Great Britain, Italy, Portugal and Spain.

oppression, and economic exploitation of Africa by Europe during the colonial period. This facilitated colonial control of territory and extraction of wealth therefrom. Further, the patchwork of European colonial dominions laid the foundation of the fragmentation and disunity of Africa as the colonies eventually evolved into independent nation states, shaping the present political landscape of the continent.

European colonialism compounded the extensive negative impact of centuries of slavery. Upon taking possession of Africa, Europe imposed an alien superstructure, dominated the base, and interrupted and distorted Africa's indigenous development. It combined European technology, knowhow, and organisation with African labour and natural resources for 'on-site' production of wealth and its direct transfer to Europe and elsewhere in the world through exportation.

In so doing, the colonial system brought Africa into dependence on the European dominated world of 'markets and market prices'. The resultant transfer of wealth and profits from Africa to Europe was done to the disservice of African interests with far reaching long-term consequences for the continent. A seminal work by Walter Rodney, *How Europe Underdeveloped Africa*, articulates Europe's major contribution to Africa's prolonged stagnation and relative underdevelopment through five centuries of slavery and colonialism that embedded the political economy of the exploitation and transfer of African resources and wealth overseas.[364]

---

[364] Rodney, Walter, How Europe Underdeveloped Africa, Bogle-L'Ouverture Publications, London and Tanzanian Publishing House, Dar-Es-Salaam, 1973.

Another work, Joseph Conrad's controversial short novel, *Heart of Darkness*, depicts the extreme cruelty and brutal atrocities that the pioneers of the European colonial project meted out to Africans in their own homeland.[365] A prominent African critic has castigated the work as a 'racist or colonialist parable' that *de-humanises* and *depersonalises* Africans, *denies* them "language and culture" and portrays them as *primitive*, "innately irrational and violent."[366] Despite the pervasive racism that features sharply throughout the narration of the story, however, the novella represents a graphic and 'powerful indictment of the evils of imperialism' and the "savage repression" of colonialism.[367]

Africa has yet to overcome the devastation that the evil duo of slavery and colonialism wrought on its physical, psychic and human geography. Colonialism rubbed salt on the gaping wounds inflicted by slavery and perpetrated a crippling injury that shackled and warped the normal development of the continent. It carved out territories, divided up peoples, tore down communities, and created, *inter alia*, the colonial state as an artificial transplant of the European state system in Africa. In the process, it cast in stone the present geopolitical map of the continent with its lasting legacy of political fragmentation, ethnic splintering,

---

[365] Conrad, Joseph, Heart of Darkness (serialized in 1899 in Blackwood's Magazine), Penguin Books Ltd.,1902.

[366] Achebe, Chinua, An Image of Africa: Racism in Conrad's *Heart of Darkness*, Chancellor's Lecture, University of Massachusetts, Amherst, February 1975 and Hugh Curtler, Achebe on Conrad: Racism and Greatness in Heart of Darkness, March 1997, Conradiana 29 (1): 30-40.

[367] Ashcroft, Bill, ed., Key Concepts in Postcolonial Studies, London, Rutledge, 1998.

irredentist movements and boundary disputes. The indelible impact of European colonialism, thus imprinted, continues to reverberate throughout the continent today.

11.2 The African Nation-State as a European Graft

"Inspired by a deep, keen feeling of nationalism" and driven by the "growth of national consciousness," the emergence of the nation-state, in diverse forms and with various types of government, has been a constant factor of political life in Europe ever since the breakup of the Roman Empire.[368] The modern nation-state has evolved from its beginnings in the Westphalian political order of the sovereign territorial nation-state[369] "that claims the monopoly of the legitimate use of physical force within a given territory"[370] to enforce rule of law and protect security of citizens. This Weberian conception of the state delegitimises the acquisition and use of force by non-state entities without authorisation or sanction from the state. In addition to the capacity to ensure

---

[368] Macmillan, Harold, *The Wind of Change*, speech to the Parliament of South Africa, Cape Town, 3 February 1960, in Edward Humphreys (ed.) Great Speeches: Words that Changed the World, London, 2010, p. 105.

[369] The Treaty of Westphalia of 1648 ended the Thirty Years' War (1618-1648) that devastated Europe and established peace by promoting a balance of power among the emerging nation-states. It marked the end of religious wars in Europe and the decisive religious and diplomatic transition from the medieval to the modern period.

[370] Weber, Max, *"Politics as a Vocation,'* *From Max Weber: Essays in Sociology*, ed. and trans. Hans Heinrich Gerth and C. Wright Mills (New York: Oxford University Press, 1958), p. 77.

the rule of law and security of citizens, the monopoly of ownership and use of legitimate force bequeaths the national state with a potent instrument of coercion to impose its authority, its will, and its ways on society, for good or ill.

Over several centuries, the progressive accumulation of capital and the concentration of the instruments of coercion catalysed state formation and reinforced the politics of nationalism in Europe, especially towards the end of the eighteenth and the beginning of the nineteenth centuries.[371] The industrial revolution in England and the political revolution in France in the nineteenth century operated to accelerate the interactive processes of state formation and nationalism that reconfigured Europe. The economic revolution produced the capitalist mode of production, the political revolution greatly strengthened the system of centralism, and the two revolutions "combined to give nationalism a new and mighty force."[372]

However, nationalism 'as the force of the future' proved a two-edged sword. Paradoxically, it carried within its kernel the seeds of both liberation and destruction. It was a powerful force of emancipation from the stultifying backwardness and serfdom of the feudal system. At the same time, it evolved into a mighty force of destruction immersing nation-states in terrible wars of reciprocal annihilation, as tragically played out in the essentially intra-European two world wars of the last century. The establishment of the European Union (EU) and the drive towards European supranationalism during the last half century have, through the gradual building

---

[371] Tilly, Charles, Coercion, Capital, and European States, AD 990-1992, Malden, MA: Blackwell Publishers, 1990.

[372] Davidson, Basil, 1989, p. 34.

up of political cooperation, an integrated internal market, and shared pan-European sovereignty, tamed the aggressive propensity of nationalism and secured the peace among the major European powers since the end of the World War II.

Essentially implanted from Europe, the colonial state system that divided Africa also gave birth to Pan-Africanism. The Pan-African movement originated in the desire to liberate the continent from the yoke of European colonial rule and build unity among the evolving and newly independent states. The idea first emerged in the black communities of African descent in the Caribbean and the United States of America (USA) as the path to unravel the deracination wrought by slavery and attain emancipation from the enduring scourge of racism through a return to the roots in Africa.[373] The Pan-Africanist project was joined in, embraced, and eventually taken over by African nationalist leaders, most notably Kwame Nkrumah, Julius Nyerere, Modibo Keita, Ahmed Sékou Touré, and Gamal Abdel Nasser, who championed the cause of African liberation from European colonial rule and advocated the unity of African states upon accession to independence.

The twin objectives of the decolonisation and unity of the continent stirred the Pan-African movement to coalesce and create an organisation of an all-African union, the Organisation of African Unity (OAU), in 1963. The OAU aimed, among other things, to "promote the unity and solidarity of the African states"; to "coordinate and

---

[373] The pioneers and most influential advocates of Pan-Africanism were Edward W. Blyden (West Indies, 1832-1812), Marcus M. Garvey (Jamaica, 1887-1940) and William B. Du Bois (USA, 1868-1963).

intensify their cooperation and efforts to achieve a better life for the African peoples"; and to "eradicate all forms of colonialism from Africa".[374] The anticolonial struggle of the African peoples, spearheaded by the nationalist movements was thus, waged to liberate and unify Africa and the Pan-African Movement and the establishment of the OAU were an essential element of that struggle.

Evolving into little more than a sort of "fraternity of heads of state", however, the OAU lacked the political will and institutional capacity to tackle Africa's most pressing problems, such as conflicts, insecurity, underdevelopment and poverty.[375] It fell short of much of its remit during three and a half decades of lackluster existence. With the entire continent virtually decolonised and apartheid approaching an end in South Africa by the onset of the 1990s, there were internal and external pressures for change in policy, strategy, and structure to enable and better advance the economic integration and political unity of Africa.

The African Economic Community (AEC) was established in June 1991 to, *inter alia*, "promote economic, social and cultural development and the integration of African economies" and "coordinate and harmonise policies among existing and future economic communities in order to foster the gradual establishment of the Community".[376]

---

[374] OAU Charter, Addis Ababa, 25 May 1963, Article II.1&2, p. 3.

[375] Babu, Abdul Rahman Mohamed, "The Eritrean Question in the Context of African Conflicts and Superpower Rivalries", in Lionel Cliffe and Basil Davidson (eds.) The Long Struggle of Eritrea for Independence and Constructive Peace, Nottingham: Russell Press Ltd., 1988, p. 47.

[376] OAU, Treaty Establishing the African Economic Community, Abuja, 03 June 1991, Art. 4.1. (a) & (d).

The adoption of the Sirte Declaration in September 1999, the Constitutive Act of the African Union (AU) in Lomé in July 2000[377] and the Durban Declaration in July 2002 marked the transition of the OAU into the AU.

African states thus launched the AU to rearrange interstate relations and reset the continent on the path to economic integration and political union based on democratic principles and institutions, good governance, and respect for human rights. The strengthening of unity, cohesion and solidarity among the states and peoples of Africa, coupled with the promotion of peace, security, and stability in the continent, would serve as the foundation for Africa's rapid development and integration. African unity, as the embodiment of the Pan Africanist ideal, offers Africa the possibility to undo the fragmentation, disunity, and interstate disputes inherited from the colonial era and strive for continental unity, solidarity, and common policies. Political union and economic integration would help Africa surmount its marginalisation, enhance its role in the international system, and tackle its pressing political, economic, and security challenges.

In the era of globalisation, regionalisation has emerged as an enduring feature of the international system. The formation of various regional groupings, with their complex interrelations, has come to dominate the prevailing global geopolitical regime. In this context, the AU strives to adopt the European model of regionalisation and to reproduce

---

[377] The Constitutive Act of the African Union was adopted by the Heads of State and Government of the Member States of the Organization of African Unity (OAU) in Lomé, Togo, on 11 July 2000.

the achievements of Europe in Africa while the EU seeks to promote, sell or even impose its model of regionalism as the ideal type for peaceful development, regional integration and political convergence in Africa.

Much as the EU seeks, in a drive to position itself as a significant player in world politics and as a global model for regional integration, to shape the AU in accordance with its "values, interests and identity,"[378] the AU strives to replicate the EU model in the pursuit of the economic integration and political union of Africa. In other words, the EU serves both as a positive 'external cogency' and as an 'extra-regional echoing' for the AU in the domains of peace and security, regional economic integration, and supranationalism.[379] The structure, internal functioning, and development of the AU have therefore been heavily influenced by its relationship with the EU and reinforced by their partnership under the Joint Africa-EU Strategy (JAES), aimed to pursue enhanced political and policy dialogue and effective technical cooperation in eight thematic areas.[380]

---

[378] Söderbaum, Fredrik and Patrik Stålgren, The EU and the Global South, in Söderbaum, Fredrik and Patrik Stålgren (eds.) The European Union and the Global South, Boulder and London: Lynne Rienner Publishers, Inc., 2010, p.1.

[379] Hänggi, Heiner, Interregionalism: Empirical and Theoretical Perspectives, Paper prepared for the workshop "Dollars, Democracy and Trade: External Influence on Economic Integration in the Americas," Los Angeles, CA, May 18, 2000, The Pacific Council on International Policy, Los Angeles, The Center for Applied Policy Research, Munich.

[380] Council of the European Union, Africa-EU Strategic Partnership: A Joint Strategy for Cooperation, Lisbon, 9 December 2007. The eight thematic partnerships are (1) Peace and Security, (2) Democratic Governance and Human Rights, (3) Trade, Regional

Upon decolonisation, the newly independent African states were, modelled essentially after the colonial metropolitan state, mere duplications of the historically evolved structure of the nation-state as a European construct.[381] Emergent Africa inherited the European state system as a central institution characterised by the exclusive possession and exercise of legitimate force within society. Further, it inherited the oppressive, exploitative, and authoritarian features of the colonial state. The African elites who championed the cause of liberation acceded to the colonial state apparatus, retained it intact, and presided over and benefited from its European dominated modern economic sector.

The African elites, who themselves were products of the colonial system of education, made no discernible attempts to restructure the colonial economy, modify the repressive features of the colonial state or integrate the postcolonial state to the indigenous sociocultural settings of African society. They lacked the will, the autonomy, and the capacity to renegotiate its dysfunctional aspects and exogenous character to suit the needs and cater to the aspirations of the African peoples. Most of the elites merely replaced the colonial rulers at the top of the hierarchy, limiting the benefits of independence to a small minority and, consequently, generating contestation to their monopoly of the possession and use of legitimate force.

Integration and Infrastructure, (4) MDGs, (5) Energy, (6) Climate Change and Environment, (7) Migration, Mobility and Employment and (8) Science, Information Society and Space.

[381] Young, Crawford, *The African Colonial State and Its Political Legacy*, The Precarious Balance: State-Society Relations in Africa, eds., Donald Rothchild and Naomi Chazan, Westview Press, Boulder, 1988, p. 52.

The East-West rivalry during the Cold War aggravated the situation of the new African states and dented the effort to build democratic, accountable, and effective governance structures, to develop the national economies, and to deliver prosperity. The East-West confrontation, the contest for global hegemony between the Soviet-led Eastern Bloc and the US-led Western Bloc, turned Africa into a battleground of ideological contention and proxy warfare. It used African regimes, and liberation and opposition movements, as pawns in the geopolitical game and fuelled interstate conflicts and civil wars. This denied much of Africa a modicum of peace, security, and stability essential to construct democratic governance and achieve sustainable development.

The ideological split between the Soviet Union and China and the consequent Sino-Soviet rivalry for protégés in Africa compounded the negative impact of the East-West rivalry. Ironically, the end of the Cold War made matters even worse for certain states which were propped up by one or the other superpower on account of their erstwhile importance in the calculus of Soviet-US competition in Africa. The fall of the Berlin Wall accelerated the weakening and eventual collapse of the states that lost their coveted roles and external support in the context of the fading strategy of East-West hostility. Notable examples of such states include Colonel Mengistu Haile Mariam's Ethiopia, General Mohamed Siad Barre's Somalia, and Mobutu Sese Seko's Zaire.

In a nutshell, slavery looted Africa of millions of its productive population uprooted in their prime years, drained the continent's creative energy and sapped its internal capacity to develop. Colonialism disrupted Africa's indigenous progression, plundered its natural and human resources, and retarded its development. The ideological battles of the Cold War fought on African soil disoriented Africa's priorities, destabilised its polities, and undermined its development. These however, were only the exogenous historical factors that contributed to the underdevelopment of Africa.

11.3 A Dysfunctional Predatory State

The disposition of postcolonial regimes to serve as pawns in the East-West conflict, domestic challenges to their undemocratic rule, and the attendant destabilisation plagued the continent and contributed to the weakness of the African state. Burdened by these historical factors, internal features diminished the capacity of the postcolonial state, often described as neo-colonial, to build functional governance structures and institutions. As a result, the typical state failed to establish enduring stability, achieve sustainable development, and deliver public wellbeing for the majority of its citizens over the course of half a century of independence.

The great struggle against European colonial domination in Africa was as much a struggle for national independence as it was one for social liberation. Attainment of self-determination would signify capture of state power and empowerment of the people. Certainly, there was much initial anticipation that the movements that spearheaded the struggle to end European colonial rule would, once triumphant, be both democratic and developmental.

The institution of a democratic state would have made the exercise of real self-determination possible for the African peoples emerging out of the darkness of colonial subjugation. Further, it would have empowered them to form governments of their choice, to actively participate in national policy and decision making processes, and to manage their own affairs. Indeed, a developmental state would have been able to establish "the economic and political relationships that can support sustained" economic development[382] and steer "investment in a way that promotes a certain solidaristic vision of national economy."[383]

Upon accession to independence and seizure of state power, however, the early promise of the nationalist project to establish a democratic and developmental state foundered. The postcolonial African state merely replicated the European colonial state. Paradoxically, the duplicate state manifests both underdeveloped and overdeveloped features.[384]

In an effort to perpetuate their hold on power, the new national ruling elites increasingly entrenched the predatory, patrimonial (neo-patrimonial), and authoritarian features of the colonial state. Such a state of affairs has given rise to the general characterisation of the postcolonial African state as "highly centralised, authoritarian and self-serving."[385] This characterisation is, in the main, consistent with its essentially predatory, patrimonial, and authoritarian features. These features underlie the dismal record of failure that has made

---

[382] Chang, Ha-Joon, The Economic Theory of the Developmental State, 1999, p. 183.

[383] Lariaux, M., *The French Developmental State as Myth and Moral Ambition*, Woo-Cumings, Meredith (ed.), The Developmental State, Cornell University Press, 1999, p. 24.

[384] Callaghy, Thomas M., *The State and the Development of Capitalism in Africa: Theoretical, Historical, and Comparative Reflections*, The Precarious Balance: State-Society Relations in Africa, eds., Donald Rothschild and Naomi Chazan, pp. 67-99.

[385] Bereketeab, Redie, 2009, p. 13.

the postcolonial African state the object of considerable debate and critical commentary.

Stepping into the shoes of their colonial predecessors upon independence, the new rulers set out to "provide public goods, such as protection," but only managed to "extort taxes for their own ends" and delivered reduced "levels of both output and popular welfare."[386] In some states, "entire sectors have been built up to feast upon public systems built originally for public purposes."[387] The predatory state sanctioned "kleptocracy" and diverted "public resources away from public goods to the pet projects of bureaucrats and politicians" rather than maximising revenue by investing money well and taxing free traders."[388] The prototype predatory state extorts at different levels of the supply chain to fill its coffers without regard to the harm that such extortion at multiple junctions does to the country, the people, and the fabric of society.

In general, predation has spanned the state system in postcolonial Africa. By definition, a predatory state "is not able to, or willing to, or even interested in, protecting the interests of its citizens" as its "primary interest is self-preservation and self-aggrandisement."[389] Frequently shared

---

[386] Moselle, Boaz and Benjamin Polak, A *Model of a Predatory State*, The Journal of Law, Economics and Organization, Vol. 17, Issue 1, Oxford University Press, 2001 http://jleo.oxfordjournals.org/content/17/1/1.abstract

[387] Galbraith, James K., The Predatory State, Free Press Publishers, 2008, p. 146.

[388] Chakraverti, Sauvik, *Predatory State – The Black Hole of Social Science*, Times of India, New Delhi, 22 September 1999 http://www.ccsindia.org/ccsindia/people_sc_predatorystate.htm.

[389] Srinivasan, Rajeev, The Predatory State (Part I of II), Rediff on Net, 16 August 2002 http://www.hvk.org/articles/0802/137.html

as a common characteristic of states "in a rudimentary state of development," the ruler of a predatory state is often "a dictator or a charismatic leader [...] or autocratic life president" who provides public goods: law and order and basic economic infrastructure, such as roads to facilitate production."[390]

In addition to being predatory, the typical postcolonial African state possesses strong patrimonial or neo-patrimonial attributes. In a patrimonial state, political power resides in and flows from the leader; and the leader considers himself as the ruler of the country and behaves as its proprietor, dispensing with the land, people and funds at his or her discretion.[391] Public and private affairs are blended and public assets and resources are widely used "by officials who manage them."[392] Under such circumstances, nepotism provides the only access to opportunity, and corruption sets in as the default mode of survival and pervades the entire state system and the whole gamut of parastatal economic enterprises.

In a patrimonial (neo-patrimonial) state, the ruler exercises absolute dominion over the political and economic life of the country and the people. The ruler's power derives literally from 'the barrel of the gun' rather than the consent of the people and is sustained by forcible repression. Based on the control of the military, intelligence, and security

---

[390] Frimpong-Ansah, Jonathan H., The Vampire State in Africa: The Political Economy of Decline in Ghana, Africa World Press, 1992, p. 46-47. http://www.amazon.com/Vampire-State-Africa-Political-Economy/dp/0865432791.

[391] Pipes, Richard, Russia under the Old Regime, New York: Charles Scribner's Sons, 1974.

[392] Hungwe, Kedmon N. & Chipo, Essay Review, Africa Works: Disorder as Political Instrument, Zambezia (2000), XXVII (ii), p. 270.

apparatuses and "the diffuse fear instilled among the masses by the security forces," the ruler's hegemony extends to "every level of government" where "formal institutions" or 'chains of command' do not reflect the real location, distribution, or exercise of power.[393] For all practical purposes, "government is personal, and government administration is an extension of the ruler."[394]

The patrimonial (neo-patrimonial) state is invariably autocratic and centrally controlled from top down. Further, the absence of "neutral" administrative institutions and "rational decision making procedures", in the form of effective, "ideal-type Weberian bureaucracies", provides for an "instrumentally profitable lack of distinction between the civic/public and private/personal spheres".[395] There are no enforceable constitutional limitations, mitigating legislative procedures or operational bureaucratic norms to impede the arbitrary exercise of authority, constrain the impulsive decisions or delimit the discretionary powers of the ruler.

The predatory and patrimonial (neo-patrimonial) state is also generally authoritarian. Political power is concentrated "in the hands of a leader or small elite that is not constitutionally responsible to the body of the people"; the leader often exercises "power arbitrarily and without regard to existing bodies of law"; and "cannot be replaced by citizens choosing freely among various competitors in elections".[396]

---

[393]   Meditz, Sandra & Merrill, Tim (eds.), Zaire - A country Study, Chapter 1: The Durability of the Patrimonial State, December 1993. http://www.country-data.com/cgi-bin/query/r-15005.html

[394]   Ibid.

[395]   Ibid.

[396]   Encyclopaedia   Britannica   http://www.britannica.com/ EBchecked/topic/44640/authoritarianism

In extreme cases, the authoritarian leader blends with the state, à la "*Moi, c'est l'État*", or I am the State.

Necessarily autocratic, the authoritarian state often usurps national symbols, monopolises total power, controls the media, strives to restrict public access to independent sources of information, and criminalises political dissent. As a rule, it relies on the armed, security forces, and the unmitigated use of violence and coercion to stay in power, frequently resorting to brutal repression in the event that intimidation proves insufficient. An authoritarian leader is usually neither freely and fairly elected by, nor accountable to, the people and, in most cases, rules according to his whims enforced by the power of the gun. This state of affairs has become a constant scourge on the African political landscape, including Eritrea's.

11.4 Challenges of the Postcolonial State

The European colonial project launched in Berlin in 1885 bequeathed Africa with a legacy of fragmentation that has fuelled conflict and insecurity throughout much of the continent. Beyond the colonial legacy, however, contemporary Africa faces several problems with multiple causes. The focus here is on the principal challenges caused or made worse by patent failures of the postcolonial state, plagued by a crippling mix of predatory, patrimonial, and authoritarian attributes, to win legitimacy, deliver democratic governance, and attain sustainable development. Willy-nilly, heads of weak governments in fragile states violate the social contract with impunity and flout legitimacy; they pursue the politics of self-aggrandisement, division, exclusion, and marginalisation of segments in society. The destabilising consequences exasperate insecurity, worsen poverty, and degrade the human condition.

The concentration of power, resources, and opportunities in the hands of a privileged few, small elite, or a minority group in the capital fuels alienation among the neglected majority in the centre or marginalised communities in the periphery. Alienation sows disaffection, fans the flames of discontent, and tends to incite resistance. The often-predictable automatic resort of authoritarian regimes to heavy-handed repression of legitimate protest or clampdown of dissent frequently backfires and provokes violent popular uprising, for repression often breeds rebellion. Armed non-state entities emerge to challenge the state's monopoly of power and the legitimacy of its use of force with a countervailing force of their own legitimised in terms of the pursuit of justice. Wars and conflicts compound the continent's challenges.

The centre-periphery dichotomy often operates to amplify existing social, ethnic, national, regional or religious divides, inflame associated tensions and antagonise conflict as marginalised segments of society whose interests autocratic regimes neglect take up arms to redress grievances. The resort to armed rebellion and the resultant civil wars and violent conflicts tend to destabilise the state and stoke human insecurity. They perpetrate underdevelopment, aggravate poverty, and hamper the campaign to eradicate common diseases. Furthermore, the devastating consequences of climate change exacerbate an already precarious human condition. Wanting in commitment, short in resources, and lacking in institutional capacity, the typical postcolonial African state is unwilling and/or unable to tackle these challenges.

Interstate wars and civil conflicts of varying intensities of violence continue to destabilise much of Africa: from the Maghreb to Zimbabwe, and Somalia to Mali; and from Darfur to the Kivus, and the Ogaden to the Niger Delta. These deadly conflicts decimate lives, destroy livelihoods, disrupt communities, and squander opportunities for development. According to a report by the United Nations Development Programme (UNDP), Sub-Saharan Africa lost over 1.5 million people between 1990 and 1999 due to armed conflict.[397]

Violent conflicts have a dreadful impact on the most vulnerable segments of society, especially women and children, with children making up half of all civilian war casualties.[398] The UNDP report estimates the astounding human toll for the decade: about 2 million children killed, 6 million permanently disabled or seriously injured, 1 million orphaned or separated from their families, 20 million forced to flee their homes to live as internally displaced persons (IDPs) or as refugees, and 10,000 killed or maimed by landmines every year.[399]

Underdevelopment breeds poverty and diseases. The prevailing state of poverty perpetrates a situation in which approximately half of the people in Sub-Saharan Africa live on less than one US dollar a day while 33 per cent of the continent's people suffer from malnutrition.[400] An estimated 20,000 Africans die every day due to extreme poverty manifested in chronic food shortages, malnutrition, hunger,

---

[397] UNDP, UN Human Development Report 2002
[398] Food 4 Africa: Facts on Poverty in Africa, 2009, 1
[399] UNDP, UN Human Development Report 2002
[400] Food 4 Africa: Facts on Poverty in Africa, 2009, 1

and affliction by common diseases.[401] The World Bank estimates that HIV/AIDS, malaria, respiratory infections, tuberculosis, measles, etc., killed about 10.8 million people in Sub-Saharan Africa in 2000.[402]

Too many Africans continue to perish from easily preventable diseases for lack of rudimentary health care or access to ordinary drugs. When not instantly fatal, common diseases, abetted by widespread hunger and chronic malnutrition, emaciate bodies, waste lives, destroy livelihoods, devastate families, and wreck communities. The great majority of people in large parts of Africa, locked in a daily struggle for survival, compete for increasingly scarce resources to eke out the food, water and energy they need to sustain life at the very margins of death. Millions of Africans subsist in an extremely precarious estate of permanent agony, as an Eritrean proverb puts it, just '*below the living and above the dead*'.[403]

Meanwhile, climate change, a serious global problem that affects all humanity, is aggravating the continent's predicament and hampering progress in its development agenda. Presently, "22 of Africa's 53 [now 54] countries are severely threatened by the direct and indirect impacts of global warming".[404] Climate change is provoking variations in rainfall patterns, causing the expansion of the Sahara Desert, destroying biodiversity, upsetting ecosystems and damaging

---

[401] The Foundation for Community Inspiration: Factsheet, 1

[402] Data available at http://www.worldbank.org

[403] *Kab zelewu ntaHti kab zimotu nlaEli.* (ካብ ዘለዉ. ንታሕቲ: ካብ ዚሞቱ ንላዕሊ.::)

[404] Shelton, Garth, FOCAC IV – New Opportunities for Africa, 22 December 2009. http://www.focac.org/eng/dsjbzjhy/t647035. htm.

the natural environment. In the continent's semiarid regions and the Sahel Belt in particular, massive deforestation, land degradation, deepening waterbed, and increasing aridity are threatening to disrupt traditional subsistence farming and pastoral grazing.

Undoubtedly, climate change is wreaking havoc to much of Africa's natural habitat and diminishing its carrying capacity. It is disrupting the ecological equilibrium and the indigenous flora and fauna that sustain sedentary agriculture, agro-pastoralism and nomadic pastoralism, the mainstays of most national economies. In effect, the degradation of the environment worsens the vulnerability of Africa's largely rural communities subsisting precariously on what they raise supplemented by what they gather from their immediate environs.

Compared to both the developed industrial countries of the Global North and the emerging economies of the Global South, Africa has the least to do with the causes but the most to endure from the effects of climate change. Accounting for "2-3 per cent of the world's carbon dioxide emissions from energy and industrial sources, and 7 per cent if emissions from land use (forests) are taken into account",[405] Africa contributes very little to greenhouse gas (GHG) emissions associated with global warming.[406] Both in absolute and relative terms, Africa as a region generates the lowest level of greenhouse gases, benefits the least from the lucrative

---

[405] UN Economic Commission for Africa http://www.uneca.org/ harnessing/chapters/chap1/Chapter1_33_38.pdf.

[406] The principal greenhouse gases emitted are carbon dioxide (CO_2), methane (CH_4), nitrous oxide (N_2O) and fluorinated gases http:// www.epa.gov/climatechange/emissions/index.html.

processes that cause their emissions, and suffers the most from their repercussions.

Meanwhile, weak national governments and impoverished communities lack the capacity to mitigate or cope up with the consequences of climate change. This has been the case to date at the level of individual countries, the Regional Economic Communities (RECs) and the continent at large. Divergent national economic interests among key member states have hampered the African Union from adopting and pursuing a coherent joint policy. The apparent lack of internal unity at the 2009 Copenhagen Climate Change negotiations, for instance, undercut the African Common Position (ACP), which took three years to evolve, and undermined the continent's bargaining position.[407] Because of the inability to sustain the common position, the African Group failed to advance its principal demands in the negotiations with the major actors.

The Conference of the African Heads of State on Climate Change (CAHOSCC) articulated five key demands as the Common Position of the African Group. These demands can be summarised as follows: 1) financial compensation; 2) adherence to the principle of common but differentiated responsibilities; 3) pursuit of two track negotiations keeping the distinction between the Kyoto Protocol and the UN Framework Convention on Climate Change; 4) implementation of the Bali Action Plan; and 5) substantial reductions of greenhouse gas emissions by developed

---

[407] Hoste, Jean-Christophe, *Where Was United Africa in the Climate Change Negotiations?* Paper presented at a conference on the Dynamics of Internal African Decision Making, Pretoria, 8-9 November 2010.

countries in two stages, specifically, by 40 per cent below the 1990 levels by 2020 and by 80 per cent to 95 per cent below the 1990 levels by 2050.[408]

The challenge is too difficult to tackle and too big to surmount by the lone efforts of individual African countries. Beyond the formal adoption of a common position to leverage the emergence of multilateral consensus for more effective global action to combat climate change and overcome its dire effects, therefore, Africa needs to develop, sustain, and implement a coherent internal strategy of its own that is national in design, continental in scope and regional in content. Success in the endeavour would depend primarily on African will, commitment, solidarity and leadership. However, it would also require generous support from Africa's development partners in the form of financial assistance, capacity building and transfer of technology.

11.5 A State in Crisis

In the beginning, the end of colonial rule in Africa raised great expectations and high hopes for a better life. Unfortunately, decolonisation did not bring about the anticipated benefits for most Africans. Half a century after independence, Africa watchers, scholars, and commentators agree that the typical postcolonial African state faces a profound crisis.

Founded on the remnants of, and maligned by, the indelible imprints of the colonial state, the postcolonial African state has been unable to cast away its inherent oppressive and exploitative features inherited virtually intact

---

[408] http://www.issafrica.org/dynamic/administration/file_manager/ file_links/3OCT09.PDF?link_id=4056&slin

from its predecessor. The colonial state aimed to serve the interests of the colonisers at the expense of the colonised peoples. It is not surprising therefore that the unreformed prototype postcolonial state in Africa, functioning under the aegis of an oppressive neo-colonial elite, has failed to provide for the needs, promote the wellbeing, cater to the aspirations and safeguard the security of the African peoples. Bereft of democratic legitimacy, pursuing the irresponsible politics of exclusion and presiding over dysfunctional institutions, it is quite apparent that several states are failing or have already failed.

Dismal performance and proven inability to deliver have alienated and rendered the typical African state irrelevant. Oblivious of the imperatives of social compact, certain states are at war with their own people. Unable to govern with the consent of the governed and scornful of their will, some states perpetrate their despotic rule and seek to enforce submission through repression and intimidation, creating a climate of fear and insecurity. As Agbese and Kieh noted:

> *The typical African state is noted more as a repressive, brutal, corrupt, and inefficient entity than a mechanism for the promotion of the collective well-being of its citizens. Consequently, the modern African state remains largely irrelevant to the needs, interests, and aspirations of the people.*[409]

There is a growing recognition that the typical postcolonial African state, grossly inept and hell-bent on self-preservation

---

[409] Agbese, P. Ogaba and Kieh Jr., G. Klay, Eds., Reconstituting the State in Africa, Palgrave Macmillan, New York, N.Y., 2007, p.4

at all cost, has proved incapable of performing the basic functions of a modern state. Further, it has been unable to overcome its *crisis of legitimacy, delivery* and *relevance* and engender its revival. Unmindful of the needs, contemptuous of the concerns, and alienated from the daily life of the people, the prototype postcolonial African state today lacks a firm social foundation and a modicum of popular support, as illustrated by recent events in North Africa that have swept away long-lasting dictatorial regimes.

The typical contemporary African state tends to be authoritarian, repressive and dysfunctional. Often characterised by gross incompetence and rampant corruption, it lacks legitimacy, accountability, and transparency in setting public policy, making decisions, and managing national resources. Unwilling and unable to govern in accordance with the rule of law and based on popular consensus, it imposes the rule of caprice and resorts to repression. Consequently, it is weak, unstable, and insecure. Such a state of affairs has rendered nation building, state construction, and socioeconomic development in Africa essentially a perpetual "work in progress" in some countries and a project for the future in others.

The postcolonial African state has, on balance, produced leaders far too few of the likes of, Julius Nyerere of Tanzania, Nelson Mandela of South Africa, and Léopold Sédar Senghor of Senegal, who willingly yielded power and allowed its peaceful transfer to new leadership. Conversely, it has produced too many of the likes of, Jean-Bédel Bokassa of the Central African Republic, Mobutu Sese Seko of Zaire, Idi Amin Dada of Uganda, Mohamed Siad Barre of Somalia, Mengistu Haile Mariam of Ethiopia, Zine El Abidine Ben Ali of Tunisia, Hosni Mubarak of Egypt, and Muammar Gaddafi of Libya. These dictators overplayed their hands and, once chased out of power, headed into exile, jail, or execution. They harmed their societies, disgraced themselves, and most ended up rendering their immediate families stateless.

There are others, like Robert Mugabe in Zimbabwe, Yoweri Museveni in Uganda, Paul Kagame in Rwanda, the late Meles Zenawi in Ethiopia, and Isaias Afwerki in Eritrea. These rulers have shown a desire to continue at the helm without the bother of definite term limits, or even to stay there for life. As revolutionary leaders of triumphant armed liberation movements that overthrew colonial or autocratic regimes, they have disappointed initial expectations that they would set the pace for democratic development, constitutional limits on the tenure of office, and the peaceful democratic transition of power.

Reluctance to yield power operates to undermine peaceful succession, invites the turbulence of unconstitutional change of government, and risks destabilisation. In terms of harshness of authoritarian rule, brutality of repression, and unwillingness to relinquish power, the great majority of postcolonial African leaders have become autocrats determined to 'die on the throne' or invite ouster by force. The adverse fallout of trying to 'stick it out' has been a significant factor of instability retarding the evolution of constitutional order in the continent and the failure to achieve economic development and advance the wellbeing of the people, especially in the countries run by the most autocratic regimes.

As stated at the beginning of this chapter, Africa is rich in natural resources. It possesses vast equatorial forests, immense tropical savannahs, huge agricultural prospects, and considerable livestock potential as well as extensive reserves of proven oil, natural gas, minerals, and marine wealth. It holds a substantial share of the world's reserves of platinum (89 per cent), diamond (60 per cent), cobalt (53 per cent), zirconium (38 per cent), gold (28 per cent), vanadium (23 per cent), uranium (15 per cent), manganese (14 per cent), and titanium (10 per cent).[410] In addition, Africa has a great human resource in its mainly young and rapidly growing population that stands at nearly one billion strong. Further, the AU and the 54 African states represent a large voice pregnant with the potential to play a powerful role in the resolution of crucial global issues in international and multilateral forums.

Yet, the continent's considerable endowment of natural and human resources has not translated into a decent standard of living for the majority of its people. Despite its great potential, Africa continues to barely subsist at the periphery of the global economy and cling on to the very margins of general world affairs and international politics. Lately, however, Africa has attracted renewed world attention that has resulted in the conclusion of a series of strategic partnership agreements with the EU and Asia's old and rising powers of Japan, China, and India. This renewed global interest in the continent may merely herald a new scramble for Africa's resources and markets, unless African leaders get their act together and turn the opportunity to generate a new impetus for Africa's development and improved role in the world.

The monopoly of political power and access to economic resources and social services in the hands of small ruling elites

---

[410] Jonah, Sam. 2005:19, quoted in Manji, Firoze, and Stephen Marks, eds.2007, African *Perspectives on China*, Nairobi and Oxford: Fahamu.

or minority groups, combined with brutal state repression and lack of balanced development have driven the majority of the African peoples into the quagmire of constant insecurity, widespread misery, and deepening despair. Mere survival has become a daily struggle for the great majority of Africans in the continent facing extreme poverty, suffering from preventable diseases, and succumbing to premature death.

The object of the exclusive focus of this chapter on the situation in Africa is to provide a general context for the present state of affairs in Eritrea, and not to single out or malign the continent *per se*, as Africa does not have a monopoly on contemporary state fragility or failure. Perhaps, varying in extent but certainly with comparable intensity, Europe, Asia, and Latin America have also produced their shares of fragile or failed states, with similar horrific repercussions on the human condition. The former Yugoslavia, Afghanistan, Yemen and Haiti stand out as extreme instances of the intercontinental reality of the phenomenon of state fragility or failure.

In the specific African setting, however, there can be no denying that the pervasive malaise troubling the continent today is deeply rooted in its colonial past. The ghost of colonial legacy continues to haunt the contemporary African state. Nonetheless, one can explain the unmitigated persistence of the malaise to date primarily as a function of the chronic dearth of democratic governance, general economic mismanagement, and rampant corruption that malign the prototype postcolonial African state. Such flaws, in turn, operate to undermine nation building, undercut state construction, hinder national development, and induce state fragility.

To be fair, there are positive steps towards the gradual introduction of democratic rule and the peaceful transfer of power in accordance with constitutional provisions and term limits taking place in some African countries, notably Botswana, Ghana, Tanzania, Cape Verde, Mauritius, Seychelles, South Africa, etc. Despite such encouraging developments however, the overall image of Africa remains negative. There prevails a tendency to cast much of the continent as if it rotates in an axis of undemocratic governance and revolves around a vicious cycle of wars, conflicts and insecurity breeding underdevelopment, environmental degradation, poverty, and diseases. Clearly, Africa is changing and making forward strides.

This chapter provides the backdrop for the analysis and commentary in the chapters that follow starting with the next one, *Eritrea: The Future of Africa that Works?* After the experience of three decades of so many 'false starts' and deep disappointments with the performance of the prototype state in post-independence Africa, there was much anticipation that Eritrea would be different. This optimistic expectation emanated from the progressive programme of the liberation movement, the resilience of the armed struggle and the total commitment of Eritrea's freedom fighters, discussed in subsequent chapters.

CHAPTER 12

Eritrea: The Future of Africa that Works

I have seen the future - of Africa [in Eritrea]- *and it works.*
- Abdulrahman Babu

Prior to the advent of colonialism, African society sustained indigenous structures of governance and cultural values of equity and justice in public administration and communal life that, in spite of colonial attempts to suppress them, have survived. This holds true also for Eritrea, which possesses codified customary laws and a rich anthology of proverbs and oral traditions that celebrate justice and equity. Although Eritrea as a state is a modern creation, the land and the people have a long history, an ancient civilisation, and a benevolent culture. Sharing strong bonds of kinship and blood, and united in diversity, the people possess a culture that values the rule of law, respects justice, and upholds fair representation. Moreover, Eritrean culture fosters affiliation and solidarity in common resistance to alien intrusion and/ or domination.

Having conquered the territory, the Italians initially retained traditional Eritrean governance structures, customary laws and cultural values virtually intact, and relied on the institutional authority of the local chief and the village assembly, or *baito*, to administer the colony.[411] As incidences of revolt against land expropriation and sporadic attacks on immigrant settlers in the countryside multiplied, however, the colonial authorities became increasingly suspicious of the loyalty of the traditional chiefs. They established new provincial administrative structures to shore up the system of indirect rule and tighten central control. In an effort to perpetuate the people's submission to alien domination, the Italians, followed by the British and the Ethiopians, attempted to distort, displace or consign Eritrean history and culture into oblivion.

12.1 The Colonialist Narrative

Consistent with general colonial practice elsewhere in Africa, successive Italian, British and Ethiopian colonial regimes, aided and abetted by a host of associated authors, misrepresented Eritrean history and exacerbated the cleavages of Eritrean society in order to justify and perpetuate their imperial domination of the country. The colonial system denied the integral character of Eritrean-ness and, in substitution, invented a narrative of fragmented subnational identities based on ethnic, regional or religious affiliation. Further, the colonialists schemed to operationalise the colonial narrative to nurture sectarian divisions and foster factional rivalry verging on open hostility.

Essentially, the colonialist narrative denies the existence of an autonomous Eritrean history, the feasibility of a discernible indigenous Eritrean culture worthy of identification and

---

[411]   *Baito* (ባይቶ) is assembly in Tigrinya. It constituted a forum of representative and participatory decision-making.

accurate analysis, or a distinct psychological makeup of Eritrea as a shared homeland of the Eritrean people.[412] It had a real motif for doing so. The fragmentation of territory and the antagonising of secondary differences aimed to weaken the struggle for self-determination while the distortion of history and the denial of culture used to justify continued colonial domination and negate the legitimacy of the demand for Eritrean independence.[413]

Armed with the colonialist narrative, imperial Britain and Ethiopia resorted, often in collusion, to intrigues and manipulations in pursuit of their respective territorial ambitions over Eritrea. In addition, Ethiopia utilised a small band of Eritrean collaborators to undermine the preponderant wish of the Eritrean people for independence and impose its domination on the country. Deploying a mixture of treachery, bribery, and coercion, the tacit alliance of British imperialism and Ethiopian expansionism nearly succeeded in inflaming the secondary divides in Eritrean society, splitting the country along religious and regional lines, and dismantling the very polity of Eritrea. Although pushed to the precipice of division and disaster, the people

---

[412] Venosa, Joseph L., Faith in the Nation: Examining the Contributions of Eritrean Muslims in the Nationalist Movement, 1946-1961, Master's Thesis, 2007, p. 12 http://etd.ohiolink.edu/sendpdf.cgi/Venosa%20Joseph%20L.pdf?ohiou1187294262

[413] See Erlich, Haggai, The Struggle over Eritrea, 1962-1978, Stanford: Hoover Institution Press, 983; Lipsky, George A., Ethiopia: Its People, Its Society, Its Culture, New Haven: Hraf Press, 1962; Reid, Richard, "The Challenge of the Past: The Quest for Historical Legitimacy in Independent Eritrea," History in Africa 28 (2001): 239-272.

effectively resisted the pressure to descend into the abyss of dismemberment and anarchy.

In concise summary, the Ethiopian expansionist narrative maintains that Eritrea, except for the brief interlude of 61 years of Italian and British occupation, had been an integral part of Ethiopia for millennia. This narrative was used as the official line propagated by successive regimes in Addis Ababa until the advent of the Ethiopian People's Revolutionary Democratic Front (EPRDF) government in 1991 and widely disseminated by several Ethiopian and non-Ethiopian writers.[414] It continues to resonate to this day among advocates of Greater Ethiopia or proponents of a unified Trans-Mereb Greater Tigray based on shared primordial identity. Several Ethiopian opposition groups have yet to come to terms with the reality of an independent Eritrea.

---

[414] See John Markakis, Ethiopia: Anatomy of a Traditional Polity. Oxford: Clarendon Press, 1974, p. 25; Harold Marcus, A History of Ethiopia, Berkeley: University of California Press, 1944, p. xiii, 91; Harold Marcus, The Life and Times of Menelik II: Ethiopia 1844-1913, Lawrenceville: Red Sea Press, 1995, p. 20; S. F. Nadel, Races and Tribes of Eritrea. Asmera: British Military Administration of Eritrea, 1943, p. 71, 78; Sylvia Pankhurst, Eritrea on the Eve: the Past and Future of Italy's 'First-Born' Colony, Essex, New Times and Ethiopia News, 1952; Sylvia Pankhurst, Why Are We Destroying Ethiopian Ports? Essex, London; Sylvia and Richard Pankhurst, *Ethiopia and Eritrea: The Last Phase of the Union Struggle 1941-1952*, Walthamstow Press Ltd., Walthamstow, 1953; Sven Rubenson, The Survival of Ethiopian Independence, London: Heinemann 1976, p. 31; John H. Spenser, *Ethiopia at Bay: A Personal Account of the Haile Selassie Years*, Reference Publications Inc., Algonac, Michigan 1987; Zewde, Bahru, A History of Modern Ethiopia 1855-1974, London: James Currey, 1991.

The Ethiopian colonial narrative holds that Eritrea's federation with Ethiopia in 1952 represented the return of the 'lost' territory to the 'mother' country. According to this perspective, annexation in 1962 completed the process of national unification, restored the territorial integrity of Ethiopia, and secured its rulers' perennial dream of direct control of the Eritrean Red Sea coast. The scheme to operationalise the expansionist narrative through annexation, however, proved to be the bane of the peoples of Eritrea and Ethiopia, causing them both three decades of war, ruin, suffering, and lost opportunity for development.

In order to justify the expansionist war, the Ethiopian colonial narrative castigated the Eritrean liberation struggle as a secessionist movement aimed to divide the country. It portrayed it as an anti-Ethiopian undertaking contrived by a handful of bandits instigated and supported by Ethiopia's traditional Arab enemies in a design to dismember the country and deprive it of access to the Red Sea. Even today, it insists that the independence of Eritrea constituted a violation of Ethiopia's territorial integrity and bemoans the EPRDF government's firm endorsement of Eritrean self-determination and formal recognition of Eritrean sovereignty as a betrayal of Ethiopian national unity. Worse still and signalling a possible menace to peaceful future relations between the two sisterly states and fraternal peoples, certain proponents of the Ethiopian expansionist narrative hanker for a re-incorporation of the "unduly severed" territory, or parts thereof, by force. The Eritrean government's current support of some of these essentially hostile groups illustrates the adage that 'politics makes strange bedfellows'.

12.2 The Eritrean Narrative

Locking horns in earnest, the Eritrean nationalist narrative mounted a vigorous challenge to the Ethiopian colonialist narrative and firmly contested its expansionist literary hegemony. The resultant confrontation between the contending Ethiopian and Eritrean narratives has been embittered by the emotive dynamics of a difficult historical relationship and the weight of destruction and suffering inflicted on the Eritrean people by a protracted colonial war. Although articulated mainly by the Eritrean nationalist movement, a number of Eritrean and non-Eritrean writers support and publicise the Eritrean perspective.[415]

In very concise terms, the Eritrean narrative affirms the existence of an *autonomous* Eritrean history and a *feasible*

---

[415] The most notable among these authors include: Dan Connell, Against All Odds: A Chronicle of the Eritrean Revolution, The Red Sea Press, Trenton, NJ: 1993; Lydia Favali and Roy Pateman, Blood, Land and Sex: Legal and Political Pluralism in Eritrea, Indiana University Press, Bloomington: 2003; James Firebrace and Stuart Holland, Never Kneel Down, Spokesman Books, 1984; Jordan Gebre-Medhin, Peasants and Nationalism in Eritrea: A Critique of Ethiopian Studies, Trenton, NJ: The Red Sea Press, 1989; Semere Haile, *Historical Background to the Ethiopia-Eritrea Conflict*, The Long Struggle of Eritrea for Independence and Constructive Peace, Lionel Cliffe and Basil Davidson (eds.), The Red Sea Press, Trenton: NJ, 1988, p. 12-13; Ruth Iyob, The Eritrean Struggle: Democracy, Resistance, Nationalism, 1941-1993, Cambridge University Press, 1995; Okbazghi Yohannes, *Eritrea: A Pawn in World Politics*, University of Florida Press, Gainesville, 1991; Roy Pateman, Eritrea: Even the Stones Are Burning, The Red Sea Press, 1990; Alemseged Tesfai, *Aynfelale*: Eritrea 1941-1950, Hidri Publishers, Asmara, 2001 and Federation with Ethiopia: From Matienzo to Tedla 1951-1955, Hidri Publishers, Asmara, 2005.

Eritrean culture that has generated a *distinctive* Eritrean national identity. It dismisses the Ethiopian assertion of 3,000 years of independent statehood as legend. It rejects the claim that Eritrea constituted an integral part, nay the core, of that historical independent Ethiopian state existing in continuous succession of the Kingdom of Axum until its forcible severance by the Italian occupation in 1890 as half-truth. Invoking the evidence of concrete historical development, the Eritrean narrative contends that both Ethiopia and Eritrea, like virtually all contemporary African states, owe their respective present geopolitical formations as distinctive nation states to the European colonial partition of the continent.

Furthermore, the Eritrean narrative holds that the federation of Eritrea with Ethiopia represented a denial of the Eritrean people's legitimate right of self-determination and served as a smokescreen for the subsequent Ethiopian annexation. It upholds the independence struggle as the embodiment of the Eritrean people's genuine aspirations for liberation. In the same vein, the Eritrean narrative celebrates independence and accession to sovereign statehood as the rectification of the historical injustice perpetrated by the UN Federal Act, the affirmation of the principle of the inalienable right of the Eritrean people to self-determination, the triumph of the will of the Eritrean people, and the fulfilment of their manifest destiny.

The general Eritrean narrative that emerged in direct confrontation with the Ethiopian narrative successfully championed, with minor exceptions, the cause of national liberation in unison and won a great many international subscribers. Indeed, the narrative of heroic resistance, taken up and expanded by many foreign supporters and sympathisers, and eternalised by countless local anecdotes, stories and songs, has become part of the collective living memory of Eritrean folklore. The anthology of the historically evolved Eritrean nationalist narrative is the crowning accomplishment of the Eritrean nationalist movement and the common heritage of the Eritrean people. Nevertheless, the Eritrean nationalist narrative is being used today by the ruling Front and the government, and propagated by regime supporters in the Eritrean diaspora, to lay exclusive claim to the remarkable achievements of the hard struggle of the Eritrean people and to glorify the prevailing dismal situation in the country.

The official narrative put forward, mostly in self-praise, by the current government poses as the direct heir and sole purveyor of the nationalist narrative. Further, it portrays present-day Eritrea as a unique example of successful nation building, state construction, and economic development in postcolonial Africa. The catchphrases of 'one people, one heart', 'independence of decision', 'state sovereignty' and 'self-reliant development' describe the central message of the narrative. Unhampered in its audacity by a modicum of respect for the truth and the presence of countervailing alternative domestic voices, the official portrayal of Eritrea stands in stark contrast to the reality or actual evolution of events on the ground. Most of the daily stories and accounts of events, activities, and developments purportedly taking place in Eritrea seem to describe happenings in another place on a faraway planet.

The principal proponents of the official narrative are the government and the state owned media at home. Moreover, a relatively small and dwindling number of hard-core government- or Front-affiliated media outlets, groups, and individuals in the diaspora continue to echo it. These overzealous advocates of the official narrative in the diaspora are well aware of the oppressive character of the regime and its blatant transgressions against the people. It is quite ironic then that they condone or acquiesce in the denial, to their compatriots at home, of the very freedoms and opportunities they themselves and their families enjoy in their host countries.

These government supporters consist mostly of people with dual citizenship whose lives are unaffected by the government's tyranny and repressive policies and practices. Their nuclear families do not suffer from the afflictions of the coupon economy, the deprivations of extreme poverty and the inadequacies of the existing system of social services inside the country. Unlike their compatriots at home, they have no obligation to bear arms and serve as *kebele* night guards. Their children are not subject to the scourge of indefinite active national service. Moreover, in contrast to Eritreans their age in the home country, the children of the diaspora supporters of the regime are not denied access to proper tertiary education. In fact, they have a chance to attend some of the finest universities in the host countries and anywhere else in the world.

In pushing the official narrative, the government mainly targets Eritreans at home and abroad as a captive audience of its well-oiled propaganda machine, painting Eritrea as a country on the move, enjoying a state of relative bliss and admirable success in a continent marred by glaring failures. The state media drum up a constant barrage of news and commentaries to paint and buttress an image of Eritrea as a unique model of successful development and good governance in Africa. They exude with claims of effective implementation of self-reliant development projects, the pursuit of independence in public policy decisions, the exemplary domestic stability and security, and the solid unity of the people. In reality, the government's policies and actions operate to undermine the meaningful pursuit of the objects of these claims.

12.3 The Eritrean Counter-Narrative

Reinforced by the ethos and triumph of the armed struggle, a unified Eritrean narrative that aspired for a democratic, developmental, and progressive Eritrean state held sway until the border war with Ethiopia. Following the end of the war however, the narrative split, as a dissenting or counter-narrative emerged to challenge the official narrative. Emanating from the same historical roots, the two versions clash in their stories about the character of the Eritrean regime, appraisals of its performance since accession to statehood, and portrayals of Eritrea's image following the first decade of sovereign independence.

As described above, two narratives, the colonial and nationalist, present contrasting and mutually exclusive versions of the history of Eritrea. Just as in the depiction of its history, so in the analysis and appraisal of its present situation and the nature of the regime in power, there are two narratives, the official and the insurgent. The official narrative makes pompous, self-flattering, and embellished claims to beautify an ugly reality. The insurgent narrative, in the main, sifts fact from fiction and portrays an undemocratic, stagnant, and regressive state which, in its brand of an "extreme version of authoritarianism" and negation of a "democratic and peaceful state," has deplorably failed to make independence beneficial for the Eritrean people.[416]

Many sympathetic Eritrea observers find it difficult to embrace the damning counter-narrative without equivocation. For instance, one such writer notes that Eritrea has "achieved a degree of non-coercive social discipline and efficiency" and a "surprisingly functional social order" unique in Africa. In the same piece, he admits to a political culture of "an almost Maoist degree of mobilisation and an almost Albanian degree of xenophobia" under a regime of harsh "political repression" and the "worst press repression in Africa."[417] The assertion that an extent of 'non-coercive social discipline and efficiency' exists under conditions of severe 'political' and 'press repression' in Eritrea today is plainly self-contradictory.

Even if one were to ignore the dysfunctional character of the regime for argument's sake, the commentary ignores the causative relationship between a uniquely 'functional social order' and a system of 'political repression' pervading the country. It reproduces and refutes the make-believe image of a peaceful, stable, and disciplined Eritrea propagated by the regime and its apologists. Its inherent self-contradiction simultaneously masks and reveals the reality of pervasive fear, deep resentment, and simmering tension that permeate Eritrean society today. After all, 'Maoist' regimentation and 'Hoxhaist' xenophobia are alien to its unbound, tolerant culture and incompatible with its

---

[416] Tafla, Bairu, Auf dem Weg zum modernen Äthiopien: Festchrift für Bairu Tafla, Lit Verlag Münster, 2005, p. 172.

[417] Kaplan, Robert, *A Tale of Two Colonies*, Atlantic Monthly, April 2003, pp. 46-53.

humanist values. Otherwise, the façade of 'social discipline and efficiency' that meets the eye and 'impresses' the casual foreign observer on first sight is built on fear, sustained by harsh repression, and enforced under an omnipresent but inconspicuous secret security apparatus spying on and brutalising the people.

The regime's harsh political repression has caused a shared feeling of profound hurt among the great majority of the Eritrean people who have sacrificed so much in the struggle for liberty. One only needs to scratch just below the surface, get a glimpse at the political developments of the last decade, and scrutinise the horrible reality of a prototype police state that is Eritrea today. The complete absence of the rule of law and due process and the prevalence of arbitrary arrests feed the climate of fear and insecurity that haunts the country. This is the outcome of arbitrary arrests; indefinite detentions; solitary confinement; routine and unaccounted disappearances; imposition of roadblocks; restriction of normal movement, including of members of the diplomatic corps and aid agencies, and goods within the country, etc.

The very same nationalist narrative has thus generated from within its organic core a burgeoning counter-narrative that contests the official narrative. The discrepancy between the government's stated policies and actual practices, accentuated by the internal rift in the historically cohesive EPLF leadership and the harsh suppression of political dissent, has reinforced the insurgent narrative. With its central message that the Eritrean people have not gotten what they fought for, this perspective epitomises the prevalent feeling of aching betrayal and profound disappointment among many former freedom fighters, the author included, that 'we didn't do it for this.'[418]

The growing number of Eritrean dissenters at home and in the diaspora as well as many international supporters of the Eritrean nationalist narrative turned critics of the postcolonial state has spearheaded the insurgent narrative.[419] The rival narratives dominate the present cyber debate on Eritrea. Briefly, the rival narrative, in its several variants and internal divisions, depicts the present Eritrean state as highly authoritarian, severely repressive, hell-bent on rent seeking, and primarily interested in self-preservation and self-aggrandisement. It contends that the dismal record of its performance during the last twenty-one years of independence makes the present Eritrean state an example of, rather than an exception to, the prototype postcolonial African state facing a crisis of legitimacy, delivery, and relevance.

12.4 Eritrea: The Future of Africa that Works

The late Abdulrahman Mohamed Babu (1924-1996), a renowned Tanzanian scholar, politician and revolutionary from Zanzibar and an ardent pan-Africanist, who visited wartime Eritrea in the summer of 1985, was positively

---

[418] Alexandra M. Dias in *'We didn't Fight for this'*: `The Twilight of the EPLF/ PFDJ's Political Project of State and Nation Building for Eritrea*, a paper presented at the 4th European Conference on African Studies (ECAS 4) in Uppsala, Sweden, 15-18 June 2011, expresses the same view.

[419] These include Redie Bereketeab, 2009; Dan Connell, Eritrea: Enough! A Critique of Eritrea's Post-Liberation Politics, 2003 and Redeeming the Failed Promise of Democracy in Eritrea, 2008; Kjeil Tronvolls, The Lasting Struggle for Freedom in Eritrea, Oslo, 2009.

impressed and greatly heartened by what he saw on the ground. On returning to London, Abdulrahman Babu stated:

> *I have just spent two weeks in the liberated areas, including the recently captured and recaptured town of Barentu. And I am not ashamed to admit that I have been overwhelmed by what I saw. Living, working and eating with these staunch revolutionaries I am tempted to echo the famous quote: 'I have seen the future - of Africa - and it works.'*[420]

As an African student in London during the early 1950s, Abdulrahman Babu had played a key role in the Movement for Colonial Freedom. Upon his return home to Zanzibar in 1957, he became Secretary General of the island state's first political party, the Zanzibar Nationalist Party (ZNP), and steered mass resistance to British colonial rule. As an aspiring Pan Africanist, "Babu participated in the historic All African People's Conference in Accra, Ghana in 1958 along with Nkrumah, Franz Fanon and Patrice Lumumba".[421]

The British colonial administration had jailed him for two years prior to the independence of Zanzibar in 1963 for his anti-colonialist activities and strong anti-imperialist

---

[420] **Babu, Abdulrahman** Mohamed, *Eritrea: Its Present Is the Remote Future of Others*, **Eritrea: The Way Forward, Proceedings of a Conference on Eritrea organised by the United Nations Association on the 9th November 1985, Russell Press Ltd., London 1986, p. 16.** The author shared the podium with Abdul Rahman Babu during the conference. The first version of Babu's address was published by *Africa Events*, October 1985.

[421] Abdulrahman Mohamed Babu, A Biographical Note http://ambabu.gn.apc.org/bioghpy.htm.

stance. Upon the formation of Tanzania by the union of Tanganyika and Zanzibar in 1964, Babu headed various ministries until 1972. But his quarrels with President Nyerere over policies of 'African Socialism' versus 'scientific socialism' led to his dismissal as Minister of Planning and landed him in prison for six years until 1978 when he was released under international pressure and forced into exile first in the US and later in the UK until his death in 1996.

Having felt the deep frustration and witnessed the general disappointment generated by the inability of the postcolonial African state to deliver emancipation and wellbeing for the African peoples, Babu envisioned Eritrea leading the way to the future of Africa. He was quite aware that his expression of enthusiasm was, in his own words, "not an easy statement to make after so many political, social and economic shocks that we went through in post-independence Africa." Yet, he was not alone at the time in his optimism and high expectations of a triumphant Eritrea blazing the path to the successful future of Africa. Suffice it to mention two contemporary observers, a European and an American, for a sample of three from three continents, who expressed similar optimism about the future of independent Eritrea.

The preeminent British Africa historian Basil Davidson, who visited Eritrea three years after Abdulrahman Babu immediately following the brilliant Eritrean military victory at Afabet in March 1988 shared Babu's perspective on Eritrea. Tempering his optimism with an admission of his human fallibility, Davidson later stated that the Eritreans and the Eritrean national liberation movement as empowered by the EPLF (Eritrean People's Liberation Front):

[H]ave achieved a wide and deepening consciousness of their own capacities, of their own place in the world, of their own responsibility for a stable peace in community with their neighbours. And this deepening consciousness, so manifest in the style and modesty of their posture and political language [...] has demonstrated the capacity of the EPLF to find common ground and promote common action [...] to create the basis for a real self-determination.[422]

A long time American friend and supporter of the Eritrean struggle for self-determination who has been a frequent visitor to the liberated areas under the EPLF and to independent Eritrea from 1983 until 2007, Richard Leonard, provided a similarly optimistic perspective with regard to the then active participation of the Eritrean people in the movement:

[T]he EPLF is a progressive national liberation front engaged in a revolutionary people's war of liberation and a revolutionary programme of national construction in which the Eritrean people actively participate.[423]

These three international friends of the Eritrean struggle, who may be taken as a sample of the many who subscribed to and strongly supported the Eritrean nationalist narrative, made, each in his own way and from his special vantage point, positive assessments of the character of the Eritrean liberation movement. They staked optimistic predictions

---

[422] Cliffe, Lionel and Davidson, Basil, eds., The Long Struggle of Eritrea for Independence and Constructive Peace, December 1988, p. 192-193.

[423] Ibid., p. 133.

or expectations on the prospects of the future independent Eritrea. The trio anticipated independent Eritrea to become the first African success story able to deliver freedom, self-determination, political participation and sustainable development in a continent where all other postcolonial states have failed to do so. Many of their contemporaries shared their enthusiastic assessments and hopeful expectations of independent Eritrea.

12.5 Golden Opportunity to Blaze a New Trail

The liberation of Eritrea in May 1991 ended one of the longest and bloodiest wars of national liberation in modern African history. The EPLF immediately established a provisional government. Subsequent to an UN-monitored referendum that allowed Eritrea as a nation the exercise of the right of self-determination, Eritrea became formally independent in May 1993, and proclaimed a transitional government intended to last for an interim period of a maximum of four years. At independence, Eritrea, Africa's then latest decolonised state, inherited, just as the other African countries that threw off the yoke of colonialism before it, the remnants of an oppressive, exploitative and dysfunctional colonial state.

Unlike elsewhere in much of postcolonial Africa, however, neither the complex legacy nor the neo-colonial ambitions of the former colonial state were in a position to encumber or obstruct the agenda of the new state. In addition, despite the horrendous human and material cost entailed, late accession to independence offered Eritrea a unique opportunity to learn from the African experience. It could avoid the mistakes and build on the experience of independent African states in nation building, state construction and socioeconomic development.

At the critical juncture of Eritrea's accession to independence, the new transitional government that succeeded the provisional government was in full political control of the situation. Starting from scratch, with complete command and overflowing popular support, availed it a clean slate to design, put in place, and forge a new statecraft that would be legitimate, democratic, and able to deliver. Late arrival or newness offered it a chance to draw lessons from the acquis and mistakes of other African countries and create viable state organs and institutions with a statutory mandate and functional authority to efficiently run the affairs of state, manage public administration, rebuild the economy, and institutionalise democratic governance.

After all, the establishment and building of an independent Eritrea with a free, democratic, just and prosperous future was the overriding objective of the protracted armed struggle for national liberation. The goals of the armed struggle, as embedded in the National Democratic Programme (NDP) of the Eritrean People's Liberation Front (EPLF) adopted in its First Congress in Fah, Sahel, January 1977, and honed and translated by the author then, were to:

1. *Establish a people's democratic state;*
2. *Build an independent, self-reliant and planned national economy;*
3. *Develop culture, education, technology, and public health;*
4. *Safeguard social rights (emphasising workers' and women's rights);*

5. *Ensure the equality and consolidate the unity of nationalities;*
6. *Build a strong people's army;*
7. *Respect freedom of religion and faith;*
8. *Provide humane treatment to prisoners of war (POWs);*
9. *Protect the rights of Eritreans residing abroad;*
10. *Respect the rights of foreigners residing in Eritrea; and*
11. *Pursue a foreign policy of peace and non-alignment.* [424]

The ideals of democracy, independence, freedom, respect for human rights, and gender equality enunciated in the EPLF's founding congress and enshrined in its eleven-point programme were among the noble aims and immortal aspirations in whose pursuit generations of Eritrean youth, men and women, fought and made untold sacrifices. Combining the pursuit of political independence with the aspirations for social liberation based on self-reliance, both in principle and in practice, the Eritrean armed struggle symbolised "an inspiring story of courage, dedication, achievement and hope, with important lessons to teach."[425]

Daily life in the field was tough, ascetic, and austere. Commitment to the cause of liberation was total, loyalty to the group selfless, discipline internalised, and faith in the justice of the struggle absolute. Eritrea's warriors of liberty were 'true believers' in their overwhelming majority. Flanked

---

[424] Eritrean People's Liberation Front (EPLF), National Democratic Programme, Fah, Eritrea, January 1977.

[425] Noam Chomsky as quoted in a comment in Dan Connell's *Against All Odds: A Chronicle of the Eritrean Revolution*, The Red Sea Press, Trenton, N.J., 1993.

by the deep blue sea in the rear and facing deadly enemy fire
in front, the watchword of the armed struggle was "*Victory
or Death!*"[426] There were to be no surrender, only triumph
or a fight to the finish. The odds were great, the sacrifices
staggering, and the aura of international acquiescence and
conspiracy of silence near total, prompting an important
regional leader to comment cynically that the Eritreans had
a just cause that was doomed to fail.[427]

Convinced of the legitimacy and inevitability of final
victory of their uphill struggle however, Eritrea's freedom
fighters persevered and won against all calculations. The
powers that be could not stop or derail the relentless forward
march of a well-organised, highly disciplined, and politically
committed liberation army whose combatants were willing to
die for a cause they truly believed to be just and invincible. In
the end, the Eritreans, in close collaboration with their then
Tigrayan allies, delivered a *fait accompli* and the world and the
Big Powers had no choice but to accommodate them willy-
nilly.

In challenging imperial Ethiopian hegemony, territorial
aggrandisement, and military occupation over the span of

---

[426] "*Victory or Death*" was the slogan of the Eritrean People's Liberation
Forces (EPLF). After the First Congress in January 1977, the slogan
of the Eritrean People's Liberation Front (EPLF) became "*Victory
to the Masses!*"

[427] After Colonel Mengistu Haile Mariam, then Ethiopia's military
dictator, publicly declared his preparations to launch the sixth and
biggest ever offensive, *Operation Red Star*, to "crush the Eritrean
secessionist bandits once and for all," the late President Anwar el-
Sadat of Egypt mused during an address over Egyptian state radio
shortly before his death in October 1981 that "the unfortunate
Eritreans have a case, but they are doomed to defeat."

half a century, Eritrean political and armed resistance gained political maturity, overcame bitter internal divisions, and successfully confronted the hostility and active opposition of the then two superpowers and their respective allies in periodically shifting alignments. It was an epic political and military struggle that gradually involved virtually the entire population of Eritrea at home and in the diaspora. The near universal commitment of the Eritrean people to the cause of liberation and their active participation in the armed struggle has very few parallels in the annals of modern history.

12.6 False Hopes and Thwarted Expectations

The armed struggle aimed to free Eritrea from Ethiopian colonial occupation and, in a stunning modern day replay of the classical David versus Goliath contest, prevailed against 'all odds' and expectations. Its ultimate success dismantled Sub-Saharan Africa's largest army, in defiance of regional conspiracies and international betrayals, to redress the historical injustice of the denial of the Eritrean people's legitimate right of self-determination. The feat enabled Eritrea to reclaim its history and secure its rightful place in the world.

Overcoming the challenge won the Eritrean struggle the admiration of friends and supporters the world over. Beyond mere national self-determination and sovereign independence however, its programmatic objectives embodied profound aspirations for self-determination as a people in the form of a government constituted by their free choice, economic emancipation, and social progress. The revolutionary transformation of Eritrean society and the rapid development of the national economy were at the heart, indeed, the core objectives of the liberation movement.

In due course, victory secured liberation, paved the way for self-determination, and affirmed the possibility to fulfil these aspirations. In the ethos of the struggle, liberation represented the necessary condition for the realisation of the age-old yearnings of an oppressed people for freedom, democracy, justice, and prosperity in a seamless nexus. In other words, liberation would be the path to independence, ushering in a sovereign state; and sovereign independence would provide the basis for the establishment of an inclusive, democratic, and prosperous state. The political vision, the economic policy framework, and the statutory principles enunciated in the National Charter, the Macro-Policy document, and the ratified Constitution drawn up soon after independence provided the compass for navigation to the Eritrea of the future.

In spite of the great opportunity and initial optimism however, the regime, oblivious of the fact that the Eritrean people waged the armed struggle for freedom, democracy, and prosperity, has abandoned the prescribed policy instruments and refused to implement the ratified Constitution. Having seized state power in the name of the revolution and exercising it in the name of the people, it has proved unwilling and unable to establish the rule of law and institute a political system that enables the people to have a voice in their government, determine their future, and manage their affairs. In reality subjected to dictate, command, and compulsion from the top down, the Eritrean people today have no say in making or influencing the policies and decisions that govern, shape, and affect their lives at the global, national, regional, or local levels.

Despite giving lip service to the ideals of participatory politics and the empowerment of the people, the government has suspended or paralysed their representative institutions at the national, regional, and local levels and denied them a voice in the governance process. Eritrea remains the only country in Africa without a functioning parliament and a working constitution. The government has disallowed the devolution of power to the regions, the emergence of an independent media or the establishment of autonomous civil society organisations. A scrutiny of independent Eritrea's experience in nation building, state construction, and development reveals a dismal record of failure. It discloses a marked divergence between policy and practice, a clear dichotomy between the promises of the government and its actual performance.

The high expectation and enthusiastic optimism that national reconstruction and socioeconomic development would build on the feat of the armed struggle for liberation have unfortunately, not materialised. In an ironic twist, the story of independent Eritrea has turned into one of broken promises, vacuous claims and abysmal failure to deliver. This is the inevitable outcome of the betrayal of the progressive programme of the liberation movement and the commitment of the freedom fighters to the cause of liberty and justice. Independent Eritrea has forfeited exceptional opportunities to set an example of success in Africa. Contrary to all hopes and expectations, the current regime has cast Eritrea down, impoverished the people, and isolated the country.[428]

---

[428] The absence of a single foreign minister or high-level foreign dignitary, except Riak Machiar of the autonomous government of South Sudan, at the funeral service of Eritrea's foreign minister,

The regime has been unable to deliver public goods and services as well as freedom, democracy, and prosperity. Such inability has impaired its legitimacy and rendered it irrelevant to the wellbeing of the people. The great expectations and initial surge of optimism of the people and the high hopes of Eritrea's friends that a future independent Eritrea would prosper and flourish have so far proven premature.

In spite of hopes, expectations, and claims, and in stark contrast to the path it charted for itself, and measured against the criteria set by its own standards, the Eritrean state has veered off course, gone astray, and ill performed. Its praxis has failed to adhere to democratic principles, advance the nation-building project, construct viable state institutions, and kick-start the economy. Like its prototype postcolonial African counterpart, the Eritrean state has proved unwilling and unable to promote the paramount national interest, deliver socioeconomic development, and improve the wellbeing of the Eritrean people.

Regrettably, the reality of post-independence Eritrea, measured against the criteria of tangible delivery of a better quality of life in terms of emancipation, empowerment, and prosperity of the people, does not represent Abdurrahman Babu's vision of *the future of Africa that works*. His enthusiastic prediction that Eritrea would blaze the trail towards real liberation, democracy, and prosperity in Africa has not come about, at least so far.

------

the late Ali Said Abdella, indicated the extent of the country's loneliness. Further, the unanimous adoption of the resolution to impose sanctions against Eritrea, in sequence, by the Inter-Governmental Authority on Development (IGAD), the AU and the UN Security Council illustrates the complete isolation of the country at the regional and international levels.

Similarly, the political, economic, and social conditions prevailing in the country do not confirm Basil Davidson's optimistic assessment of the EPLF's *demonstrated capacity to find common ground and promote common action to create the basis for a real self-determination.* Further, Richard Leonard's appreciation of the EPLF's commitment to pursue a *revolutionary programme of participatory national construction* has not materialised.

12.7 A Prototype Authoritarian State

The singular monopolisation of state power and the closure of the political space for internal debate within the Front and the government and domestic social dialogue have resulted in the imposition of authoritarian rule. In a fundamental sense, authoritarian rule signifies the weakness, not the strength, of the Eritrean state. The democratic deficit operated to hinder the interlinked processes of nation building, state construction, and sustainable development. An anaemic state, unable to govern in accordance with the rule of law, the consent of the people, and in the interest of the country, has resorted to repression, exclusion, and marginalisation to impose its authority. These generally counterproductive measures have bred widespread disaffection and further undermined the legitimacy of a weak government presiding over a fragile state.

Simmering popular discontent and latent political instability under the sway of a police state bide their time beneath a veneer of normalcy reproduced by the resort to arbitrary detentions, random disappearances, and extrajudicial killings. After all, fear and intimidation have a limited lifespan. Eventually, extreme repression is bound to delegitimise the state's monopoly of the use of violence, provoke resistance, and aggravate social conflict, the mother of all reform.

Modelled essentially after the European metropolitan state system and founded on the remnants of the old colonial state, the Eritrean state today, like the prototype postcolonial African state, is thus neither democratic nor developmental. It has abandoned the progressive objectives of the liberation movement and the transformative values of self-reliance, solidarity, and unity espoused by the EPLF during the war, which served the armed struggle for liberation so well. It merely memorialises the decisive events of that era to promote its own legitimacy and prolong its rule. Effectively, the regime has waylaid the legitimate aspirations articulated by the nationalist narrative and the optimistic predictions made by many of its international subscribers, and become a strange mélange of a prototype *predatory, patrimonial* and *authoritarian* state.

These features are manifest in the practice of the government and the reality it has created in Eritrea today. There exists great divergence between the ideals of the armed struggle and the commitments made during the first few years of independence, on the one hand, and the actual achievements delivered during the last twenty-two years of independence, on the other. The regime has failed to implement its own stated policies and win the mandate, gain the consent, meet the needs, and cater to the aspirations of the people. Its authoritarian character stands out in stark contrast to its originally declared policies and objectives.

Authoritarian rule and mismanagement have perpetrated backwardness, hampered economic development and aggravated poverty. High levels of domestic and foreign debt, spiralling inflation, and acute shortages of foreign exchange have fanned macroeconomic instability. The regime presides over a declining national economy characterised by general penury. Despite the rhetoric of economic growth it spouts and opportunities for investment it touts, it has pursued policies that decimated the private sector, inhibited autonomous private investment, and denied people any real scope for free enterprise. Starved of revenues, it extracts an assortment of taxes, levies, fees, and fines from pliant or vulnerable citizens at home and in the diaspora.

A macroeconomic climate conducive to domestic and foreign investment would have allowed the establishment of profitable enterprises and stimulated economic activity. Greater economic activity would, in turn, have created gainful employment and generated wealth to enable the government to garner income taxes from the resultant lucrative base and maximise public revenues. Instead, it minimises its predatory extraction of revenues through the constriction of private trade, industry, and agriculture. Further, it flouts public accountability for its actions and squanders the meagre public resources on unsound pet projects.

The executive branch, with its internal cohesion torn asunder by dissent and its most senior ranks depleted by detention, freezing, and exile, is weak, incompetent and dysfunctional. Long suspended, the national legislature is non-existent. In usurping the principal functions of the High Court, the Special Court, most of whose members lack basic education, rudimentary knowledge of the law, and proper legal training, has marginalised the judiciary.

It is clear that today's Eritrea does not represent *the future of Africa that works!* The trajectory of its anticipated development has atrophied. Its dismal record has not vindicated the optimistic predictions of Babu or the positive assessments of Davidson and Leonard. That Babu passed away in 1996 without the disappointment of having to witness another African story of failure where he had predicted success is no consolation to his enthusiastic vision. Davidson however, passed away in 2010 deeply disappointed that Eritrea was treading the failed political path he had witnessed in post-independence Africa. Leonard remains similarly disappointed that the then progressive movement rooted in the participation of the Eritrean people, that made military victory possible, has veered off course and forced to abandon its original purpose.[429]

Three main factors have combined to allow a few unscrupulous individuals to take control of the movement and subvert its goals for personal power and aggrandisement to the detriment of Eritrea and its people. First, the top-heavy and authoritarian political structures upon which the EPLF was built; second, the loss of so many good and capable fighters to martyrdom during the war and to relegation after independence; third, the historical context of a society lacking in social and political structures able to defend the original progressive ideals of the movement.

Independent Eritrea has duplicated the basic features of the prototype postcolonial African state. It has evolved into an authoritarian state afflicted by a profound *crisis of legitimacy, delivery,* and *relevance.* Far from being an exception, as propagated by the government and echoed by a dwindling number of apologists, therefore, today's Eritrea, Africa's second newest state, fits the prototype African mould, *par excellence.*

---

[429] Conversations of the author with Richard Leonard, Waterloo, Belgium, 14 January 2012.

CHAPTER 13

Engaging the Eritrean Diaspora

In all things that are purely social we can be as separate as the fingers, yet one as the hand in all things essential to mutual progress. - Booker T. Washington

The Eritrean diaspora, originating in the flight of Eritreans from their ancestral homeland and resettlement abroad, is essentially a product of the long war with Ethiopia. Interstate conflict, domestic repression, and the lack of opportunities at home have however, augmented its ranks, especially since the start of the border war with Ethiopia in 1998. Its emergence and growth have thus been driven by the search for refuge from the atrocities of war and opportunities for a better life. Meanwhile, the relative size, wealth, educational attainment, and close attachment to the homeland have made the Eritrean diaspora a significant player in the political, economic, and social life of the country throughout its comparatively short history of existence.

13.1 The Evolution of the Eritrean Diaspora

During the late 1960s and early 1970s, an increasing number of Eritrean students in the Middle East, Europe, and North

America opted to join the independence struggle or stay in the host countries rather than returning home or going to Ethiopia. They joined hands with Eritrean emigrant workers to organise associations and mobilise support for the liberation movement. Their numbers began to grow with the escalation of the war in the increasingly contested countryside and the intensification of repression by the Ethiopian military regime in the occupied urban and semi urban areas in the mid-1970s.

The imperial Ethiopian army launched a scorched-earth campaign in western Eritrea during the late 1960s in reprisal to the increasing military operations of the ELF, then the lone Eritrean independence organization, by burning villages and massacring villagers. The massive atrocities committed by the Ethiopian military against the civilian population displaced and drove large numbers of Eritreans into eastern Sudan in 1967, creating the first wave of refugees. The escalation of the war in scale and intensity during the second half of the 1970s generated another wave of Eritrean refugees from both the rural and urban areas into the Sudan to escape death, torture, repression, and a state of general insecurity. Many of the refugees eventually made their way into and settled in the Middle East, Europe, North America, and Australia.

Eritrean students, migrant workers, and refugees in Africa, the Middle East, Europe, and North America organised associations of students, workers, and women in support of the armed struggle for independence at home. The organisations abroad affiliated with either one of the then two fronts: the Eritrean Liberation Front (ELF) or the Eritrean People's Liberation Forces (EPLF). The General Union of Eritrean Students (GUES) and the General Union of Eritrean Workers (GUEW) had two factions each, one based in Baghdad and the other in Cairo.

The GUES and GUEW factions based in Baghdad affiliated with the ELF. On the other hand, the GUES and GUEW factions based in Cairo, Eritreans for Liberation in North America (EFLNA), Eritreans for Liberation in Europe (EFLE) and, later, the National Union of Eritrean Workers (NUEW), the National Union of Eritrean Women (NUEW), and the National Union of Eritrean Students and Youth (NUESY), affiliated with the EPLF. An attempt to unify the Eritrean student movement and bring EFLNA, EFLE, GUES-Baghdad, and GUES-Cairo under one umbrella in support of the Eritrean liberation movement in the summer of 1973 failed to bear fruit.[430]

A significant historical trend affected the social, religious, and ethnic makeup of these early Eritrean diaspora organisations. Generally, Eritreans from the Lowlands moved mostly to the Arab countries of the Middle East while Eritreans from the Highlands moved mostly to Europe and

---

[430] The author, in his capacity then as Chairman of EFLNA, participated in an effort to bring together the student movement – EFLNA, EFLE, GUES-Baghdad, and GUES-Cairo – in a meeting held on the margins of the August 1973 EFLE Congress in Pavia (Milan), Italy. The meeting of the leaders of the four groups failed to reach agreement on a common platform in support of the struggle in the field. GUES-Baghdad supported the ELF-Revolutionary Council (ELF-RC) while EFLNA, EFLE and GUES-Cairo supported the ELF-People's Liberation Forces (ELF-PLF), the forerunner of the Eritrean People's Liberation Forces (EPLF), and jointly issued the Pavia Declaration pledging to coordinate their activities and seek unity with progressive organisations.

North America, adding another feature to the complexity of Eritrean diaspora politics. The factors and patterns of fragmentation among the diaspora organisations at the time mirrored the divisions within the armed struggle in the field.

The social and political divides notwithstanding however, the Eritrean diaspora groups played an active and significant part by providing substantial material resources, including considerable financial support and hundreds of recruits, among them many cadres and several members of the leaderships of the ELF and the EPLF. Right from inception, EFLE and EFLNA worked in close coordination to mobilise vital political, material and financial support for the Eritrean struggle. During its crucial early years, in particular, they provided the EPLF with significant funds, communications equipment (walkie-talkies), and military fatigues.

The increasing ferocity of Ethiopia's scorched earth campaign and the general intensification of the war of national liberation following the fall of the Haile Selassie regime and the rise of the military junta in 1974 triggered the flight of tens of thousands of new Eritrean refugees into the Sudan. In addition, the Ethiopian regime's brutal repression, arbitrary incarceration, and constant harassment created a state of endemic insecurity and forced many Eritreans in Asmera, Addis Ababa, and other Eritrean and Ethiopian cities and towns to flee and seek refuge in the Sudan, Kenya, Djibouti or Yemen in transit to the wider Middle East, Europe or North America.

The end of the Eritrean civil war in the Field in 1981, between the two fronts, and the consequent displacement of the ELF into the Sudan generated another wave of new refugees that triggered further movement into countries outside the region. Once settled in their final destinations,

425

people brought their families and created small refugee and migrant communities, eventually giving rise to the present configuration of the Eritrean Diaspora.

The 1998-2000 border war with Ethiopia pushed more refugees into the Sudan and caused many previously repatriated and resettled Eritreans to flee again and return to their former host countries. More recently, the mixture of a general state of pervasive repression, closure of economic space for the private sector, lack of access to meaningful higher education and gainful employment opportunities for the youth, widespread impoverishment, and imposition of indefinite active national service has caused an increasing outflow of new refugees. Eritrea's youth, national service conscripts, entrepreneurs, and professionals continue to flow into neighbouring countries as potential transit points en route to other countries in Africa and the Global North as many refugees work their way out of the region. The exodus continues to swell the size of the overseas Eritrean Diaspora.

There thus exists a relatively large Eritrean diaspora scattered throughout the developed and much of the developing world today. Estimated at about a quarter of the country's total population, the Eritrean diaspora, which maintains close political, economic, and social links with the home country, constitutes a great reserve asset for Eritrea. In the heat of national excitement and patriotic fervour, Eritreans from the diaspora flocked to their liberated homeland to participate in the national economic conference; teach at the newly reinstated university; offer advisory services to the government, work in government ministries, and serve in various commissions and agencies; set up private businesses; and resettle in their country of origin. They demonstrated a general state of readiness to return to Eritrea and contribute their share in the reconstruction and development effort in any capacity or role.

13.2 The Diaspora as a Global Player

Beyond Eritrea, the age of globalisation has witnessed the emergence of the diaspora as a global phenomenon. The global diaspora has come on the world stage as a product of protracted human mobility, as a source of significant financial flows, and as an agency of rapid transfer of knowledge, skills, and technical knowhow across countries and continents. The advent of the knowledge economy has both accelerated and reinforced the growth of the global diaspora, its transnational mobility, its contribution to world political, economic and social development, and the process of multicultural interaction and exchange worldwide. Whether in the developed industrial countries of the Global North or the emerging and developing nations of the Global South, the diaspora has emerged as an important factor and a key player in the political, economic, social, and cultural development of both the host and home countries.

The diaspora possesses and has demonstrated, in many developed, emerging, and developing countries, the capacity to make a significant contribution to national political, economic, social, and cultural development. It advances political development through democratic participation in policy formulation and decision-making. It participates in human capital formation through the transfer of knowledge, skills, and expertise. It contributes to economic development through the flow of financial capital, investment, remittances, and enterprise. It helps to promote social development and welfare through engagement in the provision of education and health services as well as social safety nets. Furthermore, the diaspora has the potential to play a vital role in promoting international relations, development cooperation, and cultural diplomacy between host and home countries.

According to the World Bank, about 3 per cent of the entire population of the world, or more than 215 million people, live outside their countries of birth. The aggregate value of worldwide remittance flows in 2010 reached more than US$440 billion. Remittances to developing countries, worth US$325 billion in 2010, made up three times the total amount of official development aid to countries receiving assistance. Remittances originating in the world's top five donor countries, namely, the United States, the United Kingdom, France, Germany, and Japan, exceed the official development assistance of each of these countries.[431]

The regional concentration and relative proportion of national diaspora populations and the comparative contributions of their remittance flows to GDP may vary from country to country. However, they invariably deliver a crucial injection of hard currency to the recipient countries and help build up their foreign exchange reserves. Overall, remittances from national diasporas flowing without conditionality or strings attached, make a significant contribution to the alleviation of poverty and the enhancement of social wellbeing, particularly in the low-income and middle-income developing countries in the Global South.

---

[431] The World Bank, Migration and Remittances http://siteresources. worldbank.org/TOPICS/Resources/214970-1288877981391/ Annual_Meetings_Report_DEC_IB_MigrationAndRemittances_ Update24Sep10.pdf

Remittances benefit the economies of many developed, emerging, and developing countries. Latest World Bank estimates put recorded worldwide remittance flows to both high-income and low-income countries in 2011 at about US$483 billion, with Europe, Central Asia, and Sub-Saharan Africa leading the way. According to the same estimates, despite the continuing global financial crisis and its negative impact on the employment prospects of migrants, officially recorded remittance flows to the developing world in 2011 rose by 8 per cent over 2010, reaching approximately US$352 billion. These remittance flows are projected to grow at an estimated annual rate of 7-8 per cent to reach about US$441 billion by 2014 while worldwide remittance flows are expected to surpass US$590 billion by 2014.[432] The resolution of the on-going global financial crisis is bound to boost the growth of remittance flows to the developing world as well as aggregate remittances worldwide.

13.3 The Eritrean Diaspora as a National Actor

Immediately after the liberation of Eritrea from Ethiopian occupation, the Provisional Government of Eritrea sought to engage and facilitate the diaspora's active political participation, professional expertise, intellectual input, and financial resources in the processes of nation building, state construction, and development. In July 1991, many

---

[432] The World Bank, *Migration and Development Brief 17: Outlook for Remittance Flows 2012-14*, 1 December 2011 http://siteresources.worldbank.org/INTPROSPECTS/Resources/334934-1110315015165/MigrationandDevelopmentBrief17.pdf

Eritreans from the diaspora in Europe, North America, and the Middle East participated in an economic conference on Eritrea that gathered policymakers, practitioners, and scholars to discuss options for development strategy for an emerging independent Eritrea. The conference was originally planned to take place in the EPLF base area in Sahel but the auspicious liberation of the country made its convening at the then displaced University of Asmera possible.

The economic conference, conceived to be the first in a series to be organised in the future, signified the initiation of a democratic process in the formulation of economic policy and development strategy in the new Eritrea as well as the active involvement of Eritreans from the diaspora in that process. The idea of the conference was the brainchild of the then Secretary of the EPLF Department of Economic Planning and Coordination, Haile Weldensae (Drue),[433] while Eritreans for Peace and Democracy (EPD) in North America played an active part in its preparations and execution. The proceedings and recommendations of the conference were published in "Emergent Eritrea: Challenges of Economic Development", in 1993.[434] Some of the policy recommendations proffered by a number of the conference papers later informed the drawing up of the government's macroeconomic policy framework.

---

[433] Haile Weldensae (Drue), along with several other former senior Government and Front officials, has been under detention in solitary confinement since 18 September 2001 for criticising the president's authoritarian style of leadership and advocating reform in the manner of conduct of the affairs of state and government business.

[434] Tesfagiorgis, Gebre H., (ed.) Emergent Eritrea: Challenges of Economic Development, The Red Sea Press, 1993.

A year after the economic conference, many of the scholars returned to the same venue, along with several new comers, to participate in an international symposium on the revitalisation of the University of Asmera (UoA). The international symposium was convened in August 1992 to revitalise the newly re-established university, help chart its future, restructure its colleges and faculties, revise its syllabus, upgrade the size and quality of its faculty, and modernise its assets. As the then president of the university, I conceived and organised the symposium to help rebuild and transform the previously relegated institution into a centre of academic excellence, higher learning, and development oriented research. The overarching objective was to enable the University of Asmera to make a positive contribution to Eritrea's human resources development as the key to the success of the national effort for reconstruction and development.

Having reinstated the University of Asmera in September 1991, I immediately arranged for the return of the Eritrean members of its staff from Agarfa in southern Ethiopia. Scores of Eritrean professionals in the academia who abandoned their secure positions in Ethiopian and Sudanese universities and volunteered to return home to teach and help rebuild the newly restored university soon joined them. Together, they formed the nucleus of the faculty and played an active role in organising the international symposium to revitalise the university convened with the enthusiastic support and participation of Eritrean academics and scholars from the diaspora and international friends of Eritrea.

The symposium provided the first democratic forum to debate and chart out the structure, policy options, and strategy of tertiary education in independent Eritrea among policy makers, educators, and academics at home and in the diaspora. The original plan was to organise follow-up forums at regular intervals in the future to appraise and guide the progress of the University of Asmera as a national centre of excellence. Prof. Abraham Kidane stayed on to help synthesise and operationalise the recommendations of the symposium and initiate the process of revitalising the university and review its proposed draft charter[435] or returned later to help and teach under various short- or long-term arrangements, such as the US Fulbright Scholar Program. Moreover, Dr. Wolde-Ab Isaac replaced Dr. Araya Tsegai, in quick succession, as my successor after my precipitous departure from the university.[436]

Further, Eritreans from the diaspora played prominent roles in the organisation of the referendum and the drafting of the Constitution. Several long-time activists from the diaspora worked alongside prominent members of the EPLF and former leaders of the ELF in the referendum and constitution commissions, lining their executive and functional bodies.[437] The two national processes, which

---

[435] Professor Abraham Kidane of California State University in particular, had extended his stay on his own and played a significant catalytic role in that process. In addition, he provided invaluable advice and support in refining a draft charter for the university that I had prepared.

[436] Dr. Araya Tsegai, a returnee from the US who was initially assigned to the central bank, was put in charge of the university until he was shortly replaced by Dr Wolde-Ab Isaac who returned from Sweden to assume the post.

[437] Dr. Amare Tekle served as the commissioner for the referendum while Dr. Bereket Habte Selassie headed the constitution commission.

stimulated active participation of Eritreans at home and abroad, represented initial forums of democratic exercise. Besides, several Eritreans from the diaspora became members of the central committee/council of the EPLF/PFDJ while others assumed senior positions as cabinet ministers, ambassadors, directors general, or government advisors.[438]

The Eritrean diaspora can build on its significant engagement with the struggle for national liberation and utilise its assets to advance the political, economic, and social development of the country. This capacity was evident in its significant contribution to the success of the economic conference, the revitalisation of the university, the conduct of the referendum, the making of the constitution, and the work of government ministries and diplomatic missions.

A political and economic space more conducive to effective engagement could unleash the diaspora's tremendous creative energy and accelerate the transfer of skills, technology, knowhow, and capital from the host countries to Eritrea. Its multiple linkages could serve as a bridge to promote investment, cultural contacts, people-to-

---

[438] These include: Ahmed Haji Ali (Wedi Haji), Hagos Gebrehiwet (Kisha), Mohiedin Shengeb, Yusuf Saiq, Hamid Himed, and the late Saleh Meki, as the PFDJ CC members; Tesfai Girmatsion, Ahmed Haji Ali, Werku Tesfamicael, Saleh Meki, and Weldai Futur, as cabinet ministers; Goitom Weldemariam, Fessehaie Abraham, Zemede Tekle, Pietros Tsegai, Fessehatzion Pietros, Mohamed Suleiman Ahmed, Teclai Minassie, Musa Yassin Sheikhedin, Girmai Gebremariam (Santim), Araya Desta, Ahmed Dehli, and the late Daniel Yohannes, as ambassadors; Yemane Gebremeskel (Charlie), Teame Teweldebrhan, and Ainom Berhane, as directors general; Araia Tsegai, as a general manager; and Abraham Kidane and Girmay Abraham, as economic advisors.

people diplomacy, understanding and cooperation between the home and host countries. Its sizeable remittances could avail the country substantial foreign exchange reserves, provide a lifeline of financial support and social safety net for many households, and help alleviate poverty in the country.

In recognition of this enormous potential, there were attempts to enable, mobilise, and deploy the diaspora's considerable intellectual, financial, technical, and entrepreneurial resources in the service of national reconstruction and development. One such attempt envisaged the recruitment of about a dozen academics and professionals from the diaspora, to serve as heads of the bank's core departments or members of a board of senior government advisors, to help capacitate the bank, revitalise the financial sector, and kick-start the economy.

At the time, the former fighters turned senior government officials and public servants were working without pay, most of them housed in the barracks of the former US military communications bases at Kagnew Station and Radio Marina with their families and feeding on rations in common cafeterias, until the formal start of salaries in 1996. There were expectations for similar sacrifices from Eritreans in the diaspora for the sake of national reconstruction. However, the respective circumstances were different.

The former fighters and their families were hardened volunteers long used to serving without pay and had, during the course of the armed struggle, developed a very high tolerance for living under extremely austere conditions. On the other hand, Eritrean professionals and their families in the diaspora were accustomed to relatively higher standards of living and more prosperous lifestyles with access to state-of-the-art amenities and social services in their host countries.

They would thus be hard pressed to serve without adequate compensation, forego their relatively privileged lifestyles and give up opportunities for better education for their children and access to more advanced public health services for their families.

In my capacity as Governor of the Bank of Eritrea, I proposed to the president a scheme that would enable Eritrean professionals abroad to return home and participate in rebuilding the country, without giving up their lifestyles or affecting the situation of their families. The scheme provided for the provisional recruitment of the prospective professionals at their current salaries, adjusted by a cost of living index for Eritrea. A concessionary loan from the World Bank's International Development Agency (IDA) would secure the necessary funding for the scheme. As we had anticipated, with a high degree of confidence, the country to achieve rapid economic growth, the adjusted international level salaries would be, after a short transitional period, integrated into a comparatively upgraded national salary scale that was under consideration at the time. Under the auspices of the president, the governor of the central bank would oversee the implementation of the plan.[439]

Recognising the crucial role of reliable macroeconomic data in following up the state of health of the national economy, informing and driving public policy as well as evaluating economic performance, the central bank advocated the building of basic national microeconomic and

---

[439] Weldai Futur, the chair of Eritreans for Peace and Democracy in North America, and an employee of the International Finance Corporation (IFC), the World Bank Group, was tasked to identify and propose a shortlist of prospective candidates.

macroeconomic data. Beyond advocacy, the bank took the initiative and, in cooperation with the relevant government ministries and agencies, started compiling national economic data, such as trade and balance of payments statistics, foreign exchange reserve holdings, national income accounts, labour market figures, etc. The idea was to publish the national statistical data and make them available to policy makers, researchers and the public. Unfortunately, this, like many other good projects was also not allowed to run its course.

As part of the effort to compile and build basic economic data and trade statistics, I set up an ad hoc committee under the auspices of the Bank of Eritrea.[440] Chaired by a prominent Eritrean academic who had returned home from the diaspora, it comprised representatives of the relevant economic ministries and authorities. The committee's immediate task was to identify a basket of goods and services and their respective prices for use as a basis to compute an estimation of the consumer price index (CPI) for Asmera as a pilot project. Pending estimation for the country as a whole, which was also planned as the next step, the CPI for Asmera would serve as a rough approximation of the cost of living index (CLI) for purposes of adjusting the international salaries of the professionals who were to be recruited from the diaspora.

However, I was fired as governor of the central bank prior to the final placement of the professionals from the diaspora,

---

[440] Chaired by Professor Abraham Kidane, the committee produced the first and, regrettably, the last Consumer Price Index (CPI) for Asmera to date. In addition to serving as chair of the ad hoc committee, Professor Abraham reviewed and helped finalise the draft Bank of Eritrea Law and the draft Financial Institutions Act.

who arrived and took station at the central bank after my first departure for Brussels as Eritrea's Ambassador to the European Union (EU). The combination of inadequate appreciation of the planned objectives, insufficient preparations, lack of proper advance planning, and ineffective managerial guidance failed to avail an enabling environment for the professionals to fully utilise their expertise and effectively serve the intended purpose. Although some stayed as ministers or advisors to the government, most of them eventually returned to their former occupations in the host countries quite disappointed in the knowledge that they were unable to perform the tasks as originally conceived in the service of the central bank, the financial sector, and the government at large.

Further, scores of Eritreans had returned home from the diaspora to serve in various capacities in the public and private sectors. Engineers, architects, professors, mechanics, entrepreneurs, and businesspersons from the diaspora returned to Eritrea to settle, build a new life, and contribute their share to the reconstruction and development of the country. They came with business plans, specific projects, seed capital, and skills to invest in the various sectors of the economy. An Investment Code with relatively favourable provisions was, proclaimed and a 'one-stop shop' set up to arrange for the expeditious issuance of the needed licences to facilitate the speedy establishment of new enterprises and business ventures. However, like many things in Eritrea, this too was, shelved aside following the announcement of its introduction.

Making matters worse, the virtual monopoly position and conspicuous financial, foreign exchange, and tax privileges enjoyed by the Front's numerous parastatals squeezed small entrepreneurs, including returnees from the diaspora, out of business. The Front's routine insistence, including to potential investors from the diaspora, on the creation of joint ventures with itself as a major partner without proportionate contribution in capital and competent management personnel has driven many potential foreign investors away. The government's periodic arbitrary withdrawals of operating licences, seizures of imported equipment and merchandise on arrival at the ports of entry and customs offices, closures of shops, and shutdowns of premises have narrowed or closed the space for doing business and forced many to close shop or to interrupt investments midway.

The World Bank's Business Environment profiles ranked Eritrea 180th out of 183 countries in the Doing Business 2010 and 2011 surveys, respectively. The 2009 Enterprise Surveys list licenses and permits, political instability, and access to land as the top three constraints to investment in Eritrea. The 2011 Index of Economic Freedom shows Eritrea scoring 36.7 out of 100, making its economy one of the least free in the Index.[441] The surveys indicate that weak economic management and structural problems that include poor public finance management, underdeveloped legal and regulatory frameworks, and poor governance hamper the economic freedom of Eritreans.

The present political situation and overall macroeconomic climate in the country makes it difficult for potential investors, including those from the Eritrean diaspora, to start-up businesses, access credit facilities to finance new ventures, or sustain profitable operations. For instance, it is

---

[441] The World Bank, Country Snapshot - Eritrea http://rru. worldbank.org/BESnapshots/Eritrea/default.aspx

438

reported that it "takes at least 84 days and involves 13 separate procedures" to register a business, ranking Eritrea among the ten worst countries in the world in which to start up and do business.[442] The government's economic mismanagement and rabid hostility to private enterprise entail forfeiture of substantial potential foreign direct investment (FDI) and growth in productivity and development for the country.

In 1993, the central bank issued a directive designed to encourage the inflow of remittances and foreign exchange, promote domestic and foreign investment, reinforce the involvement of the diaspora in national political, economic, and social development, and help build the country's foreign exchange reserves. The new directive authorised the establishment of unrestricted foreign currency accounts for Eritreans at home and in the diaspora, including unrestricted non-resident foreign currency denominated accounts (FCDA) for foreigners resident in Eritrea or companies doing business in the country, in the Commercial Bank of Eritrea.

Under the bank's new directive, account holders, whether local or international and Eritrean or foreign, would be completely free to make deposits, transfers, or withdrawals to and from anywhere at their own discretion. There were to be no restrictions of any kind. The account balances would receive an annual compound interest computed at the rate of the Frankfurt Inter-Bank Overnight Rate (FIBOR) or the London Inter-Bank Overnight Rate (LIBOR), whichever is higher, plus one per cent. Within a year, the opening of thousands of foreign currency accounts resulted in a significant increase in the country's foreign exchange reserves.

---

[442] The World Bank, Doing Business 2009 http://www.hsbc.com/1/ PA_1_1_S5/content/assets/emi/gbm/business2009.pdf

Further, Eritreans in the diaspora, as their compatriots at home, are periodically, urged to donate to funds to various causes, such as national defence, martyrs' families, orphans of martyrs, etc. In addition to such recurrent contributions, they are required to pay an annual recovery tax of 2 per cent of their net income by government proclamation.[443] Apart from the US, Eritrea is the only country that requires its diaspora to pay taxes on incomes earned abroad.

This, in effect, constitutes double taxation, as diaspora Eritreans are also required to pay income taxes to their host countries. While imposing dual fiscal obligations however, the Eritrean government, unlike most other governments, does not provide political and consular protection to its nationals in cases of jeopardy; it even colludes with their victimisers under the pretext that the victims left the country illegally. Further, there are legitimate concerns of accountability and transparency concerning the end use of such funds by a government that does not operate in accordance with a transparent published budget.

Even though some Front and government officials have wrongly claimed on several occasions, that it is a voluntary contribution, the 2 per cent income tax on the diaspora often assessed based on personal income tax returns is a legal obligation and enforced by resorting to punitive measures. Failure to pay or provide formal evidence of regular and up-to-date payment entails consequences. These include the denial of consular services and access to official documents (passports, exit visas, birth certificates, marriage certificates, school transcripts, etc.); the infringement on citizenship,

---

[443] Government of Eritrea, Gazette of Eritrean Laws: Proclamation 67/1995, No.1, Asmara, 10 February 1995

inheritance, land, and property rights; the denial to arrange powers of attorney; and the discriminatory treatment of family members in the home country. Such punitive measures apply to former government officials (and family members) who resign from public service in protest of, or criticise, government policy, and opt to stay abroad for fear of 'freezing' or detention upon return home.

The various schemes to boost the country's foreign exchange reserves worked fairly well during the first decade of independence and remittances probably continued to grow in size until the advent of the new millennium. Total annual remittances from the Eritrean diaspora amounted to about US$300 million in 1994 and, according to reliable estimates, around US$400 million for subsequent years. The contribution of remittances to GNP amounted to three times that of agricultural production in the best of times up to 2003.[444] Relative to the size of the population and the scale of national economic activity, the Eritrean diaspora is one of the largest national Diasporas and its remittance flows to Eritrea "are proportionally 'the highest in the world.'"[445]

Estimated at "40 per cent of GDP,"[446] remittances constitute the single greatest and most enduring contribution

---

[444] Statement of President Isaias Afwerki in a meeting with Eritrean ambassadors, Asmera, 10 October 2003.

[445] Healy, Sally, Eritrea's Economic Survival: Summary record of a conference held on 20 April 2007, The Royal Institute of International Affairs, 2007, p. 14, quoting an IMF staff member, talking to London-based economist, March 2007 http://www.chathamhouse.org/sites/default/files/public/Research/Africa/200407eritrea.pdf

[446] Winslow, Robert, Crime and Society: Comparative Criminology Tour of the World: Africa – Eritrea http://www-rohan.sdsu.edu/

of the Eritrean diaspora to the country's foreign exchange reserves and the wherewithal of its economy. They help provide for the sustenance of a large number of households and the general welfare of an important segment of Eritrean society. Money and supplies sent home from kith and kin in the host countries represent a crucial, and in most cases, an indispensable factor relieving many thousands of families from extreme poverty. The heavy reliance of the Eritrean state and society on remittances makes the country's foreign exchange reserve position and social safety net vulnerable to fluctuations in remittance inflows. Otherwise, the crucial importance of remittances to the development finance and foreign exchange position of Eritrea is generally in line with global trends.

The Eritrean diaspora has thus been and will continue to be a major source of political support, professional expertise, foreign investment, and financial flows to the country. A more open political system, a predictable macroeconomic environment, and a climate conducive to investment would have encouraged Eritreans in the diaspora and foreign entrepreneurs to set up businesses, promote foreign direct investment, establish non-resident foreign currency accounts, and attract greater amounts of foreign exchange inflows to the country.

13.4 A Diaspora in Search of Constructive Engagement

The aftermath of the 1998-2000 border war with Ethiopia had a profound negative impact on the Eritrean state whose reverberations began to damage its relations with a significant segment of the Eritrean diaspora. In the beginning, the

---

faculty/rwinslow/africa/eritrea.html

overwhelming majority of Eritreans in the diaspora, like their compatriots at home, rallied to the support of the government and the defence of *Adebo* (Fatherland) in a wave of patriotic fervour. They lobbied host governments, civil society organisations, and media outlets for support and raised large sums of money through direct donations and the purchase of government-issued bonds to help finance the war.

After the end of the war, however, the open rupture in the top EPLF/PFDJ leadership in 2001 and the antagonistic manner of its handling caused widespread consternation and considerable disillusionment among many patriotic Eritreans in the diaspora. The ruinous events of September 2001 in particular, set a new dynamic in motion that began to corrode the hitherto symbiotic relationship between the Eritrean state and most of the Eritrean diaspora as a significant source of political, media, and financial support, and ended up bitterly dividing the diaspora itself. The extra-legal and brutal incarceration of the former senior Front, government and military officials and journalists and the concomitant closure of the private press sent shockwaves across the Eritrean public at home and in the diaspora.

The immediate and enduring response among most Eritreans in the diaspora has been a mixture of silent lamentation of the Eritrean predicament, discreet or vocal opposition to the detentions and crackdown, or slavish support for the government. Despite a hard core of vocal supporters, the regime's flagrant violation of due process and continuous transgressions against the Eritrean people with impunity have compounded growing discontent and bitter alienation among many Eritreans in the diaspora and, to a significant extent, irreversibly corroded its legitimacy in the eyes of a great many of its erstwhile veteran supporters. While the vast majority of the Eritrean diaspora has maintained stunned silence for a variety of reasons, the divisions within the activist minority have deepened and widened during the last decade, fuelling the bitter polarisation and constant fragmentation of its political, civic, and media organisations.

In the absence of access to accurate and reliable data at the national and bilateral corridor level, it is difficult to ascertain the extent to which these developments have affected the flow of remittances from the diaspora into the country. It is probable that the amount of direct flows to the regime's coffers and the scope of its centralised control of the channels and networks of money transfer might have diminished somewhat. Nevertheless, such probable decline would likely be more than offset by an increase in private remittances that provide a critical lifeline for a large number of households. Most diaspora Eritreans would not contemplate abandoning their families in these hardest of times imposed by a callous regime and a shrinking economy.

It is quite apparent that the government has alienated, antagonised, and lost the hearts and minds and, therefore, the longstanding and vital political and financial support of a great many veteran patriots and activists in Eritrea's overseas communities. The rise of a brutal dictatorship has thwarted their expectations of a free, democratic, and prosperous Eritrea. A state of general discontent with the regime has thus driven many former active supporters into quiet disengagement or discreet withdrawal. Despite the uneasy silence of the majority however, a growing number of Eritreans in the diaspora have taken up the struggle for democratic renewal as part of a broader struggle for freedom to reclaim their homeland and recover the opportunity for the Eritrean people to build a free, viable, and prosperous future.

The mobilisation of a new generation of Eritreans who are increasingly disaffected and reluctant to continue being squeezed between supporting a ruthless oppressive regime at home and an ineffective divided opposition in exile is likely to catalyse the drive to change the regime and reconstruct the state. They are keenly aware of the imperative for unity in order for the diaspora to play a vital catalytic role in the effort to bring about change and renewal in Eritrea. To be able to do so, however, the Eritrean diaspora needs to set its priorities and reset the internal discourse by engaging in *constructive dialogue within*. One way to do this would be to initiate a *platform of national conversation* aimed at constructing an *inclusive democratic frame* through the establishment of concerted local and national chapters to help bridge the divisions, mitigate the polarisation and build consensus in support of the imperative for change at home.

This would require a paradigm shift in the mentality and disposition of political, civic, and media activists in the Eritrean diaspora to give primacy to the national interest and the welfare of the people. There is an overriding need for serious soul-searching and civil discourse in the interest of critical resistance to the dictatorial regime. A stance of slavish support or blind opposition, befitting diehard football fans, would get Eritreans nowhere. There is need to beware not to be used as pawns in the geopolitics of the region under the often twisted logic of 'the enemy of an enemy is a friend' to retain credibility, legitimacy, and solidarity with the wider Eritrean public at home and abroad. Further, patriotic Eritreans have, in these extremely difficult and trying times for Eritrea and its people, a moral imperative and a historic responsibility to transcend the old ELF-EPLF divides, to rise above the petty fray and overcome the futility of fragmented and polarised politics and direct all effort to catalysing and preparing for change.

In the same vein, they have a duty to fiercely defend Eritrea's hard-won sovereign independence and territorial integrity. They should resist the divisive ploys of the regime and external forces, guard their unity, and resolutely support change from within. Perforce, changing the regime and building functional, accountable, and democratic governance in Eritrea is the task of Eritreans.

As my active engagement in the politics of Eritrean liberation started in the diaspora, where my political journey has also eventually landed me, the following chapter touches on the formative years of my life as a backdrop to discussing my role in the service of Eritrea. The purpose of the chapter is not so much to feature my service to Eritrea as to present an anecdote of personal experience that illustrates the difficulty or problem faced in the effort to render effective and conscionable public service in Eritrea under the present regime.

CHAPTER 14

In the Service of Eritrea

The reasonable man adapts himself to the world; the unreasonable one persists in trying to adapt the world to himself. Therefore, all progress depends on the unreasonable man. - George B. Shaw

For the fortunate few who escape the premature death or vicious trap of poverty that is the common lot of so many people in places like my homeland, life is a journey with many twists and turns, ups and downs, and crossroads where opportunities and choices interact to shape one's destiny. Inspired by the quest for freedom and justice, I gave up the privileged path to a life of comfort and dedicated my prime years to serving the cause of liberation, progress, and prosperity of the Eritrean people. Permanent station eluded me since early childhood. I have led the life of a global nomad, changing locales within the same country, moving from one country to another, and travelling to various corners of the world. This happened initially in pursuit of education and, later on, in the service of Eritrea and the Eritrean people.

This chapter sketches my formative years, the influences on my political orientation, and my commitment to participate in the armed struggle for the liberation of Eritrea and the progress, prosperity, and welfare of the Eritrean people. It highlights my efforts to revitalise the University of Asmera as a centre of academic excellence and build the Bank of Eritrea as a functional central bank to oversee the development of a viable financial sector and stimulate economic growth. Further, it recounts my constant efforts to build and capacitate institutions in the face of incessant presidential interference and arbitrary decisions to terminate my mandate at critical stages. This general phenomenon has subverted progress in institution building, undermined the development of functional bodies and entailed enormous waste in lost public services.

14.1 The Formative Years

I would like to recount three anecdotes to indicate the difficulty of access to education during my early schooling. First, on turning seven, which was the minimum age for school enrolment, I asked my father to let me start school. He granted my request. I went to the school and queued in one of two rows waiting to register. When my turn came, the director told me that I was "too small" to enrol and should come back in a year. Even though I had turned seven two months earlier, I looked beneath my age. I feigned to go away, turned behind the director, queued in the second row, and managed to register with the other teacher. Second, at the start of the following year, the director ordered me to redo the first grade because I was "too small" to be in the second grade. On hearing the story, my class teacher intervened to restore me to the second grade. Third, on the third year, the director turned back my younger brother because the only elementary school in the district would not enrol two children from the same family at the same time.

I thus had the luck, sealed by persistent will, to register and get the opportunity of timely access to education. I received my elementary schooling in Drco, located about midway west of the Mendefera-Adi Quala road, and attended Saint George Middle School in Mendefera. Upon finishing middle school, I started high school at the then Prince Mekonen Secondary School in Asmera, one of only two secondary schools in Eritrea and the one run by the Government of Eritrea during the federation period. After completing the ninth grade, I proceeded to the then Teachers' Training Institute (TTI) in Harar, eastern Ethiopia.

The olden and walled city of Harar seemed the edge of the world then. My parents were reluctant to let me go, but my maternal grandfather interceded on my behalf. I remember tears of love and anxiety trickling down from the corners of my mother's eyes while bidding me farewell as I boarded the bus for the three-day journey from Asmera to Addis Ababa. Leaving Eritrea at the tender age of sixteen, I lived my most formative years outside my ancestral home.

Visiting Addis Ababa for the first time in September 1962 on my way to Harar, I was struck by the relative raggedness and haphazard semi-urban façade of the Ethiopian capital, which looked like a provincial backwater compared to the tidy and superb architectural landscape of Asmera, the Eritrean capital. The two capitals have experienced marked reversal of fortunes, as Addis Ababa has flourished and Asmera decayed, particularly since 1991. After studying for two years in Harar, I left for the US in the summer of 1964 to complete my last year of high school as an exchange student under the American Field Service (AFS) programme. On my first visit to the US, I was greatly impressed by the towering skyscrapers of New York, the vast expanse of the US heartland, and the warm reception and generous hospitality of host communities in suburban America during our twenty-four hour stopovers on the way as we traversed the country by bus from New York to San Francisco. That was the longest bus trip I have ever taken to date.

I felt at home in the congenial weather and cosmopolitan milieu of the Bay Area and relished the fresh invigorating air during occasional weekend strolls in the Berkeley Hills. Politically, my arrival in the US happened in the heat of an election campaign. I witnessed an electoral process unfold for the first time and was fascinated by the fanfare and openness of US politics.

I could not help but reflect on the great contrast between the systems of government in Ethiopia and the US. In Ethiopia's backward semi-feudal political landscape, the emperor claimed and retained power by 'divine right' as 'the Elect of God'. In the developed liberal democratic state of the US, the president had to compete in an election and gain power by popular mandate. In this connection, visiting the White House with a group of fellow AFSers in July 1965 was one of the highlights of my first leg to the US; President Johnson received us in the company of his young daughters Linda and Lucy.

I supported President Johnson's stance on civil rights but strongly opposed his war policy in Vietnam. I remember participating in a panel discussion in my school, Mira Monte High School in Orinda, California, in the fall of 1964, on the presidential election campaign. I was the only one to speak in favour of Democratic candidate Lyndon B. Johnson while my fellow panellists spoke in favour of his Republican challenger, Senator Barry M. Goldwater. My host family, the Robert Blairs who were very kind and generous, were ardent supporters of candidate Goldwater and Orinda was firmly Goldwater country.[447] In supporting President Johnson's candidacy, I commended his declaration of *war on poverty*, his project of the *Great Society* and his strong support for civil rights legislation while firmly criticising his policy of war in Vietnam.

I also recall another memorable event. On a tour of the Berkeley campus of the University of California, I came face to face with a fellow Eritrean, Habteab Zerit, who was a graduate student in public health at the university. We soon became good friends and met frequently. Habteab treated me like a younger brother, showed me around and, one day, took me along to a student sit-in demonstration on campus in protest against the US War in Vietnam and heard student leader Mario Savio speak to an assembly of students and Joan Baez sing Pete Seeger's "Where Have All the Flowers Gone?" What I saw and heard then moved me very much.

At a time when the decolonisation of Africa got underway in earnest, Ethiopia had annexed Eritrea in 1962 and Eritreans were already in the throes of armed resistance. My homeland was a very poor and oppressed corner of the world. The turbulent 1960s, with the war in Vietnam and the student upheavals in Europe (Paris 1968); the anti-war

---

[447] I was once taken to a meeting of a certain John Birch Society, an extreme right wing group, where the speaker claimed that there was "a red under every bed in America" and asked the audience for financial contributions to fight the looming menace. Its founder, Robert Welch, accused Harry Truman, Dwight Eisenhower and Fuster Dulles of being part of a Soviet conspiracy and called for the impeachment of Chief Justice Earl warren.

demonstrations on university campuses and civil rights marches in the US Deep South against racial discrimination and segregation; and the struggles of the African peoples for independence from colonial domination played an important role in shaping my political perspective. I recall two incidents that cost me my dinner and have stuck in the firmament of my memory.

The first incident happened in March 1965. The evening news flashed live images of peaceful demonstrators, led by Martin Luther King, Jr., marching from Selma to Montgomery, Alabama, mistreated and clubbed by police.[448] The discussion that ensued over dinner pitted me against the rest. What I saw as a blind attempt to condone racist abuse and police violence offended my sense of justice. I left the dinner table in protest and went to my room in the basement.

Following graduation from high school, I returned home to Eritrea and, from there, proceeded to Ethiopia to continue my studies at the then Haile Selassie I University in Addis Ababa. At the end of my first year, I returned to the US to study on a scholarship at the University of Colorado in Boulder where I received Bachelor of Science and Master's Degrees within three years. I had a great time while studying in Boulder at the eastern foothills of the Rockies where the rugged mountainous terrain reminded me of my home country. I very much enjoyed driving up the winding roads

---

[448] Such abusive scenes made me sympathise with the views of Malcolm X and Eldridge Cleaver rather than those of Martin Luther King and Roy Wilkins, in the internal debate of the Afro-American community that pitted the advocates of legitimate self-defence against those of non-violent resistance as a means in the struggle for civil rights.

to the top of the nearby peaks with my friend in her MG sports car for long hikes on Sunday afternoons and skiing in Aspen on long weekends.

The second incident occurred in April 1967 in the home of a family that hosted me for dinner. The stark images of the first aerial bombing of Hanoi and Haiphong in Vietnam provoked an animated debate with my hosts that continued at the dinner table. The discussion turned into a dialogue of the deaf. There was no ambiance for rational debate. I got up, thanked my hosts, said good night and left.

In brief, support for the Afro-American civil rights movement, opposition to the war in Vietnam, and solidarity with the anticolonial struggles in the Third World stirred my deepest emotions and helped raise my awareness as an international citizen with an Eritrean identity. I was driven by a profound sense of resentment of injustice and solidarity with those who sought liberty.

The decade of the 1960s was also a time of cultural tumult in America, with rock and roll, drugs, and 'flower power' in vogue. I hated substance. I loved jazz and was particularly fond of watching the beautiful rhythm of Afro-American dancing. I also enjoyed classical and soul music. Listening to music relaxed, energised, and helped me concentrate while reading, studying or doing my homework. I would usually stack my gramophone with a pack of records playing, depending on my mood, Mozart, Beethoven, Bach, Mandel, Tchaikovsky, Aretha Franklin, Duke Ellington, Miles Davis, Barbara Streisand, Dave Brubeck, etc.

One of my best friends during my years at the University of Colorado in Boulder was a fellow Thai student of Chinese extraction. Nivot had a passion for cooking Chinese food, listening to Tchaikovsky, collecting tobacco pipes, and talking about Chairman Mao. I enjoyed his cuisine, shared his love of classical music, and kidded him for his adulation of Mao because I admired Ho Chi Minh more and preferred his poetry. My other best friends included a Norwegian (Hans), a German (Hans), and a Persian (Farouk) fellow students. We all worked hard, socialised together, and often enjoyed our respective home cooking. At the time, I shared an apartment with a fellow student from Greece, Mania Seferi. Mania was beautiful, generous, and kind. She became a professor at Harvard University and was later, killed in a tragic car accident.

Keen on a healthy lifestyle and with a knack for the good life, Mania liked to cook and introduced me to Greek and Mediterranean cuisine and a taste for vintage French wine. Our few indulgences included sipping a shot of deluxe Napoleon cognac and puffing aluminium cased Havana cigars after dinner during occasional weekend parties at home. We were deeply in love and would most probably have gotten married were it not for my hankering to join the Eritrean armed struggle for liberation and stubborn refusal to entertain the idea of going together to fight in the Field. I strongly believed, but found it hard to convince her, that it would be extremely difficult, if not very impossible, to cope up with a life of struggle in the bush.

From Boulder, I went back to Ethiopia and lectured at Haile Selassie I University for three years prior to returning to the US for the third time to pursue doctoral studies on a scholarship at Harvard University in Cambridge, Massachusetts. Boulder had its special charms for me. However, I also cherished the warm openness and cosmopolitan ambiance of Cambridge and the Boston area, which I found very much similar to those of San Francisco, and the Bay Area. Had I continued to live in the United States of America, I would probably have found it difficult to choose between the three distinctive, beautiful and hospitable locales.

In any case, I was, as a young man, driven by a profound sense of resentment of injustice and inspired by the promise of liberty for all, including the Eritrean people. Leaving the velvety comfort of Harvard University, giving up its promise of great opportunities, and going to the rugged mountains and deep ravines of Sahel to join the struggle for freedom was the right thing to do. It has been my distinct privilege to fight for the deliverance of Eritrea and the Eritrean people from foreign domination and for the birth of the Eritrean state. To the glory of the Eritrean people, the success of the armed struggle for self-determination has brought about national independence and enabled Eritrea to take its rightful place among the community of free nations. Equally as significant, it has been my distinct privilege to participate in the postliberation effort to rebuild Eritrea and advance the aspirations for freedom, progress, and wellbeing of the Eritrean people.

14.2 Dedication to the Eritrean Cause

While studying at Harvard, I linked up with some of my old friends, like Haile Menkerios, and we were all committed to serve the Eritrean struggle for self-determination and national independence. In this context, Haile and I, in particular, worked to overhaul the structure of Eritreans for Liberation in North America (EFLNA), an association of Eritrean students, workers, and women, established in 1970, that operated in close coordination with Eritreans in Europe and the Middle East to mobilise vital political, material, and financial support for the then Eritrean People's Liberation Forces (EPLF). I became the Chairman of a revamped EFLNA in 1972 and eventually gave up my studies and part-time teaching at Harvard University to devote full time to the cause of the liberation of the Eritrean people.

We were hungry for information concerning developments in the Field. We received a copy of *NHnan Elamanan* (We and Our Goals), a declaratory statement by the PLF2 leadership, and translated it from Tigrinya into English. We circulated the pamphlet in Tigrinya among members and published the English version in EFLNA's organ of *Liberation*.[449] As chairman, I travelled, always using and sharing my personal resources, often accompanied by fellow members of Executive Committee but mostly alone, to cities and towns in the US wherever there was a group of Eritreans to mobilise and organise, establish new EFLNA chapters, and raise funds and material support for the EPLF.

During the first few years of the association's existence, virtually all Eritreans in North America were affiliated with EFLNA and sympathised with or supported the EPLF. For the first time, in 1975, new arrivals from Eritrea expressed familiarity with and sympathy for the ELF and advocated that EFLNA support both fronts. Even though they managed

---

[449] EFLNA, *Liberation*, Vol. 2, No. 3, 1973, pp. 5-23. The first translation from the original Tigrinya (*NHnan Elamanan*) into English (We and Our Goals) was done by Alemseged Tesfai, Haile Menkerios, Tesfatsion Medhanie and the author, working together at Haile's and Asgedet Estifanos's apartment in Cambridge, Massachusetts, USA.

to spark lively internal debate in the association however, they remained a tiny minority, unable to change EFLNA's political stance and close affiliation with the EPLF.

I left Eritreans for Liberation in North America, Cambridge, and the US definitively in the fall of 1976 for the Field. I served as a member of the Secretariat of the First Congress of the Eritrean People's Liberation Forces (EPLF) held in Fah, then the Forces' impregnable rear base deep in the mountains of northeastern Sahel, in January 1977, and was elected member of the Front's Central Committee. Immediately after the congress, I edited and translated into English the National Democratic Programme of the EPLF as well as the resolutions and political report of the congress. I was re-elected to the Central Committee in the Second and Unity Congress of the Eritrean People's Liberation Front (EPLF) and the Eritrean Liberation Front-Central Command (ELF-CC) or *Sagem*, held in Ararb, the main rear base, in March 1987, and the Third and last Congress of the EPLF held in the EPLF's historic stronghold of Nakfa in February 1994.

During the ten years between the first and second congresses of the EPLF, I served as Deputy Secretary of the EPLF Department of Information (1977-1980) and head of foreign information (1980-1986) in the EPLF Central Bureau of Foreign Relations.[450] I also worked as a member of the Preparatory Committee and Secretariat of the Second

---

[450] The Department of Information was headed by Mahmud Ahmed (Sherifo) and the Central Bureau of Foreign Relations by Alamin Mohamed Said. Sherifo and Alamin were members of the Central Committee and the Political Bureau, the legislative and executive bodies, respectively, of the EPLF from 1977 until 1994. Later, Sherifo was one of the four former members of the EPLF Political

and Unity Congress of the EPLF. Apart from the constant mobility of life in the bush, the recurrent changes in the location of our department from Fah to Anberbeb, to Arag, and to Ararb, in response to the changing conditions of the war, accentuated the nomadic streak of life in the Field. Following the Second Congress, I served as the deputy head of the Department of Education (1987-1989) and, along with Ibrahim Idris Totil,[451] as co-editor-in-chief of *Sagem*, the Front's official organ from 1989 until the liberation in 1991. In addition, Ibrahim served as the secretary of the department of information while I served as the political commissar of the main EPLF rear base in Ararb.

On the basis of the strategy charted by the Congress, the Central Committee oversaw the conduct and developments of the war of national liberation as well as the internal dynamics and external relations of the armed and political struggle. Within the Front's overall strategy, my specific remit dealt mainly with the articulation and implementation of the EPLF's information, foreign, and education policies. My chief tasks included lettering and publishing the EPLF organs of *Vanguard* (1977), *Events* (1979-'80), *Liberation* (1980-'82), *Adulis* (1983-1986), and *Sagem* (1989-1991). I worked preparing and/or translating EPLF position papers

---

Bureau and among the seven other former senior officials detained in September 2001 and never heard from since.

[451] Ibrahim Totil, the former vice-chairman of the ELF, became a member of the central committee of the EPLF when the ELF Central Command (Sagem), a splinter of the ELF, merged with the EPLF in the Second and Unity Congress of the EPLF in 1987. Ibrahim has been 'frozen' since his dismissal as administrator of the Northern Red Sea Region in 2002 and reportedly arrested following the events of 21 January 2013 in Asmera.

and petitions and heading or deputising EPLF delegations to UN General Assembly sessions, OAU Summits, and African and Middle Eastern capitals to plead the just case of the Eritrean people for self-determination and solicit international support for their legitimate aspirations.

After Eritrea's liberation from Ethiopia in 1991, I participated in the effort to reconstruct and develop Eritrea and promote the progress and wellbeing of the Eritrean people. Driven by a deep desire to help advance the paramount interests of Eritrea and enhance the human condition of the Eritrean people, I endeavoured to institutionalise a rules-based *modus operandi*, or method of work. Further, I strove to promote prudent bilateral and multilateral economic, financial, and technical cooperation and advocated a policy of proactive and constructive engagement with the international community and Eritrea's development partners, in particular.

14.3 Revitalising the University of Asmera

At the time of liberation, Eritrea lacked a critical mass of skilled and qualified work force needed to kick start rapid reconstruction and sustainable development. During the war, most of the country's tiny educated elite had joined the ranks of the liberation army or fled into exile. Eritrean professionals, technicians, mechanics, and workers left home and Ethiopia in droves to escape repression, join the armed struggle or seek refuge in the Middle East, Europe, North America, and Australia. Many graduates and students from the University of Asmera and Ethiopian, European, and US universities flocked to the Field to fight for liberation.

In the Field, certain senior members of the EPLF political bureau viewed successful university graduates with

459

deep apprehension and disparaged independent thought. They felt more at ease and self-confident in the camaraderie of the dropouts, the less schooled, and the half-baked. In spite of the top leadership's self-serving anti-intellectual strand and general deprecation of the more learned, there is no denying that Eritrea's intellectuals, professionals, and technocrats, many of whom joined the armed struggle from outside the country, played an indispensable role in the operations, achievements, and victory of the armed struggle for liberation.

Having committed 'class suicide' in order to integrate themselves into a predominantly peasant liberation army and overcome subjection to constant suspicion, surveillance, and subordinate positions in the leading organs of the Front and the army, Eritrea's revolutionary intellectuals were instrumental in helping build the internal capacity of the EPLF, articulate the legitimacy of the Eritrean struggle for self-determination, and project a progressive image of the Front to the outside world. By the end of the war, however, the attrition of martyrdom in the Field, abetted by migration and ageing in the overall society, had significantly reduced the number of Eritrean intellectuals, professionals, and would-be technocrats at the disposal of the new state.

I thus welcomed my assignment as president of the University of Asmera in July 1991 as an opportunity to help fill in this gap by catalysing the creation of the necessary conditions to equip a new generation of Eritreans with the knowledge, skills, and expertise required to build and shape the Eritrea of the future. I set out to assess the situation on the ground and drew up an action plan to immediately re-open the university and gradually rebuild its capacity. The proposal was endorsed by the then Secretary General of the Provisional Government of Eritrea (PGE) and current president of the Transitional Government of Eritrea (TGE).

Accordingly, I reinstated the university in September 1991 literally from scratch and opened its doors to several hundred students for the 1991-1992 school year with the few members of its former faculty and personnel, comprising those who were already in Asmera and those who came back from Agarfa. During the first year of its reinstatement, I actively encouraged and recruited many leading Eritrean academics, mostly from Addis Ababa University in Ethiopia, to return to teach and help rebuild the university without salaries. Most of those who joined the faculty during the first two years served without salaries, just in return for free accommodation in the university's limited housing facilities endowed under the Ethiopian regime.

The University of Asmera was originally founded in 1958 by the *Piae Madres Nigritiae*, or the Comboni Sisters, as the Catholic College of Santa Famiglia. It had, despite years of subjection to containment and the disruption of final displacement under Ethiopian rule, retained the imprint of its ecclesiastical beginnings, especially in the parochial patronage of the remnants of most of its former staff. As a newly reinstituted national university, it had the potential to develop into a viable and fully-fledged all-Eritrea institution of higher learning and academic as well as applied research worth its name and worthy of international accreditation.

Deeply convinced that Eritrea's rapid and sustainable development depended primarily on the proper education and training of its human resources, especially its youth, I had a vision to transform the University into a citadel of quality tertiary education, equipped with modern assets and state of the art facilities. It would focus on higher learning and development-oriented research, complemented by a satellite of technical and vocational schools to train and avail the opportunity for continuing education to secondary school graduates who do not make it to the university the first time around. As symbolised by its new emblem, rebuilding and revitalising the university would enable it to develop Eritrea's human resources and make a positive contribution to the national effort for reconstruction and development in an increasingly knowledge based and high technology driven globalised world.

With the active support and participation of the university faculty and Eritrean academics from the Diaspora and international partners, I organised a Symposium on the Revitalisation of the University of Asmera in August 1992. The principal objective of the symposium was to create a forum for democratic debate on the strategy, structure, and policy options of tertiary education in the new Eritrea among policy makers, practitioners, and scholars and help chart the future of the university. The symposium came up with recommendations to restructure the colleges and faculties, revise the syllabus, upgrade the size and competence of the faculty, and modernise the assets and facilities of the emerging university.

In addition, I instituted, bringing in international expertise and pooling local competence, special training programmes and evening courses in public administration to help build managerial capacity and upgrade skills of former fighters turned government officials and civil servants. I also opened the gates of the university to eligible former fighters and government and private employees to resume their higher education. People who had no opportunity to go through or to complete the normal secondary school stream were encouraged to seat for the Eritrean School Leaving

Certificate Examination (ESLCE), or matriculation, for high school graduates and those who scored passing marks were granted admission to the university.

Further, I drew up a draft Charter of the University of Asmera to establish its legal personality, to govern its internal affairs, and to define its relations with the outside community. The draft Charter was designed to establish the legal status of the university as an autonomous institution of higher learning. It envisaged the emergence and growth of a national centre of excellence that promoted higher education in the pursuit of knowledge and applied research in the service of the country's development agenda, free from overt political interference.

The draft Charter aimed to enshrine academic freedom as an essential ingredient of unfettered intellectual development and sanction the inviolability of the premises of the university as a bastion of scientific research, critical discourse, and free exchange of ideas among the faculty, staff, students, and the larger community. In defence of this perspective, I opposed attempts to put the university under the aegis of the ministry of education and suggestions to incorporate its students into the National Union of Eritrean Students and Youth (NUESY).

The draft Charter also designated the head of state of Eritrea as the chancellor of the university. I submitted the draft Charter to the then Secretary General of the PGE and current president of the TGE and requested him to review and present it to the Provisional Eritrean National Assembly for promulgation. I also asserted that I would, in the meantime, use the structure, principles, and objectives embedded in the draft Charter as a framework to guide the effort to rebuild and revitalise the university.

As president, I considered laying a solid foundation for the transformation of the university into an autonomous national centre of excellence the core of my mission. Increasing the number and raising the quality of the academic staff represented a vital element of that strategy. As part of the preparation, I set up a select committee of senior faculty members to review the academic credentials of the faculty, to propose ways and means to upgrade their professional competence, and to establish the criteria for future recruitment.

The move was misconstrued and maligned, via the grapevine, by a few members of the old faculty who feared that professional scrutiny would adversely affect their tenure and undermine the university's clerical legacy. I later learned from a high official of the ministry of internal affairs that they had followed the case and that the grapevine on campus was joined by a smear campaign in town allegedly spearheaded by a senior official in the hierarchy of the Catholic Church in Asmera at the time. He also told me that certain senior officials in the Front and the government had joined in and added fuel to the underhanded campaign.

On the road to transformation, I set out to establish technical cooperation with international agencies, such as the Norwegian Agency for Development Cooperation (NORAD), the Swedish International Development Agency (SIDA), and UNESCO, and initiate programmes of academic cooperation, faculty and student exchange, and twining projects with universities in Africa, Europe, and the USA. These arrangements aimed to help upgrade the academic qualification and professional competence of the faculty and graduate assistants by opening up opportunities for the pursuit of graduate studies leading to master's and doctoral degrees in sister universities abroad and catalyse the revitalisation of the university and its constituent colleges. Besides, technical cooperation aimed to catalyse the transformation of the university, enhance its academic standing, and accelerate its international accreditation.

At a time when the process of revitalisation had started revving on high gear and began to gather momentum, I was relieved of my duty as president of the university. The Secretary General's impromptu decision was made amid drinking in celebration of the vote for independence in the referendum on self-determination at the Emba Soira Hotel in Asmera in the early hours of 28 April 1993. I gathered from the uninhibited side conversation that my drive to institutionalise the autonomy of the university and transform it into a national centre of excellence and academic freedom free of political interference in the conduct of its internal affairs had pricked sensitive nerves.[452]

Despite his initial nod of agreement, the Secretary General of the PGE did not present the draft Charter of the university to the provisional Eritrean National Assembly for enactment. Its formal adoption remained pending at the time I handed over the presidency of the university. My successor was unable to secure the adoption and implementation of the draft Charter as a guarantee for the independence of the university, academic freedom for its faculty and students, and a bulwark against political interference in its internal affairs.

---

[452] After my departure from the university, the government dismissed all former members of the Derg's Ethiopian Workers' Party (ኢሰፓ in its Amharic acronym), some of whom had started the smear campaign, from the faculty and posted them in other government departments and agencies.

In the fleeting moment of national ferment that enveloped the Eritrea of 2001, the government became particularly apprehensive of potential student support for the demand for change and the university was targeted for shadowing and student activities closely monitored for any signs of link with the senior officials or organised protest. The government moved quickly to quash their dissent when university students refused to sign up for the mandatory summer work programme and protested the arrest of the leader of the student union in July 2001. The president of the Student Union of the University of Asmera was arrested for making critical remarks, in a speech delivered on behalf of the graduating class of 2001 during the commencement exercises at the university, concerning the summer work programme, the interference of the government in the internal affairs of the university, and the inadequacy of the university's facilities.

The government's apprehension of the potential political activism of university students and fear of their propensity to organise, mobilise, and spearhead nationwide student demonstrations in support of the demand for reform led to a decision to dismantle the only university in the country in the name of decentralisation. The University of Asmera was finally closed in 2006. Under conditions of general resource scarcity, upgrading the university, modernising its existent assets, and gradually establishing additional colleges or institutes in other parts of the country to expand opportunities for and access to higher education would have made more economic and academic sense than closing it. After all, establishing a new institute or college worth its name takes many years and requires considerable resources:

a purpose-built physical infrastructure, a critical mass of qualified academic and administrative personnel as well as modern library, laboratory, ICT and sports facilities.

The arbitrary closure of the University of Asmera and the displacement of its colleges and faculties to makeshift and substandard militarised 'institutes or colleges', located mostly in rural areas isolated from the country's main population centres, was thus a political, not an academic, decision. The decision was primarily motivated by the desire to undermine the transformative role of higher education and, as stated above, forestall potential student protest at the cost of downgrading and trivialising the substance of higher education. The closure of the university campus in the capital and the dispersal of students in several disparate locations splinter the mass of the student body while the military style regimentation of their daily life facilitates close surveillance, monitoring, and control of their activities.

By any standards, the current hodgepodge of ill planned, poorly constructed, understaffed and inadequately equipped institutes, faculties or colleges represent inferior substitutes for what was an established university in the making. But the idea serves its purpose to fragment the student body, thwart development of quality higher education, and negate its contribution to critical thinking, political consciousness, and constructive action towards the empowerment of the people. For, in a normal academic setting, the transformative function of higher education would operate to cultivate an awareness of freedom, develop an ability to discern authoritarian propensities, and internalise a desire to connect learning and knowledge to the 'broader struggle for agency, justice and democracy'.[453] Besides negating such benefits, the demotion of higher education would lower Eritrean academic standards and research capability, deprive Eritrean intellect and talent of proper cultivation and optimal development, postpone the modernisation of Eritrea and undermine the progress and wellbeing of the Eritrean people.

In any case, after a brief period of idle suspension following my dismissal from the presidency of the University of Asmera, I was assigned as governor of the Bank of Eritrea.

14.4 Building a Functional Central Bank

Reflecting on my task as governor, I became keenly aware of the difficult challenge of building a functional central bank in a newly independent state virtually from scratch. I was equally aware of the sensitive nature of the work of the bank and its potentially crucial role in stimulating the growth and development of the national economy. Drawing a lesson from my experience at the university and keen to operate free of political interference, I had, in a one-on-one discussion with the president at the time he informed me of my assignment to the new post, proposed that the Bank of Eritrea be constituted as an independent central bank. He gave his consent to my proposal and I proceeded to constitute an independent central bank.

Accordingly, the central bank would have statutory authority over the formulation and execution of monetary

---

[453] Giroux, Henry A., "Lessons From Paulo Freire", The Chronicle of Higher Education, 22 October 2010, Vol. 57, Issue 9.

policy, the management of foreign exchange reserves, and the regulation and supervision of the financial sector in line with national development objectives and priorities. It would also have responsibility for the negotiation, with the central banks of trading partners, of clearing arrangements for outstanding current account balances in the country's international trade position. Further, in view of its principal mandate to ensure macroeconomic stability and stimulate economic growth, the central bank would have a voice in fiscal decisions concerning the size of the government's budget deficit, domestic borrowing, and external debt.

To my surprise, the president, quite uncharacteristically, offered his apologies for my removal from the university and told me how much he appreciated my dedication and professionalism. At the same time, he characteristically blamed others for misleading him into making a precipitous decision. I knew better not to be taken in by his apology or praise. For, with all due respect to the dignity of his office, he is utterly trapped in a personality that is devoid of integrity of mind, loyalty in personal relations, and prudence in the judgment of others that find expression in a penchant for hasty conclusions and rash decisions without adequate evidence, verification of the facts or concern for the consequences.

Managing a sardonic smile, I replied that the question was not just about me; that the problem was his propensity to rush to decisions on the basis of one-sided information or hearsay without reflection, without giving a fair hearing to the maligned party, without questioning the motives of eager informants or verifying the accuracy of their often mendacious intimations. I reiterated that he needed to correct this tendency so as to avoid collateral damage. His grimace and body language told me that my advice was more of an irritant than a corrective.

Immediately after the liberation, Eritrea continued to use the Ethiopian Birr (ETB) as its legal tender. What remained of the former Asmera branch of the National Bank of Ethiopia was renamed the National Bank of Eritrea.[454] On assuming my position as governor, I renamed it the Bank of Eritrea. Beyond the routine replenishment of the Birr supply in the vaults to ensure adequate currency circulation in the Eritrean economy, there was no role for the central bank or agreed mechanism to synchronize the foreign exchange, monetary, and trade finance policies and practices of the two states. An independent Eritrea needed a functional central bank to formulate its own monetary and fiscal policies in the service of its development agenda.

In close consultation and cooperation with the senior personnel, I set out to constitute an autonomous central bank and build up a critical mass of competence needed to perform its principal functions. I drew up a new emblem symbolising the bank's motto, as I had done before for the university. I planned to recruit, as explained in the preceding chapter, academics and professionals from the Eritrean diaspora in Ethiopia, Europe, and the USA to help build the capacity of the central bank and revitalise the financial sector.

---

[454] Dr. Araya Tsegai, an economist and a longtime member of EFLNA and NUESY, its successor organisation after 1978, who had returned from the US, was briefly in charge and had started to organise the former Asmera branch of the National Bank of Ethiopia into the central bank under the name of the National Bank of Eritrea.

Further, I drew up a draft Bank of Eritrea Law and a draft Financial Institutions Act. The primary aim in drafting the two documents was to establish the legal personality of, and lay the foundations for, an independent central bank and the prudent regulation of the nascent financial sector in line with the vision to turn Eritrea into a regional hub of financial services. The draft Bank of Eritrea Law and the draft Financial Institutions Act were reviewed and materially enhanced by comments and suggestions from Professor Abraham Kidane, as already mentioned in the preceding chapter, and Mr. Hans Lesshafft, my adviser from the Bundesbank.[455]

To help lay the groundwork for the plan to turn Eritrea into a centre of financial services, I had invited, with the approval of the president, a prominent German architect, Eng. Hans Fischer, to design and build a new Bank of Eritrea building and the physical infrastructure for the future financial centre in Asmera. The blueprint incorporated modern office space, living quarters, shopping malls, and green areas as well as subterranean vaults and parking floors. In addition, the subterranean structures included aqueducts to harness the abundant underground water detected during the drilling for the soil tests and cisterns to collect rainwater harvested from the buildings to be connected, upon purification, to the city's water supply system.

---

[455] Mr. Hans Lesshafft, the former president of the Nurenberg Landesbank, served as an adviser to the Bank of Eritrea on the secondment of Mr.Hans Tietmeyer, the then President of the Bundesbank, the central bank of the Federal Republic of Germany. We first met in the annual meeting of the IMF Board of Directors in Washington, DC, in the fall of 1993 and quickly struck a very warm and fruitful friendship.

The state of the art design was readily embraced by the president, the then mayor of Asmera, Sebhat Efrem, and the minister of public works, Abraha Asfaha. The buildings would be constructed in style to smoothly integrate with central Asmera's Italianate architecture. Accordingly, soil tests for the construction site were undertaken in 1994 and building projected to begin immediately thereafter and finish within a maximum of three years. The planned introduction of Eritrea's currency, the Nakfa, was the main factor in determining the timing. The value of the old buildings and properties in the area designated for the construction of the financial centre was assessed with the help of engineers from the city's urban housing unit, the rightful owners identified from municipal cadastral records, and the money set aside to pay for the compensation ahead of the planned ceremony for laying the foundation.

The Bank of Eritrea had accumulated a sizeable stock of gold through purchases from inside Eritrea and Ethiopia. Until 1993, gold extracted through artisanal mining in southwestern Eritrea used to be sold for Birr 50 per gram in Kassala, eastern Sudan, and Shire Endaselassie, northwestern Ethiopia, while its price on the world market was around Birr 100 per gram. By arranging to buy gold at Birr 65 per gram on the spot within Eritrea, the bank managed to stop the informal export of Eritrean gold to the Sudan and Ethiopia, reverse the trend, and attract a continuous and a constantly increasing inflow of gold into Eritrea.

To facilitate the informal import of the precious metal in the interest of building the country's gold reserves, the bank established a revolving fund for the RSTC, amounting to several millions of Birr, for the purchase of the gold which, upon acquisition, was recast into standard gold bars or bullions of 99.99 percent purity. After clearing the idea with the president, the Bank of Eritrea had planned to sell part of the gold reserves to secure the funds to finance the construction of the new Bank of Eritrea building and the envisaged financial centre. To that end, I had, with the help of the good offices of the architect, initiated discussions with a senior member of the management of a German corporation, Degussa, who expressed a keen interest in making the necessary funds available through direct purchase or in exchange for custody of the gold holdings as collateral at an agreed rate of annual interest.

Meanwhile, the draft Bank of Eritrea Law and the draft Financial Institutions Act were submitted to the president for review, presentation to the Transitional National Assembly, and formal adoption to establish the legal personality and supervisory mandate of the central bank. Upon my insistence, it was agreed that, pending their enactment, the draft documents would serve as the legal framework for the operations of the central bank and the supervision of the financial sector. I set out to constitute a functional central bank and develop a viable financial sector, prioritising the building of physical infrastructure, institutional capacity, and operational competence. In the end however, my work was subverted and the draft Law and the draft Act were, like the draft Charter of the University of Asmera before them, never presented to the National Assembly for adoption or enacted as proclamations.

Reneging on his endorsement of the two documents in private, the president shelved the draft Bank of Eritrea Law and the draft Financial Institutions Act and impeded their statutory adoption. This was part of an emerging pattern of contradictory and detrimental presidential behaviour: making declarations and paying lip service to the need to build institutions in formal meetings and public utterances while obstructing concrete efforts to develop and capacitate institutions or operationalise regulations and rules of procedure.

Over two decades of actual government practice demonstrates that President Isaias abhors the notion of the rule of law, detests institution building, and obstructs the institutionalisation of policy and decision making. He sees them as nuisances that would constrain his authority. In a way, institutions and the rule of law, if allowed to develop and become operational, would rein in his 'prerogative' to issue instant directives and on the spot decisions without the 'inconvenience' of due reflection and appropriate consideration of their adverse effects.

My short tenure as governor of the Bank of Eritrea offered me a chance to apply directly my academic training in economics but proved a very difficult assignment full of challenging episodes. It was a period of transition, which required the leadership of the EPLF to adapt the default command mode developed and applied in running the war of national liberation to the imperative of dialogue and consensus building in managing the affairs of state. Unlike during our time in the Field, a confidential conversation or an oral message was no longer an adequate medium or a sufficient instrument to transmit an order or implement a directive, especially when the issue involved substantial financial transactions or transfers.

There were difficulties arising from inexperience in statecraft, reluctance to separate the role of the Front and the functions of the State, and readiness to subordinate the economic and financial interests of the State to those of the Front. I will recount three incidents to illustrate the practical problems encountered in developing the work of the nascent central bank. One, a technical issue involving a bank loan to the ministry of finance; two, an interstate issue involving Eritrea's then current account surplus in its trade balance with Ethiopia; and three, a policy issue involving the privileged access of the Front to state resources.

First, the issue involving the government borrowing: The government needed money to pay for the first round of demobilisation of former fighters. This legitimate public obligation required proper fulfilment. At the close of a meeting of the Front's central committee one evening, the president invited the then minister of finance, Haile Weldensae (Drue), and I to his office and, explaining the purpose, instructed me to make money available to the minister. I agreed and, after the meeting, we drove across the street to the former colonial governor's mansion, now State House, where we shared dinner, drinks, and chitchat before retiring to our homes.

A few days later, the minister called me and asked for the transfer of the money to the treasury's account. I replied that I would readily do so but that we needed to agree on the amount and terms of the loan before I can transfer it to the treasury's account. He retorted that I had agreed to the directive to give the money and should do so forthwith. I confirmed what he said, affirmed my readiness to do so, and explained the need to fulfil certain formalities in order to transfer it; but the argument continued and ended our conversation on a sour note without agreeing.

To help resolve the issue and move forward, I prepared a raft contract between the bank and the ministry specifying the amount, duration, and terms of the loan and asked one of my deputies to hand deliver it to the minister for comments or signature. The minister refused to comment on or sign the contract and called me to confirm his refusal. I politely but firmly stated that I needed his agreement confirmed by his signature in order to transfer the money in accordance with the contract. The next day, I received a fuming phone call from the president accusing me of arrogance and insubordination. I was in the midst of a meeting with a visiting IMF delegation. Restraining my indignation with difficulty, I responded that he did not have all the facts and that he should summon both of us to a meeting together at his earliest convenience.

I took three copies each of the draft Bank of Eritrea Law, the proposed contract, and a prepared discount table to the meeting with the president and the minister. I was the last one to arrive and the atmosphere was palpably tense. After the normal exchange of greetings with a customary handshake, I handed them the extra copies and, trying to stay collected, explained that the central bank was an agency, and the banker, of the government.

Further, I stated that the money in the vaults did not belong to the bank, the government or the ministry; it belonged to the people of Eritrea held in trust in the central and commercial banks. Asserting that the bank was the lender of last resort, I explained the terms of the loan. The long grace period; the nominal interest or discount rate applied to the loan intended to maintain the present value of the money at the time of repayment; a timeframe for repayment; the bank's prerogative to unilateral reimbursement from the treasury account in the event of default; etc. After verifying that the minister had received the proposed loan contract, the president told him to sign the contract and get the money.

Second, the issue involving Eritrea's trade surplus with
Ethiopia: Almost four decades of living within the bounds of
a single sovereign state under the federation and subsequent
occupation (1952-1991) had integrated the economies
of Eritrea and Ethiopia and made them interdependent
with a unified financial system under a single currency,
the Ethiopian Birr (ETB). Prior to Eritrea's accession
to independence, Eritrea-Ethiopia trade was essentially
intrastate trade subject to Ethiopian domestic commercial
jurisdiction. Under the then prevailing domestic trade
regime, Eritrea, as an administrative region of Ethiopia, had
its prescribed quota of imports for two categories of goods
from the rest of Ethiopia, namely, foreign exchange earners,
such as coffee and leather, and goods in short supply, such
as cement and timber.

The quota system under the old trade regime continued
when Eritrea became *de facto* as well as *de jure* independent
in the early 1990s while there was no reciprocal restriction
on Eritrean exports to Ethiopia. At the same time, the
government of Eritrea had agreed, following the formal
declaration of independence, to receive payments for Eritrea's
exports of goods and services to Ethiopia, including transit
and port services fees, except in the case of cargo services
paid for in hard currency by the shipper or consignee,
in Ethiopian Birr. Eritrea also paid for its imports from
Ethiopia in ETB. In short, the ETB served as the medium
of commercial exchange and trade finance between Eritrea
and Ethiopia.

The Eritrean ports of Asseb and Massawa served as the
principal ports of transit for Ethiopia, handling the bulk of
its foreign trade. Meanwhile, the historical integration of
the two economies had created the lopsided dependence

of Eritrea on the Ethiopian market for the export of about 80 per cent of its industrial produce and 67 per cent of its total exports. At the same time, Eritrea re-exported a sizable fraction of imports from third countries, paid for in hard currency, to Ethiopia. Eritrea received the proceeds for all of its exports of goods and services to Ethiopia in Birr, the bulk of which Eritrea could neither spend in the free purchase of goods and services in the Ethiopian market nor exchange for hard currency.

Such an arrangement of bilateral trade led to the accumulation of a relatively large current account surplus in Eritrea's balance of trade with Ethiopia. The current account surplus is a measure of a country's value of exports minus the value of its imports. By early 1994, Eritrea's current account surplus with Ethiopia amounted to about ETB 1.4 b, detailed in a memo.[456]

Upon the independence of Eritrea, the governments of Ethiopia and Eritrea had agreed that Eritrea would use the Ethiopian Birr pending issuance of its own currency; and to harmonise exchange rate policies and interest rate structures, devise a mechanism to coordinate increases in money supply, and set up a scheme to synchronise foreign exchange policies in the transitional Birr zone.[457] The two states had also agreed that Ethiopia would reissue the new Birr with the insignia of the Federal Democratic Republic and Eritrea introduce its currency at the same time. However, there was no provision

---

[456] Memo from the Governor of the Bank of Eritrea to the President of the State of Eritrea, Asmera, 1994.

[457] Protocol Agreement between the Federal Democratic Republic of Ethiopia and the State of Eritrea on Harmonization of Economic Policies, September 1993, Article 1.

for the Bank of Eritrea to play a role in the formulation of the monetary policy of the Birr zone and partake of the seigniorage arising from issuing new Birr notes that accrued exclusively to the National Bank of Ethiopia.

By mid-1994, preparations for the issuance of Eritrea's currency were complete. The transitional Eritrean National Assembly had, after an unusually lively debate, adopted Nakfa as the name of the legal tender of the country and unanimously endorsed the proposed design and denomination of the notes and designations of the coins. The design of the notes, for issue in denominations of 100, 50, 10, 5 and 1 Nakfa bills, would be of identical size and colour. The 100 and 50 Nakfa notes would have very strong built-in security features to discourage potential counterfeit printing. The coins would be in designations of 100 cents, 50, 25, 10, 5 and 1 cent.

The suggestion of 'Nakfa' for the new Eritrean currency came from Peter Miovich, a visiting World Bank official over an informal dinner in Asmera to symbolise steadfastness and resilience in economic reconstruction and development as in the war of national liberation. The identical size and uniform colour of the notes of all five denominations, distinguishable one from the other only by a figure denoting the relative value, signified the determination of the new state to create a fully literate society within a very short time. The images of Eritrea's nationalities on one side of the notes and the scenes from various regions of the country on the other aimed to represent the diversity and unity of the Eritrean nation state.

At a time when preparations for the issuance of the Eritrean Nakfa (ERN) had advanced to the final stage, settling the issue of Eritrea's current account surplus assumed a new urgency as a crucial factor affecting its par value.[458] Time was running out to conclude an amicable settlement of the issue. There was an Economic Policy Board, chaired by the president and constituted of Haile Weldensae (Drue), minister of finance, Gebreselassie Yossief (Inteto), director general of the department of finance in the ministry, Yemane Tesfai, general manager of the commercial bank, and the author as governor of the central bank.

When the president dithered on the issue, I raised it to force a decision in one of the board's meetings. There was however, no decision, and the issue remained a recurring non-agenda item cropping up just prior to the adjournment of the board's meetings, with the discussion caught between the reluctance of the president to tackle the issue and my insistence to seek a resolution through formal consultation with the relevant authorities of the Ethiopian government. The president's justification for his disinclination to press the issue was that Eritrea had not only economic but also other interests, such as political and security interests, with Ethiopia.

Of course, I completely agreed with the president, and continue to appreciate deeply that Eritrea has strategic political, security, and economic interests with Ethiopia.

---

[458] There were two issues pending: selecting a printer from a shortlist and deciding whose signature would appear on the new Nakfa notes. The president wanted to put his signature on the Nakfa notes. I had suggested that it was unusual for a head of state to co-sign and that the governor's signature would normally suffice. He was unhappy with my suggestion and insisted on co-signing. In hindsight, it is probable that the desire to get his way might have been an additional factor in my dismissal as governor of the central bank.

Eritrea and Ethiopia, closely linked by geography, history and culture and bound together by a common future, share overriding reciprocal strategic interests. Therefore, what I argued for was for balance and reciprocity in safeguarding the accrual of mutual short-term benefits and sustaining the shared long-term and strategic interests of the two countries.

In brief, I insisted that Eritrea's strategic interests with Ethiopia would be better served, and cooperative bilateral relations between Eritrea and Ethiopia sustained, only if based on mutual engagement under agreed and binding commitments. I emphasised that Eritrea and Ethiopia did not have a common currency; that Eritrea was using the Ethiopian currency with Ethiopia's consent and regular replenishment of Birr to ensure an adequate level of money supply in the Eritrean economy pending the issuance of an Eritrean legal tender. I underscored that Eritrea had, otherwise, no say in the monetary and fiscal policies governing the Birr zone and had to adopt its own interest and exchange rate policies to manage its economy effectively.

Further, I contended that Eritrea's post-independence agreement to receive payments in Birr, an inconvertible currency, for its exports to Ethiopia was, in the first place, imprudent and its consequences were detrimental to Eritrea's economic and financial interests. I asserted that receipts in Birr, instead of in a convertible currency, for Eritrea's exports to Ethiopia effectively represented a balance of payments subsidy and Eritrea could not afford to continue subsidising the Ethiopian economy. I stressed that, unless settled expeditiously, the huge and growing trade surplus would depress the value of the Nakfa at birth and fan macroeconomic instability.

To remedy the situation and to settle the large current account surplus, I proposed to the president that Eritrea initiate immediate consultations with Ethiopia. I suggested that Eritrea should seek and secure Ethiopia's assent to settle the trade surplus through one or a combination of two options: Redeeming the Birr surplus in hard currency or opening up the Ethiopian market for 'foreign exchange earners' and 'goods in short supply' to allow Eritrea to spend its Birr holdings and recoup its foreign exchange earnings.

The president often betrayed irritation at my insistence and, when I finished talking, broke up the last meeting of the board in mid-session in a fit of uncontrolled anger. Apparently relenting after a few days, he delegated the then minister of finance and the governor of the central bank to raise the issue with his Ethiopian counterpart in. Our delegation, Haile Weldensae, Haile Menkerios, then our ambassador to Ethiopia, and the author, met with the then President Meles Zenawi and his economic advisors, Neway Gebreab and Kassu Ilala, in his office at Emperor Menelik's old palace in Addis Ababa.

At the beginning of the discussion, President Meles said that he saw no problem with the issue. Stating that since the Birr was Ethiopia's legal tender and the two countries had already agreed to issue the new Birr and introduce the Nakfa at the same time, he proposed that Eritrea collects all the Birr in its possession and hands it over to Ethiopia on the day of introduction of the two currencies for incineration. That would be the end of the story as far as Ethiopia was concerned. I replied that the Birr in Eritrea's possession was not Ethiopia's property but its liability; that the amount represented the "I Owe You' of the people of Eritrea on the economy of Ethiopia arising from the surplus of Eritrea's exports of goods and services to Ethiopia over its imports of goods and services from Ethiopia received in Birr. Alternately, it was Ethiopia's merchandise and services trade deficit with Eritrea.

After further discussion of the issue, including options for its resolution, we were able to reach agreement in principle. The president summed up the conclusion: Ethiopia would be willing to settle Eritrea's surplus with the proviso that reconciliation of the trade statistics of the two countries shows that Eritrea's trade surplus with Ethiopia is equivalent to Ethiopia's trade deficit with Eritrea. In other words, verify whether Eritrea's figures of its exports to and imports from Ethiopia match Ethiopia's figures of its imports from and exports to Eritrea. The President of Ethiopia had agreed to a resolution of the issue at the political level. What remained was for the President of Eritrea to endorse the proposed solution and agree to a joint technical follow-up to reconcile the indicated surplus/deficit values in the relevant data of the two countries and present the findings to the two presidents for expeditious settlement.

Upon our return to Asmera, I briefed the president and submitted detailed minutes of our meeting with President Meles and his economic advisors. The president made disparaging remarks, as he always does in speaking of third persons, about Meles's ability to grasp the issue. I disagreed and stated my impression that, if he had other ideas before, Ethiopia's president was on top of the issue now. The president then stated that we will go together to see Meles to conclude the matter. One early morning after a few weeks, the president called me to the airport, without advance notice, and we flew to Addis Ababa aboard his Challenger.

We were warmly welcomed in Addis and generously hosted at Emperor Haile Selassie's former Jubilee Palace.

President Meles would leave for his office after breakfast and re-join us in the evening while Siye Abraha,[459] kept us company and treated us to helicopter-borne sightseeing. The two presidents engaged in spontaneous discussions on various regional and global topics as the rest of us mostly listened and joined in the friendly chitchat on random issues over and after meals. As the days went by, I kept on reminding the president to seal the deal with his counterpart. He never did, at least not in my presence. On the third or fourth day, after breakfast, he told me that they were going with Meles to Kampala to see Museveni (the president of Uganda) while I was to wait for him in Addis. However, I pleaded with the president to let me return to Asmera to attend to some urgent business.

The issue of Eritrea's trade surplus remained unresolved at the time of introduction of the Nakfa in May 1997. In addition, there arose disagreements over the adoption of a payments mechanism for bilateral trade between the two countries with the introduction of the Nakfa. Eritrea favoured the establishment of a payments system that would let the Nakfa and the Birr to float and be freely convertible, and to allow bilateral trade transaction with or without opening a letter of credit (LC) with a bank. On the other hand, Ethiopia preferred the use of the US dollar as the official medium of exchange between the Birr and the Nakfa with an LC system, except in the case of cross border petty-trade not exceeding ETB 2,000 in value.

---

[459] Siye Abraha was then Ethiopian Minister of Defence and now a member of the Ethiopian opposition Unity for Democracy and Justice Party.

Given political will, the question of a trade settlements mechanism was a technical issue that could have been resolved by the central banks of the two countries, if given the mandate. A foreign exchange-based payments system, commonly used the world over, which was one of three options initially proposed by Eritrea, could have served as a basis for discussion to work out a mutually acceptable settlements mechanism. However, there seemed to have been no appetite for earnest negotiations at the top as the two governments atypically went public and resorted to using their own media to air their disagreements, defend their respective positions, and level veiled criticism at the other's proposals.

There was, right from the outset, an obvious and profound need to address the implications of Eritrea's independence on the vital economic and trade relations between the two countries. The new reality had turned the nature of Eritrea-Ethiopia trade from intrastate into interstate and would therefore, require resetting the new bilateral economic and trade relationship. Agreement on a new paradigm was the more necessary as the two states pursued divergent development policies. Eritrea's attempts to secure agreement on the free flow of goods and services with Ethiopia met resistance from the TPLF and faced obstruction at the border with Tigray/Ethiopia. When Mahmud Sherifo, in his capacity as the head of the Eritrean higher commissions, raised the issue with his Ethiopian counterpart, then Prime Minister Tamrat Layne retorted casually: "Why don't you try to resolve it with your cousins (meaning the Tigrayans)?"[460]

---

[460] In a conversation, during a secluded consultation meeting between the two leaders of the Eritrean and Ethiopian delegations of higher

There were, indeed, persistent indications of a simmering undercurrent, with its epicentre in the Tigray Regional State, flowing to transform the historical complementarity of the Ethiopian and Eritrean economies into a competitive relationship in favour of the development of Tigray. With a Tigray People's Liberation Front (TPLF) dominated government in Addis Ababa, Tigray had a chance to overcome the consequences of the region's historical neglect, marginalisation, and underdevelopment. Industrial plants, such as textile, cement, and beverage factories, whose products would substitute or directly compete against Eritrea's similar exports in the Ethiopian market, were being set up in Tigray just south of the border with Eritrea.

Further, the Eritrean government's bluff to turn Eritrea into an African Singapore, perceived in Addis Ababa as a project to develop Eritrea on the back of Ethiopia's market and resources, provoked a backlash and fanned an incipient economic rivalry. To date, the matter of Eritrea's trade surplus, the terms of Eritrea-Ethiopia trade relations, and the issue of a payments system for bilateral trade, like many other questions between the two countries, remain unresolved. These outstanding issues became part of the matrix of deteriorating relations between the two governments during the crucial period 1997-1998 preceding the border war.

Third, the issue involving the Front's access to state resources: The Red Sea Trading Corporation (RSTC) and the Front's foreign currency branch, still based in Rome, Italy, at the time, wanted to keep and use their foreign

---

commissions, with the author serving an interpreter, Addis Ababa, Ethiopia, 1994.

currency holdings outside the supervision of the central bank. At the same time, they sought to have free access to the country's foreign exchange reserves through the agency of the bank. However, I insisted on two things. First, the RSTC and the Front's foreign currency branch submit regular reports of their respective foreign exchange holdings, as part of the pool of the country's foreign exchange reserves, to the Bank of Eritrea as per the Bank's regulations. Second, the requests of the RSTC for foreign exchange be treated on par with those of other public and private sector demanders.

As a matter of prudent practice, I issued the central bank's policy decisions with the prior knowledge and express endorsement of the president. At the time, there was no consideration or mechanism to include the Front in the internal consultations, as it did not have the necessary statutory authority, professional competence, or technical expertise. Yet, the Front's Department of Economic Affairs sought to interfere in the work of the Bank of Eritrea. At times, it went to the extent of trying to reverse certain monetary and foreign exchange policy directives *ex post facto* with the connivance of the president, who played a double game.

In one instance, the president called me to his office and, to my surprise, asked me to rescind a certain policy directive a few days after its issuance. When I asked him why, he told me that the people in the Front's Department of Economic Affairs did not like it. I retorted that the people mentioned had neither the mandate nor the competence to demand the withdrawal of the directive duly issued with his prior approval and, as part of normal procedure, copied to and already in the hands of the IMF. I insisted that the policy directive should stand and managed to convince him that it would be inappropriate to withdraw it at that stage.

As in other domains of government business, the president persisted in giving the Front licence to interfere in monetary and foreign exchange policy decisions in violation of the initially agreed independence of the central bank. Consequently, the question of the Front's privileged access to hard currency remained a cause of disagreement coming to the fore on several occasions under various pretexts. The bank stuck to its position and refused to grant the requests of the RSTC for foreign exchange as long as the Corporation failed to comply with the bank's directives. The bank was aware that the president drove the RSTC's noncompliance. As a senior member of the central committee at the time, I strongly believed that the Front should focus its efforts on broad issues of state policy and general programmes and let the government do the business of governing and managing the daily affairs of the state.

Exercising its mandate with the express approval of the president, the central bank had brought the foreign exchange reserves of the country, previously held in accounts scattered in several European and US banks in the name and under the management of the Commercial Bank of Eritrea. The Bank of Eritrea had acquired title to the foreign currency reserves, after duly compensating the commercial bank with their counterpart value in Ethiopian Birr (then the legal tender in Eritrea) and consigned them in consolidated accounts with selected European and US correspondent banks. It invested, for the first time, the standing balance of the country's foreign exchange reserves in short-term placements, including overnight interbank lending, on a revolving basis through the agency of the correspondent banks at the rate of the highest bidder and, within the first year, yielded proceeds of about US$ 1.5 million.

The president had decided on an allocation of around US$70 m for the construction of a housing project in Sembel (Enda Korea) awarded without tender to a South Korean company, Keangnam Enterprises, under the ownership of the Front funded from state resources. The idea that the Front would just take and use the money, without paying its Birr counterpart value, ran counter to my effort to institutionalise public finances and foreign exchange operations. To sidestep the issue in view of the fact that the country's foreign currency reserves were now under the management of the central bank, the president instructed the general manager of the commercial bank to reclaim the long-transferred and paid out title to the country's foreign exchange holdings. The central bank refused to reverse the corrective measures duly undertaken in accordance with the bank's mandate and the president's express approval.

The issue became a buzz in the financial sector and a senior official and a mutual friend of the president's and mine in the ministry of finance, counselled me to let the president have his way. I explained the principles at stake and stressed the prudence of my position and my resolve to stand firm in view of the issue's potential implications for the bank's mandate and the overall management of the country's foreign exchange reserves. One late morning while in a meeting with two senior colleagues, Gebreselassie Yossief (Inteto) and Berhane Abrehe, finalising the crystallisation of the Macro-Policy framework in the ministry of finance, my secretary called to tell me that the president wanted to see me immediately. I excused myself from the meeting and headed straight to the president's office in an adjacent building just a few metres away.

I had no idea about the subject matter of the urgency at hand; nor did I expect what awaited me. On arrival, I found the president in the company of a group of people: Hagos Gebrehiwet (Kisha), head of the PFDJ's department of economic affairs, Yemane Tesfai, general manager of the Commercial Bank of Eritrea, Habtemariam Berhe, head of the Front's foreign currency branch, Desu Tesfatsion, general manager of the Red Sea Trading Corporation, and two operatives of the RSTC. I said hello, extended everyone the usual handshake and sat down facing the president. The eerie silence in the room with several people seated quietly together saying nothing was deafening in its stillness. I instantly understood that something was brewing and stiffened my resolve to stand firm in defence of the independence of the central bank and the proper management of nation's foreign exchange reserves, come what may.

The president broke the silence, saying, "Why didn't you give him [the general manager of the commercial bank] the money?" His tone and body language was ostentatious of authority, intended to impress his audience and intimidate the object of his feigned annoyance. I retorted, "Which money?" He said, "The dollars." Barely able to hide my indignation at his duplicity, I replied, "Because I shouldn't, and you know better why! I gave you the proposal to transfer title to the central bank in writing, executed it with your express approval, and have since provided you with daily briefs on our foreign exchange reserves position."

Unable to challenge me on the principle or on the facts, he ordered me to do it forthwith and I answered "No, I would not do it". Giving vent to his habitual impulse, he shouted, "You are dismissed; you handover the bank to Tekie Beyene."[461] I replied, "You can do as you please; but realise that you are making a big mistake." At that moment, everybody else vanished from the room in absolute silence and just the two of us were left alone staring at each other. The air vibrated with tension. He got so furious and agitated that his neck veins seemed about to burst. I was also infuriated but collected. After a long pause, he yelled at me "Get out!" I stood up, reminded him of the gravity of his mistake, and got out.

I was thus, fired as governor of the Bank of Eritrea in another off the cuff decision for trying to do the right thing. I wanted to preserve the integrity of the functional mandate of the central bank, and resist undue presidential interference to allow the Front free access to and use of the country's foreign exchange reserves without compensation or the consideration of a proper contractual arrangement. The presidential disinformation service (PDS, otherwise known as *Bado Seleste*) went into immediate operation and, as usual, leaked a contrived version of the matter. The financial sector and the business community in Asmera were instantaneously abuzz with word of my 'dismissal and arrest for insubordination to the president'.

Concerned relations and friends enquired about the situation and were relieved on learning of the story first-hand. Meanwhile certain erstwhile friends and former comrades-in-arms kept their distance. It is in the nature of the system that some colleagues estrange, turn against or even 'spy' on a colleague in order to curry favours with the regime whenever

---

[461] Tekie Beyene, then the dirctor of the Eritrean Investment Centre, was also named the bank's acting governor.

491

one gets 'in trouble' with the president or 'frozen' from active public service. It is one manifestation of the inevitable outcome of the president's policy and perfected practice of 'divide and dominate'.

The president deliberately subverted the drive to build a functional central bank with a capacity to stimulate economic growth, to revitalise the financial sector, and to help transform Eritrea into a services hub. Meanwhile, continued presidential interference has marginalised the economic, financial, and regulatory roles of the Bank of Eritrea and removed it from the frontline of development. Instead of evolving into the architect of prudent monetary and fiscal policies and the chief catalyst of economic expansion, he has reduced the central bank into a mere cash and foreign exchange guichet or window. It is quite heart-rending to see the emasculation of the central bank, the degradation of Eritrea's financial and banking sector, and the virtual collapse of the rest of its economy. What a disparity between what is and what could have been!

The following chapter describes the missed opportunities, in the context of the amicable bilateral relations following independence, to reaffirm respect for the colonial treaty border, safeguard Eritrea's territorial integrity and sovereignty, and secure durable peace with Ethiopia. Further, the chapter traces the inexorable slide towards an unnecessary war, the outbreak of armed conflict between former allies, and the effort to bring about a cessation of hostilities.

CHAPTER 15

An Avoidable War

There is no such thing as an inevitable war. If war comes it will be from failure of human wisdom. - Andrew B. Law

Much of present-day Eritrea and parts of modern Ethiopia share the legacy of the old Axumite or Abyssinian civilisation. Ethnic and linguistic kith and kin of four of Eritrea's nine nationalities, namely, the Afar, the Saho, the Tigrinya and the Kunama, comprising about 60 per cent of the country's total population, inhabit the corresponding adjacent areas across the border in Ethiopia. Linked by geography, history and culture, Eritrea and Ethiopia have a long, pervasive, and problematic relationship, heavily burdened by a difficult narrative of conquest, war, and conflict, often impacted by the intricacies of ethnic and cultural affinity straddling the common border, and closely bound by mutual economic and strategic interests.

The multiple pillars of this relationship have the potential to serve, upon the removal of the factors of the present conflict, as levers of durable political cooperation, drivers of economic integration, and anchors of regional peace and security. The restoration of peace, normalisation of relations, and fulfilment of reconciliation would open up the vast possibilities for bilateral cooperation based on a new democratic dispensation that reflects the free and express wishes of the Eritrean and Ethiopian peoples and takes into account their fundamental interests.

The Eritrean People's Liberation Front (EPLF) and the Tigray People's Liberation Front (TPLF) had, as noted in Chapter 4, forged a strong political and military alliance. Reciprocal recognition of and support for the right to self-determination of Eritrea and Tigray and common commitment to overthrow the Derg's military dictatorship formed the basis of the alliance between the two fronts. It was, however, essentially an expedient alliance troubled by incompatible visions of self-determination and state construction from the very beginning and divergent ideological leanings, war strategies, and tactical calculations later on.

National self-determination for the EPLF signified the separation of Eritrea from Ethiopia and accession to sovereign independence as a multinational (or multi-ethnic) state as delimited by its colonial borders. The EPLF viewed the final objective of the alliance as the establishment of an independent democratic Eritrea and a united democratic Ethiopia. For the TPLF, however, national self-determination meant secession from Ethiopia and the creation of a Greater Tigrayan Republic created by the redrawing of the colonial borders to incorporate the adjoining Eritrean Afar, Kunama, Saho, and Tigrinya speakers. The TPLF's advocacy of ethnic nationalism trespassing the Ethio-Eritrean colonial borders, enshrined in its *Manifesto 1976*, ran counter to the EPLF's objective of securing a multi-ethnic Eritrean state within its historically defined colonial borders, enshrined in its National Democratic Programme. Yet, the two fronts glossed over this fundamental divergence in building up and cementing their tactical alliance.

Ignoring the long-term territorial implications of this divergence, which fostered mutual suspicion and mistrust, the EPLF bolstered the alliance as a means to resolve the longstanding antagonism between legitimate Eritrean aspirations for self-determination and sovereign statehood, on the one hand, and expansionist Ethiopian ambitions for territorial aggrandisement and political hegemony, on the other. At the operational level, the blood of Eritrean and Tigrayan martyrs shed in the fields of battle both in Eritrea and in Ethiopia sealed the alliance. The liberation of Eritrea and the overthrow of the Derg's regime in May 1991, installing the two wartime allies in power in Asmera and Addis Ababa, heralded the apparent resolution of the historical Ethio-Eritrean antagonism and the advent of "a new era of durable peace and cooperation between a free Eritrea and a democratic Ethiopia".[462]

15.1 An Amicable Divorce

The 1993 referendum, made possible by military victory in the war of liberation, enabled Eritrea to exercise, via the conduct of a free and fair ballot, its right of self-determination and legitimised sovereign statehood. Ethiopia supported the referendum, endorsed its outcome, and officially recognised the State of Eritrea. An amicable divorce formalised the onset of cordial bilateral relations and signalled an auspicious

---

[462] Welde Giorgis, Andebrhan (the author), *Commentary: Border and Territorial Conflicts between Eritrea and Ethiopia: Background, Facts and Prospects*, Eritrean Studies Review, Vol.4 No. 1, 2004.

new beginning in the Ethio-Eritrean relationship. This augured well not only for democratic state construction and sustainable development in Eritrea and Ethiopia, but also for regional cooperation, peace, and security in the strategic but volatile Horn of Africa. Despite a smooth start and initial signs of close cooperation, the absence of agreement on the specific modalities of the divorce and attendant mechanisms to address its practical effects short-circuited the new Ethio-Eritrean relationship.

The independence of Eritrea dissolved the forced union between Eritrea and Ethiopia and created two sovereign states. The peaceful accommodation of this reality required Asmera and Addis Ababa to agree on a set of political, economic, and commercial arrangements to facilitate a stable transition to a friendly interstate relationship. Further, they needed to institutionalise and broaden their bilateral relations at the leadership, front, government, civil society, and people-to-people levels. Such measures would have reinforced the apparent reserve of political will to overcome the residual inertia of an uneasy historical narrative and expedient alliance and helped sustain cordial relations, close cooperation, and durable peace between Eritrea and Ethiopia.

Eritrea and Ethiopia maintained friendly relations during the seven years of peace between the liberation of Eritrea in May 1991 and the outbreak of hostilities in May 1998. They established joint commissions and signed several agreements, including a mutual defence pact, to promote closer cooperation in the political, security, economic, trade, and social spheres.[463] They started initiatives to coordinate

---

[463]   While governor of the Bank of Eritrea, the author served as a member of the Joint Eritrea-Ethiopia High Economic Commission.

diplomatic policy and political action on major regional issues of common concern, such as the civil war in Somalia, the threat of militant political Islam in the Sudan, and the revitalisation of the Inter-Governmental Authority on Development (IGAD).

The new relationship held great promise and generated high hopes that Ethiopia and Eritrea, having finally secured a stable peace between them, could serve as a nucleus for political cooperation and economic integration among the states of the Horn of Africa. Belying the outward manifestations of a close cooperative relationship however, was an undercurrent of latent discord over several crucial issues. These major issues included contention over sections of the common frontier, different visions of state construction, divergent policies of national development, disagreement over economic relations, and dispute over trade arrangements.

It is quite normal for two sovereign states to have a boundary dispute, to entertain different visions of development, to pursue divergent policies or to disagree over economic and trade issues. Such interstate problems, differences or disagreements are often unavoidable. In fact, they have been a recurrent feature of international relations since the emergence of the Westphalian system of nation-states in the seventeenth century and need not pose an obstacle to peaceful coexistence. That disputes arise between states is thus not, or should not be a problem in itself and must, in the event that they occur, be treated as a normal element of interstate relations and interaction. The question is when and how to treat or resolve them.

Ethiopia and Eritrea had a unique opportunity to address these issues of discord during the period of their close amity. Instead, their governments chose to neglect or to gloss them over to the detriment of the long-term relations between the two countries and the lament of their fraternal peoples. They failed to provide transitional measures to reset, institutionalise, and anchor the new relationship on a viable rules-based *modus operandi*. They confined policy and decision making to the leaderships of the two ruling fronts that proved unwilling or unable to resolve the piling issues of contention through earnest dialogue. These practices, coupled with the eventual exhaustion of the reserve of political will, let relations deteriorate and culminated in the sudden outbreak and hasty escalation of an otherwise unnecessary, senseless, and destructive war.

15.2 Missed Opportunities

History, whether that of nations, organisations or individuals rarely if ever, repeats itself in the same form, or offers the same scope for action. Regrettably, it is replete with instances of missed opportunity. A series of failures to seize the moment has thwarted the promise of a durable alliance between the EPLF and the TPLF and subverted the development of peaceful, stable, and cooperative relations between Eritrea and Ethiopia. Further, the unintended consequences of these failures have fanned a growing conflict, ignited a destructive war, and perpetrated an unsettled truce between the two neighbouring states.

The EPLF and TPLF missed the first great opportunity during the onset of their relationship. When the TPLF came into being in the mid-1970s, its founding *Manifesto 1976* declared its final objective as secession from Ethiopia and the creation of an independent Republic of Greater Tigray.

The Manifesto's definition of a Tigrayan as anybody who speaks Tigrinya, Kunama, Saho, Afar, etc., including those living outside Tigray, encroached on the integrity of Eritrean national identity.[464] Further, its extension of the geography of the envisaged republic to incorporate the mass of Eritrean lands, stretching from Badme in the west across the Central Plateau and the southern half of the country's Red Sea coastline to Asseb in the southeast, violated the integrity of Eritrean territory.

"Frontiers are indeed the razor's edge on which hang suspended the modern issues of war or peace, of life or death to nations".[465] The recognition of Eritrea's right to self-determination and support for its independence formed one of the major pillars of the wartime political and military alliance between the two fronts. Yet, the EPLF and the TPLF, whose relationship was permeated by constant tension and mutual suspicion, failed to address the fundamental issue of the frontier and resolve the inherent contradiction between the TPLF's expressed unequivocal support for Eritrean independence and the provocative declaration of *Manifesto 1976* that encroached on the integrity of Eritrean national identity and territory.

Whenever I raised, in private conversations during the war, the need to address the matter in good time, lest it become the cause of trouble in the future, the then secretary general and current president of Eritrea used to reply that "the TPLF is bound to abandon this infantile stance as it

---

[464] Tigray People's Liberation Front, Manifesto 1976, February 1976.

[465] Lord Curzon, Frontiers: Lecture Delivered in the Sheldonian Theatre, Oxford, 2 November 1907 (Westport, Conn.: Greenwood Press, 1976), p. 7.

matures and appreciates the long-term interests of the two peoples." I remained unconvinced. To date, I am unaware of any formal decision by the TPLF to amend the Manifesto's intrusive provisions with regard to the integrity of the people and territory of Eritrea. Nor am I aware of any formal discussion or tacit deal between the top leaders of the EPLF and the TPLF of a possible association between independent Eritrea and Tigray that would mute the boundary issue in the context of a confederal state.

Manifesto 1976 was not the only harbinger of future trouble. Following the displacement of the ELF from the area through coordinated military action by EPLF and TPLF forces in 1981, the TPLF established a presence in Badme that served as an entry point for its supply corridor from the Sudan across southwestern Eritrea. Four years later, it laid claim to the administration of the village. According to the 1902 border treaty between Italy and Ethiopia, Badme lies squarely within Eritrean territory. Yet, besides the differences in ideology and strategy that had come to the fore at the time, contestation over the administration of the village had brought EPLF-TPLF forces in the area to the brink of armed confrontation in the mid-1980s.

A military standoff then could have weakened the common fight to the benefit of the Derg's army. Perhaps apprehensive of such a diversionary effect, Isaias Afwerki, then deputy secretary general of the EPLF, who was also the Secretary General of the Eritrean People's Revolutionary Party (EPRP) and the commander-in-chief of the EPLA, directed that the EPLF units yield the administration of Badme to the TPLF in 1985. I am not aware of any discussion of the issue at the level of the central committee of the EPRP or the political bureau and the central committee of the EPLF. Nor am I aware whether there was an agreement between the leaders of the EPRP and the Marxist-Leninist League of Tigray (MLLT), the clandestine party within the TPLF, or of the EPLF and the TPLF, concerning the border issue or the nature of future relations between Eritrea and Tigray following the exercise of their respective rights of self-determination.

In any case, whatever understanding reached between the two non-state actors at the time could have no binding effect on the territorial integrity of the reconstituted Eritrean and Ethiopian states. Nevertheless, leaving the administration of Badme to the TPLF without a provision for its eventual restitution was prejudicial to Eritrean sovereignty and territorial integrity. It is baffling then that President Isaias, who directed that EPLF units yield the administration of Badme in 1985, chose to leave the matter of territorial restitution pending until 1998.

The interim period between the liberation and the declaration of independence of Eritrea, 1991-1993, presented an excellent opportunity to resolve the status of Badme and other Eritrean territories under Ethiopian administration, restore Eritrean administration and reassert Eritrea's territorial integrity. I am aware that there was no dearth of foresight in this regard. For instance, Haile Menkerios,[466] Eritrea's representative to Ethiopia, had alerted Isaias

---

[466] Conversations of the author with Ambassador Haile Menkerios, Representative of Eritrea to Ethiopia (1991-1993), Ambassador of Eritrea to Ethiopia and Permanent Representative to the OAU (1993-1996), Permanent Representative of Eritrea to the UN (1997-2001), Eritrea's Special Envoy to the Great Lakes Region (1996-1997), and currently UN Special Representative to the AU and Special Envoy for Sudan and South Sudan.

in 1992 of the need to settle the border issue and restore Badme and the other Ethiopian occupied and administered Eritrean territories to Eritrean administration prior to the conduct of the referendum, as the culmination of the process of Eritrea's decolonisation, as it would be difficult to reclaim them after formal independence.

Reluctant to press the issue, Isaias had retorted that, since the border was clearly defined on paper, all that was needed was to have it demarcated by a joint committee composed of people like Sebhat Efrem and Siye Abraha, then ministers of defence of Eritrea and Ethiopia, respectively. Meles agreed with the idea. Further, Isaias dismissed the suggested involvement of a neutral third party, like the UN, as unnecessary that would only complicate the matter.

The declaration of independence offered another great occasion. The velvet divorce in the wake of the free and fair conduct of the UN-monitored referendum in 1993 paved the way for the formal split of the Ethiopian state of 1952-1991 and the creation of two sovereign states. Eritrea's accession to independence and Ethiopia's recognition of Eritrean statehood represented the formal dissolution of the latter's forcible association with the former, or the partition of the predecessor state. As such, it imposed certain obligations on the two states to agree on the sanctity of the colonial boundary, the definition of citizenship, the sharing of state assets and debt, war reparations, trade finance, cross border movements, grazing rights, etc.

Specifically, proper succession required the formal confirmation of the colonial treaty border as the new international boundary between the two successor states. Obtaining official Ethiopian commitment to respect the integrity of Eritrean territory as established under Italian colonial rule, duly enshrined in the Federal Act and integrally maintained by both the Haile Selassie and Mengistu regimes, was of paramount importance for the security of the new state and the stability of Ethio-Eritrean relations. The stated aims of *Manifesto 1976* and, even more ominously, the TPLF's territorial claims and continued administration of Badme and other Eritrean localities, threatened the stability and continuity of the Eritrea-Ethiopia border. This made the reaffirmation of the historical colonial treaty border all the more necessary.

Furthermore, proper succession required the transfer of rights, obligations, and property from the predecessor state to the successor states. Common property eligible for equitable sharing between the Federal Democratic Republic of Ethiopia and the State of Eritrea included domestic and foreign assets, such as going concerns, monetary reserves, museum artefacts and embassies. Already in 1992-1993, the harassment of Eritrean farmers and confiscation of their property by Tigrayan authorities in the Tahtay Adiabo region adjacent to the Badme area had signalled the need to reaffirm and manage the common border. Eritrea's choice to ignore the writing on the wall, *de facto* adoption of a 'clean slate', and failure to secure Ethiopian respect for the colonial boundary treaties represented a grave mistake, as proven by subsequent events.

At the historic moment of Eritrea's declaration of independence and Ethiopia's acceptance of a sovereign Eritrean state, the governments of Ethiopia and Eritrea missed a great opportunity to codify the terms of succession in a treaty of friendship and cooperation. A transparent legal framework formally endorsing the colonial treaty border, establishing the new relationship on an equal footing, committing both governments to the pursuit of friendly relations and the peaceful resolution of all outstanding or arising issues, was in order. It could give closure to the destruction, suffering, and hurt caused by decades of conflict, war, and atrocities. Further, it could ensure the stability of the frontier and the continuity of amicable bilateral relations. They missed a historic opportunity to place the new relationship on a firm legal foundation and mutual commitment to legality in the conduct of their bilateral business at all levels.

The two governments neglected to put in place a legal framework defining the terms of the divorce, formalising the territorial dimension of the separation, and gearing their inter-front alliance to the promotion of peaceful interstate cooperation. They had another chance to reset their relationship on the solid foundation of a binding treaty. The combination of outright military victory in 1991, the velvet divorce that ushered in independence two years later and the amicable relations that ensued briefly offered Eritrea and Ethiopia a unique opportunity to peacefully resolve the pending issue of the common frontier. Frequent informal summits between President Isaias and President Meles, regular meetings between senior EPLF/ PFDJ and TPLF/EPRDF officials and periodic gatherings of joint ministerial commissions had reinforced the friendly relations and improved the prospects of a swift, amicable resolution.

The Eritrean government, in particular, had a special responsibility to bring the 'temporary' TPLF/Ethiopian administration of Badme and other Eritrean territories to an end and restore the integrity of Eritrean territory through the reaffirmation of the historical colonial treaty border as the international boundary between Eritrea and Tigray/Ethiopia. The PFDJ officials mandated by the president to address the question of Tigrayan harassment and mistreatment of Eritrean farmers in the Badme area failed to grasp and tackle the cardinal issue of the boundary in meetings with their TPLF/EPRDF counterparts. For instance, a high level PFDJ delegation failed to grasp or press the border issue in a joint meeting with senior TPLF/EPRDF officials in Addis Ababa on 21-22 July 1994 and completely missed the point in agreeing merely to strengthen the relationship and avoid misunderstandings by instructing the local communities to resolve the worsening conflict over territory among themselves through joint committees, as if it were an issue of a communal conflict within the same state.[467]

With Badme under Ethiopian control, Eritreans in the area and adjoining border villages had no legal defence from their government. When Haile raised the need to seriously address the escalating conflict as one of an interstate border rather than of local communities within a state, he was cut short by Yemane Gebreab: "You are really obsessed with this border issue, and you have been repeatedly bothering us with it." Humiliated, Haile replied: "If it is taken as just an obsession of mine, then I will never raise it again; but I know you will be forced to deal with it with much

---

[467] The PFDJ delegation led by Alamin Mohamed Said, the secretary of the Front, included Yemane Gebreab (Monkey), head of the Front's departmrnts of political affairs, Hagos Gebrehiwet (Kisha), head of the Front's departmrnts of economic affairs, and Haile Menkerios, Eritrea's ambassador to Ethiopia. The TPLF/EPRDF delegation led by Tewelde Weldemariam (Iwur), member of the Political Bureau, included Siye Abraha, Ethiopia's minister of defence and Awalom Weldu, Ethiopia's ambassador to Eritrea.

greater difficulty when it leads to wider bloodshed."[468] How prophetic!

Meanwhile, harassment, seizure of property, and expulsion of Eritreans from border villages and unilateral moving of the boundary markers (*mtrar*) deeper into Eritrean territory continued in 1995-96. As part of these activities, the TPLF established, in 1995, a marble quarry at Lij with its head office at Dichinema, both sites deep inside Eritrea, and produced marble slabs exported in an unpolished form via Massawa. The Eritrean government knew of these transgressions but refrained from making a formal protest or taking steps to redress the situation. It is common knowledge that PFDJ and TPLF officials conducted regular meetings between 1994 and 1998. It is thus mindboggling that the burning issues of the border question and violations of the integrity of Eritrean territory, sovereignty, and resources were not addressed in these meetings.

Upon independence, the government's negligence affected not just Badme but also Zalambesa, another border town. It failed to restore Eritrean administration over the two towns. It allowed Ethiopia to establish a customs checkpoint inside Eritrea, two km north of Zalambesa, set up its own checkpoint further north and left the town under *de facto* Ethiopian administration. In the context of friendly relations, Eritrea could have agreed to allow Ethiopia to locate its customs checkpoint within its own territory for reasons of administrative convenience and/or efficiency. But, there was no such agreement providing for the use or administration of sovereign Eritrean territory by Ethiopia or claim for

---

[468] Conversations of the author with Ambassador Haile Menkerios, before and after the outbreak of the war.

rent as a *quid pro quo*. Further, the government sanctioned formal correspondence and reports of the conduct of official dealings and meetings of joint bodies or committees datelined "Badme, Tigray" and "Zalambesa, Tigray".

To cap it all, Ethiopia issued a new map in 1997 singly redrawing the historical colonial treaty border between Eritrea and Ethiopia. The new map, which relocated the Eritrea-Ethiopia border roughly along what was later presented as Ethiopia's claim lines, transferred large patches of sovereign Eritrean territory in the Badme, Akhran and Irob areas, including Zalambesa and Fort Cadorna, into the Tigray Regional State. It also incorporated large swathes of Eritrean territory in the Bada and Bure areas into the Afar Regional State. Further, it embossed the new map of Ethiopia in the new Birr notes, the country's legal tender that went into circulation in the same year. There was no Eritrean protest against the Ethiopian infringement.

Ethiopia's unilateral modification of the colonial treaty border, which had remained the internationally recognised boundary between Ethiopia and Eritrea since its establishment in the 1900s under Italian colonial rule, represented a flagrant violation of the sovereignty and territorial integrity of Eritrea. Furthermore, Ethiopia moved to impose its new map on the ground by occupying the incorporated chunks of Eritrean territory. Ethiopia's actions in breach of the long established international frontier contravened the OAU's 1964 Cairo Declaration and African regional practice on the sanctity of colonial borders.

One of the basic functions of the state, duly enshrined in the National Charter and the ratified Constitution, is to safeguard the integrity of the national territory and ensure the security of the people. Eritrea had the opportunity to invoke international law, use proactive diplomacy, and capitalise on amicable relations to persuade Ethiopia to respect and abide by the colonial treaty border and rescind its new map. Further, the EPLF had the additional leverage of its historic position as the presumed 'senior partner' in the wartime alliance with the TPLF, now in power in Addis Ababa and Mekele, the capital city of Tigray Regional State bordering Eritrea, to settle the pending boundary question around Badme and the other affected areas.

The failure to deploy these vital assets as effective policy instruments in the framework of the then prevailing cooperative bilateral relationship foreclosed the chance to reaffirm the colonial treaty border as the international boundary. Inversing Clausewitz's famous maxim, diplomacy can be viewed as "an extension of war by other means".[469] This is the task of the ministry of foreign affairs, normally entrusted with the crucial functions to uphold, promote, and protect the country's sovereignty, territorial integrity, and national interest. The ministry has also the formal mandate for the overall conduct of foreign relations (including political relations, economic affairs, security matters, and social and cultural issues). Deliberate marginalisation however, undermined the ministry's capacity for proactive and functional diplomacy.

As the top diplomat, a foreign minister needs certain attributes in order to use diplomacy as an effective substitute of war in the defence of the national interest. These include: keen understanding of the intricacies of international affairs and relations among nations; a working knowledge

---

[469] Hamilton, Keith and Richard Langhorne, The Practice of Diplomacy: Its Evolution, Theory and Administration, Second Edition, Routledge, 1995, p. 185.

of an international language to personally and coherently communicate with foreign interlocutors; ability to grasp and negotiate complex foreign policy issues, monitor and analyse international developments, and formulate and propose foreign policy options to the government; authority, competence and expertise to lead, coordinate and provide guidance to the government's international dealings; and stability to establish the authority to develop and articulate foreign policy positions in defence of the national interest.

These attributes are found lacking, by design, in the majority of Eritrea's cabinet ministers and foreign ministers, appointed and dismissed in rapid succession at will by the president.[470] Each of the veteran freedom fighters serving as foreign minister had his own particular merits and could have better served the country in another capacity; most were not the best that Eritrea could offer for the post. The effects of the systematic cultivation of systemic mediocrity are accentuated by discontinuity and rapid turnover, occasioned by the constant reshuffles of cabinet ministers and senior officials. This is also the case with most of Eritrea's ambassadors and senior members of its diplomatic corps, again appointed and dismissed by the president at will. The absence of functional competence and lack of operative direction at the ministerial and ambassadorial levels has essentially reduced most of Eritrea's embassies into consular missions.[471]

---

[470] Eritrea had six foreign ministers between the liberation in 1991 and 2000: Ali Said Abdella, Mohamed Said Bareh, Mahmud Ahmed (*Sherifo*), Petros Solomon, Haile Weldensae (*Drue*) and back to Ali Said Abdella.

[471] Concern that Eritrean embassies focused on consular activities with the Eritrean diaspora rather than on diplomatic work in the

As in the case of most other ministries, deliberate instability operated to preoccupy the ministry of foreign affairs with mundane internal matters and deprived it of proper focus on the development of Eritrea's diplomatic work and the building of its capability for the defence of the country's paramount national interest. A more proficient and proactive diplomacy would have served to enhance the country's international standing and safeguard the integrity of its national territory. This handicap and the attendant mediocrity, coupled with the frequent use of even less competent Front officials to meddle in affairs normally reserved for the foreign ministry, allowed an omnipotent president to ride roughshod over Eritrea's foreign policy.

The detrimental effects of the marginalisation of the ministry of foreign affairs and its supplanting by the Office of the President and the Central Office of the Front, especially in the conduct and management of relations with Ethiopia, on national sovereignty, and territorial integrity are obvious.[472] It is not surprising, therefore, that Eritrea failed even to lodge a public protest when Ethiopia kept on moving the boundary markers deeper into Eritrea in the Badme area and issued the new map incorporating large swathes of hitherto uncontested sovereign Eritrean territory. In the absence of

---

host country was voiced by senior foreign ministry officials in a number of European capitals during bilateral discussions with our delegation headed by the late Foreign Minister Ali Said Abdella in November and December 2003. The author accompanied the foreign minister in these discussions.

[472] It is generally the case that statements, letters and communiqués released in the name of the ministry of foreign affairs are actually issued by the Office of the President, often without consultation with the minister or prior knowledge of the ministry.

formal Eritrean protest or diplomatic démarche, a strange omission in itself, Ethiopia proceeded to deploy regular and militia forces to occupy the newly incorporated swathes of territory around Bada (Adi Murug) and the Badme Plains between 19 and 26 July 1997. Further, Ethiopia continued to evict Eritrean farmers, dismantle Eritrean administration, and install Ethiopian administration in these areas.

Another PFDJ delegation, composed of Alamin Mohamed Said and Yemane Gebreab (Monkey), met with Tewelde Weldemariam (Iwur) of the TPLF political bureau in Addis Ababa on 8 August 1997 and discussed the incidents in Adi Murug and around Badme. The PFDJ delegation pleaded that Ethiopia reverse its steps and treat the matter in "a spirit of understanding" consistent with "the friendly relationship between the two sides". Far from reversing its steps or treating the matter with a spirit of understanding, however, Ethiopia staked claims to hitherto sovereign Eritrean territories. Meanwhile, the core issue of the boundary remained unresolved and Ethiopia continued to create new facts on the ground.

Apart from two hand written personal letters without letterhead or seal, dated 16 August 1997 and 25 August 1997, respectively, from "*Isaias*" to "Comrade Meles", the PFDJ and the government confined the matter to secrecy and maintained public silence. They also ignored the repeated petitions and pleas for protection from the representatives of farmers evicted from their homes and villages in parts of the 'Yirga Triangle' around Badme. Besides, they made no mention at all of a dispute in the border area around Bure on the Assab-Addis Ababa road that had almost flared up into armed confrontation in April 1997. Moreover, they kept the leading organs of the government and the public in the dark, and revealed the existence of the letters and the petitions much later, after the war broke out in 1998.

The first letter decried the "forcible occupation of Adi Murug in the Bada area by your army in the past few days" while the second bemoaned the "unjustified" expulsion of Eritrean officials and dismantling of Eritrean administration and proposed the assignment of a bilateral body of officials to "meet as soon as possible to look into these matters".[473] A joint border commission was subsequently established, convened its first meeting in Asmera on 13 November 1997 and its second and last meeting in Addis Ababa on 8 May 1998.

During the intervening period, November 1997-May 1998, Ethiopia demanded that all Eritreans living in the claimed areas acquire Ethiopian nationality and started reinforcing its military posture in the Irob region of the border between Eritrea and Tigray.[474] Surely, time was running out to settle the basic dispute over the boundary and address the attendant problems. Formed at a time when overall relations between the two fronts and governments were rapidly deteriorating, the bilateral border commission proved unable to defuse the tension and resolve the conflict.

Briefly, the president, who is also the chair of the PFDJ, proved unwilling and unable to tackle the cardinal question of the border as the root cause of the dispute in the borderlands, to protect the integrity of the national territory and to seek redress to the legitimate grievances of

---

[473] Isaias Afwerki, Letters to Meles Zenawi, dated 16 August 1997 and 25 August 1997.
[474] "The Ethiopian-Eritrean Conflict", Horn of Africa Bulletin, Vol. 3 No. 10, May-June 1998, p. 7.

the evicted population. Even as the situation deteriorated, he withheld the information and failed to brief the PFDJ central council, the Eritrean National Assembly, the cabinet of ministers, and ambassadors. Thus, like most of my senior colleagues in the Front and the government, I learned that all was not well along the Eritrea-Tigray/Ethiopia border from informal conversations with comrades and friends. In the absence of official briefing or explanation, we were unaware of the dossier of the August 1997 presidential letters or the formation of the bilateral body.

I raised concern, when I was ambassador to the EU, about the problem in the border areas and stressed the urgent need to address the root cause before the situation got worse during a meeting of Eritrean ambassadors and senior PFDJ officials chaired by the foreign minister in January 1998. The senior Front officials in the meeting shrugged off, scoffed at or downplayed the problem. They stated that the PFDJ and the TPLF, and hence Eritrea and Ethiopia, were 'strategic allies' and maintained that the alliance remained intact despite the petty snags. I disagreed with their rehearsed explanation and retorted that Eritrea has strategic interests with all its neighbours and Ethiopia, in particular; argued that strategic alliance is not an immutable concept, either in theory or in practice; and warned that the claimed strategic alliance with the TPLF was about to unravel at the seams unless immediately mended.

In his concluding remarks to the same meeting of ambassadors and senior PFDJ officials and in reply to my restated comments of concern, the president similarly downplayed the gravity of the troubles brewing along the border with Ethiopia. He stated, with ostentatious overconfidence, that there was no need to worry, as Eritrea possessed the wherewithal to ward off any threats to its security from any force. The gist of his statement heightened rather than allayed my concerns. I again raised and discussed the evolving crisis in depth in a meeting with the president during the same week before departing on a mission to Kinshasa. I shared my sense that war clouds were gathering and, stressing that war was not in our interest, reiterated that there would be war unless urgent measures were taken, with the facilitation of friendly third parties, if necessary, to defuse the tension and resolve the underlying question of the boundary.

Ethiopia moved deeper into Eritrean territory and its forces attacked an Eritrean platoon on patrol in the Badme area on 6 May 1998, killing five EDF officers.[475] Predictably, the unprovoked incident provoked a forceful Eritrean reaction and became the trigger of a bloody war. President Isaias met with senior army commanders in Keru, in the Gash-Barka Administrative Region, immediately following the incident and Eritrean troops retaliated in force on 10-13 May 1998, took Badme, pursued Ethiopian forces deeper and returned to positions along or close to the colonial treaty border. The Eritrean government remained silent as if nothing had happened while the president, having ordered the retaliatory action, left on a visit to Saudi Arabia.

There are no plausible indications that either side premeditated the all-out war that followed. It is entirely possible that the troubles in the border areas and the fateful attack on the EDF platoon could have been part of a plot hatched by opponents of Eritrean independence and rivals

---

[475] Conversations of the author with a Brigadier General of the Eritrean Defence Forces.

of the Ethiopian prime minister, seen as a friend of Eritrea, within the then factionalised top TPLF leadership stationed in Tigray since 1995. The plotters could have designed the attack to provoke Eritrean reaction and entrap the two countries in a new spiral of conflict.

In falling for the bait in his predictably reactive default mode and responding to the provocation in kind, it seems that President Isaias miscalculated and made a big gamble of his own. Egged on by the indignation of senior army commanders at his acquiescence in the TPLF's provocations, he had probably intended the forceful counter-attack as a dissuasive measure to 'teach the TPLF a lesson' and 'clip its wings'. He might also probably have succeeded in his ploy had he played his hands with the prudence of a wise leader and the flexibility of an astute strategist.

By 'going out of town', Isaias made himself inaccessible to peer pressure for reconsideration, as he often does when he gives free rein to his whims on consequential matters of national interest. In forfeiting the immediate use of the 'hotline' with Meles to cool tempers down and contain the crisis, he overplayed his hand. The 'plot' ran its course and the gambit backfired. Meles upped the ante. Taken aback, Isaias feigned deep hurt by the ferocity of the reaction of his former ally, or presumed 'junior partner', and Ethiopia's immediate declaration of war. In the absence of wise leadership and skilful diplomacy, the rash to action and counter-action sealed the fateful disruption of peaceful relations between Eritrea and Ethiopia that bore the promise of growing political cooperation and economic integration. With the seeds of animosity sown, there were to be no mutual accommodation, no turning back. The battle lines were drawn.

15.3 Allies at War

There are cases in history in which seemingly small incidents catalyse larger developments and provide the spark that fires significant events with far reaching consequences, unforeseen by the immediate actors of the moment. So goes the story of the incident of 6 May 1998 around Badme that triggered the border war between Ethiopia and Eritrea. The sudden eruption of hostilities took the world, friend and foe alike, by surprise and shattered the brief period of peace, amicable relations, and optimism ushered in in 1991. The chronology of the war's events is on the record, widely publicised often in a highly partisan manner.

Both Eritrea and Ethiopia made territorial integrity and sovereignty the *casus belli* or the core justification for the war. Ethiopia accused Eritrea of aggression and declared war on 13 May 1998, demanding a return to the *status quo ante* and, on 14 May 1997, informed the UN Security Council that Eritrea had violated Ethiopian sovereignty. In its reply the following day, Eritrea rejected Ethiopia's accusations and, belatedly, levelled its own counter-accusations.

On the same day, Eritrea announced a five-point plan. Adopted by the Cabinet of Ministers, the proposal called for the peaceful and legal resolution of the border dispute; the specification of each party's territorial claims and commitment to resolve the dispute through peaceful negotiations; the involvement of third party mediation to serve as witness and guarantor; the demilitarisation of the disputed areas under guarantee by the third party; and, in the event of failure to resolve the dispute through third party mediation, the referral of the case to international adjudication. Ethiopia rejected the proposal.

The US, then an ally of both countries, offered to mediate in the conflict right away. Ethiopia refused the US offer, insisting on the withdrawal of Eritrean forces from "Ethiopian territory" as a condition for negotiations. The second half of May saw an intense US-Rwandan effort to resolve the conflict. The joint US-Rwanda peace plan proposed a return to the *status quo ante*, the demilitarisation of the border, the deployment of an observer force, and negotiations to demarcate the boundary. Under intense US lobbying, the OAU Summit held in Ouagadougou, Burkina Faso, from the 8th to 10th of June 1998, declared its support for the US-Rwanda plan and set up a high level committee or troika, consisting of the presidents of Burkina Faso, Djibouti, and Zimbabwe and assisted by its secretary general, to mediate and help Eritrea and Ethiopia resolve the conflict. All diplomatic initiatives, including bilateral efforts by the leaders of Djibouti, Kenya, Libya, South Africa, and Uganda, proved to no avail.

In the context of Eritrea's failure to publicly protest the July 1997 incidents, the restoration of the *status quo ante* meant the withdrawal of Eritrean forces to pre-6 May 1998 positions. Otherwise, despite Ethiopia's insistence, the proposal for a return to the *status quo ante* contained in the US-Rwanda peace plan should, on account of the evolution of the sequence of actual events on the ground, have provided for a return to the pre-19 July 1997 situation. A balanced proposal would have required that neither Ethiopia nor Eritrea gained or lost territory through subterfuge or the use of force. Even then, acceptance of the US-Rwanda peace plan to avert escalation of hostilities and reach a negotiated settlement would have been in the best interest of both countries, in general, and that of Eritrea, in particular, as demonstrated by the subsequent more adverse terms that were agreed to in order to cease hostilities and end the conflict.

As it were, Ethiopia's insistent demand for the immediate restoration of the *status quo ante* as of 6 May 1998 clashed with Eritrea's adamant refusal to withdraw its forces to pre-6 May positions. These irreconcilable stances became the sticking point that doomed all diplomatic effort to resolve the crisis to fail. The conventional wisdom is that democratic governments rarely go to war as a first resort. The inherent weakness of the two governments manifest in a noticeable democratic deficit in their respective internal decision making processes and the lack of a bilateral institutional mechanism for broader dialogue to manage and resolve disputes allowed a containable incident to escalate into a major armed conflict.

The absence of prudent leadership capable of prioritising the strategic interests of the two countries and peoples recklessly gave the politics of brinkmanship free rein to disastrous effect. Otherwise, a modicum of political will and diplomacy could have given peace a chance. Clearly, the failure of leadership all along lay at the core of the outbreak of hostilities. In retrospect, the war was avoidable, unnecessary, and senseless.

First, Eritrea could capitalise on its amicable relations and the fluid political situation obtaining in Ethiopia during the crucial period of transition from 1991 to 1995 to reaffirm the colonial treaty border as the international boundary, assert its territorial integrity prior to, at, or immediately following the velvet divorce, and avoid the chain of events that led to the war.

Second, proactive Eritrean diplomacy in the service of territorial integrity could have helped the two governments to address the core issue of their common boundary. In the event that the two countries failed to reach agreement, they could have invited a friendly third party to facilitate the process. The involvement of a neutral facilitator could have persuaded Ethiopia to respect the inviolability of the colonial treaty border and dissuaded it from perpetrating the incursions or taking the provocative actions that aggravated the problem.

Third, a blink at the brink from either the president of Eritrea or the prime minister of Ethiopia in the higher interest of peace and the wellbeing of the fraternal peoples could have helped the two countries to climb down from the precipice and avert the disaster that followed. The exercise of political wisdom, foresight, and leadership in Asmera, Addis Ababa or in both capitals could have avoided the war and kept the peace between Eritrea and Ethiopia.

Finally, endorsement of the US-Rwanda peace plan as a basis for the resolution of the crisis could have prevented escalation of the conflict, refocused effort on the determination of the boundary in accordance with the colonial treaties and the record of actual administration of the affected areas, and helped preserve durable peace between Ethiopia and Eritrea.

With the die cast however, the interplay of two unstoppable impulses heading inexorably towards a bloody confrontation overtook efforts to deescalate the conflict and broker the peace. Overconfident of Eritrea's military superiority and prompted by the prospect of toppling a 'weak' former 'junior' partner grown 'recalcitrant and troublesome', President Isaias objected to the provision for the withdrawal of Eritrean forces and rejected the US-Rwanda plan.

Failing to appreciate the implications of the reality that the TPLF was at the helm of power in Addis Ababa and, therefore, in full command of Ethiopia's vastly superior resources, Isaias spoiled for war.[476] Given the deep-seated lingering division in the attitude of the senior TPLF leadership regarding relations with the EPLF and Eritrea, he also failed to appreciate that his stance antagonised and cornered the faction friendliest to Eritrea, headed by Prime Minister Meles. In a taunting display of bravado, he declared, "The world should know that pulling out of Badme would mean like the sun is dead, that the sun would not rise forever".[477]

The EPRDF government had drawn considerable fire and faced constant hostility from much of the old Ethiopian establishment, the private media, and the political opposition for its support of Eritrea's accession to independence and maintenance of close relations with Eritrea. These forces not only opposed Eritrean independence but also resented Eritrean support for the consolidation of TPLF dominance of EPRDF rule in Ethiopia during the crucial period from 1991 to 1994 when a marginalised Oromo Liberation Front (OLF) left the governing EPRDF coalition. These forces directed their hostility at both the TPLF and the EPLF.

Sensing a chance to reverse the hostile attitude, neutralise his political opponents, and mobilise public support for his government, Prime Minister Meles, once cornered, decided to co-opt the hard line, play the Ethiopian nationalist card, and whip up latent anti-Eritrean sentiment. The path offered

---

[476]   A senior Rwandan military officer informed the author in Kinshasa in June 1998 that President Isaias had told the Rwandan mediation team that he had never commanded such a large army of 100,000 men and would administer the coup de grace to the Ethiopian regime by cutting off the Djibouti-Addis Ababa lifeline.

[477]   "ምሉእ ዓለም ኪፈልጦ ዘለዎ: ካብ ባድመ ወጺእና ማለት ጸሓይ ሞይታ ማለት'ዩ፤ ጸሓይ ድሕሪ ሕጂ ኣይትበርቕን'ያ ማለት'ዩ"::

an opening to cast aside the highly politicised image of a 'junior' partner, enhance the legitimacy of his government, and consolidate his power. Further, it bore the potential to change an 'impulsive and irksome' regime in Asmera. Staking a prudent diplomatic stance, he accepted the US-Rwanda plan while reserving a military option pending the withdrawal of Eritrean forces in accordance with the declaration of a 'war of national defence'.

The belligerents missed an excellent opportunity in the US-Rwanda peace plan to deescalate and restore the peace without losing face. Ethiopia unleashed all-out war, declared an air and naval embargo, and threatened to attack all international commercial flights and shipping to Eritrea. The escalation of fighting around Badme reverberated in the areas of Zalambesa and Bure in the central and southern sectors of the over 1,000 km long common border. Joining the ground fighting, the Ethiopian Air Force carried out the first air strikes against the Eritrean capital on 5 June 1998, although Ethiopia denied that it struck first.[478] The Eritrean Air Force retaliated forthwith by bombing Mekele, the capital of Tigray Regional State. Both raids inflicted civilian casualties including, regrettably, schoolchildren in Mekele.

15.4 The Deportations

The war caused massive physical destruction and huge loss of life in both countries. In addition, it was used to justify the

---

[478] Brig. Gen. Habtezion Hadgu, the then commander of the Eritrean Air Force now languishing in jail, ascertained to the author on several occasions in 1998, 1999 and 2000 that Ethiopia initiated the air raids and that he personally led the first retaliatory strike in hot pursuit of the returning Ethiopian aircraft.

perpetration of one of the ugliest episodes in the history of relations between the two countries: the arbitrary detention and deportation of innocent civilians. Ethiopia invoked 'national security reasons' and started expelling Eritreans and Eritrean Ethiopians on 12 June 1998, and detaining over 2,000 ethnic Eritreans in remote internment camps. According to a report by Human Rights Watch (HRW), the Ethiopian government "forcibly expelled an estimated 75,000 people of Eritrean origin during the war" while the Eritrea government "forcibly expelled or took part in the voluntary repatriation of an estimated 70,000 Ethiopians", even though it persistently claimed that "it had no expulsion policy comparable to Ethiopia's".[479]

In fairness to the chain of historical events, there was a notable difference in the policies and actions of the two governments. Ethiopia's deportations were premeditated and entirely forcible whereas Eritrea's expulsions, even though regrettable, were reactive and consisted mostly of voluntary repatriation, as confirmed by independent observers, such as Amnesty International (AI), HRW, and the OAU. AI reported the voluntary repatriation of about 40,000 Ethiopians from Eritrea for economic reasons.[480] The OAU affirmed the contrasting practices of the two governments. It expressed deep concern on "the conditions in which the deportation of Eritreans were carried out by the Government of Ethiopia, the decision to extend those measures to the families of the deported persons and the fate

---

[479]   Human Rights Watch: Ethiopia & Eritrea, Vol. 15, No. 3 (A) – January 2003, p. 5.

[480]   Amnesty International news report, January 29, 1999. www.amnesty.org/news/1999/12500299.html.

of their properties" but stated that "it could not establish the reality of systematic or official action directed against Ethiopians in Eritrea."[481]

There was also a crucial distinction in the public stances of the two governments on the issue. Prime Minister Meles Zenawi defended the Ethiopian government's deportations by evoking its unrestricted right to expel any foreigner at will if it disliked the colour of one's eyes,[482] although he later showed remorse in admitting that that was not his "finest hour". In contrast, the Eritrean National Assembly guaranteed the right of Ethiopian residents to "live and work in peace" in Eritrea.[483] The sudden, systematic, and official deportations involved the forcible separation and harsh treatment of families and confiscation of their properties and financial assets. The victims of expulsion included UN and OAU staff in Addis Ababa in flagrant violation of their diplomatic privileges and immunities under the Vienna Convention.

It is one of the paradoxes of the war that the prime minister of Ethiopia who first ordered the mass deportation of Eritreans and Eritrean Ethiopians is himself an Ethiopian of mainly Eritrean ancestry and the president of Eritrea who ordered the expulsion of Ethiopians and Ethiopian

---

[481] OAU Ministerial Committee, Final Communiqué, 5 August 1998. allafrica.com/stories/199808050046.html.

[482] Prime Minister Meles Zenawi, in an interview on Ethiopia Television, aired on 9 July 1998, stated, "Any foreigner, whether Eritrean, Japanese, etc., lives in Ethiopia because of the goodwill of the Ethiopian government. If the Ethiopian government says 'Go, because we don't like the colour of your eyes,' they have to leave."

[483] Statement of the 11th Session of the National Assembly of Eritrea, 26 June 1998.

Eritreans is himself an Eritrean of mainly Ethiopian ancestry. Consistent application of their actions would have required them both to expel themselves, members of their immediate families, and some of their senior officials. In the event, the logic of power spared them, their families, and their associates from the extreme consequences of their unlawful measures.

Arbitrary detention, deportation, and confiscation constitute gross violations of human rights and fundamental freedoms duly enshrined in the Universal Declaration of Human Rights and the International Covenant on Civil and Political Rights. Furthermore, deportation constitutes a crime against humanity under customary international law. The Nuremberg Trials (1945-1949) punished perpetrators of the crime. Deportation or forcible transfer of population is also a crime against humanity proscribed under the Rome Statute.[484]

The open violations of international humanitarian law represented a frontal attack on the basic right of the victims to live, work, and enjoy the fruits of their labours in peace and security. In this regard, the UN Commissioner for Human Rights stated that "the violations of human rights of Eritrean nationals being expelled from Ethiopia...are serious violations of the rights and freedoms set forth in the Universal Declaration of Human Rights, as well as in the International Covenant on Civil and Political Rights, to which Ethiopia is a party."[485] The UN condemned Ethiopia's expulsions as "illegal, unwarranted and inhumane."[486]

---

[484] Article 7.d, International Criminal Court (ICC) Statute.

[485] Robinson, Mary, UN Commissioner for Human Rights, Statement, 1 July 1998.

[486] United Nations, Secretariat News, December 1998, p. 6.

15.5 The Evolution of the War

Although Badme and its environs was the scene of the initial clashes, once ignited, the war raged along three major fronts - Bure, Alitena-Mereb and Mereb-Setit - and the main battles waged in three rounds – May-June 1998, February-March 1999, and May-June 2000. It was a poor man's war interspersed by intermittent lulls and flare-ups in the fighting. The relatively long lulls, dotted by frequent skirmishes, probing forays and exchanges of heavy artillery fire, availed the belligerents time to regroup and build up their forces, mobilise additional troops, raise funds, procure sophisticated armaments, and replenish munitions through similar shopping sprees, mostly in the arms markets of the former Soviet Union and China.

The Ethiopian and Eritrean high commands shared familiarity with each other's array of military hardware, command structures, and combat tactics. When they erupted, the flare-ups turned the Eritrea-Ethiopia borderlands into a theatre of the fiercest set piece battles ever fought between two African armies. The full-blown conflagration turned into the world's largest conventional war of the decade as the contending armies fought each other virtually to mutual exhaustion.

The overall military balance, in terms of the size of the armed forces as well as surveillance, intelligence, and logistics capability, favoured Ethiopia. Further, several egregious factors undercut the once legendary prowess and combat effectiveness of the Eritrean Defence Forces (EDF), the proud heir of the Eritrean People's Liberation Army. These included: inability to professionalise the EDF and modernise its command and control structures, assets, and logistics; rapid turnover of ministers of defence and chiefs-of-staff; decommissioning many capable junior commanders to remove 'rebellious' officers; and dismantling of the once illustrious liberation-era military intelligence apparatus (*Enda 72*). Let me give two concrete instances.

First, there were four different ministers of defence and four different chiefs-of-staff during the short interlude of peace between the liberation of Eritrea and the border war with Ethiopia.[487] In addition, the ministry of defence had to function in makeshift headquarters that moved from one rural location to another. Beyond the destabilising effects of the lack of permanent ministry headquarters and the frequent reshuffling of ministers and chiefs-of-staff, incessant presidential interference dented the EDF's unity of command and reduced the minister of defence and the chief-of-staff into mere figureheads without effective power or influence.

---

[487]   The four ministers of defence were Sebhat Efrem, Petros Solomon, Mesfin Hagos, and then back to General Sebhat Efrem while the four chiefs-of-staff were Haile Samuel (China), Mesfin Hagos, Omer Hassen (Tewil) and Gen. Ogbe Abraha. Constant reshuffling undermined the authority of the minister and the chief-of-staff and sidetracked the transformation of the EDF from an essentially insurgent army into a professional army. In contrast, Ethiopia had two ministers of defence, Siye Abraha and Tafera Walewa, and one chief-of-staff, Maj. Gen. Tsadkan Gebretensae during the period 1991-2001. In addition, the Ethiopian military had the institutional advantages of an established ministry of defence, a unified chain of command, and an earnest effort to modernise its command and control structures, assets, and logistics. I was able to learn of the modernisation effort first-hand during a guided visit of the computerised Operations Room of the ministry by defence minister Siye Abraha in 1994.

Second, experience during the war of independence proved the crucial role of intelligence as a major factor in the successful conduct of warfare, in general, and in determining the outcome of specific military confrontations, in particular. In the time-honoured words of ancient China's Sun Tzu, "Now the reason the enlightened prince and the wise general conquer the enemy whenever they move and their achievements surpass those of ordinary men is foreknowledge."[488]

A small Eritrean liberation army equipped with inferior weapons was thus able to repeatedly rout and ultimately prevail over a large Ethiopian army possessing superior weapons thanks, to a considerable extent, to its high command's access to accurate, timely and actionable intelligence. Foreknowledge helped make possible the ultimate liberation of Eritrea, against all odds, during the war of independence. It proved crucial to the liberation of most Eritrean cities, to ten years of successful defence of Nakfa and the rear base after the strategic retreat, to countless successful ambushes and brilliant mobile operations behind enemy lines, to the spectacular commando actions against the Ethiopian air base in Asmera and naval base in Massawa.

Let me cite the instance of two events that happened ten years apart to underscore the crucial importance of reliable, actionable intelligence in deciding success or failure in battle. First, as the Derg concentrated its main forces for the defence of Keren in anticipation of a main attack there, the EPLA pulled a major surprise in the liberation of Massawa in February 1990. Second, as the EDF concentrated its

---

[488] Sun Tzu, The Art of War, New York: Oxford University Press, 1963, p. 144.

main forces for the defence of the Alitena-Mereb Front in anticipation of a frontal attack there, the Ethiopian army pulled a major surprise in puncturing and breaking through Eritrean defences on the Mereb-Setit Front in May 2000.

Throughout the border war, the Eritrean Defence Forces were seriously disadvantaged by the persistent lack of accurate, timely and actionable strategic, tactical and battlefield intelligence. Foreknowledge was lost to the disruption of military intelligence and the mediocrity of the National Security Agency that concentrated its resources and effort on spying on the people in the primary service of regime security. The debilitating lack of foreknowledge undermined the combat effectiveness of the Eritrean army, weakened its defence capability, accounted for its military reversals in crucial battles, and contributed to the adverse outcome the war.

Despite the burden of such handicaps, the Eritrean army managed, during the first round of the border war, to thwart the Ethiopian onslaught and stabilise positions established roughly along the common border that stretched across Ethiopian territory in certain sections to tie-in the frontlines with higher terrain in order to retain positional advantage. The opposing armies entrenched themselves in their respective positions and conducted random bombardment of each other's fortifications, mostly with heavy artillery, mortar, and tank shells. The EDF held mainly defensive positions along the western, central, and eastern fronts to fend off Ethiopian assaults, digging deep even in the flatlands of the rolling, forebodingly inhospitable Denkel Desert.

During the second and third rounds of the war, the Ethiopian army launched and sustained offensive operations along the three main fronts while the Eritrean army pursued a strategy of static defence. Such a strategy denied the Eritrean army, which had neither a defined objective nor a war plan, the possibility of active defence with an option for a countervailing attack and turned it into a virtual sitting duck waiting to react, leaving the initiative to the Ethiopian army. In the context of highly fortified trench warfare reinforced by the extensive use of landmines, the opposing armies employed a varying combination of dogged positional defence, waves of massive assault and counter-assault, pincer movements, and outflanking operations. In taking or facing an offensive, both sides resorted to the concentrated use of large forces on frontal attacks or defences in narrow places along several sections of the relatively stable frontlines.

The use of overwhelming force aimed to create a rapture in the other's entrenched defence positions; surprise attacks sought to puncture lightly defended positions; and pincer movements aimed to outflank the opponent's main forces. The combination of heavy conventional and high technology weapons, World War I-type operational tactics, and repeated human wave assaults, often driven by deadly friendly fire from the rear, turned the battlegrounds into open killing fields. Although on a much smaller scale of size, intensity, and casualties, the two armies fought an African version of the bloody battles of the Somme and Verdun around Badme, Adi Begi'o, Tserona, Zalambesa, Aiga, and Bure.

All along, the war defied several UN Security Council resolutions and a flurry of diplomatic efforts, involving high level missions and several special envoys from the OAU, the UN, the US, the EU, etc., to end it and settle the conflict. Despite Eritrea's rejection of the proposal as a 'dead package', the OAU summit endorsed the US-Rwanda peace plan at the urging of the US. The OAU sent a letter calling on Eritrea to return to the pre-May 6 1998 *status quo ante* in an effort to stave off an escalation of hostilities. The OAU High-Level Delegation shuttled between Addis Ababa and Asmera to plead the case for peace with the leaders of both countries. In response to the delegation's mediation efforts, Ethiopia reaffirmed its acceptance of the peace plan while Eritrea confirmed its rejection. The UN Security Council endorsed the US-Rwanda peace plan on 26 June 1998 (Resolution 1177/1998).

The OAU Mediation Committee, made up of the High-Level Delegation and the organisation's Secretary General, presented the Proposals for a Framework Agreement for a Peaceful Settlement of the Dispute between Eritrea and Ethiopia to the leaders of the two countries in November 1998. The Framework Agreement (FA), based on the US-Rwanda peace plan, provided for the withdrawal of Eritrean forces from the Badme area, the demilitarisation of the entire border pending demarcation, and the deployment of OAU and UN military observers to oversee the Eritrean redeployment. Ethiopia accepted the OAU Framework Agreement while Eritrea expressed certain reservations and asked for clarifications.

The UN Security Council unanimously endorsed the OAU Framework Agreement on 29 January 1999, welcomed Ethiopia's acceptance and, noting that the OAU had fully responded to Eritrea's request for clarifications, urged Eritrea to accept it without delay (Resolution 1226/1999). Eritrea was reluctant to oblige. Its adamant opposition to the US-Rwanda plan and the OAU Framework Agreement underscored its objection to the call for the withdrawal of its forces to pre-6 May 1998 positions. In the face of a diplomatic deadlock for which Ethiopia blamed Eritrean refusal to accept the Proposals for a Framework Agreement, both sides braced for a showdown as the former prepared for a major new offensive. The resumption of large scale hostilities preempted an OAU plan to send a mediation committee to the two countries.

During the first phase of the second round of the war in February 1999, the Eritrean army held its ground, overcoming a huge Ethiopian assault in the battle for Geza Gerehlase on the Mereb-Setit Front. Despite their apparent successes around Bure, Aiga, Alitena, Zalambesa, Tserona, and Geza Gerehlase, Eritrean forces suffered a serious setback on the Mereb-Setit Front during the second phase of the second round as a result of what the president and field commanders later described as a correctable failure of leadership. Employing an effective combination of aerial bombardments, frontal assaults, pincer movements, and outflanking manoeuvres in a campaign code-named 'Operation Sunset' to mock Eritrea's president, Ethiopian forces seized Badme on 27 February 1999. This was not supposed to happen! The Eritrean army was pushed out of Badme and the sun remained alive and continued to 'rise forever'.

The capture of Badme and the failure to recover it signalled the beginning of a shift in the military balance in favour of Ethiopia. Following the loss of Badme, Eritrea reversed position, dropped all objections, and declared full acceptance of the OAU Proposals for a Framework Agreement. The UN Security Council and the OAU welcomed Eritrea's acceptance and called for a ceasefire. In a new twist prompted by its military success in seizing Badme, Ethiopia refused to agree to a cessation of hostilities and insisted on the withdrawal of Eritrean forces from its 'occupied territories' as a condition to end the conflict.

Eritrea reiterated its readiness for a ceasefire and offered to withdraw its forces from the contested areas in accordance with the OAU Proposals for a Framework Agreement. In spite of Eritrea's reversal of position, the UN Security Council's call for an immediate ceasefire and firm support for the OAU peace process and the OAU's appeals for compliance with the Proposals for a Framework Agreement, the fighting continued unabated on all fronts. In rejecting the calls for a ceasefire, Ethiopia expanded 'Badme and its environs' to include all the Eritrean territories in the central and southern sectors incorporated in its 1997 map, in sharp contradiction to the OAU's clarifications to Eritrea.[489]

Ethiopia's new conditions for a ceasefire amounted to an abnegation of its previous acceptance of the OAU Proposals for a Framework Agreement. Spurred on by its successful seizure of Badme, Ethiopia continued its attacks in the central and southern sectors. Although Eritrean attempts to recover Badme failed, reinforced Eritrean forces on the Mereb-Setit Front managed to consolidate their positions along a new line of defence overlooking the small town.

As in the first phase so in the second phase of the second round, the Eritrean army held its ground on the Alitena-Mereb and Bure fronts. Eritrean forces repulsed all-out Ethiopian assaults around Bure, Zalambesa, and Tserona, inflicting heavy losses on the Ethiopian army in the process. The decisive Eritrean victory at the Battle of Igri Mekhel

---

[489] In response to Eritrea's request for clarifications, paragraphs 1.b and 1. c, the OAU had specified that "Environs refers to the area surrounding Badme Town" in the second paragraph of the *Responses provided by the OAU*, as communicated to Eritrea on 26 January 1999.

near Tserona in mid-March 1999, one of the bloodiest confrontations of the war, effectively ended the Ethiopian offensive of the second round, although the lull that ensued was often disturbed by aerial bombardment of several Eritrean cities and towns, including Massawa, in May 1999 and sporadic fighting along the main frontlines.

Meanwhile, the diplomatic search for peace had stalled as Ethiopia procrastinated to buy time in an effort to revise the Framework Agreement to reflect its new military edge. Whereas Ethiopia had, from the outset, accepted the OAU peace plan and Eritrea had accepted it after its setback in Badme, the former's introduction of new elements to modify the plan delayed agreement on the terms and modalities of a ceasefire. The OAU complemented the Framework Agreement with the Modalities and the Technical Arrangements (TA) for its implementation.[490]

The Modalities and Technical Arrangements provided for the sequencing of the stipulated steps with a timeframe for the implementation of the Framework Agreement. Both countries accepted the Modalities, each with its own conditions; Eritrea accepted and signed the Technical Arrangements while Ethiopia asked for clarifications. Upon receipt of the clarifications, Ethiopia refused to sign the TA, casting a new shadow over the evolving OAU peace package.

The main disagreement centered on Ethiopia's new demand for Eritrean withdrawal, and Eritrea's refusal

---

[490] Modalities for the Implementation of the OAU Framework Agreement on the Settlement of the Dispute between Ethiopia and Eritrea (12 July 1999) and the Technical Arrangements for the Implementation of the OAU Framework Agreement and Its Modalities (6 August 1999).

to withdraw, from Zalambesa and Bure. The deadlock triggered mutual recriminations as each country accused the other of preparing for a large scale offensive. A month-long intensive shuttle diplomacy between Addis Ababa and Asmera, involving EU Envoy Senator Rino Serri, US Envoy Anthony Lake, and Algerian OAU Envoy Ahmed Ouyahia between 4 February and 4 March 2000, failed to produce an accord beyond partial consensus on the Technical Arrangements. After Eritrea urged the OAU to reopen negotiations on the Technical Arrangements, President Abdelaziz Bouteflika hosted indirect talks between Ethiopia and Eritrea in Algiers from 29 April to 5 May 2000. There was no progress.

The failure of the proxy talks to produce an agreement prompted the OAU to declare that "all the efforts made by the...OAU, with the support of the representatives of the United States and the European Union, failed to soften the positions of either Ethiopia or Eritrea. As a result, the indirect talks had to be adjourned after a week of efforts".[491] The UN Security Council sent a special mission headed by US Ambassador Richard Holbrooke in a last ditch effort to resolve the sticking point and move the peace process forward. Shuttling between Addis Ababa and Asmera, the special mission met with Prime Minister Meles on 8 and 10 May and with President Isaias on 9 and 10 May 2000. As its efforts failed to break the impasse, the special mission warned of an imminent resumption of hostilities.[492]

---

[491] OAU Communiqué, 5 May 2000.

[492] United Nations Security Council, Security Council special mission visit to Eritrea and Ethiopia, 9 and 10 May 2000, S/2000/413, 11 May 2000. http://www.un.org/Docs/sc/missionreports/413e.pdf.

Two days later, on 12 May 2000, Ethiopia launched an all-out offensive against Eritrean forces on the Mereb-Setit, Alitena-Mereb, and Bure fronts. Eritrea had anticipated the brunt of the Ethiopian offensive to concentrate around Zalambesa during this final round of the war. Eritrean positions on the Alitena-Mereb and Bure fronts held firm.

Its positions on the Mereb-Setit Front, however, took a dramatic turn for the worse. In a surprise outflanking operation combined with frontal heavy artillery barrages and aerial bombardments along the main frontlines, the Ethiopian army unleashed a powerful pincer assault across the Mereb River. Deploying sizeable detachments and using the logistic support of a large pack of mules and donkeys to scale the steep cliffs of Tkhul in the mountainous ridges of Zaidekolom undetected, Ethiopian forces overwhelmed the spirited defence of the thinly spread Eritrean forces. The once famed Eritrean military intelligence had no clue and the Eritrean high command was taken by complete surprise. The advancing Ethiopian forces cut off the Mendefera-Barentu road around Molki, veered westwards to Shambuko and attacked Eritrean positions on the Mereb-Setit Front from the rear.

Caught *between a rock and a hard place*, Eritrean forces were compelled to hastily abandon their defences on 18 May 2000, fight their way out of encirclement and withdraw deeper into the interior of the country. The Ethiopian triumph dealt a serious blow to the Eritrean army and the capture of Barentu sent shockwaves across the Eritrean body politic. Pursuing their advantage, Ethiopian forces seized a vast stretch of Eritrean territory in the Western Lowlands extending all the way to Omhajer, Tessenei, and Aligidir near the border with the Sudan. It was after the shock of the capture of Barentu that a panicked President Isaias summoned his previously sidelined former comrades-in-arms and senior colleagues for what he later called an 'informal discussion within the family' in Biet Giorgis on the outskirts of Asmera.[493]

As a Tigrinya proverb states, the convening of the meeting, or 'informal family discussion', after the damage was already done was akin to "taking shelter in the cave after the rain".[494] Nevertheless, the event proved the validity of the rather sarcastic English adage of "better late than never". During the informal discussion at the meeting, Petros Solomon, Eritrea's top intelligence expert and one of its best military strategists, proposed the reorganisation of Eritrean defences to salvage the situation and reverse the EDF's declining fortunes in the western and central sectors.[495] The aim was to exchange territory for time in order to stabilise the precarious situation and chart a winning military strategy of national defence.

The move involved the withdrawal of Eritrean forces from all fixed positions in the southern borderlands and the Western Lowlands, the establishment of a new defence line along the entire southern and western rim of the Central Plateau stretching from Qohaito (south of the town of Adi Keih) in the southeast to Tunkulhas (western entrance to the city of Keren) in the northwest. The main objective of the redeployment plan was to ward off any thrust of the Ethiopian army into the core of the Central Plateau that

---

[493] Oral report of the President to the ninth meeting of the Central Council of the PFDJ held from 31 August to 2 September 2000.

[494] *Dehri mai nab beati* or ድሕሪ ማይ ናብ በዓቲ::

[495] Conversations of the author with the dissident senior officials, Asmera, June 2000.

would threaten the capital. At the same time, it sought to draw the Ethiopian army in, stretch it out over the vast vacated expanses, and bog it down with the conduct of concerted guerrilla, mobile, and special operations all over these areas. The Ethiopian high command seemed to have seen through the ruse and refused the bait.

Meanwhile on the diplomatic front, the OAU called for the redeployment of Eritrean forces from all contested areas in line with Ethiopia's demand in an effort to end the fighting. In a prompt response to the OAU's call, Eritrea started, in the early hours of 25 May 2000, to hastily withdraw its forces from Zalambesa, Aiga, Alitena, and several fortified positions in the adjacent areas. The withdrawal of Eritrean forces from the contested areas was supposed to produce an immediate ceasefire. However, Ethiopian troops pursued the retreating Eritrean forces and seized Zalambesa, Serha, Emba Soira, Senafe, Akhran, and Tserona on the Alitena-Mereb Front. The Ethiopian onslaught was eventually stopped at the northern approaches to Senafe.

Ethiopia had hedged to gain time in order to push its military advantage and continued to fight while negotiating. Three days after the withdrawal of Eritrean forces, on 28 May 2000, Ethiopian aircraft bombed the power plant at Hirgigo near Massawa and the newly established Eritrean positions around Adi Keih. On 30 May, Ethiopia and Eritrea resumed proxy talks in Algiers, with the OAU, the US, and the EU acting as mediators, and continued until 10 June 2000. On 31 May, Ethiopia affirmed its verification of the withdrawal of Eritrean forces from its 'territory', its readiness to end the war and pull its troops out of Eritrean territory upon receipt of guarantees on the redeployment of Eritrean troops. At the same time, Ethiopia launched an attack on the Bure Front on 3 June 2000 and fierce fighting continued during the following week. Ethiopia carried out air strikes on Asseb and Asmera airport; and new Ethiopian assaults on 7 June 2000 resulted in intensified fighting along all fronts.

The attempts of the Ethiopian army to advance towards Dekemhare and Mendefera and onwards to Asmera were thwarted on the foothills of the southern escarpment deep north of the Muna, Belesa and Mereb Rivers, the historical boundaries between Tigray and Eritrea's Central Plateau. Ethiopian forces seemed bent on encroaching deeper into the Eritrean highlands. Trying to push its way through well defended narrow gorges on which was trained Eritrean tank, artillery, and mortar fire from rail and cement parapet embankments fortified along commanding positions overlooking the ravines, division after Ethiopian division thrown into the fray was decimated. Ethiopia's high stakes gamble failed at a huge human cost to its army. The decisive battle at Adi Begi'o, abutting the town of Adi Quala, scuttled Ethiopia's apparent designs to carry the war to the heart of the central highlands of Eritrea, capture Asmera, and effect regime change.

Far in the isolated southeast of the country, however, the battle for the port city of Asseb that started on 3 June raged with infernal ferocity. Eritrean forces repulsed successive assaults and prevailed over Ethiopian forces on the Bure Front, valiantly defending Asseb in defiance of the president's direct orders to withdraw. As Ethiopian troops retreated, ending the attempt to breach Eritrean defences and seize Asseb, Eritrean forces there were poised to take the initiative and launch a major countervailing attack. The prospect of an imminent counter-attack raised the urgent need for the rapid reinforcement of Ethiopian positions on the Bure Front from the western and central sectors. At the same time, heavy fighting continued in the west and Eritrean forces retook the towns of Aligidir and Tessenei on 6 June 2000.

Despite its successes in the western and segments of the central sectors, the Ethiopian army was too exhausted and too vulnerable to continue fighting. Ethiopia thus abandoned its design on Asseb and began withdrawing several army units from positions in the central and western sectors to reinforce its eastern flank. In response to Ethiopian demands for an international peacekeeping force, the OAU proposed the deployment of a UN mission and the withdrawal of Ethiopian forces. Eritrea accepted the OAU proposal on 9 June 2000; Ethiopia expressed its agreement 'in principle' on 11 June 2000 and formally accepted it on 14 June 2000. The war came to an end as fighting ceased along all fronts on 13 June 2000. Eritrea and Ethiopia signed the Agreement on Cessation of Hostilities in Algiers on 18 June 2000.

The end of the war found about a quarter of Eritrea's territory, including some of the most fertile lands in the central and western parts of the country, reeling from the devastation caused by the Ethiopian advances, and about a third of the entire Eritrean population afflicted by dislocation. The summer of 2000 was thus an extremely sombre season for Eritrea and its people. It was a time of deep national distress, lament, and humiliation. The valour and resilience of the Eritrean Defence Forces, the resolute determination of the Eritrean people in the war zone and the extraordinary role of Eritrean mothers in morale-boosting combat support in the frontlines were undermined by appalling failures of intelligence and loss of compass in the Eritrean leadership and high command. Further, the outcome of the war dented the aura of invincibility of the EPLA, or the EDF, dictated its withdrawal from one-fifth of the national territory, and sanctioned the continued occupation of sovereign Eritrean territory to date.

In retrospect, the Eritrean government had missed several opportunities to secure the integrity and sovereignty of the national territory in peacetime in the context of amicable relations with Ethiopia; to establish July 1997 as the *status quo ante* through proper diplomatic demarche in line with normal international practice; and to withdraw Eritrean forces to pre-6 May 1998 positions to defuse the crisis, stabilise the situation and enable a negotiated or a legal settlement of the dispute. President Isaias had blundered into plunging the country into the abyss of senseless hostilities without prior consultation with the PFDJ Central Council, the Eritrean National Assembly, and the Eritrean cabinet of ministers. Furthermore, he had, as commander-in-chief, mismanaged the conduct of the war and dragged the country down to the indignity of disastrous military reversals and the continued occupation of its sovereign territory.

At the end of the war, both governments claimed victory. In reality, both sides lost. Truth and those who never return home to their loved ones are the immediate casualties of war. Beyond the tragedy of the massive loss of life and limb, the waste of the enormous destruction of property, and the immense cost in lost opportunity for democratic development, there persist abnormal relations, a taste of bad blood and bitter animosity between the two regimes. Moreover, neither side was able to deliver the knockout blow to undo the other.

Nonetheless, Eritrea emerged as the bigger loser while Ethiopia secured the upper hand and established itself as the predominant regional military power in the Horn of Africa. This outcome of the war is clearly reflected in the terms of the Agreement on Cessation of Hostilities, in the subsequent continued Ethiopian occupation of sovereign Eritrean territory in defiance of the *final and binding* delimitation and demarcation decisions of the Eritrea-Ethiopia Boundary Commission, and in Ethiopia's sporadic military incursions into sovereign Eritrean territory.

I remain deeply convinced that the timely settlement of the boundary issue could have avoided the incidents around Badme that triggered the senseless war and its devastating consequences for the peoples of the two countries. Seizing the moment to settle the dispute over Badme during the period of amity would have changed the course of the contemporary history of Eritrea for better in terms of the democratic development of the state, the maintenance of the territorial integrity and sovereignty of the country, and the building of a peaceful and prosperous society. Further, it would have allowed the friendly relations between the State of Eritrea and the Federal Democratic Republic of Ethiopia to deepen and thrive.

With the end of the war, there was high anticipation that the implementation of the Agreement on Cessation of Hostilities would start the process of healing and reconciliation and lay a solid foundation for the restoration of durable peace between Eritrea and Ethiopia. The following chapter addresses this issue, and describes my role as Commissioner in the effort to implement the Agreement on Cessation of Hostilities. Further, it recounts the unfolding of events that contributed to the present state of 'no war, no peace' between the two neighbours.

CHAPTER 16

An Uneasy Truce

An eye for eye only ends up making the whole world blind. -
Mahatma Gandhi

As the first of the two Algiers agreements between
Ethiopia and Eritrea,[496] the Agreement on Cessation
of Hostilities provided for, *inter alia*, an immediate end of
fighting, the deployment of a UN peacekeeping mission to
monitor the ceasefire, and the establishment of a temporary
security zone (TSZ) through the redeployment of Ethiopian
and Eritrean forces. Entirely located within Eritrean
territory adjacent to the common border, the TSZ would
serve as a buffer area separating the two belligerent armies.
Its establishment required the redeployment of Ethiopian
forces from positions taken after 6 February 1999 that were
not under Ethiopian administration prior to 6 May 1998

---

[496] The two Algiers accords comprise the Agreement on Cessation of
Hostilities between the Government of the Federal Democratic
Republic of Ethiopia and the Government of the State of Eritrea,
Algiers, 18 June 2000 and the Comprehensive Peace Agreement
between the Government of the Federal Democratic Republic of
Ethiopia and the Government of the State of Eritrea, Algiers, 12
December 2000.

and the redeployment of Eritrean forces to positions at a distance of 25 km (artillery range) from the positions of Ethiopian redeployment.

The two armies had resorted to the extensive use of anti-personnel mines as part of the defence of their respective trenches and forward positions in the areas separating their frontlines. The Agreement on Cessation of Hostilities thus required the two countries to conduct demining activities with the assistance, technical advice, and coordination of the peacekeeping mission in conjunction with the UN Mine Action Service (UNMAS). Mine clearance aimed to facilitate the speedy deployment of the UN peacekeeping mission, the safe return of the displaced population and, finally, the delimitation and demarcation of the boundary.

Further, the Agreement on Cessation of Hostilities mandated the Organisation of African Unity (OAU) and the UN to guarantee the respect for the commitment of the two countries pending "the determination of the common border on the basis of pertinent colonial treaties and applicable international law, through delimitation/ demarcation." The guarantee comprised of "measures to be taken by the international community should one or both of the parties violate this commitment, including appropriate measures to be taken under Chapter VII of the United Nations Charter by the UN Security Council."[497] Accordingly, the UN Security Council authorised, on 15 September 2000, the deployment of the United Nations Mission in Eritrea and Ethiopia (UNMEE) comprising up to 4,200 troops, including 220 military observers, to assist Eritrea and Ethiopia to implement the Agreement on

---

[497]   Ibid., para. 14, p. 5.

Cessation of Hostilities awaiting the physical demarcation of the common boundary.[498]

16.1 Implementing the Agreement on Cessation of Hostilities (ACH)

President Isaias suddenly assigned me as Eritrea's Commissioner for Coordination with UNMEE. The mandate of the Commission for Coordination with UNMEE was to facilitate UN assistance, upon the separate requests of the two countries to the Secretaries General of the OAU, the precursor of the AU, and the UN in implementing the Agreement on Cessation of Hostilities. Given a virtual *carte blanche* to establish a functional commission as a matter of urgency, I immediately constituted the commission as an autonomous body, firmly declining the president's initial suggestion to set it up in consultation with and, implicitly, under the aegis of the director of the National Security Agency.

I designated five associate commissioners in charge of, respectively, the Military Coordination Commission, Humanitarian Affairs, Resettlement and Rehabilitation of Internally Displaced Persons (IDPs), Humanitarian Mine Action, and Logistics. The associate commissioners were former mid- or high-level officials who, like me, were 'frozen' from public service for varying lengths of time. The president endorsed the proposed organisational framework, approved the appointment of the designees, and the work of the commission started forthwith.

---

[498] UN Security Council, Resolution 1320 (2000), 15 September 2000.

The UN Mission in Eritrea and Ethiopia (UNMEE) was established and its military observer mission and peacekeeping operations mandated by the UN Security Council. The host countries, Eritrea and Ethiopia, would provide UNMEE with access, assistance, protection, and freedom of movement, and facilitate the work of its mine action experts. Ambassador Joseph Legwaila, a Botswanan diplomat, became the Special Representative of the Secretary General (SRSG) of the UN, Mr. Ian Martin, a British national, the Deputy Special Representative of the Secretary General (DSRSG), and Maj. Gen. Patrick Camaert, a Ducth army officer, the Force Commander (FC). The initial peacekeeping force comprised mainly of Dutch, Indian, Jordanian, Danish, and Kenyan contingents and Italian carabineers.

The Commission had, in dialogue with its Ethiopian counterpart and in coordination with UNMEE and the Political and Military Liaison Office of the AU, to grapple with the establishment of the temporary security zone. The effort to establish the TSZ faced serious obstacles right from the beginning. The Agreement on Cessation of Hostilities stipulated that the redeployment of Ethiopian and Eritrean forces would be completed and verified within two weeks of the deployment of the UN peacekeeping mission. Upon verification of the Ethiopian redeployment, Eritrean would restore civilian administration, including police and local militia, and enable the return home of the displaced population.

At the first meeting of the parties held in Nairobi, Kenya, on 2 December 2000, UNMEE circulated the colonial treaty map of Eritrea as a basis and the two sides agreed to present their respective redeployment plans, even though Eritrea was not required to do so under the ACH, to the Force Commander, by 12 December 2000. The redeployment plans would delineate the southern and the northern confines of the TSZ upon finalisation at the next meeting of the parties in Nairobi on 28 December 2000. Accordingly, the Eritrean plan proposed to redeploy Eritrean forces to positions 25 km north of, and running parallel to, the historical colonial treaty boundary with Ethiopia, extending all the way from Eritrea's border with the Sudan in the west to its border with Djibouti in the southeast. This would form the northern limit of the approximately 25,000 km^2 buffer zone extending over 700 villages.

On the other hand, the Ethiopian redeployment plan left several swathes of Eritrean territory around Bure, Bada, Alitiena, Akhran, and Badme under the hold of Ethiopian forces, claiming that these areas were under Ethiopian administration prior to 6 May 1998. The Ethiopian redeployment plan was at variance with the Eritrean conception of the southern boundary of the TSZ. Although the redeployment of forces would not to prejudge the final status of the contested areas to be determined at the end of the delimitation/demarcation of the boundary, the establishment of the TSZ became an issue of constant contention between the two parties, fuelled by UNMEE's irresolute and inept handling of the matter.

Careful review of the two redeployment plans, due reference to the actual situation on the ground prior to 6 May 1998, and balanced consideration of the perspectives of the two sides could have helped prudently address the issue and avoided complicating UNMEE's relations with Eritrea right from the start. In adopting the Ethiopian redeployment plan, Maj. Gen. Camaert made a serious blunder whose repercussions poisoned his relations first with the Eritrean side and later with the Ethiopian side and led to his eventual expulsion as UNMEE's force commander. By allowing Ethiopian forces to retain positions taken after 6 February 1999 that were not under Ethiopian administration prior to 6 May 1998, UNMEE's adoption of the Ethiopian redeployment plan violated the terms of the Agreement on Cessation of Hostilities.

Eritrea thus objected to the declared southern boundary of the temporary security zone. At the same time, it urged the UN to fulfil its responsibility to establish the buffer zone and ensure the return of the IDPs to their home villages. The international community and the troop contributing countries, in particular, responded positively. In addition to the visits of UN Secretary General Kofi Annan and Dutch Prime Minister Wim Kok, there followed a flurry of diplomatic activity, as prominent international officials visited Asmera and Addis Ababa to plead the case for cooperation in implementing the Agreement on Cessation of Hostilities.[499]

Beyond the general historical colonial treaty border, the UN, the US, the EU, and the OAU lacked independent knowledge to help ascertain as to which specific areas in the borderlands were under Ethiopian or Eritrean administration prior to 6 May 1998. The administrative maps of Eritrea's Ministry of Local Government contained errors that placed

---

[499] These included the foreign and defence ministers of the troop contributing countries, Italian Under-Secretary for Foreign Affairs Rino Serri, Special Assistant to the President and Senior Director for African Affairs on the National Security Council Jendayi Frazer, and former US Assistant Secretary of State for African Affairs Susan Rice.

several Eritrean villages inside Ethiopia. Apart from the Eritrean and Ethiopian governments, only the people of the affected areas on both sides of the frontier, who usually lived side by side in peace and amicable interaction, knew which state administered the contested localities of the borderlands during the period extending from the Italian colonial era up to the outbreak of the border war. Nevertheless, UNMEE did not see it fit to consult the people with the greatest stake in an expeditious settlement of the dispute and learn the facts first hand.

As the impasse gained increased international attention, UN Secretary General Kofi Annan presented the leaders of the two countries, on 30 January 2001, a plan for the establishment of the TSZ, accompanied by a map clearly delineating its southern and northern boundaries. The Secretary General requested the two leaders to accept the plan without discussion or modification. Informed that the prime minister of Ethiopia had accepted the plan, the president of Eritrea followed suit on 2 February 2001, even though Eritrea had reservations, as the plan allowed Ethiopian forces to remain in positions taken after 6 February 1999, which were not under Ethiopian administration prior to 6 May 1998.

The Military Coordination Commission (MCC) adopted the Annan plan in its Nairobi meeting of 6 February 2001 and the two states, agreeing on the modalities of its implementation, started redeploying their troops accordingly. In mid-February, however, UNMEE issued a new 'operational map' under pressure from Ethiopia that removed about 50 additional villages in the subzones of Gelalo, Senafe, Tserona, Shambko, and La'elay Gash with a total of 45,000 inhabitants from the designated TSZ and placed them under Ethiopian control.[500] UNMEE's capitulation to pressure and surreptitious attempt to impose the new map for the establishment of the TSZ posed a direct threat to the integrity of the Agreement on Cessation of Hostilities. New war clouds started to gather, raising the risk of a resumption of hostilities.

I later learned, in separate informal conversations with the SRSG, the DSRSG and the FC, that the 'Annan plan' presented to the two leaders, was in fact a slightly modified version of Ethiopia's original redeployment plan handed to Kofi Annan by the prime minister. Further, Ethiopia, once again, unilaterally imposed the subsequent 'operational map' on UNMEE under the pretext that it had made mistakes in drawing up its earlier plan. In this regard, neither the Secretary General of the UN nor his Special Representative acted as honest brokers. Moreover, having acquiesced in the scheme, UNMEE tried to impose the 'operational map' on Eritrea as a *fait accompli* through subterfuge and by exploiting the simmering internal contradictions and apparent divisions within the PFDJ and the government. The Commission defied the subterfuge, protested UNMEE's machinations, and rejected the 'operational map'.

I cautioned the SRSG and the FC to insist that Ethiopia implement agreed commitments, to refrain from meddling in internal Eritrean affairs, and to work with the Commission in good faith. I stressed that the Commission

---

[500] The State of Eritrea, Commission for Coordination with the UN Peacekeeping Mission, *Compact Political and Military Report of the Effort to Implement the Agreement on Cessation of Hostilities* (Unpublished confidential report of the author as Commissioner to the President in Tigrinya), 25 July 2001, p. 4.

works independently of any ministry and that I have the final say on its decisions. As UNMEE wavered, Ethiopia reneged. Instead of completing their redeployment as agreed, Ethiopian forces returned to several positions from which they had previously withdrawn, such as Aromo, Ksad Emba, Gossomo, Adi Teklai, etc.

The Commission protested the return of Ethiopian troops and informed the DSRSG, on 21 February 2001, that Eritrea was compelled to suspend the redeployment of its forces pending the removal of Ethiopian forces from the TSZ and UNMEE's correction of its 'operational map'. Unable to secure Ethiopian accord to modify the 'operational map' or the withdrawal of its forces from positions held inside the TSZ, UNMEE opted to appease Ethiopia's intransigence and issued a press release on 28 February 2001 stating falsely that Ethiopia had withdrawn its forces from the TSZ and Eritrea was redeploying its forces according to schedule.

The Commission countered by issuing a communiqué, on 1 March 2001, refuting UNMEE's claims that Ethiopia had withdrawn its forces from the TSZ and that Eritrean forces were redeploying according to schedule. At the time, Eritrea seriously contemplated returning its forces to their vacated positions inside the TSZ and upping the ante. Only the thesis that the delimitation and demarcation of the boundary would restore these areas to Eritrea brought Eritrea back from the brink. Alarmed, UNMEE responded that it would study the situation and make the necessary amends upon the completion of its investigation.

A few days later, UNMEE claimed that it had discovered cartographic errors and would correct its 'operational map'; admitted that Ethiopian forces continued to hold several positions inside the TSZ, including areas they had initially vacated; and vowed to press Ethiopia to redeploy its forces. In a press release issued on 22 March 2001, UNMEE announced that Ethiopia had refused to redeploy its forces from the TSZ and promised to refer the matter to the UN Security Council for appropriate enforcement action.

The Commission was keen to create the necessary conditions and facilitate the return of IDPs to their home villages ahead of the rainy season to prepare their crop fields for cultivation. Taking the SRSG's pledge to press Ethiopia to redeploy its forces into account, I presented him with a *Preliminary Situation Report* on 24 March 2001 detailing the presence of Ethiopian forces in the TSZ and the location of the affected villages to which the IDPs would return. Six days later, on 30 March 2001, I informed the SRSG that Eritrea would resume the redeployment of its forces as a gesture of goodwill. In appreciation, he assured me, during the fifth meeting of the MCC in Djibouti on 6 April 2001 that he was pressing to secure the withdrawal of Ethiopian forces from positions inside the Temporary Security Zone and resolve the problems of its southern boundary taking into account the interest of the displaced population.

On 16 April 2001, I informed the SRSG of the full redeployment of Eritrea's forces in accordance with the originally agreed boundaries of the TSZ and issued a formal announcement to that effect the following day.[501] Further, I affirmed that Eritrea had fulfilled all its obligations under the ACH and would expedite the return home of the displaced population. In response, the SRSG affirmed, on 18 April 2001, that Eritrea had completed the redeployment of its

---

[501] Commission for Coordination with UNMEE, Press Release, Asmera, 17 April 2001.

forces enabling, despite the persistent problems Ethiopia caused along the southern line, the establishment of the TSZ, the restoration of civilian administration, and the return of the displaced population to their home villages.

However, UNMEE could neither secure the redeployment of Ethiopian forces as required by the ACH nor prevent their expansion into new areas from which they had initially withdrawn. As a result, we could not establish the TSZ at a uniform distance of 25 km separating the two armies, as stipulated in the agreement. In parts of the central and western sectors, the distance was as narrow as 12 km, as Ethiopia defied UNMEE's repeated demarches to redeploy and returned its forces to hold on to commanding positions up to 13 km deep inside the originally agreed buffer zone. Ethiopia went further to establish new settlements in Badme and Dembe Mengul. All these sovereign Eritrean territories remain under Ethiopian occupation to date.

16.2 Humanitarian Mine Action

Along with the establishment of the TSZ, humanitarian mine action represented an important element of the Agreement on Cessation of Hostilities. This opened a window of opportunity to rid Eritrea of an estimated two million anti-personnel and anti-tank landmines as well as unexploded ordnance leftover from World War II (1941), the war of independence (1961-1991), and the border war (1998-2000).[502] These landmines and unexploded ordnance, scattered all over the various former battlegrounds in the

---

[502] The State of Eritrea, Commission for Coordination with the UN Peacekeeping Mission, *Draft Proposal to Rid Eritrea of Landmines*

country, pose constant danger and cause immense loss of life and limb to people, livestock, and wildlife. The majority of the victims are children.

Eritrea signed the Ottawa Mine Ban Treaty on 27 August 2001, agreeing to end the use of landmines as a weapon of war and to destroy its existing stockpiles. It also signalled its desire to develop and implement an effective national programme of humanitarian mine action to rid the country of the scourge of landmines and unexploded ordnance. Accordingly, the Commission set out to design and put in place a scheme for effective mine clearance in the TSZ, and to build a national capacity for humanitarian mine action. It worked actively with the UN Mine Action Service, the Friends of UNMEE, and several international NGOs to develop programmes, initiate operations, and raise funds for the removal of all landmines in Eritrea.

In pursuing these objectives, the Commission did not start from scratch. A national agency, the Eritrean Humanitarian Demining Programme (EHDP), established with US aid in 1995, was already operational under the Ministry of Defence. Up to the outbreak of hostilities in 1998, the EHDP worked to locate and clear minefields sown by the Ethiopian and Eritrean armies during the war of independence. After the border war, it compiled, in collaboration with the EPLA's Mine Corps, comprehensive data and sketched a field map with GPS markers of the Eritrean landmines laid along the main lines of defence on the Bure, Alitena-Mereb, and Merb-Setit fronts. In August 2000, the Commission incorporated the EHDP as its arm of humanitarian mine

---

(Unpublished confidential report of the author as Commissioner to the President in Tigrinya), 23October 2001, p. 1.

action and quickly transformed it into the Eritrean Mine Action Programme (EMAP).

EMAP was designed to serve as the regulatory and supervisory authority of the Eritrean mine action sector. The Commission enabled the creation of the Eritrean Demining Agency (EDA) in April 2001 as a national non-governmental organisation (NGO) to conduct mine action operations, initially in the TSZ and eventually all over the country and the National Training Centre (NTC) to provide training in civilian humanitarian demining with international standards to clear landmines and unexploded ordnance.

The first batch of 410 trainees, demobilised fighters and national service conscripts drawn from the army's Mine Corps, began humanitarian mine action in the subzones of Senafe, Tserona, and Shambuko under the auspices of EDA. A second batch of 490 deminers worked around Shilalo, Shambuko, Tserona, Senafe, Umhajer, and Bure under the auspices of three international NGOs. In addition, Ronko, an American NGO sub-contracted by the US State Department, operated to help EDA build capacity mainly through training. It also trained dogs in mine detection, for deployment in the field alongside their trainers. Further, the Mine Action Coordinating Centre (UNMEE-MACC), UNMEE's demining arm, provided technical support, funding, and equipment to help build EDA's capacity and support its mine clearance operations.

At this stage, the Commission drew up the policy, administrative, and operational framework for the institutional development of the mine action sector. It pushed for the formal establishment of EMAP and EDA as legal entities, the streamlining of the information management system for mine action (IMSMA), and the conduct of mine census or level-1 socioeconomic impact survey. There was considerable international goodwill and promise of financing assistance. A newly set up voluntary trust fund raised USD 7.5 m by the end of 2001 while a donors' meeting held in New York on 19 November 2001 pledged USD 8.3 million. Maintaining its independence of decision and ownership of the programme, including the setting of priorities, the Commission cultivated cooperative relations with UNMAS, UNDP, UNICEF, UNMEE-MACC, and bilateral donors in a drive to rapidly build institutional capacity and expand demining operations.

The Commission combined the work to build sustainable national capability in mine action with the effort to rid the TSZ of landmines and unexploded ordnance in order to enable the restoration of civilian administration, the return of IDPs, and the physical demarcation of the boundary. Effective mine action in the TSZ required, and the Agreement on Cessation of Hostilities demanded cooperation between Eritrea and Ethiopia. Accordingly, the former belligerents reached agreement at the MCC's Nairobi meeting of 2 December 2000 to provide UNMEE with a detailed map of the location of the landmines planted by each side during the war, and of any nuisance mining that might have occurred after the end of hostilities.

In compliance with the agreement, Eritrea presented a sketch of its landmines to UNMEE on 19 March 2001. Ethiopia, on the other hand, initially claimed that it did not use landmines as it was on the "offensive"; later admitted that it had indeed used landmines but did not keep a record of their emplacements; and finally handed in a "survey of ten dangerous areas" rather than a comprehensive dossier of the landmines it implanted in the TSZ. This, however, proved too little and came too late to enable the demining of the relevant areas of the TSZ, as the approaching summer rains added urgency to the rapid return of IDPs to their home villages.

Under the circumstances, the Commission informed UNMEE, on 16 May 2001, of Eritrea's plan to return 152,000 IDPs, including 30,000 to villages still held under Ethiopian forces. The plan, worked out and operationalized in concert with all concerned government agencies, specified which IDPs would return to which villages. Further, the Commission reminded UNMEE of its responsibility to guarantee the right of return of the IDPs to their villages, to facilitate their actual return, and to ensure their safety and security once they returned home.

There were incidences of sporadic attacks carried out against targets in the TSZ by Ethiopian troops and/or armed Eritrean groups based in and sponsored by Ethiopia. When UNMEE responded that ensuring the safety and security of the population in the TSZ was not part of its mandate, we decided to restore the civilian administration and beef up the police and local militia with barely disguised EDF units to provide for a credible defence capability and to deter threats to public safety and security. Although the move prompted protests from Ethiopia and UNMEE as a violation of the Agreement on Cessation of Hostilities, Eritrea had no choice but to pre-empt the creation of a dangerous security vacuum in its own sovereign territory.

Subsequently, the Commission set out, in close coordination with the relevant government ministries, agencies and administrative zones to organise the logistics for the return of the IDPs and to arrange for the provision of necessities and essential social services following their arrival in their home villages. It also sought, in vain, UNMEE's cooperation in helping rebuild ruined villages and rehabilitate destroyed communal assets to ensure the success of the project. In the end, about 60,000 IDPs were unable to return home because Ethiopian forces held their villages or farming fields, grazing grounds, and water sources.

16.3 Pending Operational Issues

There were also other issues that remained subjects of continued discussion, most notably, the Status of Forces Agreement (SOFA) and freedom of movement for UNMEE. SOFA is a standard agreement that establishes the framework under which foreign military personnel operate in a host country and defines how the laws of civil and criminal jurisdiction of the host country apply to the personnel of the peacekeeping mission. In advance of deployment, the UN had presented Eritrea, for comments, a draft SOFA to establish the framework under which UNMEE personnel would operate and how Eritrean laws would apply to them.

A series of discussions between the Commission and a special UN delegation produced a draft SOFA amended to the full satisfaction of Eritrea's concerns. Having negotiated the final version and agreed on a date certain for the signing ceremony with the SRSG, the president told me that we would not sign the agreement. He gave me no reason when I asked him "why not?" During his visits to Asmera, Kofi Annan raised the matter twice in meetings with the president and, on both occasions, I promised the UN Secretary General right there and then, in the presence of the president, that he will see it signed on his next trip back. There was really no compelling reason not to sign the agreed SOFA but for the president's intent to spurn the UN and spite the Secretary General for the failure to put pressure on Ethiopia to resolve the outstanding issues holding up the full implementation of the Agreement on Cessation of Hostilities.

The president's strained relations with the UN Secretary General that often betrayed a noticeable deficit of normal diplomatic courtesy did not help the cause of Eritrea vis-à-vis the UN. In any case, the UN peacekeeping mission could not operate in a legal vacuum. The draft SOFA served as a framework based on a signed statement I had initially granted UNMEE giving notice that it would apply to the operations of its military and civilian personnel pending agreement on an amended version. This was a blessing in disguise for UNMEE: In comparison with the amended SOFA, the draft SOFA in operation accorded its personnel more privileges and immunity in terms of the application of Eritrean laws and jurisdiction.

The notion of freedom of movement, prone to elastic interpretation, proved quite problematic. The Commission had, right from the arrival of the first peacekeeping contingents in October 2000, assured UNMEE complete freedom of movement within the Temporary Security Zone and granted its requests to use direct land and air corridors to the TSZ and across the border to and from Ethiopia to enable it to carry out its mission. There occurred no problem until February 2001 when UNMEE claimed the right to free movement over an additional 15 km strip of Eritrean territory adjacent to the TSZ. This would have the effect of expanding UNMEE's mandated area of operations inside Eritrea to about 40,000 km², or roughly one-third of the country. This new claim, not foreseen by or provided for in the Agreement on Cessation of Hostilities, had unacceptable military and national security implications for Eritrea.

Another issue pertained to UNMEE's flight route between Asmera and Addis Ababa. Initially, UNMEE proposed the direct Asmera-Addis Ababa flight route as the shortest, fastest, cheapest, and safest air passage between the two capitals. The Commission accepted UNMEE's proposal. Ethiopia however, rejected the direct Asmera-Addis Ababa route and came up with a counter-proposal of an Asmera-Bahr Dar-Addis Ababa route that UNMEE accepted and tried to impose on Eritrea without consultation. Eritrea rejected the Ethiopian counter-proposal. The SRSG then presented a proposal suggesting that the parties choose one of three alternative routes: Asmera-Baher Dar-Addis Ababa, Asmera-Addis Ababa, and Asmera-Dire Dawa-Addis Ababa. Predictably, Eritrea chose the direct Asmera-Addis Ababa route while Ethiopia opted for either the Asmera-Baher Dar-Addis Ababa or the Asmera-Dire Dawa-Addis Ababa route.

Eritrea's choice of the direct flight route reflected considerations of cost effectiveness, flight safety, and national security. The direct route, historically used by civilian flights between Addis Ababa and Asmera prior to the outbreak of the border war, is the shortest, fastest, and cheapest of the three proposed routes. It is also the safest flight route offering the best possibility for aviation search/support/relief missions in case of emergency. Most of all, it presented the least possibility of evading Eritrea's air defence and radar surveillance system guarding Asmera.

The combination of Eritrea's small surface area, particular topographic features, and surveillance radar deployment at the time left blind spots that hindered the ability to detect hostile aircraft approaching Asmera from the southwest or the southeast before or after entry into Eritrean airspace until they reach the outskirts of the capital.

The handicap significantly increased the vulnerability of Eritrea's capital city. It is no accident that the Ethiopian aircraft that conducted bombing raids on targets in Asmera and Massawa during the border war used the Addis Ababa-Baher Dar-Asmera and the Addis Ababa-Dire Dawa-Asmera routes, respectively, to evade advance detection.

In September 2001, during the 56th session of the UN General Assembly, I appraised the UN Security Council, on behalf of the late Minister Ali Said Abdella, of Eritrea's main concerns regarding the outstanding operational issues and the situation in the TSZ. I underlined the urgent need to resolve the lingering operational questions concerning the redeployment of Ethiopian forces, mine clearance, and UNMEE's flight route between Asmera and Addis Ababa in order to facilitate the full implementation of the ACH in time for the EEBC's upcoming determination and demarcation of the boundary. Informal exchanges with Council members at the end of the meeting and later comments from friendly heads of diplomatic missions in Asmera indicated that my address was well received and able to clarify Eritrea's main concerns.

The simmering divisions within the ruling Front and the government denied my work as Commissioner the synergy and coherent perspective of a unified Eritrean stance and support in the effort to establish and stabilise the TSZ on the basis of the historical colonial treaty border. Both sides tried to interfere in the independent work of the Commission. Besides, the attendant distraction of national focus undermined Eritrea's bargaining position. Further, there was such a state of war weariness that I received unsolicited advice to show flexibility in setting the confines of the southern boundary of the TSZ. There followed veiled threats conveyed via anonymous letters slipped into the premises of my residence and an attempted car collision.[503]

Nevertheless, I stood my ground while I kept briefing the president, the 'frozen' former senior government officials, and the heads of diplomatic missions in Asmera on the sticky operational issues concerning the establishment of the TSZ. Furthermore, I had to fend off constant direct and indirect presidential interferences in the internal work of the Commission and contend with petty directives to deny UNMEE the use of certain access roads to the TSZ outside the main arteries that had no bearing on national security. I advised the president that it would serve our best interest to focus on the big picture, tackle the principal issues, and let go small things that had no impact on our strategic interests.

Upon our return from New York around the end of September 2001, the president instructed me, in the presence of the foreign minister, to assume the newly vacated American and International Organisations Desk in the Ministry of Foreign Affairs in addition to my work as Commissioner. I responded that I could not handle the two

---

[503] I had just hosted dinner for several resident ambassadors at Gidei Santa Antonio's Restaurant in Asmera. I was the last one to leave, in the company of my wife. I opened the door to get into my car, parked directly across the street on the side of the church in the direction of Radio Marina. A car that was apparently lying in wait nearby on the opposite side of the wide-open street veered off course sharply to the left and collided with mine as I mounted the driver's seat. There was some commotion as Gidei, her assistants and passers-by gathered on the scene. I was unhurt apart for minor bumps treated at the emergency ward of Halibet Hospital. A few days later, a friend told me that the culprit was a fellow security officer who feigned drunken and wanted to ask for an excuse.

posts at the same time, especially at a time when the work of the Commission was entering a critical phase with possible movement on the operational issues with the help of the UN Security Council ahead of the forthcoming delimitation decision by the Boundary Commission. As a way forward, I offered to help with the Ministry on an ad hoc basis pending the assignment of a director general to head the desk.

In the meantime, the UN Security Council had decided to visit Ethiopia and Eritrea, including the Temporary Security Zone, to underline the commitment of the international community to contribute to the successful completion of the peace process. More specifically, the Security Council's visit aimed to address the outstanding operational issues, to leverage the further implementation of the Algiers peace accords, and to urge the parties to implement all aspects connected with the Boundary Commission's determination, including mine clearance and preparations for the physical demarcation of the boundary on the ground. Moreover, the UN Security Council intended to encourage the initiation of measures to build reciprocal confidence towards the normalisation of relations between the two neighbouring states.

The work of the Commission continued to make progress and the prospect was pregnant with hope and optimism in anticipation of the planned visit of the UN Security Council and the upcoming delimitation decision of the Eritrea-Ethiopia Boundary Commission. However, there was something brewing in the president's mind. On the eve of the visit of the UN Security Council delegation to Eritrea and Ethiopia, and barely a month and half ahead of the imminent announcement of the decision of the Boundary Commission, my work as Commissioner ended abruptly in mid-February 2002. The surprise official announcement of my departure from the Commission and designation as ambassador to the EU by the state media was unusual in its step, strange in its timing, and questionable in its motive. At the time, I was on mission in the US with General Sebhat Efrem, the Minister of Defence of Eritrea, on the invitation of the US Department of Defence. The General and I had left Asmera for Washington in the midst of the last meeting of the Eritrean National Assembly.

All along, I was deeply convinced that the paramount interests of Eritrea and Ethiopia lay in peace and that real peace was achievable between them. As I left the Commission, I had two sources of concern regarding the evolution of the peace process. First, President Isaias's reactive rather than deliberative default mode that disregards adverse consequences. Second, Ethiopia's persistent violations of key provisions of the Agreement on Cessation of Hostilities, including obstructions to the establishment of the Temporary Security Zone, reluctance to provide information on its minefields inside Eritrea, establishing new settlements on sovereign Eritrean territory, and delaying the work of the Ethiopia-Eritrea Boundary Commission (EEBC). Such actions signalled disinterest in an eventual demarcation of the boundary.

I thus cautioned that, as the old Latin saying goes, "if you want peace, prepare for war." It was essential to strengthen our deterrence capability, rectify our internal situation, and consolidate our unity as the bulwark to guarantee our existence as a free people and a sovereign state with a secure future.[504] Concurrently, it was equally important

---

[504] The State of Eritrea, Commission for Coordination with the UN Peacekeeping Mission, 25 July 2001, p. 18.

to stay proactively engaged with all concerned: bilaterally with Ethiopia, regionally with IGAD and the AU, and internationally with the UN, the EU, the US, and the other permanent members of the Security Council.

The UN Security Council visited Ethiopia and Eritrea during 20-25 February 2002. The EEBC announced its 'final and binding decision' regarding the delimitation and demarcation of the boundary on 13 April 2002. The international community unanimously welcomed the final legal settlement of the position of the Eritrea-Ethiopia border as the central element of the Algiers Agreements and urged its expeditious implementation. However, the inability of the UN Security Council to help address the operational issues and the failure of the UN and the AU, the successor of the OAU, to honour their joint commitment to enforce the agreement undermined the work of UNMEE and precipitated the inauspicious termination of its mission.

The following chapter highlights the comprehensive peace agreement, the awards of the Claims Commission, and the delimitation and demarcation decisions of the Boundary Commission.

CHAPTER 17

Securing the Peace between Eritrea and Ethiopia

War is the decision to go for victory [rather] than resolution. Peacemaking is an attempt to resolve the sources of the conflict and restore a situation of balance, thereby eliminating the need for victory and defeat. - Jim Wallis

The Peace Agreement of 12 December 2000 was the continuation of the Agreement on Cessation of Hostilities of 18 June 2000. This chapter notes the key provisions of the Algiers Agreements, summarises the final damage awards by the Claims Commission, and illustrates the territorial significance of the delimitation decision of the Boundary Commission. It highlights the efforts of the Boundary Commission to carry out the physical demarcation of the boundary on the basis of the delimitation decision, appraises the respect or defiance of the Eritrean and Ethiopian governments of their obligations under the peace treaty, and the describes the virtual demarcation of the boundary. It also assesses the role of the guarantors and witnesses of the Algiers accords in fulfilling or failing to meet their commitments under the agreements.

The objective here is not to put blame or to heap praise on any party. Rather, it is to portray the salient events as they happened and consider concrete positions as they unfolded in terms of the actions, or failures to act, of the concerned parties with a view to pointing the way forward to the resolution of this seemingly intractable problem.

The comprehensive peace accord reinforced the Agreement on Cessation of Hostilities and laid a framework for a lasting solution to the boundary issue and the restoration of durable peace and normal relations between Ethiopia and Eritrea. It provided for the permanent termination of hostilities between the two countries and the renunciation of the threat or use of force against each other. It stipulated the immediate release and repatriation of all prisoners of war (POWs) and other persons detained because of the war as well as the humane treatment of each other's nationals and persons of each other's national origin within their respective territories. In addition, the accord committed the two states to the peaceful settlement of disputes and respect for each other's sovereignty and territorial integrity. Further, it provided for the establishment of three impartial and independent commissions, namely, an enquiry commission, a boundary commission and a claims commission.

Article 3 of the Agreement mandated the Enquiry Commission to conduct an investigation on the incidents of 6 May 1998 and the incidents of July and August 1997 in order to determine the origins of the conflict. It provided for the appointment of the Commission by the Secretary General of the OAU, in consultation with the Secretary General of the UN and the two parties. The Commission was required to "submit its report to the Secretary General of the OAU in a timely fashion". However, no Enquiry Commission was established, no attempt made to conduct an investigation on the incidents of July and August 1997 and May 1998 and, therefore, no determination rendered of the origins of the conflict. The omission represented the first violation of the comprehensive peace agreement prejudicial to Eritrea's case.

Article 4 of the Agreement mandated the Boundary Commission to delimit and demarcate the colonial treaty border based on the colonial treaties of 1900, 1902, and 1908 and applicable international law. It expressly denied the Commission the power to make decisions *ex aequo et bono*. It provided for the establishment of the Boundary Commission by the parties, seated in The Hague under the auspices of the International Court of Justice (ICJ) and the UN Cartographer to serve as the Secretary of the Commission. In addition, it stipulated that the Commission start work within fifteen days after its constitution and decide the delimitation of the border within six months of its first meeting.

Further, the agreement committed the two governments to respect the inviolability of the colonial borders inherited at independence, as sanctioned by the OAU resolution adopted in the 1964 Cairo Summit. Most crucially, the parties agreed the decision of the Boundary Commission to be final and binding, to accept the border so determined, and to respect each other's territorial integrity and sovereignty. They also agreed to fully cooperate with the Commission and facilitate its work during the process of delimitation and demarcation. On their part, the UN and the OAU pledged, as per the Agreement on Cessation of Hostilities, to guarantee the respect of the parties to their commitments under the agreement. In addition, the agreement provided for the UN to facilitate, upon request by the parties, resolution of issues that may arise due to the transfer of territorial control because of the delimitation and demarcation process.

Article 5 of the Agreement mandated the Claims Commission to decide, through binding arbitration, all reciprocal claims for loss, damage or injury by the two governments and their nationals, whether natural or juridical persons, against the other resulting from violations of international humanitarian law in connection with the border conflict. The mandate excluded consideration of claims arising from actual military operations or use of force. Like the decision of the Boundary Commission, the decisions and awards of the Claims Commission would be final and binding (as *res judicata*). Again, like the Boundary Commission, the Claims Commission lacked the power to make decisions *ex aequo et bono*. Fulfilment of the decisions and awards of the Commission aimed to help Eritrea and Ethiopia address the negative socioeconomic effects of the conflict on the civilian population, including deportees.

Unlike the Enquiry Commission, which never saw the light of day, the Boundary Commission and the Claims Commission were, duly established under the auspices of the Permanent Court of Arbitration (PCJ) seated in The Hague. The PCJ served as a base and as a registry for the two commissions.[505] Both commissions fulfilled their mandate and disbanded.

The Eritrea-Ethiopia Claims Commission (EECC) conducted extensive briefings and hearings, examined the claims of each party against the other, and ruled on the

---

[505] The Boundary Commission consisted of Bola Ajibola, Elihu Lauterpacht (the President), Michael Reisman, Stephen Schwebel and Arthur Watts; the Claims Commission consisted of George Aldrich, John Crook, Hans van Houette (the President), James Paul and Lucy Reed.

merits of the rival claims. Eritrea and Ethiopia filed an enormous variety of claims for compensation in damages related to the war. In addressing these claims, the Eritrea-Ethiopia Claims Commission considered several categories of issues. Such issues included the lawfulness of the initial resort to force, the treatment of prisoners of war and civilian internees, the legality of means and methods of warfare used in various localities, the treatment of diplomatic premises and personnel, the seizure and destruction of private property, and the treatment by each side of the nationals of the other.

The Claims Commission rendered its decision on fifteen partial and final awards on liability between 1 July 2003 and 19 December 2005 and its decision on the final damage awards for the global losses suffered in the war on 17 August 2009. While Eritrea and Ethiopia filed claims for about US$6 billion and US$14.3 billion, respectively, the EECC awarded Ethiopia a total of US$174,036,520 and Eritrea a total of US$163,520,865, including $2,065,865 to individual Eritreans.[506] Although awarded US$10,515,655 more than Eritrea, Ethiopia expressed dismay at the amount of its assessed compensation in light of the Commission's earlier rulings on relative liability while Eritrea accepted the decision without complaint. In concluding its decision on the two Final Awards, the Claims Commission expressed confidence that Eritrea and Ethiopia "will ensure that the compensation awarded will be paid promptly, and that funds

---

[506] Eritrea-Ethiopia Claims Commission Final Award: Eritrea's Damages Claims and Ethiopia's Damages Claims between The Federal Democratic Republic of Ethiopia and The State of Eritrea, The Hague, 17 August 2009.

received in respect of their claims will be used to provide relief to their civilian populations injured in the war".[507]

17.1 The Delimitation of the Boundary

The Eritrea-Ethiopia Boundary Commission (EEBC), fully constituted on 20 February 2001, immediately set out to "delimit and demarcate" the Ethiopia-Eritrea border. It approached the delimitation of the boundary in the Western, Central, and Eastern sectors corresponding to three colonial treaties. It received and studied written submissions and oral arguments of treaty border claims by Eritrea and Ethiopia. After examining the merits of the territorial claims of each Party based on the colonial treaties of 1900, 1902, and 1908 and applicable international law, the EEBC delivered its Delimitation Decision on 13 April 2002. The Decision defined the salient features of the boundary line and identified the key coordinates connecting it.

Map 3 shows the 1902 Treaty Claim Lines of Ethiopia and Eritrea in the Mereb-Setit section of the Western Sector of the Eritrea-Ethiopia boundary. The Ethiopian claim line stretched from the confluence of the Mereb and Mai Ambessa rivers (Point 9) in the northeast to the confluence of the Setit and Maiteb rivers (Point 3) in the southwest. Eritrea initially argued that a straight line connecting the confluence of the Mereb and Mai Ambessa rivers (Point 9) in the northeast to the confluence of the Setit and Maiten (Mai Tenné) rivers (Point 8) in the southwest delineated

---

[507] Final Award: Eritrea's Damages Claims, (Erit.-Eth.), at § IX (Aug. 17, 2009); Final Award: Ethiopia's Damages Claims, (Erit.-Eth.), at § XII (Aug. 17, 2009).

the colonial treaty border. Later, it submitted that the established boundary line ran from the confluence of the Mereb and Mai Ambessa rivers (Point 9) to the confluence of the Setit and Tomsa rivers (Point 6). Moreover, in its final submissions, Eritrea gave two different locations (7A and 7B) as the southern terminus of the straight line connecting to the confluence of the Mereb and Mai Ambessa rivers (Point 9). It also suggested that the original Treaty reference was actually to the confluence of the Setit and Sittona rivers (Point 4) linking to Point 9.[508]

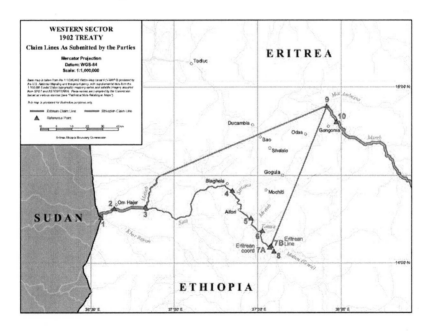

Map 3: The Ethiopian and Eritrean Claim Lines in the Western Sector (EEBC Map 2)

---

[508] Eritrea-Ethiopia Boundary Commission, Decision, 13 April 2002, p. 60.

The Boundary Commission examined the Ethiopian and Eritrean Claim Lines against the evidence. Its interpretation of the 1902 Treaty between Britain, Ethiopia and Italy established the Eritrea-Ethiopia boundary in the Mereb-Setit section of the Western Sector as a straight line connecting the confluence of the Mereb and Mai Ambessa rivers in the northeast (Point 9) with the confluence of the Setit and Maiten (Mai Tenné) rivers in the southwest (Point 8).[509] This straight line leaves Mount Tacura and the Cunama [Kunama] lands within Eritrea in accordance with the *"Terms of the Treaty"* as well as *"The object and purpose of the Treaty"*.[510]

Further, the Boundary Commission examined the rival claim lines in terms of applicable international law, considered in the context of "developments subsequent to the Treaty".[511] It found that Ethiopia's "claim to have exercised administrative authority west of the Eritrean claim line" lacked "evidence of administration of the area sufficiently clear in location, substantial in scope or extensive in time to displace the title of Eritrea that had crystallized as of 1935".[512]

The Boundary Commission's interpretation of the 1902 trilateral treaty and consideration of applicable international

---

[509] Given the nominal role of the foreign minister, Eritrea's chief counsel dealt with the president, directly or via Yemane Gebremeskel (Charlie) and Yemane Gebreab (Monkey). There was no involvement of available national expertise in preparing the case. Eritrea's later submission of a correct treaty-line map prepared by the Commission for Coordination with UNMEE in collaboration with the competent government agencies came too late to undo, in the eyes of the Boundary Commission, the damage done by its previous incorrect submissions.

[510] Ibid., p. 61-69.

[511] Ibid., p. 69-84.

[512] Ibid., p. 84.

law upheld the historical colonial treaty border in the Western Sector. Eritrea had however, submitted variable Treaty Claim Lines corresponding to different locations of the southwestern terminus at the junction of several rivers with the Setit River. The EEBC used Eritrea's inconsistency as a pretext to decide the straight line connecting the confluence of the Mereb and Mai Ambessa rivers (Point 9) with the confluence of the Setit and Tomsa Rivers (Point 6) as the international boundary in the Mereb-Setit section of the Western Sector. The submission of variable Treaty Claim Lines cost Eritrea the sliver of territory represented by the 9-6-8 triangle in Map 3, or the heavily shaded area in the Western Sector in Map 6.[513]

Map 4 shows the 1900 Treaty Claim Lines of Ethiopia and Eritrea in the Central Sector of the Eritrea-Ethiopia boundary. This sector extends from the confluence of the Mereb and Mai Ambessa rivers in the west along the Mereb-Belesa-Muna line, continues beyond the junction of the Muna and Endeli rivers at Massolae (Point 27) to Rendacoma (Point 28), and veers slightly southeast to the Salt Lake (Point 31) in the east.

Both Ethiopia and Eritrea agreed on the description of the boundary line in the 1900 Treaty as the "Mereb-Belesa-

---

[513] Map 6 (EEBC 13), reproduced by the author in June 2002 for use in a series of seminars presented to Eritrean communities in the diaspora in Frankfurt on 15 June 2002, Stuttgart on 16 June 2002, Köln on 6 July 2002, Paris on 14 September 2002, Brussels on 21 September 2002, etc. The shaded areas indicate the territorial significance of the delimitation decision of the Boundary Commission and show the new international boundary vis-à-vis the historical colonial treaty border. The shades in red signify Eritrea's loss, or Ethiopia's gain, of territory arising from the Boundary Commission's revision of the historical colonial treaty map of the boundary between the two states.

Muna" line, also depicted in a map annexed to the Treaty. They also agreed on the Treaty description of the Belesa River stretch but disputed the treaty location of its course. The task of the Commission in the Central Sector was thus, reduced to identifying the courses of the Mereb, Belesa, and Muna rivers as the delimitation line under the Treaty. Eritrea's claim line corresponded with the courses of the rivers as represented "on the 1894 map that formed the basis of the Treaty map"[514] and subsequent maps of the historical colonial treaty border between the two countries.

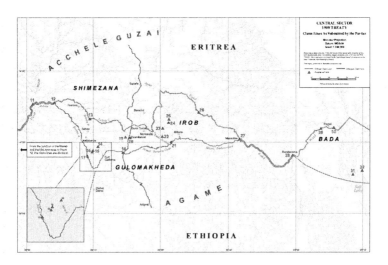

Map 4: The Ethiopian and Eritrean Claim Lines in the Central Sector (EEBC Map 3)

As a bargaining chip, Ethiopia claimed title to large swathes of territory north of the 1900 Treaty border. It contended that the Commission's task was not so much to interpret

---

[514]   Ibid., p. 18.

and apply the *de jure* geography of the Treaty's Mereb-Belesa-Muna line as it was to determine the *de facto* administrative division between the Italian controlled Akele Guzai (Eritrea) and the Abyssinian controlled Agame (Tigray) districts at the time. It challenged the geographic accuracy of the depiction of the Belesa and Muna rivers on the 1900 Treaty map. Further, Ethiopia contested that, given variations in the local nomenclature for the rivers and their main branches, the *Belesa* and, in particular, the *Muna* describe relevant rivers in the region identifiable in 1900 as located on the 1900 Treaty map.[515]

The Commission reviewed the rival claims over the identity of the Belesa and Muna rivers in the framework of what it labelled as the Belesa Projection and the Endeli Projection. In dealing with the Eritrean and Ethiopian contention regarding the identity of the course of the Belesa River in the Belesa Projection, the Commission ignored the substance of the treaty and the evidence of the map accompanying it. Instead, it resorted to an interpretation of the original intention of the parties to the 1900 Treaty, namely, Italy and Ethiopia, and the significance of the omission of the names of certain tributaries of the Belesa in the Treaty's text in order to identify the "intended" Treaty course of the Belesa River.[516]

The subsequent interpretation of original "intent" led the Commission to conclude that the parties "intended" the Tserona River, a tributary of the Belesa River flowing from the northeast, as the Treaty location of the Belesa River and that the omission of the tributary's name in the Treaty's text

---

[515] Ibid., p. 19.
[516] Ibid., p. 31-38.

was deliberate rather than an oversight or a mistake. Such a speculative conclusion left "Fort Cadorna, Monoxeito, Guna Guna, and Tserona", localities that Ethiopia's written submission described as "undisputed Eritrean places",[517] on the Ethiopian side of the Treaty line.

Ethiopia's claim of the Belesa Projection conflicted with its official admission that several localities within that area indisputably belong to Eritrea. This conflict calls into serious question the validity of the Commission's interpretation that the course of the Tserona River was the intended Treaty location of the Belesa section of the Mereb-Belesa-Muna line. It is very difficult to imagine that grasp of such an anomalous speculation escaped the learned, intelligent, and honourable commissioners of the EEBC.

Having so determined the identity of the Belesa River, the Commission proceeded to delineate the overland link between the headwaters of the Belesa (Point 19) and Muna (Point 20) rivers as the Treaty line. In addressing the Ethio-Eritrean contention with respect to the identity of the Muna River, the Commission established the Muna/Berbero Gado-Endeli-Ragali course as the Treaty line in the Endeli Projection (Irob). Cumulatively, therefore, the Boundary Commission's interpretation of the 1900 Treaty Line established the Eritrea-Ethiopia boundary in the Central Sector as the Mereb-Belesa (-Tserona)-Muna/Berbero Gado-Endeli-Ragali line continuing to its terminus at the Salt Lake in accordance with *"The object and purpose of the Treaty"*.[518]

---

[517] Ibid., p. 50.
[518] Ibid., p. 45-48. For the Commission's interpretation of the 1900 Treaty Line, see Map 7 on page 47.

In terms of applicable international law, considered in the context of "subsequent conduct", the Commission addressed the claims of the Parties in relation to the exercise of sovereign authority in, the diplomatic record or official exchanges on, and maps of the Belesa Projection, the Endeli Projection, and the Bada region and made two qualifications:

1. It modified its contentious interpretation of the 'intended' Treaty line concerning the Belesa Projection to place the bulk of the eastern part of the Belesa Projection and the town of Tserona, the Akhran region, and Fort Cadorna in the western part of the Belesa Projection in Eritrean territory. It further modified the Treaty line in the eastern part of the Belesa Projection to place the town of Zalambesa in Ethiopian territory.
2. It revised the Muna/Berbero Gado section of the Treaty line to place the southerly and easterly parts of the Endeli Projection in Ethiopian territory.

Finally, the Commission maintained the Endeli-Ragali section of the Mereb-Belesa (-Tserona)-Muna/Berbero Gado-Endeli-Ragali line continuing to its terminus at the Salt Lake as the Treaty line, leaving Bada in Ethiopian territory.[519]

Map 6 shows the territorial consequence of the Boundary Commission's modification of the 1900 Treaty line in the Central Sector for Eritrea and Ethiopia. The heavily shaded patches of territory in the western part of the Belesa Projection, around Zalambesa, in the eastern and southern parts of the Indeli Projection (Irob) and the Bada region,

---

[519] Ibid., p. 49-56.

signify areas awarded to Ethiopia by the decision of the Eritrea-Ethiopia Boundary Commission.

Map 5 shows the 1908 Treaty Claim Lines of Ethiopia and Eritrea in the Eastern Sector of the Eritrea-Ethiopia boundary. The dispute in this Sector centred mainly on the Bada area, Bure, and three technical issues. First, locating the starting point at the most westerly end; second, deciding the proper way of drawing the Treaty line running parallel to the coast at a distance of sixty kilometres inland; and third, determining the eastern terminus of the boundary or the trilateral junction of the border between Eritrea, Ethiopia and Djibouti.

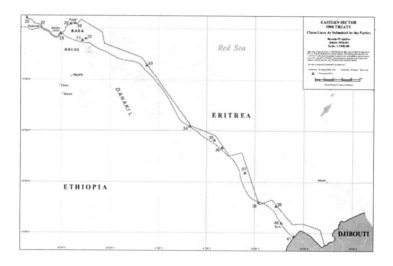

Map 5: Ethiopian and Eritrean Claim Lines in the Eastern Sector (EEBC Map 4)

In establishing the eastern terminus of the Central Sector at Point 31 at the northern edge of the Salt Lake, rather than at Rendacoma (point 28), the Commission had already decided the western terminus of the Eastern Sector. The Commission first resolved the method of drawing the inland line running parallel to the coast and determined the location of the eastern terminus atop Mount Mussa Ali. It then essentially confirmed the Treaty line with the proviso that it passes at a point, lying equidistant between the Eritrean and Ethiopian checkpoints, at Bure (Point 40) to the border with Djibouti (Point 41), as shown in Map 5.[520]

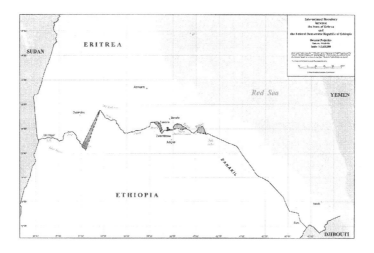

Map 6: New International Boundary between Eritrea and Ethiopia (the EEBC's Map 13; shades inserted by the author)

The Eritrea-Ethiopia Boundary Commission (EEBC) delivered its decision on the delimitation of the border between Eritrea and Ethiopia on 13 April 2002.[521] Eritrea's

---

[520] Ibid., p. 101.
[521] Eritrea-Ethiopia Boundary Commission, DECISION Regarding Delimitation of the Border between The State Of Eritrea and the

claim line generally corresponded with the historical colonial treaty border. On the other hand, Ethiopia's claim line incorporated extensive tracts of territory on the Eritrean side of that border: the 'Yirga Triangle' in the Mereb-Setit section of the Western Sector, the 'Belesa Projection' and the 'Endeli Projection' in the Mereb-Belesa-Muna line in the Central Sector, and the Bada and Bure areas in the Eastern Sector. Clearly, Ethiopia claimed large areas that did not belong to it as a bargaining chip and ended up gaining about half of its claims at Eritrea's expense.

Map 6 shows the new international boundary between the State of Eritrea and the Federal Democratic Republic of Ethiopia, with the heavily shaded areas indicating the territorial effect of the delimitation decision of the Boundary Commission on the historical colonial treaty border. The decision of the Boundary Commission effectively modified the historical colonial treaty border between the two states in favour of Ethiopia. The map depicts that the delimitation decision of the Boundary Commission, as an arbitral determination of the boundary, essentially ceded to Ethiopia the red-shaded strips of land in the Western, Central, and Eastern sectors that the colonial treaties of 1900, 1902, and 1908 had placed in Eritrean territory.

Predictably, there was a marked contrast in the immediate public reaction of the two states to the eagerly awaited announcement of the Boundary Commission's Delimitation Decision on 13 April 2002. In a swift response, the Ethiopian government declared victory and the state media in Addis

---

Federal Democratic Republic of Ethiopia, The Hague, 13 April 2002.

Ababa exuded a celebratory mood. The Eritrean government issued no official statement on that notable day; the state media merely broke the news and, in a display of uncertainty as to the territorial significance of the ruling, the country's television station kept on flashing the new delimitation line in the different sectors of the border without comment.

At the time, I was in Madrid, Spain, representing Eritrea at the Second World Assembly on Ageing. The event coincided with the beginning of my second tour of duty as ambassador to the EU and several EU Member States, including Spain. From my hotel room in Madrid, I called the Eritrean delegation that attended the Boundary Commission's announcement ceremony in The Hague and asked for details of the Delimitation Decision. I also called the President's Office in Asmera to get a feel of the official mood and find out what was happening and learned that the government was taking time to study the meaning of the Decision.

Impatient with the lack of a clear explanation, I requested Foreign Minister Ali Said Abdella, at the head the Eritrean delegation in The Hague, to send me a copy of the substantive decision. Ali faxed me the Dispositif (Chapter VIII) of the Decision and we discussed, over the phone, its attendant territorial implications for Eritrea vis-à-vis the historical colonial treaty border. We agreed on the obvious need to inform forthwith the Eritrean people at home and abroad, made the more anxious by an Eritrean silence in the face of an Ethiopian declaration of victory.

In a statement issued in the name of the council of ministers,[522] Ethiopia declared that the EEBC's decision

---

[522]   ከሚንስትሮች ምክር ቤት የተሰጠ መግለጫ (author's paraphrasing from the original Amharic), Walta Information Center -Amharic, 13

has restored all 'forcibly seized Ethiopian territories' in the three Treaty sectors to Ethiopia. It reiterated its respect for the Boundary Commission for performing its task with fidelity and a high sense of responsibility, and affirmed its acceptance of the 'just and legitimate' Decision and readiness to implement it in accordance with the Algiers Agreement. Further, it expressed its desire for the expeditious physical demarcation of the boundary, strongly urging Eritrea to honour its obligation to cooperate with the effort to demarcate the border.

Upon studying the EEBC Decision, Eritrea stated its acceptance and declared victory, despite the obvious loss of territory. Nevertheless, the unequivocal initial acceptance of the Delimitation Decision by both Parties augured well for the expeditious demarcation of the border on the ground and the successful completion of the peace process. The following section highlights the EEBC's work to demarcate the boundary.

17.2 Virtual Demarcation of the Boundary

Article 4(13) of the Algiers Agreement required the "expeditious demarcation" of the boundary. Upon delivery of its Delimitation Decision, the EEBC set out to demarcate the boundary in consultation with and the cooperation of the Secretary General of the United Nations. Just as it did with the delimitation process, the Boundary Commission approached the task in three sectors based on the colonial treaties. It had, in anticipation of the emplacement of

---

April 2002. http://www.waltainfo.com/Boundary/Ethio_Eritrea/Boundary/Amharic.htm

pillars as boundary markers along the delimitation line, already appointed a Chief Surveyor in October 2001 and established Field Offices in Addis Ababa and Asmera in November 2001. The Chief Surveyor, with a staff of assistant surveyors hired by the Commission, set up residence in Asmera on 15 November 2001. Furthermore, the EEBC appointed a Special Consultant to provide it with technical advice and assistance in May 2002 and established a third Field Office in Adigrat, northern Ethiopia, in July 2002.[523]

However, there were obstacles and ominous signs of contention on the horizon right from the start of the demarcation process. On 27 April 2002, Ethiopia forbade "further work within the territory under its control", and interrupted the work of aerial photography and ground survey to construct a 1:25,000 map of the border to serve as a basis for demarcation.[524] Furthermore, a month after issuing its clear acceptance of the Delimitation Decision, Ethiopia submitted a long Request for Interpretation, Correction and Consultation regarding the Decision.[525]

Ethiopia filed a request for comments within the 30-day period allowed in the Commission's Rules of Procedure. Eritrea characterised the Ethiopian request as an attempt at "a wholesale revision of the 13 April 2002 Decision" and called for its dismissal as "inadmissible under the Commission's

---

[523]   Eritrea-Ethiopia Boundary Commission: Order Pursuant to Article 27(1) of the Commission's Rules of Procedure, 17 July 2002.

[524]   Eritrea-Ethiopia Boundary Commission: Fifth Report on the Work of the Commission, 30 May 2002, p. 5.

[525]   The Federal Democratic Republic of Ethiopia: Eritrea/Ethiopia Boundary Arbitration, Request for Interpretation, Correction and Consultation, 13 May 2002.

Rules of Procedure" and "inconsistent with the 12 December 2000 Algiers Peace Agreement".[526] After due consideration of the Ethiopian request and the Eritrean submission in the context of its mandate, the Boundary Commission decided that, "the Ethiopian request is inadmissible and no further action will be taken upon it".[527]

The Commission also received, and duly responded to, a letter from the President of Eritrea on 17 May 2002 raising, "rather unusually in relation to an arbitral proceeding" in its view, four questions regarding the basis used, the procedures followed or any political pressures exerted in reaching the Decision and whether the Decision was final and binding.[528] The Commission replied to the Eritrean President's letter on 21 May 2002. The same day, it met with the Parties to discuss the modalities and technical aspects of the demarcation process, the role of the UN Mission in Eritrea and Ethiopia (UNMEE) and the Mine Action Coordinating Centre (MACC), and the establishment and role of field offices within Ethiopia. It also urged Ethiopia to resume cooperation immediately with the Boundary Commission in the demarcation process.[529]

---

[526]   Eritrea's Response to the Request of the Federal Democratic Republic of Ethiopia for Interpretation, Correction and Consultation (13 May 2002), 14 June 2002, p. 1 & 23.

[527]   Eritrea-Ethiopia Boundary Commission: Decision Regarding the "Request for Request for Interpretation, Correction and Consultation" Submitted by Federal Democratic Republic of Ethiopia on 13 May 2002, p. 4.

[528]   Exchange of Letters between the Presidents of Eritrea (17 May 2002) and the EEBC (21 May 2002).

[529]   Fifth Report of the Eritrea-Ethiopia Boundary Commission to the Secretary-General of the United Nations (S/2002/744), 30 May

Reminding it of its treaty obligation to cooperate without conditions, the Commission requested Ethiopia to allow the completion of the work before the start of the rainy season. Nevertheless, Ethiopia continued to prohibit fieldwork in the border areas under its control. Its refusal to lift the ban was followed by a letter, dated 15 May 2002, to the Boundary Commission from the Ethiopian foreign minister criticising UNMEE's logistical assistance to the Chief Surveyor and casting doubt about the neutrality of the Boundary Commission's Field Office".[530]

Meanwhile, Eritrea accused Ethiopia of settling its nationals in Eritrean sovereign territory around Badme as of July 2002 and requested the Commission to instruct Ethiopia to undo the new settlements.[531] The Commission, acting on a report of the findings of a Field Investigation Team[532] sent to visit the places in question, ordered Ethiopia to dismantle its new settlements by "no later than 30 September 2002" and instructed each Party to ensure that "no further population settlement takes place across the delimitation line established by the Decision of 13 April 2002".[533] When Ethiopia ignored the *Order*, the Commission reiterated that, "the Delimitation Decision of 13 April 2002 is final and binding in respect of

---

2002, p. 5-6.

[530] Seyoum Mesfin, Minister of Foreign Affairs and Agent of Ethiopia, 15 May 2002 (3-1/234/19/02).

[531] The State of Eritrea, Letter to the Eritrea-Ethiopia Boundary Commission, 7 June 2002.

[532] Eritrea-Ethiopia Boundary Commission: Report of the Field Investigation Team, Field Visit of 9-14 July 2002.

[533] Eritrea-Ethiopia Boundary Commission: Order of the Commission (Made Pursuant to Article 20 and Article 27(1) of the Commission's Rules of Procedure, 17 July 2002, p. 5.

the whole of the boundary between the Parties". Further, it ruled that, "Ethiopia, in failing to remove from Eritrean territory persons of Ethiopian origin who have moved into that territory subsequent to the date of the Delimitation Decision, has not complied with its obligations."[534]

In continuation of its preparatory steps and extensive consultation with the Parties, the Boundary Commission issued detailed *Demarcation Directions* on 8 July 2002, subsequently revised in November 2002 and in March and July 2003. The *Demarcation Directions* defined the objective of demarcation as the construction of ground pillars along the delimitation line. They indicated that the work of demarcation would be carried out through the Field Offices by the UN Cartographer, the Special Consultant of the Commission, the Chief Surveyor, and any other persons appointed for the purpose under the authority of the Commission. They also provided for each Party's nomination of a high level Liaison Representative, Deputy Liaison Representative, and two Field Liaison Officers and required each Party to allow unrestricted freedom of movement for the demarcation personnel within its territory.

Further, the *Demarcation Directions* specified that the demarcation would take place on the basis of a "1:25,000 scale map"; that "pillar emplacements shall begin in the Eastern Sector, without prejudice to the continuance of preparatory steps for pillar emplacement in the Western and Central Sectors"; that the construction of the pillars "shall be done by contractors hired by the United Nations on behalf of the Commission"; and that "the Commission has

---

[534] Eritrea-Ethiopia Boundary Commission: Determinations, 7 November 2002, p 2.

no authority to vary the boundary line. If it runs through and divides a town or village, the line may be varied only on the basis of an express request agreed between and made by both parties".[535]

Based on the Boundary Commission's initial Schedule of Activities, revised on 19 February 2003, demarcation started in the Eastern Sector in March 2003. In a final revision of the Schedule of Activities on 16 July 2003, pillar emplacement was set to begin in October and finish in December 2003 in the Eastern Sector; begin in January and finish in March 2003 in the Central Sector; and begin in March and finish in June 2004 in the Western Sector.[536] Pillar sites were determined through field assessment with the cooperation of the Parties by August 2003. The Parties received a set of marked maps indicating the location of proposed boundary pillars, stretching from the border with Djibouti in the east to the Salt Lake in the northwest, for comment. Eritrea endorsed the marked maps while Ethiopia did not reply.

When the 30-day period allowed under the Rules of Procedure for comment on the marked maps expired, "the Commission adopted specific boundary points that could serve as locations for the emplacement of pillars in that Sector". Once the Commission was set to emplace pillars in the Eastern Sector and start demarcation in the Central and Western Sectors, however, Ethiopia refused "to allow demarcation to begin in the Central and Western Sectors"

---

[535] Eritrea-Ethiopia Boundary Commission: Demarcation Directions, 8 July 2002, p. 10.

[536] Eritrea-Ethiopia Boundary Commission: Schedule of the Order of Activities Ahead as at 16 July 2003, !6 July 2003.

while Eritrea objected "to pillar emplacement in the Eastern Sector unless demarcation work was begun simultaneously in the Central and Western Sectors". In addition, Eritrea informed the Chief Surveyor that it would "withdraw its arrangements for the provision of security in the Eastern Sector if the contract then under negotiation for the emplacement of pillars did not cover the entire boundary as determined in the Delimitation Decision".[537]

Further, on 24 January 2003, Ethiopia submitted Comments stating that it had accepted the EEBC's Decision on the understanding that the "straight-line segment between Points 6 and 9 (Badme line) would be refined during demarcation" to put Badme inside Ethiopia.[538] In the view of the EEBC, Ethiopia's Comments "amounted to an attempt to reopen the substance of the April Decision". It added that: "Notwithstanding the clarity with which the Commission has stated the limits upon its authority, Ethiopia has continued to seek variations to the boundary line delimited in the April Decision, and has done so in terms that appear, despite protestations to the contrary, to undermine not only the April Decision but also the peace process as a whole." In these comments, "the Commission sees an intimation that Ethiopia will not adhere to the April

---

[537] Eritrea-Ethiopia Boundary Commission: Statement by the Commission, 27 November 2006, p. 3-5.

[538] Submission by the Federal Democratic Republic of Ethiopia, 24 January 2003, Comments Pursuant to the December 2000 Agreement, the Commission's Rules of Procedure, the Commission's Demarcation Directions and Instructions provided at the Boundary Commission's Meeting on 6 and 7 November 2002, p. 61-74.

Decision if its claim to 'refinement' of the April delimitation Decision is not accepted".[539]

Ethiopia provided additional signals of its intention not to follow the EEBC's Demarcation Directions. The UN Secretary General's 6 March 2003 Progress Report on Ethiopia and Eritrea stated that Prime Minister Meles Zenawi has intimated to his Special Representative that "if its concerns were not properly addressed, Ethiopia might eventually reject the demarcation-related decisions of the Commission" and that his "Special Representative immediately consulted with the representatives of the Guarantors and Facilitators of the peace process, as well as the group of Friends of UNMEE, in Addis Ababa and in Asmara regarding Ethiopia's position".[540]

In its Observations issued in consideration of the comments advanced by the Parties on 24 January 2003, the Boundary Commission concluded that *the Parties knew in advance, and agreed*: "that the result of the Commission's delimitation of the boundary might not be identical with previous areas of territorial administration"; "that it was not open to the Commission to make its decisions on the basis of *ex aequo et bono* considerations"; "that the boundary as delimited by the Commission's Delimitation Decision would be final"; and that the Commission is "obliged to reject the assertion that it must adjust the coordinates to take into account the human and physical geography in the border region. Moreover, the Commission firmly rejects the contention that if such

---

[539] Eighth Report of the Eritrea-Ethiopia Boundary Commission, 21 February 2003, p. 10-11.

[540] Progress Report of the Secretary-General on Ethiopia and Eritrea (S/2003/257), 6 March 2003, p.3.

adjustments are not made the Commission's work would be devoid of adequate legal basis".[541]

These contentious exchanges were capped off by a turnaround. In a complete reversal and absolute contradiction of its declaration of 13 April 2002, Ethiopia informed the UN Security Council that the Commission's Decision is "totally illegal, unjust and irresponsible". The Prime Minister's letter of 19 September 2003 went on to state that "It is unimaginable for the Ethiopian people to accept such a blatant miscarriage of justice. The decision is thus a recipe for continued instability, and even recurring wars". It further asserted that "Nothing worthwhile can therefore be expected from the Commission to salvage the peace process". Finally, the letter called on the Security Council to "set up an alternative mechanism to demarcate the contested parts of the boundary in a just and legal manner so as to ensure lasting peace in the region".[542]

In a detailed and direct response, the EEBC described Ethiopia's letter as "a repudiation of its repeated acceptance of the Commission's decision since it was rendered".[543] Similarly, the UN Security Council responded that "only the full implementation of the Algiers Agreements will lead to sustainable peace" and "that Ethiopia has committed itself under the Algiers Agreements to accept the Boundary Decision as final and binding". The Security Council urged Eritrea and Ethiopia to abide by their commitments

---

[541] Eritrea-Ethiopia Boundary Commission: Observations, 21 March 2003, p. 3-5.

[542] Letter of Ethiopian Prime Minister Meles Zenawi to UN Secretary General Kofi Annan, 19 September 2003.

[543] Eritrea-Ethiopia Boundary Commission: Letter to the Secretary General, 7 October 2003.

under the Algiers Agreements and to fully cooperate with the Boundary Commission in the implementation of its decisions.[544] It specifically called on "Ethiopia to provide its full and prompt cooperation to the Boundary commission and its field officers in order that demarcation can proceed in all sectors as directed by the Boundary Commission".[545]

The UN Secretary General welcomed Eritrea's continued cooperation with the Boundary Commission while criticising Ethiopia's failure to extend the necessary cooperation in the exercise of its mandated functions.[546] In an attempt to resolve the impasse, he appointed, on 30 January 2004, Llyod Axworthy, former Canadian Minister of Foreign Affairs, as his Special Envoy to Eritrea and Ethiopia. In direct contradiction to its *final and binding* character, Axworthy had characterised the decision of the Boundary Commission under the Algiers Agreement as "something that has to be worked at" and "needs to be developed."[547] Lacking an explicit statement of his mandate from the Secretary General to allay its suspicion, Eritrea refused to accept his good offices as an "alternative mechanism".

Meanwhile, Ethiopia declared its acceptance of the EEBC Decision "in principle" and proposed a "five point peace plan" that, in the main, called for dialogue with Eritrea to amend the 13 April 2002 Delimitation Decision

---

[544] United Nations Security Council Resolution 1507 (2003), 12 September 2003.

[545] President of the Security Council: Letter to the Prime Minister of the Federal Democratic Republic of Ethiopia, 3 October 2003.

[546] Progress report of the Secretary-General on Ethiopia and Eritrea (S/2003/1186), 19 December 2003.

[547] United Nations Integrated Regional Information Networks (IRIN), 2 January 2004.

as a condition for the demarcation of the boundary. The 'initiative' was announced by the prime minister in an address to the Ethiopian parliament on 25 November 2004.[548] On the same day the proposal was presented in the 8th Session of the ACP-EU Joint Parliamentary Assembly, in The Hague, as a 'major breakthrough'. In addition to my position as ambassador to the EU, I also served as the chief delegate of the Eritrean National Assembly to the ACP-EU Joint Parliamentary Assembly. I took the floor to comment on the new Ethiopian initiative in exercise of my right of response as the representative of Eritrea.

I stated that I have taken note of the announcement by the Delegate of Ethiopia; reminded the Joint Assembly that the Decision of the Boundary Commission is *final and binding*, to be implemented as is, as per the Algiers Peace Agreement; that the border would have long been demarcated were it not for Ethiopia's persistent obstructions; and recapped that Ethiopia had accepted the EEBC Decision in April 2002, rejected it in September 2003, and says that it has accepted it 'in principle' now in November 2005, whatever that means? I asserted that the way forward is simple and straight: Ethiopia's unequivocal acceptance of the Decision and full cooperation with the Boundary Commission to enable the physical demarcation of the boundary. Hence, time will tell whether this is a serious new 'development' leading to a real breakthrough or a mere public relations stunt. Finally, I assured the ACP-EU Joint Parliamentary Assembly that

---

[548] Speech by HE Meles Zenawi, Prime Minister of the Federal Democratic Republic of Ethiopia to Members of the House of Peoples Representatives on the Ethiopia - Eritrea Border Issue, 25th November 2004.

Eritrea will study the text of the proposal and declare its position in due course.[549]

In an attempt to end the impasse and "secure the resumption of the demarcation process", the EEBC invited Eritrea and Ethiopia, on 4 February 2005, to a meeting in London on 22 February 2005 and urged them to enable it to complete its mission. Eritrea accepted the invitation and affirmed its willingness "to meet with the Commission and Ethiopia to discuss the unconditional renewal of the demarcation process." On the other hand, Ethiopia declined the invitation to meet with the Commission and Eritrea without preconditions. In declining the invitation, Ethiopia claimed that meeting without prior "dialogue between the Parties" would be "premature", "unproductive" and could have "an adverse impact on the demarcation process".

Eritrea's insistence on "adherence to the April 2002 Delimitation Decision" as final and binding was consistent with the terms of the Algiers Peace Agreement. Ethiopia's demand for the modification of the Decision flouted the Agreement. Ethiopia's inadmissible preconditions and demand, faced with Eritrea's legitimate insistence, created an impasse and continued to disable the Boundary Commission from proceeding with the demarcation process.

The situation forced the Boundary Commission to overcome its previous reluctance "to express any legal assessment of the circumstances" which led to the "impasse" and "identify the conduct" that "prevented [it] from

---

[549] Welde Giorgis, Andebrhan, Response by the Delegate of Eritrea on Ethiopia's Announcement of Acceptance of the EEBC Decision, 8th Session of the ACP-EU JPA, The Hague, 25 November 2004.

completing its mandate" to demarcate the border as delimited by the 13 April 2002 Decision:

> *Ethiopia is not prepared to allow demarcation to continue in the manner laid down by the Commission. It now insists on prior 'dialogue' but has rejected the opportunity for such 'dialogue' within the framework of the demarcation process provided by the Commission's proposal to meet with the Parties on 22 February. This is the latest in a series of obstructive actions taken since the summer of 2002 and belies the frequently professed acceptance by Ethiopia of the Delimitation Decision. ... In view of the refusal of Ethiopia to attend the 22 February meeting, the Commission had no alternative but to cancel it.*[550]

In exasperation, the EEBC conceded that it "does not see any immediate or short term prospect of the renewal of the demarcation process" and started taking immediate steps to close down its Field Offices. At the same time, it reaffirmed its readiness to reactivate them and resume its ground work if the deadlock is resolved:

> *These [Field Offices] can be reactivated (though subject to some months of lead time) if Ethiopia abandons its present insistence on preconditions for the implementation of the demarcation. As for the Commission, it remains ready to proceed with and complete the process of demarcation whenever circumstances permit.*
>
> *The Commission must conclude by recalling that the line of the boundary was legally and finally determined*

---

[550] Sixteenth Report of the Eritrea-Ethiopia Boundary Commission (S/2005/142), 24 February 2005, p. 10.

by its Delimitation Decision of 13 April 2002. Though undemarcated, this line is binding upon both Parties, subject only to the minor qualifications expressed in the Delimitation Decision, unless they agree otherwise. Conduct inconsistent with this boundary line is unlawful.[551]

Subsequently, the UN Security Council called on Ethiopia "without preconditions, to start the implementation of demarcation, by taking the necessary steps to enable the Commission to demarcate the border completely and promptly".[552] Yet, Ethiopia remained unwilling to accept the Delimitation Decision without equivocation, enable the physical demarcation of the boundary or meet its financial obligations to the Boundary Commission. Faced with Ethiopia's refusal to budge and persistent reluctance to cooperate, an exasperated Boundary Commission announced, on 30 May 2005, that it had suspended all its activities, closed its Field Offices, and placed its field assets in the custody of UNMEE due to Ethiopia's refusal to cooperate with its efforts to demarcate the boundary.[553] The situation remained unchanged and no demarcation activity was conducted during the rest of the year.

In an effort to break the impasse, the witnesses to the Algiers Agreement and the President of the Security Council issued similar statements on 22 February 2006 and 24 February 2006 (S/PRST/2006/10), respectively. The witnesses and the President reminded Eritrea and Ethiopia of their agreement to accept the delimitation and demarcation decisions of the

---

[551] Ibid., p. 16-17.

[552] UN Security Council Resolution 1586 (2005), 14 March 2005.

[553] Eritrea-Ethiopia Boundary Commission: Seventeenth Report on the Work of the Commission, 30 May 2005.

Eritrea-Ethiopia Boundary Commission as final and binding and called on them to respect their commitments and cooperate with the Boundary Commission to implement its decision without further delay. In addition, they urged the Commission to convene a meeting of the Parties for technical discussions, and the Parties to attend the meeting and abide by the decisions of the Boundary Commission, in order to successfully conclude the demarcation process.

In the context of realpolitik, however, the scores of resolutions of the UN Security Council and the numerous statements of its rotating Presidency, underlining "unwavering commitment" to the peace process, to the full and expeditious implementation of the Algiers Agreements, and to the final and binding delimitation and demarcation determinations of the Eritrea-Ethiopia Boundary Commission, lacked coherent internal support and substantive authority to effectively persuade Ethiopia to cooperate with the Boundary Commission.[554] The UN Security Council lacked the convergence of interest, the unity of purpose, and the political will to honour its commitment and enforce its resolutions vis-à-vis the Eritrea-Ethiopia peace process.

The US, as the principal architect of the Algiers Peace Agreement, one of its witnesses, and the predominant

---

[554]   S/RES/1398 (15 March 2002), S/RES/1430 (14 August 2002), S/RES/1466 (14 March 2003), S/RES/1507 (12 September 2003), S/RES/1531 (12 March 2004), S/RES/1560 (14 September 2004), S/RES/1586 (14 March 2005), S/RES/1622 (13 September 2005), S/RES/1640 (23 November 2005), S/RES/ 1661 (14 March 2006), S/RES/ 1670 (13 April 2006), S/RES/1678 (15 May 2006), S/RES/1681 (31 May 2006), S/RES/1710 (29 September 2006), S/RES/1741 (30 January 2007), S/RES/1767 (30 July 2007), S/RES/1798 (30 January 2008) and S/RES/1827 (30 July 2008).

actor of the Permanent Members (P5) of the UN Security Council, had initially supported the physical demarcation of the boundary on the basis of the Delimitation Decision. Caught up in the mix of a close regional alliance with Ethiopia in the 'war on terror' and tense relations obtaining with Eritrea originating basically in the latter's refusal to address the issue of the continued detention of two Eritrean employees of the US embassy in Asmera, the US reversed its position, instructed Ethiopia not to allow the demarcation of the boundary,[555] and used its dominant position and enormous clout to abet Ethiopia's non-compliance with its treaty obligations under international law.

It seems that the policy reversal was not without its sceptics within the administration. For instance, the then US Permanent Representative to the United Nations, Ambassador John Bolton stated, that "For reasons I never understood, Frazer [US Assistant Secretary for African Affairs] reversed course and asked in early February [2006] to reopen the 2002 EEBC decision, which she had concluded was wrong, and award a major piece of disputed territory to Ethiopia. I was at a loss to explain that to the Security Council, so I didn't".[556] Having persuaded Ethiopia not to implement demarcation and issued her internal directive referred to by the ambassador, Jendayi Frazer publicly suggested that 'just

---

[555] Conversations of the author with senior EU officials in Brussels privy to the dossier revealed that Meles had agreed to allow the physical demarcation of the boundary until Jendayi Frazer told him otherwise, to spite Isaias.

[556] Bolton, John, Surrender Is Not an Option: Defending America at the United Nations, Threshold Editions, November 2007, p. 347.

and reasonable adjustments' be made to the EEBC's *final and binding* delimitation decision in demarcating the border.[557]

In any case, the Commission sought, in consideration of the advice of the witnesses of the Algiers Agreement and the President of the Security Council, to arrange a meeting with the Parties to try to secure their consent to the resumption of the demarcation process, interrupted in 2003, in early March 2006.[558] The meetings took place on 10 March and on 17 May 2006. At both meetings, the Boundary Commission operated on the premise that both states were "committed without condition or qualification to the full implementation of the Boundary Commission's delimitation decision of 13 April 2002".[559] At the March meeting, the Boundary Commission stressed the need to resume and complete the demarcation process without further delay to prevent the possible deterioration in the situation due to the deadlock. At the May meeting, the Commission advised the Parties of its intention to reopen immediately its field offices in Addis Ababa and Asmera as a first step to resume the demarcation process.

At the political level, the resumption of the demarcation process would require the full cooperation of the Parties with the Boundary Commission and their assurance of security for its field personnel. At the technical level, it would require re-staffing the offices, rehiring the surveyors, concluding contracts for the construction of the boundary pillars, and re-establishing the security arrangements to ensure the

---

[557] Jendayi Frazer, US Assistant Secretary for African Affairs, the Voice of America, 1 February 2006.

[558] Eritrea-Ethiopia Boundary Commission: Twentieth Report on the Work of the Commission, 27 February 2006.

[559] Eritrea-Ethiopia Boundary Commission: Letter from the President to the Secretary-General, 21 May 2006.

safety of the Commission's field personnel, surveyors and contractors. Since Eritrea had submitted its security plan on 14 October 2003, the Commission repeated its request to Ethiopia to submit its security plan by 19 May 2006.

Further, at the 17 May 2006 meeting, the Commission proposed to resume demarcation once:

> *(a) The Commission can be assured that UNMEE will be retained in the area at a level sufficient to enable it to continue to provide the services to the field staff on at least the same scale that it has hitherto; (b) The parties can provide or, if already provided, confirm their proposed security arrangements; (c) Contracts can be concluded with the surveyors and the on-site contractors; (d) And most important of all, both the parties should cooperate fully with the Boundary Commission's representatives in the field; (e) The Boundary Commission has set 15 June 2006 for a further meeting with the parties in the hope that this will help to develop the momentum.*[560]

There was, however, no momentum. The Commission had to cancel the proposed 15 June 2006 meeting because Eritrea declined to attend it on the grounds that "Ethiopia still had not accepted the delimitation decision without qualification".[561] On the same day, the Commission held an internal meeting, discussed the next steps, decided to reopen the field offices in Asmera and Addis Ababa as soon as possible, invited Eritrea and Ethiopia to a meeting on 24 August 2006, and asked them to reply by 10 August 2006.

---

[560] Ibid.

[561] Twenty-first Report of the Eritrea-Ethiopia Boundary Commission, 8 September 2006.

The Commission sent teams in early August 2006 to reopen the field offices in the respective capitals. The team in Addis Ababa was denied formal reception and the team to Asmera was refused entry visa. Nevertheless, the field office in Addis Ababa was reopened with UNMEE's assistance while that in Asmera remained closed.

Both Eritrea and Ethiopia failed to respond to the Commission's invitation to meet on 24 August 2006. The lack of real progress in the demarcation process caused growing exasperation. Eritrea informed the Commission that Ethiopia's public and unequivocal acceptance of the final and binding Delimitation Decision was necessary to work out the procedures of and arrangements for demarcation and avoid "another round of fruitless meetings".[562] The Commission held an internal meeting from 22 to 24 August 2006 and scheduled another one in November 2006 to examine the situation and consider the best way forward to demarcate the boundary and conclude its mandate. Its efforts to resume the demarcation process were frustrated as Eritrea persisted in its demand for the demarcation of the boundary as delimited and Ethiopia stuck to its insistence for the modification of the Delimitation Decision prior to demarcation.

Under the circumstances, the UN Security Council adopted, on 29 September 2006, resolution 1710 (2006) calling on the Parties to "cooperate fully with the EEBC" and "to implement completely and without further delay or preconditions the decision of the EEBC and to take concrete steps to resume the demarcation process". Specifically, the resolution demanded that "Eritrea reverse, without

---

[562]   Letter from President Isaias Afwerki to the President of the Eritrea-Ethiopia Boundary Commission, 21 August 2006.

further delay or preconditions, all restrictions on UNMEE's movement and operations" and that Ethiopia "accept fully and without delay the final and binding decision of the Eritrea-Ethiopia Boundary Commission and take immediately concrete steps to enable, without preconditions, the Commission to demarcate the border completely and promptly".[563]

Further, the President of the Security Council issued a Press Statement, on 17 October 2006, expressing the Council's "unwavering commitment to the peace process, including the full and expeditious implementation of the Algiers Agreements and implementation of the final and binding decision of the EEBC".[564]

Subsequently, the Commission, in a letter dated 6 October 2006, asked the Parties "of the actions which each proposes to take to comply with the Council's specific requests" and to respond by 22 October 2006. Ethiopia gave no reply while Eritrea's reply on 22 October restated its previous position that Ethiopia's unqualified acceptance of the EEBC's Decision of 13 April 2002 was necessary for progress and insisted on the expeditious execution of the Award on the basis of the Commission's Demarcation Directions. Again, both sides refused, Ethiopia in a letter dated 13 November 2006 and Eritrea in a letter dated 16 November 2006, the Commission's 8 November 2006 invitation to meet on 20 November 2006 "to consider the further procedures to be followed in connection with the demarcation of the

---

[563] United Nations Security Council Resolution 1710 (2006), 29 September 2006.

[564] President of the UN Security Council: Press Release on Eritrea-Ethiopia, 17 October 2006.

boundary between Eritrea and Ethiopia".[565] Ethiopia's letter contained criticisms which the Commission deemed necessary to answer.

In a direct response to Ethiopia's letter of 13 November 2006 on 27 November 2006, the President of the Boundary Commission provided conclusive assessment of Ethiopia's conduct in the demarcation process:

> It is a matter of regret that Ethiopia has so persistently maintained a position of non-compliance with its obligations in relation to the Commission. ... Ethiopia has by its conduct on many occasions repeatedly obstructed the Commission's field personnel and prevented them from carrying out the necessary investigations in the field and made a 'cooperative process' impossible.[566]

With its work frustrated by Ethiopia's persistent non-cooperation, the Boundary Commission, by November 2006, abandoned its original plan to emplace boundary markers on the ground and decided to demarcate the boundary by a list of precise coordinates representing "the locations at which, if the Commission were so enabled by the Parties, it would construct permanent pillars" along the entire length of the boundary. Applying the concept of 'institutional effectiveness', relying on the authority of 'international law', and 'guided by significant authority in State practice', the Boundary Commission adopted 'virtual demarcation' as a viable legal option to circumvent the deadlock caused

---

[565] Twenty-second Report of the Eritrea-Ethiopia Boundary Commission, 21 December 2006.

[566] Letter from the President of the Boundary Commission to the Foreign Minister of Ethiopia, 27 November 2006.

by persistent non-cooperation and effect the demarcation of the boundary. Having affirmed the legal basis of virtual demarcation as a technique, the Commission asserted its terrestrial accuracy as follows:

> *Modern techniques of image processing and terrain modelling make it possible, in conjunction with the use of high resolution aerial photography, to demarcate the course of the boundary by identifying the location of turning points (hereinafter called "boundary points") by both grid and geographical coordinates with a degree of accuracy that does not differ significantly from pillar site assessment and emplacement undertaken in the field. The Commission has therefore identified by these means the location of points for the emplacement of pillars as a physical manifestation of the boundary on the ground.*[567]

The Commission provided the Parties with the list of the boundary turning points accompanied by forty-five 1:25,000 scale maps illustrating the boundary points; gave the Parties 12 months up to the end of November 2007 to demarcate the border; and advised that:

> *If, by the end of the period, the Parties have not by themselves reached the necessary agreement and proceeded significantly to implement it, or have not requested or enabled the Commission to resume its activity, the Commission hereby determines that the boundary will automatically stand as demarcated by the boundary points listed in the Annex hereto and that the mandate of the Commission can then*

---

[567] Eritrea-Ethiopia Boundary Commission: Statement by the Commission, 27 November 2006, p. 8-10.

be regarded as fulfilled. Until that time, however, it must be emphasised that the Commission remains in existence and its mandate to demarcate has not been discharged. Until such time as the boundary is finally demarcated, the Delimitation Decision of 13 April 2002 continues as the only valid legal description of the boundary.[568]

In the definitive assessment of the Boundary Commission, Ethiopia's conduct in the demarcation process, both at the political and technical levels and particularly, its systematic and persistent non-cooperation, obstructed the physical demarcation of the boundary. Its non-cooperation constituted a clear violation of its commitment to accept the delimitation and demarcation decisions of the Boundary Commission as final and binding under the Algiers Agreement.

For its part, Eritrea initially cooperated fully with the Boundary Commission. It later started to raise obstacles mainly in reaction to Ethiopia's conduct and in protest of the Security Council's failure to address effectively Ethiopia's obstructions. In response to Ethiopia's refusal to allow fieldwork in the Central and Western Sectors, Eritrea objected to demarcation in the Eastern Sector unless it continued in tandem with the work planned along the entire boundary. It also imposed restrictions on UNMEE's freedom of movement that affected the Mission's ability to provide necessary assistance to the Commission's field staff.[569]

Given the character and impact of the comparative obstructions, the Boundary Commission put the blame for its inability to demarcate the boundary by emplacing permanent

---

[568] Ibid., p. 10.
[569] Eritrea-Ethiopia Boundary Commission: Statement by the Commission, 27 November 2006, p. 5-6.

604

pillars on the ground squarely on Ethiopia's conduct. In indirectly conceding its non-compliance with the terms of the Algiers Agreement, Ethiopia complained that Eritrea was also guilty of the same obstruction. In the matter of appraising the actual conduct of the Parties and apportioning blame for disabling the Boundary Commission to demarcate the boundary on the ground as delimited by the 13 April 2002 Decision, it is illustrative to quote at length from the commission's letter responding to Ethiopia's complaints:

> One of the elements in Ethiopia's complaints is that Eritrea is guilty of the same obstruction. Eritrea's non-cooperation with the Commission only really developed after Ethiopia insisted that the boundary should be altered to meet with what Ethiopia chose to call 'anomalies and impracticalities', despite the clear statements of the Commission that this could not be done. When asked to confirm its continuing acceptance of the delimitation Decision, Ethiopia repeatedly qualified its position by saying that it wished negotiations to take place regarding such 'anomalies and impracticalities'. Eritrea's insistence on strict adherence to the terms of the Delimitation Decision was a position which it was entitled to adopt in accordance with the Algiers Agreement.
>
> You place great emphasis on the 'need for dialogue and support by neutral bodies to help the two Parties make progress in demarcation and normalisation of their relations'. Of course, 'the normalisation of relations' is a desirable objective but that is a matter that falls outside the scope of the Commission's mandate, which is solely to delimit and demarcate the border. The scope for 'dialogue' is limited to what is necessary between the Commission and the Parties to further the actual process of demarcation on

the ground. There is no room within the framework of the Algiers Agreement for the introduction of 'neutral bodies' into the demarcation process.

You ask 'Why has the Commission abruptly and without notice chosen to abandon the process for demarcation embodied in its rules, instructions and decisions?' The answer is that the Commission has been unable to make progress, initially, because of Ethiopia's obstruction and, more recently, because Eritrea has followed a similar course.

Your letter seeks to blame the Commission for Ethiopia's failure to meet its obligations under the Algiers Agreement. Such blame is entirely misplaced. The truth of the matter appears to be that Ethiopia is dissatisfied with the substance of the Commission's Delimitation Decision and has been seeking, ever since April 2002, to find ways of changing it. This is not an approach which the Commission was empowered to adopt and is not one to which the Commission can lend itself.[570]

The UN Secretary General fully shared the assessment of the EEBC of Ethiopia's singular failure to respect its commitments under the Algiers Agreement and cooperate with the Commission in the demarcation process in accordance with the Delimitation Decision:

Ethiopia's refusal to implement - fully and without preconditions - the final and binding decision of the Boundary Commission remains at the core of the continuing deadlock". I therefore strongly urge the Government of Ethiopia to comply with the demand of the Security Council, expressed

---

[570]   Letter from the President of the Boundary Commission to the Foreign Minister of Ethiopia, 27 November 2006.

in resolution 1640 (2005) and reiterated in resolution 1710 (2006). Full implementation of the latter resolution remains key to moving forward the demarcation process and to concluding the peace process.[571]

The EEBC made a final attempt to revive the demarcation process by convening a meeting with the Parties on 6-7 September 2007 "to consider how pillars may be erected along" the *boundary points* of the November 2006 line of virtual demarcation.[572] In preparation for the meeting, the Commission had, on 27 August 2007, circulated to the Parties an Agenda specifying the conditions each Party was required to satisfy in order to enable it to resume its activities.

Eritrea was required "to lift restrictions on UNMEE insofar as they affect the EEBC; to withdraw from the Temporary Security Zone (TSZ) insofar as the present position impinges on EEBC operations; to provide security assurances; to allow free access to pillar locations." For its part, Ethiopia was required "to indicate its unqualified acceptance of the 2002 Delimitation Decision without requiring broader ranging negotiations between the Parties; to lift restrictions on movement of EEBC personnel; to provide security assurances; to meet payment arrears; to allow free access to pillar locations."[573]

In his opening statement, the President of the Commission reminded the Parties of "the list of locations identified by the

---

[571] Report of the Secretary-General on Ethiopia and Eritrea (S/2007/33), January 22, 2007, p. 7.

[572] Letter from the President of the Commission inviting the Parties to meet in New York, 10 July 2007.

[573] Twenty-fifth report of the Eritrea-Ethiopia Boundary Commission(S/2007/645), 28 September 2007.

Commission for boundary pillars using coordinates accurate to within one metre, which took into account the observations of the Parties"; observed that had the Commission "been able to go on the ground in the way originally planned, this is where the pillars would have been fixed, subject to the processes outlined in the Demarcation Directions"; expressed "hope that this indication of the adjusted line would enable the Parties to take a more positive approach to demarcation on the ground as they would see what [we] had in mind"; noted that the Parties had "less than three months now" left out of the previously given "twelve months to consider their positions and seek to reach agreement on the emplacement of pillars;" and acknowledged that Eritrea's letters of 5 September 2007 "contain significant indications of willingness to see the process of demarcation resumed."

In the trilateral exchanges during the meeting, Eritrea affirmed its readiness to meet the stated conditions required to enable the Commission to resume its activities while Ethiopia failed to do so and presented, instead, a series of observations which did not directly respond to the specified agenda items.[574] The meeting ended without progress. In his concluding remarks, the President of the Commission reminded the Parties that "the demarcation by coordinates identifying with precision the locations where pillars should be in place will become effective at the end of November unless in the interval the Parties act so as to produce a new situation" and stated that "we greatly regret that we could not take our work through to its full conclusion, but at least we leave you with a line that is operable".[575]

---

[574] Ibid.

[575] Ibid.

The 30 November 2007 deadline arrived with no progress attained towards the construction of boundary pillars in the manner anticipated by the Commission. Ethiopia declined the EEBC's request to appoint a substitute for Sir Arthur Watts, one of the EEBC's Commissioners originally appointed by Ethiopia, who died on 16 November 2006, as required by the Commission's Rules of Procedure. It also remained, in defiance of repeated requests by the Commission to meet its financial obligations, in arrears in payment of its share of the Commission's expenses in breach of the Algiers Agreement.

The Commission was "obliged to reaffirm the considerations of fact and the statements of law set out in its Statement of 27 November 2006. The Delimitation Decision of 13 April 2002 and the Statement of 27 November 2006 remain binding on the Parties". In conclusion, the Boundary Commission reiterated that the boundary automatically stood as demarcated by the boundary points given on 27 November 2006, officially sent signed copies of the maps illustrating the points identified in the annex to the 27 November 2006 Statement to the Parties, considered its mandate fulfilled and decided to disband itself on 30 November 2007.[576]

Eritrea accepted the virtual demarcation of the border; Ethiopia rejected it as "legal nonsense". Despite the failure to expedite the physical demarcation of the boundary, the Boundary Commission's validation of virtual demarcation rendered UNMEE's continued presence in the TSZ untenable, as its mandate was coterminous with the demarcation of the boundary. Under pressure of incremental restrictions of free movement and support facilities from Eritrea, UNMEE's

---

[576] Twenty-sixth report of the Eritrea-Ethiopia Boundary Commission, 7 January 2008.

activities and size steadily diminished until it was officially disbanded by the UN Security Council on 30 July 2008.

In its twenty-seventh and final report, the EEBC declared the end of its activities and the termination of its mandate. The report also noted that Ethiopia had refused, and the UN Secretary General had not exercised his power, to appoint a substitute Commissioner for the deceased Sir Arthur Watts; that Ethiopia continued to be in arrears of its share of the Commission's expenses; and that the EEBC has deposited on 17 January 2008 a copy of the maps illustrating the boundary points of the demarcation with the UN Secretary General and a copy for public reference with the UN Cartographer. Further, the Commission stated that it had communicated to the Parties on 18 June 2008 that the boundary stands demarcated in accordance with the coordinates annexed to its Statement of 27 November 2006.[577]

The next section underscores the imperative to complete the peace process so as to end the prevailing state of *cold war* between Eritrea and Ethiopia, help create the conditions necessary to normalise their bilateral relations, and contribute to regional peace, stability and security in the strategic but volatile Horn of Africa.

17.3 The Imperative of Durable Peace

As stated above, the June and December 2000 Algiers Agreements produced a ceasefire that ended the 1998-2000 border war between Eritrea and Ethiopia and specified a mechanism to settle the conflict. The full and expeditious

---

[577] Twenty-seventh report of the Eritrea-Ethiopia Boundary Commission, 25 August 2008.

implementation of the Algiers accords aimed to accomplish the delimitation and physical demarcation of the boundary, address the socioeconomic impact of the war on the civilian populations, and set the stage for the restoration of peaceful and cooperative relations between Eritrea and Ethiopia.

However, reality did not match the intended aims. As highlighted in the preceding section, Ethiopia's persistent non-cooperation obliged the Boundary Commission to circumvent its effort to emplace boundary pillars on the ground by adopting the technique of virtual demarcation, or demarcation by coordinates, of the border in order to fulfil its mandate and terminate its work. The Eritrea-Ethiopia boundary thus stands virtually demarcated by the boundary points connecting the boundary line.

Nearly thirteen years have passed since the signing of the peace agreement, over eleven years since the delimitation, and over six years since the virtual demarcation of the boundary between the two countries, and more than three years since the decision on the final damage awards. Yet, the successful completion of the peace process has eluded Eritrea and Ethiopia and the two states remain locked in a bitter *cold war* with no end in sight. Ethiopia has an obligation to respect Eritrea's territorial integrity. It must unconditionally accept the boundary as virtually demarcated by the Boundary Commission and enable the construction of boundary pillars in fulfilment of its treaty obligations under the Algiers Peace Agreement. Ultimately, Ethiopia's reaffirmation of the rule of law in international relations remains an essential condition for the establishment of durable peace and cooperative relations between Ethiopia and Eritrea.

In the diagnosis of the Boundary Commission, Ethiopia's dissatisfaction with the substance of the delimitation Decision lay at the heart of its non-cooperation with the Boundary Commission in clear violation of its commitment under the Algiers treaty and in defiance of international law. It is in the nature of the arbitral process, more often than not, that an arbitration arrangement awards each party at least part of its submitted claims. As the claims are invariably mutually exclusive, it is generally inconceivable that each party is awarded all its claims. Territorially, therefore, the outcome of arbitration is 'zero-sum', in which one party's gain is the other party's loss, although the relative gain or loss of territory may vary.

In the specific Eritrea-Ethiopia case, the Delimitation Decision of the Boundary Commission divided the 'contested' areas between the two 'claimants'. This distribution effectively modified the hitherto existing political boundary, i.e., the original colonial treaty border, between the two states in favour of Ethiopia. Accordingly, Ethiopia gained and Eritrea lost territory in all the three treaty sectors of the common boundary, as indicated in the map of the international boundary (Map 6) between the two neighbours reproduced on page 579 above.

Effectively, the arbitral determination of the precise position of the international boundary as final and binding on the basis of the Commission's interpretation of the pertinent colonial treaties and applicable international law ceded to Ethiopia swathes of territory in the three sectors that the colonial treaties of 1900, 1902, and 1908 had placed on the Eritrean side of the border. Win or lose, however, each party had agreed in advance to accept the decision and was obligated by treaty to implement the determination as final and binding.

Despite gaining swathes of territory at the expense of Eritrea, Ethiopia's failure to respect the terms of the Agreement has rendered stable peace an unfinished business between the two neighbours. The prevailing state of 'no war, no peace', the conduct of the parties to date in respect of their treaty obligations, and the causes and impact of the unresolved crisis at the national and regional levels have been the subject of considerable commentary by the states themselves, interested parties, and neutral observers. There are, of course, other issues of contention between Eritrea and Ethiopia besides the boundary question, including disputes over political, economic, trade, and security issues. With a modicum of political will and reciprocal consent, earnest bilateral negotiations could resolve all such disagreements to mutual satisfaction through independent of the boundary question.

Leaving the respective positions of the Eritrean and Ethiopian governments on the other outstanding issues aside, Ethiopia has clearly demonstrated bad faith in failing to fulfil its obligations with respect to the boundary issue and would set a dangerous precedent of flouting international law if allowed to get away with it. The bottom line is that Ethiopia, despite its treaty commitment to the contrary, equivocated on the Boundary Commission's Delimitation Decision, disobeyed the Commission's Demarcation Directions, and obstructed the Commission's efforts to undertake the physical demarcation of the boundary. In addition, it has established new settlements on the Eritrean side of the delimitation line in July 2002 and defied the Commission's subsequent Order to dismantle them. Finally, having obstructed physical demarcation, it has also rejected virtual demarcation.

Ethiopia remains in occupation of sovereign Eritrean territory north of the international boundary as demarcated by the Boundary Commission. Hostile relations with the current government cannot justify the continued violation of the territory and sovereignty of the State of Eritrea. Ethiopia must unconditionally accept the final and binding character of the delimitation and demarcation decisions of the Boundary Commission and effectively respect Eritrea's sovereignty and territorial integrity.

Another wrong requires righting in order to secure peace and tranquillity within Eritrea itself. The announcement of the Eritrea-Ethiopia Boundary Commission's April 2002 delimitation decision coincided with a difficult domestic situation that has perpetrated a constant state of insecurity and tension in the country. The consolidation of autocratic rule had prompted the abandonment of the national agenda to establish a constitutional order and the suspension of the internal process towards democratic development. The resultant transgression of domestic rule of law, democratic deficit, and introversion, compounded by diplomatic ineptitude, closed vital windows of opportunity for engagement and cornered the regime into isolation. This contributed to neutralise the country's legal moral high ground and abet international acquiescence in Ethiopia's failure to cooperate with the Boundary Commission, accept virtual demarcation, and end its occupation of sovereign Eritrean territory in defiance of international law.

Unable to defend the national territory in war, recover it from occupation in peace, or address the domestic political repercussions of the war, the enfeebled government vented its wrath on the people, in general, and its critics, in particular. It has used the frozen conflict as a pretext to close the political space tighter, stiffen internal repression, impose indefinite active national service, and rationalise the vagaries of the coupon economy. All this has turned Eritrea into a dysfunctional garrison state. To date, the government continues to hold the Eritrean people and the future of Eritrea hostage to its impotence.

Truly, the government's domestic policy response to the immediate aftermath of the war, to the frozen conflict, and to Ethiopia's continued occupation of sovereign Eritrean territory and the international appeasement of its behaviour has, over and above the occupation itself, been the source of the greatest suffering for the Eritrean people since 2001. Above all, it continues to pose the most serious threat to the country's long-term prosperity, security, and stability. Only a new homegrown democratic dispensation can abort the looming existential threat to Eritrea's future.

In the context of international law, the restoration of peace between Eritrea and Ethiopia requires Ethiopia to respect Eritrea's territorial integrity and end its unlawful occupation of several swathes of sovereign Eritrean territory in fulfilment of its obligations under the Algiers peace accord and in compliance with the UN Charter. The issue is not one of territorial adjustment by modifying the delimitation line or the international boundary as it stands demarcated. Even if there were a compelling reason for its contemplation, which there is not, neither country can unilaterally impose territorial adjustment. If ever need be, it can come about only by mutual agreement of the two states. Nor is the issue one of the wilful reciprocal pursuit of regime change in Asmera or Addis Ababa. Regime change is the internal business of the Eritrean and Ethiopian peoples. The real issue at stake is the overriding interests and future relations of the fraternal peoples of the two states and the region at large.

In the first place, the peoples of Eritrea and Ethiopia share a history of close relations that embraces complex political, economic, social, and cultural elements shaded by the dynamics of a troubled historical memory, including the most vivid reminders of the last war. Further, shared strategic interests connect the fraternal peoples while common aspirations for peace, progress, and prosperity unite them. To continue to scratch the scars of the historical memory of destructive wars of territorial aggrandisement detracts from these shared interests and aspirations. Moreover, the bonds of mutual interests and aspirations that bind the future of the Eritrean and Ethiopian peoples extend to the kindred peoples of the region.

At present, there appear no real prospects of change in the entrenched positions or political disincentive of the current governments in Addis Ababa and Asmera to end the state of 'no peace, no war'. I am not sure of what changes, if any, the recent premature death of the late Prime Minister Meles Zenawi would bring about in the Ethiopian stance. To date, international efforts have lacked the necessary convergence of interest, unity of purpose, and coherence of policy to help Eritrea and Ethiopia achieve peace and build a framework of rapprochement and mutual understanding. I wonder whether it is in the Abyssinian stars that undoing the deadlock and securing the peace must await the advent of new political will, courage, and leadership past both current regimes in Asmera and Addis Ababa!

As European political leaders adopted the Westphalian principle of 'forgetting the sins of the past' to promote peaceful coexistence in an earlier era, a new crop of Eritrean and Ethiopian political leaders must forgive, not necessarily forget, the failings of the past. Otherwise, they lose sight of the lessons learned to move beyond the present impasse into a new era of stable peace, normal relations, political cooperation, and regional integration. Beyond Eritrea and Ethiopia, the stalemate has been a significant factor of instability stoking other conflicts in the Horn of Africa where each state aligns with the local and regional opponents of the other. The regional impact of the stalemate has been most clearly evident in the crisis in Somalia. Resolving the deadlock, securing the peace, and restoring normal relations would thus serve the interests of both countries and that of peace, security, and stability in the region.

The present state of affairs between Eritrea and Ethiopia is abnormal. The hard border hampering the age-old interface between two of the closest peoples in the Horn of Africa and sustaining the artificial severance of exchange between two essentially complementary economies represents an anomaly. The political, economic, and social consequences of the *cold war* between Eritrea and Ethiopia and the hostile relations fanned by mutual antipathy and spite at the top detract from the wellbeing of the fraternal peoples. The vital interests of the Eritrean and Ethiopian peoples require the speedy resolution of the seemingly intractable conflict and the restoration of peace leading to a return to normalcy and the resumption of mutually beneficial cooperative relations in a future of open borders that serve as bridges for the free passage of peoples, goods, and services. Surely, reconciliation and cooperation are the way forward to the future, a future of peaceful development, amicable neighbourly relations, and shared prosperity.

In the face of the mismatch between the goals and ideals of the armed struggle, on the one hand, and the present predicament of Eritrea and the Eritrean people, on the other, the next chapter expresses the sense of profound deception and deep disappointment shared by many veterans of the war of independence, the author included.

CHAPTER 18

We Didn't Do It for This!

You were good fighters in the Field. We were very proud
of you and full of hope. You won the war and brought us
independence. We were elated. However, a dozen years on,
you have made our life more miserable! Having lived under
Italian, British, federal and Ethiopian administrations, let
me tell you, my son, that your administration is incompetent,
your manners uncouth and your currency worthless. It is a
cruel irony that we are worse off today under the rule of our
own children.[578]

These measured words of a wise elder carry considerable
weight in a society long reluctant to criticise the
'government of its children'. They express widespread popular
discontent, indicate deep disappointment, and represent
a powerful indictment of the character and performance
of the government. In spite of its indigenous identity, the
regime has become the blight of Eritrea and the scourge of
its people. Devout, patient, and stoic, the Eritrean people

---

[578] Conversation of the author with an Eritrean elder, Sheka Yohannes
Weldeabzgi, Asmera: 25 January 2004 (author's translation from
the original Tigrinya).

seek deliverance from their current predicament and aspire to build a better future. They yearn for the freedom to be left alone to conduct their affairs without forcible conscription and indefinite active national service; the freedom to lead normal family life and manage the upbringing of their children; and the freedom from want, poverty, and the indignity of the coupon economy.

The government holds, and strives to retain, the exclusive ownership of the instruments of violence and their legitimate use within the society. At the same time, it breaches the rule of law and keeps its citizens on edge in a permanent state of insecurity through the unrestrained use of the instruments of violence to carry out arbitrary arrests and perpetrate indefinite detention, torture, and extrajudicial killings. It applies brute force without the procedural or substantive restraint of the law or recourse to redress to coerce unquestioning submission to its authority and irrational random directives. As a replica of an alien construct in historical, conceptual, and institutional terms, it bears the oppressive and predatory hallmarks of the colonial state. Even in replacing Ethiopian rule, the regime has retained key features of the Derg's order, such as the *kebele* system of local administration, intact as a means of social control.

Further, the regime has retained the repressive features inherited from the colonial state and failed to adapt its functioning to the specific sociocultural conditions or traditional governance structures of Eritrean society. It has been unable to reform the moribund structural relationship between the public and private sectors and apply the precepts of its declared economic policy framework. Unable to align its policies and actions with the basic interests of the people and driven by the desire to hold on to power as an end in itself, the state, like many of its counterparts elsewhere in Africa, has taken on a distinctly patrimonial and predatory character. As such, it has relegated the needs, aspirations, and welfare of the people to the back burner.

18.1 So Much for So Little

The protracted and tortuous path to Eritrea's independence was paved with the blood, flesh, and bones of its martyrs and the toil, sweat, and sacrifices of its people. The triumph of liberation and the inauguration of sovereign statehood, greeted with immense public jubilation, were the crowning achievements of the Eritrean people's political and armed struggle for emancipation from foreign domination and the right to determine their own affairs. As a historic moment, the advent of independence was pregnant with policy choices and decision alternatives concerning the future of the new nation and the destiny of its people.

Given its record of effective delivery of rudimentary social services in the liberated areas and programmatic commitment to the fundamental transformation of Eritrean society during the war, the EPLF's accession to state power upon independence was greeted with excitement, hope, and optimism, both at home and abroad. There were great expectations from the Eritrean people as well as the friends of Eritrea that the EPLF government would successfully shoulder the huge responsibility to establish democratic governance, pursue sustainable development, and expand the realm of freedom, opportunity, and security for the people.

The Eritrean people share a culture of respect for the rule of law, a practice of fair representation, and a tradition of consensual decision-making. There has evolved a body of customary laws to adjudicate their political, economic, and social affairs via the representative and participatory forum of the *baito* in the Central Plateau (*Kebessa*). The *Baito Adi* (village assembly), presided over by a village judge, or *tchqa adi*, and advised by a committee of three elders representing the main kinship or social groups, determined land allocation for purposes of residence, agriculture, grazing and forestry, and adjudicated over civil and criminal cases involving members of the village community. In the Western Lowlands (*Metaht*), Northern Highlands, and Coastal Plains, Sharia served as a common basis to adjudicate over matters of family and personal status.

Pre-colonial Eritrean society thus owned indigenous governance structures that respected legal and cultural norms that valued fairness, equity, and justice embedded in the various customary laws and common practices of the people. In addition, Eritrea's brief experience of autonomous government during the federation functioned in accordance with a Constitution that provided, in principle, for a democratic order and guaranteed the basic rights and fundamental freedoms of the people.[579] Despite its inherent structural flaws and ultimate undoing, the first Eritrean Government of the early 1950s set a precedent of a parliamentary system of government in the framework of competitive pluralist politics and a clearly defined delimitation of powers as to between its legislative, executive and judicial branches.

---

[579] Eritrean Constitution adopted by the Eritrean Assembly on 10 July 1952, ratified by the Emperor of Ethiopia on 11 Sep 52 and put into effect with the inauguration of the Federation between Eritrea and Ethiopia.

Upon independence, the EPLF had thus the opportunity to embed the developed European state model on home-grown administrative structures, existing in a rudimentary state of development, and integrate innovative techniques of political participation with historical modes of governance and cultural values to construct a viable state that is modern, functional, and democratic. The Front could have capitalised on its nationalist credentials and revolutionary legitimacy to build and consolidate a state that embodies democratic development with a capacity to sustain freedom and deliver prosperity for the people. Instead of availing itself of the great opportunity to democratise and modernise Eritrea, the Front allowed the emergence of an essentially regressive state with a melange of predatory, patrimonial, and authoritarian features.

The Transitional Government subverted the planned process of transition to a democratic system of government in order to consolidate its domination and perpetuate itself in power. It abandoned the commitment to reconstruct and develop the national economy, heal the gaping wounds of war, and remedy the severe disruption of a war-torn society. Consistent with the practice of kindred autocratic regimes, it arrogated the political prerogatives of the people, usurped absolute state power, monopolised the country's resources and productive assets, and seized control of the national news media. Twenty-two years past *de facto* independence, the hopes and expectations of the people for a better life have not materialised.

As Chapter 10 above explains, Eritrea's record of sovereign statehood to date shows a huge contrast between the laudable objectives set in the troika of documents and the degraded human condition prevailing in the country. Like its prototype African counterpart, the Eritrean state has failed to provide for the needs, meet the aspirations, and promote the interests of the people. Independence has thus brought about neither a democratic government nor a developmental state. Lack of liberty, opportunity, and prospects of improvement continues to afflict the people and drive its youth out of the country. Furthermore, the mix of harsh political repression, persistent economic stagnation, and malignant social regression threatens to destroy the very foundation of Eritrean society - the nuclear family - and disrupt the essential fabric that holds it together - the civilised values of fairness, justice, and tolerance in civic and public affairs.

Forged under the colonial experience, Eritrea endured successive foreign conquest, occupation, and annexation. It also waged a protracted war of resistance. The Eritrean people endured the difficult struggle in stride, rising to the challenge with patient resolve and perseverance. The story of Eritrea's thirty-year war of independence is one of great endurance, stoic self-sacrifice, and remarkable resilience driven by abiding faith in liberty, justice, and a bright future, in defiance of superior forces and the odds. It is an amazing story of great human endeavour, heroic personal choices and selfless sacrifice: people abandoned families, interrupted careers, gave up education, and forfeited livelihoods to fight for freedom. Multiple generations of Eritreans in their tens of thousands freely offered toil, life, and blood, and readily endured deprivation, harm and pain. Others gave food and shelter, donated money and jewellery, and raised funds and essential materials to provide the wherewithal to wage the struggle for liberation.

As the core message of this book celebrates, the war was fought for freedom, democracy, progress, and prosperity.

Victory was made possible through active, wide, and deep popular participation and at the price of enormous sacrifices. Indeed, the extent of the human toll and physical damage of the war was staggering. Despite the enormous human and material cost sustained in its quest however, real freedom remains elusive. The ascent of a brutal dictatorship has exposed the people to jeopardy and deprived them of their intrinsic right to 'life, liberty and the pursuit of happiness'. The present reality does not correspond with the abiding hopes of the fighters and the profound aspirations of the people for a free, democratic, and prosperous Eritrea. Nor does it vindicate the huge sacrifices made during the armed struggle.

To the anguish of the people, the government has betrayed the promises of liberation, abandoned the commitments made at independence, and failed to safeguard the integrity of the national territory on land and sea.[580] Eritrea's surface area is smaller, its territorial waters lesser, and its islands fewer today than in 1991-1993. The regime has diminished Eritrea, brought all kinds of indignity on the Eritrean people, and undermined their unity. Unable to perform its principal state functions and unwilling to undertake the construction of a functional state, it has weakened the historically evolving process of nation building, presided over a stagnant and/or a declining economy, and further impoverished the country.

---

[580] Having arrogantly rejected a French mediation offer, accepted by Yemen, that would have secured Eritrea the islands of Great Hanish, Little Hanish and Seyul Hanish and the associated territorial waters, Isaias ended up ceding the Jabal al-Tayr, Jabal Zubayr, and Zuqur-Hanish Archipelagos, and their associated territorial waters, to Yemen.

In retrospect, few peoples in the annals of modern African history have suffered so much for so long under the callous rule of so many and fought as hard to be free as have the Eritreans. Yet, they are not free. Independence has merely replaced foreign domination by domestic oppression. The present reality does not represent the vision of the free, democratic, and prosperous Eritrea for which its people aspired and generations of its young men and women made sacrifices, fought and died. Indeed, few peoples have paid so much for so long in return for so little!

18.2 Serenading in the Past

The pledge to cultivate participatory politics and construct a democratic system of government based on 'Eritrean cultural values' has been totally discarded and supplanted by the reality of a highly 'centralised, authoritarian and self-serving' state alien to Eritrean cultural values and devoid of democratic governance structures. The state of general contempt for the rule of law, denial of basic liberties, and forcible suppression of political dissent expose the authoritarian character of the state and fan the growing contestation of its legitimacy. The closure of opportunities for meaningful higher education, for the optimal development of Eritrea's human potential, and for a better future for its youth depicts the regime's regressive features.

These salient attributes of the dysfunctional state underlie its dismal record of failure to deliver on the promises of liberation. Obsession with centralised control, systemic incompetence, gross mismanagement, and rampant corruption have hampered its ability to promote economic growth, produce public goods and services, and attain social progress necessary to meet the basic needs of the people. Preoccupation with the preservation of its rule at any cost in total neglect of the public wellbeing have alienated and divested the regime of any relevance.

Lacking concrete achievements to show for the present in terms of a higher standard of living and a better quality of life for the people, the regime endeavours to live off past glories. It conducts elaborate commemoration ceremonies of yesteryear's events while banishing the values that made the feats possible and condemning many of the chief architects, engineers, and makers of the very same glorious events to languish behind prison bars in its hidden *Gulags*. Even if that were not the case, serenading in the past, as the regime orchestrates in a constant exhibition of bouts of vanity, cynicism, and extravagance does Eritrea and the Eritrean people no good. Instead of clinging to the laurels of the past to divert attention from the misery of the present and the desperation of the future, the regime should have directed its attention to facing the challenges of today and striving to build for a better tomorrow.

In essence, the winning of independence constituted a historic achievement that enabled Eritrea to become a sovereign state and join the community of free nations and paved the way for a better future. As a people, we made history with our toil, sweat, and blood. We are very proud of the history we made, and it has been my distinct privilege to be part of that historic journey amongst many of my generation, martyred and living. We are not however, so nostalgic as to wish to live in that history. We do not relish dwelling in our past as a substitute for our present and as a 'pie in the sky' for our future. Equipped with and relishing the glory of our history, we want to move on to overcome the misery of our present and to traverse the path to the prosperity of our future through the pursuit of rational political, economic, social, and security policies.

Mere propaganda cannot sustain the people. They want real and tangible improvements in their living conditions. They yearn for freedom, justice, and dignity. They need jobs, food, medicines, education, and housing. They want access to clean water, electricity, and affordable sources of energy. They desire to live in peace, create wealth, and achieve prosperity, like other peoples the world over. Instead, in addition to enchaining the youth and stultifying their boundless creative energy in the vast wastelands of open-ended active national service, the regime has forced every citizen, including septuagenarians, exempting only the acutely disabled and the chronically sick, to bear arms with inadequate military training. Under the pretext of providing local security and guarding neighbourhoods, probably aimed to tighten its control over the daily life of the people, it is fanning a dangerous proliferation of small arms in its twilight years.

Self-serving claims aside, the regime's actual record illustrates an inability to deliver sustainable economic growth, democratic development, and general prosperity. This incapacity endangers the real national security and undermines the effective sovereignty of the State of Eritrea. Indeed, the authoritarian, predatory, and dysfunctional state, with its extremely repressive features, has become the main enemy within. Its familiar penchant for blunder, propensity to lick its wounds and urge to scratch the scars have led to the deepening of the domestic political, economic, and social crisis and the progressive isolation of the country, and earned the regime the reproach of the Eritrean people and the ostracism of the international community.

Essentially, Eritrea exhibits the distinctive features of the typical postcolonial African state and, as a consequence, faces a deep crisis of legitimacy, relevance, and delivery. A state of alternating economic stagnation and decline has foreclosed opportunities for normal human development, multiplied and worsened extreme poverty, and generated large-scale malnutrition. A marked democratic deficit has disconnected public policy and action. Severe repression, combined with the chronic shortage of essential goods and services, has disaffected the people. The high hopes that Eritrea would avoid the general malaise afflicting the continent and shine as an inspiring beacon of an African success story have been dashed by the rise of tyranny and the dismal failure of the government to provide for the needs and promote the wellbeing of the people.

Indeed, the closing years of the first decade of independence witnessed the rapid contraction of the political space for internal debate within the ruling Front and the Government, the dimming of Eritrea's prospects for democratic governance, and the inexorable consolidation of predatory, authoritarian rule. The unhappy outcome has been routine violations of fundamental freedoms and basic rights, including arbitrary arrests, disappearances, and indefinite detentions in solitary confinement. Counting the shipping containers, subterranean cells, and detention centres that dot the country, it is a shame that there are probably more jails than schools in Eritrea today, earning the country the notoriety of "the world's biggest prison".[581]

---

[581] The Guardian, Eritrea: The World's Biggest Prison, 17 April 2009. http://www.guardian.co.uk/commentisfree/2009/apr/17/eritrea-human-rights#start-of-comments

The regime's political repression, economic mismanagement, and limitless military conscription have caused an unprecedented exodus of Eritrean professionals and youth. The exodus has caused massive depletion of productive work force and substantial brain drain that operate to undermine Eritrea's national development, compromise its future regional competitive position, and harm the wellbeing of its people. Eritrea is lagging behind its neighbours in key areas that have a significant bearing on its future prosperity, such as local entrepreneurship and foreign direct investment (FDI), port services development, tertiary education, and professional training, so essential for the acquisition of knowledge, new technology, and knowhow.

The state of governance, the level of development, and the human condition epitomise a rabidly dismal situation. Preoccupied with its jingoistic ventures, the regime has failed to meet the aspirations of the people for peace, freedom, democracy, and prosperity. The prevailing bleak economic, political, and social reality contradicts the ideals and objectives embedded in the EPLF National Democratic Programme and the objectives enunciated in the National Charter, articulated in the Macro-Policy paper, and enshrined in the ratified Constitution.

The government has abandoned the promise of freedom, democracy, and prosperity of the armed struggle and imposed a virtual state of siege on the people. It is a national tragedy that Eritrea's brief experience in sovereign self-government has produced a ruthless dictatorship sustained through harsh repression and systematic intimidation. The regime operates an unrestrained killing machine that wastes away the productive lives of a large number of citizens without the restraint of due process. The people did not pay such a high price in order to enact a lethal one-man show on the political screen. In particular, a great number of Eritrean youth did not spend their prime years, endure untold hardships, and make immense sacrifices during the struggle for liberation in order to enthrone a brutal dictator who engineers the mass detention, mass exodus, and mass suffering of the people and drags the country into ruin.

It is crystal clear that independent Eritrea's actual record has thwarted all optimistic expectations, let its people down, and disappointed its friends. The regime has bitten the hand that fed the struggle and nourished its victory. The disparity between the noble aspirations that inspired and sustained the hard struggle and the dismal reality that exudes poverty, despair, and misery has become the hallmark of Eritrea today. This has been the cause of much agony to the people and the source of great distress for many veterans of the armed struggle, including the author. The following section elaborates the depth of anger and the sense of hurt shared by many Eritrean patriots that find common expression in the apt but sad retort: *we didn't do it for this!*

18.3 On a Personal Note

As a veteran of the war of liberation and a founding member of the EPLF Central Committee, I admit a profound sense of disappointment and a painful awareness of shared responsibility in the betrayal of the programmatic objectives of the armed struggle, the promises of liberation, and the expectations of statehood. As Eritrea embarks on the third decade of independence, it is quite heartrending to find shards of broken promises, broken expectations, and broken hopes littering its political, economic, social, and cultural landscape. The country reels under tyranny, the people languish in poverty, and the youth continue to flee in droves. Dictatorial, incompetent, and predatory, the regime perpetrates domestic repression, thrives in regional confrontation, and provokes international isolation. It has betrayed the *raison d'être* of the armed struggle, despoiled the sacrifices of our martyrs, and miscarried the vision of building a free, democratic, and prosperous Eritrea that stands out as a bright star in the African constellation.

It deeply pains me to acknowledge that Eritrea's experience of the first two and half decades of full self-government has been a failure in terms of the human condition of its people, its political situation, and its international standing. It is not independence, *per se*, but the the PFDJ leadership and the government that are on trial for this failure. The PFDJ regime has failed to respect the human rights, raise the material standards of living or promote the human security of the Eritrean people. Our collective failure has resulted in the emergence of an autocratic regime akin to and, in certain respects, even worse than the colonial regimes that ruled Eritrea in the past. What seemed unthinkable during the era of the struggle has transpired: betraying the cause, violating the trust, and desecrating the memory of our martyrs!

We in the leadership of the former Eritrean People's Liberation Front (EPLF), and the successor PFDJ, have allowed a once progressive revolutionary movement, embedded in the participation of the people that made military victory possible and socioeconomic transformation conceivable, to be subverted and turned away from its original purpose. Immersed in our routine tasks and unmindful of our higher political duty, we succumbed to a devious policy of 'divide and rule', allowed the systematic sidelining of the key Front and government organs, and facilitated the accumulation and abuse of power by the president. Passive complicity, abetted by petty rivalries and squabbles, and the secretive, top-heavy, and dictatorial structures upon which the EPLF was built enabled a handful of clever, unscrupulous, and ruthless individuals, under the aegis of a determined power-hungry dictator, to take control of the movement and distort its fundamental objectives for personal aggrandisement at the expense of the people.

We failed in our mission to complement the historic exercise of the right of the Eritrean people to choose national independence and establish a sovereign state with the exercise of the equally significant right to choose their government and constitute a democratic state. Our programmatic commitment to create the conditions that would enable the Eritrean people to determine freely the status and evolution of the Eritrean state and to manage their political, economic, and social affairs has miscarried. To our collective grief, we have failed our country, let our people down, and disappointed our friends and supporters. The inability to empower the people to construct a democratic, accountable, and effective state and engender a free, progressive, and prosperous Eritrea has been the cause of the greatest disappointment of my life.

I had the honour and privilege to serve with Eritrean patriots across generations whose personal courage in the struggle for self-determination, political commitment to the cause of liberation, and concern for the welfare of the people remain unequalled. Like many of them, I recognise, with profound distress, that we did not fight the struggle for liberation and make the attendant sacrifices for the kind of Eritrea we have today: oppressed, impoverished, laggard, and isolated. With its people mistreated, enchained, and brazenly abused, Eritrea has sadly become a country whose youth flee it in droves at great risk to their lives and whose people lack food, water, medicine, and electricity. As a founding member of the Central Committee of the EPLF, the Central Council of the PFDJ, and the transitional Eritrean National Assembly, and a former senior public servant and diplomat, I bear my share of the blame, responsibility, and pain for Eritrea's present predicament.

18.4 Crossing the Rubicon

As a veteran fighter for freedom, I must admit that I was deeply troubled by the murky events of September 2001, the arbitrary and sweeping arrest of several of my former comrades-in-arms, colleagues, and friends. That the arrest of the former senior officials happened without due process, in violation of their parliamentary immunity as members of the transitional Eritrean National Assembly, and that there were no formal charges against them made their detention in flagrant violation of their rights even more troubling. Most of them were, like me, among the few surviving members of the first central committee of the EPLF, elected in its first congress, and members of the central council of the PFDJ, elected in the third and last EPLF congress.

The arrests had stunned the Eritrean body politic and pervaded the country with profound indignation. Paralysed by division, the PFDJ leadership was too impotent to react as a body. I could not however remain silent. In conversations with the president, I discreetly pleaded the prudence, carefully couched in terms of our paramount national interest, of either a 'credible' trial before a court of law or a 'magnanimous' clemency. The first time in December 2001 while, in my capacity as Commissioner for Coordination with UNMEE, I briefed him on the outcome of my meetings with the heads of diplomatic missions in Asmera and with several visiting foreign dignitaries. The second time in March 2002 while discussing, in the presence of the late foreign minister Ali Said Abdella, a statement I had drafted for presentation to the 4th Session of the ACP-EU Joint Parliamentary Assembly held in Cape Town, South Africa. The third and last time in September 2005 while, we met one-on-one. My pleading proved to no avail.

The bottom line is that every Eritrean citizen, detained under any pretext, has the inalienable right to due process and to a fair trial before a court of law irrespective of the nature of the accusations levelled against him or her. The thought of the fateful end of the former senior officials and journalists in open-ended incarceration under solitary confinement, of the agony that befell their families and children, and of the omens for the political future of Eritrea became a constant source of personal distress. The existential contradiction between the values I cherish and the sense of guilt I felt from continued association with a government whose actions I detested gnawed my conscience and denied me inner peace.

My position as ambassador made matters worse. I found myself in a paradoxical and increasingly untenable situation. My continued representation of the State and concomitant obligation to defend the government's abusive and disagreeable transgressions as a matter of professional duty clashed with my deep conviction that the detentions were wrong and indefensible. They also conflicted with my long struggle for and personal commitment to the pursuit of democratic development, respect for human rights, the rule of law, and answerable government. I firmly believed at the same time and still do, that these values must be cultivated in the home soil to germinate, flourish, and bear fruit to transform the State, uplift the human condition, and enhance the wellbeing of the people. They could otherwise, not be imposed by outside dictation or external intervention.

To cut a long story short, I believed in the principal aims of the EPLF, which I helped articulate and disseminate, and there was a time when I trusted Isaias, the current president. The EPLF has unfortunately degenerated into the PFDJ and, in the process, turned from an instrument of liberation into a tool of oppression. What has become the bane of Eritrea has long forfeited my trust for his deep contempt of the people, objective hostility to and subversion of the real development, progress, and wellbeing of the country, and bestial cruelty to his former comrades-in-arms. Despite profound disappointment with the rise of dictatorship and the reign of misery in Eritrea however, I am very proud to have dedicated my life to the struggle for liberation and to the cause of the emancipation, progress, and prosperity of the Eritrean people, as a freedom fighter during the war and as a public servant after independence.

We fought the war for justice, freedom, and prosperity. We paid dearly in sweat, opportunity, life, and limb for our victory. Having gained independence, however, we have failed to construct a functional, accountable, and democratic state based on the rule of law, to empower our people, and to engender a free, peaceful, and prosperous Eritrea. Sadly, we ended up with the opposite of what we fought for. The contradiction hurts like a permanent cut with a blunt knife.

My ambassadorial functions included the duty to explain the numerous and unceasing infractions of 'my' government of its initial commitment to the Eritrean people, to its partners, and to the international community at large. My hosts summoned me to periodic meetings where officials, including close and long-time friends of the Eritrean struggle for self-determination, grilled me with critical questions. This happened in the several host foreign ministries, in the EU Development Commission, and in various political and parliamentary forums, including the European Parliament and the ACP-EU Joint Parliamentary Assembly, where I represented Eritrea. I duly submitted summary reports of the discussions, detailing the main questions raised, to the Ministry of Foreign Affairs and the Office of the President.

Further, I discreetly suggested, on several occasions and at the highest level, the need to take up a bold political initiative to rectify our internal situation, renew our commitment to our people, and address the unresolved issues of concern to our partners in order to reverse our country's avoidable but accelerating slide towards international isolation. In a meeting of ambassadors and senior government and PFDJ officials held in Asmera in January 2005, I argued for a reappraisal of the misconstruction that the entire international community was arrayed against Eritrea and suggested that proactive engagement rather than feigning victim would better serve our national interest, as 'it takes two to tango'. Although only one fellow ambassador spoke in support of my argument during the ensuing heated exchange with three Front and government officials, several participants commended my contestation afterwards. Even one of the eager beavers who vocally opposed my suggestion at the meeting admitted later, in private, that he agreed with me.

Diplomacy is a two-way street that involves reciprocal engagement. I decided to push for a proactive approach in a four-hour *tête-à-tête* with the president on 5 September 2005 when I was in Asmera for the funeral of the late Foreign Minister Ali Said Abdella. The conversation started with a question on the state of EU-Eritrea relations. In response, I explained the concerns of the EU with the continued detention of the former senior officials, the ban on the private press, the delayed national elections, the non-implementation of the constitution, the stalled EU-Eritrea political dialogue, etc. The discussion digressed to the situation in the region, relations with the Sudan, and the latest developments regarding the demarcation of the border with Ethiopia. Moving on to Eritrea, the conversation touched on the domestic nexus of Eritrea's declining external standing and focussed on the need for policy renewal to set the country back on track, improve its image, and reverse its growing regional and international isolation.

I came up with an idea that seemed feasible. I had given it a lot of thought and discussed it privately with certain senior colleagues in the government and the relevant Belgian and EU officials in Brussels and Asmera. The president would pay a state visit to Belgium and his itinerary would include meetings with senior EU officials from the Council, the Commission, and the Parliament, and the inevitable encounter with the press, followed by similar visits to the capitals of key EU member states. Its success would require certain groundwork.

In advance of the visit, the Government of Eritrea would on its own initiative, resolve the case of the detained former officials and journalists via either a presidential pardon or formal charges in a court of law. It would also lift the ban on the private press. Further, it would announce a general timeframe for the application of the ratified constitution, and the conduct of regional and parliamentary elections. The move would send positive signals, pre-empt the otherwise inevitable negative international media coverage, and turn the visit into an effective charm offensive. Cumulatively, I explained, the outcome of the measures would enhance the president's stature, reverse Eritrea's isolation, and promote its national interest.

After a while, the discussion went on in circles. His interruptions and body language signalled discomfort and irritation. It was already past lunchtime and about time to take a break. As we walked out of the office, I suggested that we continue the discussion after lunch. He replied that he was too tired and wished to sleep in the afternoon, as he had just returned from Nakfa in the morning. I then asked him if we could meet the next day. He said *mashi* (okay) and asked me when I will return to Brussels. I replied that I would take the night flight the day after.

The following day, instead of the expected meeting, I received a note, copied to the Ministry of Foreign Affairs and the Bank of Eritrea, assigning me as the Governor of the Bank of Eritrea. I went immediately to see the president but found out that he had left for an 'inspection tour' in the Gash-Barka Region. I had thought, quite naïvely then, that there was a narrow window of opportunity to reset Eritrea's domestic agenda and international engagement without losing face. However, the president would entertain none of the idea. To my dismay, I soon realised that he let me speak out in order to gauge where I stand and connived to shut me up from expressing such views anymore as part of my work as a diplomat.

I saw the assignment as an act of spite and malicious provocation. I would have considered any other post that would take me back home, hoping to stay engaged in possible efforts for reform from within. I would have returned despite the steady tightening of the political space in the country and the increased risk of advocating or pushing for reforms. But going back to the central bank after the way I was fired in 1994 would be, as an Eritrean saying goes, tantamount to "licking one's puke". I thus faced a real dilemma, much more troubling than an on-going medical condition I was grappling with at the time.

In this connection, even though the relative circumstances were quite different, I remembered what had happened after my abrupt and whimsical recall as ambassador from Brussels in September 1999. Except for being sent on a sundry of *ad hoc* missions of 'damage control' and 'crisis management' abroad, I remained 'frozen' from active public service for nearly a year until my sudden assignment as Commissioner for Coordination with the UN Mission in Eritrea and Ethiopia (UNMEE) in August 2000. From a professional perspective, formally imposed idleness is a stultifying, wasteful, and humiliating experience. The companionship and solidarity of my dear family and friends and the pastimes of reading, tennis, and frequent swimming in the warm waters of the Red Sea redeemed me from boredom, provided diversion from my predicament, and helped make life bearable in an otherwise distressful situation.

Well aware of Isaias's increasingly merciless reprisal to defiance of his directives and orders, I suspected that declining the post would certainly land me in 'freeze land' or in detention. I wanted to dissociate from the regime but retain the ability to return home. As I pondered a way out of the dilemma, I decided that I would no longer stay part of the regime but would always serve the interests of my country and people. In a polite letter, I declined the post and requested a two-year sabbatical leave or early retirement to complete an on-going personal and family medical treatment. I waited in vain for the president's response.

Once in the Front or the government, there is no space for dissent or consensual exit. My fancied solution proved an illusion. Still, I wanted to help keep the torch of liberty and hope aflame via a critical discourse to restore the ideals of freedom, democracy, and progress that inspired the armed struggle. I crossed the Rubicon. It was the most agonising personal decision of my life, for I did not spend my prime years in the struggle to free my homeland only to end up in exile later! I left the regime, but not my country, people, former comrades-in-arms, and colleagues.

Like many of my closest friends and former comrades-in-arms in the EPLF/EPLA, I am, as mentioned earlier, a product of the early Eritrean diaspora. I lived my formative years as a student and political activist in the United States during the turbulent late 1960s and early 1970s. Moreover, like several of my close friends and former comrades-in-arms, the quirks of cruel betrayal have compelled me to become a reluctant émigré and re-join the resistance to the regime in the effort to bring about the democratic transformation of the Eritrean State.

In spite of the present all-round paralysis, the state of play in Eritrea is bound to change and make a radical break with the trajectory of the last decade and a half. The state cannot overcome its internal crisis and external isolation, build capacity to perform its essential functions, and deliver public welfare without transforming its basic character. Quite aware that its days are numbered, the regime totters on the brink of collapse. Only an internally driven and all-inclusive reform process, guided by effective political initiative to reconstruct the State on a new basis, would rectify the prevailing bleak state of affairs and reverse Eritrea's on-going comprehensive decline ensure a bright future for the Eritrean people. Internal reforms would discard the failed policies of the government and imbed a radical shift in political orientation designed to deliver the Eritrean state from the rule of men to the rule of law.

There is, of course, no silver bullet formula for basic reform to re-launch the Eritrean state on a democratic path. Nevertheless, basic structural reform is both necessary and possible to discard the rotten head and retrieve the untainted body of both the PFDJ and the State. Internal reform could allow the Front to cast away the persistence of its dogmatic ideological origins and morph into an inclusive democratic force that sanctions political competition in the framework of pluralism and enable Eritrea to reinvent itself. Several East European states have successfully blazed the path following the breakup of the former Soviet bloc.

In the context of the undeveloped Eritrean State, a hybrid model that synthesises the developed architecture of the European state system, the mother of the modern nation state, with the legacy of indigenous cultural values and traditional governance structures offers a viable way forward to its reconstruction.[582] Such a reconstructed state would combine the best elements of the African and European worlds and integrate the principal attributes of the European state model with indigenous Eritrean governance structures, customary

---

[582]   Bereketeab, Redie, 2009, pp. 17-19.

respect for the rule of law and cultural values of justice. The model of an Afro-European hybrid, carefully calibrated to fit the historical and sociocultural specifics of the country, bears the promise of re-launching the Eritrean state and restoring its legitimacy, relevance, and capacity to deliver.

The struggle to effect change and transform the Eritrean state would be extremely hard. The calculus of external interests would further complicate the process. There is a paramount need to chart an independent path guided by a cautious and objective appraisal of the alignment and correlation of national forces. A successful strategy must ensure that the downfall of the regime does not produce the destruction of the state. The overall stability, security, and sovereignty of the Eritrean State merits top priority. The construction of an inclusive *grand coalition* of all those who desire, and are willing to work for democratic change would be essential for the success of the reform project. In this context, the premise that the core of the PFDJ and the government is entirely beyond redemption through internal reform and, therefore, should be crushed with the intervention of outside forces is untenable and risks the creation of a destabilising power vacuum that could prove catastrophic for Eritrea under the prevailing geopolitical reality.

Undeniably, there are a handful of 'rotten apples' in the Front, the government, and the army high command. Yet, there is no question that, as recent events have confirmed, disaffection runs deep and wide at all levels and that the 'rotten' handful are far too few to irrevocably contaminate or to justify the blanket condemnation of the core organic bodies. Moreover, when change happens and internal reforms begin, it would be possible to identify, neutralise, and isolate the handful of corrupted henchmen. Otherwise, the vast majority, deeply aggrieved by the predicament that has befallen Eritrea and the Eritrean people, are good people who have demonstrated their ardent patriotism, readiness to make the supreme sacrifice, and firm commitment to serve the common good through action. Thus, besides the effective mobilisation of the Eritrean people at home and abroad, an internally driven process of regime change and an orderly transition to democratic governance would require the agency and active participation of major elements of the Front, the government and the army.

Surely, the Isaias regime has failed and shall fall sooner than later. The time has come for Eritrean patriots and democrats at home and abroad to join hands and work together, in the pioneering spirit of unity of purpose of Ibrahim Sultan and Weldeab Weldemariam, to accelerate the advent of change and prepare for the transition in a manner to say *Never Again* to dictatorship. Lessons drawn from experience must prevent the recurrence of the mistakes of the past. It would be absolutely imperative to re-launch the Eritrean State on the basis of the rule of law, democratic principles, respect for human rights, and the commitment to the progress, prosperity, and wellbeing of the people as its *raison d'être*. Rectification would also provide coherent guidance to enable successful nation building, state construction, and democratic development in Eritrea and, through the force of example, in much of Africa.

18.5 Towards a Functional State

The existential imperative to overcome the country's years of oppressive rule, reclaim its present, and secure its future has acquired special urgency. There is a paramount need and a palpable desire for change to reconstitute a constitutional state and an inclusive democratic regime, reform the security apparatus to protect the people, and rationalise the civil service to build delivery capacity. The restoration of the historical legacy of representative institutions and adherence to legal precepts could, once revamped and enhanced, serve as an anchor to build a modern state founded on the rule of law and committed to a constitutional order.

This would help usher in a democratic system of government able to transform the state into an effective vehicle of delivery of freedom, prosperity, and security for the people. The institution of a new democratic dispensation would avert the clear and present danger of implosion, with its attendant political disaster. Further, it would pave the way for the reconstruction of the state, the renewal of society, and the revival of our cultural values.

A viable project of state reconstitution requires internal change of direction committed to basic reforms designed to open up the country's political space, transform its national economy, and rationalise its external action. The Chinese experience since the 1980s and the Eastern European experience since the fall of the Berlin Wall in 1989 illustrate that change is feasible and doable. Deng Xiaoping's bold 'open door policy' and economic reforms lifted China out of the morass of Maoist dogma, the devastation of the cultural revolution, and the cocoon of international isolation. China has emerged as a global economic powerhouse and a rising world power whose economic transformation is bound to drive corresponding political reforms. Most of the states of Eastern Europe have undergone democratic development as thriving members of the EU. In spite of the great difference in the specific conditions, the reforms in China and Eastern Europe proffer significant lessons for change in Eritrea.

The reconstitution of the Eritrean State commences with putting the ratified Constitution into effect to establish the rule of law, reorganise the state apparatus, affirm functional balance among the three branches of government, and legitimise state authority. The creation of a constitutional government would restore sovereignty to the people, operationalize a democratic system of government, allow political pluralism, and facilitate participatory politics. It would depersonalise power, end the arbitrary rule of men, and reorient the security forces toward the protection of the Eritrean people within the framework of a constitutional order. Reform of the security apparatus, revitalisation of education, and rationalisation of the civil service would reinforce the successful re-launching of the State. Further, political reform would create an essential condition for national renewal and help Eritrea rationalise its external action, overcome its international isolation, and pursue constructive engagement with the region and the world at large.

Economic reforms would capacitate the regulatory and supervisory functions of government to launch a developmental state, set the dynamic role of the private sector as the engine of growth, and free the creative energies of the people. Gainful employment, sufficient food on the family table, adequate housing, and access to electricity, clean water, basic drugs, meaningful education, and improved public health care delivery would replace pompous state propaganda and constant exhortations for endless donations of funds and labour. China's meteoric rise may be out of bounds for small Eritrea. However, it would not be out of reach for a reformed Eritrea to replicate, on a small scale,

China's remarkable progress in achieving relative prosperity and improved standard of living for a large and growing proportion of its huge population.

As the book goes to press, Eritrea finds itself at a crossroads. Whatever the origins of their conception or the manner of their organisation, the events of 21 January 2013 in Asmera have exposed more fractures within the ruling Front, the government, and the army and put the country in the limelight of international focus.[583] Notwithstanding the divisive designs underlying the regime's patently sectarian manoeuvres that ensued, the legitimate demands raised by a group of army officers and soldiers for the release of political prisoners and the implementation of the ratified Constitution to pave the way for a democratic government represents an essential catalyst that heralds the onset of a tipping point towards imminent change. As John F Kennedy once said, "Those who make peaceful change impossible will make violent revolution inevitable". Burdened by a volatile history and a tormented present, Eritrea cries for change to

---

[583] Following the event, reports from Asmera indicated the arrest of several officials and army officers. Detained senior officials include: Abdella Jaber, member of the PFDJ executive committee and head of its organisational affairs; Alamin Saleh Sheikh (Wedi Sheikh), member of the PFDJ executive committee and former regional administrator; Ibrahim Idris Totil, member of the PFDJ central council and former regional administrator; Ahmed Haji Ali, member of the PFDJ central council and minister of mines and energy; and Mustafa Nurhussein, member of the PFDJ central council and regional administrator. Army officers put under house arrest include Maj. Gen. Omer Hassen (Tewil), member of the PFDJ central council, former army chief of staff and commander of the southern zone; and Col. Saleh Osman, division commander.

secure the people's aspirations for democracy, freedom, and justice.

Lifting Eritrea out of the muddle of its general crisis would take a colossal effort. Once set in motion, the reconstruction of a constitutional, democratic, and functional state would require the creation of an inclusive regime that values assertive citizenship capable of holding it to account through conscious and organised political and civic action. This would enable active, informed, and organised political participation of citizens, directly and via truly representative organs, in the processes of policy formulation and decision-making. It would also help build national cohesion based on consensus forged through autonomous conciliation of social and political conflicts. Further, it would help mobilise domestic resources in pursuit of an integrated national development programme, based on self-reliance and ownership, with the complement of cooperative international relations.

Bibliography

Abbay, Alemseged, Identity Jilted or Reimagining Identity? The Divergent Paths of the Eritrean and Tigrayan Nationalist Struggles, The Red Sea Press, 1998.

Adams, John, A Defence of the Constitutions of the United States of America, London, 1787.

Agbese, Pita Ogaba / Kieh Jr., George Klay (eds.), *Reconstituting the State in Africa*, New York: Palgrave Macmillan, 2007.

Adejumboli, Saheed A., The History of Ethiopia, Westport, Connecticut & London: Greenwood Press, 2007.

Almedom, Astier M., Re-reading the Short and Long-Rigged History of Eritrea 1941-1952: Back to the Future, *Nordic Journal of African Studies* 15(2): 103–142 (2006).

Amnesty International, Annual Report 2011, The State of the World's Human Rights: Eritrea.

Andall, Jacqueline, and Duncan, Derek, (eds.) Italian Colonialism: Legacy and Memory, Peter Lang AG, European Academic Publishers, Bern 2005.

Association Swisse-Erythrée (ASE), *Eritrea-Ethiopia Conflict: Analysis of Causes and Events*, A report prepared by Spyros Demtriou and Awet Gebre-Medhin, Octber 2002.

Ayyiteh, Georges, *Indigenous African Institutions*, Dobbs Ferry, New York: Transnational Publishers, 1991.

Azarya, Victor, *Reordering State-Society Relations, Incorporation and Disengagement*, The Precarious Balance: State-

Society Relations in Africa, Rothchild & Chazan (eds.), 1988.

Bayart, Jean-François, *The State in Africa: The Politics of the Belly*, London & New York: Longman, 1993.

Bereketeab Redie, *State Building in Post-Liberation Eritrea: Challenges, Achievements and Potential*, Adonis and Abbey Publishers Ltd, London, May 2009.

Brown, David, Palmerston and the Politics of Foreign Policy, 1846-1855, Manchester: Manchester University Press, 2002.

Calhoun, Craig, Nationalism, Open University Press, Buckingham, 1997.

Callaghy, Thomas M. *The State and the Development of Capitalism in Africa: Theoretical, Historical, and Comparative Reflections*, The Precarious Balance: State-Society Relations in Africa, eds., Donald Rothchild and Naomi Chazan, Westview Press, Boulder, 1988.

Caulk, Richard, *Black snake, white snake: Bahta Hagos and his revolt against Italian overrule in Eritrea, 1894*, in Donald Crummey, *Banditry, Rebellion, & Social Protest in Africa*, African Writers Series, 1986.

Chabal, Patrick & Jean-Pascal Daloz, *Africa Works: Disorder as Political Instrument*, The International African Institute and Indiana University Press, Indianapolis, 1999.

Chakraverti, Sauvik, *Predatory State - The Black Hole of Social Science*, Times of India, New Delhi, 22 September 1999.

Chang, Ha-Joon, The Economic Theory of the Developmental State, 1999.

Clinton, Hillary Rodham, Living History, Simon & Schuster, 9 June 2003.

Connell, Dan, Against All Odds: A Chronicle of the Eritrean Revolution. Lawrenceville: Red Sea Press, 1993.

Connell, Dan, *Inside the EPLF: The Origins of the 'People's Party' and its Role in the Liberation of Eritrea*, Review of African Political Economy (September 2001), Vol. 28, No. 89.

Constitution of Eritrea, 23 May 1997.

Constitution of the Federal Democratic Republic of Ethiopia, 1995.

Copnall, James, *Eritrea: The land its citizens want to forget*, BBC News, 21 December 2009.

Conrad, Joseph, Heart of Darkness, Penguin Books Ltd., 1902.

Curzon, George (Lord Curzon), Frontiers: Lecture Delivered in the Sheldonian Theatre, Oxford, 2 November 1907 (Westport, Conn.: Greenwood Press, 1976).

Danish Ministry of Foreign Affairs, *Policy Paper for Denmark's Engagement in Somalia*, August 2009.

Davidson, Basil, Modern Africa: A Social & Political History, Second edition, Longman Group UK Ltd 1989.

Davidson, Basil, *The Blackman's Burden: Africa and the Curse of the Nation-Sate*, New York: Times Books, 1992.

D'Avray, Anthony, Lords of the Red Sea: The History of a Red Sea Society from the Sixteenth to the Nineteenth Centuries, Wiesbaden, Harrassowitz, 1996.

Denison, Edward, RenGuang Yu and Gebremedhin, Naigzy, Asmara: Africa's Secret Modernist City, Merrell, London and New York, 2003.

Del Boca, Angelo, *The Myths, Suppressions, Denials, and Defaults of Italian Colonialism* in Patrizia Palumbo, (ed.) A Place in the Sun: Africa in Italian Colonial Culture from Post-Unification to the Present, University of California Press, Berkeley, Los Angeles, London: 2003.

Dias, Alexandra Magnólia, The Conduct of an Inter-state War and Multiple Dimensions of Territory: 1998-2000 Eritrea-Ethiopia War, *Cadernos de Estudos Africanos*, 22/2012, 31 January 2012.

Dorman, Sara R., Eritrea's Nation and State-building: Re-assessing the impact of 'the struggle', *QEH Working Paper Series - QEHWPS105*, April 2003.

Duffield, Mark, *Global Governance and the New Wars*, London: Zed Books, 2001.

Ellis, Stephen, 'What has happened to the Colonial State in Africa?' Unpublished paper, presented at The End of the Post-Colonial State in Africa: Perspectives from the Great Lakes Region, a conference organised by the North/South Priority Research Area, University of Copenhagen, Koge, 5-7 December 2001.

Encyclopaedia Britannica.

Eritrean People's Liberation Front (EPLF), A National Charter for Eritrea: For a Democratic, Just and Prosperous Future, Third Congress, Nakfa, February 1994.

Eritrean People's Liberation Front (EPLF), National Democratic Programme, January 1977.

Eritrean People's Liberation Front, Proposals for a Referendum in Eritrea, 21 November 1980.

Eritrean People's Liberation Front (EPLF), Vanguard, Official Monthly Organ, August 1977, Volume II, No. 5.

Fanon, Frantz, The Wretched of the Earth, New York: Grove Press, Inc., 1963, p. 73.

Finaldi, Giuseppe, *Italy's Scramble for Africa from Dogali to Adowa* in John Dickie, John Foot & Frank M. Snowdon (edts.) Disastro!: Disasters in Italy since 1860: Culture, Policy and Society, PALGRAVE™, New York, 2002.

First, Ruth, *Colonialism and the formation of the African States*, States and Societies, David Held et al(eds.), Oxford, 1983.

Frimpong-Ansah, Jonathan H., The Vampire State in Africa: The Political Economy of Decline in Ghana, Africa World Press, 1992.

Galbraith, James K., The Predatory State, Free Press Publishers, 2008.

Gebre Hiwot Tesfagiorgis ed., *Emergent Eritrea: Challenges of Economic Development*, Trenton, NJ: Red Sea, 1993.

Gebremedhin, Naigzy, Asmara, *Africa's Modernist City*, African Perspectives: Dialogue on Urbanism and Architecture, The Faculty of Architecture, TU, Delft 6-8 December 2007.

Giroux, Henry A., "Lessons From Paulo Freire", The Chronicle of Higher Education, 22 October 2010, Vol. 57, Issue 9.

Government of Eritrea, Department of External Affairs, Asmara, 1993.

Government of the State of Eritrea, *Macro-Policy*, November 1994.

Governments of Ethiopia and Eritrea: Transit and Port Services Agreement between the Transitional Government of Ethiopia and the Government of the State of Eritrea, 29 September 1993.

Haggai, Erlich, *The Struggle over Eritrea 1962-1978*, Washington, D.C.: Hoover Institution Press, 1983.

Haile, Semere, *Historical Background to the Ethiopia-Eritrea Conflict*, The Long Struggle of Eritrea for Independence and Constructive Peace, Lionel Cliffe and basil Davidson (eds.), Trenton, NJ: The Red Sea Press, 1988.

Hamilton, Keith and Richard Langhorne, The Practice of Diplomacy: Its Evolution, Theory and Administration, Second Edition, Routledge, 1995, p. 185.

Harris, Joseph E., Africans and their History, Revised Edition, New York and Scarborough, Ontario: New American Library, 1987.

Healy, Sally, Eritrea's Economic Survival: Summary record of a conference held on 20 April 2007, The Royal Institute of International Affairs, 2007.

Henze, Paul B., *Horn of Africa: From War to Peace*, Macmillan, 1991.

Herbst, Jeffrey, *State and Power in Africa*, Princeton: Princeton University Press, 2000.

Horn of Africa Bulletin, Vol. 3 No. 10, May-June 1998.

Horne, Sir Alistair, A Savage War of Peace: Algeria 1954-1962, Viking Adult (First Edition), 27 March 1978.

Hoste, Jean-Christophe, *Where Was United Africa in the Climate Change Negotiations?*

Human Rights Watch, State Repression and Indefinite Conscription in Eritrea, 16 April 2009.

Hungwe, Kedmon N. & Chipo, Essay Review, Africa Works: Disorder as Political Instrument, Zambezia (2000), XXVII (ii).

IMF, *Executive Board Concludes 2009 Article IV Consultations with the State of Eritrea*, PIN No. 09/13, December 11, 2009

International Commission of Jurists, *Review of the International Commission of Jurists*, No. 26, June 1981.

International Herald Tribune, 8 October 2008.

Jacquin-Berdal, Dominique /Plaut, Martin (eds.), *Unfinished Business: Ethiopia and Eritrea at War*, Trenton & Asmara: The Red Sea Press, 2004.

Johnson, Chalmers, MITI and the Japanese Miracle: The Growth of Industrial Policy 1925-1975, Stanford University Press, 1982.

Jonah, Sam. 2005:19, quoted in Manji, Firoze, and Stephen Marks, eds.2007, African *Perspectives on China*, Nairobi and Oxford: Fahamu.

Journal of Eritrean Studies, "The 25 July 1949 Declaration of the Eritrean Independence Bloc against US-UK-Ethiopia Conspiracies at the United Nations", JES, Vol. 1, No. 1, Summer 1986.

Kaplan, Robert, "A Tale of Two Colonies," *Atlantic Monthly*, April 2003.

Killion, Tom, *Historical Dictionary of Eritrea*, Scarecrow Press, 1998.

Langohr, Vickie, Colonial Education Systems and the Spread of Local Religious Movements: The Cases of British Egypt and Punjab.

Lariaux, M., *The French Developmental State as Myth and Moral Ambition*, Woo-Cumings, Meredith (ed.), The Developmental State, Cornell University Press, 1999.

Levin, Victor, "African Patrimonial Regimes in Comparative Perspective", Journal of Modern African Studies, vol. 28, no. 4, 1980.

Li Cunxin, Mao's Last Dancer, Penguin Books Australia, 2003.

Longrigg, Stephen, *A short History of Eritrea*, London: Clarendon Press, 1945.

Longrigg, Stephen H., Half Yearly Report by the Military Administrator on the Occupied Enemy Territory of Eritrea: From the Period 1st January to 30th June 1942, Asmara: Eritrea, 29July 1942.

Lovejoy, Paul E., Transformations in Slavery: A History of Slavery in Africa, Cambridge University Press, 2000.

Mamdani, Mahmood, *When Victims Become Killers: Colonialism, Nativism and the Genocide in Rwanda*, Princeton University/Oxford: James Currey, 2001.

Marino, Lt CDR Francesco (Italian Navy), Military Operations in the Italian East Africa, 1935–1941: Conquest and Defeat, USMC Command and Staff College, 15 April 2009.

Markakis, John, National and Class Conflicts in the Horn of Africa, Cambridge, 1987.

Mazrui, Ali, *Francophone Nations and English-Speaking States: Imperial Ethnicity and African Political formation*, States Versus Ethnic Claims: African Policy Dilemma, Rothchild & Olorunsola (eds.), Westview Press, Boulder, 1983.

Mebrahtu, Simon, Eritrea: Constitutional, Legislative and Administrative Provisions Concerning Indigenous Peoples, Country Report of the Research Project by the International Labour Organisation and the African Commission on Human and Peoples' Rights, 2009.

Meditz, Sandra & Merrill, Tim (eds.), Zaire - A Country Study, December 1993.

Ministry of Information of Eritrea, Eritrea: A Country Handbook, 2002.

Mo Ibrahim Foundation, *The Mo Ibrahim Index*, 2001-2007 (2009).

Moselle, Boaz and Benjamin Polak, *A Model of a Predatory State*, The Journal of Law, Economics and Organization, Vol. 17, Issue 1, Oxford University Press, 2001.

Munro-Hay, Stuart, *Aksum: A Civilization of Late Antiquity*, Edinburgh: University Press, 1991.

Nadel, S.F., *Land Tenure on the Eritrean Plateau*, Africa: Journal of International African Institute, 1946, 16(1).

National Assembly of Eritrea, *Election Proclamation of Eritrea*, January 2002.

National Assembly of Eritrea, *Draft Proclamation of Political Parties and Political Organisations of Eritrea*, February 2001.

N'Diaye, Boubacar, *"Beyond the 'Berlin Conference / OAU Framework': A Pan-African Analysis of Africa's Security Crisis"*, Journal of African Policy Studies, vol. 7, no. 1, 2002.

Organization of Eritrean Americans (OEA), A Chronology of the Eritrea-Ethiopia Conflict and Peace Process, August 2008.

Oudes, Bruce, Zimbabwe Independent, 4-10 February 2011.

Pankhurst, Sylvia, *Eritrea on the Eve*, New Times and Ethiopia News Books, Walthamstow Press Ltd., Walthamstow, 1952

Pankhurst, Sylvia, *Why Are We Destroying Ethiopian Ports?* New Times and Ethiopian News Books, Woodford Green Essex, London: 1952.

Pankhurst, E. Sylvia and Pankhurst, Richard, *Ethiopia and Eritrea: The Last Phase of the Union Struggle 1941-1952*, Walthamstow Press Ltd., Walthamstow, 1953

Parkinson, Cyril Northcote, *The Evolution of Political Thought*, Boston, Houghton Mifflin Co., 1958.

Pateman, Roy, Eritrea: Even the Stones Are Burning, Red Sea Press, 1990.

Pollera, Alberto, The Native Peoples of Eritrea, Red Sea Press, 2001.

Pool, David, *From Guerrillas to Government*, James Currey, Oxford and Ohio University Press Athens, 2001.

Poscia, Stefano, Eritrea: Colonia Tradita (Eritrea: A Colony Betrayed), Roma: Edizione Associate, 1989.

Provisional Government of Eritrea, *Gazette of Eritrean Law: Proclamation 21/1992, No. 3*, Asmera, 6 April 1992.

Provisional Government of Eritrea, *Gazette of Eritrean Laws: Proclamation 23/1992, No.5*, Asmera, 22/5/1992.

Provisional Government of Eritrea, *Gazette of Eritrean Laws: Proclamation 37/1993, No.6*, Asmera, 19 May 1993.

Provisional Government of Eritrea, *Gazette of Eritrean Laws: Proclamation 42/1993, No. 8*, Asmea, 1 July 1993.

Provisional Government of Eritrea, *Gazette of Eritrean Laws: Proclamation 67/1995, No. 1*, Asmera, 10 February 1995.

Provisional Government of Eritrea, *Gazette of Eritrean Laws: Proclamation 82/1995, No. 11*, Asmera, 23 October 1995.

Rashid, Ahmed, Descent into Chaos: How the War against Islamic Extremism Is Being Lost in Pakistan, Afghanistan and Central Asia, the Penguin Group, London, 2008.

Reid, Richard, The Trans-Mereb Experience: Perceptions of the Historical Relationship between Eritrea and Ethiopia, Journal of Eastern African Studies, Vol. 1, Issue 2, July 2007.

Rodney, Walter, How Europe Underdeveloped Africa, Bogle-L'Ouverture Publications, London and Tanzanian Publishing House, Dar-Es-Salaam: 1973.

Rousseau, Jean-Jacques, "On the Social Contract", quoted in C. Northcote Parkinson, *The Evolution of Political Thought.*

Rovighi, Alberto, *Le Operazione in Africa Orientale*, Vol. 1, Officio Storica SME, Rome, 1995; *Gli Italiani in Africa Orientale*, Vol. 3.

Santoianni, Vittorio, *Il Razionalismo nelle colonie italiane 1928-1943 La «nuova architettura» delle Terre d'Oltremar.*

Shelton, Garth, FOCAC IV – New Opportunities for Africa, 22 December 2009.

Smis, Stefaan, *The Legal Status of International Land Boundaries in Africa*, in Politics of Identity and Economics of Conflict in the Great Lakes Region, Ruddy Doom & Jan Gorus (eds.), Brussels: VUB Press, 2000.

Somit, Albert and Steven A. Peterson, *The Failure of Democratic Nation Building: Ideology Meets Evolution* by Palgrave Macmillan, 2005.

Spenser, John H., *Ethiopia at Bay: A Personal Account of the Haile Selassie Years*, Reference Publications Inc., Algonac, Michigan 1987.

Srinivasan, Rajeev, The Predatory State (Part I of II), Rediff on Net, 16 August 2002.

Sun Tzu, The Art of War, New York: Oxford University Press, 1963.

Steer, George L., Sealed and Delivered: A Book on the Abyssinian Campaign, London: Hodder and Stoughton, 1942.

Tesfai, Alemseged, *Aynfelale*: Eritrea 1941-1950 (ኣይንፈላለ: ኤርትራ 1941-1950), Hidri Publishers, Asmara, 2001.

Tesfagiorgis, Gebre Hiwet, Self-Determination: Its Evolution and Practice by the United Nations and Its Application to the Case of Eritea, Wisconsin International Law Journal, Vol. 6, No. 1, June 1988.

Tesfai, Alemseged, Federation with Ethiopia: From Matienzo to Tedla 1951-1955 (ፌደረሽን ኤርትራ ምስ ኢትዮጵያ፡ ካብ ማቲየንሶ ክሳብ ተድላ 1951-1955) Hidri Publishers, Asmara, 2005.

Tilly, Charles, Coercion, Capital, and European States, AD 990-1992, Malden, MA: Blackwell Publishers, 1990.

Trevaskis, G.K.N., *Eritrea, A Colony in Transition: 1941-1952*, Oxford University Press, London, 1960.

Tronvoll, Kjetil, *The Lasting Struggle for Freedom in Eritrea: Human Rights and Political Development 1991-2009*, Oslo: HBO AS, Haugesund, 2009.

Tronvoll, Kjetil, "The process of nation-building in post-war Eritrea" *JMAS* 36, 3 (1998).

Turchin, Peter and Jonathan M. Adams and Thomas D. Hall: *East-West Orientation of Historical Empires*, University of Connecticut, November 2004.

2012 Global Hunger Index: The Challenge of Hunger: Ensuring Sustainable Food Security under Land, Water and Energy Stresses.

UNDP, *Human Development Report 2002*.

Vestal, Theodore M., *Consequences of the British Occupation of Ethiopia during World War II*, Rediscovering the British Empire, Barry Ward (eds.), Melbourne, FL: Krieger, 2001.

Villalon, Leonardo/ Huxtable, Phillip (eds.), *The African State at a Critical Juncture, Between Disintegration and Reconfiguration*, Boulder, CO: Lynne Rienner Publishers, 1997.

UN Resolution 390(A), 1950.

UN General Assembly Resolution 1514 (XV), 14 December 1960.

United Nations Food and Agriculture Organisation (FAO) Country Briefs, 7 July 2011.

UN Human Rights Council, Report of the Special Rapporteur on the situation of human rights in Eritrea, Sheila B. Keetharuth, 28 May 2013.

UN Security Council, Resolution 1320 (2000), 15 September 2000.

United Nations Security Council Resolution 1907(2009), 23 December 2009.

US Department of State, Incoming Telegram Control 8528, No. 171, 19 August 1949.

US Library of Congress, *Singapore Country Studies: Two Decades of Independence.*

Venosa, Joseph L., Faith in the Nation: Examining the Contributions of Eritrean Muslims in the Nationalist Movement, 1946-1961, Master's Thesis, 2007.

Wallis, Jim, The Soul of Politics: A Practical and Prophetic Vision of Change, London: Fount, 1994.

Weber, Max, Politics as a Vocation, Munich: Munich University, 1918.

Welde Giorgis, Andebrhan, *Commentary: Border and Territorial Conflicts between Eritrea and Ethiopia: Background, facts and Prospects*, Eritrean Studies Review, Vol.4 No. 1, 2004.

Wikileaks, Diplomatic Cables.

Woo-Cumings, Meredith (ed.), The Developmental State, Cornell University Press, 1999.

World Bank, *Indicators Database: Eritrea Country Profile*, September 2009.

Woodward, Peter, *US Foreign Policy and the Horn of Africa*, Ashgate Publishing Ltd., Hampshire, England, 2006.

Wrong, Michela, *I Didn't Do It for You: How the World Betrayed a Small African Nation*, London and New York: Fourth Estate, 2005.

Yohannes, Okbazghi, Eritrea: A Pawn in World Politics, University of Florida Press, 1991

Young, Crawford, *The African Colonial State and Its Political Legacy*, The Precarious Balance: State-Society Relations in Africa, eds., Donald Rothchild and Naomi Chazan, Westview Press, Boulder, 1988.

Young, Crawford, The African Colonial State in Comparative Perspective, Yale University Press, New Haven, 1994.

Young, William C., The Rashayida Arabs vs. the State: The Impact of European Colonialism on a Small-Scale Society in Sudan and Eritrea, Journal of Colonialism & Colonial History, Baltimore: Fall 2008, Vol. 9, Issue 2.

Lightning Source UK Ltd.
Milton Keynes UK
UKOW03f0816020514

230997UK00001B/65/P